GENERAL CORRESPONDENCE

VOLUME II

CRITICAL EDITION OF THE COMPLETE WORKS

(Texts and Words)

OF

SAINT THÉRÈSE OF LISIEUX

Centenary Edition

(1873–1973)

SAINT THÉRÈSE OF LISIEUX

GENERAL CORRESPONDENCE

VOLUME II

1890–1897

Translated by

John Clarke, O.C.D.

Typos
815 Bold type

INSTITUTE OF CARMELITE STUDIES

A critical edition of all the letters written by St. Thérèse according to the autographs, and, for the letters that are lost, according to copies; these are accompanied by all the letters from her correspondents and by letters shedding light upon her life and thought.

This edition was prepared by Sister Cécile, Lisieux Carmel, with the assistance of Sister Marie-Ange, Lisieux Carmel, Sister Geneviève, O.P., Clairefontaine monastery, Sister Anne, Boulogne Carmel, Pères Albert Patfoort, O.P., Bernard Bro, O.P., Guy Gaucher, O.C.D., Jeanne and Jacques Lonchampt.

ST. THÉRÈSE OF LISIEUX GENERAL CORRESPONDENCE II
is a translation of *Correspondance Générale* II
(Les Editions du Cerf-Desclée De Brouwer, 1974)

Copyright © by Washington Province of Discalced Carmelites, Inc. 1988
ICS Publications
2131 Lincoln Road, N.E.
Washington, D.C. 20002

Library of Congress Cataloging in Publication Data
(Revised for vol. 2)

Thérèse, de Lisieux, Saint, 1873-1897.
  General correspondence.

  Critical edition of the complete works of Saint Thérèse of Lisieux.
  Translation of: Correspondence générale.
  Includes bibliographical references.
  Contents: v. 1. 1877-1890—v. 2. 1890-1897.
  1. Thérèse, de Lisieux, Saint, 1873-1897. 2. Christian saints—France—Lisieux—Correspondence. 3. Lisieux (France)—Biography. I. Clarke, John, 1917-   . II. Thérèse, de Lisieux, Saint, 1873-1897. Works. English, 1982. III. Title. BX4700.T5A4   1982   282'.092'4 [B]   81-6474
  ISBN 0-9600876-9-9 (pbk. : v. 1)
  ISBN 0-935216-10-3 (pbk. : v. 2)

CONTENTS

ABBREVIATIONS 689

PRESENTATION, CONVENTIONAL SIGNS,
  AND GUIDE 694

Fifth Period
NOVITIATE
THE HIDDEN YEARS
(September 1890–February 1893)

The hidden years 701
  "In the darkness of the night"
  (September 1890–October 1891) 705
  "The winter is passed"
  (October 1891–October 1892) 736
  "Jesus told me to descend"
  (October 1892–February 1893) 757

Sixth Period
THE PRIORATE OF MOTHER AGNES OF JESUS
(February 1893–March 1896)

The priorate of Mother Agnes of Jesus 773
  Repose in the valley
  (February–September 1893) 777
  "Our souls remain free"
  (September 1893–June 1894) 818
  "As gold in the crucible"
  (June–September 1894) 856
  "How sweet is the way of love"
  (October 1894–March 1896) 885

v

Seventh Period

THE NEW PRIORATE OF MOTHER MARIE DE GONZAGUE
(March 21, 1896–September 30, 1897)

The new priorate of Mother Marie de Gonzague 941
    "To forget myself for the glory of God and the salvation
    of souls"
      (March–September 1896) 947
    "Love...the key to my vocation"
      (September–December 1896) 985
    "I have the hope that my exile will be short"
      (December 1896–April 1897) 1025
    "I am not dying, I am entering into life"
      (April–September 1897) 1077

COMPLEMENTARY DOCUMENTS

Extracts From Letters About Thérèse 1197
Printed Documents 1277
Biographical Guide For Proper Names 1283
Chronology 1297
Table of References 1331
Index 1339

ABBREVIATIONS

ACL Archives du Carmel de Lisieux.
(Lisieux Carmel Archives).

AL *Annales de sainte Thérèse de Lisieux* (revue).
(Annals of St. Thérèse of Lisieux).

CE I, etc. Copie des Ecrits, 1910 (CE I, II, III, IV).
(Copy of the Writings, 1910).

CF *Correspondance familiale*, Lettres de Zélie Martin
(1863–1877).
(Family Correspondence, Letters from Zélie Martin,
1863–1877).

CG I *Correspondance generale*, tome I, 1972*
General Correspondence, volume I, 1972 (first
volume of this work).

ChrIG Cahier de M. Isidore Guérin, contenant des gén-
éalogies et chronologies de sa famille.
(Copybook of M. Isidore Guérin, containing his
family genealogy and chronology).

CJ "Carnet jaune" de Mère Agnès de Jésus.*
("Yellow notebook" of Mother Agnes of Jesus).

CMG I, etc.	Carnets manuscrits de soeur Geneviève (CMG I, II, III, IV).
	(Manuscript Notebooks of Sister Geneviève).
CSG	*Conseils et Souvenirs*, publiés par soeur Geneviève, 1952.*
	(Counsels and Reminiscences, published by Sister Geneviève, 1952).
DCL	Documentation du Carmel de Lisieux.
	(Lisieux Carmel's Documentation).
DE	Sainte Thérèse de l'Enfant-Jésus et de la Sainte-Face, *Derniers Entretiens*, 1971.
	(Saint Thérèse of the Child Jesus and the Holy Face, *Last Conversations*, 1971).
DE/G	Derniers Entretiens recueillis par soeur Geneviève.
	(Last Conversations set down by Sister Geneviève).
DE/Meu	Derniers Entretiens recueillis par soeur Marie de l'Eucharistie.
	(Last Conversations set down by Sister Marie of the Eucharist).
DE/MSC	Derniers Entretiens recueillis par soeur Marie du Sacré-Coeur.
	(Last Conversations set down by Sister Marie of the Sacred Heart).
G/NPHF	Soeur Geneviève, *Notes préparatoires à l'Histoire d'une Famille.*
	(Sister Geneviève, Preparatory Notes for *The Story of a Family)*.
Ha 98, etc.	*Histoire d'une âme*, édition 1898 (07 = 1907; 53 = 1953).*
	(Story of a Soul, 1898 edition).
IM	*Imitation de Jésus-Christ*.
	(Imitation of Christ).
LC	Lettres des correspondants de Thérèse.
	(Letters from Thérèse's correspondents).

LD	Lettres diverses des correspondants entre eux. (Diverse letters from the correspondents).
LT	Lettres de Thérèse (Letters from Thérèse)
LT 1948	*Lettres de sainte Thérèse de l'Enfant-Jésus*, édition 1948.* (Letters of St. Thérèse of the Child Jesus, 1948 edition).
LTS	Lettres supplémentaires de Thérèse. (Supplementary letters from Therese).
Ms A	Manuscrit autobiographique dédié à Mère Agnès de Jésus (1895).* (Autobiographical manuscript dedicated to Mother Agnes of Jesus, 1895).
Ms B	Lettre à soeur Marie du Sacré-Coeur, manuscript autobiographique (1896).* (Letter to Sister Marie of the Sacred Heart, autobiographical manuscript, 1896).
Ms C	Manuscrit autobiographique dedié a Mère Marie de Gonzague (1897).* (Autobiographical manuscript dedicated to Mother Marie de Gonzague).
Mss I, etc.	Trois volumes du P. François de Sainte-Marie, acompagnant l'édition en fac-similé (1956) des *Manscrits Autobiographiques* (Mss. I, II, III). (Three volumes of P. François de Sainte-Marie, accompanying the facsimile edition (1956) of the Autobiographical Manuscripts).
NPPA	Notes préparatoires au Procès Apostolique. (Preparatory notes for the Apostolic Process).
NPPO	Notes préparatoires au Procès de l'Ordinaire. (Preparatory notes for the Bishop's Process).
OCL	Office Central de Lisieux (maison d'éditions). (Central Office of Lisieux, publishing house).

P   Poésies de sainte Thérèse de l'Enfant-Jésus (num-
                érotage de Mss I).
                (Poems of St. Thérèse of the Child Jesus, according
                to the Mss I numbering).

PA   Procès Apostolique, 1915–1916 (d'après Sum II).
                (Apostolic Process, 1915–1916, according to the
                second volume of the Summary).

PO   Procès de l'Ordinaire, 1910–1911 (ibid.).
                (The Bishop's Process, 1910–1911 (ibid.).

PST   *Le Père de sainte Thérèse de l'Enfant-Jésus* (1953).
                (The Father of Saint Thérèse of the Child Jesus,
                1953).

RP   "Recreations pieuses" de sainte Thérèse de l'Enfant-
                Jésus (numerotation de Mss I).
                ("Pious Recreations" of St. Thérèse of the Child
                Jesus, according to the Mss. I numbering).

VT   *Vie Thérésienne*, Lisieux (revue).
                (Theresian Life, Lisieux).

VTL   *Visage de Thérèse de Lisieux* (1961), en deux
                volumes.*
                (Face of Thérèse of Lisieux (1961), in two volumes).

Works already translated:

1. *"Carnet jaune" de Mère Agnès de Jésus: St. Thérèse of Lisieux, Her Last Conversations*, trans. by John Clarke, O.C.D. (Washington, D.C.: ICS Publications: Institute of Carmelite Studies, 1975), "Yellow Notebook," pp. 35–207.

2. *Conseils et Souvenirs*, 1952: Sister Geneviève of the Holy Face (Céline Martin), *A Memoir of my Sister, St. Thérèse*, authorized translation by the Carmelite Sisters of New York (New York: P.J. Kenedy & Sons, 1959).

3. *Sainte Thérèse de L'Enfant Jésus et de la Sainte-Face, Correspondance Génèrale*, tome I, 1972: *Saint Thérèse of Lisieux, General Correspondence*, volume I, trans. by John Clarke, O.C.D. (Washington, D.C.: ICS Publications, 1982).

4. *Histoire d'une Ame*, edition 1898: *Soeur Thérèse of Lisieux, An Autobiography*, edited by T. N. Taylor (London: Burns & Oates, Ltd., 1912). Also: *Saint Thérèse of Lisieux, The Little Flower of Jesus*, revised translation by Rev. Thomas N. Taylor (New York: P.J. Kenedy & Sons, 1927).

5. *Lettres de sainte Thérèse de l'Enfant-Jésus*, édition 1948: *Collected Letters of Saint Thérèse of Lisieux*, trans. by F. J. Sheed (New York: Sheed & Ward, 1949).

6. *Manuscrit autobiographique dédié à Mère Agnès de Jésus* (1895): *Story of a Soul, The Autobiography of St. Thérèse of Lisieux*, a new translation from the original manuscripts by John Clarke, O.C.D. (Washington, D.C.: ICS Publications, 1972); see Ms. A, pp. 13–182.

7. *Lettre à soeur Marie du Sacré-Coeur, manuscrit autobiographique* (1896): see *Story of a Soul, The Autobiography of St. Thérèse of Lisieux*, Ms. B, pp. 183–200.

8. *Manuscrit autobiographique dédié a Mère Marie de Gonzague* (1897): see *Story of a Soul, The Autobiography of St. Thérèse of Lisieux*, Ms C, pp. 201–259.

9. *Visage de Thérèse de Lisieux* (1961): *Photo Album of St. Thérèse of Lisieux*, trans. by Peter-Thomas Rohrbach, O.C.D. (New York: P.J. Kenedy & Sons, 1962).

PRESENTATION
CONVENTIONAL SIGNS AND GUIDE
FOR USING THIS VOLUME

General Correspondence is presented in two volumes, following a continuous pagination:

Volume I: Introduction. Correspondence from April 4, 1877 to September 24, 1890 (the day Thérèse received the Veil).

Volume II: Correspondence from September 28, 1890 to September 30, 1897 (the day of Thérèse's death). Appendices and Index.

The texts of the letters (LT, LC, LD) are clarified by introductions, captions, and footnotes.

THE TEXTS OF THE LETTERS

1. *Letters from Thérèse* (LT)

The text of Thérèse's letters was transcribed according to the entire content of the autograph. The French editors scrupulously respected her spelling, use of capital letters, and abbreviations. Surprising irregularities resulted from this, but this is to be expected in a critical edition. In cases of doubt (for example, when certain words in the autograph were almost illegible), they gave Thérèse the benefit of the doubt. It was impossible, of course, in a translation to duplicate Thérèse's occasional errors in spelling; however, I did capitalize the words she capitalized, such as Divine, Heavenly, Sun, etc.

The editors applied the same rigor to Thérèse's punctuation, although her use of the "period" and "comma" was difficult to distinguish at times. Her marks of suspension and exclamation were also introduced by them into the printed text. Here, again, it was not possible to observe Thérèse's punctuation, but I did duplicate her marks of suspension and exclamation.

Very frequently when writing, Thérèse emphasized her point by underlining certain words. These underlinings were interpreted in the following way: a single underlining: *italics*; a double underlining: small capitals; a triple underlining: LARGE CAPITALS; anything beyond this: LARGE CAPITALS and a footnote to indicate their exact number.

2. *Letters from correspondents* (LC, LD)

The original text was followed as closely as possible. Since these letters were not the main object of the critical edition, the editors corrected the spelling errors and a *minimum* of the errors in punctuation in order to facilitate the reading.

INTRODUCTIONS

The "introductions," printed in italics, divide the text in a very free manner, making no attempt to point out the minor incidents in the Saint's life but simply its important stages. Volume II deals with:

     5. novitiate
     6. the priorate of Mother Agnes of Jesus
     7. the new priorate of Mother Marie de Gonzague

These "introductions" encourage the reader to make a comparison between the event actually written about in the letters (LT, LC, LD) and the rereading of this same event as it was explained years later by Thérèse in her *Story of a Soul* (Ms. A, B, C). For if the letters by their very nature serve to complete and confirm the *Story of a Soul*, inversely, the *Story of a Soul* is indispensable for completing the letters. (For this reason, at the end of these "introductions" the editors have carefully pointed out the corresponding passage in Ms.

A, B, and C.)

In spite of their appearance, the "introductions" make no attempt to fill in the normal "gaps" in any correspondence. They are simply rough outlines, "guideposts," and they have no other purpose but that of aiding the reader to situate Thérèse's letters within their historical and psychological context, as well as within the context of the Saint's spiritual development.

CAPTIONS AND FOOTNOTES

The "captions" (beneath the heading of some of the letters) and the "footnotes" are mainly historical and documentary in nature. Biographical accounts are rare and not developed at length: a "Biographical Guide For Proper Names" is provided in the Appendix of this volume and completes the information, especially with regard to the letters of St. Thérèse.

The sources, certain or probable, of thoughts expressed by Thérèse were indicated whenever it was possible to trace these sources. The editors were conscious of the fact that St. Teresa of Avila's influence on Thérèse would call for a deeper study, especially since the Carmelite nuns at Lisieux at this time (1888–1897) were very much imbued with St. Teresa's spirit and writings.

As for references to Thérèse's other writings (*Story of a Soul, Poetry*, and so on), only the more apparent similarities are noted. From 1893, especially, the possibilities for cross-references are so frequent that they go beyond the limits required by these notes. For the final six months, references are made in the notes to *Derniers Entretiens (Last Conversations)*. These bring to light the coherence existing between Thérèse's words and her writings.

CONVENTIONAL SIGNS

The following "conventional signs" will aid the reader to know precisely where he is in the correspondence. At the top of each page, along with the date, the reader will see the abbreviations LT and LC. An abbreviation in Roman type corresponds to the letter which appears on the page. Two abbreviations in roman type naturally indicate that there is one or several letters of each category on the page.

The *title* of each letter (bold-faced for LT and *italics* for LC, LD) makes mention of the sender and the recipient. It is sometimes followed by the words: "Fragments" or "Extracts" in parentheses. In the first case, it must be understood that the editors found only an incomplete document but that they cited it integrally. In the second case, *and this has reference to the LD exclusively*, curtailments were made in order to prevent developments which were of no interest for this edition.

The *date*, at the beginning of each letter, sometimes has a question mark. Depending on its position, uncertainty has reference to the day, the month, or the year.

Immediately under the date, the arrow (→) indicates a direct link between two documents. Thus, LT 254 responds to LC 178, which was cited some fifty pages before. The reader may be interested in going back to this document before reading the response, especially when these two documents are far apart.

The words "LT *lost* (or LC) mean that the letter in question has certainly been destroyed by its recipient (P. Pichon, for example), or that letters have disappeared or been destroyed (we often don't know by whom), or that letters have not been found up to this day.

Immediately after the text of the letters, and before the "footnotes," the *source of the document* is indicated (preceded by an asterisk).

J.C.

R.I.P.

The Institute of Carmelite Studies dedicates this volume of Saint Thérèse's writings to our late collaborator and brother, John Clarke, o.c.d.

After completing his translation of all the letters and all the supplementary sections in this book, Father John Clarke died of cancer on February 15, 1985. In spite of our sense of loss, we take consolation from his enduring presence among us in his excellent translations of the works of Saint Thérèse.

FIFTH PERIOD

NOVITIATE

THE HIDDEN YEARS

(September 1890 — February 1893)

THE HIDDEN YEARS

"The desert where God willed that I go to hide myself also . . . ": This is how Carmel appeared to Thérèse as a child (Ms. A, p. 58), and how it revealed itself to her in all its austerity after her Profession.

The large black veil hiding her face from the people on the morning of September 24, 1890, was more than a symbol. Henceforth, very few were those who saw her features again, except her sisters and the Guérins. The human and spiritual destiny of Sister Thérèse of the Child Jesus and of the Holy Face was played out more than ever "in the interior" — of the cloister and her hidden life.

If we confine ourselves to the Story of a Soul, *the thread of events is extremely tenuous for the years 1890-1893, years in which she was perfecting her religious formation in the novitiate, according to the customs of the time. In order that the* Correspondence *may sketch a portrait of Thérèse on the threshold of her twentieth birthday, it is important to present here some biographical data. First, we should place her within her family and Community relationships.*

There was no longer any possible communication with her father, who was in a mental home since February 1889 (LD, August 24, 1891). "Silence settled more and more around the venerated name of him whom we loved. In the Community where, until then, it had enjoyed a kind of prestige, if we pronounced it, this was in a whisper as though it were the name of a man almost in disgrace" (Mother Agnes of

Jesus, Souvenirs intimes, *p. 83).*

Exchanges with her sister Léonie were reduced to the usual visits at the Carmel. There is not a single letter during these three years.[1] *A little older than twenty-seven, Léonie is still in search of a path among "the sandy paths" mentioned by Uncle Guérin (LD, October 15, 1886).*

Thérèse's whole solicitude was centered upon Céline. It bordered on an uneasiness, a fear of losing this other "self," who formed a "single flower" with her (LT 134). It was not because she suspected a premature death for Céline, though this eventuality was not excluded (LT 124, note 1). But was not Céline about "to give herself to a mortal being"? (Ms. A, p. 176.) Her sister's marriage was the only thing Thérèse could not accept (ibid.). This intelligent and vivacious brunette was attractive to young men (LT 130, note 2), and, in spite of her plan for a consecrated life, there was nothing stilted in Céline's conduct. She was at ease with the happy and charming young people around her, among whom weddings followed one after another: four in five years in the Guérin-Maudelonde families (1889–1894). With a mother's instinct rather than that of a sister (Ms. A, p. 176), Thérèse felt that Céline's heart remained disputed territory. This explains in part her apologia *on virginity, her insistence on "Jesus alone," present in the greater part of her letters to Céline.*

Uncle and aunt Guérin's attention was taken up henceforth with the doings of their newlyweds: Jeanne and Francis La Néele (October 1, 1890). Marie Guérin received a confirmation of her own Carmelite vocation on the day of Thérèse's reception of the Véil. However, it was for Céline that Marie Guérin reserved her confidences more and more. Thérèse experienced once again, with regard to the Guérin family, the effacement of her childhood years (Ms. A, p. 82).

Within the Carmel, circumstances set up certain barriers between Thérèse and her two older sisters, Pauline and Marie. In February 1891, a change of work deprived her of the daily contacts with Sister Agnes of Jesus in her office as refectorian. In the following July, Sister Marie of

*the Sacred Heart left the novitiate quarters, her religious
probation being terminated. Thérèse did not seek to compensate for this separation from her "little mothers" of years
gone by (LT 129, note 1; LD, 10-12/September 1891, note
1).*

*On the other hand, she developed a more confiding open-
ness with her mistress in the novitiate: "I was here perhaps
for two years when God brought to an end my trial regarding Sister Marie of the Angels, and I was able to open my
soul to her.... In the end, she really consoled me" (CJ
2.9.2).*

*She clasped, too, "the maternal hand so capable of
leading and consoling us" (LT 129): the hand of her prioress,
Mother Marie de Gonzaque. The prioress was not sparing,
at least on paper, in her expressions of tenderness for her
"little lamb" (LC 143 and 144).*

*Besides her superiors and the chaplain, l'abbé Youf, two
other religious made up the narrow circle of her daily contacts:[2] Sister Saint-Stanislaus, a little bustling and kindly
religious whom Thérèse helped in the sacristy work; Sister
Martha of Jesus, her companion in the novitiate, who was
communicative but not too intelligent, very much attached
to Mother Marie de Gonzague "like a dog to its master"
(Ms. C, p. 236). A postulant, Sister Marie-Madeleine, joined them in July 1892.*

*Such was the context within which the newly-professed
Thérèse was invited to advance "as a strong and vigorous
soul" (LC 144).*

*In the absence of external events, it is possible to adopt
the retreats of October 1891 and 1892 as the decisive steps
in this advance. This period can be organized as follows:*

*1) October 1890–October 1891: a difficult ascent "in the
darkness of the night" (p. 705);*

*2) October 1891–October 1892: a more joyful advance:
"the winter has passed" (p. 736);*

*3) October 1892–February 1893: the descent into the
valley: "Jesus told me to descend" (p. 757).*

A threshold is crossed with the election of Mother Agnes of Jesus as prioress, February 20, 1893.

A more careful examination of the Correspondence, *grouping together thirty-four letters in thirty months, including nineteen from Thérèse, sheds light on these stages.*

---

1. Unless Léonie destroyed these letters; see *Introduction*, p. 82.
2. The novices shared in the Community recreations twice each day.

"In the darkness of the night" (LC 145)
(September 1890 — October 1891)
Age seventeen and eighteen

> *Eighteen letters or notes sketch the outline of the first stage:*
>
> 1) *ten from the hand of Thérèse,* including six to Céline;
> 2) *two notes carrying her signature;*
> 3) five others addressed to her;
> 4) *a fragment reporting one of her conversations.*
>
> *At first, Thérèse appears to us in her freshness as spouse of Jesus: "The heart of my Spouse is mine alone, just as mine is His alone" (LT 122). The example of her married cousins, Francis and Jeanne La Néele, is an incentive for her (Ms. A, p. 168); however, this "delightful heart to heart" (LT 122) is of short duration.*
>
> *The eclipse of the paternal* sun *(see LT 130) is accompanied by a kind of interior eclipse: "Jesus is far off" (LC 143). Sadness invades her at each moment: Is she truly loved by God[1] (Ms. A, p. 169), by this Father, to whom she may henceforth "really say: 'Our Father, who art in heaven'"? (LT 127).*
>
> *Uprooted from "the foreign land" (LT 127), she directs her longings to "our native land" (LT 130), this beautiful heaven which seemed to her within hand's reach on the night of her Profession (Ms. A, p. 167). But here again, the ground is taken from under her feet: Is there really a heaven? She wonders about this at times (Ms. A, p. 173).*
>
> *Her best guide in this trying ascent is Saint John of the Cross, whose spritual works make up her only "spiritual nourishment" (Ms. A, p. 179). The "testament" which she drew out by lot on November 24 sheds light retrospectively on the lesson of the doctor of the nights, in this year of 1891: "My daughter, I leave you my interior annihilation. The soul who wills to possess God totally must renounce all in order to give herself totally to this great God!" (Autograph copy of the note drawn by Thérèse, November 24, 1891.)*
>
> *A real Carmelite, this she was still, and above all through*

her apostolic zeal, which she communicated to Céline. She gets her sister interested in a salvation more difficult than that of Pranzini: the conversion of the ex-Carmelite, Hyacinthe Loyson, "renegade monk," the newspapers said, "our brother," Thérèse said (LT 129, note 6).

Like fire under ashes, the flame burning in her heart begins to dispense light and warmth unobtrusively. The chaplain one day made a reflection about it to Sister Agnes of Jesus. Entering the cloister several times a week to bring Holy Communion to the ailing Mother Geneviève, he observed the young sacristan walking by his side, wearing her large veil: "When I see your sister close to me in the cloister as I carry the Blessed Sacrament, she always reminds me of those blessed candles burning in churches, the sight of which draws one to prayer and recollection." (Mother Agnes of Jesus, NPPA, Reputation for sanctity.)

1. According to the context of this quotation in Ms. A, p. 169, Thérèse went alone to see Mother Geneviève in the infirmary for her customary little visit; this seems to imply a date posterior to September 8, 1890. Usually a novice could not go alone on such visits.

LT 121	**From Thérèse to Sister Marie-Joseph of the Cross.**
September 28, 1890	This correspondent shared the life of Thérèse as a child and young girl for several years: she is
→ LC lost	none other than Marcelline Husé, servant of the Guérins from 1880 to 1889. Internal criticism leads to certain reservations regarding the attribution of this text to Thérèse; see note 3.

J.M.J.T.

Carmelite Monastery,
September 28, '90

Jesus †

Dear Sister,

I was very much touched by your letter, and I thank you for the prayers you offered for me. As for me, I have not forgotten you, and I have recommended all your intentions to God.

Here I am at last all for Jesus; in spite of my unworthiness, He has willed to take me for His little spouse. Now I must give Him proofs of my love, and I count on you, dear Sister, to help me in thanking Our Lord.

Both of us have received great graces, and soon I hope the same bond will unite us forever to Jesus.[1]

I had the happiness of receiving the blessing of the Holy Father for the day of my Profession. The religious who obtained it for me wrote me about how numerous were the enemies of the Church; at Rome, the struggle never ceases for an instant with regard to our Holy Father, the Pope. It is sad.[2]

How good it is to be a religious in order to pray and to appease God's justice; yes, the mission which is entrusted to us is very beautiful, and eternity will not be long enough to thank Our Lord for the lot He has given us.[3]

Dear Sister, I recommend to your prayers my dear Father, so tried by the cross and so admirable in his resignation. I dare, also, to recommend myself to the prayers of your holy Community.

Please believe, dear Sister, in the entire religious affection of her who is so happy to call herself,

Your little Sister,
Thérèse of the Child Jesus
rel. carm. ind.[4]

*   Autograph
1. Having entered the Benedictines at Bayeux, July 1889, Sister Marie-Joseph made Profession, August 10, 1892.
2. See LC 134.

3. The vocabulary of this paragraph is unusual for Thérèse. The style of the letter as a whole is that of Sister Agnes of Jesus. In this instance, it is not impossible that Thérèse had solicited the help of her sister, even "a little rough draft"; see LT 70 and 112.

4. According to the testimony of Sister Marie-Joseph, Thérèse corresponded with her on other occasions (before or after this date): "After the year 1889, I no longer had any contacts with the Servant of God, except an exchange of some letters." (PA, 49.) The present autograph alone has been preserved.

LT 122	**From Thérèse to Céline.**
October 14, 1890	The second centenary of Blessed Margaret Mary's death, October 17, 1890, attracted crowds to Paray-le-Monial. Léonie, whose spiritual home was still the Visitation, was eager to share in the celebrations. Céline went there not because of any personal attraction but for Léonie's sake.

J.M.J.T.

Jesus †   October 14, '90

Dear Céline,

I do not want to allow Marie's letter to leave without adding to it a note for you. Our dear Mother is allowing me to come make my prayer with you.... Céline, is this not what we are *always* doing together?...

Dear Céline, I *always* have the same thing to say to you. Ah! Let us pray for priests;[1] each day shows how few the friends of Jesus are.... It seems to me this is what He must feel the most, ingratitude, especially when seeing souls who are consecrated to Him giving to others a heart that belongs to Him in so absolute a way.... Céline, let us make of our heart a little garden of delights where Jesus may come to rest...let us plant only lilies in our garden, yes, lilies, and let us allow no other flowers, for other flowers can be cultivated by other souls, but it is virgins alone who can give lilies to Jesus....

"Virginity is a profound silence from all cares of this earth,"[2] not

only from useless cares but from *all cares*.... To be virgin we must
think only of the Spouse, who allows nothing around Him that is
not virgin "since He willed to be born of a virgin mother, to have
a virgin precursor, a virgin foster-father, a virgin favorite, and finally
a virgin tomb."[3] He wants also a little virgin spouse, His Céline?...
It is said: "Each one naturally loves his native land, and since the
native land of Jesus is the Virgin of virgins and since Jesus was born
by His will of a Lily, He loves to find Himself in virgin hearts."[4]
And I seem to be forgetting your trip...no, my heart is following
you there. I understand all you are experiencing...I understand
all... All passes away. The trip to Rome with its heartrendings[5] is
past...our life of years gone by is past... *Death* will pass also, and
then we shall enjoy life not for centuries, but millions of years will
pass for us like a day, and other millions of years will follow them
filled with repose and happiness.[6]...Céline....

Pray to the Sacred Heart; you know that I myself do not see the
Sacred Heart as everybody else.[7] I think that the Heart of my Spouse
is mine alone, just as mine is His alone,[8] and I speak to Him then
in the solitude of this delightful heart to heart, while waiting to contemplate Him one day face to face...

Do not forget your Thérèse over there; whisper only her name,
and Jesus will understand. So many graces are attached there,
especially for a heart that is suffering. ...I would really like to write
to Léonie, but this is impossible. I do not even have time to read
this over. Tell her how much I think of her, etc., etc. I am sure the
Sacred Heart will give her many graces, etc., etc. Tell her all, you
understand....

Your Thérèse of the Child Jesus of the Holy Face
rel. carm. ind.

* Autograph
1. On the matter of prayer for priests, see LT 94, note 7.
2. The first part of this quotation was placed in parentheses instead of
   quotation marks. See *Introduction*. The quotation has not been
   identified.
3. An almost identical enumeration appears in a book of Meditations
   of the time: *L'homme d'oraison, ses lectures spirituelles pendant tout
   le cours de l'année ou Dévotion envers Notre Seigneur Jésus-Christ,*

souverainement bon, souverainement grand, souverainement saint,
by Jacques Nouet, S.J. (Thibaud-Landroit, Clermont-Ferrand, 1837,
ten books in five volumes; two copies in the library of the Lisieux
Carmel, with many other works by the same author.) However, it is
doubtful whether Thérèse is referring to P. Nouet here, for the
preceding quotation (note 2) does not appear in this author, and the
following one is formulated by him in a notably different manner.
In fact, this was a current theme in the preaching of the time; see l'abbé
Youf, *Sermons*, book 4, p. 404, manuscript text, undated; P. Lemonnier, *Retreat* of 1894, sixth day, notes of Sister Marie of St. Joseph,
p. 15; etc. We recognize in it an echo of the preaching of St. Am-
brose, St. Bernard, Bossuet, on Christian Virginity.

4. A similar thought in P. Nouet, op. cit., t. 13, p. 13. See also Leo
   the Great: "Christ chose to be born of a virgin," quoted in the sixth
   lesson of the Divine Office, October 12, 1890, second Sunday of October, feast of the *Maternity of the Virgin Mary*. Thérèse's expression: "It is said," may be a reference to an instruction in a retreat.
   In 1890, the retreat was preached by P. Godefroid Madelaine,
   Premonstratensian, future sponsor of the *Story of a Soul*. We do not
   have any notes from this retreat, and we do not know its exact date.
   See following letter, note 1.

5. The heartrending experiences at the audience with Leo XIII; see pp.
   350ff.

6. See Arminjon, *Fin du monde présent et mystères de la vie future*, ed.
   1882, p. 316.

7. "Crowned with thorns, with a big cross set up in the center," as Sister
   Marie of the Sacred Heart wrote to Céline on October 13, quoting
   P. Pichon.

8. See Canticle of Canticles 2:16.

LD   *From Marie Guérin to Céline.   (Extracts.)*
October 15, 1890

I was at the Carmel yesterday,[1] and Thérèse began her visit by
scolding me, telling me that I was not sufficiently detached. She does
not understand that I am sad at having given you up for five days;[2]
however, I pointed out to her that I was sad because I knew you
were unhappy. She answered that you were much more detached than
I am and that you were not as sad as all that. Then I told her she

was heartless, and she closed the grille in my face,[3] opening it again after a minute.

Both of us had a very nice visit for three quarters of an hour; Mother Marie de Gonzague was unable to come. Thérèse told me something that I had not dared tell you in my last letters, believing this would annoy you. She said, as I do also, that certainly there was not another person on the pilgrimage who made it with as much merit as you.[4] ... Thérèse told me yesterday that surely you will receive some consolations from the Sacred Heart just as the Blessed Virgin gave you some at the Grotto. You had not told me that you received consolations at Lourdes;[5] you tell me absolutely nothing but your sorrows, so I am always sad,[6] but it is so sweet for me to share in the sorrows of my *Mimi.*

Your little sister who loves you always more and more,
Marie

* Autograph
1. To wish Thérèse a happy feast. Must we deduce from this that the Community retreat was over? Visits were generally prohibited during a retreat. Most frequently at this time, the retreat immediately preceded October 15. For the year 1890, the monastery chronicle simply notes: "The preached retreat was conducted by R. P. Godefroid, Premonstratensian" (Foundation III, p. 173).
2. A statement to be interpreted in the wide sense. According to ChrIG, p. 39, the departure took place on October 8, and the date of return was not specified. In the present letter, Marie feels she is "not half way through her days of exile." It seems that Céline and Léonie had left Paray-le-Monial on the 16th in order to avoid the crowds of the 17th.
3. This is the inside shutter which doubled the grille, the outside grille being stationary.
4. Because Céline went there reluctantly; see her letter of October 6 to Jeanne La Néele: "I tell you I do not like pilgrimages at all; I find it very difficult to be recollected in them. I do not like crowds for praying; I like solitude."
5. The preceding May; see LT 106.
6. The letters of Marie Guérin to Céline were sentimental and tearful at this time.

LT 123   **From Thérèse to Mme. Guérin**
October 15, 1890

J.M.J.T.

Jesus †   October 15, 1890

Dear Aunt,

I was much touched by all you sent me for my feast day, and I do not know how to thank you or where to begin.

First, dear little Aunt, you sent me your charming Marie,[1] who wished me a happy feast in the name of all those I love.

The two pretty pots of flowers offered by my two dear little sisters pleased me very much; they are placed near the little Jesus, and each hour of the day, they beg for my two little sisters as many graces and blessings as each branch contains little flowers.

Finally, dear little Aunt, your delicious cakes came to crown the feast and to fill your little Thérèse's heart with gratitude to you who are giving all these treats.

I am touched all the more because I know, dear little Aunt, how ill you are, and in spite of this, you are still thinking of your little Thérèse. But if you are thinking of her, she is thinking, too, very often of you, and she does not cease praying to God so that He may return a hundredfold to you all you are doing for us. I pray also for my dear little Jeanne that God may make her happy insofar as one can be happy on this earth. I beg Him to console you for the great void that this dear sister's departure must cause.[2] I am not forgetting dear Uncle either, and I beg you to hug him tightly for me.

I am leaving you, dear little Aunt, or rather I am leaving my pen which is so poorly carrying out the mission entrusted it by my heart; as for my heart, it is not separated from you for one moment.

Your little daughter,
Sister Thérèse of the Child Jesus
rel. carm. ind.

*   Autograph.
1.   See preceding LD.

2. Since her marriage to Dr. La Néele, October 1, Jeanne was living at Caen, some fifty kilometers from Lisieux.

LT 124   **From Thérèse to Céline.**

October 20, 1890

J.M.J.T.

Jesus †　　　　　　　　　　　　　　　　　　October 20, 1890

Dear Céline,

Your Thérèse comes to wish you a happy feast!... For a long time she has been thinking of it, so this year she will not be the last. Céline, this is perhaps the last time your feast will be celebrated on earth![1]... Perhaps!... What a sweet hope...next year the little *Céline flower*, unknown on earth, will perhaps be placed upon the Heart of the divine Lamb. But the enraptured eyes of the angels will then contemplate, instead of a poor little flower without beauty, a lily of dazzling whiteness!... Céline, life is very mysterious; we know nothing...we see nothing...and yet Jesus has already revealed to our souls what the eye of man has not seen!... Yes, our heart has a presentiment of what the heart would be unable to understand[2] since at times we are without *any thoughts* to express something ineffable which we feel in our soul!...

Céline, I am sending you *two Célines*[3] for your feast; you will understand their language.... One stem carries them, one same sun made them grow together, the same ray made them bloom, and undoubtedly the same day will see them die!...

The eyes of creatures do not dream of looking at a little *Céline-flower*, and yet its white corolla is filled with mystery. It carries in its heart a great number of other flowers, no doubt the children of *its soul* (souls), and so its white calyx is red on the inside, one would say purpled with its own blood!...

Céline...The sun and the rain can fall upon this unknown flower without wilting it! No one dreams of plucking it!... But is it not virgin too?... Yes, since Jesus alone has seen it, since it is He who has created it for Himself alone!... Oh! then, it is more blessed than the brilliant rose that is not for Jesus alone!...

Céline, I am wishing you a happy feast in an uncommon way, one may say; but you will understand the incoherent words of your Thérèse!...

Céline, it seems to me that God has no need of *years* to carry out His work of love in a soul,[4] a ray from His Heart can in one instant make His flower bloom for eternity!...

Your Thérèse of the Child Jesus
and of the Holy Face
rel. carm. ind.

* Autograph.

1. Céline was suffering from heart trouble (see LT 104, note 2) which became more serious in the following months. In March 1891, Mme. Guérin wrote: "This poor Céline was very sick yesterday at your home.... We decided now not to allow her to go so frequently to see her father, and she was the first to agree to this. She is getting so emotional that her health is really being affected. I think it is time to remedy this" (to Mme. La Néele, March 18, 1891). And again: "I am really worried about all these little setbacks she is having" (to the same, March 20, 1891). "The problems were such that Dr. La Néele did not want to take sole responsibility for his diagnosis, and he had Dr. Notta come, who prescribed a strong treatment and recommended especially the avoidance of emotional upsets" (Note of Sister Geneviéve, September 19, 1940).

2. See I Corinthians 2:9.

3. Two flowers of the common aster (the "Céline-flower," see LT 98, note 7), carried on one stem. They are still pinned to the word "Jesus," on the autograph.

4. The same thought in LT 114, suggested by the same eventuality: Céline's premature death. This hope of seeing love "supplying for a long life" (LT 114) was valid especially for Thérèse herself. We know, through later confidences (CJ 31.8.9 and its parallel in NV 31.8.2), how much she was urged on, in 1890-1891 probably, by this text read in St. John of the Cross: "It is vital for a person to make acts of love in this life so that in being perfected in a short time, he may not be detained long, either here on earth or in the next life, before seeing God." *Living Flame of Love*, stanza I, explanation of verse 6. See *The Collected Works of St. John of the Cross*, trans. Kieran

Kavanaugh, O.C.D., and Otilio Rodriguez, O.C.D., (Washington, D.C.: ICS Publications, Institute of Carmelite Studies, 1973), p. 594.

LT 125   **From Thérèse to Mme. Guérin**
November 17, 1890

J.M.J.T.

Jesus †   Carmel, November 17, '90

Dear Aunt,

With what joy I come to wish you a happy feast!... For a long time I have been thinking of this beautiful day, and I am delighted to come to dear Aunt to tell her how much her last, her littlest daughter loves her. In everything she wants to be the last and the littlest, but in affection and tenderness never will she allow herself to be surpassed by her elder sisters.... And, then, is it not a Benjamin's right to love more than others?...

How many memories for me there are in this date of November 19. For a long time in advance I used to take delight in it, first, because this date was dear Aunt's feast day, and also because of the nice treats I was given on this day. Now time has passed by, the little birds have grown, they have spread their wings and have flown from the very sweet nest of their childhood. But, dear little Aunt, while I was growing up, your little daughter's heart was growing also in tenderness for you, and now especially it understands all it owes you.... To pay my debt I have only one means. Being very poor and having as my spouse a powerful and very rich King, I entrust Him with pouring out in profusion on dear Aunt the treasures of His love and thus making return to her for all the motherly acts of kindness with which she surrounded my childhood.

Dear Aunt, I am not saying *adieu* to you, for I count on remaining all day with you, and I hope you will divine your little daughter's heart.

Thérèse of the Child Jesus
rel. carm. ind.

* Autograph.

LC 143 *From Mother Marie de Gonzague to Thérèse*
End of 1890— Uncertain date; see notes 1 and 2
summer 1891 (?)
→ LT lost

† J.M.J.T. I am really making my dear little lamb[1] wait to give it a poor little drop of milk without any sugar, but I know my child is generous and that she is looking only for the Cross of her Beloved, who was abandoned by all.

Oh, beloved child, I am not abandoning you in my heart, for you are really deep within it. We are suffering, Jesus is far off, but nevertheless how close I see Him to the heart of His spouse,[2] and all the closer, for she is living totally in this infinite Love....

How *little* creatures have to say, is this not true, child, their words are insipid; the silence of Jesus, while making us suffer, speaks so much more.... Let us think of heaven, there only we shall taste joy; the earth is a desert which was not made to delight the exiled soul. We need the thought of the homeland, we who are seeking only the truth!...and want only Jesus. At times the Beloved leads us to Tabor but more frequently to Calvary; it is there He gave us to His Mother as her children.[3]

Yes, spouse of Jesus and this up to death and for eternity, follow the Lamb, singing the canticle which virgins *alone* will have the right to sing.[4]

I envy your lot, dear child....

* Autograph.
1. Recourse to a written communication proves that Mother Marie de Gonzague was on retreat or sick. In the first instance, this note could have been written in November 1890, the usual time of her retreat (however, there is no date indicated for her retreat in 1890); in the second instance, the note could have been written during her illness of June-July 1891; see LT 129.
2. The word "spouse" permits us to place the note after Thérèse's Profession date (September 8, 1890). Would the next to the last paragraph suggest that this event was still recent?

3. See John 19:27.
4. See Apocalypse 14:3-4.

LC 144   *From Mother Marie de Gonzague to Thérèse*
End of 1890-   This note appears to be contemporaneous
summer of   with the preceding.
1891 (?)

→ LT lost

†J.M.J.T.

Dear little Lamb,

How I love the suffering of my dear daughter, for this is the way the Beloved treats His privileged ones. Sugar is good for children, but we are now at port,[1] and we must walk with a strong and vigorous soul.

I do not believe my little lamb is without faults, far from it; I know very well that she has her failings, and these are what make our life a meritorious life, an apostolic life, because it is the victories won over our faults that obtain all we desire!!! souls, souls for Jesus!! A soul is so beautiful, dear child. Ah! if we could only understand its grandeur in God's plan at the moment of its creation and in its end also, redeemed as it is at the price of all the blood of a God! What mercy.... Let us love Jesus, child of His tenderness, let us live by love in order to die from love. Since our Holy Mother had this desire,[2] we can walk in our Mother's footsteps! We shall love so much in heaven, let us begin our heaven here below.... This earth is not for the soul who has God as Spouse. Alas! our nature attaches us always to this life's material things, but let us cut the thread still holding us back and fly to Him who has given us so much; it does not matter what we shall offer Him, for His gifts will form our offerings since we possess nothing whatsoever.

How good it is to enjoy the absence of joys, oh, dear child. In these privations you will discover a gold mine that you will increase a hundredfold. Do not be disturbed by the prayer of St. Peter.[3] This great apostle, who nevertheless loved His divine Master very much, fell asleep near Him at the moment of our Jesus' agony[4] in the sorrowful garden where He was sweating blood and water because of His terrible grief at the sight of the bitter chalice accepted even to the last dregs for our souls!!! I do not know what I have written on this sheet of paper, dear child; I have lost track of what I was saying, and it is late.

I bless you in the Heart of Jesus; let us suffer together in order to rejoice together....

   *   Autograph.
   1. When making her Profession, Thérèse definitively "cast anchor" in Carmel.
   2. Possible reference to St. Teresa of Avila's poem; *I die because I cannot die*. On the death of love, see DE, pp. 432-433, note 7.
   3. Thérèse used to sleep during her prayer (like St. Peter during the agony of Jesus in the garden). This drowsiness, due to insufficient sleep because of the Carmelite Rule, accompanied her throughout her religious life; see Ms. A, p. 165. The chaplain, l'abbé Youf, was not as indulgent with her as was the prioress regarding such failings; see LT 112, note 3.
   4. See Matthew 26:40.

LC 145	*From Sister Marie of the Angels to Thérèse*
Autumn 1890 or 1891 (?) → LT lost	Uncertain date; see notes 1 and 3. This note is the last of the eight notes from Sister Marie of the Angels that have been preserved.

J.M.J.T.!

Dear little Benjamin,

I just read your lines[1] which tell me that your soul is more and more dear to Jesus!... You will never be able to thank Him enough, dear little child, for the graces He is giving you, for , believe your poor little Mistress, your way is very pleasing to your Beloved; it is much more enviable than every other way of joy and consolation. Jesus is doing His share; He is taking all for Himself because He knows that His little child is generous and He knows that He can act freely with her without any fear that she may leave Him and make even the smallest complaint to Him!. . . Let Him do all He wills with His little grain of sand, and do not doubt Him. You are winning for Him, each day and each hour of the day, many souls who quench His thirst and answer His *sitio* on Calvary![2] Adore this thirst of your Spouse,[3] honor it especially by thinking of it at each moment and by offering your entire being to Jesus for the salvation of souls that have cost Him so dearly! It is necessary that they cost you dearly too, for the redemption of a soul can be brought about only through suffering and sacrifice. Make yourself more and more a little victim, the holocaust of Jesus, and without your seeing them, many souls will owe their heaven to you and you will be in this way a real Carmelite[4] in the hiddenness of the desert, in the darkness of the night, and in the bitterness of the exile! Courage, confidence, Jesus is pleased, He loves you, all goes well, and your crown is being made each day.

Your poor little Mistress, who is carrying you in her heart and who wants you to be a great saint.[5]

Sister Marie of the Angels

* Autograph.

1. This response was motivated either by the retreat of the mistress of novices (there are no indications of the date for any retreat of Sister Marie of the Angels), or by Thérèse's retreat; in the latter instance, this note would have to be put ahead to September 1891.

2. See John 19:28; and LT 141, note 15.

3. Thérèse is then "spouse" (professed)? The note would be written, then, after September 8, 1890.

4. See prayer suggested by Thérèse to Sister Marie-Madeleine in 1894: "Saint Teresa, my Mother, teach me how to save souls in order that I may become a real Carmelite." (Notebook written by Thérèse in view of her companion's Profession, November 20, 1894.)

5. A desire which confirms Thérèse in her own aspirations; see LT 107, note 8 and at the end.

LC 146 *From P. Pichon to Thérèse.*
February 16, 1891
→ LT lost

† Hôtel-Dieu
February 16, '91

My dear and blessed Child
in Jesus Christ,

How I bless this *grippe* which, when confining me to a hospital room, finally obtains for me the happiness of answering you! Thanks to the good Master for not extending any longer this long Lent of my pen![1]

Oh! yes! the alliance is concluded and it will be eternal. You have all the rights, all the privileges of a real spouse. My congratulations for your honeymoon trip to Calvary![2] Were you not very much spoiled by receiving the Holy Father's blessing?... Oh! you were spoiled in so many ways. I was deeply moved when seeing your crown of white roses blessed by the venerable Patriarch and placed on his white head.[3]

What gives prestige to your Profession is the seal of the Cross. Your sisters can envy you this and the elect of heaven are jealous because of it.

Jesus has given you his Childhood and His Passion. How fortunate you are! What an incomparable dowry![4] Make the child in the crib smile, and console the Crucified on Calvary. Did the Blessed Virgin have a more beautiful mission?

If ever I wept over my exile and suffered from these fifteen hundred leagues of the Atlantic, it was on September 8. But in spite of everything I was close to you, and no one was closer to you than I. And I offered you to Jesus in the happiness of my heart.

How I congratulate you for seeking and finding your happiness in the bitterness of your divine Spouse.

Jesus enjoyed Himself to the full on September 24 by having you drink His bitter gall.[5] How good it is to console Him at your own expense!

Yes, yes, may the desire of saving souls and the thirst of being an apostle by aiding apostles increase and develop more and more in your heart. If you only knew how my Canadian apostolate counts on you and depends on your prayers, your tears, your sacrifices!

I understand the silence of your soul. I see the depths of your heart. I can read and read again your unexpressed thoughts.

When advancing toward heaven, you will see better and better that to suffer is to love and to love is to suffer! Listen to Jesus when He reveals this admirable secret to you.

Keep calm and serene in your whole exterior even when your interior is tossed by the tempest. This is a holy hypocrisy.

You are blessed, dear little Lamb of God, at no longer finding any pleasure outside of Jesus. Jesus alone! What riches!

Do not ask martyrdom for yourself without asking it for me. This would be selfish. In the meanwhile, live the martyrdom of the heart,[6] the daily martyrdom of pinpricks.

Let us feel our nothingness and rejoice in being only a poor little nothing; this is a great grace. Profit from it!

This ambition for a more exiled exile,[7] I will pray to Our Lord about it. Before answering you on the matter, I must pray. I bless you from my heart.

Almire Pichon

*　Autograph.

1. The last letter from P. Pichon to Thérèse goes back five months (August 29, 1890). Had he kept the silence of Lent, which began on February 11, his letter would have been put off until March 29 (Easter).

2. Thérèse's retreat in preparation for her Profession; see LT 110, 112, 115.

3. See LD, September 5, 1890; and the talk given by Mother Marie de Gonzague on the morning of the Profession: "Come, crown your head with this crown which is so precious in your eyes. . .it was blessed and rested on the white head of your good and venerable Father."

4. A reference to the symbolic invitation composed by Thérèse before her reception of the Veil; see LT 118, note 2, end.

5. Because of the absence of M. Martin, her father; see LT 120.

6. See the prayer of Thérèse, September 8: "Jesus, may I die a martyr for You, martyrdom of the heart or the body, or rather both of them" (*Billet de Profession*, Ms. A, p. 275).

7. A departure for the Sáigon Carmel, envisaged very early by Thérèse:

Ever since my entrance into the holy ark," she wrote in Ms. C, p. 216. P. Pichon gave no answer to this desire, repeated in 1893; see LC 157.

LT 126   **From Thérèse to Céline.**
April 3, 1891

J.M.J.T.

Jesus †   April 3, 1891

Dear little Céline,

We saw Marguerite M.[1] this afternoon. I do not have time to speak to you in detail about this visit, and I cannot tell you the good it did to my soul.... Ah, Céline, how blessed we are for having been chosen by the Spouse of Virgins!... Marguerite confided to us intimate secrets that she tells no one. We really must pray for her, for she is exposed to danger.... She says that no book does her any good. I thought that the mysteries of the future life[2] would do her some good and would strengthen her faith which, alas, is really endangered!... She told us she could read books without her husband's knowing it.

You should give her that book, telling her that we thought it would interest her, but to begin it only at the third chapter where there is a little holy picture, because the first three chapters would have little interest for her. I believe it would be better if you did not seem to be acquainted with this book and to be simply carrying out a request, for she would be embarrassed if she knew we had spoken one word of her confidences. We would prefer that Mme. Maudelonde and Aunt do not know that we are lending this book to Marguerite. However, do the best you can, and tell her to keep it as long as she wants.... If you cannot give it to her without being seen, it would perhaps be better to do nothing; try at least to speak to her about it. As for myself, I have the greatest desire[3] that she read a book in which she will really find the answer to many doubts![4]... I believe this will be a work very pleasing to God. He gave this idea to me, but you know Thérèse can do nothing without Céline; the two are needed to do a complete work, so it is up to Céline to finish what Thérèse has begun!... Céline...if you only knew how I love you and how my love for you is pure!...

Dear Céline, your little Thérèse remains always with you since you are in her heart, and you are half her heart....

> Thérèse of the Child Jesus of the Holy Face
> rel. carm. ind.

*   Autograph.
1. Marguerite-Marie Maudelonde, niece of Mme. Guérin, married eighteen months to René Tostain. The latter while giving proof of a great moral rectitude, said he was an atheist. Thérèse prayed for him up to her last months, offering "especially" for him her trial against faith; see CJ 2.9.7.
2. Arminjon's Work; see LC 86, note 1.
3. In her hurry, Thérèse wrote *"le le plus desir"* corrected to *"le plus grand desir"* in CE II, p. 83.
4. In 1898, the *Story of a Soul* provided something better than an answer to Marguerite-Marie Tostain: "You recall that a few days after Thérèse's death I wrote you that I reached a point of doubting the existence of a second life? Since then I doubted even more, I doubted *everything*. Well! the life of Sister Thérèse has done me much good. She, too, suffered as I do, but she did not reason it out; she submitted to the trial God was sending her by means of this temptation. And I can do as she did; instead of thinking and losing myself in suppositions of all kinds, I can also think that if the faith God placed in us appears to be darkened at times, this is a trial to which I must submit while continuing to act as though I had before my eyes a dazzling light" (to Mother Agnes of Jesus, November 18, 1898).

LT 127   From Thérèse to Céline.
April 26, 1891

J.M.J.T.

Jesus †   Carmel, April 26, '91

Dear Céline,

For the fourth time Thérèse is coming from the solitude of Carmel
to wish you a happy birthday.... Oh! how these wishes little resemble those of the world,... It is not health, happiness, fortune, glory,
etc., that Thérèse desires for her Céline; oh, no, it is exile; our heart
is there where our treasure is,[1] and our treasure is up above in the
homeland where Jesus prepares a place[2] near Himself. I say *one place*
and not places, for no doubt the same throne is reserved to those
who on earth have always been only one soul.... Together we grew
up; together Jesus instructed us in His secrets,[3] sublime secrets that
He hides from the mighty and reveals to the little ones;[4] together
we suffered at *Rome*. Our hearts were closely united then, and life
on earth might have been the ideal of happiness if Jesus had not
come to make our bonds even tighter. Yes, by separating us, He has
united us in a way unknown up to that time to my soul, for since
that moment I can desire nothing for myself alone but for us both....
Ah, Céline!... Three years ago[5] our souls had not yet been broken;
happiness was still possible for us on earth, but Jesus cast a glance
of love on us, a glance veiled in tears, and this glance has become
for us an ocean of suffering, but also an ocean of graces and love.
He took from us the one whom we loved with so much tenderness,
in a way still more painful than when He had taken from us our
dear Mother in the springtime of our life. But was it not so that we
could truly say' "Our Father, who art in heaven"? Oh! how consoling are these words, what infinite horizons they open to our
eyes.... Céline, the foreign land has for us only wild plants and
thorns,[6] but is this not the portion it has given to our divine Spouse?
Oh! how beautiful for us too is this portion that is ours, and who
will tell us what eternity reserves for us?... Dear Céline, you who
used to ask me so many questions when we were little,[7] I wonder
how it happened that you had never asked me this question: "Why

did God not create me an angel?'' Ah, Céline, I shall tell you what I think. If Jesus did not create you an angel in heaven, it is because He wants you to be an angel on earth; yes, Jesus wants to have His heavenly court here below just as up above! He wants angel-martyrs, He wants angel-apostles, and He has created a little unknown flower,[8] who is named Céline, with this intention in mind. He wills that His little flower save souls for Him; for this, He wills only one thing: that His flower *look at* Him while suffering her martyrdom.... And it is this mysterious look exchanged between Jesus and His little flower that will effect marvels and will give Jesus a multitude of other flowers (above all, a certain Lily faded and withered,[9] which He will have to change into a rose of love and repentance!)...

Dear Céline, do not be vexed if I tell you that up above we would have the same place, for, do you not see, I think that a poor little daisy can really grow in the same soil as a beautiful lily dazzling in its whiteness, or, again, a little pearl can be mounted by the side of a diamond and borrow its brilliance from it!...

Oh! Céline, let us love Jesus to infinity, and from our two hearts let us make only one so that it may be greater in love!...

Céline, I shall never come to an end with you; understand all I would like to tell you for your twenty-two years!...

Your little sister who is only one with you....

(Do you know that we two are now forty years old. It is not surprising that we have already experienced so many things. What do you think of that?)

Thérèse of the Child of Jesus of the Holy Face
nov. carm. ind.[10]

---

* Autograph.
1. See Matthew 6:21
2. See John 14:2.
3. Recalling their intimacy in 1887; on the word "together," see vol. I, p. 263, note 1.
4. See Matthew 11:25.
5. The alteration "three" which we read on the autograph is of doubtful origin; in any case, the first writing "four years" harmonizes with the context, for it was in 1887 that the life of the two sisters was one of *"ideal happiness"* (Ms. A, p. 106).
6. See Genesis 3:18.

7. Thérèse mentions one of these questions in Ms. A, p. 27.
8. Sister Agnes of Jesus wrote the following day to Céline: "Your heart is like a little consecrated flower." She develops the allegory: sap, perfume, corolla, etc. We are not sure if either is borrowing from the other. Sister Marie of the Sacred Heart's letter for this same birthday is of a totally different inspiration.
9. Père Hyacinthe Loyson, concerning whom Thérèse writes at length in her next letter (LT 129).
10. Distracted, Thérèse wrote "novice" instead of "religious" in her signature.

LC 147   *From Brother Simeon to Thérèse.*
June 12, 1891
→ LT lost

J.M.J.

College Français
Saint-Joseph   June 12, 1891
des
Frères des Ecoles Chrétiennes
Place d'Espagne
ROME

Dear Sister,

I am informing Madame, your venerable Superior, that I am sending her some relics[1] today, not many, but with a real hope of being able to obtain others. I did not forget that, in pleasing your venerable Mother, I was pleasing you, too, love for you both sustained my efforts.

You will see by the authentic documents that there is one which has come from Parma. Today, it is very difficult to obtain these holy and venerable remains of the Servants of God. The relics of the true Cross are given only to bishops. Among my personal relics, I found one of St. Teresa, Sister's patroness; I willingly deprive myself of it for you. You will pray a little for a certain Sister who is in need of prayers.

I am saddened by the continued painful condition of your very worthy and venerable father.[2] God is reserving for him a great crown in which you will be a beautiful little flower, I trust.

Pray and have the other Sisters pray for me, dear Sister, and accept my humble greetings in Jesus, Mary, and Joseph.

Brother Simeon

* Autograph.

1. The other letter from Brother Simeon was not preserved. In 1891 the third centenary of the death of St. Aloysius Gonzaga was being celebrated, and Thérèse's request was no doubt made in order to enhance the feast day of Mother Marie de Gonzague, June 21.

2. Sister Geneviève's (Céline) notebooks have not preserved a single detail on M. Martin's state of health in 1891. We encounter details only rarely in the correspondence; see LT 130 and LD, August 24, 1891. Céline and Léonie paid a visit to their father at *Bon Sauveur* at Caen on June 27, before their vacation at La Musse (according to a letter from Mme. Guérin to Jeanne, August 26, 1891).

LT 128   **From Thérèse to Sister Marie of the Sacred Heart.**

July 5, 1891   Inscription in pencil on the back of a picture in lace entitled: *Jesus' Cradle* or the *Joyful Stabat Mater in Contemplation*.

Souvenir offered to my dear Sister on the feast day of the Precious Blood[1] for her departure from the novitiate.

Sister Thérèse of the Child Jesus of
the Holy Face
rel. carm. ind.

* Autograph.

1. The feast of the Precious Blood was celebrated on the first Sunday in July; in 1891, Sunday, July 5. This is the date on a holy picture given in exchange by Sister Marie of the Sacred Heart to Thérèse.

LT 129   **From Thérèse to Céline.**

July 8, 1891   The Guérin family was spending six weeks on
→ LC lost   vacation at La Musse (June 29 — August 13, according to ChrIG, p. 39). Léonie and Céline
joined them.

J.M.J.T.

Jesus †   July 8, 1891

Dear Céline,

Your short note spoke volumes to my soul;[1] it was for me like
a faithful echo repeating all my own thoughts....

Our dear mother is still very sick; it is sad to see those whom we
love[2] suffering in this way. However, do not be too grieved; though
Jesus intends to enjoy in heaven our dear Mother's presence, He
will be unable to refuse to leave on earth her whose maternal hand
can lead and console us so well in the exile of life.[3]... Oh! what
an exile it is, the exile of earth, especially during these hours when
everything seems to abandon us.... But it is then that it is precious,
it is then that the day of salvation dawns;[4] yes, dear Céline, suffering alone can give birth to souls for Jesus.... Is it surprising that
we are so favored, we whose only desire is to save a soul that seems
to be lost forever?[5]... The details interested me very much,[6] while
making my heart beat very fast.... But I shall give you some other
details that are not any more consoling. The unfortunate prodigal
went to Coutances where he started over again the conferences given
at Caen. It appears he intends to travel throughout France in this
way.... Céline.... And with all this, they add that it is easy to see
that *remorse* is gnawing at him. He goes into the churches with a
huge Crucifix, and he seems to be making great acts of adoration....
His wife follows him everywhere. Dear Céline, he is really culpable,
more culpable than any other sinner ever was who was converted.
But cannot Jesus do once what He has not yet ever done? And if
He were not to desire it, would He have placed in the heart of His
poor little spouses a desire that He could not realize?... No, it is
certain that He desires more than we do to bring back this poor stray
sheep to the fold. A day will come when He will open his eyes, and

then who knows whether France will not be traversed by him with a totally different goal from the one he has in mind now? Let us not grow tired of prayer; confidence works miracles. And Jesus said to Blessed Margaret Mary: *"One just soul* has so much power over my Heart that it can obtain pardon for a thousand *criminals."*[7] No one knows if one is just or sinful,[8] but, Céline, Jesus gives us the grace of feeling at the bottom of our heart that we would prefer to die rather than to offend Him; and then it is not our merits but those of our Spouse, which are *ours*, that we offer to Our Father who is in heaven, in order that our brother, a son of the Blessed Virgin, return vanquished to throw himself beneath the mantle of the most merciful of Mothers....

Dear Céline, I am obliged to end; divine the rest, there remain *volumes* to be divined!...

Kiss everybody for me, and all that you would like to tell them as coming from me is what I am thinking!...

Thérèse of the Child Jesus of the Holy Face

* Autograph.
1. A revealing detail of Thérèse's discretion regarding Céline's confidence. Sister Marie of the Sacred Heart wrote the latter on July 15: "I hope the next time you write, the note will be for me. Thérèse of the Child Jesus did not give me hers, and I remain, so to speak, without any news from you."
2. A biographical digression: We may wonder if the incident concerning "the keys of the Communion grille" occurred during this illness of Mother Marie de Gonzague. According to the account in Ms. C, p. 223, Mother Marie de Gonzague was prioress and Thérèse was still in the novitiate: the incident is then anterior to February 1893. It is also posterior to February 1891 since Thérèse is sacristan. The illness of the prioress (she had bronchitis) seems distinct from the influenza of the 1891-1892 winter. This is pointed out only as an assumption.
3. See Mother Marie de Gonzague's notes, LC 143 and 144, which could tie in here chronologically.
4. See II Corinthians 6:2.
5. A reference to Père Hyacinthe Loyson, sixty-four years old. Successively Sulpician, Dominican, Carmelite, then separated from his Order and from Rome just before Vatican I (1869), married civilly to a Protestant widow, founder at Paris of a "Catholic Gallican

Church" (1879), he was travelling throughout Normandy at this time (summer of 1891).

6. Details regarding Père Hyacinthe Loyson, undoubtedly collected from local newspapers. We found among Thérèse's papers four excerpts from *La Croix du Calvados*, a supplement to *La Croix de Paris*: Nos. 9-16, 16-23, and 23-30, July 1891, and no. 3-10, September. The articles anonymous or signed *Tête de Loup*, attacked the "renegade monk" sarcastically. On the third clipping, a light pen stroke similar to those of Thérèse underlined this sentence: "If the Church [says Loyson] were to prove me wrong, *I will gladly acknowledge my error and take my place once again humbly in Christian unity.*"

In January 1911, the Carmel sent Père Loyson a copy of the *Story of a Soul*. On February 5, he thanked them for the "beautiful book containing the *Life* and *Poems* of Sister Thérèse of the Child Jesus and of the Holy Face, a religious of the Lisieux Carmel. Some notes written in pen indicated that this beautiful soul had offered to God her prayers and sufferings for what she called 'my conversion,' that is, my submission to the teachings imposed by the Pope on consciences that surrender themselves into his hands.... I insist on telling you that I was touched, very much touched, by many of the things I read in this book. I must add that I am far from being convinced, and I cannot refrain from applying to Sister Thérèse what Saint Paul said of the good Jews, his contemporaries and adversaries: 'They are zealous for God but not according to knowledge.' I can be mistaken, Reverend Mother, I have been mistaken more than once in my life, but I am convinced that what God condemns in man is not error when this is sincere, but selfishness, pride and hatred. I believe I can say, in the very face of death and before God, that such were never the motives of my mind and my life. Very respectfully, Hyacinthe Loyson, former superior of the Paris Carmel." (Geneva, February 5, 1911, to the Mother Prioress.)

Sister Geneviève answered him on February 9, 1911 (the rough draft is still in the Carmel archives). Then she began a correspondence with him on July 18, saying she was sending the *Articles* on the cause of the Servant of God. Père Loyson answered her personally, saying he "was touched, not shaken" by his correspondent's arguments, and added: "I promise to read the book of the *Articles* which you sent me. Because of all I know about her, your good and heroic sister is far from being a stranger to me, and, without giving approval to everything concerning her, I admire her and am grateful to her" (Paris, July 21, 1911). He added to his letter a copy of one addressed, April 17, 1911, to the Carmelites of Turin, in which he repeated his attach-

ment to "what is true, great, and fruitful, in the tradition of Saint
Teresa of Avila, and even more so in that of Saint John of the Cross."
    He died at Paris, February 9, 1912, whispering, "My sweet Jesus!"
7. *Vie et Oeuvres de la Bienheureuse Marguerite-Marie Alacoque*, vol.
    I, *"Vie par ses Contemporaines,"* p. 159. The statement is made in
    this way: "A just soul can obtain pardon for a thousand criminals."
    The same quotation is in the *Petit Bréviaire du Sacré-Coeur de Jésus*,
    p. 27.
8. Sister Marie of the Angels testified: "The Servant of God had a great
    fear of the lightest faults, and this saying: 'No one knows whether
    he is worthy of love or hatred' caused her to shed tears one day, until
    she was consoled by the explanation given her" (PA, 1171). Probably
    this was done by Père Alexis Prou on the first day of the retreat, Oc-
    tober 7, 1891, in his second instruction. See *Vie Thérèsienne*, April
    1965, pp. 108-111: *Piat, Quelques précisions sur le Père Alexis Prou.*
    We find here, too, an article of P. Alexis quoted and published in
    the *Annales du Tiers-Ordre* (Franciscan) of March 1892, developing
    at greater length the commentary of the saying: "No one knows
    whether he is worthy of love or hatred."

LT 130   **From Thérèse to Céline.**

July 23, 1891
→LC lost

J.M.J.T.

Jesus †   Carmel, July 23, '91

Dear Céline,

    I am again entrusted with answering you.... Mother Geneviève
was much touched by your letter, and she has really prayed for her
little Céline; what a grace to have the prayers of such a saint and
to be loved by her!... Yesterday's feast[1] was delightful, and it was
truly a foretaste of heaven.... All the gifts pleased us very much,
the fish, the cherries, the cakes; thank Aunt and tell her all you like
that is nicest....
    Dear Céline, your two letters spoke volumes to my soul, they made
my tears flow....

The *solicitor*[2] really made me laugh. We must *admit* that he is not shy to come seeking the King of heaven's fiancée, but the poor man has undoubtedly not seen "the seal which the Spouse placed on your forehead,"[3] the mysterious seal that Jesus alone contemplates and the angels, too, who make up His royal court.... Céline, why this extraordinary privilege, why?... Ah, what a grace to be a virgin, to be a spouse of Jesus. It must be very beautiful, very sublime, since the purest, the most intelligent of all other creatures preferred to remain a virgin rather than to become the Mother of God.[4]... And this is the grace Jesus grants us. He wants us to be His spouses, and then He promises that we shall be His mother and His sisters, for He says this in the gospel: "He who does the will of my Father, he is my Mother, my brother, and my sister."[5] Yes, the one who loves Jesus is His whole family. He finds[6] in this *unique* heart, which does not have its LIKE, all that He desires; He finds His heaven there!...

Dear Céline, let us always remain the lilies of Jesus; the favor I ask from Him is that He withdraw them from this world before the pernicious wind of the earth has detached a single particle of the pollen from their stamens, pollen that could yellow a little the brilliance and the whiteness of the lily. Jesus must be able to find in His lilies all that He desires to find in them, purity which seeks Him alone, which rests only in Him....

Alas, there is nothing so easy to tarnish as the lily.... Well, if Jesus said of Magdalene that "one loves more to whom more has been forgiven,"[7] we can say it with more reason when Jesus has forgiven sins *in advance*![8]... Céline, do you understand?... And when the tears of Jesus are the smile of a soul,[9] what has the soul to fear? I think that these mysterious pearls have the power to whiten lilies, to preserve their brilliance.... Dear Céline, the image of this world is passing,[10] the shadows are lengthening,[11] soon we shall be in our native land, soon the joys of our childhood, the Sunday evenings, the intimate chats...all this will be restored to us forever and with interest. Jesus will return to us the joys which He has deprived us of for one moment!... Then from our dear Father's radiant head, we shall see waves of light coming forth, and each one of his white hairs will be like a sun that will give us joy and happiness![12]... Life is then a dream?[13]...and to think that with this dream we can save souls!... Ah! Céline, let us not forget souls, but let us forget

Lk. 7.47 (margin note)

ourselves for them, and one day Jesus will say, when looking at us: "How beautiful is the chaste generation of virgin souls."[14]

I hug tightly little Marie, Léonie, and all, and as for you, Céline, you know where your place is in my heart!...

Thérèse of the Child Jesus of the Holy Face
rel. carm. ind.

* Autograph.
1. Mother Geneviève's sixtieth anniversary of religious Profession; see vol. I, p. 669, note 1.
2. Henry Maudelonde (1864-1937), attorney-at-law in Caen. He frequently met Céline at the home of their aunt, Mme. Guérin. In 1909, Sister Geneviève (Céline) recalled this "true military type of man, who had renounced this career only for the sake of his parents". She goes on to say: "Either at his house or ours, he always had to be near me. Since he demanded this boldly when he was not, we ended up by placing him definitively next to me at table in order to avoid scenes. Dinner over, he used to take me in his arms, whether I liked it or not, and made me dance.... My cousin Marie, who loved me very much, believed she was pleasing me by reporting certain conversations that she had had with her cousins: 'If you only knew how much Henry loves you; he is crazy about you.' Ah! I had no need of anyone's telling me this, I was well enough aware of it!... What struggles!... I belonged to Jesus alone, I had given Him my pledge, but I found the marriage vocation beautiful also; I had, so to speak, two vocations, two attractions.... I would have to speak only one word, give only one look! When I think back on it, I am seized with fright, my vocation was so close to foundering! It seems it was holding on only by a thread." (*Souvenirs autobiographiques*, pp. 95-99.) When Céline declined his advances, the young man married Marie Asseline, April 20, 1892; see LT 134.
3. Liturgical Office of St. Agnes, third antiphon of Matins.
4. The same thought is repeated in: *Why I love you, oh, Mary!* (p. 51, May 1897, stanza 3). See also LT 137, note 7.
5. See Matthew 12:50. Thérèse quoted these words again in LT 142 and 172, and in the Poem quoted *above*, in stanza 20. She wrote them (in 1896-1897, according to the handwriting) on two pictures of her breviary, representing the Nativity scene, placing emphasis on the word "Mother".
6. We notice the change of subject, which is henceforth Jesus, right up

to the end of the paragraph; see *Introduction*, vol. I, p. 68, note 32.
7. See Luke 7:47.
8. See Ms. A, p. 84 and *Jesus at Bethany* (RP 4, July 29, 1895).
9. An allusion to the poem composed by Céline: *The Divine Charm*; see LT 120, note 1.
10. See I Corinthians 7:31.
11. See Canticle of Canticles 4:6. These two scripture quotations are to be found several times in the *Reflections* of de Lamennais, commenting on the *Imitation*. On the theme: "the shadows are lengthening," see LT 120, 141, 142, 156.
12. There is a comparable reflection by Thérèse in February 1890: "In heaven one of his white hairs will illumine us!" (Appendix, p. 1145.) We cannot state whether there is here, as in LT 60, a recall from Arminjon, who compares the elect to "a new sun of the city of God" (*op. cit.*, p. 312).
13. Concerning "the dream this miserable life is" (Saint Teresa of Avila), see LC 93, notes 3 and 4.
14. See Wisdom 4:1, according to the Vulgate; text quoted in the Office of Virgins.

LD   *From Sister Marie of the Sacred Heart to M. Martin.*

August 24, 1891 (?)   This note bears the autograph signature of Thérèse; uncertain date; see note 1.

Jesus!   Lisieux, August[1]

Dear little Father,

Your three Carmelites come to wish you *a happy feast*. They love you and are praying for you and ask Jesus that He give you His graces and after the trial of this life that He unite us all one day in His beautiful heaven![2] . . .

          Sister Marie of the Sacred Heart
          Sister Agnes of Jesus
          Sister Thérèse of the Child Jesus of the Holy Face

Il veut que nous soyons ses épouses et
ensuite il nous promet encore d'être
sa Mère et ses sœurs; car Il le
dit dans son évangile + Celui qui fait la
volonté de mon Père, celui-là est ma
Mère, mes frères et mes sœurs » Oh! Celui
qui aime Jésus est toute sa famille
Il trouve dans ce cœur unique qui
n'a pas son semblable, tout ce qu'il
désire. Il y trouve son Ciel ...
Céline chérie, restons toujours les lys de
Jésus: la grâce que je lui demande
c'est qu'il les retire de ce monde avant
que le vent pernicieux de la terre
ait fait se détacher une seule des
poussières de leurs étamines, poussière qui
pourrait jaunir un peu l'éclat et
la blancheur des lys. Il faut que Jésus
puisse trouver dans ses lys tout ce qu'il

LT 130, rear of 2nd page. July 23, 1891
Original format: 13.5 x 10.3 cm.

Ma Céline chérie, réjouissons nous de notre sort
elle est si belle..... Pauvres donnons à Jésus soyons
avares pour les autres mais prodigues pour Lui...

Jésus est un trésor caché, un bien inestimable
que peu d'âmes savent trouver car il est caché
et le monde aime ce qui brille. Ah si Jésus
avait voulu se montrer à toutes les âmes avec
ses dons ineffables sans doute, il n'en est pas une
seule qui l'aurait dédaigné, mais Il ne veut pas
que nous l'aimions pour ses dons, c'est Lui
même qui doit être notre récompense....
Pour trouver une chose cachée il faut se cacher
soi même..., notre vie doit donc être un mystère
il nous faut ressembler à Jésus à Jésus dont
le visage était caché..... Voulez vous apprendre
quelque chose qui vous serve dit l'Imitation
aimez à être ignoré et compté pour rien....
et ailleurs. Après avoir tout quitté il faut surtout
se quitter soi même..... Que celui ci se
glorifie d'une chose celui là d'une autre pour
vous ne mettez votre joie que dans le mépris
de vous même.) Que ces paroles donnent
de paix à l'âme.., ma Céline, tu les
connais, mais tu ne sais pas tout ce que je voudrais
te dire!.... Jésus t'aime d'un amour
si grand que si tu le voyais tu serais dans un
extase de bonheur qui te donnerait la mort
mais tu ne le vois pas et tu souffres...
Bientôt Jésus se lèvera pour sauver tous
les doux et les humbles de la terre)!.....

LT 145, front 1st page. August 2, 1893
Original format: 21.2 x 13.2 cm.

J.M.J.T.   Le 26 Avril 1894

Jésus †   Chère petite Lyre de Jésus
pour chanter tes 25 ans je t'envoie une petite poésie
que j'ai composée en pensant à toi !.....
Céline ! je suis sure que tu vas comprendre tout ce
que mon cantique voudrait te dire, hélas il faudrait
une autre langue que celle de la terre pour
exprimer la beauté de l'abandon d'une âme entre
les mains de Jésus. mon cœur n'a pu que balbutier ce
qu'il ressent.... Céline l'histoire de Bébé (la Sainte
de l'abandon) est aussi ton histoire ! Jésus a placé près
de toi un ange des cieux qui te garde toujours.
il te porte entre ses mains de peur que ton pied ne
heurte contre la pierre, tu ne le vois pas, et cependant
c'est lui qui depuis 25 ans a préservé ton âme qui
lui a conservé sa blancheur virginale, c'est lui qui
éloigne de toi les occasions de péché.... C'est lui qui s'est
montré à toi dans un rêve mystérieux qu'il t'a
envoyé dans ton enfance, tu voyais un ange
portant un flambeau qui marchait devant notre
Père chéri, sans doute il voulait te faire comprendre
ta mission que tu aurais plus tard à remplir
c'est toi maintenant qui es l'ange visible de celui
qui bientôt ira s'unir aux anges de la cité céleste
Céline ne crains pas les orages de la terre.... ton ange
gardien te couvre de ses ailes et dans ton cœur repose

LT 161. April 26, 1894 (fragment)
Original format: 21.4 x 13.3 cm.

N'ayez pas de peine ma petite Mère chérie que votre petite fille ait semblé vous cacher quelque chose, je dis semblé car vous le savez bien, si elle a caché un petit coin de l'enveloppe elle ne vous a jamais caché une seule ligne de la lettre et qui donc la connaît mieux que vous cette petite lettre que vous aimez tant! Aux autres on peut bien montrer l'enveloppe de tous les côtés puisqu'elles ne peuvent voir que cela mais à vous!!! ... Oh! petite Mère vous savez maintenant que c'est le Vendredi saint que Jésus a commencé à déchirer un peu l'enveloppe de votre petite lettre, n'êtes vous pas contente qu'il s'apprête à la lire cette lettre que vous couvez depuis 24 ans! Ah! si vous saviez comme elle saura bien lui dire votre amour pendant toute l'Éternité

(2ème petit mot)   LT 232

J'ai mis mon petit mot dans la main de Sr Geneviève comme elle me donnait le votre je regrette maintenant d'avoir mis ma lettre à la poste mais je vais payer un double port pour vous dire que je comprends bien votre chagrin je désirais plus que vous peut être ne rien vous cacher, mais il me semblait qu'il fallait attendre, si j'ai mal fait pardon, dites moi et croyez que jamais je n'ai manqué de confiance en vous! — Ah je vous aime trop pour cela! ... Je suis bien contente que vous ayez désiré avoir moi — Je ne me rappelle pas avoir caché autre chose de l'enveloppe à ma petite Mère. Et je la supplie après ma mort de point croire ce qu'on pourra lui dire Oh! ma petite Mère la lettre est à vous je vous en prie continuez de l'écrire jusqu'au jour où Jésus déchirera complètement la petite enveloppe qui vous a fait tant de chagrin depuis qu'elle est faite! ...

LT 231 and LT 232. May 30, 1897
Original format:
LT 231: 9.1 x 6.3 cm.; LT 232: 9.1 x 8.4 cm.

* Autograph.

1. A tear in the paper between these two words took away the date. They used to celebrate M. Martin's feast on the feast of Saint Louis, August 25. We cannot be certain of the year. Thérèse's handwriting seems to date from 1891. In 1892 she was using purple ink; see vol. I, p. 62. August 25, 1891, Sister Agnes of Jesus wrote Céline: "We are sending you a little letter and some pictures for our dear little Father! How sweet our remembrance of him, even though it is sorrowful!" This letter could be this present document.

2. In 1891—if this is really the date of this note—M. Martin's condition was still not good and his return to Lisieux was postponed: "Poor little Father is upset at times. He was unable to make the trip in the carriage into the countryside as he did last year...." (Information received from Sister Costard and transmitted by Sister Marie of the Sacred Heart to Céline at La Musse, July 23, 1891.) Another report: "Jeanne wrote a nice letter to Sister Marie of the Sacred Heart; news of Papa was good. Dear little Father! He was saying, leaning on Francis' arm: 'With a support like yours, I could go to the end of the world....' And Jeanne added: 'He seemed so happy to be supported and loved.' But as for bringing him home, let us be in no hurry!" (Sister Agnes of Jesus to Céline, early August, 1891.)

LD	*From Sister Agnes of Jesus to M. and Mme. Guérin.*
September 10-12 1891	This note signed by Thérèse also could have been for the occasion of M. and Mme. Guérin's silver jubilee of wedding (September 11, 1866-1891), celebrated on Sunday the 13th, judging by the correspondence of the time.

J.M.J.T.

Dear Uncle and dear Aunt,

My picture will express my whole heart to you or rather all our hearts! I finished it at this very moment, which allows me to send you only a few words.

The little angel, who is on retreat,[1] joins us in offering you her good wishes. She is praying for you! I would not be able to say your parcel pleased her, but it did her some good.[2]

> Your child who loves you,
> Sister Agnes of Jesus
> r.c.ind.
> Sister Thérèse of the Child Jesus
> r. carm. ind.

* Autograph.

1. Thérèse. At the request of Sister Martha of Jesus, Thérèse postponed her private retreat beyond September 8, anniversary of her Profession for the years 1891, 1892, and 1893, in order to make it coincide with that of Sister Martha which began a little later; see PA, 1282. With Mother Marie de Gonzague's permission, the two Carmelites spent the time of the Community recreations together. This was an occasion of mortification for Thérèse, who preferred a more solitary retreat. It was probably at the end of this retreat of 1891 that Thérèse took her place next to the first religious to show up at recreation, without even bidding a *bonjour* to Sister Agnes of Jesus. Mother Geneviève heard about this and reproved Thérèse, telling her "This was not understanding true charity." (Testimony of Sister Marie of the Angels, PA, 1187.)

2. We do not know what this was.

"The winter is passed" (Ms. A, p. 34)
(October 1891 - October 1892)
Age eighteen and nineteen

> *Is the mysterious little flower "which has grown and blossomed almost in one act," not in spite of but because of the rigors of winter, a symbol only of Céline (LT 132)? We may doubt it: Thérèse can be repeating here: "you are myself." Like an unexpected blossoming, consolations[1] have returned to strew her path.*
>
> *Nothing, it is true, in the correspondence of October-*

November gives any inkling of the graces received during the Community retreat of October 7-15. Thérèse was at grips with "great interior trials of all kinds" (Ms. A, p. 173). Then suddenly she "is understood in a marvelous way and even read into" by the retreat master, Père Alexis Prou, a Franciscan. He launched her "full sail on the waves of confidence and love," assuring her that her faults "did not grieve God" (ibid.).

Is it at this time that she is bold enough to say to the subprioress, Sister Fébronie: "Sister, you want God's justice, you will have God's justice. The soul receives exactly what it expects from God"?[2]

On November 24, Bishop Hugonin entered the cloister for the celebration of St. John of the Cross' centenary. The bishop was most paternal to "his little daughter" and bestowed on her "a thousand caresses" (Ms. A, p. 156) in the presence of the Community; she saw in this a reflection of God's own tenderness.

On December 5, Mother Geneviève died: it was the first time Thérèse assisted at a death. The spectacle appeared "delightful" to her (Ms. A, p. 170). The sight of the coffin brings her back fourteen years, face to face with her mother's coffin. But at this moment joy completed the healing of her childhood wound (Ms. A, p. 34). Shortly afterward, she received in a dream the maternal inheritance: the foundress leaves Thérèse her heart (Ms. A, p. 171).

The day after Christmas, the influenza epidemic struck the Carmel, causing the death of three religious in eight days. The three youngest remained in good health, including Thérèse. The "little Sister ainsi soit-il," as she was nicknamed at times,[3] *gave herself fully through her devotedness and composure, to the point of making the superior, M. Delatroëtte, shake off his persistent prejudice against her.*

The elections were to have taken place in February 1892. The Community, weakened by the epidemic, sought and obtained an extension of offices for one year. Sister St. Raphael was named subprioress to replace Sister Fébronie, who had died during the epidemic.

With the coming of spring, Thérèse at last saw her sun appear once again: M. Martin returned to his family on May 10, 1892. He was certainly an obscured sun, and the last visit to the Carmel on May 12 was an emotional meeting. From the depths of his dimmed consciousness, the sick man was able to snatch only these few words: "In heaven!" The "little queen" will be the first to arrive at this paternal rendezvous, *five years later. For the immediate present, she experienced "a very sweet consolation" (LT 138) in the realization that her father was surrounded by his own family at Lisieux.*

Her spiritual life was nourished more and more from the source of Revelation: Scripture and "especially" the gospels: "I am always discovering new lights in them, meanings hidden and mysterious" (Ms. A, p. 179). Céline was the first confidante of her discoveries (LT 135).

Thérèse's correspondence is sparse during this year (only five letters), but there comes from it a sweetness hitherto unknown. Without losing sight of the fact that suffering remained the dominant note of her first five years in Carmel (Ms. A, p. 149), up to the spring of 1893, we see that Thérèse was able to anticipate its closing date by stating with reference to this period: "All my trials had come to an end, and the winter of my soul had passed away forever" (Ms. A, p. 34).[4]

Read: Ms. A, pp. 169-173.

1. This word or the word *"consoling"* is encountered in her writings to describe each of the events recalled here.
2. According to a letter from the Lisieux Carmel to the Compiègne Carmel, without date or signature; copy transcribed by Sister Marie of the Angels in her NPPA, 1915.
3. She was nicknamed: "little Sister *ainsi soit-il*" (Sister Amen) with reference to her slowness but not with an unkind nuance; it originated with Sister St. Stanislaus, who loved Thérèse (DCL).
4. A sentence written in 1895, before the great "trial of faith," which began in early April 1896.

LT 131   **From Thérèse to Mme. La Néele (Jeanne Guérin)**
October 17, 1891
→ LC lost

J.M.J.T.

Jesus †   Carmel, October 17, '91

Dear little Jeanne,

I do not know how to thank you for your kind attention.

I was very much touched when seeing that the name of Francis accompanied that of Jeanne in wishing me a happy feast, so it is to both of you that I am sending my thanks.

I am entrusting the payment of my debt to my divine Spouse; since I am poor because of Him, it is only right that He not refuse me what I am asking for those whom I love.

I assure you, dear Jeanne, that if you are not forgetting the littlest of your sisters, she, too, thinks very often of you, and you know that for a Carmelite to remember and especially to love is to pray. My poor prayers undoubtedly are not worth much, however, I hope that Jesus will answer them, and, instead of looking at her who is addressing them to Him, He will rest His eyes on those who are their object, and thus He will be obliged to grant me all my requests. I hope that soon God will send a little Isidore as perfect as his Papa or else a little Jeanne resembling exactly her Mamma.[1] . . . I am asking that the pharmacy may be finally sold.[2] I would like nothing to be lacking to the perfect happiness of my dear little sister and that of my good cousin. But on earth there will always be some little cloud since life cannot go on without it, and since in heaven alone joy will be perfect. However, I desire that as much as possible God may spare those whom I love the inevitable sufferings of life, even if it means taking upon myself, if necessary, the trials He is reserving for them.

Sister Marie of the Sacred Heart asks me to thank you very much for what you have sent for the empty pocket; it is really too kind on your part, and this all the more since our Mother was happy to be able to offer you this little work. I have only enough space left to say again thanks from myself and my sisters and to send you and our dear cousin as well the assurance of the affection of the last of your sisters, who is not the littlest in the tenderness she has for you....

Sister Thérèse of the Child Jesus
rel. carm. ind.

* Autograph.
1. Mme. La Néele never had a child, and this was a great suffering for her. After seven years of disappointed hopes, the reading of the first edition of the *Story of a Soul* finally brought her peace in this trial.
2. M. Guérin wrote to his daughter, March 20, 1891: "Does Francis know that the law on the practice of medicine has been voted on and it prohibits the retaining of two professions? It is evident that the law will provide a morally necessary extension of time so that those in his situation may be able to dispose of their pharmacy; however, I do not believe this will be in his favor regarding the sale price. Knowing he is forced to sell, the buyer will take advantage of the situation." Dr. La Néele's pharmacy was sold on November 26, 1891, according to ChrIG, p. 39.

LT 132   **From Thérèse to Céline.**
October 20, 1891

J.M.J.T.

Jesus †   Carmel, October 20, 1891

Dear Céline,

This is the fourth time I am coming to wish you a happy feast since I am in Carmel....

It seems to me that these four years have tightened even more the bonds that united us so closely. The more we advance the more we love Jesus, and as it is in Him that we cherish each other, this is why our affection becomes so strong that it is rather *unity* than union which exists between our two souls!... Céline, what must I say to you, do you not know everything?... Yes, but I want to tell you why the *Célines* have blossomed earlier this year. Jesus made me feel it this morning for your feast. You have undoubtedly noticed that never had winter been so rigorous as last year,[1] consequently, all flowers were retarded in their blossoming. This was very natural, and no one dreamed of being astonished by it. But there is a little mysterious flower that Jesus has reserved for Himself in order to instruct our souls. This flower is the Céline-flower...contrary to the other flowers, it blossomed one month before the time of its blossoming.... Céline, do you understand the language of my dear little flower...the flower of my childhood...the flower of our memories?!!!!... Wintry weather, the rigors of winter, instead of retarding it, made it grow and blossom.... No one paid any attention to it; this flower is so little, so unattractive...only the bees know the treasures that its mysterious calyx encloses, made up of a multitude of little calyxes, each one as rich as the others.... Thérèse, like the bees, understood this mystery. Winter is suffering; suffering misunderstood, misjudged, looked upon as useless by profane eyes,[2] but as fruitful and powerful in the eyes of Jesus and the angels who, like the vigilant bees, know how to gather the honey contained within the mysterious and multiple calyxes that represent souls or rather the children of the virginal little flower.... Céline, I would need volumes to write all I am thinking about my little flower...for me it is so perfect an image of your soul. Yes, Jesus has made wintry weather pass over it instead of the warm sun of His consolations, but the effect expected by Him has been produced; the little plant has grown and has blossomed almost in one act.... Céline, when a flower has blossomed, we have only to pluck it, but when and how will Jesus pluck His little flower?... Perhaps the pink color of its corolla indicates that this will be by means of martyrdom![3]... Yes, I feel my desires are reborn. Perhaps after having asked us love for love, so to speak, Jesus will want to ask us blood for blood, life for life.... In the meantime, we must let the bees draw out all the honey from the little calyxes, keeping nothing, giving all to Jesus, and then we shall say like the flower in the evening of our life: "The night, behold the night."[4] Then it will be finished.... And to the wintry blasts will succeed the gentle rays of the sun, to the tears of Jesus, eternal smiles....

Ah, let us not refuse to weep with Him during one day since we

shall enjoy His glory throughout an eternity!...
Dear little flower, do you understand your Thérèse?...

* Autograph.
1. On January 10, 1891, for example, Mme. Guérin wrote to Jeanne: "It is preferable that you do not come, the weather is so bad; today we have fourteen below zero at our house."
2. Some of Sister Geneviéve's confidences shed light on one aspect of this "useless suffering": Was it not pure loss when she obstinately took care of her father? "Devotedness to him held the greatest place in the visits I was making there [at Caen]. I was often there alone, for dear little Léonie, finding her presence useless, took advantage of the trips by going to the Visitation.... But my dear little Father needed me, a need that was well contested, it is true, for I was unable to console him in anything, he was too sick ordinarily even to enjoy my visits. However, I did not fail to make them in order that he might see that he was supported and loved, if, alas! he could still take any delight in these pleasures!" (*Souvenirs autobiographiques*, pp. 87, 105.)
3. The vicious anti-clericalism of this epoch did not make the assumption of a persecution unlikely. In September 1891, a Congress of the Masonic Lodges called for the resumption of the religious war. During the same autumn, a French pilgrimage of twenty thousand workers to Rome was the occasion of an incident, slight in itself, but exploited by the Italian anticlericals. Fallières heckled the French bishops. He drew a vehement reply from Bishop Gouthe-Soulard, and Leo XIII had to intervene to pacify minds.
4. A quotation from the poem by Céline: *La Rosée*. Thérèse preserved a fragment of it (twelve alexandrins) in one of her books. We read: *Le soir, voici le soir! ainsi comme la fleur — Nous dirons ce refrain, ô suprême bonheur! — Un jour aussi comme elle au soir de notre vie — Fatiguée des combats l'âme toute ravie — S'élancera chantant dans la splendeur du ciel.*
The night, behold the night! thus like the flower —
We shall sing this refrain, oh, great joy!
One day, too, like it, in the evening of our life
Tired out by combats, the soul all enraptured
Will spring forth, singing, into heaven's splendors.
   Sister Geneviève transcribed this poem, with some alterations, into her notebook: "*Notes intimes* I"; partly on p. 35, integrally on pp. 170-171. She states: "A poem composed while I was still in the

world in 1889. Thérèse liked it very much...she knew passages by heart."

LT 133   From Thérèse to Mme. Guérin.

November 16, 1891

J.M.J.T.

Jesus †   Carmel, November 16, '91

Dear Aunt,

It is very sweet for your littlest daughter to come with her older sisters to wish you a happy feast day.

Each year, I see the date of November 19 return with joy, and if it is filled with sweet memories for me, it is also rich with hope for the future....

The more I go on in life the more I appreciate how sweet a mother's feast day is. Alas, in my childhood God seemed to take from me forever a joy I had never experienced. But from the height of heaven she who could no longer bestow her caresses on me awakened in a maternal heart, dear to her, the tenderness of a mother for her poor little child, and since then she was able to feel the sweet joys one experiences in honoring a dear mother!...

Dear little Aunt, since she has been on the mountain of Carmel, your little Thérèse feels still more deeply, if that be possible, the affection she has for you; the more she learns to love Jesus, the greater, too, becomes her tenderness for her dear relatives.

The little gift[1] which our good Mother was happy to have made for your feast will tell you better than I, dear Aunt, what I am powerless to tell you. My heart is filled with emotion when seeing this poor hair which undoubtedly has no other value but the delicate workmanship and the gracefulness of its arrangement, but which nevertheless was loved by him whom God took away from us.[2]...

Dear little Aunt, do you understand? I am happy when seeing it is to her—who is dearest to me in this life, after my Father—this hair is offered, which he would have received with so much pleasure.

Dear little Aunt, this letter hardly resembles a feast day letter in which one must speak only of joy and happiness. But I myself cannot speak except with my heart, it alone guides my pen; and I am sure the maternal heart I am addressing will be able to understand me and even guess at what I cannot express. . . .

Dear Aunt, I am obliged to terminate my letter, but first I want to send you all my kisses, and I beg you to tell your little daughters it is they whom I entrust with giving them to you for me. I am sure they will be charmed by the mission I confide to them and that they will carry it out perfectly. . . .

Your little daughter is sending you all her best wishes, and I beg you, dear little Aunt, to believe in all the tenderness of her childlike heart. . . .

Sister Thérèse of the Child Jesus
rel. carm. ind.

*   Autograph.
1.   A card on which was placed some of Thérèse's hair (cut after her reception of the Habit) and arranged in such a way as to represent a branch of lilies. It was given later to Mme. La Néele (Jeanne Guérin), who left it to the Benedictine Abbey at Lisieux; it was evidently destroyed during the bombing of 1944.
2.   See LT 77; M. Martin was very proud of his "little blond rascal's" hair.

LC 148   *From Mme. Guérin to Thérèse.*

November 16, 1891
→ LT 133

November 16, 1891

Dear little Thérèse,

I read and reread your nice letter, and I really do not know how to respond to so much thoughtfulness. I am very much moved when seeing all the affection you are showing me and of which your sisters and yourself have already given me so many proofs.

What have I done, then, that God has surrounded me with such loving hearts! I did nothing but answer the last look of a mother whom I loved *very much, very much.* I believed I understood that look which nothing will be able to make me forget.[1] It is engraved within my heart. Since that day, I have tried to replace her whom God had taken away from you, but, alas! nothing can replace a Mother!...

However, God has willed to bless my feeble efforts, and today He permits me to receive the affection of these young hearts. He willed that the mother who guided your early childhood be raised to a more sublime glory and enjoy heavenly delights. Ah! it is because, little Thérèse, your parents are among those we may call saints and who merit bringing forth saints.[2]

When I consider this good father, venerable Patriarch we are pleased to call him, bent under the weight of his trial, dragging his cross painfully, and when I remember him as so kind, so happy among his children, taking his dear little queen by the arm, I say to myself: "There must be a beautiful heaven where all this will be rewarded. This good father has given three of his children to God, and there remains nothing in return...."

All these reflections came to me, dear little Thérèse, when reading your nice letter and receiving your beautiful hair so artistically and delicately arranged. I am very happy to possess this souvenir which is very precious to me, and you will thank your good Mother for me until I can do so myself.

I have not written your sisters, dear little Thérèse; you will be my messenger to them, telling them of all the pleasure their affectionate letters gave me, thanking them for their prayers for me and mine, which I beg them to continue.

Remember me to Reverend Mother Marie de Gonzague. I am very appreciative of the remembrance of the entire Carmel. Remember me to Mother Geneviève. In a word, little Thérèse, remember me to all the Sisters, telling them of my gratitude.

I kiss you with my whole heart and your two dear sisters as well.

Your very devoted aunt,
Céline Guérin

*   G. copy.
1.   This took place on August 27, 1877, the night before Mme. Martin died.
2.   Not an authentic sentence. Sister Geneviève destroyed the autograph. The copy written by her (in 1926?) has an illegible erasure and three lines written over it, in a much later handwriting.

LD   *From Céline to Mme. La Néele.   (Extracts.)*
January 5, 1892
                                                 January 5, 1892

Dear little Jeanne,

The poor Carmel is right now a prey to the influenza epidemic, the plague is raging there in full force. This morning we were at the burial of the religious who died on Saturday, and on Friday we shall return for another burial, that of the Mother Subprioress, who died last night. There are still two of the three sick ones whom they despair of saving, among them Sister Madeleine, aunt of Madame St. Benoît at the Abbey, and another religious whom I do not know. Up until now, it is the older ones who are leaving, but the young are also very sick.[1] Pauline has been in bed for a few days now; she was seized with a violent headache and is bleeding profusely from the nose. We are very much upset because Pauline, who was already very weak, will have trouble getting the upper hand. It will be, I think, only a question of time and once on her feet the tonics will restore her. No one is worried about her. But we pity the Carmel very much. It is upsetting to see the desolation that reigns there; the religious are dying not in the infirmary but on their beds, not surrounded by their Sisters but assisted only by one or two religious who are there by chance. We must hope that God will finally put an end to their trial and bring the plague to an end.

Is it the same at Caen as at Lisieux? We talk only about the influenza epidemic....

                                                 Your Céline

*   Autograph.

1. See Thérèse's account of the epidemic in Ms. A, p. 171; and the account in the monastery chronicle: "The influenza epidemic raged in our region with force. On December 28, Holy Innocents, several of our Sisters had to take to their beds. When we saw our good Sister St. Joseph, eighty-three, seized by this terrible sickness, we had no doubt that the Lord would find her ripe for heaven. We then mourned the departure of Mother Subprioress, Sister Fébronie of the Holy Childhood, and Sister Madeleine: three coffins in less than eight days!... Our Reverend Mother was very sick, all our Sisters confined to bed; never in the annals of our Carmel had we seen the like. At the burial of our two Sisters, hardly six or seven were present, and then at the cost of a great effort on their part! Only the three youngest of the entire Community were not stricken by this epidemic.... What Community life! no more office in choir, no prayer, no reading in the refectory, no bells rung for religious exercises. Death was hanging over us!...." (Foundation III, p. 206.) The three youngest were: Sister Marie of the Sacred Heart, infirmarian, Thérèse, sacristan, and Martha, cook (DE, p. 481).

LT 134

April 26, 1892

From Thérèse to Céline.

This letter was written six days after the marriage of Henry Maudelonde (LT 130, note 2), on the occasion of Céline's unsuccessful attempt to dance (see CSG, pp. 136-137). "This incident, unique in its kind...." (Ms. A, p. 178) made Thérèse conscious of her spiritual twinship with Céline. The story of the twofold daisy takes on its beauty in this light.

J.M.J.T.

Jesus †   April 26, 1892

Dear Céline,

The meadow of Carmel supplies me this year with a symbolic gift that I am happy to offer you for your twenty-three years.[1]... One day, in the grass all-whitened by simple daisies, I seemed to see one of them with a long stem, and it surpassed them in beauty; coming close, I saw with surprise that instead of one daisy there were two very distinct ones. Two stems so tightly joined together put me in mind immediately of the mysteries of *our souls.* . . . I understood that, if in the order of nature Jesus is pleased to sow beneath our feet marvels so delighful, it is only to aid us in reading into more hidden mysteries of a superior order that He is working at times in souls. . . . Céline, I feel that you have already understood your Thérèse, already your heart has guessed at what is taking place in this other heart to which yours is so tightly united that the sap nourishing them is the same! . . . However, I want to speak to you about some of the hidden mysteries in my little flower. Jesus has created a multitude of little daisies to give joy to our eyes and to instruct our souls. I see with surprise that, in the morning, their pink corollas are turned[2] in the direction of the dawn, they are awaiting the rising of the sun; as soon as this radiant star has sent toward them its warm rays, the timid little flowers open up their calyxes, and their dainty leaves form a sort of crown which, uncovering their little yellow hearts, give immediately to these flowers a great resemblance to what has struck them with its light. Throughout the whole day, the daisies do not cease gazing on the sun, and they turn like it until the evening;[3] then when it has disappeared, they quickly close again their corollas, and from white they become pink. . . . Jesus is the divine Sun, and the daisies are His spouses, the virgins. When Jesus has looked upon a soul, He immediately gives it His divine resemblance, but it is necessary that this soul not cease to fix its eyes upon Him *alone.* To develop the mysteries of the daisies, I would have to write a volume; however, my Céline understands all, so now I want to speak to her about the whims of Jesus. . . . In His meadow, Jesus has many daisies, but they are separated, and they receive the rays of the Sun each one separately. One day, the Spouse of virgins bent down to earth; He united tightly two little buds scarcely open, their stems were merged into a single one, and one look made them grow up. Together these little flowers, *now only one flower,* blossomed, and now the double daisy, fixing its eyes on the divine Sun, accomplishes its mission which is one. . . . Céline, you alone can understand my language; in the eyes of creatures, our life seems very different, very much separated, but I myself know that Jesus has joined our hearts in so marvelous a way that what makes one heart beat also makes the other heart throb.... "Where your treasure is there is your heart also."⁴ Our treasure is Jesus, and our hearts make only one in Him. The same look has ravished our souls, a look veiled in tears, which the double daisy has resolved to dry; its humble and white corolla will be the calyx in which precious diamonds will be collected to be poured out on other flowers that, less privileged, will not have fixed upon Jesus the first glances of their hearts.... Perhaps, in the evening of its life, the daisy will offer the divine Spouse its corolla, become pink.⁵

Adieu, dear Céline, the little flower I am sending you is a relic, for it has rested in the hands of our saintly Mother Geneviève,⁶ and she has blessed Céline and Thérèse.....

Thérèse of the Child Jesus of the Holy Face
rel. carm. ind.

*   Autograph.
1. Thérèse made two cuts in the paper for inserting the stem of the daisy, plucked in the spring of 1891 (see note 6) and allowed to dry out.
2. "sont tournées"; Thérèse had used the singular number instead of the plural.
3. This whole piece calls to mind, with regard to its content and vocabulary, a poem composed the preceding March 31 by Sister Agnes of Jesus: the poem asks Mother Marie de Gonzague to preserve the daisies in the meadow which some wanted to uproot. We may wonder which sister inspired the other. It is possible both felt the same way, the older one being capable of expressing herself in poetry; Thérèse composed her first poem only six months later, February 1893.
4. See Matthew 6:21; already quoted in LT 127.
5. Reference to possible martyrdom; see LT 132.
6. Mother Geneviève died on December 5, 1891. The discovery of the daisy dates then to the spring of 1891.

LD   *From Mme. Guérin to Mme. La Néele.* (Extracts.)
May 10, 1892   Day of M. Martin's return to Lisieux.

Dear little Jeanne,

Your father went today to Caen to get your uncle. He lunched at your place,[1] and he brought back good M. Martin at four o'clock. The trip went along very well.[2] His morale is as good as it can possibly be, but his limbs can no longer support him.[3] He had to be carried into the carriage. He cried all the time and appears so happy to be among his children. He has been placed in the bedroom on the second floor, but he would not be able to come down,[4] he would be incapable of doing so. Céline and Léonie are really happy. They have wanted to see this day for so long a time.

Above all, profit by your trip; I am very happy your husband is taking this little vacation, he needs it.

Your very devoted mother,
Céline Guérin

* Autograph.
1. At Caen; Doctor and Mme. La Néele just left on a pilgrimage to Saint-Anne-d'Auray to obtain the favor of having a child. A few days before, Mme. Guérin had written her daughter: "Céline has spoken of your intention to her sisters at Carmel; they approve very much and find this is very good.... Thérèse even said that if you received the favor requested, it could be a privileged soul" (April 24, 1892).
2. Marie Guérin recalled the trip three years later: "When Papa brought him back from Caen, Uncle was very much moved, touched to see Papa caring for him in this way; at this time, he still had lucid moments and he began to weep and say: 'I will repay all this, you will see....' These words really affected Papa" (to Mme. La Néele, March 3, 1895).
3. "His poor limbs were as though stuck together and lifeless, and he was able to move his arms only partially. His mind was affected in part and as a result of the seizures he had undergone there was a gentle childishness about him, and still not entirely childish, for he understood and felt what children do not understand and feel; we noticed the grief he experienced at not being able to express himself in the manner he would have liked. His servant helped him to eat, and when it was necessary to lift him or sit him down or place him

in his wheelchair, he put his arms around the servant's neck, who then carried him'' (G/NPHF, p. 577).

4. "He remained a few weeks at M. Guérin's home, rue Paul Banaston, then we rented a house on rue Labbey, close to Uncle's house. We had only to cross the street to enter my uncle's house by the carriage gate in the garden. I hired a maid and a manservant'' (Sister Geneviève, CMG IV, p. 210).

LD   *From Mme. Guérin to Mme. La Néele.* (Extracts.)
May 15, 1892
                                              Lisieux, May 15, '92

Dear little Jeanne,

   Your uncle is always as well as possible. He spends all his afternoons seated in the garden. He walks with the help of two persons. He is very easy to take care of and wants all that we want. Nevertheless, his condition is really sad. He recognized all the members of the family, but it was touching at the Carmel. We took him there on Thursday,[1] and one would say the day was very special, and in fact, I believe God blessed it because it was the best day he has had. He seemed to be aware of everything that was taking place.[2] The Carmelites were happy to see their father again, but afterward the tears they held back flowed freely. They found him very much changed,[3] and nevertheless here we find him less changed than we might have thought. However, all of us are very grateful. It was touching to see the way they expressed their gratitude to your father.

                            Your very devoted mother,
                               Céline Guérin

* Autograph.
1. May 12
2. Mother Agnes of Jesus wrote this account in the first edition of the *Story of a Soul*: "During the two years preceding his death, the paralysis became generalized and my uncle kept him close to himself, bestowing all sorts of attention on his painful old age. Because of the state of his infirmity and weakness, we saw him only once in the

speakroom during the whole course of his illness. Ah! what a visit that was! When he was about to leave us, as we were bidding him *"au revoir,"* he raised his eyes and pointing to heaven with his finger, he remained this way for a long time, with only these words to express his thoughts, spoken in a voice filled with tears: *"au ciel*!!!" (Ed. 1898, p. 136-137.)

3. "In his mortal state, our father was well-built; when sick, he was very thin" (G/NPHF, p. 685). The 1892 documents give very few details on the sick man's condition. We have this letter from Céline: "Papa is fairly well, I do not dare say very well, for he has had several very sad days. He went through some pitiful agonies and some crying spells which tore my heart out. Today, he is happy, so I am breathing freely. Oh! how I pity him and sympathize with his ills! Yesterday, he was saying to me: 'Oh, children, really pray for me!' Then he told me to ask Saint Joseph that he may die a holy death." (To Mme. La Néele, July 25, 1892.)

LT 135	**From Thérèse to Céline.**
August 15, 1892	Céline was on vacation at La Musse with the Guérin family (from August 11-23, according to the documents of the time), while Léonie took care of her father at Lisieux.

J.M.J.T.

Jesus †   August 15, 1892

Dear Céline,

I cannot allow the letter[1] to leave without joining a note to it. For this, I must steal a few moments from Jesus, but He does not hold it against me, for it is about Him that we speak together, without Him no discourse has any charms for our hearts.[2] . . . Céline, the vast solitudes, the enchanting horizons opening up before you must be speaking volumes to your soul? I myself see nothing of all that, but I say with Saint John of the Cross: "My Beloved is the mountains, and lonely, wooded valleys, etc."[3] And this Beloved instructs my soul, He speaks to it in silence, in darkness. . . . Recently, there came a thought to me which I have to tell my Céline. It was one day when I was thinking of what I could do to save souls, a word of the gospel gave me a real light. In days gone by, Jesus said to His disciples when showing them the fields of ripe corn: "Lift up your eyes and see how the fields are already white enough to be harvested," and a little later: "In truth, the harvest is abundant but the number of laborers is small, ask then the master of the harvest to send laborers." What a mystery!... Is not Jesus all-powerful? Are not creatures His who made them? Why, then, does Jesus say: "Ask the Lord of the harvest that he send some workers"? Why?... Ah! it is because Jesus has so incomprehensible a love for us that He wills that we have a share with Him in the salvation of souls. He wills to do nothing without us. The Creator of the universe awaits the prayer of a poor little soul to save other souls redeemed like it at the price of all His Blood. Our own vocation is not to go out to harvest the fields of ripe corn. Jesus does not say to us: "*Lower* your eyes, look at the fields and go harvest them." Our mission is still more sublime. These are the words of our Jesus: "*Lift* your eyes and see." See how in my heaven there are empty places; it is up to you to fill them, you are my Moses praying on the mountain, ask me for workers and I shall send them, I await only a prayer, a sigh from your heart!...

Is not the apostolate of prayer, so to speak, more elevated than that of the word? Our mission as Carmelites is to form evangelical workers who will save thousands of souls whose mothers we shall be.... Céline, if these were not the very words of our Jesus, who would dare to believe in them?... I find that our share is really beautiful, what have we to envy in priests?... How I would like to be able to tell you all I am thinking, but time is lacking, understand all I could write you!...

On the feast day of Jeanne,[7] wish her a happy feast for us with a little bouquet. The Rule does not permit us to do it, but tell her that we shall be thinking even more of her. Kiss everybody for me, and tell them all the nicest things you can think of. If you were to find some heather, I would be pleased.

> Your little Thérèse of the Child Jesus
> rel. carm. ind.

*   Autograph.

1. A letter of Sister Agnes of Jesus, written on the 14th: "Your little Thérèse is not writing you, for she is too busy in the sacristy; however, I would have liked her to write you a note. Oh! what a soul pleasing to God and enlightened by His divine light!" August 14 was the date chosen by the Carmel of Lisieux for its day (night included) of Perpetual Adoration.

2. See Imitation of Christ II, 8:1 and III, 34:1.

3. *Spiritual Canticle*, stanza XIV; *Collected Works*, p. 412.

4. See John 4:35.

5. See Matthew 9:37-38. In 1896, it seems, Thérèse transcribed this verse and the preceding one on a picture of the Holy Family in Egypt by Müller. She completed the verses with Luke 12:49: "I have come to bring fire on the earth." and these verses of her poem: *Jésus mon Bien-Aimé, rappelle-toi*!: "So that the harvest may soon be gathered — Each day, oh, my God, I immolate myself and I pray — My joys and my sorrows are for Your harvesters — I would like, oh, my God, to carry Your fire afar! (P 21, stanza 12.)

6. See Exodus 17:8-13.

7. Mme. La Néele, whose feast day was on August 21.

LC 149   *From Céline to Thérèse.*

August 17, 1892   In the copybook serving as the source of this text,
→ LT 135   Sister Geneviève wrote: "Foreseeing I would be able to pursue my vocation without much delay, P. Pichon considered me for a foundation he was planning to make. He had forbidden me to speak of it to anyone, not even to Thérèse, and this made my conversation with her restrained and sad. Since I would have no hope of entering the Carmel—the Superior having vowed that a fourth sister would not be admitted there—I was trying to make the Carmelites understand the confused state of my soul so that they might lead me on another way."

La Musse, August 17, 1892

Dear Thérèse,

I, who yesterday, in the letter to our Mother,[1] was asking for a short response, was not expecting such a surprise. Oh! if you only knew what good your short note did me! I did not grow tired of reading it, of meditating on it. And I find Our Lord is so good to you, He gives you so many lights that I go no further.... I love to contemplate the miracles of graces, the strange mysteries taking place in the soul of my Thérèse. This does me good.

You speak to me about beautiful nature which is presented to my gaze, about infinite horizons unfolding before me. Alas! the eye becomes accustomed to everything, even to the most beautiful things, and the attraction of all that is not our "Divine Charm"[2] pales and wears out. I question immensity, I dream at night when gazing on the stars, or rather I try to dream, for my soul is downcast and nothing gives me any response. I would like to think of beautiful things, and I think of nothing. I am like a little donkey that goes grazing on the highway without knowing what it is doing. Right now, my state is to see without seeing, to understand without understanding. I would be unable to stop at anything tangible. I go on "supported without any support!"[3]

Oh, Thérèse, yes, "we have in our Beloved, the lakes, the mountains, the breezes, the wooded solitary valleys."[4] In Him, we find all that, while in all that we do not find Him, unless He gives life to these pale objects by His glance and His presence.

Thérèse! if you only knew the strange effect the things of earth have on me.

Formerly I would have contemplated La Musse with pleasure, thrilled before its eloquent structures, its slender spires and graceful steps; I would have sauntered along the pathways of the park while meditating upon the vanity of earthly riches; my heart would have leapt for joy at the thought that Jesus was making me disdain the futility that others prize so highly. Right now, my thoughts do not linger long enough to come to such a conclusion. My spirit is as though flattened out, a plain without highs or lows, just a flat surface throughout. Even though I look about and say to myself: "Why do you not admire these marvelous vistas, and fill yourself with such magnificence," I cannot work up any enthusiasm as I have lost the power to distinguish between the beautiful and the ugly. Something within me forces me to see all in the same perspective, as though all had been covered by the same veneer.

My Thérèse, your Céline at present is going through a succession of voids, or rather *one* mysterious void....

It is true, I am in darkness, reduced to the state of the log; I hardly think of Jesus, but perhaps, without noticing it, the log is being consumed under the ashes....

I would not be able to tell you either, oh, my beloved Thérèse, whether I am thinking of souls; no, I repeat it, I am thinking of nothing. I am in the most total incapacity.

Tell my dear little Pauline that her letter did me much good. I am not answering her because I know that she will be more pleased that I write you in preference to herself. She is so good, Pauline! Kiss my dear little Marie for me, and especially my dear Mother; tell her that I am grateful to her for having allowed you to write me.

Your little Céline

P.S. Tell Pauline not to worry about the picture;[5] if she does not paint it, it will be all right just the same. Let her do what she wants. I do not understand why Léonie did not send the chocolate for the feast;[6] Aunt was depending on her. Marie kisses her Mother and her little sisters. She would be happy to receive a word from her dear Mother at my address...but we do not ask this![7]

* G. copy.
1. Letter to Mother Marie de Gonzague was not preserved.
2. Title of a poem by Céline; see LC 128, note 1.
3. John of the Cross, St., *Glosa a lo divino*, see *Collected Works*, p. 734. Céline copied out this poem in one of her notebooks when she was still young; it is difficult to ascertain the date, but in 1893 it seemed to her it was a long time ago; see LC 154.
4. John of the Cross, St., *Spiritual Canticle*, see *Collected Works*, stanza XIV, p. 412.
5. A photographic reproduction of a painting by Müller for P. Pichon, according to Sister Agnes' letter to Céline, August 14, 1892.
6. For August 15; the chocolate mentioned in the same letter by Sister Agnes of Jesus, "the provisor," that is, the one in charge of provi-

sions for the meals.

7. "Marie wrote our Mother a very long letter, a real little diary, which pleased Mother very much. She feels she has everything necessary for holiness; tell her this because I doubt if Mother will write her today on account of her duties." (Sister Agnes to Céline, in same letter.) Regarding Marie Guérin's letters to Mother Marie de Gonzague, preserved by Thérèse but later on destroyed, see Introduction, p. 94, note 12.

"Jesus told me to descend...." *(LT 137)*
(October 1892 - February 1893)
Age nineteen and twenty

"You want to climb a mountain, and God wills to have you descend to the bottom of a fertile valley" (CSG, p. 26). This truth which Thérèse will one day attempt to teach Céline, now her novice, was first a lived experience for herself. The Story of a Soul *makes no mention of it. Thanks to the* Correspondence, *it is possible to determine the time of this "conversion": it took place during her private retreat of 1892 (LT 137). The Carmelite nun is on the verge of discovering her own contemplative style: renouncing the sublime, she chooses to descend to serve as* an abode *for Jesus. An orientation which was confirmed throughout the years to come.*

Concerning this "time of graces" at the end of 1892, the Story of a Soul *retains only one incident: the conversation with Sister Martha of Jesus around December 8 (Ms. C, p. 235). Thérèse had decided to open the eyes of her companion who was too assiduous in her attentions towards Mother Marie de Gonzague. She measured the risks in her undertaking and confided in Sister Agnes of Jesus. "I still seem to see her in the evening in the sacristy," testified the latter. "She said to me in a serious tone of voice: 'Pray very*

*much for me. The Blessed Virgin has inspired me to
enlighten Sister Martha. I am going to tell her this evening
what I think of her.' I said: 'But you are running the risk
of being betrayed. Then our Mother will not be able to stand
you, and you will be sent away to another monastery.' She
answered: 'I know that, but since I am now certain it is my
duty to speak, I must not consider the consequences'''
(NPPA, Virtue of Fortitude). Thus the "little brush" was
beginning her work in souls. The outcome was encouraging.*

A chance reference to the Mother of God, in a letter to
Céline *(LT 137)*, opens up a vista on her contemplative life
at this time. Without ceasing to be Thérèse *of the* Holy Face,
she has discovered a new intimacy with the Child Jesus. She
will express this soon in the first of her poems: La Rosée
divine ou le lait virginal de Marie, The divine Dew or Mary's
virginal milk, *February 2, 1893.*

On the family level, a certain relaxation has set in. M.
Martin's "three years of martyrdom" have come to an end
(Ms. A, p. 173): the great humiliations give way to "a very
gentle childishness" *(LD, May 10, 1892, note 3)*. Thérèse
herself has also gone beyond "the sad years" *(LT 138)*, and
she resumes once again "the memories of her youth" *(LT
139)*. Her playful nature is evidenced once more *(LT 139
and 136)*, carrying its "joyful echoes" even to Canada *(LC
151)*.

Thus Thérèse "mystic and comic" of 1893 (see p. 778)
is on her way.

LT 136   **From Thérèse to Marie Guérin.**
October 16, 1892
→ LC lost

J.M.J.T.

Jesus †   Carmel, October 16, '92

Dear little Marie,

Since you were entrusted with offering me wishes for a happy feast from the whole family, I think I must entrust you with the mission of thanking dear Aunt, first, for her little letter and the large package of chocolate which really delighted our little provisor,[1] and, secondly, for the delicious coffee cream, and then above all for the dear and amiable little letter from her nurse,[2] who will soon restore dear little Aunt's health, I have no doubt. I beg also the little Doctor[3] of *rue de l'Oratoire* to offer my thanks to the Big Doctor and his dear little Jeanne, who, in spite of her convalescence, thought of my feast, which really touched me....

The slight relapse, which fortunately has had no ill effects on Jeanne's health, gave me a thought I shall confide to my dear little Doctor. It seems to me the good Saint Anne felt she was being forgotten somewhat,[4] so she hurried to make us think of her! I assure you, henceforth I am always mindful of her. When I am in spirit near my dear little sister at Caen, immediately the good Saint Anne returns to my memory, and I entrust the one whom I love to her.

I see with pleasure, dear little Marie, the air of the city of Caen is causing you no melancholy, and your cheerfulness, I have no doubt (even more than your knowledge as Doctor), will soon quickly restore our two dear patients.

The patties made by a pastrycook as distinguished as yourself seem to me a very delicate dish for Carmelites, but could you not prove your talent by making some pies so light that Jeanne may devour them not only with her eyes but eat them without experiencing any bad effects?...

I close, dear little Doctor, begging you to excuse my ugly handwriting. Hug very tightly for me the whole family and thank them for all the treats sent to me in such abundance that I fear I forgot to mention some of them.

Tell dear Aunt I am begging her to place a big kiss from me on your little cheeks and believe in the tenderness of your little sister,

Thérèse of the Child Jesus
rel. carm. ind.

* Autograph in twenty-seven fragments.
1. Sister Agnes of Jesus; see LC 149, note 6.
2. Marie Guérin. Her mother was sick at her daughter's home at Caen.
3. Marie Guérin, who was given this title later on in the Carmel; see DE, p. 756. The big doctor was Francis La Néele, whose office was on 26, *rue de l'Oratoire*, Caen (section destroyed by the 1944 bombing of Normandy).
4. Since the pilgrimage to Auray in May (LD, May 10, 1892, note 1).

LT 137   **From Thérèse to Céline.**
October 19, 1892

J.M.J.T.

Jesus †   Carmel, October 19, 1892

Dear Céline,

Formerly, in the days of our childhood, we used to enjoy our feast because of the little gifts we mutually exchanged. The smallest object had then an incomparable value in our eyes.... Soon, the scene changed. Wings grew on the youngest of the birds, and it flew away far from the sweet nest of its childhood, and all illusion vanished! Summer had followed spring, life's reality, the dreams of youth....

Céline, was it not at that decisive moment that the bonds which joined our hearts were tightened? Yes, separation united us in a way that language cannot express. Our childlike affection was changed into a union of feelings, a unity of souls and minds. Who, then, could have accomplished this marvel?... Ah! it was He who had ravished our hearts. "The Beloved chosen among thousands, the odor alone of his ointments suffices to draw us after him.[1] Following his steps, young maidens run lightly on the road."[2] (Canticle of Canticles.)

Jesus has attracted us together, although by different ways; together He has raised us above all the fragile things of this world whose image passes away.[3] He has placed, so to speak, *all things* under our feet. Like Zachaeus, we climbed a tree to see Jesus.[4]... Then we could say with Saint John of the Cross: "All is mine, all is for me, the earth is mine, the heavens are mine, God is mine, and the Mother of my God is mine."[5] With regard to the Blessed Virgin, I must confide to you one of my simple ways with her. I surprise myself at times by saying to her: "But good Blessed Virgin, I find I am more blessed than you, for I have you for Mother, and you do not have a *Blessed Virgin to love*.[6]... It is true you are the Mother of Jesus, but this Jesus you have given entirely to us...and He, on the Cross, He gave you to us as Mother. Thus we are richer than you since we possess Jesus and since you are ours also. Formerly, in your humility, you wanted one day to be the little servant of the happy Virgin who would have the honor of being the Mother of God,[7] and here I am, a poor little creature, and I am not your servant but your child. You are the Mother of Jesus, and you are my Mother." No doubt, the Blessed Virgin must laugh at my simplicity, and nevertheless what I am telling her is really true!... Céline, what a mystery is our grandeur in Jesus.[8]... This is all that Jesus has shown us in making us climb the symbolic tree about which I was just talking to you. And now what science is He about to teach us? Has He not taught us all?... Let us listen to what He is saying to us: "Make haste to descend, I must lodge today at your house."[9] Well, Jesus tells us to descend.... Where, then, must we descend? Céline, you know better than I, however, let me tell you where we must now follow Jesus. In days gone by, the Jews asked our divine Savior: "Master, where do you live?"[10] And He answered: "The foxes have their lairs, the birds of heaven their nests, but I have no place to rest my head."[11] This is where we must descend in order that we may serve as an abode for Jesus. To be so poor that we do not have a place to rest our head. This is, dear Céline, what Jesus has done in my soul during my retreat.[12]... You understand, there

1 Cor 7:31

Lk 19:5

Jn 1:38

Mt 8:20

is question here of the interior. Besides, has not the exterior already
been reduced to nothing by means of the very sad trial of Caen?...
In our dear Father, Jesus has stricken us in the most sensitive exterior part of our heart; now let us allow Him to act, He can complete His work in our souls.... What Jesus desires is that we receive
Him into our hearts. No doubt, they are already empty of creatures,
but, alas, I feel mine is not entirely empty of myself, and it is for
this reason that Jesus tells me to descend.... He, the King of kings,
humbled Himself in such a way that His face was hidden,[13] and no
one recognized Him...and I, too, want to hide my face, I want my
Beloved alone to see it, that He be the only one to count my
tears..that in my heart at least He may rest His dear head and feel
that there He is known and understood!...

Céline, I cannot tell you all I would like, my soul is powerless....
Ah, if only I could!... But, no, this is not in my power...why be
sad, do you not always think what I am thinking?... Thus all I do
not tell you, you divine. Jesus makes you feel it in your heart. Has
He not, moreover, set up His abode there to console Himself for
the crimes of sinners? Yes, it is there in the intimate retreat of the
soul that He instructs us together, and one day He will show us the
day which will no longer have any setting....

Happy feast. How sweet it will be one day for your Thérèse to
wish it to you in heaven!...

* Autograph.
1. See Canticle of Canticles 5:10; 1:3-4.
2. John of the Cross, St., *Spiritual Canticle*, stanza XXV *Collected
   Works*, p. 413.
3. See I Corinthians 7:31.
4. See Luke 19, 4.
5. John of the Cross, St., *Prayer of the Soul enkindled by love, Collected Works*, p. 668. See also LT 182, note 23.
6. Thérèse shared these reflections during recreation; see CJ 11.8.4.
7. Same idea in RP 6, *Flight into Egypt*, January 21, 1896. Among other
   possible sources for this opinion, let us cite the *Année liturgique* by
   Dom Guéranger (Advent December 9, ed. 1858, p. 398). This whole
   development on the Mother of Jesus is to be considered in the light
   of Sister Thérèse of Saint Augustine's remarks; see LC 153, note 5.
   This meditation should be set several weeks or months before February
   2, 1893.

8. A spontaneous exclamation or a reference to the book of Msgr. de Ségur? At the end of October, Sister Agnes of Jesus wrote to Céline: "If you would like to lend me the 2nd and 3rd little volumes of *Nos grandeurs en Jésus*, this would please me much, but if you are using one of the two, send me only one." (Undated letter, October 30-31, 1892, judging by its content.) The Lisieux Carmel library has three volumes: *La Piété et la Vie intérieure* - Vth treatise: *Nos Grandeurs en Jésus*, by Msgr. de Ségur (Tolra, Paris, 5th. ed., 1886). To be noted also are the different books of P. D'Argentan on the "grandeurs" of God, Mary, the Christian, etc.

9. See Luke 19:5.

10. See John 1:38.

11. See Matthew 8:20. Words commented on in P 21, stanza 8 of *Jésus, mon Bien-Aimé, rappelle-toi*! See LT 144.

12. Private retreat postponed to please Sister Martha (LD September 10-12, 1891, note 1). In 1892, the Community retreat was preached in November by P. Déodat de Basly, Franciscan, who had conducted the St. John of the Cross triduum in November 1891.

13. See Isaias 53:3; LT 108.

LT 138   **From Thérèse to Mme. Guérin.**

November 17,   For her feast day.
1892

J.M.J.T.

Jesus †   Carmel, November 17, 1892

Dear Aunt,

The littlest of your daughters feels powerless to tell you again of her affection and all the prayers she is offering for you. However, a mother's heart easily divines what goes on in her child's soul, so, dear little Aunt, I shall not try to express these sentiments which you have known for a long time.

This year, God filled my heart with a very sweet consolation by recalling my dear Father from his exile. When I go over in my mind the sorrowful years just passed, my soul is overflowing with gratitude. I cannot regret the sorrows that are passed and that have completed and embellished the crown God intends to place soon on the venerable head of him who loved and served Him so faithfully....

And then these sorrows have taught me to understand better the treasures of tenderness hidden in the heart of the dear relatives whom God has given me.... "The most beautiful masterpiece of God's Heart is the heart of a mother."[1] I am experiencing how true this saying is, and I thank the Lord for having made me have this sweet experience.

Dear little Aunt, I assure you, though you have a maternal heart for us, your little daughter has one that is very filial, so she is begging Jesus to bestow on you all the favors of which a child's heart can dream for its dear mother. Frequently, only silence can express my prayer, however, this divine Guest of the Tabernacle understands all, even the silence of a child's soul filled with gratitude!...

Though I shall not be present on dear Aunt's feast day, my heart will really be near her, and no one will give her more tenderness than I.

I beg you, dear Aunt, to kiss good Uncle and my dear little sisters for me.

I leave you, dear Aunt, while remaining united to you as a daughter to her mother.

Your child who loves you,

Sister Thérèse of the Child Jesus
rel. carm. ind.

---

*   Autograph.
1. Msgr. Dupanloup, *Conférences aux femmes chrétiennes,* 9th conference: *"La Mère."*

LT 139   **From Thérèse to M. and Mme. Guérin.**
December 30, 1892

J.M.J.T.

Jesus †   Carmel, December 30, 1892

Dear Uncle and dear Aunt,

It is very sweet for your little Benjamin to come to offer you her wishes for the New Year about to begin.

I am not going to attempt to tell you here all the wishes I am making for my dear relatives; it would take too long, and then the heart has aspirations that words are powerless to express. There are desires God alone can understand or rather divine. It is, then, to Him I want to entrust the wishes my heart is making for those who are so dear to me.

Frequently, when I am at the feet of Our Lord, I feel my soul overflowing with gratitude when I think over the grace He granted me in giving me relatives like the ones I have the happiness to possess.

I am not forgetting that January 2 is dear Uncle's birthday.[1] I am proud to have been born on the same day as he, and I hope he will not forget to pray for his little Thérèse, who will soon be an old girl of twenty.[2] How time flies!... It seems only yesterday that good Uncle used to bounce me on his knees, singing the romance of Blue-Beard, with terrible eyes that almost made me die of fright.[3]... The little *tune of Mirlitir* was more to my taste.... The remembrance of this song is enough to make me laugh still.

You see, dear Uncle and Aunt, the weight of years[4] has still not taken away your little daughter's memory; on the contrary, she is at an age when memories of childhood have a particular charm....

I beg you, dear relatives, to offer all my wishes to those whom I love; I am naming no one, for the remainder of my paper would not be sufficient, but all the names are inscribed in my heart and hold a large place there.

Your OLD Niece, who loves you with all her heart,

Sister Thérèse of the Child Jesus,
rel. carm. ind.

    * Autograph.
    1. M. Guérin was fifty-two years old, January 2, 1893.
    2. The word "twenty" is enlarged.
    3. A memory recalled in Ms. A, p. 42.
    4. Thérèse made a similar statement to P. Pichon; see LC 157.

LC 150   *From Sister Marie of the Sacred Heart to*
                    Thérèse.

January 2, 1893

   Dear little sister, I spent the whole time of silence looking for a
little picture, and my heart is very sad at not being able to find it.
I have nothing, then, to give my little girl for her twentieth birthday! What poverty! But my heart is filled with riches and with
tenderness for her.... It is nine o'clock. Twenty years ago at this
same hour, Mamma was saying to us: "Go and rest, children, it is
time to go,"[1] and at her mysterious look we were rejoicing in advance at the imminent arrival of our little sister, now a Carmelite,
now the dear little spouse of Jesus, the King of heaven.... Oh! how
He loves her and is proud of her beauty!...

    * Autograph.
    1. Little Thérèse was born on January 2, 1873, at eleven-thirty at night;
    see *Correspondance Familiale*, p. 141, letter 84.

LC 151   *From P. Pichon to Thérèse.*

January 20, 1893
→ LT lost

Sister Thérèse
of the Child Jesus   † Lavaltrie

                                              January 20, '93

Dear little Lamb of the Child Jesus,

I can see no longer except with four eyes![1] But my heart never
loses sight of you, and our souls are forever inseparable in Jesus.
You are really to be pitied if my silence is as painful to you as it
is to me.

You speak to me, and I am answering you in the adorable Heart
of the Beloved. Do you understand me as I understand you? All the
echoes of your soul are joyous to me.

What should I wish for you this year when the Sacred Heart of
Jesus wills to be your Protector and your Patron.[2] Is there any greater
happiness than to be spoiled by the Heart of love?

Close to the Sacred Heart one sigh is very much; one sigh is sufficient for Him to open His Heart entirely to you. Dare, then, to complain again at having only a sigh!

Dear Child of my soul, listen to what I am about to tell you in
the name and on the part of Our Lord: No, no, you have not committed any mortal sins. I swear it.[3] No, we cannot sin gravely without
knowing it. No, after absolution, we must not doubt about our state
of grace. To your Mother St. Teresa, who was praying one day for
souls, who were deluding themselves, Our Lord answered: "My
daughter, no one is lost without knowing it perfectly."[4] Banish, then,
your worries.[5] God wills it, and I command it. Take my word for
it: Never, never, never, have you committed a mortal sin. Go quickly
to kneel before the Tabernacle to thank Our Lord. Fall asleep, tranquil and serene in the arms of Jesus. He has never betrayed you;
He will never betray you.

Not having written you on Christmas day was a very great sacrifice
for me. I had promised myself to do so, but Jesus makes sport of

all my little plans. Let us be a toy in the divine Child's hands.
Oh, my dear little Lamb, all my heart blesses you and my whole
soul is yours lovingly in the Most Sacred Heart.

Almire Pichon

Pray for my fifty years.[6]

* Autograph.

1. In 1892, P. Pichon complained of his failing sight. It became worse
   as time went on; see LD, January 1, 1896, note 1. The progress of
   this infirmity has no doubt something to do with the spacing of
   Thérèse's letters; see LT 142, note 16.

2. On January 1, each Sister drew by lot a piece of paper bearing the
   name of a patron Saint for the coming year; Thérèse had written to
   P. Pichon, then, on this date or shortly afterward.

3. This was an assurance given *viva voce* to Thérèse in May 1888; see
   Ms. A, p. 149. It is the only positive intervention of P. Pichon which
   Thérèse seems to have retained; see CJ 4.7.4: "P. Pichon used to treat
   me too much like a child; however, he did me some good, too, by
   telling me I had never committed any mortal sins."

4. See St. Teresa of Avila: "With regard to the fear about whether or
   not I was in the state of grace, He told me: 'Daughter, light is very
   different from darkness. I am faithful. Nobody will be lost unknow-
   ingly." (See *Collected Works* of St. Teresa of Avila, trans. Kieran
   Kavanaugh, O.C.D. and Otilio Rodriguez, O.C.D., vol. I, p. 332.)

5. P. Pichon is answering several letters here, for his last letter goes back
   twenty-three months. It is impossible to be precise, then, about the
   time of these confidences from Thérèse on this matter. We know there
   is a little autograph note in the Carmel archives. Thérèse wrote on
   it an answer from l'abbé Baillon, extraordinary confessor around the
   beginning of 1892: "If you do not act against your conscience, even
   though there would be a sin, you would not be sinning." The slanted
   handwriting and black ink *suggest* a date in 1893. Regarding these
   dates, we must weigh carefully Mother Agnes of Jesus' testimony:
   "From this retreat (1891), Thérèse surrendered herself totally to confidence in God" (PO, 1496).

6. The following February 3.

SIXTH PERIOD

THE PRIORATE OF MOTHER
AGNES OF JESUS

(February 1893 — March 1896)

THE PRIORATE
OF MOTHER AGNES OF JESUS

"It was especially since the blessed day of your election that I have flown on the ways of love...." (Ms. A, p. 174.) *It was thus that Thérèse expressed herself at the end of 1895 when Mother Agnes' term of office was about to end. We run the risk of forming, on the strength of this statement, an idyllic image of the priorate in question, or of attributing to the change in prioress the spiritual development that took place in Thérèse. The* Correspondence, *once again, dissipates these optical illusions.*

When we follow the documents step by step, without any a priori *outline, it appears that the years 1893-1896 present a diversified itinerary, even though they are placed under the sign "of peace and love" (LT 143).*

The first months of Mother Agnes' priorate passed by in a kind of euphoria. For Thérèse it was "repose in the valley" (p. 777). A new spring of poetry and tenderness flowed for Thérèse with the return of her "little Mother," to whom she was one day to say: "You are a lyre, a song, for me" (CJ 11.9.2). The spring and summer of 1893 are to be numbered among the most lyrical of Thérèse's existence.

However, an interior call soon snatched her away from her oasis. The autumn and winter of 1893-1894 were

*witnesses to a vigorous effort at detachment on her part,
even including certain liberations (p. 821). It was certainly
not due to chance that the vertical direction of her handwriting, until then slanted, occurred at this time (January
1894).*

*The route of her exodus passed through a new "desert,
arid and without water" (LT 165). Many types of suffering
purified her "as gold in the crucible" (p. 856).*

*Though the death of M. Martin (July 29, 1894) had no
direct effect upon Thérèse's correspondence, nevertheless,
Céline's entrance into the cloister, six weeks later (September
14), modified the character of this correspondence and even
impoverished it. Moreover, the correspondent herself
withdrew deliberately into her littleness (p. 888). These two
family events manifested to her, each in its own way, God's
"immensity of love" for her (CJ 16.7.2 and Ms. A, p. 177);
this was an intimate experience soon to be sanctioned by
the Word of God which set her definitively on her "little
way."*

*But the paradoxical efficacy of this withdrawal was shown
without delay, just as it will happen again in 1896: "Lowering myself into the depths of my nothingness, I raised myself
so high that I was able to attain my goal" (Ms. B, p. 194).
A summit is effectively attained in 1895. From this "mountain (see Mark 3:13, quoted in Ms. A, p. 13), the Carmelite
could survey the panorama of her past existence. Now it is
at this precise moment that she was invited by Mother Agnes
of Jesus to write her* Story of a Soul. *For one who has
followed Thérèse since April 4, 1877, the date of her first
"letter," it would be good to stop in order to reread here
the* Story of a Soul *in which are recapitulated eighteen years
of the* Correspondence.

*This in-depth survey brings out the astonishing coherence
of an itinerary, the course of which the* Letters *have detailed.*

It especially justifies the importance attached by Thérèse to her "conversion" of Christmas 1886 (General Correspondence, vol. I, p. 259). The Thérèse alone of 1895 could, in fact, reveal the meaning of this basic event, "day of graces among all others" (LT 201). The warlike vocabulary that its description borrows (Ms. A, p. 97) seems to imply a likening of her spiritual adventure (1886-1895) to the heroic exploits of Joan of Arc (p. 820), advancing from "victory to victory" (but, first, from combat to combat, including wounds and fear). However, more so than Joan of Arc, the Thérèse of 1895, now clothed in "the waves of infinite tenderness," was in a position to evaluate the stakes of such a loving liberation for the total victory of "consuming and transforming love" (LT 197).

With regard to herself, this liberation (from self, from her sensitivity) was born on the "night of light" at Les Buissonnets (Christmas 1886). Thérèse will not cease to conquer it and to defend it right up to the day when—three months before her death—she will write: "I already enjoy the reward promised to those who fight courageously. I no longer feel it necessary to refuse myself all consolations of the heart, for my soul is strengthened by Him whom I wanted to love alone. I see with joy that in loving Him, the heart grows, it can give incomparably more tenderness to those who are dear to it than if it were centered in a selfish and unfruitful love" (Ms. C, p. 237). Up to this time, there was no tenderness received or given that had not passed through the crucible of trial for her. Better than any other document, the Correspondence *of 1893-1896 illustrates this law, which was applied first to those who were dearest to Thérèse: her "little Mother," and her "twin-sister" Céline (without mentioning her "dear King," whom she had to lose in so many ways during the preceding years).*

A Carmelite at age fifteen thanks to Pauline, Thérèse never swerved from the ideal she had formed at the age of nine: "I wanted to go to Carmel not for Pauline's sake but for Jesus alone" (Ms. A, p. 58). She continued acting this way, even when Jesus restored "her mamma" in person (LT 106), who was now "consecrated" (LT 140) and identified, so to speak, with Him: on February 20, 1893, did not Pauline become her "living Jesus"? (Ms. A, p. 174.) The rediscovered harmony of nature and grace promoted in her an incontestable development. The forty-six Letters written during this priorate do not permit (in content and handwriting) any doubt in this matter. Thérèse did not allow herself to be enchained. Furthermore, when, in spite of all expectations, this priorate turned into a storm (see LT 156, note 7), she surmounted with strength of soul the filial and fraternal compassion that each confrontation between Mother Marie de Gonzague and Mother Agnes of Jesus made her endure.

The suffering endured when she left her inseparable Céline, April 9, 1888, was nothing compared with the eventuality "of the great sacrifice. . . very painful for Thérèse (Ms. A, p. 177): the project of her sister's departure for Canada. And nevertheless she will have to lose this very dear sister for a time in a way far more difficult for her "maternal" heart. "These pages" are among the number of those that Thérèse thought "would never be read on earth" (Ms. A, p. 160), and of which the Correspondence *nevertheless allows us to see some scattered words.*

For having kept her heart pure, *not allowing it to become enclosed in a selfish and sterile affection, Thérèse of the Child Jesus and of the Holy Face made herself capable of "knowing" Love, a Love whose "characteristic is to lower Itself" (Ms. A, p. 14). For having attached herself to "remaining in love," to "living by love," by remaining little, the contemplative merited* to see God: *"To me He has given His infinite Mercy, and it is through it that I contemplate and adore the other divine Perfections!" (Ms. A, p. 180.)*

Repose in the valley *(see LT 142)*
(February–September 1893)
Age twenty

The first months of Mother Agnes' priorate witnessed the development, with regard to the Correspondence, *of a dialogue of unusual compactness between Thérèse and Céline. The richness of the letters in July especially is too obvious to need any emphasis. The exchanges between the two sisters take up more than half of the seventeen documents of this period, and, by way of exception, their ten letters are in direct response to each other. A glance at both writers will lead to a better reading of their letters.*

The election of Pauline was a real blessing for both of them. Thérèse expressed her sentiments with tenderness and reserve on that same evening to Mother Agnes (Lt 140). Céline confided her own feelings to her cousin Jeanne: "I was very much moved; Pauline's election proved to me once again how God is interested in His own and how, after trial, He can exalt them" (to Mme. La Néele, February 23, 1893).

In the absence of any photographs, two portraits give us a description of Thérèse at the age of twenty:

1) *A symbolic self-portrait painted by her brush on the wall of the oratory during the summer of 1893. Among a dozen little angels as guard of honor for the Monstrance, a sleeping child (without wings) presses a lyre and a lily to its heart. The sleep of abandonment, the brilliance of the* Lily of the Valley *(Jesus), the vibrations of the* lyre, *these are so many themes easily discernable in Thérèse's letters at this time.*

2) *A sketch, contemporaneous with the preceding, from the pen of Sister Marie of the Angels. We must give in its entirety this classic from Theresian literature: "Sister*

Thérèse of the Child Jesus, twenty years old. Novice and jewel of the Carmel, its dear Benjamin. Office of painting in which she excells without having had any other lessons than those of seeing our Reverend Mother, her dear sister, at work. Tall and strong, with the appearance of a child, a tone of voice, an expression, hiding within her a wisdom, a perfection, a perspicacity of a fifty-year-old. Soul always calm and in perfect possession of itself in all things and with everybody. Little innocent thing, to whom one would give God without confession, but whose head is full of mischief to play on anyone she pleases. Mystic, comic, everything. . .she can make you weep with devotion and just as easily split your sides with laughter during our recreations." (To the Visitation at Le Mans, 1893.)

The former prioress, Mother Marie de Gonzague, was named mistress of novices, and Sister Marie of the Angels was elected subprioress. Oldest in the novitiate, Thérèse was invited by Mother Agnes "to watch over her two companions, Sister Martha and Sister Marie-Madeleine" (NPPA, Virtue of Prudence). Mother Marie de Gonzague agreed "to be aided by her in correcting and occasionally instructing them" (ibid.). There was nothing new in this regarding Sister Martha. As for Sister Marie-Madeleine, Thérèse never succeeded in winning over this gloomy companion, marked by an unhappy childhood.

Céline, now twenty-four years old, was going through a complicated crisis. In spite of her filial tenderness—we should call it: maternal—for her sick father, it was difficult for her to be unable to realize her vocation. Léonie left her in order to enter the Visitation once more: Marie Guérin made her decision to enter Carmel. Céline felt that she was cast aside, a family stray. Moreover, P. Pichon had placed her in a compromising situation regarding her sisters, asking her to keep secret his plan for a religious foundation in Canada. Finally, Mother Agnes feared for her "little

Céline" the intoxication of a somewhat worldly form of life: parties at the Guérin home, many servants, etc. In order to neutralize these attractions, she had recourse to the "little lyre player," Thérèse, who wrote Céline with unusual frequency (one letter a week in July-August 1893).

Though Céline's boat was "out at sea," "lost on the stormy waves," that of Thérèse was gliding gently with the current, following closely the meanderings of an opulant valley. The collection of letters for these six months reminds us of a pastoral symphony, very cool and peaceful, revealing many themes that were to be developed two years later in the Story of a Soul.

Read: Ms. A, pp. 173-174.

LD   *From Mme. Guérin to Mme. La Néele.*
February 20, 1893   (Extracts.)

Dear little Jeanne,

I have great news to announce to you today, so I shall not await your letter to answer it. Today was the election of a new superior for the Carmel, and Mother Marie de Gonzague could not be reelected.[1] Can you guess who was named superior?... It was your cousin Pauline. So you would be unable to believe the state of emotion she is in today. Your papa went to see her, and our two little girls[2] went there also. She was unable to say anything to her sisters, poor Pauline, she was so much touched. All they heard were little sobs; your papa went to see her also in order to encourage her in her new charge. Fortunately, she will have Mother Marie de Gonzague to guide her, for a heavy weight has fallen upon her shoulders, young as she is.[3] The visit of the young girls was not gay, and this even more so because the situation was very delicate for them. Mother Marie de Gonzague was present, and this required very much tact. It is certain that our dear little Pauline has everything necessary to make a good superior, but she is so timid, so easily moved, her health is weak,[4] and she is very young. Once she has overcome her feelings and has been broken into her charge, I am sure she will be all right. I think, dear little Jeanne, it will be good for you to write her a little letter, but you should keep in mind that Mother Marie de Gonzague may see it,[5] and so you will keep a certain reserve.

Before leaving you, I beg for a little remembrance in your prayers for our dear little superior. You will not receive a letter from the Carmel informing you of the election, for Mother Marie de Gonzague asked us to inform the whole family. I forgot to tell you that our little Pauline was elected by a unanimous vote.[6] It seems it is very rare to see an election turn out in this way. They saw the finger of God in this.

Your very devoted mother,
Céline Guérin

1. She was in charge since February 3, 1886, having had two successive priorates (the maximum canonically), with the extension of one year because of the epidemic in the winter of 1891-1892.
2. Marie Guérin, Léonie, and Céline (average age was twenty-five).
3. Pauline was thirty-one and a half years of age.
4. She wrote "*faible*," but first "*n'est pas bonne.*"
5. Because Mother Agnes will undoubtedly show it to her. Later on, she will assume an independent attitude in these things, conformably with her right as prioress.
6. Statement needing qualification. The register of the monastary simply records the stereotyped statement: "Her election was made canonically," without any other precise details. In 1910, Sister Aimée of Jesus stated at the Beatification Process: "At the election of Mother Agnes of Jesus, her sister, to the priorate of 1893, the votes were very much divided; Sister Thérèse of the Child Jesus never showed any animosity towards the nuns who had not voted for Mother Agnes of Jesus, the secret of the votation not having been well kept" (PO, 2220). Sister Saint Stanislaus expressed herself in guarded words: "At her sister's election as prioress, her conduct was admirable; she experienced a moment of sadness which I alone noticed, and I was very much edified by her" (*Memoire* of 1906). See LT 140, note 6.

LT 140   **From Thérèse to Mother Agnes of Jesus.**
February 20, 1893

J.M.J.T.

Jesus †   February 20, 1893

Dear *Mother*,

How sweet it is for me to be able to give you this name!... For
a long time already you were my *Mother*,[1] but it was in the secret
of my heart I was giving this sweet name to her who was at once
my *guardian Angel*[2] and my *Sister*. Today God has *consecrated*
you...you are truly my Mother and you will be this during all eternity.... Oh! how beautiful this day is for your child!... The veil
Jesus has cast over this day[3] makes it more luminous in my eyes,
it is the seal of the Adorable Face, the perfume of the mysterious
bouquet[4] that is poured out on you. No doubt, this will always be
the same. "He whose face was hidden,"[5] He who is still hidden in
His little white Host and who communicates Himself to souls only
as *veiled*, will be able to spread upon the entire life of the beloved
apostle of His divine Face a mysterious veil which He alone can
penetrate!...

Yes, Mother Geneviève's spirit lives entirely in you,[6] and her prophetic word has been realized.[7] At *thirty* you have begun your public
life. Is it not you who gave to all the Carmels and to so many pious
souls the consolation of the touching and *poetic* account of our
Saint's life?... But already Jesus had cast on my dear Mother His
veiled look, and He did not allow her to be recognized,[8] for her face
was hidden!...

If this day is already so beautiful on earth, what is it in heaven?
I seem to see our saintly Mother looking with joy on her Pauline
(the one whom she loved, the one who attracted her);[9] she sees her
becoming in her turn a Mother, Mother of many virgins, among
whom are her own sisters. What a mystery....

Now you are about to penetrate into the sanctuary of souls; you
are going to pour out upon them the treasures of grace with which
Jesus has filled you. No doubt, you will suffer.... The vessels will

be too little to contain the precious perfume you will want to place in them. However, Jesus Himself has only very small musical instruments on which to play His melody of love, and yet He can use all those we present to Him. You will be like Jesus!... Little Sister, dear Mother, my own heart, the heart of your child is a very *little* lyre. When you are tired of making the harps resound, you will come to take up your *little* lyre, and hardly will you have touched it when it will produce the sounds you desire...at the touch alone of your *consecrated* fingers,[10] it WILL UNDERSTAND and its feeble melody will mingle with the song of your heart....

Oh, Mother! how many things I would like to say...but, no, you know all.... One day, when the shadows will have passed, I shall rest on your heart, and I shall repeat this sweet name

Mother

* Autograph.
1. Since the death of Mme. Martin; see Ms. A, p. 34.
2. In two years, Thérèse will dedicate the poem to her: *To my dear Mother, the Beautiful Angel of my Childhood* (P 19, September 7, 1895); see LT 156, last paragraph, and LT 159, 229, 230.
3. First writing: "on my Mother." This veil was first the tears of the new prioress, due to her emotions (see preceding LD); perhaps, too, other circumstances of her election which have not been revealed.
4. Allusion to the symbolic prayer to the Holy Face, composed by Sister Agnes of Jesus in 1890; see p. 610, vol. I.
5. Isaias 53:3; see LT 108.
6. Thérèse is recalling Canon Delatroëtte's exhortation to the new prioress at the obedience ceremony in the choir: "Your saintly Mother Geneviève will aid you, you will apply yourself to imitating the precious example she left you. I can tell you without failing in discretion that if the greater part of your Sisters thought of giving you their votes, it is because they noticed you are trying to practice the virtues you saw practiced in her." (Notes taken down by Thérèse; without taking part in the election, she had heard the exhortation, along with the Community gathered together for the announcement of the names of the religious elected.)
7. We have found no written text on this "prophecy."
8. At the end of the second notebook in which Mother Agnes transcribed Thérèse's manuscript (see Mss. I, p. 25), she also copied this letter,

and noted: Mother Marie de Gonzague had asked me to make a circular [biographical sketch after death] for our saintly Mother Geneviève. She was prioress, and she signed this circular as she had the right and the duty." (Notebook, p. 541.) This note dates from 1936. Mother Agnes did not hide from certain ones how this *incognito* pained her in 1892, the time of the writing of the biographical circular.

9. Mme. Martin had a preference for her daughter, Pauline, who resembled her very much; see p. 1125, her letter to Pauline, November 19, 1876. A short time before her death, Mme. Martin expressed her love to her daughter: "She held my hands, kissed them, and she said: 'Oh, Pauline, you are my treasure. I know you will be a religious, that you will become a saint. I am not worthy to have a daughter like you; you are my glory and my honor.' These are not her exact words but they express their meaning." (*Souvenirs intimes*, pp. 41-42.) M. Martin had a preference for his oldest daughter Marie; in his letters he referred to her as "my big one, my first, my beloved." See *Le Père de sainte Thérèse de l'Enfant-Jésus*, pp. 112-118. Expressions Thérèse used in RP 8 (August 1894, the month after M. Martin's death): *Rappelle-toi ta bien-aimée Marie — Ta fille aînée, la plus chère à ton coeur. (Remember your beloved Marie — Your oldest daughter, the dearest to your heart.)*

10. We read here: "maternal," a correction by Mother Agnes of Jesus.

LT 141   **From Thérèse to Céline.**

April 25, 1893   For Céline's twenty-fourth birthday. It is possible that Thérèse had observed, that very morning, the drops of dew "that sparkled on the tips of blades of grass in the meadow," while the procession in honor of St. Mark was in progress in the garden of the Carmel.

J.M.J.T.

Jesus †   Carmel, April 25, '93

Dear Céline,

I am going to tell you a thought that came to me this morning, or rather I am going to share with you the desires of Jesus concerning your soul.... When I think of you in the presence of the one friend of our souls, it is always simplicity that is presented to me as the distinctive characteristic of your heart.... Céline!...*simple* little *Céline*-flower, do not envy garden flowers. Jesus has not said to us: "I am the flower of the gardens, the cultivated rose," but He tells us: "I am the *flower of the fields* and the Lily of the valleys."[1] Well, I thought this morning near the Tabernacle, that my Céline, the little flower of Jesus, had to be and to remain always a *drop of dew*[2] hidden in the divine corolla of the beautiful Lily of the valleys. A drop of dew, what is more simple and more pure? It is not the *clouds* that have formed it since, when the blue of the sky is star-studded, the dew descends on the flowers; it is not comparable to the rain that it surpasses in freshness and beauty. Dew exists only at night; as soon as the sun darts its warm rays, it distills the charming pearls that sparkle on the tips of blades of grass in the meadow, and the dew is changed into a light vapor. Céline is a little drop of dew that has not been formed by the clouds but has descended from the beautiful heaven, its homeland. During *the night* of life, its mission is to hide itself in the heart of the *Flower of the fields*; no human eye is to discover it there, only the calyx possessing the little drop will know its freshness. Blessed little drop of dew that is known only by Jesus!... Do not stop to consider the course of resounding rivers that cause admiration in creatures. Do not even envy the clear brook winding in the meadow. No doubt its murmur is very sweet, but creatures can hear it...and then the calyx of the flower of the fields would be unable to contain it. It could not be for Jesus alone. To be His, one must remain little, little like a drop of dew!... Oh! how few are the souls who aspire to remain little in this way![3]... "But," they say, "are not the river and the brook more useful than the drop of dew, what does it do? It is good for nothing except to refresh for a few moments a flower of the fields which is today and will have disappeared tomorrow."[4]... Undoubtedly these persons are right, the drop of dew is good only for that; but they do not know the wild flower that willed to live on our earth of exile and to remain there during the short night of life. If they did know it, they would understand the reproach that Jesus made in days gone by to Martha.[5]... Our Beloved has no need of

our beautiful thoughts[6] and our dazzling works. If He wants sublime
thoughts, does He not have His angels, His legions of heavenly spirits
whose knowledge infinitely surpasses that of the greatest geniuses
of our sad earth?. . . It is not, then, intelligence and talents that Jesus
has come to seek here below. He became the flower of the fields
only in order to show us how much He cherishes simplicity. The Lily
of the *valley* longs only for a little drop of dew. . . . And it is for
this reason He has created one whose name is Céline!. . . During
the night of life, she will have to remain hidden from every human
glance, but when the shadows begin to lengthen,[7] when the Flower
of the fields becomes the Sun of Justice,[8] and when He comes to
carry out His giant's race,[9] will He forget His little drop of dew?. . . *PS.18.6*
Oh, no! as soon as He appears in glory, the companion of His exile
will appear there too.[10] The divine Sun will cast on her one of His
rays of love, and immediately to the eyes of the dazzled angels and
saints will be shown the poor little drop of dew that will sparkle like
a precious diamond which, reflecting the Sun of Justice, will have
become like Him.[11] But this is not all. The divine Star, gazing at
His drop of dew, will draw it to Himself; it will ascend like a light
vapor[12] and will go to place itself for eternity in the bosom of the
burning furnace of uncreated love,[13] and it will be forever united
to Him. Just as on earth it had been the faithful companion of His
exile, His insults, in the same way it will reign eternally in heaven. . . .

Into what astonishment will be plunged those who, in this world,
had considered the little drop of dew as useless!. . . No doubt, they
will have an excuse: *the gift of God*[14] had not been revealed to them;
they had not brought their heart close to that of the *Flower of the
fields*, and they had not understood those stirring words: "Give me
to drink.'[15] Jesus does not call all souls to be drops of dew; He wills   *Jn.4.7*
that there be precious liqueurs that creatures appreciate and that console them in their needs, but He keeps for Himself a drop of dew.
This is His only desire. . . .

What a privilege to be called to so lofty a mission!. . . But to respond to it, how *simple* we must remain. . . . Jesus knows very well
that on earth it is difficult to preserve oneself pure, so He wills that
His drops of dew forget themselves. He is pleased to contemplate
them, but He alone looks at them, and, as for themselves, not realizing their value, they deem themselves as beneath other creatures. . . .

That is what the Lily of the valleys desires. Has the little drop of dew, Céline, understood?.... That is the purpose for which Jesus has created her, but she must not forget her little sister. She must obtain for her the favor of realizing what Jesus made her understand, so that one day the same Ray of love may distill the two drops of dew, and that together, after having been only one on earth, they may be united for eternity in the bosom of the divine Sun.

Thérèse of the Child Jesus of the Holy Face
rel. carm. ind.

*   Autograph
1. See Canticle of Canticles 2:1. Thérèse loved to refer to Jesus under one or other of these names, especially in letters and poems destined for Céline; see LT 142, 143, 183; P 13, 16, 21; RP 2, 5.
2. *Dew* is a theme meaningful to both sisters: see Céline's poem in 1889 (LT 132, note 4); Thérèse's first poem: *La Rosée divine ou le lait virginal de Marie* (the divine Dew or the virginal milk of Mary), sent to Céline during the first days of March 1893 (letter of Mother Agnes of Jesus to Céline, p. 1147; here *dew* is used as a symbol of life hidden in God with Christ (see note 10); poems and other compositions use it to symbolize the tears and blood of Jesus (P 21, RP 2) or Baptism (P 45, RP 2).
3. The first time the expression "to remain little" appears under the pen of Thérèse, destined to become an important point in her spirituality; see Ms. C, pp. 207-208. Perhaps Sister Agnes of Jesus was the first to make use of it in her poem of March 31, 1892 (LT 134, note 3): *Ainsi fait une Carmélite, — La pâquerette de Jésus.... Elle cherche á rester petite — Pour lui plaire de plus en plus....* (Thus does a Carmelite act — The daisy of Jesus — She seeks to remain little — To please Him more and more.) See LT 154, note 2.
4. See Matthew 6:30.
5. See Luke 10:41-42.
6. See Ms. C, p. 234: "I understood a long time ago that we should not depend on them."
7. See Canticle of Canticles 4:6.
8. See Malachi 3:20.
9. See Psalm 18:6.
10. See Colossians 3:4.
11. See I John 3:2.
12. See Thérèse's statement to Mother Agnes of Jesus in 1897: "God will

sip you up like a little drop of dew" (CJ 7.4.1).

　　In Saint John of the Cross: "God, in the omnipotence of His fathomless love, absorbs the soul in Himself more efficaciously and forcibly than a torrent of fire would devour the drop of morning dew, which usually rises and dissolves in the air!" (*Spiritual Canticle*, explanation of stanza XXXI; see *Collected Works*, p. 531.) It is difficult to know if Thérèse was inspired here by Saint John of the Cross.

13. Thérèse uses the words "*amour incréé*": This is the only time it appears in her writings; regarding "*foyer brûlant*," see Ms. B, p. 199.

14. See John 4:10. Thérèse was soon to inscribe these words: "If you knew the gift of God!" on the walls of the oratory where she painted a fresco in June.

15. See John 4:7. In 1889-1890, the thirst of Jesus which Thérèse desires to quench is that of the Crucified, John 19:28 (LC 145). In 1893, she is thinking more of the episode of the Samaritan woman (dear to St. Teresa of Avila). In 1895, giving an account of her July 1887 grace, she combines both themes (Ms. A, pp. 99 and 101); she recalls them in her poem of October 21, 1895: *Jésus, mon Bien-Aimé, rappelle-toi!* (stanzas 10 and 24); in 1896, she inscribes them, among other gospel texts, on a picture of Jesus on the Cross: "I thirst... Give me to drink!" with explicit reference to John 19:28 and 4:7. See also LT 196, Ms. B, p. 189.

LC 152　　　　　　　*From Céline to Thérèse*
April 28, 1893
→ LT 141

　　　　　　　　　　　　　　　　Caen,[1] April 28, 1893

Dear little Thérèse,

　　I am writing you because Francis is going to answer Pauline,[2] I believe, so dear little Pauline will not be vexed with my not addressing my letter to her since she will be receiving one. Tell her that her missive did me too great a good for me to be able to express it. I think of it constantly and this encourages me. Oh! how beautiful and consoling the things she said to me.

　　Thérèse, my own dear Thérèse! If you only knew all I am thinking and how I am meditating a long time and several times a day on what you are whispering to your Céline's heart. . . .

"To be the dew, the drop of dew of the Flower of the fields. . ." Oh, Thérèse, how deeply I understand it, how my soul is plunged into unfathomable depths. . . if you only knew! No, never would I be able to tell you what is going on in me regarding this matter. Now I no longer want anything, nothing pleases me any longer, except to be the drop of dew refreshing the calyx of the Flower of the fields. Each word of your dear letter is a world to my heart. . . .

But I am going to be silent, for I prefer to meditate in silence to speaking about what has no words. The little drop of dew is always and in all things powerless, except to give drink to the Flower of the fields. . . . Thérèse! Both, both of us, are we not two little drops of dew in the calyx of the Flower of the fields? You know that two drops of dew cannot be next to each other, very close to each other, without intermingling and forming only *one single* drop of dew. The Flower of the fields is satisfied with the drop of dew "Thérèse-Céline," with this *single* drop that is an ocean for Him![3]

Pauline tells me in her letter that "Céline's love is more precious to Jesus than the hatred of the wicked is bitter to Him, and that a single note of the wailing of her soul helps Him forget the blasphemies of sinners."[4] It is then, really true that *a single* drop of dew *is sufficient* for Jesus, a single one! He is both consoled and His thirst quenched. . . . Thérèse, dear Thérèse, I could not tell you all that I feel, it is too much. I am explaining myself poorly, but read into my thoughts!

My soul is now stronger, your letters have been a heavenly melody for it.

Dear Thérèse, I love you and I kiss you with my whole heart, and dear little Pauline and Marie also.

Céline

If you know of anything I can bring back to our Mother,[5] but I see nothing at the fair or elsewhere; I would, however, be happy to please her.

Regarding flowers, if you do not answer me or if you are undecided, I favor the large daisies; never have I seen them so well made and not expensive.

There are some delightful pink carnations, red and yellow roses at thirty and twenty *centimes*, etc.; buttercups, greens, etc., etc., the lilies are stiffer. If Pauline wanted anything for her Holy Face picture, I would buy it for her, but it would be better to write and tell me what you want, for example: two red roses, six carnations, six or twelve branches of tall daisies (three daisies to each branch),[6] twenty *centimes* a branch, the carnations, fifteen centimes. If you want something, tell me the number, for I am hampered by not knowing where you want to place them. With no answer, I will buy nothing. However, I would like to give you some, you who love flowers so much and simple flowers.

* G. copy.

1. Céline was at Caen since April 25, with Léonie and Marie Guérin, having been invited there by Mme. La Néele in view of the fair held in that city. She returned to Lisieux, May 2.

2. April 26, Mother Agnes wrote Céline: "If Francis cannot give us any news about Mlle. Troude, I beg you to write me quickly. Ah! if you could only see her, but I fear this is not possible." Mlle. Troude was the niece of Sister Marie-Philomène.

3. Thérèse commented on these expressions in her next letter (LT 142).

4. April 26, 1893. Mother Agnes wrote: "The love of His little dove is more precious to Him," etc. Almost the entire letter develops the allegory of the dove: plumage, nest, song, and cooing.

5. This refers to Mother Marie de Gonzague, they called her "*grand mère*" (see p. 1173). She became very ill in this month of April. Mother Agnes wrote Céline: "The asthma attack has passed.... How frightened we were yesterday evening! How sick she was.... She looked like a dying person to me; I was broken, I wept! She told me God would help me, that she was no longer necessary for me, that Mother Geneviéve would be with me, etc..... And she was giving me her last words of advice.... Imagine my sorrow" (undated, after April 14, 1893).

6. Céline chose the daisies. Mother Agnes wrote her, May 11: "Sister Thérèse of the Child Jesus is in bliss. If you only saw her little Jesus! It is a real gem and the daisies are the admiration of the whole Community.... There are several Sisters who are *smitten with envy!*"

LC 153
1893 (?)

From Sister Thérèse of St. Augustine to Thérèse

Date uncertain. We place this note at this time because of the reference to "virginal milk" (see note 5). Sister Thérèse of St. Agustine is evidently on retreat: anniversary of her Profession, May 1, 1877, or on retreat for the Ascension, May 11-21, 1893.?

J.M.J.T.

I thank you, *dear little Sister*,[1] for your kindness, it pleased me very much. My little Jesus, having no flowers whatsoever, saw with satisfaction the cornflowers and daisies from His little *Sister* Thérèse of the Child Jesus,[2] and I am sure this very gracious charity merited one of the sweetest smiles from my little King for the dear donor.

May the divine flower of the fields[3] be more and more the bond of our hearts; let us be His little daisies,[4] nothing more delightful then simplicity, and nothing better rewarded, for it is Jesus Himself, who gives Himself with more love and familiarity.

Pray for your little *sister*, you understand this word, and may Mary's arms be the place of our *rendex-vous*. We shall find our little Brother there. May we, like Him, receive the virginal dew[5] and the delightful kiss, presage of the heavenly one. . . .

---

*   Autograph.
1.   The emphasis placed on various words is to be interpreted with regard to this Sister's affection for Thérèse. She was thirty-six. "As soon as we met we experienced an irresistible attraction for one another" (*Souvenirs d'une Sainte Amitíe*, p. 1; written a few months after Thérèse's death). Thérèse revealed at the end of her life the nature of this attraction: "Ah! what attracted me was Jesus hidden in the depths of her soul. . . Jesus, who makes sweet whatever is most bitter. . . ." (Ms. C, p. 223.) She had written in this same Ms. C, a few lines above: "There is in the Community a Sister who displeases me in all things, her ways, her words, her character, all seem very disagreeable to me." See also DE, pp. 786-789, on the relationship between them.
2.   Did this sharing of flowers come from Céline's gift a few days earlier? See LC 152, note 6.

3. See Canticle of Canticles 2:1; LT 141, note 1.
4. "Close to the scented flower that Jesus was soon to gather up, the divine Master had placed a little daisy. His Heart was the Sun of these two dear flowers. The little wild flower, image of my poor little soul, was the only one to profit from this blessed union" (*Souvenirs*, op. cit., p. 1).
5. "We loved the Child Jesus...taking at His mother's breast nourishment during the first months of His exile. Our souls were plunged into this delightful mystery, hidden from the greater number but revealed to our hearts by Jesus and His holy mother. We loved to receive together the virginal milk" (ibid., p. 2). We have here a reminder of the poem bearing this title and composed by Thérèse at Sister Thérèse of St. Augustine's request. Her share in the composition is very probable in this quotation and in many passages from these *Souvenirs*. It is true, however, that Thérèse shared in this devotion, following especially the example of Sister Marie of the Angels, who was a disciple of the Carmelite of Tours; see *Vie de Soeur Saint-Pierre*, by l'abbé Janvier (Tours, 1881, ch. XIX, pp. 327-351, *La maternité divine*.)

LD   *From Céline to Mother Agnes of Jesus, Sister Marie of the Sacred Heart, and Thérèse.*

July 3, 1893   Letter written from La Musse, where the Guérin family went on June 27.

Last week Uncle wrote a letter to Léonie which must have reached her on Saturday,[1] but a letter I would never have expected, it was so paternal and gentle.

He is allowing her to remain at the Visitation,[2] congratulates her on her plans, and goes as far as to tell her she is not to worry about the void she is causing with regard to Papa, for with God's help, he and Aunt hope to make his life so nice that they will take her place insofar as this is possible.

I was very much surprised by this language. I had seen Uncle so oppositely disposed, and I do not doubt God has placed His hand on Léonie's boat. All obstacles broke down at the same time.

Dear little sisters, oh! if you only knew how torn my heart was when reading this letter from Uncle; it was the consummation of the offering, it was the *first*! I wept...my heart was sad for a long time.... I was thinking of Léonie, my companion in misfortune who was abandoning me!... There is no longer anyone on earth,[3] a void was formed around me, and for a moment I considered myself with heartbreaking dizziness as the last stray of the family.... Oh! life seemed so sad to me, so sad!...

My whole life with dear Léonie came back to me in all its details to deepen my regrets. I went back into my bedroom sadly, and I read this passage from the psalms: "Lord, you are my inheritance and all my good; it is you who make firm my lot. The lot that has fallen to me is delightful, and what I possess is infinitely pleasing to me!" (Psalm XV). Poor little Céline's heart was consoled.

Dear little sisters, I do not want to speak only about myself, for I know the joy you experience when receiving news about Papa.

He is always well,[4] but the day when I had written our Mother[5] was exceptional. I had never seen him like that, and for the rest of my life I shall remember his beautiful face when in the evening as night was falling, deep in the woods, we stopped to listen to a nightingale. He was listening...with such an expression in his eyes! It was like an ecstasy, an indescribable something of the homeland was reflected on his features. Then, after a long moment of silence, we were still listening, and I saw tears rolling down his dear cheeks. Oh! what a beautiful day!

Since then he is not so well; this extraordinary consolation could not last. And still, in spite of everything, how sweet his last days are, who would have thought it?... God is treating us with inexpressible kindness.[6]

Dear little sisters, I am thinking of you, and I am trying to take your place at Papa's side. I am doing my best, I assure you, for I realize the sacrifice it is for you not to assist our dear little Papa in his last days. I am the one who has this wonderful consolation. God is not asking as much from me as He is from you! No doubt, I would not have the fortitude. Oh! pray for your poor little Céline! I am doing so little for God and for you; you are giving Him so much.[7] I think you are so good and I am so bad!...

Dear little sisters, you know I love you with my whole heart.

I kiss you tenderly,

                              Your little Céline

*   CMG.
1. July 1; letter not preserved.
2. Léonie had first asked to make a retreat at the Visitation instead of going to La Musse on vacation. Céline was displeased about this; see this letter from Mme. Guérin to her daughter: "Good Léonie was very sad this morning when she received Céline's letter; she gave it to me, and I tried to console her. She told me that if the boredom she experienced at going to La Musse was more pleasing to God than the happiness she has at going to the Visitation, she would gladly sacrifice the latter and would not even want to hear it mentioned. Now the poor girl is no longer crying; I think she is very good. She wrote this morning to Thérèse about what Céline said to her." (To Marie Guérin, April 27, 1893; the letter to Thérèse is lost.) The Carmelites supported Léonie in her plans; see Mother Agnes of Jesus to Céline: "The more I think about Léonie, the more I feel we cannot hold her back. Sister Thérèse of the Child Jesus is of my opinion. What do you expect? We cannot complain of the blessings of God on our very privileged family" (May 6, 1893).
3. Céline saw she was on the point of losing her cousin and friend, Marie Guérin, who wanted to enter Carmel. Three letters from Mother Agnes, in April and May, speak of Marie's plans: "Let little Marie take courage. . . . I desire and find it even *necessary* that she write the pastor of St. Jacques to let him know of her plans and speak to him of her step, but that she is not, above all, to give the impression of thinking he could make any difficulties because she is our cousin." (To Céline, April 1893.) "Our Father Superior spoke to M. Youf [chaplain of the Carmel] and highly sang the praises of Marie and Uncle. I cannot get over it, for usually he is so cold and even more than cold!. . . Dear little Marie, then, will soon take her flight to the mountain of Carmel!. . . And you, little Céline, you who are going to be all alone once again. Be convinced you are the privileged of the priviledged." (To the same, May.) "What do you think of Marie's situation? I found Uncle admirable. He reminds me of Papa. . . . You put me in mind of St. Sebastian while I am waiting for you to be a prisoner of love in Carmel. You seem to be serving the world, but your work is to fortify and visit the martyrs while awaiting martyrdom yourself." (To the same, May-June.)
4. In 1893, the Guérins decided to take M. Martin to La Musse. "Our trip went along very well. It was not possible to desire better. M. Martin was very good, and he allowed himself be led like a little child. . . . If you had only seen him during the trip looking at my husband. He really understood my husband was his protector, and he was looking

at him with a smile and never took his eyes off him.'' (Mme. Guérin to Mme. Fournet, June 28, 1893.) ''Uncle is radiant ever since he is here; he likes it better here than at Lisieux, he says. Céline and I have him take outings in the woods, but what pleases him very much is to look at the beautiful view. The other day he never grew tired of gazing at it, and he was laughing all day.'' (Marie Guérin to Mme. Le Néele, June 30, 1893.)

5. Mother Marie de Gonzague, see LC 152, note 5; letter not preserved.
6. The last six words are a later alteration over an erased passage; the first text is illegible.
7. In her answer (LT 142), Thérèse places matters in perspective regarding ''merit.''

LT 142   **From Thérèse to Céline**
July 6, 1893
→LD, July 3, 1893

J.M.J.T.

Jesus †   Carmel, July 6, 1893

Dear Céline,

Your two letters[1] were like a sweet melody for my heart. . . . I am happy to see Jesus' predilection for my Céline. How He loves her, how He *looks tenderly* upon her!. . . Now here we are, all five of us, on our way. What joy to be able to say: ''I am sure of doing God's will.'' This holy will is clearly manifested with regard to Céline. She is the one whom Jesus has *chosen* among us all to be the crown, the reward of the holy patriarch who has delighted heaven by his fidelity. How dare you say you have been forgotten, less loved than the others? I say you have *been* CHOSEN by privilege, your mission is all the more beautiful because, while remaining our dear Father's visible angel, you are at the same time the spouse of Jesus. This is true, perhaps Céline thinks, but I am doing less than the others for God. I have more consolations and consequently less merits. ''My thoughts are not your thoughts,'' says the Lord.[2] Merit does not consist in doing or in giving much, but rather in receiving, in loving

I Saiah
55.8

much. . . . It is said, it is much sweeter to give than to receive,[3] and it is true. But when Jesus wills to take *for Himself the sweetness of giving*, it would not be gracious to refuse. Let us allow Him to take and give all He wills. Perfection consists in doing His will,[4] and the soul that surrenders itself totally to Him is called by Jesus Himself "His mother, His sister," and His whole family.[5] And elsewhere: "If anyone loves me, he will keep my word (that is, he will do my will) and my Father will love him, and we will come to him and make our abode with him."[6] Oh, Céline how easy it is to please Jesus, to delight His Heart, one has only to love Him, without looking at one's self, without examining one's faults too much. Your Thérèse is not in the heights at this moment, but Jesus is teaching her to learn "to draw profit from everything, *from the good* and *the bad* she finds in herself."[7] He is teaching her to play at the bank of love, or rather He plays for her and does not tell her how He goes about it, for that is His affair and not Thérèse's. What she must do is abandon herself, surrender herself, without keeping anything, not even the joy of knowing how much the bank is returning to her.[8] But after all she is not the prodigal child, it is not worthwhile for Jesus to set a banquet for her "since she is always with Him."[9] Our Lord wills to leave the faithful sheep in the desert.[10] How much this says to me!. . . He is *sure to them*; they could no longer go astray, for they are captives of love. So Jesus takes away His tangible presence from them to order to give His consolations to sinners. If He does lead them to Tabor, it is for a few moments, the valley is most frequently the place of His repose. "It is there He takes his rest at midday."[11] The morning of our life has passed, we have enjoyed the perfumed breezes of the dawn. Then everything smiled at us, Jesus was making us feel His sweet presence,[12] but when the sun became hot, the Beloved led us into His garden, He made us gather the *myrrh*[13] of trial by separating us from *everything* and from Himself. The hill of myrrh has strengthened us with its bitter scents, so Jesus has made us come down again, and now we are in the valley. He leads us beside the waters.[14] . . Dear Céline, I do not know too well what I am saying to you, but it seems you will understand, divine what I would like to say. Ah! let us be always Jesus' *drop of dew*.[15] In that is happiness, perfection. . . . Fortunately, I am speaking to you, for other persons would be unable to understand my language,

Mt.
12:50

Lk 15:
31

Mt.
18:12

Mk 9:
2-8

PS 22.2

and I admit it is true for only a few souls. In fact, directors have others advance in perfection by having them perform a great number of acts of virtue, and they are right; but my director, who is Jesus,[16] teaches me not to count up my acts.[17] He teaches me to do *all* through love, to refuse Him nothing, to be content when He gives me a chance of proving to Him that I love Him. But this is done in peace, in *abandonment*,[18] it is Jesus who is doing all in me, and I am doing nothing.

I feel very much united to my Céline. I believe God has not often made two souls who understand each other so well, never a discordant note. The hand of Jesus touching one of the lyres makes the other vibrate at the same time. . . . Oh! let us remain hidden in our divine Flower of the fields until the shadows lengthen;[19] let us allow the drops of *liqueur* to be appreciated by creatures. Since we are pleasing *our Lily*, let us remain joyfully His drop, His *single* drop of dew! . . . And to this drop that has consoled Him during the exile, what will He not give us in the homeland? . . . He tells us Himself: "He who is thirsty, let him come *to me* and drink,'[20] and so Jesus is and will be our *ocean*. . . . Like the thirsty hind we long for this water[21] that is promised to us, but our consolation is great: to be the ocean of Jesus also, the ocean of the Lily of the valleys! . . .

Your heart alone will be able to read this letter, for I myself have difficulty in deciphering it. I have no more ink, I was obliged *to spit* into our inkwell to make some. . . is this not something to laugh about? . . .

I kiss the whole family, but especially my dear king,[22] who will receive a kiss from my Céline from his queen.

Sister Thérèse of the Child Jesus of the Holy Face
rel. carm. ind.[23]

* Autograph
1. The second letter could have been addressed to Mother Marie de Gonzague; see note 5 in preceding letter.
2. Isaias 55:8.
3. See Acts of the Apostles 20:35.
4. Same definition in Ms. A, p. 14.
5. See Matthew 12:5; see LT 130, note 5.
6. See John 14:23. Thérèse will comment on these words next year; see LT 165, note 8.

7. John of the Cross, St., *Glosa a lo divino*, see *Collected Works*, p. 735. Same thought in Ms. A, p. 178, and P. 26, stanza 3.

8. See CSG, p. 71. "To play bank" was a game spoken about by the Guérin-La Néele families; see letter of Jeanne La Néele to Léonie, March 1893; "I played bank and did absolutely nothing but lose, which showed me once again the truth of the axiom: *qui n'a pas de chance au jeu en a en ménage*," (unlucky at games, lucky in marriage.)

9. See Luke 15:31. See Ms. A, p. 180 and P 21 (these two texts are almost contemporaneous, end of 1895), *Jésus, mon Bien-Aimé, rappelle-toi!*, stanza 26: *Avec amour tu recois le prodigue — Mais les flots de ton Coeur pour moi n'ont pas de digue!* (With love You receive the Prodigal — But the waves from Your Heart for me have no dike!)

10. See Matthew 18:12.

11. See Canticle of Canticles 1:7

12. Thérèse was no doubt thinking of the year 1187; see LT 127, note 5.

13. See Canticle of Canticles 5:1.

14. See Psalm 22:2. The Prologue of Ms. A, in January 1895, takes up this psalm. Thérèse commented on it again on her deathbed as a spiritual last will and testament for P. Pichon.

15. See LT 141.

16. Thérèse wrote four times to P. Pichon between January and September 1893; see LC 157. But did she still consider him as her director? See Ms. A, p. 151; and with reference to the October 1891 retreat: "God willed to show me that He alone was the director of my soul" (Ms. A, p. 173).

17. Soon Thérèse will begin using again a "chaplet of practices" (chaplet for keeping track of little acts of mortification) to help Sister Martha; see LT 144, note 10.

18. First appearance of the word *abandon* in her *Letters*.

19. See Canticle of Canticles 4:6.

20. See John 7:37.

21. See Psalm 41:2.

22. Last use of the name *king* in her *Letters*, written this time without a capital; see *Introduction*, p. 68, note 30.

23. Mother Agnes of Jesus adds: "I am on retreat, pray for me, little godchild. Sister Agnes of Jesus, r. c. ind." Céline was Pauline's godchild in Confirmation.

LC 154   *From Céline to Thérèse*
July 12, 1893
→ LT 142

La Musse, July 12, 1893

Dear little Thérèse,

Your beautiful letter pleased me very much, it is food for my soul. But I see God is leading us by the same way, for I am in such aridity that I no longer see clearly. I even wonder if I shall come to the end, filling these four pages. Yes, no doubt, but on condition that I do not speak of my soul, for it is plunged into death. There is nothing, no, nothing to say about it. And this state is not fleeting, it lasts for months.[1]

Within me, there is always nothing, always the dark night. Where then is the time when, so transported, so strong, so courageous, I used to read St. John of the Cross,[2] and I was flying so high, my soul filled with joy! The time is past for "weaving garlands with flowers and emeralds chosen on cool mornings...."[3]

Thérèse, you understand me so well, and your soul is so faithful an echo of mine! Yes, the morning of life is past, now it is noon, so heavy, so crushing....

However, a thought comes to me: Saint John of the Cross does not say: "the soul weaves garlands *during* the cool mornings, but with flowers chosen during the cool mornings." It is, then, at present, during midday that the soul weaves the flowers chosen during the cool mornings....

Now it no longer has anything to offer its Beloved except the bouquet already gathered, it can no longer do anything else but to tie it "with one of its hairs...."[4]

Dear Thérèse, you believe, then, that this one hair of our love suffices?... You believe that God is not asking me to choose new flowers and new emeralds, to practice many virtues, to produce "aspirations divinely scented,"[5] but only to tie with love the flowers of the cool mornings?... And you believe that now love alone suffices?[6] Oh! this thought does me some good, it came to me suddenly when writing you, for I was interpreting these words in a different way altogether.

In fact, midday is so hot for my poor soul that this is no longer the time to gather. I would like to but I cannot do so. I am incapable of "doing good," absolutely. I can only "desire good." It seems to me I am descending always lower, that nothingness invades me more each day. But since one single hair suffices for finishing the bouquet!

Dear Thérèse, I feel your soul responds so fully to my soul that you divine all I do not say to you.... I kiss you, with what love!

Your little Céline

Shower with kisses dear Mother,[7] Pauline, Marie. The letter from my dear Marie[8] gave me inexpressible joy, it thrilled my soul.

Pauline must take care of her teeth; if she is suffering from her gums, she should use some alum. From time to time, one puts some of this alum solution in the mouth for a few moments, then spits it out. Alum is not expensive and tightens the gums. This soothed me very much when I was suffering from my mouth.

As for the seltzer water, Francis has an apparatus, but it is in poor condition; he will check it later and give it to you with directions. Marie is not to worry, and she is to get some siphons;[9] they are very inexpensive, three *sous* only, and I can pay for them!

Papa is always well, but there is nothing new to tell you, in spite of my questioning myself to find some interesting detail. On Sunday, he had a very good day.

   *   G. copy.

1. "Trial relating to P. Pichon's appeals, due also to the *malaise* of living in a half-worldly atmosphere in which I was courted. When rereading, after fifty years, these letters whose tone is rather sad, I find no other explanation except this since, as our directors and confessors used to tell us: "We all had joyful souls." (Note of Sister Geneviève on page twenty of her typewritten notebook.) See also LC 149.

2. Perhaps in 1890, at Thérèse's suggestion? See LC 149.

3. John of the Cross, St., *Spiritual Canticle*, stanza XXX; see *Collected Works*, p. 527.

4. Same stanza as above.

5. John of the Cross, St., *Spiritual Canticle*, stanza XXV; see *Collected Works*, p. 506.
6. The statement heralds that of Thérèse when she was dying: "It is love alone that counts" (NV 29.9.6). With the destruction of the autograph we cannot state with certitude that this reflection of Céline is original, although this does seem to be in the process of development.
7. Mother Marie de Gonzague.
8. Letter from Sister Marie of the Sacred Heart, July 7; she must have read Thérèse's letter since she wrote: "I believe little Thérèse's letter is enough for you."
9. Answer to a question from Sister Marie of the Sacred Heart: "If you could show us the way to make Seltzer water. This, it seems, would be less expensive than having siphons. It seems one can make a siphon for one *sou*; ask Uncle." (July 7, 1893.) These siphons were for Mother Marie de Gonzague, who was sick, notes Sister Geneviève (copybook, p. 22); also, no doubt, for feast of St. Martha, July 29.

LT 143　　　　　　**From Thérèse to Céline**
July 18, 1893
→ LC 154

J.M.J.T.

Jesus †　　　　　　　　　　　　　　　Carmel, July 18, 1893

Dear Céline,

　　I was not counting on answering your letter this time, but our Mother wants me to add a note to hers.[1] What things I would have to tell you! But since I have only a few moments, I must first assure the little drop of dew that her Thérèse understands her.... After having read your letter, I went to prayer, and taking the gospel, I asked Jesus to find a passage for you, and this is what I found: "Behold the fig tree and the other trees, when they begin to bear tender leaves, you judge that summer is near. In the same way, when you will see these things taking place, know that the kingdom of God is near.'[2] I closed the book, I had read enough; in fact, *these things* taking place in my Céline's soul prove the kingdom of Jesus is set up in her soul.... Now I want to tell you what is taking place

Luke 21.29

in my *own* soul; no doubt, it is the same things as in yours. You have rightly said, Céline, the cool mornings have passed for us, there remain no more flowers to gather, Jesus has taken them for Himself. Perhaps He will make new ones bloom one day, but in the meantime what must we do? Céline, God is no longer asking anything from me...in the beginning, He was asking an infinity of things from me. I thought, at times,[3] that since Jesus was no longer asking anything from me, I had to go along quietly in peace and love, doing only what He was asking me.[4]... But I had a light. St. Teresa says we must maintain love.[5] *The wood* is not within our reach when we are in darkness, in aridities, but at least are we not obliged to throw little pieces of straw on it? Jesus is really powerful enough to keep the fire going by Himself. However, He is satisfied when He sees us put a little fuel on it. This *attentiveness* pleases Jesus, and then He throws on the fire a lot of wood. We do not see it, but we do feel the *strength* of love's warmth. I have experienced it; when I *am feeling* nothing, when I am INCAPABLE *of praying*, of practicing virtue, then is the moment for seeking opportunities, *nothings*, which please Jesus more than mastery of the world or even martyrdom suffered with generosity. For example, a smile, a friendly word, when I would want to say nothing, or put on a look of annoyance, etc., etc.

Céline, do you understand? It is not for the purpose of weaving my crown,[6] gaining merits, it is in order to please Jesus.... When I do not have any opportunities, I want at least to tell Him frequently that I love Him; this is not difficult, and it keeps the *fire* going. *Even though* this fire of love would seem to me to have gone out, I would like to throw something on it, and Jesus could then relight it. Céline, I am afraid I have not said what I should;[7] perhaps you will think I always do what I am saying. Oh, no! I am not always faithful, but I never get discouraged;[8] I abandon myself into the arms of Jesus. The little drop of dew goes deeper into the calyx of the flower of the fields,[9] and there it finds again all it has lost and even much more.

Your little Sister Thérèse of the Child Jesus of the Holy Face
re. carm. ind.

* Autograph
1. No doubt, the same day Mother Agnes of Jesus wrote to Céline: "It is little Pauline's turn to write you. Alas! she has hardly any time or thoughts! It will be a poor meal for dear little Céline! But soon the heavenly lyre of Thérèse of the Child Jesus will play again; oh! then Céline's heart will be satisfied!" Then, at the end of four pages: "Finding my letter very foolish, I begged the little player of the lyre to send you some of her tunes."
2. See Luke 21:29.
3. First writing: "*longtemps*" (for a long time).
4. Sister Geneviève (Céline) added in pencil on the autograph: "formerly"; see *Introduction* p. 65, note 14. This addition was written in at the Process (CE II, p. 97).

   She also erased on the original the words: "*en faisant seulement ce qu'Il me demandait. . . .*" She omitted the ending in CMG IV, p. 101.
5. *The Book of her Life*, chapter 30. Perhaps Therese was reading the *Life of St. Teresa of Avila*; see LT 150, par. 4. See Volume One, *The Collected Works of St. Teresa of Avila*, trans. Kieran Kavanaugh, O.C.D. and Otilio Rodriquez, O.C.D. (Washington, D.C.: ICS Publications, Institute of Carmelite Studies, 1976), p. 202, par. 20.
6. To follow Thérèse's development of thought regarding this matter, see, in particular, LT 43 and 94; P 13, December 25, 1894: *Jesus will weave your crown — If you want only His love*; LC 161; *Act of Oblation to Merciful Love*, June 9, 1895; LT 182; LC 183; DE, p. 690, letter 14.
7. Sister Geneviève inserted the word "*dit*" to complete Thérèse's meaning; the addition was written in at the Process and in CMG
8. See Thérèse's resolution when making her First Communion: "I will not be discouraged." Quoted in Mss. I, p. 27.
9. See LT 141.

LD   *From Céline to Sister Marie of the Sacred Heart.*

Around July 20,
1893

When entering Papa's room one night, I was surprised to hear him singing, for Désiré[1] was not helping him. He had only intoned the *Kyrie*, and Papa was continuing it with his beautiful voice, very precise but a little muffled.

Frequently Papa and Désiré sing psalms and all kinds of church hymns in this way. This pleases Papa very much.

Dear little Father is my little baby...you cannot imagine, dear Marie, all the affection I have for him. Would you believe it? Each night, when I leave him, after saying *bonsoir*, I bless him without his noticing it, and the night is always very good afterward. It is as though I had become his mother, and the efficacy of my sign of the Cross touches me very much as coming from God.

* CMG.
1. Céline's manservant. See above, LD, May 10, 1892, note 3.

LT 144   **From Thérèse to Céline.**

July 23, 1893
→ LC or LD
(?) lost

J.M.J.T.

Jesus †   Carmel, July 23, 1893

Dear little Céline,

I am not surprised that you understand nothing that is taking place in your soul. A LITTLE *child all alone* on the sea, in a boat lost in the midst of the stormy waves, could she know whether she is close or far from port? While her eyes still contemplate the shore which she left, she knows how far she has gone, and, seeing the land getting farther away, she cannot contain her childish joy. Oh! she says, here I am soon at the end of my journey. But the more the shore recedes, the vaster the ocean also appears. Then the little child's KNOWLEDGE is reduced to nothing, she no longer knows where her boat is going. She does not know how to control the rudder, and the only thing she can do is abandon herself and allow her sail to flutter in the wind.... My Céline, *the little child* of Jesus, is all alone in a little boat; the *land* has disappeared from her eyes, she does not know where she is going, whether she is advancing or if she is going backward.... Little Thérèse knows, and she *is sure* her Céline is on the *open sea*; the boat carrying her is advancing with full sails toward the port, and the rudder which Céline cannot even see is not without a pilot. Jesus is there, *sleeping* as in days gone by, in the boat of the fishermen of Galilee.[1] He is sleeping...and Céline does not *see* Him, for night has fallen on the boat.... Céline *does not hear* the voice of Jesus. The wind is blowing...she *hears* it; she *sees* the darkness...and Jesus *is* always *sleeping*. However, if He were to awaken only for an instant, He would have only to command the wind and the sea, and there would be a great calm.[2] The night would become brighter than the day.[3] Céline *would see the divine glance* of Jesus, and her soul would be consoled.... But Jesus, too, would no longer be sleeping, and He is so FATIGUED![4]... His divine feet are tired from going after sinners, and in Céline's boat Jesus is sleeping so peacefully. The apostles had given Him a *pillow*[5]. The Gospel gives us this detail. But in His dear *spouse's* little boat Our Lord finds another pillow much softer, Céline's *heart*. There He forgets all, He is at home.... It is not a stone which supports His divine head (that stone for which He longed during His mortal life),[6] it is the heart of a *child*, the heart of a *spouse*. Oh, how happy Jesus is! But how can He be happy while His spouse is suffering, while she *watches* during the time He is sleeping so peacefully? Does He not know that Céline sees only the night, that His divine face remains hidden from her, and even at times the weight she feels on her heart seems heavy to her?... What a mystery! Jesus, the little child of Bethlehem whom Mary used to carry as a light burden, becomes heavy, so heavy that St. Christopher is astonished by it.... The spouse of the Canticles also says her Beloved is a bundle of myrrh and that He rests on her heart.[7] Myrrh is *suffering*, and it is in this way that Jesus rests on Céline's heart.... And nevertheless Jesus is happy to see her in suffering. He is happy to receive all from her during the *night*.... He is awaiting the dawn and then, oh, then, what an awakening will be the awakening of Jesus!!!...

Be sure, dear Céline, that your boat is on the open sea, already perhaps very *close to port*. The wind of sorrow that pushes it is the *wind of love*, and this wind is swifter than lightning....

How *touched* I was when seeing that Jesus had inspired you with the idea of little sacrifices; I had asked it of Him, not counting on writing you so soon. Never yet has Our Lord refused to inspire you with what I begged Him to tell you.[8] He is always giving us together the same graces. I am even obliged to have a chaplet of practices;[9] I did it out of love for one of my companions.[10] I will tell you this in detail, it is very amusing.... I am trapped in the nets that do not appeal to me but are very useful to me in my present state of soul.

* Autograph.

1. See Matthew 8:24 and Mark 4:38, where Thérèse finds the detail of the pillow (note 5).
2. See Matthew 8:26.
3. See Psalm 138:12.
4. See John 4:6.
5. See Mark 4:38.
6. See Matthew 8:20 and LT 137, note 11.
7. See Canticle of Canticles 1:13.
8. See LT 137, par. 4; LT 149, par. 2; CJ 13.7.9.
9. As in her childhood days; see LC 24.
10. Sister Martha of Jesus, whom she must help especially "in keeping her eyes lowered in the refectory," according to the existing monastic custom and according to the resolution expressed in the prayer: *Glances of love toward Jesus*; a prayer composed by Thérèse for her companion, July 16, 1893, it seems. We read there, among other things: "We ask You to reward us with a *glance* of love each time we deny ourselves the lifting of our eyes; and we even beg You not to refuse us this gentle *glance* when we shall have failed since we expect these failures." In fact, Sister Martha noted down these failures in the column marked "Refectory," on three sheets of "practices," prepared by Thérèse (December 1893, January 1894, Lent 1894).

   Sister Marie of the Eucharist wrote about Thérèse's strictness on this point (in 1896-1897): "She used to have me make the resolution "not to raise my eyes." And as I was almost always next to her, each time she saw me looking around, I was sure of being called to order by a little flick of her finger cleverly and gently given.... When I was very rebellious, my little sister used to raise her eyes to heaven and made sighs and ahs!... This made me more recollected. She told me: 'You will never succeed if you do not mark on your chaplet of practices each time you fail. This is the only way.... You are not willing, then, to lower your eyes out of love for God?... Think that you are making an act of love each time you do not raise them, that you are saving a soul!' " (*Souvenirs de soeur Marie de l'Eucharistie, annexés par Mère Agnès de Jésus à sa déposition en 1910.*)

LC 155   *From Céline to Thérèse.*
July 27, 1893
→ LT 144

La Musse, July 27, 1893

Dear little Thérèse,

I kept the best till last for you, and I do not know if I am going to have the time to write you all I would like. However, I would really like to tell you a lot of things.

You will perhaps think that your letter, written to console me, did not attain its purpose since I wrote Pauline that Jesus was consoling me.[1] Oh! nothing of the kind. Your letter consoled me over again, and it did me so great a good that I thanked Our Lord for it. I do not understand this, but you always tell me exactly what you should tell me. . . .

The comparison of the *child* on the open sea gives me very much to think about; and this: "Jesus is happy to receive all during the night. . . . He is awaiting the dawn, oh! then what an awakening will be the awakening of Jesus!!!. . ." This, Thérèse, enraptures me.

I was touched, very much touched, by the coincidence of your little sacrifices. Yes, Jesus is asking these from me, and I am not rebelling. I feel drawn to: "since Jesus is not giving to me," give without counting and take advantage of opportunities.

Dear Thérèse, I said Jesus has consoled me because I am no longer discouraged, but as for having any consolations, I do not have any, in spite of drinking in with delight what my dear little sisters write me.

Pauline told me: "Whether our soul be sad or joyful, disturbed or calm, is not important *if* we turn our eyes to heaven, *if* we always have confidence, *if* all things of the earth appear to us as contemptible."[2] (However, what to do if everything is the contrary?)

These words of Marie comforted me: "You are really blessed to be sought out by such a friend, to be the object of His divine whims."[3]

Oh! yes, Jesus is good for having made Himself our Friend! Who, then, would have been able to be the friend of our souls, our very souls?

Your Céline

I shall make you smile by a detail which is neither mystical nor elevated but which will sound the note of my isolation: the other night, I was considering the moon in the immensity of space; it was veiled by a light cloud. The earth was in shadow. I was walking and suddenly saw at my side faithful Tom.[4] He had heard me and he came, I had only him! Thérèse, oh, understand your Céline!

* G. copy.

1. To this letter, not preserved, written no doubt on the 24th, Mother Agnes answered on the 25th: "I just received your last letter. What a joy that Jesus has come to console you." On the 25th, too, Sister Marie of the Sacred Heart thanked Céline for the letter to herself (see above LD, July 20, 1893). From this datum, Thérèse's letter of the 23rd (LT 144) was kept back two days before being sent, and Céline received three letters from the Carmel at one time, July 26.

2. Textual quotation from Mother Agnes' letter of the 25th.

3. Textual quotation from Sister Marie of the Sacred Heart's letter of the 25th.

4. Thérèse's spaniel, named "Tom." See LTS 18a, p. 238, note 4.

LT 145   **From Thérèse to Céline.**
August 2, 1893
→ LC 155

J.M.J.T.

Jesus †   Carmel, August 2, '93

Dear little Céline,

Your letter filled me with consolation. The road on which you
are walking is a royal road, it is not a beaten track, but a *path* traced
out by Jesus Himself. The spouse of the Canticles says that, not having found her Beloved in her bed, she arose to look for Him in the
city but in vain; after having gone out of the city, she found Him
whom her soul loved![1] . . . Jesus does not will that we find His
adorable presence in repose; He hides Himself; He wraps Himself
in darkness. It was not thus that He acted with the *crowd* of Jews,
for we see in the gospel that the people were CARRIED AWAY when
He was speaking.[2] Jesus used to charm weak souls with His divine
words, He was trying to make them strong for the day of trial. . . .
But how small was the number of Our Lord's friends when He was
SILENT before His judges![3] . . . Oh! what a melody for my heart
is this silence of Jesus. . . He made Himself poor that we might
be able to give Him love. He holds out His hand to us like a *beggar*
so that on the radiant day of judgment when He will appear in His
glory, He may have us hear those sweet words: "Come, blessed of
my Father, for I was hungry and you gave me to eat; I was thirsty,
and you gave me to drink; I did not know where to lodge, and you
gave me a home. I was in prison, sick, and you helped me.["4] It is
Jesus Himself who spoke these words; it is He who wants our love,
who *begs* for it. . . . He places Himself, so to speak, at our mercy,
He does not want to take anything unless we give it to Him, and
the smallest thing is precious in His divine eyes. . . .

Dear Céline, let us take delight in our lot, it is so beautiful. Let
us give, let us give to Jesus; let us be miserly with others but prodigal with Him. . . .

Jesus is a *hidden* treasure,[5] an inestimable good which few souls

*Lk
19:48*

*✻
see below*

*Mt 25:
34-36*

✻ *See Mt 25: 34-36 (in fol.) "He made himself
poor."*

can find, for it is *hidden*, and the world loves what sparkles. Ah!
if Jesus had willed to show Himself to all souls with His ineffable
gifts, no doubt there is not one of them that would have despised
Him. However, He does not will that we love Him for His gifts, [6] *Gn.15.1*
He Himself must be our *reward.*[7] To find a hidden thing one must
hide oneself;[8] our life must then be a *mystery*. We must be like Jesus,
Jesus whose *face was hidden*[9]... "Do you want to learn something
that may be of use to you?" says the Imitation. 'love to be unknown
and accounted for *nothing*...."[10] And elsewhere; "After you have
left everything, you must above all leave yourself;[11] let one man boast
of one thing, another of something else; as for you, place your joy
only in contempt of yourself."[12] What peace these words give to the
soul, Céline. You know them, but do you not know all I would like
to say to you?... Jesus loves you with a love so great that, if you
were to see it, you would be in an ecstasy of happiness that would
cause your death, but you do not see it, and you are suffering.

   Soon Jesus will stand up to save all the meek and humble of the
earth![13]...

* Autograph.
1. See Canticle of Canticles 3:2-4.,
2. See Luke 19:48.
3. See Matthew 26:63. See Prayer: *Glances of love for Jesus* (LT 144,
   note 10): "When this impious prince [Herod] was mocking You, oh,
   Infinite Beauty, no complaint came from Your lips."
4. See Matthew 25:34-36.
5. See Matthew 13:44; quoted by Saint John of the Cross in the passage
   mentioned below, note 8.
6. This is the basic teaching of the *Imitation of Christ II*, 11, a verse
   which Thérèse will quote in a moment.
7. See Genesis 15:1; quoted implicitly in the *Imitation of Christ III*, 49,
   also mentioned by Thérèse. This text from Genesis was very dear to
   M. Martin; see LT 182, note 18.
8. John of the Cross, St., *Spiritual Canticle*, explanation of the first verse
   of stanza 1: "Where have You hidden?" See Collected Works, p. 419,
   par. 9.
9. See Isaias 53:3. This is the last time, until February 1896 (LT 183),
   that Thérèse quotes this text in her *Letters*. We find it again in her
   poems and plays: RP 2, December 25, 1894; P 21, stanza 23, October
   21, 1895; RP 6, January 21, 1896.

10. See Imitation of Christ I, 2:3.

11. *Ibid*. II, 11:4.

12. *Ibid*. III, 49:7. We shall find two of these three quotations from the *Imitation* brought together in this way in LT 176 and in Ms. A, p. 152.

13. See Psalm 75:10, and CJ 25.9.1. This letter seems to be incomplete. In the blank space at the bottom of the page, Mother Agnes added: "*Bonjour*, little Céline. I kiss you with all my heart; impossible to write you today, I am overloaded with work. Kiss little Marie for me. Thank you for your nice letter; it did not upset me, on the contrary." Céline's letter has been lost.

LT 146   **From Thérèse to Mme. Guérin.**

August 10, 1893

→ LD lost

J.M.J.T.

Jesus †   Carmel, August 10, '93

Dear Aunt,

I saw with pleasure that you were able to divine your little daughter's heart. However, I do not want my *beautiful* handwriting to lose the honor of being admired at the *chateau de la Musse*! So I was happy when our good Mother entrusted me with the sweet mission of answering your letter.

Oh! dear Aunt, each of the lines you wrote reveals your heart to me, that of the most loving of mothers, but your little daughter's heart, too, is a child's heart filled with love and gratitude....

I am begging God to cure dear Uncle.[1] Truly it seems to me this prayer cannot fail to be answered since Our Lord Himself is interested in this cure. Is it not for His glory that Uncle's hand never grows tired of writing these admirable pages which must save souls and make demons tremble?[2]

I hope we are already answered and that you are enjoying in peace the last days remaining to you to be spent in your beautiful chateau.[3] How happy Jeanne must be when enjoying at her ease Francis' presence, she who is so deprived of it at Caen![4] I have really prayed so that the ugly sprain may disappear completely, for this must have been a heavy cloud in Jeanne's blue heaven.

I am thinking, too, of my little sister Marie. It seems to be that since she has placed her abode in the *treetops*,[5] I must appear to her very little and insignificant. When approaching the heavens, we discover marvels that are not met in the humble valley. She will say I am naughty, but this will not stop me from receiving Holy Communion for her *Highness* on her feast day....

I cannot tell you, dear Aunt, the joy I experience when thinking my dear Father is in your midst, laden with affection and care. God has done the same for him as for His servant Job; after having humbled him, He is showering His favors upon him,[6] and it is by means of you that all these good things and this affection are given to him.

Dear little Aunt, I still have many things to tell you, but I have no more space, and it is not respectful to end in this way across a letter.[7] Pardon me, dear Aunt, and understand all the things I would like to write, as well as to the whole family.

Mother Marie de Gonzague and our Mother send you a thousand regards. They are happy to think Madame de Virville will be meeting you.[8]

I kiss you with my whole heart, dear Aunt, and I am always,

> Your respectful little daughter,
> Sister Thérèse of the Child Jesus
> rel. carm. ind.

---

*   Autograph.
1. M. Guérin was suffering rheumatism in the arm.
2. Retired from business, December 1888 (thanks to the inheritance from M. A. David and the sale of his pharmacy), M. Guérin was quick in offering help to the newspaper *Le Normand* by means of contribution and collaboration in writing articles. We see his initials for the first time only on October 17, 1891, at the end of a necrological article for his friend, Dr. Pierre Colombe. On October 20, Sister Agnes of Jesus wrote to Céline: "Congratulate Uncle on behalf of the whole Community for his magnificent article on M. Colombe.... Alas! Jesus alone will write our dear little Father's obituary, but why say

'alas!' Are not heaven's journals worth more than those of earth?''
M. Guérin entered the arena officially on October 20, entitling his
first editorial: *Fear and trembling*. He attacked the anticlerical boasting
of his former student in his pharmacy, Henri Chéron, whom he
spiritedly refuted on November 3, 1891: *Two questions to be resolved*.
He worked with *Le Normand* until 1896. In 1893, eighty-one articles
were signed by him. M. Guérin felt that journalism could be "considered as a priestly service by those who wish to use it only as a vehi-
cle for spreading noble, generous, and unselfish goals" (November
5, 1892). He dealt with the most diversified subjects: internal, foreign,
colonial politics; international and social questions; fiscal problems,
etc. He carried this out as a cultured gentleman, gifted with a color-
ful, often lyrical, style. He was a kind of Catholic conservative, an
uncompromising monarchist, an anti-dreyfusard, and he was unknow-
ingly and clearly falling short of Leo XIII's directives to French
Catholics. Probably, Thérèse was not reading his newspaper. Aware
of current events, she approached them at a different level. She put
her sentiments into the mouth of Joan of Arc in a play composed
the following winter: [Germaine] "You must be bored, not knowing
the news?... I know some very interesting things.... Do you know
what is taking place at Orleans?" [Joan of Arc]: "No, I know
nothing.... I do not want to know what is happening at Orleans or
anywhere else.... While remaining humble and hidden, I can be more
useful to our country than by seeking to know things which do not
concern me" (RP, January 21, 1894).

3. The return to Lisieux was set for August 18.
4. Doctor La Néele, because of his profession, had to be away frequently.
5. Marie Guérin was attracted especially to one of the oaks in the park
    (according to one of her letters to Léonie, July 27, 1892).
6. See Job 42:10-12.
7. In fact, from this time, Thérèse ceased to cross her already written
    lines in her letters (writing transversally), with the exception of some
    of them to Céline. See *Introduction*, p. 63.
8. Mme. Alexandre de Virville, sister-in-law of Mother Marie de Gon-
    zague, had been chosen as *godmother* for Sister Marie-Madeleine's
    reception of the Habit. The clothing was set for September 7. M. Gué-
    rin was godfather; see pp. 860, 922, and 1256. On this occasion, Mme,
    de Virville and her daughters visited the Guérin family.

LT 147   **From Thérèse to Céline.**
August 13, 1893

J.M.J.T.

Jesus †   Carmel, August 12, '93

Dear little Céline,

All the problems you are having with your maid have upset us.[1]
Our Mother was not counting on sending you a letter before your
return, but she is so kind, she loves her Céline so much, and realizing she is sad, she wants to give her a little consolation by allowing
your Thérèse to write a note.

We do not know what you should do regarding the house;[2] you
must rely on Uncle. We shall find good whatever he will decide, and
besides we will speak to you about it *viva voce.* Your poor maid
is very unfortunate in having such a bad habit, especially in being
deceitful, but could you perhaps convert her as you did her husband?[3]
For every sin, mercy, and God is powerful enough to give *stability*
even to people who have none. I will really pray for her; perhaps
were I in her place, I would be still less good than she is, and perhaps,
too, she would have been already a great saint if she had received
one half the graces God has granted to me.

I find that Jesus is very good in allowing my poor letters to do
you some good, but, I assure you, I am not making the mistake of
thinking I have anything to do with it. "If the Lord does not build
the house, in vain do those work who build it."[4] All the most
beautiful discourses of the greatest saints would be incapable of making one *single* act of love come from a heart that Jesus did not
possess. He alone can use His lyre, no one else can make its har-
monious notes sound; however, Jesus uses all means, all creatures
are at His service, and He loves to use them during the night of life
in order to hide His adorable presence, but He does not hide Himself
in such a way that He does not allow Himself to be divined. In fact,
I really feel that often He gives me some lights, not for myself but
for His little exiled dove, His dear spouse.[5] This is really true. I find
an example of it in nature itself. Here is a beautiful peach,[6] pink

and so sweet that all confectioners could not imagine a taste so sweet. Tell me, Céline, is it *for the peach* that God has created this pretty pink color, so velvety and so pleasing to see and to touch? Is it for the peach that He has given so much sugar?... No, but for us and not for it. What belongs to it and what forms the *essence* of its life is its *stone*; we can take away all its beauty without taking from it *its being*. Thus Jesus is pleased to shower His gifts on some of His creatures, but very often this is in order to attract other hearts to Himself, and then when His end has been attained, He makes those external gifts disappear,[7] He despoils completely the souls dearest to Him. When seeing themselves in so great poverty, these poor little souls are fearful, it seems to them that they are good for nothing, since they receive all from others and can give nothing. But it is not so: the *essence* of their *being* is working in secret. *Jesus* forms in them the seed which must be developed up above in the celestial gardens of heaven. He is pleased to show them their nothingness and His power. In order to reach them, He makes use of the *vilest* instruments so as to show them that He alone is working. He hastens to perfect His work for the day when the shadows having vanished,[8] He will no longer use any intermediaries but an *eternal Face to Face!*[9]...

Our Mother thanks Marie for her little letter, Mother Marie de Gonzague also; they are delighted.

> Sister Thérèse of the Child Jesus of
> the Holy Face
> rel carm. ind.[10]

* Autograph.
1. Marie, Désiré's wife, looked after Céline's house, rue Labbey (see above LD, May 10, 1882, notes 3 and 4). She went to La Musse with the Guérin-Martin families, and they had just learned Marie was an alcoholic.
2. Because of Léonie's departure, there was question of Céline's living again at the Guérin's when they returned from la Musse.
3. Désiré had returned to the practice of his religion after Céline made a novena to St. Joseph, March 1893. He had been moved by a picture of the Virgin and Mary Magdalene painted by Céline in 1888, now on exhibition at Les Buissonnets; see Piat, *Céline, soeur et tèmoin de sainte Thérèse de l'Enfant-Jésus*, p. 53.

4. See Psalm 126:1.

5. A truth Thérèse tried to convince Sister Geneviève of during the latter's novitiate without fully succeeding in doing so while she was alive; see CSG, pp. 158-162, *Instruments de Dieu.*

6. One of the fruits preferred by Thérèse; see CJ 24.7.1.

7. In this parable destined to comfort Céline, an experience Thérèse had during these weeks could be surfacing. We read in Mother Agnes of Jesus' notes: "Then [after serving as sacristan] she worked at painting and was, at the same time, helper to the bursar. She was very much humbled by several Sisters who never ceased repeating that she was doing nothing, that she seemed to have come to Carmel to amuse herself." (NPPA, Outline of her tasks.)

8. See Canticle of Canticles 4:6.

9. Arminjon, *op. cit.*, p. 290. We find these two quotations joined in this way at the end of the *Act of Oblation to Merciful Love* (June 9, 1895).

10. In the margin, in Mother Agnes' handwriting: "Sister Marie of the Sacred Heart kisses her little Céline and thanks her for her remembrance for the 15th."

LT 148   *From Thérèse to Léonie.*   (BOLD TYPE)

August 13, 1893   Having gone to the Visitation at Caen on June 24 to make an eight-day retreat, Léonie asked to remain definitively; see LD, July 3, 1893. The following letter is the first of eleven Thérèse addressed to her sister during her second stay at the Visitation.

J.M.J.T.

Jesus †   Carmel, August 13, '93

Dear Léonie,

Perhaps you are thinking your little Thérèse is forgetting you? Oh, no! you know her heart too well to think that. I would have liked to write you at the same time as our Mother and Sister Marie of the Sacred Heart, but there was a misunderstanding, and their letter left earlier than I thought. Today, I am coming to take my revenge and to spend a short moment with you.

If you only knew, dear little Léonie, the thanksgivings I am sending to heaven for the favor that God has granted to you. At last, your desires are fulfilled. Like the dove released from the ark, you could find on the soil of this world nowhere to rest your foot[1] you flew for a long time, seeking to reenter the blessed home in which your heart had forever fixed its abode. Jesus made you wait, but finally the moanings of His dove touched Him, and He extended His divine hand, and taking His fiancée, He placed her on His Heart in the tabernacle of His love.

The prediction of our holy Aunt[2] is, then, now realized. The child of Blessed Margaret Mary[3] is at the Visitation, and she will be the spouse of Our Lord forever.

Oh! no doubt my joy is entirely spiritual, since from now on I must no longer see here below my dear Léonie, I must no longer hear her voice or pour my heart into hers. But I know this earth is the place of our exile, we are voyagers who are travelling toward our homeland. What does it matter if the route we follow is not the same since the only goal will be heaven. There we shall be reunited never to leave each other, there we shall taste family joys eternally. We shall find our dear Father again, who will be surrounded with glory and honor for his perfect fidelity and especially for the humiliations that were showered upon him; we shall see our good Mother, who will rejoice at the trials that were our lot during life's exile; we shall take delight in her happiness as she contemplates her five religious daughters, and we shall form, along with the four little angels who await us up above, a crown adorning the heads of our dear Parents.

Dear little Sister, you see the share I am taking in your joy. I know that it is great but also that sacrifices do not fail to accompany it; without them, would the religious life be meritorious? No, certainly not. On the contrary, it is the little crosses that are our whole joy; they are more common than big ones and prepare the heart to receive the latter when this is the will of our good Master.

I beg you, dear Léonie, to remember me to your Reverend Mother, for whom I have retained a filial affection since the day I had the honor of meeting her.[4] Am I not a little part of her family since you are her daughter and I your unworthy little sister?...

Our Mother, Mother Marie de Gonzague, and Sister Marie of the Sacred Heart want to be remembered to *Mother Superior* and send their dear Léonie best wishes for your happiness.

Do not forget in your prayers, dear Sister, the littlest Carmelite, who is really united to you in the heart of the Blessed Virgin.

Sister Thérèse of the Child of the Holy Face
rel. carm. ind.[5]

* Autograph
1. See Genesis 8:8-9.
2. Sister Marie-Dosithée, sister of Mme. Martin and Visitandine at Le Mans. She wrote, April 28, 1869: "As for little Léonie, I cannot refrain from believing that she will become a little Visitandine" (to Mme. Martin; see VT, October 1970, p. 247).
3. Reference to Léonie's cure as a child; see LC 56, note 4.
4. Mother Marie de Sales Lefrançois, whom Céline and Thérèse saw on the occasion of a visit to Léonie during her first stay at the Visitation (July 16, 1887-January 6, 1888).
5. In the margin, Mother Agnes of Jesus wrote: "Little Léonie, I will write you soon; in the meanwhile, your poor little sister and Mother sends you her affectionate regards. Sister Agnes of Jesus."

LC 156   *From Léonie to Thérèse.*

August 27, 1893
→ LT 148

Visitation, August 27, 1893

Very dear little Thérèse,

Your letter pleased me; if you only knew how much I wanted a letter from Carmel!

You compare me to the little dove of the Ark. I have thought of it very frequently, for this is my story, in fact. I compare myself also to the prodigal child: I have returned once more to throw myself into God's arms but again and especially into His divine Heart. I am perfectly happy. Céline, however, will give you some news; we talked together for a long time.[1] This dear little sister has a big place in my heart. Her generosity in the trials that God is sending her touches me deeply. She is a very beautiful soul, and she is highly esteemed and loved at the Visitation.

Tomorrow is the anniversary of our dear Mother's death;[2] she sees us from the heights of heaven, she is praying for us, very surely she has a more tender look, a more tangible protection for her little Céline left alone in the world to carry out her filial and very sweet duty to our dear Father.

I leave you, dear Thérèse, or rather I do not, for we are always very much united in the Heart of Jesus. There only we are loved with a tenderness which will last not only in this short life but also during the blessed eternity.

Your poor little sister who loves
you with her whole heart.

*   MSC copy.
1.   Upon her return from La Musse (August 18), Céline went to pay a visit to Léonie, whom she had not seen since June 24.
2.   Sixteenth anniversary of Mme. Martin's death (August 28, 1877).

"Our souls remain free" *(LT149)*
(September 1893 - June 1894)
Age twenty and twenty-one

> *The return of the Guérin-Martin families from la Musse put an end to Thérèse's letter exchanges with Céline. Their conversations were continued in the speakroom of the Carmel. Letters from other correspondents: the Guérin family, Léonie, a so-called "cousin" or "aunt," have not been preserved. The* Correspondence *of the following nine months is presented, then as a monologue of sixteen letters*

from Thérèse, completed by two letters from P. Pichon (LC 157 and 158).

The external incidents that gave rise to these responses were centered around various events having no great bearing on her interior life: good wishes and thanks on the occasion of the usual feast days, Léonie's reception of the Habit, Céline Maudelonde's wedding, Céline's domestic worries, etc.

The community situation no longer offered her any matter for narration (this aspect is almost totally absent from her letters). Her time in the novitiate expired on September 8, 1893, but Thérèse herself asked that it be extended. For that matter, she would not have been able to enjoy her rights as a capitular nun (active and passive voice) because of the presence of her two older sisters in the conventual chapter.

Because of Thérèse's extended stay in the novitiate, Mother Agnes of Jesus counted on a beneficial effect for the two other novices: Sister Martha, whose novitiate was to terminate only in September 1894, and Sister Marie-Madeleine, who had just received the Habit. However, with regard to the latter, Thérèse was to see all her efforts end in failure (see LC 157, note 8).

Thérèse's assignments remained unimportant: painting (holy pictures, decoration of church objects or ornaments); office of "tierce," perhaps; at least she had not yet received the assignment as second turn-Sister. If so, she would have been helper to Sister Saint Raphael, a religious who was fifty-three years old, interim subprioress in 1892-1893, gentle and kind, but with little odd ways "that would try the patience of an angel" (PO, 2138).

Undoubtedly, this section of the Correspondence *offers many statements worthy of appearing in an anthology. However, it does retain, on the whole, an appearance of unimportance that runs the risk of misleading the reader, prompting him to pass on to something else. Now, at this very moment, Thérèse was entering a critical phase in her human and spiritual development. In a few months, she was to recall this period in her life with an unusual vivacity (LT*

167).

The *"kernel," "the essence of her life" (see LT 147), continued its secret growth. Beyond their banality, the letters make us aware of a kind of centrifugal thrust in Thérèse* which is seeking some kind of outlet:

1) *The resurgence of her desire to leave for the Carmel of Saigon, thus withdrawing herself from the distracting comforts of family affection (see LC 157, note 4);*
2) *after a delaying answer from P. Pichon, coinciding, within a few days, with the October retreat, there is an attempt to escape* up above, *a longing for heaven (see LT 151 and already 149;*
3) *then there is a more pressing longing for martyrdom: either through the shedding of her blood, following the example of St. Cecilia or the victims of the French Revolution, the sixteen Carmelite nuns of Compiègne whose centenary was celebrated in 1893-1894; or through her sickness which was already attacking the young Carmelite's body, and this more effectively because of undernourishment (she was now observing a strict fast because she was twenty-one).*

Thérèse's real vitality during these winter months cannot be fully appreciated until one reads one of her contemporaneous writings: The Mission of Joan of Arc or The Shepherdess of Domrémy listening to her voices *(RP I, January 21, 1894). When writing this little book in prose and poetry for her Community, Thérèse was participating in a current event: on January 27, 1894, Pope Leo XIII declared Joan of Arc "Venerable," and his initiative aroused the enthusiasm of French Catholics. It is difficult, however, to measure the significance, for Thérèse, of her own identification with Joan of Arc (she plays the role of the French heroine in the above-mentioned play). However, to which of the heroines was the injunction, repeated throughout the play, addressed: "I must leave"? Did this demand, which had at first frightened the Shepherdess of Lorraine, also shake the Carmelite of Normandy? Will the latter have the boldness to make the necessary departures outside the beaten track (see LT 145)? Her entire liberation, and that of a whole spiritual kingdom, demanded this price. Her change in hand-writing is proof of her courageous determination—and she needed this when daring to go beyond the form of writing inherited from Pauline (see LT 155, note 3)! Thérèse took things into her own hands. January 1894 confirmed the Christmas grace of 1886 and set her off once more on her "giant's race" (Ms. A, p. 97).*

LC 157   *From P. Pichon to Thérèse.*
September 21, 1893
→ LT lost

† Lachenaie, September 21, '93

Dear Benjamin,

You speak to me of the weight of years[1] and you are twenty years old! Twenty years, oh! I wish sixty more years for you, filled with good sacrifices, all perfumed with myrrh and incense to console the Heart of your divine Spouse at your own expense.

To experience the exile, to be bruised by all the thorns along the way, to drink down the gall, and, with an ever increasing delicacy, to feel one's heart beat and quiver concerning things that others pass over thoughtlessly...all this is a beautiful portion. Oh! how priv-ileged you are to have a heart so well fitted for suffering.[2]

In spite of everything, your four[3] letters are filled with joy from the Tabernacle and gladness from heaven.

May Jesus always keep for you this *ideal of the exile*[4] which your eyes can discover and your soul taste. The Saints loved so much everything that was amiable in the works of God: flowers, nature, above all souls, and holy affections.

Cherish your Céline: she deserves it. I know her better than you do. Our Lord is leading her to heights by a rugged and steep path.[5]

Jesus and I really love our little lamb and the entire, dear family of Les Buissonnets. Do not despair of seeing me again. I myself am counting on this!⁶

Could a spoiled child like you ever hesitate to abandon herself, to fall asleep peacefully in the arms of her Jesus, never fearing to be betrayed?

Sursum corda! Let us lift up our hearts! Let us soar more and more far away from what is earthly and human. Let us climb up to the Heart of Jesus. This is heaven before heaven; the heaven of heavens.

Long live peace, joy, confidence. Always smile for the divine Spouse.

My congratulations on your assignment as *Tierce.*⁷ Stay, stay in the novitiate.⁸

I bless you, you who are my youngest child, with a thousand privileged blessings.

Almire Pichon

* Autograph
1. See LT 139.
2. We know some of Thérèse's sufferings at this time: humiliations regarding her use of time (see LT 147, note 7), anxiety regarding the clashes between Mother Marie de Gonzague and Mother Agnes of Jesus (see LT 156, note 7).
3. Word erased; first writing: three. Perhaps Thérèse's most recent letter could have been dated for the feast of Saint Almire (September 11) sent at the beginning of this month.
4. The desire to leave for the Carmel of Saïgon, already expressed at the time of her Profession; see LC 146, note 7. To be noted is the frequency of the word "exile" in preference to "mission" each time Thérèse mentions this departure; see LT 221.

    Sister Geneviève (Céline) later interpreted this desire as coming from a disappointment. The permanence of *her family* within the cloister and at the doors of the Carmel of Lisieux could have frustrated Thérèse in the *eremitical* life she had dreamed about. See VT, April 1963, p. 85.
5. The *Correspondence* sheds light on the various trials of Céline at this time. In a note written in 1951, Sister Geneviève relates very explicitly this sentence to temptations against chastity she was undergoing then.
6. He was referring to his return to France; this took place only in 1900, after Thérèse's death.

7. According to CJ 13.7.18, Thérèse was *"tierce* of the econome" during the two months (June-July) of 1893. This office consisted of accompanying the bursar, then Mother Marie de Gonzague, each time workmen entered the monastery.

8. Asking for an extension or prolongation of the novitiate was not something exceptional at this time. It was even considered as virtuous. Thérèse sought this favor for different motives according to the sayings of certain witnesses at the Process; "out of humility" (Mother Agnes, PA, 378); "in order not to be freed from the restraints of the novitiate" (Sister Geneviève, PO, 487); and also "out of zeal" with regard to her companions because she "knew that once she left the novitiate, it would have been impossible for her to be associated with the novices," because of the touchy character of Mother Marie de Gonzague (Mother Agnes of Jesus, NPPA, Virtue of Prudence).

Her devotedness was directed first to Sister Martha, who had an additional year in the novitiate because she was a lay Sister; in other words, four years after having made her Profession (September 23, 1890-1894). With regard to Sister Marie-Madeleine, Mother Agnes wrote: "I could not even make you understand to what a degree Sister Marie-Madeleine is estranged from Sister Thérèse of the Child Jesus, because she feels herself divined (read into) to the very depths of her soul, and she is obliged, as a consequence, to wage war with her nature. When I was prioress, I had obligated her for a period of one year to go to Thérèse for one-half hour on Sundays, and I know what this is all about" (to the Guérins; see p. 924). This obligation was imposed on Sister Marie-Madeleine, very likely, during her canonical year of novitiate, between the reception of the Habit (September 7, 1893) and her Profession November 20, 1894); a constraint poorly accepted as this Sister later on testified at the Process; "When she told me to go with her at an hour agreed upon, I often used to go and hide instead of going with her. Then she would look for me and when she could not find me and we later met, she would say: 'I looked for you and I could not find you,' I would answer coldly: 'I was busy.' In these cirumstances, she retained her calm and smiling face." (Sister Marie-Madeleine, NPPO.)

LD

October 8 (?), 1893

From Mother Agnes of Jesus to Céline.

(Extracts.)

Thérèse's letter to Céline (LT 149) for her feast day remains an enigma for one who does not know the context. These lines from Mother Agnes, written shortly before, give us a hint of it.

J.M.J.T.

Little Céline, did you receive a letter from Father, the day before yesterday? Each one got a note here (this is not too much in a year). He said he will write you soon![1]...

Do not cry! Your soul is in the hands of God, like a beautiful white rose, which must give all its scent to the Creator. Put aside the vain work of painting,[2] that is, do not take up the brush except with detachment of spirit....

Dear little one! Believe us!... It is true, we have given up worldly ideas.... But we do have light from heaven. And you, too, possess this light, but the atmosphere in which you are living presents more than one mirage, and at times you could think we are the ones who are in darkness....

Darling, you whose soul is like a cloud, a light vapor, a springtime breeze, do not be dissipated, do not mix with the poisoned breath of the world.... The world is only folly, only nothing!... Oh! beautiful little dove, fly away, rest in the crevice of the solitary rock which is none other than Jesus living and resting in your heart!

How I love you!!!

Your little Mother who lives on the summits *of truth*.

Sister Agnes of Jesus

Are you not having a grand dinner today, if I have understood correctly? Well, let my little dove recall the words of St. Teresa,[3] and let her consider in spirit the table of heaven at which the guests are the angels and saints and the nourishment God Himself...and let her desire ardently to see herself seated at this blessed banquet.

We are on retreat.[4] Thérèse of the Child Jesus kisses HER CÉLINE and Sister Marie of the Sacred Heart and Mother Marie de Gonzague do the same.

    *   Autograph.

    1. The only extant letters from P. Pichon are to Thérèse (LC 157) and to Sister Marie of the Sacred Heart (see LT 156, note 7). Sister Geneviève mentioned two letters of eight pages received in 1893: one, November 4 (see Mss. II, p. 57), not found after her death; the other, April 17, from which only a short fragment remains. We read there: "As for dancing, I approve your line of conduct. Have I not always told you that your theology is according to my taste!" A possible reference to the discussion between Céline and Thérèse in 1892; see LT 134, caption.

    2. Céline was passionately fond of painting. Marie Guérin wrote her sister: "Last night, Céline had an excellent idea. Since we are always reproaching her or rather telling her that what is lacking in all her paintings is that she has never had any lessons from a great master, she thought of Krug, who is painting the cupola at the Abbey and who does portraits very well. He is a student of Flandrin. . . . Papa went to see l'abbe Domin; he saw Krug, and he is willing to come at least to give Céline some advice, he will perhaps even give her some lessons. . . . Céline is delighted. All are charmed by this idea" (to Mme La Néele, Jeanne Guérin, September 15, 1893).

    3. Teresa of Avila, St., *Avis XL*. Peers vol. 3, p. 258.

    4. See LT 151. Terminating October 15, the retreat began on October 7 or 8; hence the date we suggest for the undated letter.

LT 149   **From Thérèse to Céline**

October 20 (?),   For Céline's feast day. Without being too ex-
1893   plicit, with prudence lest she contradict Mother
                     Agnes, Thérèse sets about consoling her sister for
                     "the most bitter sorrow, that of not being
                     understood," especially by Pauline.

J.M.J.T.

Jesus †

Dear Céline,

I am entrusting *Jesus* with wishing my little Sister Marie of the
Holy Face[1] a happy feast for me. . . . *Jesus is the one* who must be
our divine link. He alone has the right to penetrate the sanctuary
of His spouse's heart. . . . Oh, yes! *He alone* understands when
nothing answers us.[2] . . . *He* alone arranges the events of our life of
exile. It is He who offers us at times the bitter chalice. But we do
not see Him, He is hiding. He veils His divine hand, and we can
see only creatures. Then we suffer since the voice of our Beloved
does not make itself heard and that of creatures seems to misunder-
stand us. . . . Yes, the most bitter sorrow is that of not being
understood. . . . But this sorrow will never be Céline's or Thérèse's,
never, for their eyes see higher than the earth, they are raised above
what is created. The more Jesus hides Himself, the more, too, they
feel that Jesus is close to them. With *exquisite delicacy*, He walks
before them, throwing aside the stones on the road,[3] removing the
reptiles, and this is not all. He makes the voices of friends resound
in our ears; these voices warn us not to walk with too much securi-
ty. . . . And why? Is not Jesus the one who has traced out our route
Himself? Is He not the one who enlightens us and reveals Himself
to our souls? . . . Everything brings us to Jesus. The flowers growing on the edge of the road do not captivate our hearts;[4] we gaze
on them, we love them, for they speak to us about Jesus, about His
power, about His love, but our souls remain free. Why disturb our
sweet peace in this way? Why fear the storm when the heavens are
serene? . . . Oh, Céline! my dear Céline. . .it is not the precipices we

must avoid, we are in the arms of Jesus. And if the voices of friends advise us to fear, it is our Beloved who *wills it* so, and why?... Ah! in His love He chooses for His spouses the same road He chose for Himself.... He wills that the purest joys be changed into sufferings so that not having, so to speak, even the time to breathe at ease, our heart may turn to Him who alone is our Sun and our joy....

The *flowers by the roadside* are the *pure pleasures* of life.[5] There is no evil whatsoever in enjoying them, but Jesus is *jealous* of our souls, He desires that all pleasures be mingled with bitterness for us.... And yet the *flowers on the roadside* lead to the Beloved, but they are a roundabout way, they are the plaque or mirror reflecting the Sun, but they are not the Sun itself.... I am not telling my dear Céline what I would like to tell her, I am explaining myself so poorly.... Perhaps she will understand without any explanations, Jesus is so skilled at delivering the messages of His poor Thérèse![6]...

There is a passage in the *Canticle of Canticles* which suits perfectly poor little exiled Céline. Here it is: "What do you see in the spouse except choirs of music in an army camp?"[7] Oh, yes. My Céline's life is really a field of battle.... Poor little dove, she sighs on the banks of the rivers of Babylon, and how could she sing the songs of the Lord in a foreign land?[8]... And nevertheless she must sing. Her life must be a *melody* (a choir of music). Jesus is the one who holds her captive, but He is at her side... Céline is the little lyre of Jesus.[9]... Is a concert complete when no one sings?... Since Jesus is playing, must not Céline *sing*?... When the tune is sad, then she *will sing* the song of the exile, and when the tune is joyful, her voice will make the strains of the *homeland* heard.... All that takes place, all the events of life, will be only distant sounds that will not make the little lyre of Jesus vibrate. Jesus alone has the right to place His divine fingers on it, creatures are *means*, instruments, but it is the hand of Jesus that conducts *everything*. We must see Him alone in *everything*.... I cannot think without delight of the dear little *St. Cecilia*; what a model for the little lyre of Jesus.... In the midst of the world, plunged into the center of all dangers, at the moment of being united with a young pagan who longs only for profane love, it seems to me that Cecilia would have had to tremble and to weep...but, no, while hearing the sounds of the instruments that were celebrating her nuptials, *Cecilia was singing in her heart.*[10]...

What abandonment!... She *was hearing* no doubt other melodies besides those of earth, her divine Spouse *was singing* too, the angels were making resound in Cecilia's heart the sound of their celestial concerts.... They were singing as in years gone by at the cradle of Jesus: "Glory to God in the heavens and peace on earth to souls of good will"[11] The glory of God! Oh, Cecilia divined that her divine Spouse thirsted for souls, and she desired already that of the young Roman, who was dreaming only of earthly glory. Soon she will make a martyr of him and multitudes will walk in his footsteps.... She does not fear, for the angels have sung: "*Peace* to souls of good will." She knows that Jesus is obliged to guard her, to protect her virginity, so what a reward!...

Yes, the chaste generation of virgin souls is beautiful.[12] The Church sings of it often, and these words are still true today as in the time of the virgin Cecilia....

Oh, dear Céline, what pleasure Jesus has with His little lyre! He has so few of them in the world, allow Him to rest near you, do not grow tired of *singing* since Jesus never grows tired of playing.... One day, up above in the homeland, you will see the fruits of your works.... After having smiled at Jesus in the midst of tears, you will enjoy the rays of His divine Face, and He will still play on His little lyre. He will play throughout eternity new tunes which *no one* will be able to sing except Céline![13]...

* Autograph.
1. Regarding this name, see LT 98, note 3.
2. A sentence currently attributed to St. Augustine.
3. See Ms. A, p. 84.
4. A possible reference to the *Spiritual Canticle* of St. John of the Cross, stanza III, v. 3; "I will not gather flowers"; see *Collected Works*, p. 427.
5. For Céline, painting took first place in these pure pleasures; see above, LD, October 8 (?), 1893, note 2.
6. See LT 144, note 8.
7. See Canticle of Canticles 7:1; commented on in the same way in LT 165.
8. See Psalm 136:4.
9. Henceforth, in the *Correspondence*, Thérèse applies this symbol only to Céline; here and in LT 161.

10. Office of St. Cecilia, November 22, first response of Matins. When a novice, Thérèse mentioned this "melody of Cecilia" (LT 54; LT 55, note 3; LT 87, note 9). We note the change of tone. At the end of 1893, Thérèse is more aware of the heroic abandonment of the Roman virgin in an extreme situation, of her apostolic intrepidity founded on the certitude that God "thirsts for souls." She develops these thoughts in the following spring (LT 161 and P 3 on this theme), and she condenses them in a definitive way in her *Story of a Soul* in the autumn of 1895 (Ms. A, p. 131). No doubt, she is enriching here the sentiments of the adolescent of 1887, according to a subsequent deepening of these sentiments over a period of eight years. Finally, on her deathbed, she makes this terse statement: "I prefer the saints who feared nothing, like St. Cecilia, who allowed herself to be married and feared nothing...." (CJ 30.6.1.).

11. See Luke 2:14.

12. See Wisdom 4:1.

13. Incomplete letter. A "t" was about to begin a new sentence. No signature.

LT 150   **From Thérèse to Mme La Néele.**
October 22, 1893
→ LC lost

J.M.J.T.

Jesus †   Carmel, October 22, '93

Dear Jeanne,

It is my turn to make excuses, for I am very late in thanking you for all your treats, but I had a faint hope of expressing my gratitude *viva voce* and I put off writing you for this reason.

Oh, no! I did not have the nasty thought that my little sister was forgetting me, but I found it very natural that she was content to offer a prayer for her little Thérèse, and I was more touched than I could tell you when receiving your amiable letter. The wishes from my dear cousin were also much appreciated. Finally, the jars of jam came to crown all your acts of kindness toward me!... Our Mother

St. Teresa was so grateful that she used to say: "One could win her heart with a sardine."[1] What would she have said had she known Francis and Jeanne?...

But heaven is not so far from earth that she cannot see them and bless them. I am even confident that she loves my dear Jeanne particularly.

Our Holy Mother also had a sister by the name of Jeanne, and I was really touched when reading her Life to see with what tenderness she watched over her little nephews. So, without leaving aside good Saint Anne,[2] I am praying to St. Teresa to obtain through her intercession the favor of being an aunt myself.[3] I do not doubt that she will answer me by sending to my dear little Jeanne a blessed family that will give to the Church some great saints.[4]

The delay does not discourage me, for I know much time is required at the court of Rome to make saints, and I cannot bear God any grudge for placing all His care and His love into the preparation of little souls whom He will one day entrust to my Jeanne.

I beg you, little sister, to offer a prayer to St. Teresa. I am sure St. Anne will be happy with this; union gives strength, and together they will obtain the grace we are asking.

I beg you, dear Jeanne, speak to Francis on my behalf, thanking him for his kind wishes, and I kiss you with all my heart with all the tenderness of a little sister.

> Thérèse of the Child Jesus
> re. carm. ind.

Our Mother and Sister Marie of the Sacred Heart send you a thousand tokens of affection, and they do not cease praying that dear little Jeanne's desires be fully answered.[5]

* Autograph.
1. Letter to *María* de San José, September 1578.
2. See LD, May 10, 1892.
3. First cousin once removed.
4. See LT 131, note 1; LT 152, note 3, etc.
5. Marginal addition by Mother Agnes: "Dear Jeanne, will you let us know the time of your next trip, for Mme Pays, sister of Mother Marie de Gonzague, is to send us some apples, and she will take advantage

of the occasion. I kiss you as a dear sister. Regards to Francis. Sister
Agnes of Jesus.''

LT 151   **From Thérèse to Léonie**
November 5, 1893
→ LC lost

J.M.J.T.

Jesus †   Carmel, November 5, '93

Dear Léonie,

   I am overjoyed at your happiness; your nice little letters are a real
joy to me. I see, without any doubt, that you are where God wills
you to be.
   How good Our Lord is to our family! He has not permitted any
mortal being to become the spouse of a single one of us.
   We just listened to a beautiful retreat to prepare us for the feast
of our Holy Mother [St. Teresa of Avila]. The good Father[1] spoke
especially about union with Jesus and the beauty of our vocation.
He pointed out to us all the advantages of the religious life, especially
the contemplative life. He gave us a comparison that charmed me.
He said: ''Look at the oaks in our countryside, how deformed they
all are; they spread out their branches to the right and left, nothing
hinders them, so they never reach a great height. On the contrary,
look at the oaks of the forest, hemmed in on all sides; they do not
see the light except from *on high* so their trunks are without all these
deformed branches that draw away the sap necessary to go upward.
The oaks see nothing but the sky above, and all their strength is
turned in that direction, so soon they attain a prodigious height. In
the religious life, the soul like the young oak is hemmed in on all
sides by the Rule, all its movements are hampered and thwarted by
the trees of the forest. . . . But the soul has *light* when it looks upon
HEAVEN, there alone it can rest its gaze, never must it fear climb-
ing too much in this direction.''

Dear little Sister, I think I am pleasing you by talking about these things; our joy is to speak of spiritual matters, to plunge our hearts into infinity!...

I beg pardon for sending you letters *so poorly written*,[2] but, you see, dear little Sister, I prefer allowing my pen to run under the influence of my heart to turning out beautiful sentences and sending you *a page of real penmanship.*

I beg you to remember me respectfully to Mother Superior.

Do not forget me in your prayers; think of me in the presence of Jesus as much as I think of you.

I leave you, dear Léonie, remaining truly united with you in our divine Spouse's Heart.

Your unworthy little Sister,

> Thérèse of the Child Jesus of the Holy Face
> rel. carm. ind.

* Autograph.
1. Père Armand Lemonnier, *Missionnaires de La Délivrande* (Calvados). We have found no notes from his retreat. He preached a retreat at the Carmel in 1894 and 1895; see LD, June (?), 1895.
2. Thérèse's letters to Léonie manifest a more careful penmanship; see *Introduction*, p. 75, note 39.

LT 152　　　　　**From Thérèse to Mme Guérin.**
November 17, 1893

J.M.J.T.

Jesus †　　　　　　　　　　　　　Carmel, November 17, '93

Dear Aunt,

How sweet for your little Thérèse to come each year to offer you her wishes for a happy feast!

I have nothing new, however, to say to you; you know, for a long time now, how much I love you.

Dear little Aunt, when repeating it, I have no fear of boring you, and this is the reason making me think this way. When I am before the Tabernacle, I can say only one thing to Our Lord: "My God, you know that I love You."[1] And I feel my prayer does not tire Jesus; knowing the helplessness of His poor little spouse, He is content with her good will. I know, too, that God has poured something of the love overflowing His Heart into the hearts of mothers.... And the one to whom I am speaking has received such a large measure of maternal love that I cannot have any fear of being misunderstood....

Jn. 21,15

Besides, my helplessness will not last eternally; in the heavenly homeland, I shall be able to say many things to dear little Aunt that cannot be expressed in human words.

In the meanwhile, I beg Our Lord to leave for a *very, very long time* on earth the one who can work so well for His glory, and I want her to see the *children* of her *grandchildren*.[2] Perhaps my little sister Jeanne would laugh if she were to read these lines, but I have much more confidence than she has, and I am awaiting the *great saint* and the *great pontiff*,[3] followed by a great number of other little angels.

Dear Aunt, tomorrow I will offer my Holy Communion for you and also for Madame Fournet, I think very often of her and beg our Lord to preserve her a long time still for your sake.[4]

I beg you, dear Aunt, to kiss Uncle for me, and I ask him as well as my little sisters to give you the most tender caresses for me.

Your little *Benjamin*, who is proud of her title.

> Sister Thérèse of the Child Jesus
> re. carm. ind.

* Autograph.
1. See John 21:15.
2. See Psalm 127:6, integrated at this time into the marriage liturgy.
3. "Thérèse makes a reference here to a dream Jeanne had some time after her pilgrimage to Auray.... Jeanne dreamt her prayers were answered and that a mysterious voice spoke these words: 'He will be a great saint and a great pontiff.' " (Note of Sister Geneviève (Céline) in CMG III, p. 242.) Thérèse quoted these words in her poem: *Confidence de Jésus à Thérèse,* dedicated to Jeanne (P 34, stanza 6); see

LC 168. The same in LT 255.

4. Mme Fournet was recovering from a heart attack: "Good Mamma is always very weak. No trouble last night, but she had a very restless night" (Mme. Guérin to her daughter, Mme. La Néele, November 7, 1893).

LT 153   **From Thérèse to M. Guérin.**

December (?),   Approximate date; see note 1.
1893

J.M.J.T.

Dear Uncle,

Our Mother is doing much better,[1] but she is very *weak* even though she says the opposite.

Thank you, thank you, for all the care you are giving her. I hope she will be very obedient, it would be very bad not to obey *so paternal* an Uncle!... Mother Marie de Gonzague is very much touched by your attention; she thanks you and is giving all her motherly care to her dear little Prioress.

Pardon me, dear Uncle, I am in such a hurry that I do not know what I am saying to you, but I hope you will divine our *gratitude*. We are praying *very much* for Madame Fournet.[2]

I kiss you for your three little Carmelites, Aunt, too.

Sister Thérèse of the Child Jesus
rel. carm.[3]

* Autograph.

1. Mother Agnes of Jesus. Two undated notes from her to Céline make reference to this illness. When arranging the correspondence from Mother Agnes, in 1950, Sister Geneviéve suggested the date of February 1894 for these notes. In an explanatory note, she writes: "Sick probably from influenza rampant since the beginning of January, end of December." However, the slanted handwriting of Thérèse in the above note would date it in 1893. On the other hand,

CMG III, p. 237, transcribes this letter at the beginning of the 1893 collection (before that of August 10. But the reference to Mme Fournet suggests a date close to that of LT 152.

2. See LT 152, note 4. November 23, 1893, Mme Guérin wrote her daughter Marie: "Mamma's health is holding out. Yesterday, her night was not too good, restless in her sleep, but there was no crisis."

3. Mother Marie de Gonzague adds this P.S.: "Little Mother Prioress will write tomorrow to thank her beloved uncle for the rice which arrived just now."

LT 154   **From Thérèse to Léonie.**

December 27, 1893
→ LC lost

J.M.J.T.

Jesus †   Carmel, December 27, 1893

Dear Léonie,

I am happy to come to offer my best wishes for '94. The wish I am making at Jesus' cradle is to see you clothed again soon in the holy Habit of the Visitation. I say to see you, but I know I shall have this joy only in heaven; what a joy, then, to find each other once more after the exile of life!...

What things to tell each other! Here below, words are powerless, but up above one single glance will suffice to understand one another, and I believe our happiness will be greater than if we had not been separated from one another.

Your dear little letter pleased me very much. I see that you are truly happy, and I do not doubt that God is giving you the grace of remaining forever in the holy ark. We are reading, in the refectory, the Life of Saint Chantal.[1] It is a real consolation for me to listen to it; this brings me even closer to the dear Visitation that I love so much, and then I see the intimate union that has always existed between it and Carmel. This makes me bless God for having chosen these two Orders for our family. The Blessed Virgin is truly

Our Mother since our monasteries are dedicated particularly to her.

Dear little Sister, do not forget to pray for me during dear little Jesus' month; ask Him that I remain always little, *very little*![2] . . . I will offer the same prayer for you, for I know your desires, and I know humility is your preferred virtue.

Do not forget, dear Léonie, to offer my respectful good wishes to your revered Mother, and believe in the sincere affection of the last and *littlest* of your sisters.

> Thérèse of the Child Jesus of the Holy Face
> rel. carm. ind.

* Autograph.

1. Abbé E. Bougaud, *Histoire de sainte Jeanne de Chantal et des Origines de la Visitation*, Paris, 1865, 3rd. ed., two volumes.

2. See LT 141, note 3; and this sentence written at this same time: "I want to remain always little, very humble, in order to resemble Jesus and to merit that He make His abode in me. . . ." (RP 1, January 21, 1894.) Thérèse was to use only in 1895 (LT 178) and especially in 1896 (LT 182) her definitive expression: "to remain a child, to remain a little child."

LT 155   From Thérèse to M. and Mme Guérin.
December 29, 1893

J.M.J.T.

Jesus †   Carmel, December 29, 1893

Dear Uncle and dear Aunt,

I have only a few minutes to offer you my wishes for a happy New Year. Our Mother just told me her letter[1] must be delivered tomorrow morning. But I do not need a lot of time to repeat to my dear relatives the wishes my heart is making for their happiness. I would like, were this possible, the New Year to reserve only consolations for them. But alas! God, who knows the rewards He is reserving for His friends, often loves to have them win His treasures by means of sacrifices. Our Holy Mother Teresa said smilingly to Our Lord these very true words: "My God, I am not surprised You have so few friends, You treat them so badly."[2]

However, even in the midst of the trials He sends, God is filled with tenderness. My dear Father's illness is an evident proof of this for me. This cross was the greatest I could have imagined, but after we had tasted its bitterness, Our Lord came to sweeten, by means of our dear relatives' hands, the chalice of sorrow He had offered us and which I was expecting to drink to the last dregs....

O, dear Uncle and dear little Aunt! if you only knew how loving and grateful is your little Thérèse's heart!... I cannot tell you all I would like, it is the hour for Matins. Pardon me for the incoherence of my letter and my *spidery handwriting*[3]...look only at your child's heart.

> Thérèse of the Child Jesus
> rel. carm. ind.

I beg you to give Madame Fournet sincerest wishes from her little daughter.

*   Autograph.

1. Mother Agnes of Jesus' letter, December 29, 1893, deals for the first time with the matter of Marie Guérin's Carmelite vocation and its approaching realization. See LD, July 3, 1893, note 3.

2. Thérèse could have read these words in the *Histoire de sainte Thérèse* by the Carmelites of Caen, according to the Bollandists (vol. II, p. 362; Ed. Retaux-Bray, Paris 1885, two vols.). However, the retort is legendary, but it does fit in with Teresa of Avila's character.

3. This letter is the last from Thérèse written in her slanted handwriting. The "schoolteacher" of Les Buissonnets, Pauline (Mother Agnes), finally authorized her former pupil to free herself from the rules she had received: "She had a greater facility in writing "vertically" than otherwise; her handwriting (slanted to) the right was ugly; but I told her that this was an affectation [writing vertically], and I did not allow her to take on this kind of penmanship until the last years of her life" (Mother Agnes of Jesus, NPPA, Virtue of Fortitude). See *Introduction*, pp. 75-76.

LT 156   **From Thérèse to Mother Agnes of Jesus.**

January 21, 1894   First of the letters in which Thérèse adopts her
                     new vertical handwriting.

    The allegory which follows was inspired by
several poetic compositions of Mother Agnes:
Les vertus au berceau de Jésus (Christmas 1884);
Le premier Rêve de l'Enfant Jésus (Christmas
1889; see vol. I, pp. 594 and 606); finally, the
Prayer to the Holy Face (1890).

    To its first purpose: "to please" Mother Agnes
on her feast day (hence the flowery style) was
added another which Thérèse was soon to reveal:
to express her own life of faith (LT 160).

J.M.J.T.

The Dream of the Child Jesus[1]

    While playing in His crib with the flowers His dear spouse brought
Him, Jesus is thinking of what He will do to thank her.... Up
above, in the celestial gardens, the angels, servants of the divine
Child, are already weaving crowns His Heart has reserved for His
beloved.

    However, the night has come. The moon sends out its silvery rays,
and the gentle Child falls asleep.... His little hand does not let go
the flowers that delighted Him during the day, and His Heart continues dreaming about the happiness of His dear spouse.

    Soon, He sees in the distance strange objects bearing no
resemblance to the springtime flowers. A cross!...a lance!...a
crown of thorns![2] And yet the divine Child does not tremble; this
is what He chooses to show His spouse how much He loves her!...
But it is still not enough; His infant face is so beautiful. He sees
it disfigured, covered with blood![3]...unrecognizable!...Jesus knows
that His spouse will always recognize Him,[4] that she will be at His
side when all others abandon Him, so the divine Child smiles at this
bloodstained image, He smiles at the chalice filled with the wine giving birth to virgins.[5] He knows that, in His Eucharist, the ungrateful
will desert Him; but Jesus is thinking of His spouse's love, her at-

tention. He sees the flowers of her virtues as they scent the sanctuary, and the Child Jesus continues to sleep on peacefully.... He awaits the shadows to lengthen[6]...the night of life to give way to the bright day of eternity!...

Then Jesus will give back to His beloved spouse the flowers she had given Him, consoling Him on earth.... Than He will lower His divine Face to her, radiant with glory, and He will allow His spouse to taste eternally the ineffable sweetness of His divine kiss!!!...

Dear Mother,

You have just read the *dream* that your child wanted to reproduce for your feast day. But, alas! only your artistic brush could paint such a sweet mystery!... I trust you will look only upon the good will of her who would be happy to please you.

It is you, Mother, these virtues are yours that I wanted to represent by the little flowers that Jesus is pressing to His Heart. The flowers are really for Jesus alone! yes, my dear Mother's virtues will always remain hidden with the little Child in the crib; however, in spite of the humility that would like to hide them, the mysterious perfume coming from these flowers gives me a presentiment already of the marvels that I shall see one day in the eternal homeland when I shall be allowed to contemplate the treasures of love that you are now giving to Jesus.[7]

Oh, Mother, you know it. Never shall I be able to tell you of my gratitude for your having guided me like an angel from heaven[8] along the paths of life. You are the one who taught me to know Jesus, to love Him; now that you are doubly my Mother, oh, lead me always to the Beloved, teach me to practice virtue, so that in heaven, I may not be placed too far from you and that you may recognize me as your child and your little sister.

> Thérèse of the Child Jesus of the Holy Face
> re. carm. ind.

*   Autograph.
1.   Thérèse commented on this picture which she had painted. It was a reproduction of a picture in lace, squared off by her in view of an

enlargement: a Child Jesus reclining, *The Crib, the first Altar of Sacrifice under the New Law of Love* (Letaille, pl. 489, Boum ard editeur). But whereas her model presented a three-quarters portrait, looking toward the instruments of His Passion, Thérèse painted it as fullface, the Child's eyes closed. It is impossible to obtain the original expression on the face, for in 1927 Sister Geneviéve (Céline) had the painting returned from the Visitation at Le Mans to Lisieux, and she retouched the Child Jesus' face drastically. The older religious at Le Mans recalled that it resembled much more a "baby" with rather strong features, not too graceful. See the letter of Mother Agnes regarding this "painting," pp. 1257 ff., and LT 160.

2. On the same painting, we see in the background: sponge, whips, and reed.

3. A Veronica Veil, with the Holy Face, is fastened to the Cross; see the painting described on April 28, 1890 (LT 102, note 1).

4. See Isaias 53:3.

5. See Zacharias 9:17.

6. See Canticle of Canticles 4:6.

7. A reference to the clashes of character between Mother Agnes and Mother Marie de Gonzague. September 18, 1893, P. Pichon wrote to Sister Marie of the Sacred heart: "I know the souls of my daughters (the strong and the weak) much better than you think; you are telling me nothing. My heart senses the delicate position set up by Jesus for the dear Lamb, and I am not unaware of all the help she is receiving from heaven to face up to it. My thought goes deeper than your pen, and I feel it is in agreement with your thought.... When reading the story of the little and great storms your pen so filially confides to me, I am reminded of this beautiful saying of Fenelon: 'God polishes a diamond by means of another diamond!' I am thinking of that quietly. Dear little shepherdess, help her smile at the bundle of myrrh!'' Mother Agnes wrote later, regarding this matter: "Poor Mother Marie de Gonzague! She was the one, however, who worked for my election, but she could not stand my taking too much authority. She would have liked to have me always under her control. How I suffered and wept during those three years! However, I know this yoke was necessary for me; it matured me and detached my soul from honors" (*Souvenirs intimes*, p. 69).

8. See LT 140, note 2.

LT 157   **From Thérèse to Céline.**

March or May,   Uncertain date; see notes 1 and 5.
1894

J.M.J.T.

The *codfiches*[1] please our Mother *very much*. She would like to write a note to thank her dear Céline, but she cannot do it. She is also very happy about Marie's letter.[2]

Let the little exile be sad *without being sad*,[3] for if the tenderness of creatures is not concentrated on her,[4] the *tenderness* of Jesus is totally CONCENTRATED on her. Now that Céline is without a home, Jesus Himself is well lodged. He is content to see His dear spouse *wandering*, this pleases Him! Why?... I myself know nothing about it.... This is Jesus' secret, but I believe He is preparing very beautiful things in His little house.[5]... He has to work so much that He seems to forget His dear Céline...but, no, without being seen by her, he is looking at her through the window.[6]... He is pleased to see her in the desert, having no other duty but to love[7] while suffering, without even *feeling* that she *loves*!... Jesus knows that life is only a dream, so He is taking delight in seeing His spouse weeping on the banks of the river of Babylon![8] Soon the day will come when Jesus will take His Céline by the hand and will have her enter her little house which will have become an eternal palace.... Then He will say: " 'Now, my turn.'[9] You have given me on earth the *only home* that every human heart is unwilling to renounce, that is, *yourself*, and now I am giving you as a dwelling my eternal substance, that is, "Myself." This is your house for all eternity. During the night of life, you have been homeless and solitary, now you will have a companion, and it is I, Jesus, your Spouse, your Friend, for whom you sacrificed all, who will be this Companion, who must fill you with joy from age to age!..."

*   Autograph.
1.   From the English word "codfish" (*morue*), given improperly in Normandy to *coquilles Saint-Jacques*. In CMG IV, p. 89, Sister Geneviève thus annotated her copy: "The season for *coquilles Saint Jacques* or "*codefiches*" begins in March." The vertical handwriting of this note

is certainly that of 1894: handwriting in transition, from the first
months of this year. Some letters are still uncertain, especially the "d"
which has not as yet received its characteristics loop; this becomes
constant from May 1894.

2. Marie Guérin was suffering from a "mucous fever from the beginning of January to April" (ChrIG, p. 68), which will delay her entrance to Carmel.

3. In February 1894, Céline composed a poem: La Mort, filled with
nostalgia (*Notes intimes*, notebook I, pp. 168-169).

4. Céline Maudelonde's wedding (LT 159) could have accentuated
Céline's feeling of being alone.

5. We know that, as a general rule, Thérèse's symbolism arises from concrete things: events, environment. The succession of the words: *asile,
errer, maison, demeure,* could be a reference to some family events
taking place in May, which would prompt us to postpone this note
by several weeks. In fact, according to the Guérin correspondence,
May 18, 22, 26, and June 7, the rather frequent bouts of intoxication
of Auguste, Céline's new servant, caused worries for the safety of
Céline and her father. M. Guérin considered bringing back Céline and
her father to his own home. For this purpose, he would "arrange his
laboratory quarters into a bedroom for M. Martin, with a bedroom
above which he would make in the attic for the servant" (letter of
Mme Guérin to Mme Le Néele, May 22, 1894). This move took place
on June 7 and 8.

6. See Canticle of Canticles 2:9.

7. John of the Cross, St., *Spiritual Canticle,* stanza XXVIII, see *Collected Works,* p. 520.

8. See Psalm 136:1.

9. See Arminjon, LT 57, note 5. The termination of the letter is inspired
by the same author: "If I have my servants and friends enter my
house...it is to quench their thirst and their desires superabundant-
ly...but this is not enough for the satisfaction of my divine Heart....
I owe them more than Paradise, more than the treasures of my
knowledge, I owe them my life, my nature, my eternal and infinite
substance" (*op. cit.,* p. 290).

LT 158   **From Thérèse to Léonie.**
March (?), 1894   Date inserted by the recipient: "March 1894."

J.M.J.T.

Jesus †

Dear Léonie,

I cannot tell you my happiness when learning that you were received for the taking of the Habit![1]. . . . I understand how happy you
must be, and I am sharing greatly in your joy.

Dear little Sister, how well God has rewarded your efforts! I recall
what you were telling me in the speakroom before your entrance into the holy ark: that it meant nothing for you to remain always the
last, to receive the Habit without any ceremony. . . . It was Jesus
alone you were seeking, and for Him you were renouncing all consolation. but as our dear father used to repeat often to us: "God
does not allow Himself to be outdone in generosity." So He did not
will that you be deprived of the joy of becoming His fiancée public-
ly, while waiting for you to be His spouse. It seems to me that the
years of exile you spent in the world served to adorn your soul with
a precious garment for the day of your espousals. The sad winter
days have been followed by the radiant days of spring, and Jesus
is saying to you as to the spouse in the Canticles: "For winter is now
past, the rain is over and gone. Arise, my beloved, my dove, and
come. . . . Behold I am at the door, open to me, my sister, my love,
for my Face is full of the dew and my locks of the drops of the
night."[2] For a long time you longed for the visit of Jesus, and you
were saying to Him as the spouse: "Who will grant me, my Beloved,
to find you *alone outside* so that I *may give you a kiss* and that in
the future no one may despise me!. . ."[3]

Here at last is this day so much desired. . . . You have not yet encountered Jesus, dear little Sister, in the presence of people, but you
have sought Him with great care, and now He Himself is coming
to you. . . . You consented to find Him *alone outside*, but He wants
to give you *a kiss before everybody* so that all will know that He
has placed His seal on your forehead and that never will you receive

any other lover but Him.[4]

Dear Léonie, I am forgetting to thank you for the letter; I should have begun with it, but you understand, do you not, that it is the joy I feel at your great happiness that alone causes this forgetfulness.

I hope your wishes will soon be fulfilled and your good chaplain[5] will be quickly cured. I beg you, dear little Sister, to remember me respectively to your good and revered Mother.[6] Like you, I am very happy that she is the one giving you the holy Habit. . . .

I leave you, remaining united with you in the divine Heart of Jesus. Your unworthy little sister,

> Thérèse of the Child Jesus of the Holy Face
> rel. carm. ind.

*   Autograph.
1. No document of the time has preserved the announcement of this news. Thérèse's handwriting is very much like that of the following letter (LT 159), but it still has the "d" of the transition. The ceremony of Léonie's reception of the Habit took place on April 6.
2. See Canticle of Canticles 2:11, 10; 5:2. See LT 108, note 7.
3. See Canticle of Canticles 8:1.
4. Divine Office for feast of St. Agnes, third antiphon of Matins: "He has placed His seal on my forehead in order that I may never receive any other lover but Him." This quotation appears on page 8 of the copy made by Thérèse, precisely at the beginning of 1894 (according to the handwriting), of the "Play composed in 1888 by our Mother Agnes of Jesus"; see LT 53.
5. L'abbé Enault, who became chaplain in 1893; he remained there until 1928.
6. Mother Marie de Sales Lefrançois (see LT 148, note 4); she gave up the office of superior on Pentecost 1894. See LT 163, note 5.

LC 158   *From P. Pichon to Thérèse.*
March 19, 1894
→ LT lost

† Lachine, March 19[1]

Dear Benjamin,

How I congratulate you for walking in the valley of humility. Jesus is to be found only there!

Peace! Peace! This is the Master's heritage. At the cradle, the angels gave no other enticement to the little shepherds of the countryside.[2]

Let Our Lord nourish you with His Gospel:[3] this is a royal dish.

Do not be in too much haste to arrive at the eternal face to face.[4] Wait patiently for your hour of martyrdom. But desire it for me as for yourself.

How I enjoyed this little glimpse of your soul, your religious life![5] This "Jesus alone" will have to be your supreme rule right up to death. Oh! the good portion which is yours! Outside Jesus, only bitterness! Feel how well you are provided for! *Alleluia!*

Let the divine Spouse make use of His little nothing![6] Grant Him this whim. Be the most pliant of His toys.[7]

Your soul appeared very limpid to me, very transparent. God be blessed! Keep all your holy ambitions and your hopes.

With Jesus, I bless you with all my heart.

Almire Pichon

* Autograph.
1. Date determined from a letter of P. Pichon to Sister Marie of the Sacred Heart, identical in appearance, carrying the same heading: "Lachine, March 17." The recipient added: "March 1894."
2. See Luke 2:14.
3. See Ms. A, p. 179. On March 17, P. Pichon wrote also to Sister Marie of the Sacred Heart: "I gladly pardon you for not liking books. All is simplified within our soul as we advance toward eternity. Enjoy, enjoy the Gospel, more and more."
4. See LT 147, note 9.

5. From this sentence, we could conclude that Thérèse wrote once to P. Pichon since his last response (LC 157), and very likely between Christmas and New Year's day.
6. Probable reference to Thérèse's role with her two companions.
7. Recall of a frequent theme in the *Correspondence* in 1887-1889; see LT 79, note 2. We do not know if P. Pichon is content here with merely repeating something from Thérèse's recent letter.

LT 159   **From Thérèse to Céline Maudelonde.**
March 26, 1894
→ lost

J.M.J.T.

Carmel, March 26, 1894

Dear little Céline,

I would have liked to answer earlier your letter which gave me much joy; Lent prevented me from this, but at last this is Paschal time,[1] and I can tell my dear little cousin[2] the share I am taking in her happiness.[3]

The great peace you are experiencing is to me a manifest sign of the will of God, for He alone can pour peace into your soul, and the happiness you are enjoying under His divine glance can come only from Him. Dear little Céline, I cannot show you my affection in the way I would if I were still in the world, however, it is not less strong for that reason. On the contrary, I feel that in solitude I will be more useful to you than if I had the consolation of being near you. Carmel's grilles are not made to separate hearts that love one another only in Jesus, they serve rather to make the bonds uniting them stronger.

While you are following the path God has traced out for you, I will pray for my Céline, the companion of my childhood.[4] I will beg that all her joys be so pure that she may always be able to enjoy them under the eyes of God. I will ask, especially, that she may experience the incomparable joy of bringing back a soul to Our Lord, and that this soul be the one that must soon form only one with hers.

I do not doubt this grace will soon be granted to you, and I would be happy if my weak prayers had contributed a little bit to it.

I hope my dear little Hélène is now cured, the moment for being sick would be very poorly chosen!... I beg you to hug her tightly for me, and I ask her to give my dear Céline all my most tender kisses; I am sure I cannot choose anyone better for carrying out this sweet mission....

Mother Marie de Gonzague joins your three cousins in Carmel by taking delight in your happiness. They beg you, dear Céline, to remember them respectfully to *Monsieur* and *Madame* Maudelonde.

I leave you, dear Céline, always remaining united to you in heart.

Your little cousin who will love you all her life and will not cease praying for your happiness.

Sister Thérèse of the Child Jesus
re. carm. ind.

P.S. The Mother Prioress of the Saïgon Carmel[5] has sent us a great number of Chinese objects, among which is a charming little drawing-room suite. Our Mother thought of raffling them off for the benefit of our Community. The tickets are fifty *centimes*. We are offering them to all the friends of our Carmel. If you want any, we shall be happy to send you some.[6]

* Autograph.
1. In 1894 Easter fell on March 25.
2. There was no blood relationship between the Martin and Maudelonde families, but the name "cousins" was an accepted thing among the children for a long time. "Pauline wants Marguerite [Maudelonde] absolutely as her cousin; she says that since Jeanne [Guérin] is her first cousin and also Marguerite's cousin, it is impossible that the letter be nothing to her. It is agreed then that Marguerite is cousin to all!" (Mme Martin to Mme Guérin, *Correspondence familiale*, August 20, 1873.)
3. Her coming marriage with M. Gason Pottier, notary at Fervaques (Calvados). The ceremony took place June 19, 1894; see LT 166.
4. See Ms. A, p. 54. Thérèse had spent Thursday afternoons dancing—without any enthusiasm—with Céline and Hélène Maudelonde at the

848   April 1894   LT 160/*LC 158*

Guérin cousins' home.

5. Mother Philomena of the Immaculate Conception (d. 1895), one of the Lisieux Carmelites, who sailed on July 9, 1861, to make the foundation at Saïgon, the first mission Carmel.

6. "In 1894, we decided to complete the decorations of the chapel and to replace the windows of the dome. But how cover all these expenses? We set up a little lottery among our Carmels and families, and this helped us, along with some donations, to meet the expenses." (*Foundation of Carmel of Lisieux*, III, p. 216.)

LT 160 **From Thérèse to Sister Marie-Aloysia Vallée.**

April 3, 1894 Mother Agnes of Jesus gave her former teacher
→ LC lost at the Visitation in Le Mans a picture painted
by Thérèse during the preceding January; see LT
156 and p. 1257.

J.M.J.T.

Jesus †   April 3, 1894

Dearest Sister,

I am unable to tell you how much your kind letter touched me. It was a great joy for me to know the painting of the little Jesus pleased you, and I was rewarded beyond all my hopes.... Dear *Aunt*,[1] allow me to give you this name, I was thinking of you when I was meditating on the gift I wanted to offer our Reverend Mother for her first feast day as Prioress.

I knew she would be happy to send you a little souvenir, so I put all my heart into composing *The dream of the little Jesus*. But, alas! my unskilled brush was not able to reproduce what my soul dreamed about. I *watered* my little Jesus' white dress with my *tears*, which did not bring down a heavenly ray on His little face![2]... In my grief, I promised myself to say nothing of the thought that had inspired me to undertake my work. In fact, it was only after seeing our good Mother's indulgence that I confided my secret to her. She was willing to look at my heart and my intention rather than at her child's skill, and to my great joy my little Jesus has gone *for me* to meet

good Aunt at Le Mans. I painted this divine Child in order to show what He is in my eyes.... In fact, He *is* almost always *sleeping*....
Poor Thérèse's Jesus does not caress her as He used to caress her Holy Mother.[3] This is very natural, for the daughter is so unworthy of the Mother!... However, Jesus' little closed eyes speak volumes to my soul,[4] and since He does not caress me, I take care to please Him. I know well that His Heart is always watching[5] and in the homeland of the heavens He will deign to open His divine eyes...
Then when seeing Jesus, I shall also have the happiness of contemplating my good Mothers of the Visitation, next to Him. I trust they will be willing to recognize me as their child. Are they not my Mothers, in fact, those who fashioned the hearts of the *two* visible *angels* who served me as real *Mothers*?[6]...

I remember perfectly my trip to the Visitation at Le Mans at the age of three;[7] I have repeated it many times in my heart, and Carmel's grille is not an obstacle preventing me from visiting dear Aunt and all the revered Mothers who love little Thérèse of the Child Jesus without knowing her.

I beg you, *good Aunt*, to pay your *little niece's* debt of gratitude by thanking your Reverend Mother and all your dear Sisters, especially Sister Joseph de Sales,[8] whose affectionate regards really touched me.

VERY DEAR AUNT, I would like to talk with you for a long time, but I am at the end of my paper, and I am obliged to leave you, begging your pardon!...

> Sister Thérèse of the Child Jesus,
> Your unworthy *little niece*

* Autograph.
1. "In order to please me, she gave this title to my former teacher, whom I loved very much. Sister Agnes of Jesus, r.c.i." (Note of Mother Agnes on the autograph.) See LC 1 and 2.
2. See LT 156, note 1.
3. A few days afterward, Thérèse gave Céline an illuminated picture on which was glued a vignette depicting St. Teresa of Avila being embraced by the Child Jesus; see LT 162.
4. Concerning the "sleep" of Jesus, see LT 144, 161, and 165.
5. See Canticle of Canticles 5:2.

6. Marie and Pauline, Thérèse's two teachers, had retained a deep impression of their years at the Visitation boarding school at Le Mans (1868-1877). See the *"Archives de Famille,"* which published from October 1969 in *Vie Thérésienne* the correspondence of Sister Marie-Dosithée Guérin and her nieces. Concerning Sister Marie-Aloysia's influence, see VT, April 1972, letter 230.
7. March 29, 1875; see Ms. A, p. 23, and VT already cited, letter 223. Thérèse was two years and three months old.
8. Louise Gasse (1861-1914), companion and friend of Pauline at the boarding school, 1873 to 1877; she entered the Visitation in 1884.

LT 161   **From Thérèse to Céline.**

April 26, 1894

J.M.J.T.

Jesus †   April 26, 1894

Dear little Lyre of Jesus,

To sing your twenty-five years I am sending you a little poem[1] that I composed when thinking of you!...

Céline! I am sure you will understand all my canticle would like to tell you, alas, I would need a tongue other than that of this earth to express the beauty of a soul's abondonment into the hands of Jesus. My heart was able only to babble what it feels.... *Céline, the story of Cecilia* (the *Saint* of ABANDONMENT) is your story too! Jesus has placed near you an angel from heaven who is always looking after you; he carries you in his hands lest your foot strike against a stone.[2] You do not see him, and yet he is the one who for twenty-five years has preserved your soul, who has kept its virginal whiteness; he is the one who removes from you the occasions of sin.... He is the one who showed himself to you in a mysterious dream that he gave you in your childhood. You saw an angel carrying a torch and walking before our dear Father. Undoubtedly, he wanted to have you understand the mission that you would later carry out. You are now the visible angel of him who will soon go to be

united to the angels of the heavenly city!... Céline, do not fear the
storms of earth.... Your guardian angel is covering you with his
wings, and Jesus, the purity of virgins, reposes in your heart. You
do not see His treasures; Jesus is sleeping and the angel remains in
his mysterious silence. However, they are there with Mary, who is
hiding you also under her veil!...

Do not fear, dear Céline, as long as *your lyre* does not cease to
sing for Jesus, never *will it break*.... No doubt it is fragile, more
fragile than crystal. If you were to give it to an inexperienced musician, soon it would break; but Jesus is the one who makes the lyre
of your heart sound.... He is happy that you are feeling your
weakness; *He* is the one placing in your soul sentiments of mistrust
of itself. Dear Céline, thank Jesus. He *grants* you His choice *graces*;
if always you remain faithful in pleasing Him in *little* things He will
find Himself OBLIGED to help you in GREAT Things.... The
apostles worked all night without Our Lord and they caught no fish,
but their work was pleasing to Jesus. He willed to prove to them
that He alone can give us something; He willed that the apostles *humble themselves*. "Children," he said to them, "have you nothing to
eat? [13] "Lord," St. Peter answered, "we have fished all night and
have caught nothing. [14] Perhaps if he had caught some *little fish*,
Jesus would not have performed the miracle, but he had *nothing*,
so Jesus soon filled his net in such a way as almost to break it. This
is the *character* of Jesus: He gives as God, but He wills *humility
of heart*....

Jn. 21:5

Lk 5:5

Before Him, the whole earth is like this *little grain of sand* which
hardly gives the slightest motion in a scale or like *one* drop of the
morning dew which falls upon the earth (Wisdom, chapter 11). [5]

*Wisdom
11:22*

(Dear Céline, if you can read me, it is very extraordinary, but I
do not have the time to look twice at what I am writing you. [6]...)

Time passes like a shadow, soon we shall be reunited up above.
Has not Jesus said during His Passion: "Nevertheless, you will soon
see the Son of Man seated at the right hand of God and coming on
the clouds of heaven...." [7]

We shall be there!...

Thérèse of the Child Jesus

* Autograph.
1. *The Melody of Saint Cecilia* (P 4): thirty stanzas of four alexandrines. To this letter was attached the picture which follows (LT 162).
2. See Psalm 90:12.
3. See John 21:5.
4. See Luke 5:5.
5. See Wisdom 11:22. The underlining of "*one* drop of dew" is a recall of LC 152 and LT 142.
6. This letter has many underlinings and alterations, especially on the reverse side.
7. See Matthew 26:64. The Son of Man's return on the clouds of heaven is a theme dear to Thérèse; see LT 117, 118, P21 *Jésus, mon Bien-Aimé, rappelle-toi!*, RP 6 *La Fuite en Egypte*, and a picture of the Breviary of the *Ecce Homo*, with this text in her handwriting.

LT 162

April 26, 1894

From Thérèse to Céline.

In this same letter, Mother Agnes writes Céline: "Sister Thérèse of the Child Jesus is sending you something delightful for your twenty-fifth birthday! How happy you will be!... Ah! I beg you, consider Sister Thérèse of the Child Jesus' little gifts as coming from me also, this will console me" (April 27, 1894). These gifts are the poem on St. Cecilia (LT 161, ote 1) and a little picture of St. Teresa of Avila (see LT 160, note 3).

Text on the picture

Jesus, what has made You so little? Love.[1]

Text on the envelope

Little picture
painted by
Little Thérèse
for the 25 years
of *little* Céline

with the permission of
Little Mother Prioress

*   Autograph.
1.   "The greatest of all beings has become the littlest. What has worked
this prodigy? Love!" (*Oeuvres de Saint Bernard*, vol. 5, *Traité de la
charité,* ch. VI, p. 202; translation by A Ravelet, L. Guérin edit., Bar-
le-Duc, 1870.) Thérèse transcribed this text on a picture of her
Breviary.

LT 163   **From Thérèse to Sister Thérèse-Dosithée
(Léonie).**

May 20, 1894
→ LC lost

J.M.J.T.

Jesus †   Sunday, May 20, 1894

Dear little Sister Thérèse,

What joy your letter gave me!... I cannot thank God enough for
all the graces He is bestowing on you.

Céline has told us in minutest details about the beautiful celebration of April 6.[1] How our little Mother in heaven must have rejoiced
on that day!... And Aunt of Le Mans,[2] with what love her eyes
were fixed on you!

I am very happy my Mother Teresa has become your mother; it
seems to me that this is a link uniting us together even more closely.

I cannot, dear little Sister, tell you all I would like, my heart cannot translate these intimate feelings in the cold language of this
earth.... But one day in heaven, in our beautiful homeland, I *shall
look*[3] at you and in my *look* you will see all I would like to say to
you, for *silence* is the language of the blessed inhabitants of
heaven![4]...

In the meanwhile, we must merit the homeland of heaven.... We
must suffer, we must fight.... Oh! I beg you, pray for your little
Thérèse that she may profit by the exile of earth and by the abun-

dant means she has for meriting heaven.

Céline has informed us of the results of your elections. I suffered when seeing you being deprived of a Mother whom you loved, but I was consoled when thinking that the one replacing her is truly worthy of her predecessor,[5] and I am very sure that you now have to guide you to Jesus *two Mothers*, who merit this sweet name.

I leave you, dear little Sister, without ever being far from you in my heart, and I beg you to remember me respectfully to your good Mothers.

Sister Thérèse of the Child Jesus of the Holy Face
rel. carm. ind.

* Autograph.
1. Léonie's reception of the Habit. Several documents, including ChrIG, assign erroneously April 5 as the date of this ceremony.
2. Sister Marie-Dosithéé Guérin (d. 1877), whose name the novice took in part.
3. Concerning the intuitive communication hoped for by Thérèse, see DE, p. 482.
4. At the entrance to the dormitory (corridor of the cells) where Thérèse slept at this time, Mother Agnes had painted in 1887 the sentence: "Silence is the language of the angels!"
5. In the elections at Pentecost, Mother Marie de Sales Lefrançois, superior for six years, and Mother Jeanne-Françoise Le Roy, novice mistress, exchanged offices.

LT 164　　　　**From Thérèse to Sister Thérèse-Dosithée (Léonie).**

May 22, 1894
→ LC lost

J.M.J.T.

Jesus †   May 22, 1894

Dear little Sister,

My Sunday note will reach you at the same time as this one, and you will see that already I was rejoicing in your happiness.... Thank you for your little letter which pleased me very, very much!...

You are very much blessed, dear little Sister, that Jesus is so jealous of your heart. He is saying to you as to the spouse of the Canticle: "You have wounded my heart, my sister, my spouse, by one of your eyes and by one strand of your hair fluttering on your neck."[1] Jesus is very much pleased with you, I feel it. If He is still allowing you to see infidelities in your heart, I am very sure that the acts of love He is gathering are more numerous.

Which of the Thérèses will be the more fervent?... The one who will be more humble, more united to Jesus, more faithful in performing all her actions through love!... Ah! let us pray for one another in order to be equally faithful.... Let us wound Jesus by our eye and by a single hair, this is, by the greatest thing and by the littlest. Let us not refuse Him the least sacrifice. Everything is so big in religion...to pick up a pin out of love can convert a soul. What a mystery!...

Ah! it is Jesus alone who can give such a value to our actions; let us love Him with all our strength....

Your little Sister who loves you,

Thérèse of the Child Jesus
re. carm. ind.

*   Autograph.
1. See Canticle of Canticles 4:9, taken and commented on by Saint John of the Cross in stanza XXI of his *Spiritual Canticle*. See Collected Works, p. 532. See LT 191.

"As gold in the crucible" *(LT 165)*
(June — September 1894)
Age twenty-one

    Repeated heart attacks, in May and June, announced the approaching end of M. Martin, who died at La Musse (Eure), July 29, 1894. As at the death of her Mother, Thérèse kept to herself "the deep sentiments" she experienced (Ms. A, p. 33); she listened in silence (see LD, July 29, 1894, caption). However, joy prevailed over sorrow: once again she "found" her father (LT 169 and 170) "clothed in joy," after having been tried "as gold in the furnace" (see M. Martin's death card).

    At this same time, she prepared herself to meet her Céline once again. "The most intimate of her desires, the greatest of them all," the entrance of her childhood companion into the same Carmel as her own, "an unlikely dream" (Ms. A, p. 176), was about to be realized. So she thought. However, she had planned without the dream of another who also claimed her Céline: Père Pichon! (see LT 168, note 3.) He already visualized her enrolled under the standard of Saint Ignatius, as foundress of a secular institute (see LC 159, note 5). The Carmelite nuns turned a deaf ear to this plan. The Correspondence *traces out the events of the swift counter-offensive they launched for the recapture of Céline. From this letter trial, Thérèse's affection for her sister comes forth "purified as gold in the crucible" (LT 168).*

    Other trials[1] chiselled away at her, body and soul, during these same weeks:
    1) Her illness made evident by a persistent hoarseness (see LC 159, note 8), necessitating cauterization.
    2) Difficulties at the beginning with her "daughter," who entered on June 16 (see LT 167, note 10). The "wild rabbit" mannerisms of this twenty-year-old postulant—the future Sister Marie of the Trinity—disconcerted at first the little, well-reared, middle-class girl from Les Buissonnets.

Thérèse quickly recovered, understanding that she had to tone down her methods under pain of incurring a half-checkmate as she had experienced with Sister Marie-Madeleine.

3) *More trying than these "exterior crosses," was the turmoil or at least the darkness" (LT 165). Hardly has she set out on her exodus along an unknown route (see p. 726), when she is groping along: "I no longer knew where I was" (LT 165). However, every now and again, a gentle voice is heard, a voice more gentle than the springtime breeze.[2] "Return, return." The Holy Spirit groans within her (ibid.). The hour is approaching for her great discovery.*

Read Ms. A. pp. 176-177.

1. This word appears sixteen times in four letters (LT 165, 166, 167, 168: trials of Jesus, Thérèse, others).
2. See A. Soumet in his *Joan of Arc*: "And his voice resembled a springtime breeze." (Poem introduced by Thérèse in the second part of her *Joan of Arc*; the voice Soumet was referring to was that of Saint Michael.)

LD   *From Céline to Mother Agnes of Jesus, Sister Marie of the Sacred Heart, and Thérèse.*

June 5, 1894

Dear little Sisters,

This morning again, Papa had an extremely violent attack while I was at Mass;[1] they came to get me. This attack was no longer a paralytic attack like the last one,[2] it was a heart attack.

Uncle told me that Papa had a very pronounced heart ailment which will carry him off, and he considers his condition as very serious, although it no longer appears so this evening. Two hours after the attack, one would never have said that Papa had been so sick, and when I had left for Mass, he was doing very well. It happens all of a sudden.

It appears that dear little Father turned blue and that his heart was no longer beating; Uncle believed that I was going to get back too late. It was only a question of the time of/the trip;[3] running it, I could find him either cured or dead. God willed that I was not deprived of assisting him in his last moments; help me, dear little Sisters, to thank Him for this! Oh! pray for both of us, Papa and myself!... My heart is constantly upset. However, Papa is doing well this evening. He is resting.

I kiss you,
Céline

P.S. I do not know when I shall see you again; I do not dare go out.[4] Léonie writes me that she is suffering from her eczema on her head, caused by the headdress worn night and day;[5] I am worried about her.

(Lisieux, June 5, 1894)

  * CMG.

1. "At the time when they were about to wake him up, he had become black. Désiré believed it was the end; he called your Papa, who rushed in with some ether, and the crisis passed.... It seems his pulse was no longer beating.... His condition is becoming more serious, and from one moment to the next we must expect a crisis." (From Mme. Guérin to her daughter, Mme. La Néele, June 5, 1894.)

2. The attack of Sunday, May 27: "While I was at Caen helping Jeanne arrange her temporary altar, Papa had a serious paralytic attack; he was administered the last sacraments. When I received the telegram that my uncle sent me, I rushed to him, begging God that I might arrive in time to receive his last breath. When I arrived, the crisis was over." (Sister Geneviéve, CMG IV, p. 219.) On May 28, Mme Guérin wrote her daughter Jeanne: "Dr. de Corniére came, and he found M. Martin's condition much better than yesterday. He hopes that since the paralysis has settled in his left arm, it will be arrested in this way."

3. The distance between the cathedral of Saint-Pierre of Lisieux and M. Guérin's house on *rue Paul Banaston*.

4. For this reason Céline did not attend the wedding of Céline Maudelonde, June 19 (according to CMG IV, p. 221).

5. "Dear little Céline, would you ask Uncle for a remedy for eczema which has come back to me and is making me suffer very much" (Léonie to Céline, MSC I, p. 15).

LD

June 13 (?),
1894
→ LD lost

From Mother Agnes of Jesus and the Community to M. and Mme Guérin.

Thérèse's signature appears as fourteenth on the list. Approximate date; see note 3.

J.M.J.T.

Long live St. Anthony of Padua[1] and the dispensers of his blessings...
Thank you, thank you! I cannot believe my eyes.[2]...
Mother Marie de Gonzague is so pleased that she wants to read your note from the pulpit in the refectory during dinner.
And we shall thank St. Anthony and beg him to grant you his favors. Oh! how I love you, dear Relatives! How we all love you, all the Carmelite nuns.[3]

Signed:
Sister Agnes of Jesus, Prioress
Sister Marie de Gonzague
Sister Marie Emmanuel
Sister Anne of the Sacred Heart
Sister Thérèse of Jesus, may St. Anthony grant
 you his blessings
Sister Saint John of the Cross
Sister St. John the Baptist
Sister Marie of Jesus
Sister Marie of St. Joseph
Sister St. Stanislaus of the Sacred Heart
Sister Marie of the Angels
Sister Marie of the Sacred Heart
Sister Aimée of Jesus
Sister Thérèse of the Child Jesus

Sister Marguerite Marie
Sister Marie Philomène of Jesus
Sister Heart of Jesus of the Imm. Concept.
and St. Joseph
Sister St. Pierre of St. Teresa
Sister St. Raphael, zealous for devotion
to St. Anthony
Sister Saint Vincent de Paul
Sister Thérèse of Saint Augustine
Sister Marie of the Incarnation
Sister Martha of Jesus
Sister Marie Madeleine, M. Guérin's god-
daughter

* Autograph
1. At the approach of the seventh centenary of his birth, Saint Anthony of Padua (1195-1231) enjoyed a renewal of fame. He is mentioned several times in the Guérin correspondence. Furthermore, Mother Marie de Gonzague's family claimed ties of relationship with this Saint. "Our dear Mother numbered real Saints in her family, among whom was SAINT ANTHONY OF PADUA, whose famous name is on pious lips in our day." (*Circulaire n*écrologique, p. 1, written by Mother Agnes, December 20, 1904.)
2. We do not know the nature of the gift motivating this gratitude.
3. The Community signed this as a group. Because of the absence of Sister Marie of the Trinity's name, formerly, Sister Marie-Agnes of the Holy Face, who entered June 16, we may deduce this letter was anterior to this date. The vertical handwriting of Thérèse is after April 1894 (loop of the "d" as in *delta*). Hence this date is suggested with reservations: June 13, feast of Saint Anthony.

LT 165   **From Thérèse to Céline.**

July 7, 1894   Letter addressed to La Musse, where the Guérin
→ LD lost   family arrived on July 4, accompanied by M.
                 Martin and Céline.

J.M.J.T.

Jesus †   July 7, 1894

Dear Céline,

Léonie's letter[1] is disturbing us very much....

Ah! how unhappy she will be if she returns to the world! But I admit that I hope this is only a temptation; we must pray very much for her.[2] God can very well give her what she is lacking....

Our Mother is on retreat. It is for this reason that she is not going to write you; she is thinking of you and Marie, and she will pray very much for her two little girls.

I do not know if you are still in the same frame of mind as the other day, but I will tell you just the same about a passage from the Canticle of Canticles which expresses perfectly what a soul is when plunged into aridity and how nothing delights or consoles it. "I went down into the garden of nuts to see the fruits of the valley, to look if the vineyard had flourished, and if the pomegranates had budded.... I no longer *knew* where I *was*...my soul was all troubled because of the chariots of Aminadab" chap. 6, vv. 10 and 11).[3]

This is really the image of our souls. Frequently, we descend into the fertile valleys where our heart loves to nourish itself, the *vast field of the scriptures*[4] which has so many times opened before us to pour out its rich treasures in our favor; this *vast field* seems to us to be a desert, arid and without water.... We *know no longer* where *we are*; instead of peace and light, we find only turmoil or at least darkness.... But, like the spouse, we know the cause of our trial: our soul is troubled because of the chariots of Aminadab.... We are still not as yet in our homeland, and *trial* must purify us as gold in the crucible.[5] At times, we believe ourselves abandoned. Alas! the chariots, the vain noises that disturb us, are they within us or outside us? We do not know...but Jesus really knows. He sees our sadness and suddenly His gentle voice makes itself heard, a voice more gentle than the springtime breeze: "Return, return, my Sulamitess; return, return, that *we may look at* you!..." Cant. chap. 6, v. 12.) What a call is that of the Spouse!... And we were no longer daring even *to look at ourselves* so much did we consider ourselves without any splendor and adornment; and Jesus calls us, He wants to *look at* us at His leisure, but He is not alone;

with Him, the two other Persons of the Blessed Trinity[6] come to take possession of our soul.... Jesus had promised it in days gone by when He was about to reascend to His Father and our Father.[7] He said with ineffable tenderness: "If anyone *loves* me, he *will keep* my *word*, and my Father *will love* him, and *we* will come to him, and *we* will make in him *our* abode.'[8] To keep the *word* of Jesus, that is the sole condition of our happiness, the proof of our love for Him. But what, then, is this word?... It seems to me that the *word* of Jesus is *Himself*...He, *Jesus*, the *Word*,[9] the *Word* of *God*! He tells us further on in the same gospel of St. John, praying to his Father for His disciples, He expresses Himself thus: "Sanctify them by your *word*, your word is *truth*.'[10] In another place, Jesus teaches us that He is the way, the *truth*, the life.[11] We know, then, what is the *Word* that we must keep; like Pilate, we shall not ask Jesus: "What is *Truth*?'[12] We possess *Truth*. We *are keeping* Jesus in our *hearts*!... Often, like the spouse, we can say: "Our Beloved is a bundle of myrrh,"[13] that He is a Spouse of blood for us.[14]... But how sweet it will be to hear one day this very sweet word coming from the mouth of our Jesus: "You are the ones who have always remained with me in all the trials I have had, so I have prepared my kingdom for you, just as my Father has prepared it for me.'[15] The trials of Jesus, what a mystery! He has trials then, He too?... Yes, He has them, and often He is alone in treading the wine in the wine press; He looks for consolers and can find none.[16]... Many serve Jesus when he is consoling them, but *few* consent to keep company with *Jesus sleeping* on the waves[17] or suffering in the garden of agony!... Who, then, will be willing to serve Jesus for Himself?... Ah! we shall be the ones.... Céline and Thérèse will unite always more and more; in them, will be accomplished this prayer of Jesus: "Father, that they may be one as we are one.'[18] Yes, Jesus *is* already *preparing* His kingdom for us, just as His Father prepared it for Him.[19] He prepares it for us by leaving us in the *trial*. He wills that *our face be seen* by creatures, but that it be *as though hidden*[20] so that no one *recognize* us but Himself alone!... But what joy, too, to think that *God*, the entire *Trinity*, is looking at us, that It is within us and is pleased to *look at* us. But what does *It* will to see in our heart if not "choirs of music in an army camp"? (Canticle, ch. 8, v. 1.) "How, then, shall we be able to sing the Lord's canticles in a strange land?... For a long time, our harps were hung on the willows of the shore.*²¹* We were not able to use them!... Our *God*, the *Guest* of our soul, knows it well, so He comes to us with the intention of finding an abode, an EMPTY *tent*, in the midst of the earth's field of battle. He asks only this, and He Himself is the Divine Musician who takes charge of the *concert*.²²... Ah! if only we were to hear this ineffable harmony, if one single vibration were to reach our ears!...

"We do not know how to ask for anything as we ought, but the spirit pleads within us with unutterable groanings" (St. Paul).²³ We have, then, only to surrender our soul, *to abandon* it to our great God. What does it matter, then, if our soul be without gifts that sparkle exteriorly since within us the King of kings shines with all His glory! How great must a soul be to contain a God!... And yet the soul of a *day-old* child is a Paradise of delights for Him;²⁴ what will it be, then, for our souls that have fought and suffered to delight the Heart of our Beloved?...

Dear Céline, I assure you, I do not know what I am saying to you, it must have no coherence, but it seems to me you will understand just the same!... I would like to tell you so many things!...

Do not answer me in a long letter speaking to me about your soul; a single note will suffice for me. I prefer that you write an *amusing* letter for *everybody*. God wills that I forget myself in order to please.²⁵

I kiss good Uncle, dear Aunt, and my little sister.²⁶ *As for Papa*, I *smile* at him and *watch over* him by means of his VISIBLE *angel* to whom I am so intimately united that we form only one!...

Thérèse of the Child Jesus of the Holy Face
rel. carm. ind.

* Autograph.
1. Undoubtedly the letter, not preserved, from Léonie to M. Guérin at La Musse on the 6th and sent without delay to the Carmel: "Yesterday, we received a letter from Léonie to your father which left us with some anxiety. She is telling him with filial trust all her trials, her struggles, her combats, and even tells him that if she were not helped by her mistresses, she would be with us.... I assure you it is not encouraging; what will she do in the world? She cannot bear it, she is

not happy in it.... Céline will write the Carmel to ask for their prayers." (Letter of Mme Guérin to Mme La Néele, July 7, 1894.) It is possible that Céline's letter reached Lisieux this same day, July 7.

2. On July 11, 1894, Mme Guérin was thanking her daughter Jeanne (Mme La Néele) for a letter regarding Léonie, which she said: "has really encouraged us.... Céline thanks you; she is going to set her mind at rest somewhat regarding her sister."

3. Besides the explicit reference to the *Canticle of Canticles* 6:10-11, Thérèse cannot fail to be recalling the commentaries of Saint John of the Cross on these same verses, which we encounter as many as seven times in his *Works*.

4. See Imitation of Christ III, 51:2.

5. See Wisdom 3:6. Expression used again in LT 168, par. 2.

5. The Trinity, already mentioned in LT 118, will be mentioned also in LT 169, 182, and 183. *L'Hommage à la Trés Sainte Trinité* composed for Sister Martha of Jesus dates from May-June 1894 or 1895. Though the autograph of this prayer has disappeared (see Mss. I, p. 22 and HA 1953, pp. 255-256), we have at least the two pages on which Thérèse and Sister Martha added up their acts of virtue during a four-week period.

7. See John 20:17. The possessives "his" and "our" are emphasized; the same further down: "our abode." In this letter, Thérèse also underlines the plural number, recalling the three divine Persons.

8. See John 14:23. Quoted without any commentary the preceding year (LT 142, note 6), this text is fully developed in her peom *Vivre d'Amour* (P 15, February 26, 1895), the fifteen stanzas of which detail Thérèse's manner of "abiding in love."

9. See John 1:1.

10. See John 17:17.

11. See John 14:6.

12. See John 18:38.

13. See Canticle of Canticles 1:13.

14. See LT 82 and note 1.

15. See Luke 22:28-29.

16. See Isaias 63:3 and 5.

17. See Matthew 8:24; LT 160, note 4.

18. See John 17:21.

19. See Luke 22:29.

20. Like that of the *Suffering Servant*; see LT 145, note 9.

21. See Psalm 136:4 and 2.

22. Compare with Ms. A, pp. 172-173, in which Thérèse describes how she prepared herself to receive Holy Communion.

23. See Romans 8:26.
24. See RP 2: *Les Anges à la Crèche de Jésus*: "The littlest soul that loves
     Me — Becomes a Paradise for Me." (Christmas 1894.)
25. "To forget myself in order to please": in these terms, in the follow-
     ing year, Thérèse explained her Christmas grace of 1886 (Ms. A, p. 98).
26. Marie Guérin. In the sentence following, the *visible angel* is Céline.

LT 166   **From Thérèse to Mme. Pottier (Céline**
                                Maudelonde).
July 16, 1894
→ LC lost

J.M.J.T.

Jesus †   Carmel, July 16, 1894

Dear little Céline,

Your letter gave me real joy. I marvel at how the Blessed Virgin
is pleased to answer all your desires. Even before your marriage,
she willed that the soul to whom you were to be joined form only
one with yours by means of an identity of feelings. What a grace
for you to feel you are so well understood, and, above all, to know
your union will be everlasting, that after this life, you will still be
able to love the husband who is so dear to you!...
   They have passed away, then, for us both the blessed days of our
childhood! We are now at the serious stage of life; the road we are
following is different, however, the goal is the same. Both of us must
have only one same purpose: *to sanctify* ourselves in the way God
has traced out for us.[1]
   I feel, dear little friend, that I can speak freely to you; you understand the language of faith better than that of the world, and the
Jesus of your First Communion has remained the Master of your
heart. In Him, you love the beautiful soul who forms only one with
yours, and it is because of Him that your love is so tender and so
strong.
   Oh! how beautiful is our religion; instead of contracting hearts

(as the world believes), it raises them up and renders them capable of *loving*, or *loving* with a love *almost infinite* since this love must continue after this mortal life which is given to us only for meriting the homeland of heaven where we shall find again the dear ones whom we have loved on earth!

I had asked for you, dear Céline, from Our Lady of Mount Carmel the grace you have obtained at Lourdes. How happy I am that you are clothed in the holy scapular![2] It is a sure sign of predestination, and besides are you not more intimately united by means of it to your little sisters in Carmel?...

You ask, dear little cousin, that I pray for your dear husband; do you think, then, I could fail in this?... No, I could not separate you in my weak prayers. I am asking Our Lord to be as generous in your regard as he was formerly to the spouses at the wedding of Cana. May He always change water into wine![3]... That is to say, may He continue to make you happy and to soften as much as possible the trials that you encounter in life.

Trials, how could I place this word in my letter, when I know everything is happiness for you?...

Pardon me, dear little friend; enjoy in peace the joy God is giving you, without disturbing yourself regarding the future. He is reserving for you, I am sure, new graces and many consolations.

Our good Mother Marie de Gonzague is very appreciative of your kind remembrance of her, and she herself is not forgetting her dear little Céline. Our Mother and Sister Marie of the Sacred Heart are also very happy because of your joy, and they ask me to assure you of their affection.

I dare, dear little *cousin*,[4] to beg you to offer my respectful regards to *Monsieur* Pottier, whom I cannot refrain from considering also as my *cousin*.

I leave you, dear Céline, remaining always united to you in my heart, and I shall, throughout my life, be happy to call myself,

Your little sister in Jesus,
Thérèse of the Child Jesus
rel. carm. ind.

 *   Autograph.

1. See the last message of Thérèse to Mme. Pottier, sent by Sister Marie of the Eucharist (Marie Guérin): "God is calling her to be a real saint in the world, and He has plans and a very special love for her" (DE, p. 718, letter of July 20, 1898).

2. "Wear the scapular of Mount Carmel; it will be a great joy for me, and we shall be united by still greater spiritual bonds" (Marie Guérin to Céline Maudelonde, undated letter, a little before June 19, date of her marriage).

3. See John 2:7-9.

4. See LT 159, note 2.

LC 159   From Céline to Thérèse.

July 17, 1894

→ LT 165

July 17, 1894

Dear Thérèse,

I am going to write you in haste, for these days I do not have time to turn around. Joseph de Cornière[1] is here, and we are busy doing photography. We dress up and are making a whole story of travellers in living pictures;[2] it will be very amusing. In the meanwhile, however, I am beginning to get enough of it. My days seem insipid to me, no more reading, no time to write, hardly any time to make meditation; we are always on the go.[3]

Dear Thérèse, oh! I would be unable to tell you how this life weighs on me.... When I received your letter, I was again recollected, I enjoyed and relished your letter...but at present I am like a piece of wood, there is no longer anything to draw on from within me. When I received your letter, dear Thérèse, my soul was not sad but filled with fervor to be good and practice virtue, and it is again to you that I owed this feeling. Your book by P. Surin[4] is extraordinary, and certainly I shall buy a copy of it. It is really this type of language that I need to sustain myself.... I say the same thing for each book that you lend me, but I believe I have never found any that may do me as much good as the evangelical counsels. Thérèse!... Oh!

I have made meditations on yourself from this book, on our affection for one another!.... And it seemed to me—I would be unable to tell you this very well—it seemed to me that you were too much for me...that you were a support for me that was allowing me too much support...that I was relying on you too much and was basing myself too much on you...in a word, guess at the rest!.... And it seemed to me that to be totally for God, I would have to leave you.... I took a glimpse into the future, and I believed that I had to separate myself from you in order that I might see you again only in heaven.⁵... Finally, oh, dear Thérèse, I was afraid, and I had a kind of presentiment of a sacrifice surpassing all other sacrifices... Each day my heart is trembling, but my soul is inundated with graces that I must have to accustom myself to this thought. Since I saw you last, I have had deep thoughts on a multitude of subjects.... The cross appeared to me all bare and with it many realities...certainly, God is making strange appeals to my soul, in its innermost depths, and this is in the midst of an incredible peace and tranquility of soul. Oh, Thérèse! what can I not tell you!... And yet I would be able to say nothing to you, I have nothing to say to you....

Thérèse! oh! understand your Céline, without her talking to you, without her telling you a single word!... Oh, life, life! And I find life is so short, and that we shall be so happy when meeting one another up above!... All appears to me like a dream. I stop....

Thérèse! your letter was a heavenly song for me, a sweet melody...oh! understand all I have understood! But I love you too much, you see?... Oh, Thérèse, my heart tortures me, and it is for this reason that I have a kind of inner certitude that God will have to break it in order to reign over me; I need the cross and the most bitter tribulation...Thérèse!

Lately, I have been going out of myself, and I am suffering much from this, a continual *malaise.* Furthermore, we spend our days in uncontrollable laughter, enough to split our sides, and I am thirsting for solitude. I can no longer breathe. Then I am unhappy...not being accustomed to living with boys,⁶ it seems strange to me to be spending my days in their company. As holy and pure and candid as they are, I cannot get used to it. Oh, Thérèse, understand what I mean.... These past days, I have scruples,⁷ and everything all mixed up, with the privation of my spiritual exercises, makes me dry and sad. . . .

I hug tightly my *dear little sisters* and our Mother. Oh! how I love my dear little sisters!. . . Above all, take care of yourself,[8] this is a duty of conscience. . . . The stalks of daisies are on loan,[9] Pauline is not to keep them any longer than a month. Marie of the Sacred Heart has not sent me: "the only thing for today."[10] And your girl, the little C.,[11] I am worried about the news!. . .

Papa is coming along.[12]

* Autograph.

1. L'abbé Joseph de Cornière (1874-1939), older son of the Carmel's doctor; still a seminarian. He was invited by the Guérins to La Musse, arriving there on July 14, with Doctor La Néele and his wife.

2. *Voyage excentrique aux Cordillères des Andes*: title inspired by l'abbé Cornière by his stay in Chili in 1892-1893 as a Redemptorist novice (a vocation he did not pursue). On this theme, he composed twenty-eight humorous quatrains, adapted to the actors: himself, Francis and Jeanne La Néele, Céline Martin, and Marie Guérin.

3. The twenty-seven photographs illustrating this happy voyage made use of various sites at La Musse (forty hectares): river, woods, abandoned quarry, cabin of a forest-ranger, approaches to the chateau, etc.

4. Probably *Les Foundements de la vie spirituelle tirés du livre de l'Imitation de Jésus-Christ*, 1732; described in Mss. II, p. 51; see Ms. A, p. 158. We found a short excerpt from this work (book 5, chap. 11) in Céline's notebook of notes and readings. In October 1896, Marie Guérin, novice of Thérèse, advised its reading to Mme Pottier (Céline Maudelonde).

5. Céline's confidence was brought about by a recent letter from P. Pichon, June 20: "Our future! Jesus is preparing it! He has thought of it from Calvary, Bethlehem, oh! ever since eternity. Why be agitated, worried? Jesus will settle the matter. In Carmel or at Bethany!. . . The contemplative life is the most perfect, you say. Who taught you that? The holy doctors teach me differently, St. Thomas at their head. They state the mixed life (half contemplative, half active) as the more excellent. . . . Bethany will be neither a boarding house or hospital, but a type of religious life altogether different, the most apostolic type I might think of for a woman. . . . My daughters will follow the Rule of St. Ignatius on every point, and I have not decided as yet on giving them a religious Habit. They will be somewhat like the *frances-tireurs* of an army." (Excerpts from pp. 5-8 of this letter, June 20, 1894, the first four pages of which were destroyed

by Céline.) Thérèse and her sisters were unaware of this plan which, in certain ways, did correspond with Céline's active temperament...it gave her some support: "To go far away, to Canada! To leave all those whom I loved, to found a work, all this was a marvel to me; God 'had plans for me'; no doubt, I was a great soul, a saint in the making, why not?" (Sister Geneviève, *Souvenirs autobiographiques*, p. 215.) See VT, April 1968, pp. 123-133.

6. Dr. La Néele (Francis), thirty-six, and l'abbé de Cornièrs, twenty.

7. The word is used in the general sense attributed to it by the Martin and Guérin families; see LC 113, 114, and 130.

8. Thérèse was examined by Doctor La Néele, July 1: "At Carmel, they expect Francis on Sunday, who will see Thérèse, who has a persistent sore throat, hoarse voice, and some pains in her *chest*. They would have liked Francis to examine her, but this is a very delicate matter with Dr. D.... [de Cornière]. (Marie to Mme La Néele, June 28, 1894.

9. Painting models requested by Pauline (Mother Agnes); see LT 167 *bis*.

10. *Mon chant d'aujourd'hui* (P 5, June 1, 1894). On May 20, Sister Marie of the Sacred Heart told Céline: "I will give you on my feast day (for I will not have it before that) a nice little poem little Thérèse is actually composing for me. It will be for both of us." She finally sent this poem to Mme Guérin.

11. "little Castel," or Sister Marie of the Trinity, see LT 167, note 10.

12. On July 11, Mme Guérin gave this news: "M. Martin is not too well these past few days, he is bent double and swallows with difficulty" (to Mme La Néele, July 11, 1894).

LT 167   **From Thérèse to Céline.**
July 18, 1894
→ LC 159

                    J.M.J.T.

Jesus †   July 18, 1894

Dear Céline,

    I am not surprised at your trials; I passed through this *last year* and I *know what it is*[1]... God willed that I make my sacrifice; I made it and now, like you, I have felt calm in the midst of suffering.

But I felt something else, that frequently God wants only *our will*; He asks *all*, and if we were to refuse Him the least thing, He loves us too much to give in to us; however, as soon as our will is conformed to His, as soon as He sees we seek Him alone, then He conducts Himself with us as in the past He conducted Himself with Abraham②... This is what Jesus is making me feel interiorly, and I think that you are on TRIAL, that *now* the cutting off is taking place which you feel is necessary.... It is *now* that Jesus *is breaking* your *nature*, that He is giving you the cross and tribulation. The more I go on, the more I have the inner certitude that one day you will come here. Mother Marie de Gonzague advises me to tell you this③She was so kind when reading your letter, if you had seen her you would have been touched!...

Gen. 22.12

Fear nothing. Here you will find more than anywhere else the cross and *martyrdom*!... We shall suffer together, as in the past the Christians who used to join together in order to give each other more courage in the hour of trial.[4]...

And then Jesus will come, He will take one of us,[5] and the others will remain for a *short time* in exile and tears.... Céline, tell me, would the suffering be as great if we were, one at Lisieux and the other at Jerusalem?... Would the Blessed Virgin have suffered as much if she had not been at the foot of the Cross of her Jesus?...

You perhaps believe I do not understand you?... And I assure you that I am reading into your soul.... I read that you are faithful to Jesus, willing only His *will, seeking only His love; fear nothing. In the present trial* God is purifying what might be too human in our affection, but the *foundation* itself of this affection is too pure for Him to break it. Listen well to what I am going to say to you. Never, never, will Jesus separate us. If I die before you, do not believe I shall be far from your *soul*, never shall we have been more united! It is perhaps this which Jesus wills to make you feel when speaking to you of separation? But, above all, do not worry, I am not sick; on the contrary,[6] I have iron health, however, God can break iron just like clay.... All this is childishness, let us not think of the future (I am speaking about myself, for I do not look upon the trial visiting my dear Céline's soul as something childish).

Exterior crosses, what are they?... We might be far from each other without suffering, if Jesus were to comfort our souls.... What is a real cross is the martyrdom of the heart, the interior suffering of the soul, and this, which no one sees, we shall be able to bear without ever being separated.

I know well that all I am saying to you and [saying] nothing are absolutely the same thing; your interior trial will cease only on the day set by Jesus, but since He wills to make use of me at times to do good to your soul, perhaps my words are the expression of His will.... It is incredible how we always have the same trials! A little earlier or later, we have to drink of the same cup.[7]

When the storm is very strong on the land, everybody says: "There is no longer anything to fear for the ships, for the storm is no longer raging on the sea."[8] Well, I say to Céline: The storm has passed over my soul, it is now visiting hers, but I do not fear, soon the calm will be restored, "a great serenity will follow the storm."[9]

You want to know some news about my girl.[10] Well, I believe she WILL STAY; she was not brought up like us; it is very unfortunate for her, her education is the cause of her *unattractive* ways, but basically she is good. Now she loves me, but I am careful to touch her only with *white silk gloves*.... However, I have a title which gives me a lot of trouble:[11] I am a little hunting dog, I am the one chasing the game all day long. You realize the hunters (mistresses of novices and Prioresses) are too big to slip into the bushes, but a little dog...it has a *sensitive nose* and it *slips in everywhere*!... So I am watching my girl closely, and the *hunters* are not unhappy with their little dog.... I do not want to do any harm to my little rabbit, but I *lick* it, telling it with *compassion* its fur is not *sleek* enough, its *appearance* is too much that of a *wild rabbit*, in a word, I am trying to make it such as my hunters want it to be: a very simple little rabbit which is to be busied only with the little grass it has to graze on. I am jesting, but basically I think the little rabbit is worth more than the little dog...in its place, I would have been *lost* forever a long time ago in the vast forest of the world!!!...

I thank you for your two little photographs,[12] they are *charming*.

Thérèse of the Child Jesus

I beg you to give my kindest regards to all the dear travelers who are enjoying themselves so much there. I understand what you feel regarding the boys. . . . But this is only for a passing moment, one day you will not see too much of them. Console yourself!. . .

I am sending you two little canticles I composed;[13] show them to dear little Marie. Tell her I love her and am praying for her. . . . Oh! may suffering ennoble her soul and bring it close to its goal!. . .

Mother Marie de Gonzague is not writing her because the letter is addressed to Aunt; she will write the next time!. . . Ask Aunt for *My Song for Today*; Sister Marie of the Sacred Heart wanted to send it to her.

* Autograph.

1. See p. 726.
2. See Genesis 22:12.
3. Mother Marie de Gonzague's influence on the superiors and the Community was the determining factor in Céline's favor.
4. See Ms. C, pp. 215-216. Let us note, regarding companionship in martyrdom, that July 17 marked the centenary of the execution of the Carmelite nuns of Compiègne. In view of this celebration, Thérèse had helped Sister Thérèse of Saint Augustine in the making of banners: "She was beside herself with joy: 'What joy,' she said to me, 'if we were to have the same lot, the same grace!' " (Sister Thérèse of Saint Augustine, PO 1970.)
5. Thérèse was not alone in speaking this way. Excusing herself for incessantly calling upon the reserves of Céline's purse, Sister Marie of the Sacred Heart wrote Céline: "A day will come when you will be able to dispose of nothing, you will be like us, and we will no longer have our little Céline as a plank of salvation. However, we shall have her with us, which will be still better or who knows? One of us will have returned to her homeland, and this will perhaps be myself" (May 20, 1894). At this time, Marie and Thérèse were putting together the thoughts for expressing *Mon chant d'aujourd'hui*.
6. Probably on July 20 Mother Agnes wrote Céline: "Sister Thérèse of the Child Jesus is not too bad, but she is always having her bouts with sore throat; in the morning and evening, around half past eight, she gets them and is a little hoarse. We are taking care of her as well as we can" (undated letter).
7. See Matthew 20:23.
8. A local saying.
9. See Matthew 8:26. + *Mk 4:39*
10. Marie-Louise Castel (1874-1944), who had already made an attempt

of two years (1891-1893) at the Paris Carmel, *avenue de Messine* (today at *Boulogne-sur-Seine*). Around Pentecost (May 13, 1894), Mother Agnes wrote Céline: "When will you tell me the little postulant has gone to your house, I would be so happy! Besides, you will be able to tell better what you think of her." The postulant entered on June 16, under the name of Sister Marie-Agnes of the Holy Face. At her Profession (April 30, 1896), they named her Sister Marie of the Trinity in order to avoid confusion with the name of Mother Agnes.

11. Thérèse's function regarding the new arrival was poorly defined: "Mother Agnes of Jesus gave her to me as "angel," according to the custom of our Order, so that she might initiate me into the external practices of the Rule. At the same time, she recommended that I take her counsels for my formation as though she were the mistress of the novitiate" (Sister Marie of the Trinity, PA, 47). It is not certain whether Mother Marie de Gonzague, novice mistress, had been informed of this arrangement: and so Thérèse found herself in a delicate situation.

12. Probably pictures of Céline and Marie Guérin, those of the "voyage," having hardly been developed as yet?

13. The first edition (LT 1948, p. 278) offers two titles: *Cantique pour obtenir la Canonization de Jeanne d'Arc* (P 4, May 8, 1894), dedicated "to the *Valeureux chevalier C. Martin*"; and *Mon Chant d'aujourd'hui*. We must exclude this second title, just as Thérèse points out when ending her letter. As for the first, it is surprising that she might have waited two months to send this copy to her sister. The handwriting is, moreover, anterior to that of LT 167. The critical edition of the *Poems* alone will shed light on this matter.

LD

July 29, 1894

From Céline to Mother Agnes of Jesus, Sister Marie of the Sacred Heart, and Thérèse.

A telegram sent on Sunday morning to Lisieux transmitted the news of M. Martin's death at La Musse. Sister Marie of the Sacred Heart recounted later: "In the afternoon, Mme. Maudelonde asked to see us in the speakroom. I can still see Thérèse; she was pale, she followed behind us, without saying anything; in the speakroom, she said almost nothing either. This was her way, we did not pay any attention to her because she was the little one.'' (Conversation of July 29, 1926, notebook of Sister Marie of the Incarnation, p. 109.)

When answering the letter which followed on July 31, Mother Agnes ended in this way: ''I am alone in answering you, but you understand that our hearts are very much united to your own in these sad moments! Sister Thérèse of the Child Jesus told me this morning: 'No, I could not write Céline!' Her heavenly and profound look made it sufficiently plain that the very lofty sentiments of her soul could not be expressed!...'' (Letter to Céline, July 31, 1894.)

Dear little sisters,

Papa is in heaven!... I received his last breath, I closed his eyes.[1]... His handsome face took on immediately an expression of beatitude, of such profound calm! Tranquility was painted on his features.... He expired so gently at fifteen minutes after eight.

My poor heart was broken at the supreme moment; a flood of tears bathed his bed. But at heart I was joyful because of his happiness, after the terrible martyrdom he endured and which we shared with him....

Last night, in a sleep filled with anguish, I suddenly awakened; I saw in the firmament a kind of luminous globe.... And this globe went deeply into the immensity of heaven.

. . . .

Today, St. Martha, the saint of Bethany,[2] the one who obtained the rescurrection of Lazarus....

Today, the Gospel of the *five* wise virgins.[3]...

Today, Sunday, the Lord's day....

And Papa will remain with us until August 2, feast of Our Lady of the Angels.[4]...

Your little Céline

P.S. We shall arrive probably tomorrow. Yesterday evening, Papa received Extreme Unction, Absolution, and the application of the Indulgences. Uncle told me he had never seen so peaceful a death.[5]

* CMG.
 1. Sister Geneviève (Céline) published her memories relative to July 28 and 29 in *La Père de Sainte Thérèse de l'Enfant-Jésus*, pp. 96-98.
 2. See John 11:1. The name "Bethany" had a special significance for Céline; see LC 159, note 5.
 3. See Matthew 25:1-13. Céline was thinking of herself and her four sisters, all consecrated to God.
 4. Date of his burial in the Lisieux cemetery, after the Office of the Dead in the cathedral of Saint-Pierre. In October 1958, the remains of M. and Mme Martin were taken to the chapel of the Basilica of Lisieux.
 5. On September 30, 1897, Sister Geneviève (Céline) could not refrain from making a comparison between the death of M. Martin and that of Thérèse: "I, who had said at the death of my father, who fell asleep so gently in the Lord: 'How beautiful it is to die!' was thinking with anguish: 'How frightful it is to die!...'" (NPPA, quoted in DE, p. 144, note 103.)

LD   *From P. Pichon to Mother Agnes of Jesus, Sister*
                   Marie of the Sacred Heart, and Thérèse.

July 30, 1894

Dear Daughters in Jesus Christ,

Heaven has taken the beloved Patriarch from us. Shall we have the courage to weep over his happiness? After such a life, he must have been so well received up above. I can see him smiling gently from the eternal shore on which we shall rejoin him tomorrow, from the homeland in which he has found once again those who were awaiting him for a long time.

Picture him, dear children, picture him, your beloved Father, in the arms of your saintly Mother, surrounded by his heavenly family. You will have to smile at Jesus, then, who is taking him from you only to beatify him. I shall dare to say that now more than ever he is more yours; oh! much more yours than during these six years of his long purgatory[1] when we saw him dead to earth and not living in heaven.

I do not know what sweet emotion took hold of me yesterday night when the cablegram reached me. I threw myself down to pray for him, the holy old man, and to pray to him. This morning I celebrated the Holy Sacrifice for him. Tomorrow I will renounce in his favor the Mass in honor of St. Ignatius which I reserve for myself each year. My Chalice will be offered entirely for him insofar as I can dispense its merits.

I bless each and all of you[2] in the name of Our Lord, of the venerable Patriarch, and in my own name.

Almire Pichon

*   G. copy.
1.   This "purgatory," his illness, had begun in 1888. P. Pichon had been a witness of M. Martin's painful condition at Le Havre, November 3, 1888; see LC 92.
2.   At the same time as he had written to the Carmelites, P. Pichon wrote to Céline; see HF, ed. 1965, p. 369.

LT 168   **From Thérèse to Céline.**

August 5-10, 1894   Shortly after M. Martin's burial, August 2,
→ LD lost   Céline revealed P. Pichon's plans to her sisters:
                       he was calling her to Canada to be a foundress.
                       There was a unanimous outcry of indignation.
                       On August 7 or 8, Céline wrote to the superior
                       of the Carmel, Canon Delatroëtte, begging for
                       admission, at least as a lay Sister. The superior
                       answered kindly on August 9: "...but I fear the
                       entrance of a fourth sister is against the spirit and
                       even the letter of the Rule; however, we shall
                       look into this grave and very important matter
                       with the one in authority" (Canon Delatroëtte
                       to Céline, August 9, 1894). It seems Céline in-
                       formed P. Pichon about her decision at this time.
                       Probably it was this letter that Céline gave to her

Carmelite sisters.

J.M.J.T.

Jesus †

Dear Céline,

Your letter is *delightful*; it made us shed many sweet tears!...
Fear nothing, Jesus will not misguide you. If you only knew how
your *docility*, your childlike *candor* delights Him!... As for me,
my heart is *torn apart*.[1]... I suffered so much for you that I hope
I am not an obstacle to your vocation. Has not our affection been
purified like gold in the crucible?... We have sown the seeds, weeping, and now we shall soon return *together*, carrying the sheaves in
our hands.[2] I am not going to write Father today; I believe it is better to await his letter to see what he will say?[3]... If you prefer that
I write to *justify* you, tell me when you come, and I shall not be
embarrassed!... I am *heavy* at heart!!!...

But I thank God for this trial which He Himself has *willed*, I am
sure, for it is impossible that Jesus misguide *a little child like you*.

All three of us love you still better than before if this is possible.
Your look spoke volumes to us. If you were to hear Sister Marie
of the Sacred Heart, I assure you she would astound you!... She
does not hesitate to say that her beloved Father is mistaken.... But
he was only the docile instrument of Jesus, so little Thérèse is not
vexed with him![4]...

Thank Aunt for her letter. *If she knows* that I have written you,
tell her that we are deeply touched.

Mother Marie de Gonzague has wept, too, when reading your letter. Poor Mother, she knows nothing at all[5]...see how discreet we
are!

---

* Autograph
1. Sister Geneviève [Céline] was to note later: "Thérèse told me that in
   all her life she had not wept so much; she had such a violent headache
   that she wondered if she were on the verge of becoming ill." (*Souvenirs
   autobiographiques*, p. 213.) The handwriting in this note is much much

troubled and manifests not only an emotional upset but physical exhaustion
2. See Psalm 125:6.
3. P. Pichon answered on August 20 (Céline wrote at the latest on August 10): "Yes, yes, I give my Céline to the Carmel, to St. Teresa, to the Blessed Virgin. Can I offer them anything more attached to my heart? But God wills it!.... I have no doubt, I hesitate no longer. God's will appears evident to me."
4. She did make some reproaches to P. Pichon, judging by the answer he gave her (LC 161).
5. P. Pichon's plans? An obscure remark which no contemporaneous document explains in any satisfactory manner.

LC 160   *From Céline to Thérèse.*

August 19, 1894   Céline went with the Guérins to pay a visit to
                     Doctor and Mme La Néele at Caen, August 14
                     to 22; from there they made a trip to the coast;
                     Luc, Saint-Aubin, Lion, Cabourg" (Guérin
                     Chronicle).

August 19, '94

Dear little Thérèse,

I am not going to write you at length, for Marie[1] will give you a multitude of details she knows moreover better than I; I want simply to tell you the sorrow caused me by this war that is going on in an underhanded way.

Jeanne and Francis are really dead set against me, they are talking with great bitterness. They reproach me with many things, and when Marie has pinned them down on one point, they find another complaint. First, they say that I do not have a vocation, that I was destined to be the mother of a family, that I should have spoken earlier about this attraction to the religious life, that I am foolish to decide so quickly, that if they were to offer me a good match, I would take it, that it is an impulse, out of desperation that I am entering the convent, etc.; afterward, it is about yourselves [the Carmelites], you are monopolizers, and you and I are low in their estimation, etc.; afterward, it is because I am ungrateful to be leaving so quickly after Papa's death! I should have finished my time of mourning in the world, strengthened my vocation, and given at least one year to Uncle and Aunt out of gratitude, etc., etc. It never comes to an end...and I could not tell you how worked up they are. Never would I have believed that my vocation, already so much tried, would have met with so much anger. I am twenty-five years old, I know what I am doing, and they should know that never have I appeared inclined to marriage; they should have guessed that immediately after the departure of our dear Father, my first care was to settle down, and they should not blame me for this. Finally! Since that is how it is! And they are pitiless when it comes to souls consecrated to God; it seems that religious deserve everything when it comes to contempt and trouble, and Jeanne would have preferred to see me go to Jerusalem[2] rather than to Lisieux.

Thérèse! do you know what I think? I am already a daughter of St. John of the Cross and St. Teresa since my lot is "to suffer and to be despised."[3] The glory surrounding such a step on the part of a young girl is being refused to me. But I look upon this as a grace and a pledge of predilection. Uncle is admirable; he is making much of me, caresses me, and I see that he is broken-hearted.[4] Francis and Jeanne are careful not to make their statements in front of him.

I thought that *M. le Curé de St. Jacques* would perhaps be on retreat for the week of September 14; maybe you could inform him about the date I have chosen so that he would leave the first week, the week of the 3rd. I would be very sad if I had to give up the date of September 14.[5] I see Léonie every day. I go to the ocean every day. Yesterday, we fished for crabs, and I did not see one. I prayed to Papa, and they were plentiful, a real miraculous catch, more than one hundred, and I was the one who saw the most.... If you can write me a word, I will be delighted, but we are returning on Wednesday night, so write me immediately...should I have my picture taken?

* Autograph.
1. Marie Guérin brought this letter when passing through Lisieux.
2. At the Carmel called *Pater Noster*, founded in 1874 by Mother Xavier of the Heart of Jesus (1836-1889), professed at Lisieux, co-founders of the Saïgon Carmel (LT 159, note 5). At this time, Mother Marie

de Gonzague was carrying on a correspondence with the Prioress of the Jerusalem Carmel, Mother Aloysia. Thérèse had occasion to write this Carmel (the date is unknown, the document lost; this information was given in 1948 by a Carmelite nun who had known Mother Aloysia).

3. Sentence from Saint John of the Cross, dear to Céline and Thérèse; see LT 81, note 5.

4. M. Guérin was to blame himself for giving his consent too easily for this departure: "For the past two days, I am very much disturbed, and I am sorry for not having tried Céline; I fear I have not done my duty." (Words reported by Marie Guérin in a letter to Céline, end of September-beginning of October, 1894.)

5. The *Semaine religieuse de Bayeux* (August 26, 1894, p. 533) announced two sacerdotal retreats for the weeks beginning September 3 and 10. Céline had to renounce not the date of the 14th but the presence of Canon Delatroëtte. P. Lemonnier blessed her at her entrance into Carmel (according to a letter from P. Lemonnier to Sister Geneviève, February 24, 1895).

LT 169   From Thérèse to Céline.
August 19, 1894
→ LC 160

J.M.J.T.

Jesus †   August 19, 1894

Dear little Sister,

This is the last time, then, that I am obliged to write you while you are in the world!... I did not know I spoke so truly in the letter I sent you at La Musse, promising you that you would soon be in Carmel.[1]

I am not surprised at the storm raging at Caen. Francis and Jeanne have chosen a road so different from ours that they cannot understand the sublimity of our vocation!... But they laugh best who laugh last.... After this life of one day, they will understand who will have been the most privileged, *we* or *they*....

How sweetly the miraculous catch of the fish touched us.... How much these little delicacies make us feel that our dear Father is close to us! After a *death* of five years, what a joy to find him once more always the same, seeking out ways to please us as he did in days gone by. Oh! how he is going to return to his Céline the cares she lavished on him!. . . He is the one who carried off your vocation in so little time;[2] now that he is a pure spirit, it is an easy thing for him to go find priests and bishops, so he has not had as much trouble over his dear Céline as over his poor little queen!. . .

I am very happy, dear little Céline, that you are not experiencing any perceptible attraction in coming to Carmel.[3] This is a favor from Jesus, who wills to receive a *gift* from you. He knows it is much sweeter to give than to receive.[4] We have only the short moment of this life *to give* to God. . .and He is already preparing to say: "Now, my turn. . ."[5] What a joy to suffer for Him who loves us unto *folly* and to pass as *fools* in the eyes of the world. We judge others as we judge ourselves, and since the world is senseless, it naturally thinks we are the ones who are senseless!. . . But, after all, we are not the first; the only crime with which Jesus was reproached by Herod was that of being *foolish*,[6] and I think like him!. . . Yes, it was *folly* to seek out the poor little hearts of mortals to make them His *thrones*, He, the King of Glory, who is seated above the Cherubim[7]. . . He, whom the heavens cannot contain[8]. . He was *foolish*, our Beloved, to come to earth in search of sinners in order to make them His friends, His intimates, His *equals*, He, who was perfectly happy with the two adorable Persons of the Trinity!. . . We shall never be able to carry out the follies He carried out for us, and our actions will never merit this name, for they are only very rational acts and much below what our love would like to accomplish. It is the world, then, that is senseless since it does not know what Jesus has done to save it, it is the world which is a *monopolizer*, which seduces souls, and which leads them to springs without water.[9]. . .

We are not *idlers*, squanderers, either. Jesus has defended us in the person of the Magdalene. He was at table,[10] Martha was serving, Lazarus was eating with Him and His disciples. As for Mary, she was not thinking of taking any food but of *pleasing* Him whom she loved, so she took a jar filled with an ointment of great price and poured it on the *head* of Jesus, after *breaking the jar*, and the whole house was scented with the ointment, but the APOSTLES

[handwritten margin note:] acts 20:35

[handwritten margin note:] I - III Kings 8:27

complained against Magdalene.... It is really the same for us, the most fervent *Christians, priests*, find that we are *exaggerated*, that we should *serve* with Martha instead of consecrating to Jesus the *vessels* of our *lives*, with the ointments enclosed within them.[11]...
And nevertheless what does it matter if our *vessels* be broken since Jesus is *consoled* and since, in spite of itself, the world is obliged *to smell* the perfumes that are exhaled and serve to purify the empoisoned air the world never ceases to breathe in.

. . . .

The infirmarian would be pleased if you found at Caen one half bottle of antihemorrhagic Tisserant Water, two francs, fifty. If there are only the large bottles, do not take them, there are some here at Lisieux.

Sister Marie of the Sacred Heart would like to have seven or eight nut-crackers.

*   Autograph.
1.   See LT 167.
2.   See Ms. A, p. 177: "My dear King, who on earth never liked delays, hastened to arrange the muddled affairs of his Céline."
3.   "Once I made the resolution to enter Carmel as early as possible, disgust invaded my soul, repugnance for the religious life became a real torture.... I wondered with anguish what was this unknown, hidden life, what was this tomb in which I was about to bury myself.... I, too, was going to be a "good Sister" and share in the disgrace which surrounds them! Why am I not a man!... On the eve of my leaving the world, my interior troubles redoubled in intensity and my apprehensions were so great that I spent the night without sleep. I pictured the religious as huge specters who were going slowly through the cloisters, reciting the *De Profundis* in a monotonous tone. This picture filled me with terror, and really it was inexcusable in me, who visited so many religious, to be forming such ideas, but in my eyes my dear sisters were my sisters and nothing else; I truly believe I had not thought of them as religious." (*Souvenirs autobiographiques*, pp. 215-216.)
4.   See Acts of the Apostles 20:35.
5.   See Arminjon, *op. cit.*, p. 290, see LT 57, note 5.
6.   Thérèse was no doubt thinking of Luke 23:11.
7.   See Psalm 79:2.
8.   See III Kings 8:27: "He whom the heavens cannot contain."

9.   See Jeremias 2:13.
10.   Thérèse combines Mark 14:3-6 and John 12:1-8.
11.   See *Vivre d'Amour*! (P 15, February 26, 1895, stanzas 12 and 13.)

LT 170   **From Thérèse to Sister Thérèse-Dosithée**
August 20, 1894   (Léonie).

J.M.J.T.

Jesus +   August 20, 1894

Dear little Sister,

I would like to write you a long letter, but I have only a few minutes to spare, they are waiting for my note in order to mail it.

I am thinking more than ever about you ever since our dear Father has gone up to heaven; I believe you are experiencing the same feelings as ourselves. Papa's death does not give me the impression of a death but of a real *life*. I am finding him once more after an absence of six years, I feel him around *me*, looking at me and protecting me.[1]...

Dear little Sister, are we not more united now that we gaze on the heavens to find there a Father and a Mother who offered us to Jesus?... Soon their desires will be accomplished, and all the children God gave them are going to be united to Him forever....

I understand the void Céline's departure will cause you, but I know how generous you are with Our Lord, and then life will pass by so quickly...afterward, we shall be reunited never to be separated, and we shall be happy for having suffered for Jesus....

Dear little Sister, pardon me for this ugly letter, look only at the heart of your Thérèse, who would like to say so many things which she cannot express....

I beg you to pay my respects to Mother Superior and to your dear Mistress.

I would like you to give the letter to Céline[2] as early as possible when she comes to see you.

Adieu, dear little Sister; do not forget to pray for the *littlest* and the most *unworthy* of your sisters.

Thérèse of the Child Jesus of the
Holy Face
rel. carm. ind.

    * Autograph.
    1. In the month of August, Thérèse composed the nine stanzas of the
       Prayer of a Saint's Child (P 8); the last four stanzas have reference
       to herself.
    2. The preceding letter, LT 169.

"How sweet is the way of love" (Ms. A, p. 179)
(October 1894 - March 1896)
Age twenty-one and twenty-two

> *After a separation of six years, Céline and Thérèse were
> once again under the same roof, September 14, 1894. For
> them, correspondence lost its* raison d'être; *the* Conseils et
> Souvenirs *of Sister Geneviève (Céline) has given us the
> substance of their new relationship.*
>
> *A more copious number of letters made its way to the
> Visitation where Léonie was pursuing her solitary route.
> Then this correspondence ended abruptly: July 20, 1895, for
> the third time, Léonie left the convent; she returned to the
> Guérin home at Lisieux.*
>
> *Marie Guérin's entrance into the Carmelite family, August
> 15, 1895, gives rise again to letters from Thérèse to her aunt
> and cousins, pending the time when the presence of the
> "Benjamin" (Marie) furnished her with a pretext to
> withdraw more and more.*
>
> *There was a brief appearance of a new correspondent at
> the end of 1895: l'abbé Bellière, a seminarian with a weak
> vocation. The adoption of this spiritual brother was a joy
> to Thérèse (Ms. C, p. 251), but an exchange of letters did*

not take place until a year later, under the priorate of Mother Marie de Gonzague.

The rhythm of the Correspondence *slowed down during the end of Mother Agnes' term of office. We count fifteen letters from Thérèse in eighteen months, as against thirty-one in the preceding same lapse of time. The cause or consequence of this decline: Thérèse's literary activity unfolded on other levels.*

Fifteen poems (P 10 to 24), totalling more than twelve hundred verses, were composed for novitiate celebrations (Professions, receptions of the Habit) or feast days of her own sisters. In fact, though she did not receive the title, Thérèse had become the Community's poetess.

The entrances of three young women, full of life, stimulated her talent as "producer of plays" for occasions, such as Christmas, the prioress' feast, or Saint Martha. During the months of most interest to us just now, Thérèse composed five plays (Récréations Pieuses, nos. 2 to 6), including her second Joan of Arc *(RP 3, January 21, 1895): on this occasion, she reached the "apogee of glory" in her group (see Sister Marie of the Trinity, Mss. II, p. 56).*

But, above all, she began in January 1895 the writing of her Story of a Soul, *which she wrote in her free time throughout the year. The origin of this writing is well known (Mss. I, pp. 43-45): Sister Marie of the Sacred Heart's intervention, Mother Agnes' hesitation, Thérèse's surprise and acquiescence. No one at this time imagined that these "childhood memories" would one day go outside the family circle.*

We have already pointed out the significance of the rereading of her existence by Thérèse, precisely in 1895. The comparison between the Correspondence *and the* Story of a Soul *would suggest another remark: the* Letters *leave in the shadows entire areas of the Carmelite's life during this year of spiritual fullness.*

The mysterious voice guiding her groping progress for a year (pp. 820 and 857) has just pronounced her name through "the mouth of Eternal Wisdom: If anyone is little, let him come to me" (Ms. C, p. 208). This little one is Thérèse herself, "the littlest . . . the last" (LT 173). "Then I came" (Ms. C, p. 208). She has just discovered her "little way," a short cut to sanctity and to heaven.

In this winter of 1894-1895, there is really a question of "her going to heaven." Since her father's death especially, she longed with her whole being for the "homeland" where "more than half her family now enjoyed the sight of God" (LT 173). Moreover, she realized that her illness was sapping away her strength insidiously, that "this can become serious from one day to the next, and then there will no longer be any remedy" (p. 892). She observes the symbolic "little white flower" that she had received from her father on Pentecost Sunday, 1887: "Now the stem is broken away very close to the root" (Ms. A, p. 108). In all these signs, she has a presentiment of the imminence of the end, the realization of the great dream conceived since her encounter with Saint John of the Cross: to be consumed rapidly by Love (CJ 27.7.5; 31.8.9). Mourir d'Amour *(To die of love), that is her "hope" (P 15, February 26, 1895).*

The invitation of Jesus on the morning of June 9, 1895, feast of the Blessed Trinity, "to accept His infinite Love," finds her instantly available. She offers herself as "victim of holocaust to Merciful Love." Thus He will be "happy not to hold back the waves of infinite tenderness" closed up within His Heart (Ms. A, p. 181). And Thérèse will be "the joyful victim" consumed more rapidly still than she had dared to hope. As during the time in the belvédère at Les Buissonnets (Ms. A, p. 103), beyond what now separates the two sisters (LT 173, note 6), Céline is the first to be affected by the "touch of the spark" enflaming and "wound-

ing" Thérèse (see pp. 904-907).

> *But this fire was smoldering under the embers. Thérèse buried herself deliberately in "littleness" and insignificance. A sort of withdrawal, a refusal to influence others, is perceptible in many an autograph during 1895, as also in the greater number of the eighteen photographs – in which Thérèse appears, unknown among her companions in the Carmel.*

> *Read: Ms. A, pp. 174-182; Ms. C, pp. 206-207; p. 241; p. 251.*

1. VTL, nos. 9 (November 1894) to 26 (March 17, 1896); concerning their dating, see LT 176, note 1.

LT 171   **From Thérèse to Sister Thérèse-Dosithee**
October 11, 1894 (Léonie).

J.M.J.T.

Jesus †   October 11, 1894

Dear little Sister,

How happy I am your feast day is now on the same day as mine.... I am sure Saint Teresa will grant you her graces on the 15th; I will pray very much to her for you and also to Blessed Margaret Mary.[1]...

If you only knew, dear little Sister, how much we are praying for you!...and especially how we are offering *sacrifices*, I believe you would be very much touched.... Since we know about your trials,[2] our fervor is very great, and I assure you, all our thoughts and prayers are for you.

I have great confidence that my dear little Visitandine will come off victorious from all her *great trials* and she will one day be a model religious. God has already granted her so many graces, could He abandon her now when she seems to have reached port?... No, Jesus is sleeping while His poor spouse is fighting against the waves of temptation, but we are going to call Him so tenderly that He will awaken soon, commanding the wind and the storm, and calm will be restored.[3] ...

Dear little Sister, you will see that joy will follow trial and that later on you will be happy for having suffered; moreover, God is sustaining you visibly in the persons of you KIND Mothers, who never cease to lavish their cares and their tender and maternal counsels on you.

I beg you, *dear* Sister, to remember me to them, and you, dear *Thérèse, believe in the ever growing love of your little Sister,*

*Thé*rèse of the Child Jesus
rel. carm. ind.

* Autograph.
1. Her feast day was on October 17; in the family, they always attributed Léonie's cure as a child to Blessed Margaret Mary.
2. By means of Mme. Guérin, no doubt; see LD, October 20, 1894, and LD, October 21, 1894.
3. See Matthew 8:26.

LD   *From Mme. La Néele to Sister Marie of the Holy Face, Céline.* (Extracts.)

October 20, 1894

Yes, dear little Céline, I accept with all my heart the sacrifices God is asking from me. If He asks the sacrifice of motherhood, I offer Him this sorrow for His greater glory.[1] ... I have thought often of what you wrote me: "Our Lord will not ask us if we had children, this is not the goal of our life; our goal is to do the will of our Father who is in heaven...." I would have like to go to see you on Sunday to wish Thérèse a happy feast; I had the intention of wishing her this *viva voce*, this is why I had not written her. Then a difficulty arose, and the little cakes alone spoke for me. Kiss our dear little Thérèse, and tell her how much I love her and that I am praying to her little Jesus whom she adores to grant all the wishes I am making for her....

I just saw Léonie. She has not cried for three days; she is better since the feast of Blessed Margaret Mary. I had a long one-hour conversation with the mistress of novices. I will report this to Marie, who will speak to you about it on her next visit. Besides, she did not tell me anything more than what Mamma told you from her last trip. She told me. . . we had to pray relentlessly, for she was not accountable for our dear Léonie's perseverance.

Adieu, dear, I kiss you. How I love you and your three sisters as well.

Your Jeanne

   *   Autograph.
   1. This sacrifice had to be renewed more than once; see LT 178, note 10, LC 168.

LCS 160a

From Sister Marie of the Holy Face (Céline) to Thérèse

October 20-21
1894

Date deduced from the content; see note 2. For the first time since 1887, Thérèse and Céline were together for their feast days (October 15 and 21). Céline celebrated the event by preparing a surprise for her sister: stuffed birds arranged in a nest in the midst of flowers and branches, photographs of the family. These gifts were prepared with the help of Marie Guérin, who wrote Céline on October 20: "I am sending the feast day gifts to little Thérèse: I shall arrive during the octave, it could have been worse. Hug her tightly for me" (October 20, 1894). A message from Céline's hand accompanied the gifts: one of her allegorical descriptions which Céline loved to write.

I, the little bluebird,[1] was entrusted with a mission very dear to my heart. . . . In memory of my joyful and too short life at Les Buissonnets, I sought the honor of being the fortunate messenger.

Leaving my spouse to enjoy eternal rest, I came down from the celestial heights to greet you on God's behalf and that of the inhabitants of His kingdom.... I did not have ears enough to hear everything, nor eyes big enough to see everything, but my little heart understood everything, divined everything.

First, there was the family: Papa,[2] Mamma, the four cherubs, who kiss and love their little Thérèse; they would really like the family to be already complete in the homeland. The four rascals were so happy that when playing with the Holy Innocents they discovered a nest. A nest! No sooner seen than seized, they left nothing, neither the father, the mother, nor the little ones;[3] they even plucked the branch and carried me off in my wagon, laughing and babbling with delight.

St. Joseph brought the moss.... The angels hurried to harness my brothers, the little hummingbirds, telling them to make the trip quickly.... All the saints were there, looking at the whole retinue; they wanted to talk to me, so reading their thoughts, I made a sign with my head showing that I understood. I think, too, that each of them gathered a twig of moss....

When we were about to leave, your friends, the virgins, ran, carrying bunches of Céline-flowers[4] that they had just gathered from the fields of heaven.

Then the Blessed Virgin, with motherly heart, prepared a little package.... I think it is the most beautiful gift.... Perhaps it is made up of some portraits[5]...some views from Paradise...some scenes from up above.... I do not know, and perhaps I am talking too much! So I will stop....

Then God blessed us and made us immortal, and we shall remain with you on earth; this is the gift He is offering to his Thérèse.... And we shall be happy to adorn her altars!...

*   Autograph.
1. One of the birds (the male) bought by Thérèse for Céline at the exhibition at Le Havre in June 1887; see LT 25, and on p. 1140 a fragment from a letter of June 28.
2. Since M. Martin is mentioned as an inhabitant of the "celestial heights," this is proof the message was written after July 29, 1894, when he died. Céline dated it: October 1888 by mistake.
3. "I had placed in it some hummingbirds tinted in gold, which had

adorned one of Aunt's hats'' (note of Céline).
4. Asters, traditionally part of Céline's feast day celebration.
5. Photographic prints of M. and Mme. Martin done by Marie Guérin (according to a letter from Marie to Céline, October 20).

LD   *From Marie Guérin to Sister Marie of the Holy*
                          Face, Céline. (Extracts.)
October 21, 1894

Happy feast once more, pretty little white wolf.... Jeanne has been to see Léonie. For the last three days, there has been an improvement. The mistress of novices is beginning to lose courage, and if this improvement is not maintained, I do not know what will happen. Poor Léonie is also having temptations about the Eucharist, she is doubting the Real Presence. I have really prayed for her, for I really feel sorry for her. From the moment the mistress of novices pays no attention to her during the Divine Office, it seems she follows it as poorly as she can.... But let us hope the improvement will continue. It is ever since the feast of Blessed Margaret Mary that there has been some progress....

May little Thérèse take good care of herself; I found her voice very much changed yesterday,[1] so I spoke to Francis[2] about her. It is absolutely necessary that she take care of herself ENERGETICAL-LY. For the moment there is nothing serious, but it can become so from one day to the next, and then there will be no longer any remedy. Right now she can very well be cured, but for this she must take care of herself without letting up. Let her especially use a lot of *gillete*[3] (I do not know how to write this noun, it is not in the dictionary). Little Thérèse would have to be very obedient to the doctor. Francis is a specialist for these illnesses, so I believe him and have great confidence in him. He cured M. Ferouelle[4] from a sickness which was very grave, he will also cure little Thérèse. I am going to promise a very large sum to my little St. Anthony purse so that in six months my little sister may be entirely cured and in good health. She will gain some benefit from this, for this will be St. Anthony's money for her.

Are you thinking of the novena I asked you about, yesterday?

I hug you all tightly.

Your dear little
Marie

Papa advises Thérèse to take care of herself; when I speak about her to him, he seems to be disturbed. How is dear Mother?[5]... I inquire about her from the little turn-Sister.[6]

* Autograph.
1. Saturday, October 20. In the letter of that day already cited, Marie Guérin told Céline: "I am going to see you this afternoon at three o'clock in honor of your feast; you know, you must give me a nice visit." Thérèse took part in this visit.
2. He arrived at Lisieux with Jeanne on Saturday night, the 20th. He had already examined Thérèse the preceding July 1; see LC 159, note 8. We can imagine he continued to take care of her unofficially, but without entering the cloister for a real examination, until Doctor de Cornière took charge of the patient; see LT 192.
3. From the Normandy patois "*giler*": to project a liquid forcefully (see Moisy, *Dictionnaire de patois normand,* Caen 1887, p. 341: "*faire giler quelque chose*": *le faire sortir discrètement* (Le Vavasseur, *Nouvelles remarques sur quelques expressions usitées en Normandie, et particulièrement dans le département de l'Orne,* Alençon, 1891, p. 81). It was a matter of spraying a medicinal liquid into the throat with an atomizer or nebulizer: see CSG, p. 126. We have not identified the product used for these sprayings.
4. Lieutenant Louis-Marie-Gustave Férouelle, childhood friend of Francis La Néele. He died of consumption two years later. In his discourse given at the grave, December 20, 1896, Dr. La Néele recalled the "cure" of 1894: "Two years ago, having survived after long months of rest and care the first effects of his illness, he put on uniform and sword once again, and though his heart was affected, he asked to leave for Madagascar."
5. Mother Marie de Gonzague, who was sick. It is probable that the prescriptions from Dr. de Cornière, October 19, November 5, 7, 18, 1894, were for her (copybook of prescriptions for the Community).
6. Thérèse was the turn-Sister; see p. 819.

LT 172   From Thérèse to Mme. Guérin.
November 17, 1894

J.M.J.T.

Jesus †   November 17, 1894

Dear Aunt,

It is with soul still fragrant from Uncle's beautiful letter to Sister Marie-Madeleine[1] that I come to wish you a happy feast.

Oh, dear little Aunt! if you knew how proud I am to have relatives like you!... I am happy to see God so well served by those whom I love, and I wonder why He gave me the grace of belonging to such a beautiful family....

It seems to me Jesus comes to rest with delight in your home just as He did in the past at Bethany. It is truly "the divine Beggar of love" who is asking hospitality and who says "thank you" by always asking more and more in proportion to the gifts He receives. He feels the hearts to whom He directs Himself understand "that the greatest honor God may bestow on a soul is not to give it much but to ask much from it."[2]

So how sweet it will be one day for you, dear Aunt, to hear yourself being given the name *mother* by Jesus Himself!... Yes, you are truly His *mother*; He assures us of this in the Gospel in these words: "The one who does the will of my Father is my mother.[3] And you have not only done His will, but you are giving Him six of your children to be His spouses!... Thus you are His mother *six* times over, and the angels of heaven might address these beautiful words to you: "You will rejoice in your children because *all* will be blessed and they will be reunited in the Lord."[4] Yes, *all* are blessed, and in heaven, oh, dear Aunt, your crown will be made up of roses and Lilies....

The *two* roses[5] which will sparkle in the middle will not be its least ornament. These are the ones who on earth have copied your virtues in order to perfume this sad world and that God might still encounter here below some flowers that charm Him and hold back His arm which would punish the wicked....

Dear little Aunt, I wanted to speak to you at length...but they are coming to get my letter; I have time only to assure you again of all my love. I am thinking, too, of our dear Grandmamma's[6] feast day, and I beg you to hug her tightly for me.

Your little *daughter,*
Thérèse of the Child Jesus
rel. carm. ind.

* Autograph.
1. This letter was not preserved. M. Guérin was "godfather" at Sister Marie-Madeleine's reception of the Habit; see LT 146, note 8. The latter was preparing to make her Profession on November 20. To prepare her for it, Thérèse composed a *Little Collection of Aspirations* (title given to it in CE IV, pp. 71-72). It covers a two-week period and is entitled: *Mystical Flowers for making up my Wedding Gift.* Thérèse took up again the method she used in 1884 to prepare for her First Communion; see *General Correspondence*, pp. 181-182. On Thérèse's role regarding this novice see LC 157, note 8.
2. P. Pichon, sermon of investiture of Sister Marie of the Sacred Heart, March 19, 1887. Thérèse could have read again this thought in the notebook brought by Céline when she entered Carmel. In this notebook, Céline had recopied in their entirety, around Christmas 1890, P. Pichon's retreats of 1887 and 1888; see VT, January 1968, pp. 63-64, no. 10. In LT 213, Thérèse quoted this thought again, attributing it to a "Saint."
3. See Matthew 12:50; see LT 130, note 5.
4. See Tobias 13:13. This text appears on the back of M. Martin's death card. According to an oral tradition, it was Thérèse who had chosen the texts for this picture, collaborating with her sisters in Carmel.
5. Francis and Jeanne La Néele.
6. Mme. Fournet.

LT 173   **From Thérèse to Sister Thérèse-Dosithée**
January 1895   (Léonie).
→ LC lost

J.M.J.T.

Jesus †

Dear little Sister,

With great joy I come to offer you my wishes at the beginning
of this New Year. The one which has just passed away has been very
fruitful for heaven: our dear Father has seen what "the eye of man
cannot contemplate." He has heard the music of the angels...and
his heart understands, His soul is enjoying the rewards God has
prepared for those who love Him![1]
Our day will come also...perhaps we shall not see end the year
which is beginning! Perhaps one of us will hear the call of Jesus
soon![2]...
Oh! how sweet it is to think we are sailing towards the eternal
shore!...
Dear little Sister, do you not find, as I do, that our Father's departure has brought us close to heaven? More than half the family now
enjoys the vision of God, and the five exiled on earth will not be
long in flying away to their homeland. This thought of the brevity
of life gives me courage, it helps me bear with the weariness of the
road. What does a little work on earth matter (says the Imitation)[3]...we pass away and we have not here a lasting dwelling! Jesus
has gone before us to prepare a place in the home of His Father,
and then He will come and He will take us with Him so that where
He is we also may be.[4]... Let us wait, let us suffer in peace, the
hour of rest is approaching, the light tribulations of this life of a
moment are preparing us for an eternal weight of glory.[5]...
Dear little Sister, how much your letters pleased me and did *some
good to my soul*. I rejoice when seeing how much God loves you
and is granting you His graces.... He finds you worthy of suffering for His love, and it is the greatest proof of affection that He

Hope

may give you, for suffering makes us like Him....

O, dear little Sister! do not forget the last, the *poorest* of your sisters. Ask Jesus that she be *very faithful*, that she be like you, happy to be everywhere the littlest...the last![6]...

I beg you, offer my best wishes to your kind Mothers and assure them that I am united to them in the Heart of Jesus.

Your poor little Sister,

Thérèse of the Child Jesus
rel. carm. ind.[7]

* Autograph.
1. See I Corinthians 2:9, commented on by Arminjon, *op. cit.*, pp. 284-285. See LT 68, note 1.
2. See LC 161: "Is it true you are so eager to go to heaven?" In her poem *Vivre d'Amour!*...: "I have the hope, my exile will be short" (P 15, February 26, 1895); "For I feel it, my exile is about to end" (*ibid.*, stanza 14). In April, she confided to Sister Thérèse of Saint Augustine: "I shall die soon" (PO, 1945).
3. See Imitation of Christ III, 47 *Reflections*. The quotation is continued to the end of the paragraph. See LT 87, note 5.
4. See John 14:3.
5. See II Corinthians 4:17. We note in transcribing the *Reflections* of Lamennais, Thérèse omits these four words: (the light tribulations) *nous elevant sans mesure* (lifting us beyond measure).
6. This sentence may be understood on two levels:

   1) As an echo of the recent discovery, in the scripture notebook brought by Céline to the Carmel, of two texts which reveal to Thérèse her "little way": "Whoever is a *little one*, let him come to me" (Proverbs 9:4), and: "As a mother caresses her child, so will I comfort you; I will carry you on my breast, and I will rock you on my knees" (Isaias 66:13, 12). Regarding this discovery, see Ms. C, p. 208; regarding the time of this discovery: very probably at the end of 1894. See Conrad de Meester, *op. cit.*, pp. 81-85. Learned substantially at this time, the "little way" is explained on two occasions: in September 1896, where Ms. B, p. 188 (LT 196) takes up the two texts from the Old Testament; in June 1897, where the *account* of the discovery incorporates the word "elevator," the symbol used by Thérèse (LT 229, note 3).

   2) As an expression of an existential situation, accentuated by Céline's

entrance into the cloister. Céline, it is true, has "left all in a noble way, in a generous way" (P. Lemmonier to Sister Geneviève, February 24, 1895). However, this gift itself was not exempt from some search for glory. Daily reality was not long in manifesting it, and some inglorious beginnings upset the "knight Céline." They made her sadly conscious of the distance separating her henceforth from her sister. In her *Souvenirs autobiographiques*, p. 261, Céline (now Sister Geneviève) wrote: "There was more of a difference between Thérèse and Céline than formerly at the time of the first flights, they were no longer equal these two sisters." This difference became a source or increasing anguish and temptation for Sister Geneviève right up to the death of her younger sister. The necessity to teach was combined, then, with the interior call, inviting Thérèse to make herself littler regarding Céline. Not having an official role regarding her, except that "of angel," Thérèse acted—or saw herself treated—as the "littlest, the last" (as formerly at Les Buissonnets) in spite of her seven years of religious life. See LT 191, note 1.

7. The fourth page is taken up with a letter from Mother Marie de Gonzague.

LT 174   **From Thérèse to Sister Geneviève (Céline).**

End of January,   In 1889 (see LT 98, note 3), Thérèse had given
1895   her sister the name "Marie of the Holy Face."
                         It was still under this title that, on January 13, 1895, M. Delatroëtte congratulated Céline for her coming reception of the Habit. But at the end of the month, the superior expressed the desire that the name of the Carmel's foundress, Mother Geneviève of St. Teresa (d. 1891), be perpetuated. The matter was ratified one evening during recreation: "Both of us were stupified" (CMG IV, p. 273). As for Thérèse: "she had no words" (note of Sister Geneviève, March 17, 1936). After coming out of recreation, on a little piece of paper she found in her pocket, Thérèse wrote these words in pencil to comfort her sister:

Sister Geneviève of Saint Teresa,
little Thérèse is the first to write it![1]...

* Autograph.
1. On the back of the autograph, we read, in Sister Geneviève's handwriting: January 1895, the evening of the day when our Mother
changed my name." Concerning this change, see LT 183, note 4.

LT 175   **From Thérèse to Sister Thérèse-Dosithée**
February 24, 1895 (Léonie).
→ LC or LD lost

J.M.J.T.

Jesus †   February 24, 1895

Dear Léonie,

I was very happy to receive news from you; I trust you are continuing in good health and your dear Sisters are on the road to
recovery.[1]
I have only a little time to give you, but I want to recommend
myself to your prayers before Lent,[2] and I promise I will think of
you more, if that is possible, and I will come to sing *Alleluia* at great
length with you to make up for not being able to do so today....
I mean after Easter, but I am explaining myself so poorly that you
might believe I will sing the *Alleluia* during Lent.... Oh! no, I shall
content myself with following Jesus on His painful way; I shall hang
my harp on the willows on the shores of the rivers of Babylon.[3]...
But after the Resurrection, I shall take up my harp again, forgetting
for a moment I am exiled; with you I shall sing the joy of serving
Jesus and living in His house, the joy of being His spouse for time
and Eternity!...
Dear little Sister, offer, I beg you, my respectful wishes to your
kind Mothers, and believe in my *great* affection.

Your *very little* Sister,
Thérèse of the Child Jesus

P.S. When you write, will you tell me the *year* of your First Communion?[4]

* Autograph.
1. Influenza came to try the Visitation at Caen, taking four victims in February.
2. Lent began on February 27, Ash Wednesday.
3. See Psalm 136:1-2.
4. Léonie made her first Communion on May 23, 1875. When asking for this information, was Thérèse seeking it for the writing of her "childhood memories"?

LC 161   *From P. Pichon to Thérèse.*

February 25,   Last letter addressed personally to Thérèse dur-
1895   ing her lifetime.

† February 25[1]

Sister Thérèse of the
Child Jesus

Dear Child,

Is it true you are so eager to go to heaven?[2] I love you too much to fight against your joy. However, I have a selfish desire to see you once again here below. And something deeply interior promises me this.

And you have your Céline! What an overindulgence on God's part. And what can He not ask from you since He is giving you so much?

If Jesus comes to get you, you will remain my little daughter in heaven, will you not, and I shall not lose any of my paternal rights. Count on my Mass, for it is yours forever.

Yes, allow your divine Spouse the care of weaving your crown;[3] be content with pleasing Him. In this way, you will take Jesus through His Heart.[4]

Thank you for your feast day wishes,[5] your delightful poems. Everything coming from the little lamb to me is very good for my heart.

I am grateful to the good Master for inspiring you with so much confidence!

The very touching miracle worked by God to give you the assurance of the Patriarch's entrance into heaven really touched me[6] and I am adding my *Deo gratias* to your own.

No, no, the secret imposed on Céline[7] was not a lack of confidence. One day I will explain it to you. Take revenge by praying very much for my little work[8] which appears to me destined to save many souls and is already saving some.

Sleep in abandonment on God's Heart.

I bless you with all my heart.

Almire Pichon

* Autograph.
1. The "year" was written in by Thérèse on the autograph.
2. See LT 173, note 2.
3. See LT 143, note 6.
4. Thérèse takes up this expression in LT 191 and 258. See in a comparable sense: "to take Jesus through caresses" (NV, July 17, no. 2). On his part, P. Pichon used to use this expression; see VT, October 1967, letter of April 29, 1882, p. 191.
5. For St. Almire, September 11; for this occasion, at the request of Sister Marie of the Sacred Heart, Thérèse composed an acrostic on the name "Almire" (P 9).
6. This was the unhoped for change of mind of Sister Aimée of Jesus, at the beginning of August 1894; until then she was opposed to Céline's entrance into the Carmel of Lisieux; see Ms. A, p. 177.
7. Regarding her eventual departure for Canada, see LT 168; see also Ms. A, p. 177: "Her Céline had hidden a secret from her for *two years*."
8. "Bethany"; see LC 159, note 5.

LT 176   **From Thérèse to Sister Thérèse-Dosithée**
April 28, 1895   (Léonie).
→ LC lost

J.M.J.T.

Jesus †   Sunday, April 28, 1895[1]

Dear little Sister,

I would have liked to thank you sooner for your letter which
pleased me, but our Mother answered you immediately, and I was
unable to write you the same time as she.

Dear little Sister, I am interiorly convinced you are in your vocation, not only as a Visitandine but as a *Caen* Visitandine. God has
given us so many proofs of this that we are not permitted to doubt
it.... I consider this thought of your going to Le Mans as a temptation, and I am begging Jesus to deliver you from it. Oh! how much
I understand the delay of your Profession must be a trial for you,
but this is such a great grace that the more time we have to prepare
for it, the more we rejoice too. I recall with pleasure what took place
within my own soul a few months before my own Profession. I saw
my year of novitiate pass by, and no one was busied about me
because of our Father Superior, who considered me too young. I
assure you, I was very sad,[2] but, one day, God gave me to understand that there was a great self-seeking in this desire to pronounce
my holy vows. Then I said to myself: For my reception of the Habit,
I was robed in a beautiful white dress adorned with lace and flowers,
and who was thinking, now, of giving me any dress for my wedding?... This dress I must prepare *all alone*; Jesus wills that no one
help me except *Himself*, so with His aid I was going to set myself
to the task, to work with fervor.... Creatures will not see my efforts which will be hidden in my heart. Taking care *to forget myself*,
I shall want no other look but that of Jesus.... What does it matter
if I appear poor and destitute of mind and talents?... I want to
put into practice this counsel from the Imitation: "Let this one take
glory in one thing, another in something else, but as for you, set
your joy only in *contempt of self*, in My will and My glory."[3] Or:

"Do you want to learn something that will help you: Love to be unknown and counted as nothing!...."[4] When thinking this over, I felt a great peace in my soul, I felt that here was *truth* and *peace*! I was no longer disturbed about the date of my Profession, thinking that on the day when my wedding *dress* was finished, Jesus would come seeking His poor little spouse....

Dear little Sister, I was not mistaken and even Jesus was content with my desires, my total abandonment. He saw fit to unite me to Himself much earlier than I dared hope.... Now God continues to direct me by the same road, I have only one desire, that of doing His will.[5] Perhaps you remember how in the past I used to love calling myself "Jesus' little plaything."[6] Even now I am happy to be this; however, I have thought that the divine Child had many other souls filled with sublime virtues who call themselves "His toys." I thought, then, they were His *beautiful toys* and my poor soul was only a *little* toy without any value...to console myself, I said: Often little children are more pleased with *little toys* that they can *leave* aside or *take up, break* or *kiss* at their whim than with others of a greater value which they almost dare not touch.[7]... Then I rejoiced at being *poor*, I wanted to become this more and more each day, in order that Jesus may take more delight *in playing* with me.

Dear little Sister, now that I have given you my spiritual direction, pray that I may put into practice the lights Jesus is giving me.

Remember me respectfully to your kind Mothers.

Your *very little* Sister who loves you,
Thérèse of the Child Jesus
rel. carm. ind.

* Autograph.
1. Feast of the Good Shepherd. We may recall that three photographs (Community groups where Thérèse is present) were taken on that day or the eve: VTL, nos. 21, 22, 23. Today it is possible to be more exact about the dates of seven other pictures of the same period, thanks to the dates inserted by Mother Agnes of Jesus and found after the death of the editor, P. François de Sainte-Marie (d. 1961). We have this chronology:
   1) Easter Monday, April 15: VTL, nos. 18, 19, 20;
   2) Friday, April 19: VTL, nos. 24, 25 (Community doing the wash;

3) Saturday, April 20: VTL, nos. 16, 17 (recreation under the chestnut-trees).
2. See Ms. A, p. 160.
3. See Imitation of Christ III, 49:7; see LT 145, note 12.
4. See Imitation of Christ I, 2:3.
5. See *Act of Offering to Merciful Love* (June 9, 1895), and Ms. A, pp. 14 and 177.
6. See LT 34, note 2.
7. See Ms. A, p. 136 (which does not point out the stages in the meaning attached to the symbol: toy).

LD   *From P. Lemonnier to Sister Geneviève.*

June (?), 1895   "After our offering to Merciful Love, June 1895" (Sister Geneviève's note).

Dear Child,

You can see my happiness over your joy! and I sense your joy is very profound. Rejoice in this bliss, surrender yourself totally without any look elsewhere but on Jesus. Jesus! who is all for you. Yes, my child, you are victim[1] but not alone, Jesus is there, immolating Himself in you and through you. How good it is to offer oneself totally to Jesus so that He may continue as adoring, expiating Victim, but above all as loving Victim! Dear little flower[2] who will console Jesus for so much ingratitude He receives from creatures.

Dear child, I bless you with all my heart, you and your Angel of the Child Jesus.[3] I bless you, and I ask you to stir up one another in good, and that you not only be good and holy religious but that you do good, that your zeal may be a fire spreading itself[4] and causing a real conflagration in your dear Carmel.

You will pray, my child, you and your dear sister, for the Father who has the most paternal interest in you.[5]

May Jesus bless you and keep you in these sentiments all through your life.

                                        A. Lemonnier

* Autograph.

1. The "victim" theme was brought up several times in P. Lemonnier's retreat, October 1894, judging by Sister Marie of St. Joseph's note; see, for example: "How do we love our divine Spouse? . . . By making ourselves Victim with Him for poor sinners. . . . By offering Him the fragrant roses of our love without ceasing" (first day, notes, p.6).

2. In the same retreat, the preacher compares the Carmelite to "the little fragrant flowers, whose sweet scent Jesus loves to breathe, the little flower He will come one day to gather to transport it to the delightful thickets where virgins follow the Lamb everywhere" (fourth day, theme: "The thought of death," notes, p. 7). This preaching could have inspired in part the play composed shortly afterward by Thérèse: *The Angels at the crib of Jesus* (RP 2, December 25, 1894), one of the major themes of which is the comparison of the human soul to a flower. We know, too, that P. Lemonnier loved to call Thérèse "the little flower" (while she was still living; testimony of Sister Marie of the Angels, PA, 2871).

3. Sister Thérèse of the Child Jesus, "angel" of Sister Geneviève in the Carmel.

4. In June-July, Thérèse convinced Sister Marie of the Sacred Heart to offer herself as she did; see LT 197, note 6. In October, Mother Agnes of Jesus consulted P. Lemonnier concerning the advisability of making known to others this *Oblation* and asked him to examine the text "to see if one could give it as a formula of consecration to religious who desired to make it" (P. Lemonnier, PO, 2325). Thérèse was then invited to substitute "immense desires" for "infinite desires"; see LT 230, note 4. She suggested the *act of offering* to Sister Marie of the Trinity, November 30, 1895; the novice made it the following day.

5. This is P. Lemonnier, who took an interest in Céline since the summer of 1894; see LC 160, note 5. After the August 1894 crisis, in fact, the correspondence with P. Pichon declined. Sister Geneviève noted later that she received five letters in 1895 and 1919, the year of P. Pichon's death.

LC 162   *From Mother Marie de Gonzague to Thérèse.*

Toward mid-June Conjectured date; see notes 2, 5, and 6.
1895 (?)

† J.M.J.T. According to what they told me this evening, I am fortunately mistaken, my *double* novice and beloved daughter[1] has

nothing that is tiring her. *Deo gratias*. . . .

I prefer the wounds made on my daughter[2] to the dart of dear Mother St. Ephrem.[3] Oh, child, how many illusions there are in those heads filled with great things. . . . How blessed we are to prefer the gaiety, the simplicity, of our Holy Mother[4] to all these devotions which tire us, even when hearing about them. See how she was able to join to her grand ways the amiability that charms the heart; she knew how to love and make herself loved! *Long live her drum and her flute*. . . . These lines were begun last night, but our beloved little Mother[5] came to rest on the heart of her poor and unworthy old daughter; I left my daughter in favor of my Mother, while loving each from the depths of my heart.[6]

Let us be saints but not made by any false devotion.

Your poor Mother

* Autograph.
1. After having received the Habit and made Profession during Mother Marie de Gonzague's priorate, Thérèse "redoubled" her novitiate gladly under her direction since 1893; see LC 157, note 8.
2. Are these the wounds of Community life? "The wound of love" experienced a few days after her Oblation to Merciful Love? See HA 1898, p. 231; CJ 7.7.2 and DE, p. 456. Thérèse's confidence regarding this matter had deeply moved Mother Agnes of Jesus, who feared seeing her sister becoming involved in extraordinary ways. (Oral tradition in the Lisieux Carmel.) Did Mother Agnes seek advice from Mother Marie de Gonzague? The date of this note is uncertain, and consequently the question we have just asked is presented as an assumption. But it is not without some probability.
3. Not identified thus far.
4. Saint Teresa of Avila.
5. Mother Agnes of Jesus. From this sentence we can deduce with certitude that the note was written between February 20, 1893 and March 21, 1896.
6. The visit of Mother Agnes to Mother Marie de Gonzague and the written communication to Thérèse are explained either by the fact of a private retreat (no information on Mother Marie de Gonzague's retreat in 1895), or by an illness of the former prioress. On a photograph of April 27-28, 1895 (VTL, no. 21), Mother Agnes wrote in pencil: "grandmother is sick." Prescriptions of May 13, June 6, and July 10, could have been for her.

LT 177   **From Thérèse to Marie Guérin.**

July 7(?), 1895   For the last time before her entrance into
                       Carmel, August 15, Marie was spending her
                       vacation at La Musse (June 27 - August 6, ac-
                       cording to the ChrIG, p. 42).

To my dear little Sister[1] from her little Thérèse, who is *thinking
very much* of her!...and who above all is hoping (while trembling)
that her dear Marie is keeping to her promises, remaining as calm
as a little child in its mother's arms....

I am praying very much for you, dear little sister, and for all the
dear inhabitants of La Musse, who must be making, at this moment,
rapid progress in perfection since they are accepting so generously
the sacrifice of the separation!...

I *love* and *pray* for *dear Uncle* and *dear Aunt more and more.*
I do not know how far this will go since my affection is growing
each day!...

* Autograph.
1. Was a picture to be added to the note? It could have been sent shortly before July 10, with some mail from the three other sisters to M.
   and Mme. Guérin.

LT 178   **From Thérèse to Mme. Guérin.**

July 20-21, 1895   This letter was interrupted by the arrival at the
                       Carmel of Léonie, who had left the Visitation
                       on July 20.

J.M.J.T.

Jesus †   July 20, 1895

Dear little Aunt,

I was really touched when seeing you were thinking of your little
Thérèse;[1] she, too, is thinking very much about you, and although
she has not yet written her dear Aunt, it is not through indifference,

but because her heart is so filled with tenderness and affection that she does not know how to express her thoughts....

I must, however, make an attempt at the risk of saying to little Aunt some things that will displease her. Does not truth come out of the mouths of children? Well, you must forgive me if I speak the truth, I who am and want to remain always a child.[2]

I am going to give you my little spiritual direction and show you how *good* God is to me. I love the reading of the lives of the saints very much, the account of their heroic deeds sets my courage on fire and attracts me to imitate them; but I admit that, at times, I happen to envy the blessed lot of their relatives who had the joy of living in their company and of enjoying their conversations. Now I have nothing to envy, for I am in a position to contemplate at close quarters the actions of saints, to see their struggles and the generosity with which they submit themselves to God's will.[3]

Dear little Aunt, I know it would displease you if I were to say that you are a saint, however, I really want to do so...but if I do not say it to you, I can tell you something which you must not tell Uncle because he would love me no longer, this thing you know better than I. It is that he is a saint such as are few on earth and his faith can be compared to that of Abraham.... Ah! if you only knew with what sweet emotion my soul was filled yesterday when seeing him with his angelic little Marie.[4]... We were plunged into a very great sorrow because of our dear Léonie, it was like a real agony. God, who willed to try our faith, was sending us no consolation whatever, and, as for me, I was unable to offer any other prayer but that of Our Lord on the Cross: "My God, my God, why have You abandoned us!"[5] Or like that in the garden of agony: "My God, may Your will be done and not ours,"[6] Then to console us, our divine Savior did not send us the angel who sustained Him in Gethsemani but one of His *saints*, still a traveler on earth and filled with His divine strength. When we saw his calm, his resignation, our anxieties were dispelled, we felt the support of a paternal hand.... Oh, dear little Aunt! how great are God's mercies on His poor children!... If you only knew the sweet tears I shed when listening to the heavenly conversation of my holy Uncle.... He seemed to me already transfigured, his language was not that of a faith that hopes but a love that possesses. At the moment when trial and humiliation came to visit him, he appeared to forget everything in order to think of nothing but to bless the divine hand which was taking from him his *Treasure* and, as a *reward*, was testing him like a saint.... St. Teresa was very right in saying to Our Lord, who was loading her with crosses when she was undertaking great works for Him: "Ah! Lord, I am not surprised that You have so few friends; You treat them so badly!"[7] On another occasion, she said that to souls whom God loves with an ordinary love He gives some trials, but on those He loves with a love of predilection He lavishes His crosses as the most certain mark of His tenderness.[8]

(July 21)

I had left aside my letter yesterday without finishing it, for Marie arrived with Léonie; our emotion was very great when seeing her. We were unable to make her say a word, she was crying so much; finally, she ended up by looking at us, and everything went off well. I am not giving you any other details, little Aunt, because you can obtain all through Marie, who was a really *valiant woman* during the painful circumstances that had just taken place. We told her this, but I really saw that the compliment did not please her, so I called her "little angel." She told me, laughing, that this pleased her more than "valiant woman." She has a gaiety about her that could make a cat laugh, and this distracts her poor companion. We served them on the earthenware plates just like Carmelites, and this really amused them.[9]

Ah! what virtue your little Marie has.... The control she has over herself is surprising. It is not always *energy* that one lacks in becoming a saint, and yet it is a most necessary virtue; with energy one can easily reach the summit of perfection. If she could only give a little of hers to Léonie, your *little angel* would still have enough, and it would do no harm to the latter.... Dear little Aunt, I notice that my sentences are not clear; I am hurrying up in order to give my letter to Marie, who did not want me to write you, saying that she was going to deliver my messages or else give me *three sous* to get a stamp. But I did not want to wait any longer to send dear Aunt something other "than a look"; expressive as this may be, she would be unable to see it from so far away.

I wanted to speak to you about Jeanne and Francis, but I do not have the time. All I can say is that I count them in the number of the *saints* I am permitted to contemplate at close range on earth and that I rejoice at seeing them soon in heaven in the company of *their children*,[10] whose bright crowns will augment their own glory. . . .

Dear Aunt, if you cannot read me, it is Marie's fault; to scold her kiss her for me and tell her to hug you tightly for me.

Your *very little* daughter,
Thérèse of the Child Jesus
rel. carm. ind.

*   Autograph.

1.   On July 18, Mm. Guérin wrote to Mother Agnes: "Little Sister Thérèse of the Child Jesus said nothing to me on my last visit; this does not matter because I see her very sweet little face, but here I do not see her, and I would really like her to say something to me."

2.   First appearance, in the *Correspondence*, of the expression "to remain a child"; see LT 154, note 2 and LT 173, note 6.

3.   M. and Mme. Guérin had just written on July 18 two admirable letters to Mother Agnes of Jesus regarding the approaching departure of their daughter.

4.   They were going to Caen to bring Léonie home. To be noted is the adjective "angelic." This is exceptional under Thérèse's pen when applied to a human being (unlike the habit of Mother Agnes). Perhaps it is because of a recent letter from Marie to Sister Geneviève: "Mme. Lahaye said the other day to Jeanne that she really thought I would be a Carmelite because I have an angelic look" (an expression which made Marie laugh; letter of July 12, 1895).

5.   See Matthew 27:46.

6.   See Mark 14:36.

7.   See LT 155, note 2.

8.   See *Way of Perfection*, vol. II, *Collected Works of St. Teresa of Avila*, ch. 18 (first paragraph) p. 102, translation by Kieran Kavanaugh, OCD—Otilio Rodriguez, OCD.

9.   Léonie and Marie Guérin returned alone from Caen, M. Guérin continuing on his way to *La Délivrande*, for the pilgrimage of the Saint Vincent de Paul Conference (ChrIG, p. 42). The Guérin home on *rue Paul Banaston* was deserted: the family and servants were at Le Musse. The young girls took their meals, by way of an exception, in the refectory of the Extern Sisters. Thérèse could have shared in this service

in her position as second turn-Sister.

10.   On June 12, Jeanne La Néele had written to Céline: "I had a thought this afternoon, perhaps the Holy Spirit gave it to me. I shall say first that I am frequently praying to my holy Uncle [M. Martin] and very often I obtain what I ask for. I had the thought, then, of making a novena to Our Lady of Lourdes, and at the same time saying a prayer each day to my holy Uncle. Surely, he is in heaven, surely he will answer our prayers and especially those of his four Carmelites.... Will you kindly begin the novena tomorrow, Thursday, *Corpus Christi*, feast of the *Nocturnal Adoration* which Uncle loved so much. I am asking always for the same thing: my complete cure and a baby." (Mme. La Néele to Sister Geneviève, June 12, 1895.) These prayers were never answered...

LC 163   *From Mme. Guérin to Thérèse.*
July 28, 1895
→ LT 178

July 28, '95

Dear little Thérèse,

I want to write you on this sorrowful anniversary. It is already a year since your good father finished this sad life of exile.[1] Everything here speaks to us of him and the last moments he spent in our midst. But do you know how I always like to picture him: taking the arm of his little Benjamin. Undoubtedly, that time is far distant, but it was the moment of his happiness. His little Thérèse!... How proud he was to have her close to him, and did he not have the appearance of a holy Patriarch? That time is already far away and the child has really grown up, and the virtues instilled at so young an age in her heart have grown with her! How happy this good father must be now; if, as I hope, he is in heaven, the sight of his dear children must be a joy to him.

We just returned from High Mass, and M. le Curé announced the anniversary for M. Martin for tomorrow morning.

And her I am forced to be unable to assist at it; I have to remain at home[2] for several days, and we must postpone our return to Lisieux. This is an inconvenience, but if you were with me, you would

say: "Little Aunt, God is permitting it this way, do not be upset."
Ah! dear little Thérèse, it is because I am far from having the perfection you imagine me to have. On the contrary, I see myself filled with faults, my self-love causes me much trouble in everything, it tortures me. You, you know so well how to pray to little Jesus, ask Him to cure me of *this malady*.[3] I would need the gaiety of the Carmelite, and to attain it I do not know how to conduct myself. I count on you, little Thérèse, to obtain this grace for me. Tell me how to go about it, but not with just a look.... Ah! you want to call me a saint; you would do well not to dare, for I am a strange saint. I am turning to you, dear little Benjamin, so that you teach me how to become a saint! I would also like to see my little Marie walking in your footsteps. You will be her model! Poor child! how hard these last days are for her! And when she has entered, how will she be? Who will really tell me?... It seems to me the time will never come, and yet it is approaching in great strides. I beg God that she may be a holy religious like yourself, Thérèse. I fully realize that she will have much to suffer, for the little happy faces in the speakroom say nothing of the interior sorrows and sufferings within the cloister. But God will sustain her, I hope, just as He has sustained her dear cousins. I place all my confidence in Him.

Let us speak now about our dear Léonie.[4] Well! really in conscience I do not find her too badly off. The first days she had her ups and downs. Very cheerful for two or three days, she then became very sad. We distracted her and we have done everything to stop her from daydreaming. Marie has entertained her, and she has had a tough one to deal with. Yesterday, Léonie pleased me: she wanted to try doing a crochet design for an altar cloth that she found in a magazine. She has not yet succeeded, which does not surprise me, because it is very difficult and I would not have done better than she, but she has put a lot of time into it, and at least her mind is occupied during this time, and she is not up in the clouds. She is not bored at La Musse any longer, and she seems to be content to remain here a few more days. In a word, the news I have to give you about Léonie is good; tell this to Pauline and my *other two dear daughters*. If you only knew, Thérèse, what a storm we had on Friday at six in the evening. We were at dinner. Lightning flashes followed each other without interruption, when one flash brighter than all the others lighted up the room, and the clap of thunder resounded almost at the same time. Jeanne was frightened and held on to her father and Marie. Struck by the commotion, I jumped up and cried out: Ah! this time it is the end!'' Then I sat down again and said very calmly: "But do not be frightened, we saw the flash, there is no longer any danger." The picture was so funny (if I add here that Léonie, who was not afraid and, dying with hunger, was not missing a bite) that your uncle began to laugh heartily. Then everything came out: my words, my tone of voice, my actions were all reproduced in all kinds of ways. I must add to this that Maria,[5] who died from fright in her kitchen, threw herself in panic on the first person she met, and this was Alexandre![6] You have now a painting of a storm scene at La Musse.... However, I must add that the lightning struck a tree at La Musse outside the wall of the park on the St. Sebastian side (Céline will understand) and Mother Simon, who was milking her cows at *La Vieille Musse*, felt the shock and was still upset by it yesterday. Her cows were dancing.

I leave you, dear little Thérèse, kissing you with all my whole heart. Tell little Céline that I am not forgetting her, that she is not to be sad if I have not written her. She was my companion last year, and I am not forgetting her. Hug her *very, very* tightly for her godmother. Thank good Marie of the Sacred Heart for her very affectionate letter, and tell little Pauline that I love her *very much, very much*. Kiss both of them for me and offer my respectful wishes to Mother Marie de Gonzague. Your very devoted aunt,

Céline Guérin

Jeanne and Léonie ask me to give their love. Uncle kisses all of you with his whole heart.

I am forgetting to tell you that it was at Navarre[7] that we learned the lightning struck La Musse. M. Le Curé said to me: "It seems that lightning struck a poplar tree on your property." I answered: "No! M. le Curé." When we returned, we examined the trees, and discovered a poplar struck by lightning. We have to go far away to learn the news about home! It is not surprising then that Mother Simon had felt the shock, for she was not very far. And the poor cows that were dancing!... I should have given my pen to Marie to paint the whole picture for you, she would have painted from life and made you laugh.

*   Autograph.
1. July 29, 1894; see LD, July 29, 1894.
2. The same day, Marie Guérin wrote Céline: "Mamma is ailing and cannot travel for some time" (July 28, 1895).
3. Mme. Guérin always had a tendency to scruples; see VT, July 1971, p. 181; October 1971, p. 247; January 1972, p. 70.
4. She joined the Guérin family at La Musse, while waiting to go to live at Lisieux until her definitive departure for the Visitation in 1899.
5. Maria Cosseron, worked for the Martin family from Pentecost 1888 until the summer of 1889, when she began working for the Guérin family for many years.
6. Alexandre Mariette began working for the Guérins on June 27, 1892.
7. At Saint-Germain-de-Navarre, suburb of Evreux. The pastor was l'abbé Auguste Levasseur, with whom the Guérins became friendly in 1895. He was Marie Guérin's spiritual director.

LT 179   **From Thérèse to Sister Geneviève.**

After September   Note written in colored pencil in eight different
8, 1895   tints; date uncertain.

Demoiselle,[1] is she content?
Pauvre Monsieur really hurried to satisfy her.[2]

*   Autograph.
1. *"Mademoiselle Lili"* (Céline) and *"Monsieur Toto"* (Thérèse): a recall of *L'arithmétique de Mademoiselle Lili à l'usage de M. Toto pour servir de préparation à l'arithmétique du grand-papa,* by Jean Macé (Hetzel éditeur), a book the two sisters had known at Les Buissonnets. The name appears again in LT 182, 207, 208, 209, 214, 228. Thérèse makes use of these nicknames in 1896-1897, a fact which could place this note at a later date. See DE, pp. 596, 606, and especially 602, where Thérèse reveals the reason for the title *"Demoiselle."*
2. On the back of the note, Sister Geneviève wrote: "She had placed my mark on my socks." The novice received on September 8, 1895, her symbolic mark (LT 54, note 7): the monogram IHS which had been given to Mother Geneviève of St. Teresa, the foundress. The note is posterior to this date.

LT 180   **From Thérèse to Mme. La Néele.**
October 14-17, 1895
→ LC lost

J.M.J.T.

Jesus †   October 14-15, and 17, 1895

Dear Jeanne,

I seem to see and hear you while reading your letter; it gives me great pleasure to learn of the loving sickness that Uncle and Aunt came to bring you from Lisieux, and I hope that you are not yet cured of your attack of gaiety...this is probable since the famous member of the Faculty,[1] in spite of his universal knowledge, cannot find any remedy for his dear little Jeanne. If by chance he were to discover one, I beg him not to forget our Carmel, for the whole novitiate is stricken by the contagion since the entrance "of the little *rascal* who deepened the wrinkles and whitened the hair" of her dear *Fifine*.[2]

It is a great consolation for me, the *old* senior of the novitiate,[3] to see so much gaiety surrounding my last days;[4] it rejuvenates me and, in spite of my seven and a half years of religious life, my gravity often breaks down in the presence of the charming rascal who delights the whole Community.[5] If you had only seen her the other day with your photograph and that of Francis, it would have made you laugh!... Our Mother had brought them into our recreation and was having them passed around to each Sister; when Sister Marie of the Eucharist's turn came, she took the photographs one after the other, giving them her most *gracious smiles* and saying to each: "*Bonjour, Fifine.... Bonjour, Séraphin.*" These expressions of tenderness made all the Carmelites laugh, who are very happy to have so nice a postulant. Her beautiful voice is the joy and delight of our recreations, but what delights my heart especially, more than our dear angel's talents and exterior qualities, is her disposition to virtue.

The sacrifice God has just asked from you is very great, dear Jeanne, but has He not promised: "to the one who for Him leaves

father or mother or *sister* . . . a hundredfold in this life" [26] Well, for
His sake, you did not hesitate to separate yourself from a sister dear
beyond all that can be expressed! Ah! Jesus will be obliged to hold
to His promise. . . . I know that usually these words are applied to
religious souls, however, I feel in the depths of my heart that they
were spoken for the generous parents who make the sacrifice of
children dearer to them than they are to themselves. . . .

Have you not already received the hundredfold promised? . . . Yes,
already your little Marie's sweet peace and happiness have escaped
the cloister grilles to be diffused into your own soul. . . . I have an
interior conviction that soon you will receive a richer hundredfold,
a little angel will come to delight your home and receive your maternal kisses. . . .

Dear little sister, I should have begun by thanking you for the gift
you want to offer me for my feast day; I was really touched by it,
I assure you. But pardon me if I express my taste very simply. Since
you want to please me, I would prefer, instead of the *fish*, a model
of floers.[7] You will think I am very selfish, but, you see, Uncle is
spoiling his dear Carmelites, and they were really assured of not dying from hunger. . . . Little Thérèse, who never *liked things to eat*,[8]
loves, however, things useful for her Community. She knows that
with some models we can earn money to buy some *fish*. Is this not
a little like the story of Perrette? However, if you give me a branch
of *eglantine*, I shall be very content. If there is none, then some
periwinkles, buttercups, or even any other *common* flower would
please me. I fear I am being tactless; if I am, pay no attention to
my request, and I shall be thankful for the fish you will give me,
especially if you want to add to them the *beads* you spoke about
the other day. . . . You can see, dear Jeanne, that I am converted,
and far from keeping silence I am talking like a *magpie* and am too
bold in my requests. . . . It is so difficult to keep a happy medium! . . .
Fortunately, a sister pardons everything, even a little Benjamin's
importunities. . . .

I have interrupted my letter so often that it has no continuity. I
was thinking of some very beautiful things regarding the *hundredfold* that I was speaking about at the beginning, but I am obliged
to keep the *beautiful things* in the bottom of my heart and to beg
God to make them a reality for you, for I do not have the time to

enumerate them. I must go "to the washing" to listen, while scrubbing the linens, to the dear little imp who no doubt is going to sing: "*Ce lavage, doit nous conduire au Rivage sans Orage....*"[9]

Our two good Mothers and all your little sisters send you and Francis their love. I am not forgetting that tomorrow we celebrate the feast of St. Luke, one of his patrons,[10] so I will offer my Holy Communion for him, and I will ask Jesus to reward him for the trouble he is taking to find remedies for me.[11]...

I kiss you from my heart, dear little Jeanne, and I assure you of the love and gratitude

of your *very little* sister,
Thérèse of the Child Jesus
rel. carm. ind.

*   Autograph.

1.   Francis La Néele, doctor.

2.   The "rascal" is Marie Guérin, now Sister Marie of the Eucharist; *Fifine* is Jeanne, *Séraphin* is Francis.

3.   See LD, December 20-25, 1895, note 2.

4.   An expression half-joking, half-serious, Thérèse alone being aware of its significance; see note 11.

5.   With time, Thérèse judged it necessary to tone down this novice's exuberance. Sister Marie of the Eucharist wrote down Thérèse's counsels for her: "In recreation, practice virtue, be lovable towards all, no matter with whom you are speaking; be happy out of virtue not whim. When you are sad, forget yourself and show cheerfulness.... Take pleasure, but especially out of love for others.... There is a foolish gaiety about you at times, do you believe it pleases the Sisters?... They laugh at your foolishness, it is true, but it does not edify them." (*Souvenirs de soeur Marie de l'Eucharistie*, annexed by Mother Agnes of Jesus to her own testimonies at the Process, PO).

6.   See Matthew 19:29.

7.   This was for doing works of art, sold for financial aid for the Community.

8.   See CJ 31.8.5: "And to say that all through my life eating was a torment for me."

9.   Couplet from Sister Marie of the Eucharist's composition. They retained for a long time the custom of singing during long sessions of doing the Community laundry. See LT 192, note 5.

10. Patron of Christian doctors. October 18 was the thirty-seventh birth-
    day of Dr. Francis La Néele.
11. These remedies have not been identified. Mention of this shows she
    was still being attended to unofficially by her cousin; see LD, Oc-
    tober 21, 1894.

LD   *From l'abbé Maurice Bellière to Mother Agnes*
                          of Jesus. (Extracts.)

October 23,   On October 17, in the laundry, Mother Agnes
1895   took Thérèse aside; she held in her hand a letter
                          from a seminarian (written Tuesday evening on
                          the 15th), asking for a spiritual sister; see Ms.
                          C, p. 251, LC 191. The prioress chose Thérèse,
                          but not wanting her to engage in this cor-
                          respondence she answered the letter. L'abbé
                          Bellière established a first contact with the young
                          Carmelite through the mediation of Mother
                          Agnes.

                                       †
                          Major Seminary - Sommervieu

                                       Wednesday, October 23, '95

    How I thank you, Mother, for having exercised so much charity
toward me. . . you who were so kind as to comply with my desperate
request. . . . Whom have you given me as a Sister? A saint, an angel,
as you express it yourself! I knew there were only saints among you,
but I did not dare imagine that a saint among saints would become
my sister. Oh, Mother, you are treating me like a son, permit me
to consider myself as such, and to come into your family to pour
out my sorrows and joys.[1] Permit me to write you or to come and
tell you all that will happen to me, the good and the bad, with the
various events in a life to be rebuilt and which is just beginning. Allow
me to speak with you about the things of God, and to draw at your
side strength and virtue, in all the simplicity of a child and a "spoiled
child" as the world says.

I would also be happy to tell Sister Thérèse of the Child Jesus how touched I was by her charity, her devotedness, drawn from the purest fountain of divine Love. The rules of your order, no doubt, do not permit me to write her, and so I am asking you, Mother, to be my intermediary with her, as you already have been with so much success and joy. Tell her, Mother, that I thank, with emotion, the divine goodness that has chosen this Sister to aid me in doing the work of Jesus Christ, that I read with deep feeling the inspired prayer which she composed[2] and is saying each day for me, and that I am asking you to give her this emblem of the Sacred Heart which seals our divine association—it lacks only her signature[3] since you, Mother, and God have already approved it first. Tell Sister also that my promise holds and will hold eternally since in heaven for us priests[4] there will be a *perpetual Mass*: She will always have a place in the *memento*, as well as yourself, Mother, and your Community.... In the Eucharist, I will return thanks to her for these prayers and these sacrifices which she is offering in my favor.[5] But her great desire will be realized also: I shall be a priest, an apostle after God's own Heart; I feel it, and together we shall save the dear souls of Jesus Christ.... I shall be the instrument, and you, Sister, will do the converting....

A Dieu, Mother *à Dieu*, Sister; always in the Sacred Hearts. Thank you also for the golden *Ave Maria*.

Your respectful and grateful son and brother forever,[6]

> M. Barthélemy-Bellière
> *Enf. de Marie et Joseph*
> *garde d'honneur de S.C.*
> *Asp. Miss.*

---

* *Autograph.*
1. *The later correspondence will stress on both sides the family* aspect of their relationship. L'abbé Bellière, twenty-one years old, was an orphan at age three. He was reared by his aunt, Mme. Barthélemy, hence the double name of his signature.
2. Text published in the appendix of *Histoire d'une Ame*, ed. 1953, pp. 262-263. Thérèse dates it October 15, but she did not write it until October 17 at the earliest.
3. Thérèse signed the back of the emblem (a badge of the Guard of Honor

of the Sacred Heart, to which l'abbé Bellière was affiliated). He had already written: "seal of union in apostolic and fraternal love in the Sacred Hearts of Jesus and Mary. Signed: M. Barthélemy-Bellière, child of Mary and Joseph, missionary aspirant. October 24, 1895." Under the usual emblems of the Sacred Heart, on the front side, appears the printed motto: "There is only mercy and love!" See LT 266.
4. L'abbé Bellière was ordained on June 29, 1901.
5. In the prayer mentioned above, Thérèse wrote: "I offer you with joy for the soul of the missionary all the *prayers and sacrifices* of which I may dispose." The exclusive character of this offering explains Thérèse's hesitation in May 1896 when faced with a second offer of spiritual brother; see Ms. C, p. 253 and LT 189.
6. See in VT, October 1963, pp. 179-180, complementary excerpts from this letter, as well as in that of October 15, 1895 to Mother Agnes of Jesus. Thérèse described the present letter of October 23 as: " a charming letter full of emotion and noble sentiments" (Ms. C, p. 251).

LD   *From l'abbé Bellière to Mother Agnes of Jesus and Thérèse.*

November 12, 1895   After the October letter, "my little brother gave me no sign of life until the following month of July, except that he sent a card in the month of November to say he was entering the barracks" (Ms. C. p. 251).

November 12, Tuesday

L'Abbé Barthélemy-Bellière
(Langrune)

comes to greet his Mother in Carmel and his Sister Thérèse of Jesus (*sic*) before entering the barracks[1] today at two o'clock.

He recommends to your prayers the seminarian-soldiers and their sad families.

Always in union of prayers and graces in the Sacred Hearts. Let us do good, and may God's Kingdom come!

* Autograph.
1. At Caen, 5th. line, 4th Company.

LT 181   **From Thérèse to Mm. Guérin.**
November 16, 1895

J.M.J.T.

Jesus †   November 16, 1895

Dear little Aunt,

Your very little daughter comes to join her feeble voice to the delightful concert her big sisters are making heard on the occasion of your feast.

What remains for me to wish you, dear Aunt?... I feel that after all the wishes addressed to you I have only to say with all my heart: "Amen!..."

I repeat this to you every year, on earth I find no words capable of expressing the sentiments of my soul, so I am happy to join my three older sisters and especially our dear Benjamin[1] in offering you my feast day wishes.

I do not have time to write you at length, dear little Aunt, but I am certain you will read all the feelings of affection that overflow from my heart.

On the day of your feast, I will offer my Communion for you and for our dear Grandmamma.

I beg you, dear Aunt, to give kisses to all whom I love, especially to dear Uncle, and I ask him to give you a thousand other kisses for your little daughter.

Thérèse of the Child Jesus
rel. carm. ind.

*   Autograph.
1. Sister Marie of the Eucharist.

LD

From Sister Marie of the Eucharist to M. and Mme. Guérin. (Extracts.)

December 20-
25, 1895

Reception of a Child Jesus in wax for the Community crib (see note 1). No doubt, this little statue was used on the night of December 25 for: *The divine little Christmas Beggar* (RP 5) and on January 21, 1896, for *The Flight into Egypt* (RP 6). A note in pencil, signed by the six "novices."

...What a great surprise I had this afternoon!... What to do to thank you.... Had you only seen my joy, I was unable to control myself.... The reception of the case was an odd scene: all the little novices around the case, the dormitory[1] was filled with our cries. Who would unpack the case: one was shouting: "I see a hand," another: "Oh! a pretty little head," and Sister Marie of the Sacred Heart was objecting and crying out in despair: "You will see, they will break it, they will not be satisfied until they do!"

It was a real comedy, or to express it better an impossible uproar. We could not be quiet until we each gave vent to our joy.

I say a thousand times "thank you" and send the best kisses from your little daughter.

And the little novices send their thanks to generous Papa and Mamma.

Sister Thérèse of the Child Jesus, old senior novice
Sister Martha of Jesus, old senior novice[2]
Sister Marie-Agnes of the Holy Face,[3] baby of the novitiate
Sister Geneviève of St. Teresa, artist, who finds the little Jesus delightfully artistic
Sister Marie of the Eucharist, little Benjamin
Sister Marie-Madeleine, goddaughter.[4]

---

*   Autograph.
1. The Saint Elias dormitory (a corridor) which led into the Chapter room where the crib was set up. "It was very impressive: there were a number of trees, the facade was in rock paper. Sister Marie of the Sacred Heart arranged little paths of moss undergrowth; she excelled in this" (Sister Geneviève, *Recueil des travaux artistiques*, I, p. 28).
2. Having entered four months before Thérèse, Sister Martha of Jesus merited the title of "old senior novice" even more so than Thérèse.

At the Process she explained her extended stay in the novitiate: "The Servant of God wanted to remain in the novitiate out of humility, even after the usual period of her novitiate had been completed. I remained with her until 1895, and even after this date I never ceased seeking advice from the Servant of God" (Sister Martha of Jesus, PO, 513; see LC 157, note 8).

3. Provisional name given to Sister Marie of the Trinity; see LT 167, note 10; she was the youngest (twenty-one) and the most "childlike" in character. See LT 212.

4. Goddaughter of M. Guérin when she received the Habit; see LT 146, note 8.

LD   *From P. Pichon to Mother Agnes of Jesus, Sister*
Marie of the Sacred Heart, Sister Geneviève,
Thérèse, and Mother Marie di Gonzague.

January 1, 1896

To my five beloved daughters   † Montreal
in the Sacred Heart   January 1, '96

Dear Children in Jesus Christ,

My first lines are to you, just as you had this morning my first blessings and my first Mass. I feel very close to you in the Heart of the Master, united to your souls. The father and his favorite daughters make up but one.

But, alas! my sight is failing, always failing.[1] My two bad eyes are not worth one good one; they are no longer any good for correspondence. How I envy the days when I could read and write! Do not pout with God. I even count on you all to teach me to be generous.

It is really my hope to answer each of you; but in the meantime, it was too difficult to allow the new year to pass by without having you hear a cry from my heart.

May '96 be a year of the Sacred Heart for us! It was thus that I baptized it this morning, and you subscribe to this, do you not?

I bless you with my most loving blessings.

Almire Pichon

1. See LC 151, note 1. November 3, 1896, in a letter to Sister Marie of the Sacred Heart, P. Pichon begged his writers to write him "letters of two pages at the most, in large characters."

LT 182

February 23, 1896

From Thérèse to Sister Geneviève.

No external celebration accompanied the "demoiselle's wedding": Sister Geneviève's Profession, set for February 24, took place within the intimacy of the monastery, according to the bare essentials of the Ceremonial of the time. In compensation, the novice asked her sister to describe "the celebration in heaven" for her. Thérèse responded to this desire by adapting herself to Céline's taste for the marvelous and the overly embellished; she adopted, too, Céline's style (see LCS 160a, October 20-21, 1894). Perhaps she intended to console Céline for some recent troubles (see note 15). However, Thérèse remains herself in setting up the plan: she is yesterday's storyteller, captivating her listeners at the Abbey with her continued stories (Ms. A, p. 81); she is today's spiritual mistress, clear and picturesque, using stories to inculcate the lessons she wants to teach (CSG, p. 9); while waiting to become tomorrow's heroic patient, who will often tell "little stories to her sisters to cut short their lamentations (CJ 29.6.1).

Although by preference she sounds the family note particularly dear to Céline (see LCS 160a: "First, there was the family"), it was for the purpose of enlarging her sister's horizon: "The wedding will be composed of one great and identical family"; and of making her aware of the cosmic harmony awakened by the "incomprehensible mystery" of the union between God and His creature: "All is *ours*, all is *for us*, for in Jesus we have all!" (see note 23.) All of which recalls the teaching of the Apocalypse.

Better advised as to the literary genre of such a piece, the Roman censor might have been less critical when reading it (see notes 12 and 21).

With this letter, Thérèse inaugurates her combination of vertical and slanting handwriting with a variety that defies typographical transcription (see p. 67). The autograph copy is very condensed because the entire text is crowded into four pages.

J.M.J.T.

Jesus †   February 23, 1896

Dear little Sister, you have asked me to tell you how things will go in heaven on your wedding day. I will try to do this, but I feel in advance that I shall not even outline the celebrations which cannot be described, since "the eye of man has not seen, his ear has not heard, and his heart has not conceived what God is reserving for those whom He loves!"[1]

1 Cor 2,9

On February 24, at midnight, St. Peter will open the portals of heaven, and immediately the angels and saints will go forth with incomparable joy to form the court of the King and His fiancée.

The Virgin Mary, immediately preceding the Adorable Trinity, will advance, carrying the royal adornment of the spouse, her dear daughter. With an all-motherly care, she will open the abyss of purgatory before descending to earth. Instantly, innumerable multitudes of souls will fly toward their liberatrix, desiring to thank her and to learn the reason for their unexpected deliverance. The gentle Queen will answer: "Today is my Son's wedding. On the earth of exile, He has chosen from all eternity a soul that charms and delights Him, among the millions of others whom He has nonetheless created according to His image. This chosen soul offered this prayer to me: 'On the day of my wedding, I would like all suffering to be banished from my Bridegroom's kingdom.' Answering her appeal, I am coming to deliver you... take your place in our cortege, sing with the blessed the favors of Jesus and Céline.''

Then all heaven will descend to earth, and it will find the happy fiancée prostrate before the Tabernacle.[2] Rising at the approach of the cortege, she will graciously greet the angelic hosts and the multitude of saints; then, approaching Mary, she will present her forehead so that Mary's motherly kiss may prepare her to receive soon the seal and kiss of her Bridegroom.... Jesus will take His dear Céline's hand and lead her into the poor little cell in the corridor of St. Elias[3] so that she may rest for a few hours. The whole heavenly court will crowd into this narrow enclosure, and the angels will want to begin their concerts immediately, but Jesus will whisper to them: "Do not awaken my beloved,[4] leave Me alone with her, for I cannot be separated from her for one instant.''

The gentle Queen of heaven will understand her divine Son's wish, and she will have the bright cortege leave and will lead it to the wedding hall.[5]

Immediately beginning the preparation for the celebration, myriads of angels will weave such crowns as are not found on earth. The cherubim will prepare coats of arms more brilliant than diamonds, and their delicate brushes will trace out in indelible strokes the armorial bearings of Jesus and Céline.[6] They will set these up everywhere: on the walls, on the arches of the cloister, in the refectory, the choir, etc.... There will be so many artists that their masterpieces will find no room, and the innocent group of little children will come and offer to hold them up all day long before the Bridegroom and the bride. Smiling, the angels will refuse to give up their shields, for they will need them to *embellish* all the saints and to embellish themselves in order to show they are the humble servants of Jesus and Céline. To console the little children they will give each a charming *little* coat of arms so that they may be part of the celebrations, and, sending them off to remove petals from roses and lilies, they will continue with their splendid preparations....

The pontiffs and doctors will have a great mission to carry out. At their request, the *Lamb* will open the Book of Life,[7] and they will take from this *book* precious documents concerning *Céline's life*, and to honor her Bridegroom they will write down all the choice graces, all the *hidden* sacrifices, they find traced out in golden letters by the hand of angels. A great number of standards will be made up in this way by the doctors, and they will reserve to themselves the honor of carrying these before the royal cortege....

The apostles will gather together all the souls Céline has already brought forth to eternal life, and they will even gather the spiritual children she will bring forth in the future for her divine Bridegroom.

The holy martyrs will be careful not to be idle. Incomparable palms and fiery arrows will be arranged with touching care along the entire route of the royal procession. They want to render homage to the martyrdom of *love*[8] which is to consume the life of the joyful bride in a short time.

I would need too much time to describe the many occupations of the holy confessors, hermits, etc., and all the holy women. Let it suffice to say that each will use his whole genius, all his care, to celebrate worthily such a beautiful day.... However, I cannot leave in oblivion the canticle of the *virgins*, the palms and Lilies they will offer with inexpressible joy to their dear sister Céline. I already see Cecilia, *Geneviève*, Agnes with her companion Joan, the shepherdess, dressed in her warrior costume. I see *Céline*, our bride's patroness, offering her a bouquet of flowers which has her name on it.[9]

I see especially the whole Order of Carmel sparkling with a new glory. At its head, St. Teresa, St. John of the Cross, and Mother Geneviève. This splendid wedding is really their celebration because Céline is their beloved daughter....

And the delightful crowd of little Innocents, will it be a stranger to the glory of this beautiful day?... No, I see them playing with the *crowns* they did not *win*, they are getting ready to place one on the head of her who wants to resemble them and not *to win a crown*. They are proud as kings and toss their blond heads gracefully, for they glory at seeing their big sister taking them as models.... Suddenly, a *Mother* of incomparable beauty comes among them, she stops, and taking *four* charming cherubs by the hand she dresses them in clothes whiter than lilies and in diamonds glistening like dew in the sunlight.... A venerable Old Man with silvery hair is there, too, who bestows caresses on them, and all the other children are surprised at such preference. One of them timidly comes to little Thérèse,[10] asking her why this beautiful Lady is dressing them so richly. Little Thérèse answers in her silver-toned voice: "It is because we are the sisters and brothers of the happy fiancée of Jesus, the King. Hélène and I will be bridesmaids, and our two little Josephs will hold us by the hand.[11] Papa and Mamma, whom you see near us, will lead us, along with our little sisters still exiled on earth, and, the entire family reunited, we shall rejoice with unequalled joy." In the excess of her joy, little Thérèse will begin clapping her pretty little hands whiter than the wings of swans, and she will cry out, jumping on the necks of Papa and Mamma: "Oh! how beautiful, how beautiful! our dear sister's wedding. . . . We have come already three times to celebrations like this for Marie, Pauline, and *Thérèse (the little thief, who took my name), but never did I see such great preparations, I can see that Céline* is the last!"

Little Hélène and the little Josephs will make some delightful remarks on their joy at belonging to the family of the Queen of so beautiful a celebration. Then some little children who have been listening, gravely supporting their chins in their hands, will stand up and will say that they, too, are *Céline's brothers*, and to prove it they will explain why and from what line this illustrious relationship comes to them. Then will be heard more than just cries of joy, and the Blessed Virgin will be forced to come and restore calm to the childlike group.[12] All the saints will come running, too, and learning the cause of this extraordinary jubilation, they will find the idea so charming that each will hasten to set up a genealogy showing his *close kinship* to Céline. Thus all the pontiffs, the glorious martyrs, the warriors (at their head, St. Sebastian),[13] in a word, the whole heavenly nobility will take glory in giving the spouse of Jesus the name of sister, and the wedding will be composed of one great and identical family.[14]

However, let us return to the handsome Old Man, the beautiful Lady, and the four cherubs. All dressed up, they will come into the Chapter room. The angels will bow when seeing them pass by and will show them the magnificent thrones prepared for them on each side of the lowly chair destined for *dear* little Mother. It is into her hands that, in a few hours, the indissoluble bonds uniting Jesus and Céline will be made, and so this *Mother, little* in the eyes of creatures[15] but great in the eyes of Him whose place she takes, will receive most abundant blessings from her dear parents to place on the head of her sister and beloved child. . . .

Each saint, each angel will come to congratulate the venerable
Patriarch and his happy spouse. They will shine with a new glory,
and their children will cry out in admiration: "Oh, Papa! oh, Mamma!
how beautiful you are! how unfortunate Céline does not see
you!... Let her see you just for today."

"*Leave me alone*, children," Papa will answer. "You do not
realize that though I am hiding myself today it is because I know
how great a reward my *brave one*[16] will draw from remaining without
any consolation. In days gone by, I suffered much, and Céline was
then my only support, so now I want to be here, but do not imagine
I want to take the merit of suffering from her. Oh! no, I realize its
value only too well.... God will not allow Himself to be outdone   Gn 15.1
in generosity.[17] He is already my great reward,[18] and soon He will
be my *faithful* Céline's." "It is very true," Mamma will say. "It
is better not to show ourselves to her in the *foreign land* since Céline
is exiled there only for one *instant* in order *to combat and to die.*[19]
The day will come soon when Jesus will be truly the Master and my
little daughter the *Mistress*. She said this to me when she was very
little,[20] and I see she was right!..." The family conversation will
be interrupted by the angels, who will come to announce with great
pomp that the fiancée is ready to attend the Nuptial Mass. The procession will line up in perfect order and precede Jesus and *Céline*
surrounded by her family from heaven and earth. I cannot describe
Jesus' transports of love for Céline, her radiant beauty (for she will
be clothed in the adornment which *Mary herself* has brought). I do
not know if the inhabitants of heaven have ever seen a celebration
so beautiful, but I do not believe so, and as for myself, I say to my
dear sister that I have never seen one so sweet to my heart!...

I shall not speak of the *moment itself* of the *union*, for words cannot express this incomprehensible mystery to be revealed to us only
in heaven.... I know only that at this moment the Trinity will descend into the soul of my dear Céline and *will possess* it entirely, giving it a splendor and and innocence *superior* to that of Baptism.[21]...
I know the Blessed Virgin will become the *Mamma* of her privileged
child in a more intimate and *motherly* way than in the past....

I know that poor little Thérèse already feels in her heart a joy so
great at the thought of the beautiful day soon to begin that she is
wondering what she will feel when it actually arrives!...

Dear little Sister, my soul has very poorly expressed its feelings....
I was thinking of so many things concerning the heavenly celebration that it was impossible for me to give only an outline on the
subject....

I have no wedding present to give my Céline, but tomorrow I will
take up into my arms the *charming cherubs* I have spoken about,
and it is they themselves whom I will offer to her. Since we want
to remain as children, we must unite ourselves to them, and in this
way I shall be *demoiselle's* bridesmaid,[22] carrying a beautiful bouquet of lilies. All is *ours*, all is for *us*, for in Jesus we have all![23] ...

Céline's little *sister*,
Thérèse of the Child Jesus of the Holy Face

I forgot to say that when she wakes up, Céline will find by her
side Jesus, Mary, and *good Saint Joseph*, whom she loves so much,
along with Papa, Mamma, and the little angels. They will get her
ready. I forgot, too, to express the joy of Jesus when He hears Céline
pronounce[24] for the first time the words of the *Office*,[25] which will
be her *task*, the spouse of His Heart being entrusted with charming
Him in the midst of the camps![26] ...

*   Autograph.
1.   See I Corinthians 2:9; see LT 68, note 1.
2.   It was customary to pray in the choir until midnight, on the eve of
      one's Profession: "Like the warriors of old who spent the night in
      prayer before becoming armed knights, so the little fiancée of Jesus
      is preparing herself to receive her titles of nobility" (Sister Marie of
      the Sacred Heart to Céline, February 23, 1896).
3.   Sister Geneviève occupied the last cell at the extremity of this dor-
      mitory (corridor), next to the library. See DE, p. 820, plan of the first
      floor of the Carmel. In August 1894, shortly before her sister's en-
      trance, Thérèse had changed her cell for another adjacent to the
      Chapter room, two doors from Céline's.
4.   See Canticle of Canticles 2:7.
5.   The Chapter room.
6.   Regarding the Coat of Arms, see LT 183.
7.   See Apocalypse 20:12.
8.   See *Act of Offering to Merciful Love* made by Thérèse and Céline,
      June 11, 1895; and the meditation written by Céline, November 1,

1895: "*My Knight*!..." "I want to be a *martyr* of Love! I want to live by love and die from Love!..."

9. Asters; see LT 98, note 7.

10. Marie-Mélanie-Thérèse Martin, died at two months old (1870).

11. Recalling the three other children: Hélene, who died at the age of five and a half (1870); Joseph-Louis who died at the age of five months (1866); Joseph-Jean-Baptiate, who died at the age of eight months (1867). On the designation of the children as bridesmaids and best men, see Sister Agnes of Jesus' description for Thérèse's Profession, vol. I, p. 670.

12. The Roman censor of *The Writings of the Servant of God* noted in 1912: "much imagination, with no rapport to the truth!" (Sum II, p. 8, following the Testimonies.) To which the lawyer answered that though this fiction is devoid of ontological truth, it is not lacking a certain charm (*ibid.*, p. 80).

13. "I loved St. Sebastian very much, that brave soldier who deserved for his courage two palms of martyrdom since he suffered twice, and I used to ask him to give me one of them, I who no doubt would not have the honor of shedding my blood for Jesus" (a later note of Sister Geneviève, in CMG IV, p. 332). See also the letter of Mother Agnes of Jesus to Céline, LD, note 3, July 3, 1893; the prayer composed by Thérèse for Céline: "Oh! glorious soldier of Christ!" (HA, 1953, pp. 258-259.)

14. In the months following, Thérèse never ceased going thoroughly into this "Communion of Saints" forming one family of all the Blessed; see Ms. B, p. 191 and 194; LC 169; CJ 13.7.12 and 15.7.5, etc., and note 23 below.

15. A reference to the difficult circumstances preceding Sister Geneviève's Profession because of Mother Marie de Gonzague's character. Mother Agnes of Jesus was the main target, but Thérèse was equally implicated in this affair. See p. 1182: the circumstantial exposé of this frequently distorted episode. It is not unlikely that this matter encouraged Thérèse in embellishing "the celebration in heaven" surrounding this Profession in order to help her sister forget about the earthly clouds.

16. One of Céline's nicknames.

17. A saying dear to M. Martin; see LT 158.

18. See Genesis 15:1: "I shall be your reward exceedingly great." Sister Geneviève wrote: "Several times, surprising our dear Father in his belvédère, we saw him, his gaze plunged into infinity, repeating with a deep tone these words of Sacred Scripture which delighted him: 'Ego sum merces tua magna nimis.' This is why we had this text written on his death-card" (G/NPHF, p. 214).

19. See Lamartine: *Réflexion* in *Recueillements poétiques*: "Exiled for a moment in the foreign land — We live on earth to combat and to die." Céline had copied this excerpt in her copybook of poetic fragments; see LC 83, note 1. Thérèse quotes elsewhere one of the verses from this poem: "Time is your barque and not your home" (Ms. A, p. 88).

20. See CF, letter 105, July 9, 1873.

21. Another objection of the Roman censor (see note 12), who refutes Thérèse's statement but concedes that the one being professed "by reason of the intensity of the love with which she offers herself to God, and in virtue of her preceding merits, could reach a degree of sanctifying grace superior to that of a child recently baptized." The lawyer agreed, deeming that Thérèse was "the best witness" of her sister's dispositions.

22. "*Demoiselle Lili*"; see LT 179, note 1.

23. See St. John of the Cross, *Prayer of the soul on fire with love*. See *Collected Works*, pp. 668-9. See LT 137, note 5. The final verse of this prayer "filled Thérèse with joy and hope," expressing for her "that admirable Communion of Saints which was her delight" (Sister Geneviève, DE, p. 615).

24. Thérèse misspells the verb "*prononcer*."

25. According to the custom of the time, the newly professed presided at the Divine Office on the day of her Profession, that is, intoned various parts of the Office as hebdomadarian.

26. See Canticle of Canticles 7:1; see LT 149, note 7.

LT 183　　　　　**From Thérèse to Sister Geneviève.**

February 24,　　　On the eve of her Profession, Sister Geneviève
1896　　　　　　found in her cell a very large envelope contain-
　　　　　　　　ing an illuminated parchment, and Céline's coat
　　　　　　　　of arms, with this motto: "Who loses wins." The
　　　　　　　　text which followed borrowed her symbol and
　　　　　　　　a number of expressions in her meditation: "*My
　　　　　　　　Knight*!" written on November 1, 1895.

CONTRACT OF MARRIAGE
OF JESUS AND CELINE

I, JESUS, ETERNAL WORD, THE ONLY SON OF GOD AND

OF THE VIRGIN MARY, espouse today CELINE, exiled princess, poor and without titles.[1] I give Myself to her under the name of KNIGHT OF LOVE OF SUFFERING AND CONTEMPT.[2]

My intention is not to give My Beloved her homeland, her titles, and her riches now. I will that she share the lot it pleased Me to choose on earth.... Here below, My Face is hidden,[3] but she can recognize Me when others despise Me. In return, I am placing on her head today the helmet of salvation and grace so that her face may be hidden like Mine.... I will that she hide the gifts she has received from Me, allowing me to give them to her or take them back, just as I please, not attaching herself to a single one, forgetting even all that can make her great in her own eyes and in those of creatures.

My beloved will henceforth be named GENEVIEVE OF SAINT TERESA (her more glorious title, that of MARIE OF THE HOLY FACE will remain hidden on earth[4] so that it may shine in heaven with incomparable brilliance). She will be shepherdess of the one Lamb, who is becoming her Bridegroom. Our union will bring forth souls more numerous than the stars in the firmament, and the family of the seraphic Teresa will rejoice in a new splendor to be given to it.

Geneviève will bear patiently the absence of her Knight, leaving Him to combat alone so that He alone may have the honor of the victory; she will be content to handle the sword of Love. Like a sweet melody her voice will delight Me in the midst of the camps.[5] The lightest of her sighs of Love will set on fire with a totally new ardor my elite troops.

I, the Flower of the Fields, the Lily of the Valleys,[6] will give My Beloved for her nourishment the Wheat of the Elect, the Wine that brings forth Virgins.[7]... She will receive this food from the humble and glorious Virgin Mary, the Mother of us both....

I want to live in My Beloved, and, as proof of this Life, I am giving her My Name;[8] this royal emblem will be the mark of her omnipotence over My Heart.

TOMORROW, THE DAY OF ETERNITY, I shall lift My helmet.... My Beloved will see the brightness of My Adorable Face.... She will hear the NEW NAME I am reserving for her.[9]... She will receive for her Great Reward[10] the BLESSED TRINITY!...   Gn 15.15

After having shared the same hidden Life, we shall enjoy in our kingdom the same GLORIES, the same THRONE, the same PALM, and the same CROWN. . . . Our two hearts, united for eternity, will love with the same ETERNAL LOVE!!!. . .

Given on the Mountain of Carmel, under our signature and the seal of our arms, on the feast of My Agony,[11] *the 24th day of February, in the year of grace 1896*

THERESE OF THE CHILD JESUS, EDITRESS OF THE DIVINE KNIGHT

Contract

*   Autograph.
1.   Compare these titles with those in LT 118.
2.   Regarding the meditation entitled *My Knight*, Sister Geneviève wrote in 1946: "I have learned that after fifty years it was always the echo of my soul, and it is with jubilation that I would still sign it."
3.   See Isaias 53:3.
4.   See LT 174. Because of her later work on the Holy Shroud, Sister Geneviève took back her title "of the Holy Face" in 1916, becoming definitively: "Geneviève of the Holy Face."
5.   See Canticle of Canticles 7:1.
6.   See *ibid*. 2:1; LT 141, note 1.
7.   See Zacharias 9:17.
8.   Reference to the monogram IHS; LT 179.
9.   See Apocalypse 2:17.
10.   See Genesis 15:1.
11.   At this time, they used to celebrate on each Tuesday of Lent an Office relating to the Passion of Our Lord: The Agony, the Crowning with Thorns, the Holy Shroud, the Holy Cross, etc. In 1896, because of the leap year, the feast of St. Matthias, Apostle celebrated on February 24, was transferred to Tuesday the 25th, so that on Monday, the 24th, they celebrated the feast of "the Prayer of Our Lord in the Garden of Olives."

LT 184   **From Thérèse to Sister Geneviève.**

February 24,   On the night of December 5, 1891, Thérèse had
1896   gathered up the "last tear of a saint" (Ms. A,
                        p. 170), that of the foundress of the Lisieux
                        Carmel, who had just died. This was the relic
                        Thérèse offered Céline in Mother Geneviève's
                        name.

J.M.J.T.

To you, dear child, I give as wedding present the *last tear* I shed
on this earth of exile. Carry it on your heart and remember that it
is through suffering that a Sister Geneviève of Saint Teresa can reach
sanctity. You will have no trouble in loving the Cross and the tears
of Jesus if you think often of this saying: "He loved me and He
gave Himself up for me!"[1]

Gal. 2,20

Mother Geneviève

*   Autograph.
1.   See Galatians 2:20. The day after Mother Geneviève's jubilee (LT 130,
     note 1), Sister Marie of the Sacred Heart wrote Céline: "This even-
     ing, Mother Geneviève called me and said: 'This is what you will tell
     your little Céline for me, that she meditate on these words: 'He loved
     me and He gave Himself up for me'" (Letter of July 23, 1891).

LT 185   **From Thérèse to Sister Geneviève.**

February 24-   A holy picture for her Profession and reception
March 17, 1896   of the Veil. Entitled *The divine Choice* (Pannier,
                        pl. 109), it depicts the Child Jesus standing on
                        His Mother's lap, holding a bouquet of lilies in
                        one hand, signing the forehead of a young girl
                        with the other. She presses a crown of thorns to
                        her heart while four little angels contemplate the
                        scene.

(on the front in black letters)
POSUIT SIGNUM IN FACIEM MEAM![1]
St. Agnes, v.m.

(on the reverse side)

Souvenir of the most beautiful of days...the day containing and confirming all the graces Jesus and Mary granted their beloved Céline....

Through love, Céline will henceforth press to her heart the thorns of suffering and contempt, but she has no fear because she knows from experience that Mary can change into milk the blood flowing from wounds made by Love.[2]...

Céline is pressing the thorns with her left hand, but with her right she is embracing Jesus, the divine bundle of myrrh resting on her heart.[3]

Céline will bring forth souls for Him alone, watering the seeds with tears, and Jesus, always joyful, will carry the sheaves of Lilies in His hands.[4]...

The four little cherubim, whose wings hardly touched the earth,[5] run and contemplate their dear sister with delight. They hope to share in the merits of her sufferings[6] by coming close to her, and, in return, they are making the immaculate brightness of the innocence and all the gifts the Lord gave them gratuitously reflect on her.
February 24 - March 17, 1896.[7] Thérèse of the Child

Jesus of the Holy Face
rel. carm. ind.

* Autograph.
1. "He has set His seal on my face": response in the Office of St. Agnes, used in the Ceremonial for the reception of the Veil.
2. At the end of one of Céline's notebooks (CMG I), we read in her *curriculum vitae*: *Dream - Drop of Blood - Milk* (feast of the Maternity of the Blessed Virgin) 1893. There is a reference to the same thing in *Céline's Canticle*, composed by Thérèse for Céline's twenty-sixth birthday (P 16, April 28, 1895, stanza 21).
3. See Canticle of Canticles 1:13.
4. Transposition of Psalm 125:6.

5. Her little sisters and brothers; see LT 182.
6. On the meaning of "sharing," see LT 250, note 2.
7. See in Appendix pictures offered to Thérèse by Sister Geneviève on February 24, 1896, and by Sister Marie of the Eucharist on March 17, 1896, the day of her reception of the Habit.

SEVENTH PERIOD

THE NEW PRIORATE OF MOTHER MARIE DE GONZAGUE

(March 21, 1896 – September 30, 1897)

THE NEW PRIORATE
OF
MOTHER MARIE DE GONZAGUE

"No one,' Jesus said, 'lights a lamp and puts it under a measure but upon the lampstand that it may give light to ALL in the house.' It seems to me that this lamp represents charity which must give light and joy not only to those who are the most dear to us but to 'ALL who are in the house' without excepting anyone" (Ms. C, p. 220). At the stage of the *Correspondence which we have reached, this lamp could represent Thérèse herself, a burning lamp but hidden up until now, and henceforth placed on the lampstand.*

In the autumn of 1895, four months after her Offering to Merciful Love, *which resulted in her being clothed by Love, Thérèse paraphrased the gospel verse: "I have come to cast fire upon the earth" (Luke 12:49). She could sing in truth: "This Fire from heaven, You have placed it in my soul - I, too, want to spread its ardors - A feeble spark, oh, mystery of life - Suffices to set on fire an immense conflagration"* (Jesus, my Beloved, remember! *P. 21, stanza 19).** The *Correspondence of the last eighteen months of her life was witness to this conflagration which grew little by little.*

Statistics (see vol. I, p. 91) take on symbolic value here. Under the priorate of Mother Agnes (1893-1896, thirty-seven months), the forty-six letters from Thérèse were reserved to the family alone. One half of the eighty-one letters she wrote during the priorate of Mother Marie de Gonzague (March 1896 - September 1897) go outside the family circle. Certainly, circumstances explain this extension of her relationships with others. However, at this time, circumstances were in a large part due to the doings of the prioress of the Carmel. In the year 1896 precisely, Thérèse takes on a renewed consciousness of the providential role of "creatures" (LT 190) and events (LT 201) in her advance toward God. In order to better situate the letters during this period, it is important to cast a careful glance upon both "creatures" and "events": the state of her Community in the spring of 1896, Thérèse's position regarding her Sisters and her relationship with her new prioress.

Composed of twenty-four members, the Community of Lisieux experienced a rejuvenation during the two preceding years. Three vacancies had been made in its ranks: Sister Saint-Pierre's death (November 10, 1895), the invalid upon whom Thérèse bestowed so much attention when she was a novice (Ms. C, p. 247); Sister Anne of the Sacred Heart's return to Saïgon, her Carmel of origin (July 1895); the hospitalization of Sister Marguerite-Marie at Bon Sauveur in Caen (March 14, 1896). To make up for these vacancies, three young women between the ages of twenty to twenty-five brought their youthful strength to the monastery (p. 886). On March 21, 1896, the sixteen chapter nuns (those who voted) were called upon to elect a new prioress. A majority decision was reached with difficulty at the end of seven ballotings; Mother Marie de Gonzague was barely elected. Sister Marie of the Angels was reelected as subprioress, and Mother Agnes of Jesus and Sister Saint Raphael were elected as counsellors.

The nomination of the mistress of novices was the right of the prioress. Mother Marie de Gonzague's glance fell upon Thérèse, who had aided her in this charge during the former priorate. Twenty-three years old, not even a Chapter nun (she would not be voting on the novices), and aware

*of the prioress' touchiness, Thérèse declined the title.
However, she did remain as aid to the novice mistress
(Mother Marie de Gonzague was novice mistress as well as
prioress) until her strength gave out. After Thérèse's death,
her prioress wrote the following: "An accomplished model
of humility, obedience, charity, prudence, detachment, and
regular observance, Sister Thérèse carried out the difficult
charge of mistress of novices with a wisdom and perfection
that was equalled only by her love for God" (Mother Marie
de Gonzague, autumn 1897, in the margin of the saint's act
of Profession).*

*From the election onward, Thérèse used to gather together
each day the five young Sisters—including three professed—for half an hour. "There was no conference properly so-called, nothing systematic...." (CSG, P. 6), but
rather a lively exchange in which Thérèse excelled. She went
deeper with the novices into the Rule of Carmel, the Con-
stitutions; she instructed them in the various customs which
codified every detail of the religious life at this time. She
answered their questions, corrected their faults, "spoke in-
formally to them on what might be of interest at the moment regarding their spiritual life or even some work in progress" (ibid.). Editions of the* Story of a Soul *published
"Counsels and Reminiscences" collected by her novices. In
1896-1897, Marie Guérin's (Sister Marie of the Eucharist)
letters to her family were filled with expressions inspired by
Thérèse's teachings, even though the latter was not named
(see p. 1263–64).*

*The remainder of Thérèse's time was spent in her sacristy
work, now under the direction of Sister Marie of the Angels;
the task of painting, in which she furnished her share of articles to be sold; linen room work, for which she volunteered
in order to help Sister Marie of Saint Joseph, a temperamen-
tally unstable religious (p. 988).*

In an enclosed milieu, which was furthermore feminine,

every change in authority was laden with consequences for individual development. After the incidents of January-February 1896, the Martin sisters were not without some apprehension regarding the outcome of the election. Thérèse made up her own mind quickly: Mother Marie de Gonzague was fully acceptable as far as she was concerned. Formerly, "the vivifying water of humiliation" was not spared her, but "now it is the sun" (Ms. C, p. 206). Following the documents in their chronological sequence, without any preconceived notions, we even get the impression that a change in superiors represented a "blessing" for Thérèse at this time. Since the personalities of the two prioresses is in question here, a brief sketch of each of them is essential at this point.

In continuity with a life "hidden from outside influences" which Thérèse had always known at Alençon (see l'abbé Dumaine, PA 82) and at Les Buissonnets in Lisieux, "with no mundane company" (P. Pichon, PO, 316), Mother Agnes of Jesus placed an emphasis on the hidden life, fidelity to asceticism, the quality of love, including a reparatory intention in the name of sinners. Very significant in this regard was the program of sanctity she offered "her little girl" in March 1888: become "a center of love and virtues" (LC 78), but a hidden center, which is not to be "admired by anyone in the world" (LC 76). In the spring of 1896, Mother Agnes' ambition was almost fulfilled: "It seems to me that Love penetrates and surrounds me," Thérèse confided to her shortly before (Ms. A, p. 181). And Mother Agnes, when reading this Ms. A, was astonished: "How unknown she is here!" (CV, V, p. 128.)

Upon her return as prioress, Mother Marie de Gonzague opened doors and windows. She had a congenital need for relationships. Enriched by fifteen years of experience in governing, and moreover "grande dame," she does not allow herself to become enslaved by the letter of the law. There is room in her life for both the missionary and the mystical spirit. The best of these aspirations she finds in Thérèse. When she fostered their development, she was promoting, consciously or not, the work of the Holy Spirit in this young religious, helping her to discover her full stature. When she assigned to Thérèse a concrete objective for her apostolic zeal (taking charge of the novices and praying for her spiritual brothers), Mother Marie de Gonzague was permitting her to surmount the twofold trial that had overtaken her at Easter 1896, in contrast with the calm of the previous months:

1) the onslaught of tuberculosis, the spitting up of blood (April 2-3), at a time when, as she wrote: "Never did I feel so strong" (Ms. c, p. 210);

2) her sudden entrance into the "tunnel" at the very moment when she was marveling at her peace: "Really, I do not have any great exterior trials, and as for having any interior ones God would have to change my way. I do not believe He will do it, but I cannot live always in repose like this . . . what means, will Jesus find to try me? The answer was not long in coming" (Ms. C, p. 250).

There was no longer any rest for Thérèse right up to her death: "I must walk right up to my last moment," she one day answered in jest (LT 239); this was a spiritual rather than a physical necessity. The Correspondence *traces out this uninterrupted march:*

1) March - November 1896: Apparently restored by an invigorating diet, during her private retreat she experienced hours of a real spiritual depth (p. 985). Meditating upon the graces of the preceding months, she consigned them to "pages burning with love for Jesus" (LC 170): her incomparable "letter to Sister Marie of the Sacred Heart" or Manuscript B.

3) December 1896 - April 1897: With the first cold of winter a definitive relapse began; instead of a possible depar-

ture for the Saïgon Carmel, she now had to face up to death within a brief space of time. Will her desires for a world-wide apostolate be answered beyond space and time (pp. 1025-27)?

4) April – September 1897: *With courage and abandonment, Thérèse faced her final combat. Up to the very end, she used her strength to communicate her "way of confidence and love" (p. 1093) by means of letters, her last copybook (Manuscript C), and her "last conversations." She was now convinced that the spread of her "little way" was at the heart of her posthumous mission: "My mission to make God loved as I love Him... of spending my heaven in doing good on earth" (CJ, July 17).*

* Ce Feu du Ciel, tu l'as mis en mon âme Je veux aussi répandre ses ardeurs Une faible étincelle, ô mystère de vie Suffit pour allumer un immense incendie.
1. See in the Appendix pp. 1154 and following, several extracts which concern her personally or wit her sisters. The whole of this Guérin correspondence recreates an atmosphere which is found in the notes of and introductions to this volume.

"To forget myself for the glory of God and the salvation of souls"
(LT 193)
(March - September 1896)
Age twenty-three

On the basis of the exceptional documentation from March to September of 1896, the historian will one day be able to write one of the most compact chapters of the Saint's life. This documentation includes the following: confidences of Thérèse in her autobiographical accounts (Ms. B and C); poetical writings (twelve poems, dated for the most part, and a scenic play); prayers; photographs (five of Community groups, VTL, nos. 32, 33, 34, 35, 36, and three of her alone, VTL, nos. 29, 37, 38, including the classic "Thérèse with the Lily"); many chronological data, personal or family; finally, correspondence (eight letters from Thérèse, five addressed to her, about twenty others coming from her family).

We must content ourselves here with a brief outline:

1) April 2-3: *During the night of Holy Thursday - Good Friday, and again on the night of Good Friday, she experienced her spitting up of blood. Thérèse was filled with joy, for she sensed the Bridegroom's arrival: "It was like a sweet and distant murmur which announced the Bridegroom's arrival" (Ms. C. p. 211).*

A few days afterward, in contrast to the joy of Easter (April 5), she felt herself "invaded by the thickest darkness," the thought of heaven becoming for her "a subject of combat and torment" (Ms. C, p. 211). "The storm rumbles very strongly" in her soul during the following months" (Ms. B, p. 190).

2) April 30: *Sister Marie of the Trinity's Profession, soon followed by the reception of the Veil (May 7). In her novice's name and more so in her own, Thérèse sings with St. John of the Cross: "Supported without any support - Without light and in darkness - I am being consumed by Love" (see Collected Works, p. 734).* *

3) May 10: *A flash of lightning tears through her night; she received in a dream a visit of the Spanish foundress of Carmel in France. The feeling is restored to her for a time: "that there is a heaven and it is peopled with souls who love me" (Ms. B, p. 191). This favor is only "the prelude to greater graces" (ibid.). In fact, from this moment, Thérèse appeared to be more and more drawn outside herself, led into regions of love "which embrace all times and places," as she was soon to write (Ms. B, p. 194). In this ascent, every occasion is turned to account; she used them as so many "steps to lift herself" to her Beloved (LT 190 and 191).*

4) May 30: *Mother Marie de Gonzague entrusted her with the "spiritual interests of a missionary, who was to be ordained a priest and to leave shortly for the missions" (Ms. C, p. 253), Pére Roulland.*

By means of prayer, the Carmelite accompanied her "brother" on his farewell tour, then on to Natal, which brought him to Su-Tchuen, China. This association revived within her a latent vocation of the priest and missionary (Ms. B, p. 192).

5) June 21: *For the feast of the prioress, Thérèse prepared a scenic play entitled* The Triumph of Humility. *This play was based on a current theme. The extraordinary destiny of a Miss Diana Vaughan, ex-priestess of Lucifer, "converted" a year earlier (June 13, 1895), writer of strange Memoirs, gave rise to very strong emotions in many throughout France (LT 192, note 5). Diana Vaughan had revealed that Lucifer was declaring war to the death on the convents and especially on the Order of Carmel. The spiritual posterity of Elias, that champion of the Lord God of Hosts, would enter the duel. What were its weapons to be? Humility, which "sets hell in a rage." Such was the theme of Thérèse's play:* The Triumph of Humility *(RP 7).*

There was another irresistible weapon of Thérèse: the offering up of little sacrifices symbolized by the unpetalling of flowers before the Christ in the courtyard of the Carmel.

The Correspondence *has more than one reference to her poem* To Throw Flowers!

Outside the novitiate, Thérèse's influence was felt by the other religious. One indication of this was the many requests for poems (including that of the caustic Sister Saint Vincent de Paul). The prioress even treated Thérèse as an "equal" (LT 190), accepting her spiritual advice.

6) July - August: *Love never ceases to move back the limits of her desires, laying claim to "a wider space" (LT 193). Her excessive aspirations made her suffer "a real martyrdom" (Ms. B, p. 193). Instinctively, she sought an answer from the two geniuses of the Old and New Testaments: Isaias and Paul.*

While her Mother, Teresa of Avila, disposed her to "offer a thousand lives to save a single soul," St. John of the Cross taught her the fruitfulness for the whole Church of the "smallest act of pure love."

Without the letters from the correspondents, we would forget that this spiritual development has as its backdrop the illness of Thérèse. By means of her sisters and her cousin, Marie Guérin, we learn that Thérèse does not look well, that she coughs, that she suffers from her chest. They begin to overfeed her. Progress was noticed in July, and this permitted her to cut short, gently but firmly, inquiries from her family: "I am in excellent health" (LT 192). Her courage was misleading.

Read: Ms. B, pp. 190-192; Ms. C, pp. 208-212; pp. 216-217; p. 250; pp. 252-254.

* Appuyée sans aucun appui Sans lumieère et dans les ténèbres Je vais me consumant d'Amour

LD   *From Sister Marie of the Eucharist to M. Guérin.*
                    (Extracts.)

April 3, 1896   Feast day greetings signed by Thérèse on the
                    same day as her first spitting up of blood.

Our Mother asks me to tell you that she is joining in this little
family celebration,[1] and she is sending you her feast day gift: the
photograph of your five little Carmelites and your dear little imp
on the day of her espousals[2] (the one in which I am alone in white
is marked). She realizes how this little gift will please you, and you
cannot imagine with what *motherly kindness* she ordered us to do it.

Your *five little* Carmelite *daughters* offer you their wishes and
greetings for your feast day.

> Your little Marie of the Eucharist
> Sister Agnes of Jesus
> Sister Marie of the Sacred Heart
> Geneviève of St. Teresa
> Thérèse of the Child Jesus

* Autograph.
1. Saint Isidore (April 4), M. Guérin's feast day, the first since Marie's
   entrance into the Carmel (August 15, 1895).
2. There is a reference here to: 1) one of the photographs, VTL, no.
   30 or 31, taken under the chestnut trees, after Marie Guérin's clothing
   (March 17) and no doubt before the elections (March 21); 2) the
   photograph of Marie in her wedding dress on the day she received
   the Habit, standing next to Sister Geneviève, who received the black
   veil on the same day (March 17).

LT 186   **From Thérèse to Léonie.**

April 11, 1896   Date written in by the recipient.

J.M.J.T.

Dear Léonie,

Your very little Sister cannot refrain from coming to you also to

tell you how much she loves you and is thinking of you especially
on this your feast day. I have nothing to offer you, not even a *picture*; but I am mistaken, I will offer you tomorrow the divine *Reality*,[1] Jesus-Victim, YOUR SPOUSE and mine.... Dear little Sister,
how sweet it is that we can, all five, call Jesus "Our Beloved." But
what will it be when we shall see Him in heaven and follow Him
everywhere, singing the same canticle only virgins are permitted to
sing![2]

Then we shall understand the value of suffering, and, like Jesus,
we shall repeat: "It was really necessary that suffering should try
us and have us come to glory."[3]

Dear little Sister, I cannot tell you all the deep thoughts my heart
contains concerning yourself; the only thing I want to say is this:
I love you a thousand times more tenderly than ordinary sisters love
each other, for I can love you with the *Heart* of our celestial Spouse.

In Him we are living the same life, and in Him for all eternity
I shall remain.

Your very little sister,
Thérèse of the Child Jesus
rel. carm. ind.

* Autograph.
1. See LT 86. Is Thérèse thinking of Colossians 2:17?
2. See Apocalypse 14:3-4.
3. See Luke 24:46. The pericope of the disciples of Emmaus was read
   a few days earlier (Easter Monday, April 6). Among the trials affect-
   ing Thérèse at this moment, we must not forget, in the first place,
   her temptation against faith. Is she perhaps also recalling her father's
   illness, a suffering for the whole family? This gospel quotation appeared on M. Martin's death-card.

LT 187	**From Thérèse to Sister Marie of the Trinity.**
April 30, 1896	A note placed by Thérèse on the young nun's bed which she had covered with forget-me-nots.

Dear little Sister,

I would like to have some *immortelle* flowers to offer you as a remembrance of this beautiful day,[1] but it is only in heaven that flowers will never fade away!...

These forget-me-nots will at least tell you that in the heart of your little sister will remain engraved forever the remembrance of the day when Jesus gave you His Kiss of *union*, which must terminate or rather be accomplished in heaven!...

Thérèse of the Child Jesus
of the Holy Face
rel. carm.

*   Autograph.
1. "April 30, 1896, Profession of Sister Marie of the Trinity": date written in pencil on the autograph by the recipient. Thérèse said of this Profession: "I am reminded of Joan of Arc assisting at the coronation of Charles VII" (Circular of Sister Marie of the Trinity, p. 7). The perseverance of this young Carmelite, after a difficult novitiate was the work of Thérèse in large measure. See VTL, no. 32; poems; P 25 and 26, composed for the occasion.

LTS 187a	**From Thérèse to an unknown recipient.**
Spring-summer 1896 (?)	Approximate date according to the handwriting.

To my little Sister a THOUSAND MILLIONS OF TIMES LOVED!!!!!!!

*   Autograph.

LT 188   **From Thérèse to Sister Marie of the Trinity.**

May 7, 1896   Texts placed on a picture of Saint John of the
                        Cross on the occasion of Sister Marie of the
                        Trinity's reception of the Veil.

(On the front)
Through Love, to suffer and to be despised.[1]

(On the back)
Thoughts from Our Father St. John of the Cross.[2]

The affection [for the creature] is purely spiritual if the love of
God grows when it grows, or if the love of God is remembered as
often as the affection is remembered, or if the affection gives the
soul a desire for God—if by growing in one, the soul grows also
in the other.

He who walks in the love of God seeks neither his own gain nor
his reward, but only to lose all things and himself for God; and this
loss he judges to be his gain.

In the evening of life, they will examine you on love. Learn then
to love God as He wills to be loved and forget yourself.

Souvenir of May 7 of the year of grace 1896. Offered to dear little Sister Marie of the Trinity and of the Holy Face.

> Sister Thérèse of the Child Jesus
> of the Holy Face
> rel. carm. ind.

* Autograph.
1. Answer of Saint John of the Cross to the *Christ of Segovia*, see LT
   81, note 5. Thérèse adds the word: "through love." The *souvenirs*
   of Sister Marie of the Trinity make clear how much this saying was
   a necessary encouragement for her: her exterior conduct caused un-
   favorable judgements regarding her.
2. The three thoughts which follow are extracts from the *Maximes et
   Avis spirituels de notre Bienheureux Père Saint Jean de la Croix* (see
   DE, p. 844), maxims 129, 103, and 70. Thérèse wanted to be
   photographed with this book, June 1896; see VTL, no. 36. She read

it very much up to the end of her life; see DE, p. 519, par. 1. In her testimonies at the Process, Sister Marie of the Trinity brought to light Thérèse's devotion to Saint John of the Cross and the rooting of the "little way" in his doctrine. See *Collected Works*, pp. 305, par. 7, 526, par. 11, 672, no. 57.

LD

June 20, 1896

From P. Roulland to Mother Marie de Gonzague

Letter kept by Thérèse in her personal collection and dated by her in pencil (see note 2).

P. Roulland recounted the genesis of his correspondence with Thérèse in this way: "I was about to leave for the missions. R. P. Norbert, a Premonstratensian of Mondaye, diocese of Bayeux, my compatriot, intervened at my request with the Lisieux Carmel to obtain permission from the prioress that a religious of the monastery be chosen to pray specially for me and my mission. Sister Thérèse, whom I did not know until then, was chosen" (PA, 55). This took place on May 30, 1896. After some objections, Thérèse accepted this second spiritual brother (see Ms. C. p. 253). P. Norbert transmitted Mother Marie de Gonzague's affirmative answer. A few days later, the missionary aspirant wrote to the prioress.

R. Ap.[1]   †
Foreign Missions
128 rue du Bac
Paris

Reverend Mother,

I have learned with joy that you are willing to give me a helping angel for my apostolate. Sister Thérèse of the Child Jesus will pray specially for the success of my apostolic work. Thanks to the prayers which will be offered for me at the Carmel, I shall win over some souls for our God.

I would be happy to give you some details about my future mission, but I do not know it as yet. We do not choose: our Directors send us into the mission where they believe we are best suited to work for God's glory and the salvation of souls, and they do not let us know about their decision until the night of our ordination to the priesthood.

I shall enter upon my retreat on Monday night, June 22.[2] Pray and have prayers said for me and my confrères.

I shall be ordained a priest on Sunday, June 28, and on the 29th I shall offer, at the holy altar, your intentions to Our Lord.

During this same week, I shall go to Normandy to pay my farewell visits to my family.[3] I shall be passing through Lisieux, and I had the thought, if this is acceptable to you, to stop there a few hours in order to say Mass in your chapel with which I am acquainted. It would be a real joy for me to give Sister Thérèse of the Child Jesus the God of the Eucharist, the beloved Lord Jesus. I would be unable to celebrate Mass after seven o'clock, Friday, July 3. If you see no difficulties in the realization of my plan, please let me know by next Sunday.

Please, Reverend Mother, accept my sentiments of deep respect with my sincere gratitude.

A. Roulland
missionary aspirant

* Autograph
1. Abbreviation for *"Regina Apostolorum"* (Queen of Apostles).
2. The letter reached Lisieux on June 21 or 22; the date of the 20th, written in by Thérèse, is then the date when it was written.
3. P. Roulland was born at Cahagnolles, near Bayeux, a village about ten kilometers from the Abbey of Juaye-Mondaye.

LT 189

June 23, 1896
→ LD
June 20, 1896

From Thérèse to P. Adolphe Roulland.

Answering the first letter of the aspirant missionary, Mother Marie de Gonzague invited Thérèse to join her. This letter is the first of the seven Thérèse will address to her "spiritual brother."

J.M.J.T.

Jesus †

June 23, 1896
Lisieux Carmel

Reverend Father,

I thought it would please our Good Mother to give her on June 21 for her feast day a corporal and a purificator, along with a pall, that she might have the pleasure of sending them to you for *the 29th*.[1] I owe this reverend Mother the interior joy of being united to you by the apostolic bonds of prayer and mortification, so I beg you, Reverend Father, to aid me at the holy altar to pay her my debt of gratitude.

I feel very unworthy to be associated in a special way with one of the missionaries of our adorable Jesus, but since obedience entrusts me with this sweet task,[2] I am assured my heavenly Spouse will make up for my feeble merits (upon which I in no way rely), and that He will listen to the desires of my soul by rendering fruitful your apostolate. I shall be truly happy to work with you for the salvation of souls. It is for this purpose I became a Carmelite nun; being unable to be an active missionary, I wanted to be one through love and penance just like Saint Teresa, my seraphic Mother.... I beg you, Reverend Father, ask for me from Jesus, on the day He deigns for the first time to descend from heaven at your voice, ask Him to set me on fire with His Love so that I may enkindle it in hearts.

For a long time I wanted to know an Apostle who would pronounce my name at the holy altar on the day of his first Mass.... I wanted to prepare for him the sacred linens and the white host destined to veil the King of heaven.... The God of Goodness has

willed to realize my dream and to show me once again how pleased
He is to grant the desires of souls who love Him alone.

If I did not fear to be indiscreet, I would ask you, Reverend Father,
to make each day at the holy altar a memento for me.... When the
ocean will separate you from France, you will recall, when looking
at the pall which I painted with so much joy, that on the mountain
of Carmel a soul is praying unceasingly to the divine Prisoner of
Love for the success of your glorious conquest.[3]

I want, Reverend Father, our apostolic union to be known only
to Jesus,[4] and I beg one of your first blessings for her who will be
happy to call herself eternally,

> Your unworthy little Sister in
> Jesus-Victim,
> Thérèse of the Child Jesus
> of the Holy Face
> rel. carm. ind.

* Autograph.
1. Date of P. Roulland's first Mass, ordained on June 28.
2. See Ms. C, p. 253, in obedience to Mother Marie de Gonzague: "I
   asked you if obedience would double my merits. You answered yes."
   Thérèse felt that the undertaking of such a correspondence required
   "the *express permission* of authority" (Ms. C, p. 252). See her thought
   on this subject in CJ 8.7.16.
3. The main theme of the pall represents a boat heading out to the open
   sea; in the foreground, on a rock jutting out over the sea, a dove
   (Thérèse) gazes on a radiant host (see Ms. B, the little bird gazing
   on the sun). Shields on the side bear the initials of the missionsary
   and the Carmelite: AR and TJ.
4. Mother Marie de Gonzague told Thérèse to keep this correspondence
   secret. In the eyes of the Community, P. Roulland was "our Mother's
   missionary" (see LT 221). In May 1897, Thérèse was permitted to
   speak only to Mother Agnes of Jesus; see CJ 1.5.2.

Ex. 17.
9-13

LT 190

June 20, 1896

From Thérèse to Mother Marie de Gonzague.

As the weeks passed by after the difficult election of March 21, Mother Marie de Gonzague became conscious of a change in spirit in some of the Sisters during Mother Agnes of Jesus' priorate. The exceptional glamour given to the feast of Saint Aloysius Gonzaga on June 21 could not hide the ambiguity of the situation. "For this feast, we must turn everything upside down," wrote Sister Marie of the Eucharist on March 17. Thérèse received, in spite of herself, the confidences, complaints, and tears of her prioress, who envisaged at times her resignation or even her departure for the Carmel of Saigon. Thérèse suffered when feeling that the prioress was bogged down in human considerations. Through the roundabout way of a parable, she tried to make her face the truth by helping her realize that "her cross came from heaven and not from earth." According to Mother Agnes: "Mother Marie de Gonzague was not upset by Thérèse's advice. Basically, it was in Thérèse alone that she had any confidence; the other nuns seemed to be traitors to her" (NPPA, Reputation for sanctity during her life, p. 8).

J.M.J.T.

June 29, 1896

Legend of a very little Lamb.

In a cheerful and fertile meadow, there lived a happy shepherdess. She loved her flock with all the tenderness of her heart, and the sheep and the lambs loved their shepherdess too.[1] . . . But perfect happiness is not to be found in this valley of tears. One day, the beautiful blue sky of the meadow was covered with clouds, and the shepherdess became sad; she no longer found any joy in taking care of her flock. And must I say it? The thought of separating herself from it forever came into her mind.... Fortunately, she loved a very little lamb, and often she took it up in her arms, caressed it, and as though the lamb were her equal, the shepherdess confided to it her troubles and at times shed tears with it.

Seeing its shepherdess crying, the poor little lamb was upset; it sought vainly in its very little heart the means of consoling her whom it loved *more than itself*....

One night, the little lamb fell asleep at its shepherdess' feet. Then the meadow...the clouds...everything disappeared before its eyes. It was in a country infinitely more vast and more beautiful. In the midst of a flock that was whiter than the snow, it saw a Shepherd resplendent with glory and gentle majesty.... The poor lamb did not dare to advance, but, coming to it, the Good, the Divine Shepherd took it up on His knees, kissed it as its sweet shepherdess had done in the past, and then He said: "Little Lamb, why do these tears glisten in your eyes, and why does your shepherdess *whom I love* often shed tears?... Speak, I want to console both of you."

"If I am crying," answered the lamb, "it is only when I see my dear shepherdess weeping. Listen, Divine Shepherd, to the reason for her tears. In the past, she believed she was loved by her dear flock; she would have given her life to make it happy, but because of Your commands she was obliged to absent herself for some years; when she returned, it seemed she no longer recognized the same spirit that she had loved so much in her lambs. You know, Lord, it is to the flock that You have given the power and the freedom of choosing its shepherdess. Well, instead of seeing herself chosen unanimously as in the past, it was only after having deliberated seven times that the flock placed the staff in her hands.[2]... You, who in the past *wept* on our earth, do You not understand how much my dear shepherdess' heart must be suffering?...

The Good Shepherd smiled, and bending over the lamb He said: "Yes, I understand...but let your shepherdess be consoled. I am the one who has *not permitted* but *willed* the great trial that has made her suffer so much." The little lamb answered: "Is it possible, Jesus! I believed You were so good, so gentle.... Could You not, then, have given the staff to another, just as my dear Mother[3] desired, or if You wanted absolutely to place it again in her hands, why did You not do so after the *first* deliberation?..." "Why, little lamb?

It is because *I love* your shepherdess! Throughout her life I have watched over her with jealous care; she had already suffered very much for Me in her soul, in *her heart*. However, there was lacking the *special trial* that I have just sent her after I had *prepared* it from *all* eternity."

"Ah, Lord! I can see now that You do not know the greatest sorrow of my shepherdess...or else You do not want to confide it to me!... You think also that the primitive spirit of our flock is going away.... Alas, how would my shepherdess not think so?... There is so great a number of shepherdesses who deplore the same disasters in their sheepfolds...." Jesus replied: "It is true. The spirit of the world is creeping even into the midst of the most distant meadows, but it is easy to be mistaken in the discernment of intentions. I, who see all, who know the most secret thoughts, I tell you: The flock of your shepherdess is *dear to Me among all others*, and it has served me only as an *instrument* to accomplish My work of sanctification in your dear Mother's soul."

"Ah! Lord, I assure You that my shepherdess does not understand all You are telling me...and how would she understand it since no one judges things in the way You are showing them to me?... I know some sheep who are doing much harm to my shepherdess with their *mundane* reasoning.[4]... Jesus, why do You not tell these sheep the secrets You are confiding to me, why do You not speak to the heart of my shepherdess?..." "If I were to speak to her, her *trial would disappear*, her heart would be filled with so great a joy that her staff would never have seemed so light...but I do not want *to take her trial away* from her, I want only that she *may understand the truth* and recognize that *her cross* is coming from *heaven* and not from earth."

"Lord, speak then to my shepherdess. How do you expect her to *understand* the *truth* since she hears only falsehood around her?..."

"Little lamb, are you not the favorite of your shepherdess?... Well! repeat to her the words I am speaking in your heart." "Jesus, I shall do it, but I would prefer if You gave this charge to one of the sheep whose reasoning is *mundane*.... I am so little...my voice is so weak, how will my shepherdess believe me?..."

"Your shepherdess knows that I am pleased to hide my secrets

1 Chron 28:9

from the wise and the prudent, she knows I reveal them to the *lit-tlest ones*,[5] to the simple lambs whose white wool is not soiled by the dust on the road. . . . She will believe you, and if tears still flow from her eyes, these tears will no longer have the same bitterness, they will adorn her soul with the austere brightness of suffering loved and accepted with gratitude."

"I understand You, Jesus, but there is still a mystery I would like to fathom: Tell me, I beg You, why have You chosen the *dear sheep* of my shepherdess to try her?[6] . . . . If You had chosen strangers, the trial would have been sweeter. . . ." Then showing the lamb His feet, His hands, and His heart, adorned with luminous wounds, the Good Shepherd answered: "Look at these wounds; they are the ones *I received in the house of those who loved Me!*[7] . . . This is the reason why they are so beautiful, so glorious, and why for all eternity their brilliance will revive the joy of the angels and saints. . . .

"Your shepherdess wonders what she has done to estrange her sheep, and *I*, what had I done to My people? . . . . In what had I made them sad?[8]

"Your dear Mother, then, must rejoice in having a share in My sorrows. . . . If I am removing from her human support, it is only to fill her *very loving* heart! . . .

"Blessed is the one who places his support in Me, for he is setting up in his heart steps which will lift him up to heaven. Notice, little lamb, that I am not saying that one must separate himself *completely* from creatures, despise their love, their kindness, but, on the contrary, one *must accept* them in order to please Me, and to use them as so many *steps*, for to separate oneself from creatures would serve only one thing: *to walk* and go astray on the paths of this earth. . . . To lift oneself up one *must place his foot* on the *steps* of creatures and attach himself to Me only. . . . Do you understand, little lamb?"

"Lord, I believe it, but above all I *feel* that Your words are the truth, for they bring *peace*, joy to my *little* heart. Ah! may they enter sweetly into the *very big* heart of my shepherdess! . . .

"Jesus, before I return to her, I have a prayer to make to You. Do not leave us languishing on this earth of exile for a long time, call us to the joys of the heavenly meadow where You will lead our dear flock eternally through flowery paths."

The Good Shepherd replied: "Dear little lamb, I will answer your request. *Soon*, yes soon,[10] I shall take the shepherdess and her lamb; then throughout eternity you will be grateful for the blessed suffering that will have merited so much happiness, and I Myself will dry all tears from your eyes![11] . . .

*   Autograph.

1.   The roles are easy to distinguish: the shepherdess, Mother Marie de Gonzague; the sheep, the professed nuns; the lambs, the young Sisters in the novitiate; the little lamb, Thérèse. See Ms. C, p. 209, which recalls the first weeks after the election of 1896.

2.   Mother Agnes of Jesus pointed out in 1932: "The election, moreover, was not canonical. One would have had to be a witness to what took place because of the ignorance of the Superior" (*Souvenirs intimes*, p. 70, marginal note). Canon Maupas, pastor of Saint-Jacques at Lisieux, had begun to function as superior of the Carmel only in January 1896, and he was not sufficiently acquainted with the procedures of an election. According to our present knowledge, we can shed no light on this question.

3.   Did Mother Marie de Gonzague desire the reelection of Mother Agnes of Jesus? On April 23, 1896, she wrote to the Carmel of Compiègne: "A little prayer for the poor *old woman* upon whose shoulders they have placed the staff again in the mouth of March. She would have so much preferred to remain in her dear solitude because the burden seems heavier to her than in the past. The three years in the cell appeared to me like three days! . . ." She was sixty-two and in poor health; see LT 193, note 13, and LT 201, note 21.

4.   No document thus far permits the identification of the religious concerned.

5.   See Matthew 11:25.

6.   According to all probability, Thérèse's older sisters are to be numbered among the "dear sheep" whose attitude disappointed Mother Marie de Gonzague.

7.   See Zacharias 13:6.

8.   See Micheas 6:3; see the Reproaches on Good Friday.

9.   See Psalm 83:6. A sentence inscribed on the wall (in 1887) at the foot of the stairs which Thérèse climbed every day to return to her cell. Concerning the absence of support, see the *Glosa a lo Divino* of Saint John of the Cross set in verse by Thérèse shortly before (P 26, April 30, 1896).

10.   See Thérèse's question to Mother Anne of Jesus, seen in a dream on May 10, 1896: " 'Tell me if God will leave me a long time on earth. . . .

Will He come soon to get me?...' Smiling tenderly, the Saint
whispered: "Yes, soon, soon.... I promise you" ' (Ms. B, p. 190).
Mother Marie de Gonzague died on December 17, 1904.
11.   See Apocalypse 21:4.

LC 164   *From Léonie to Thérèse.*

July 1, 1896   This letter was given to Thérèse after a delay of
                    ten days; see LT 191, note 2.

V + J!¹

La Musse, July 1, 1896

(for Sister Therese of the Child Jesus)

Very dear little Sister,

If you only knew how I am always thinking of you, and remembrance of you is so sweet for me. It brings me close to God, and
I understand your desire to go to see Him soon in order to lose
yourself eternally in Him.² I myself, too, desire it like you; I love
to hear death spoken about, and I do not understand persons who
love this life of suffering and of continual death.

As for yourself, my dear, you are ready to go to see God. Surely
you would be well received, but I, alas, would arrive with empty
hands, and yet I have the boldness not to be afraid, do you understand? It is incredible; I know it, I confess it, but I am unable to
stop acting otherwise.

How are you? Dear little sister, on this subject alone I have no
confidence in you, for you always tell me that you are well or better, and I believe nothing at all.³

When you write me, tell me above all the real truth and speak
to me of God and about all that I can do to advance in virtue. This
is the only think that really pleases me and that I expect from the
beloved Carmel.

If you only knew how necessary it is that I be helped not to allow
myself go after the pleasures and vanities of the world, for, in spite

of all the good will possible, we allow ourselves to be drawn insensibly toward these, and if we do not find death in them, at least piety and pure love for Jesus are impaired. We no longer have anything to offer the dearly Beloved except faded flowers;[4] how many times have I not offered Him some. Dear Sister, you will stop me, will you not, from continuing to do so? I am so weak. You know I am depending on you.

How happy I am for not going to the wedding;[5] thanks! thanks! for what you know always stops your little *runaway horse*.

A thank-you to dear little Mother Agnes for her good letter; I hug all very tightly; how I love you.

I beg you, ask God especially for me that He may free me from my scruples; always drawn in upon myself, I am terribly harmed by this and held back very much from perfection. Be certain that I am placing my finger on the wound in order to show it to you.

Your little sister, who loves you with all her heart.

Léonie
child of Mary

Remember me to our good Mother.

I fear Marie of the Eucharist is forgetting the scapular for Madame St. François de Sales;[6] two large pieces of her dress, no embroidery, only pictures.

---

* Autograph.

1. "*Vivre Jesus!*" (Long live Jesus!): a heading in use in the Visitation convents and retained by Léonie, who was always a Visitandine at heart.

2. A desire no doubt expressed *viva voce* during a visit prior to the departure of Léonie and the Guérins for La Musse (June 10); unless it is a reference to the poem: *What I shall see soon for the First Time* (P 29), composed by Thérèse for the feast of Sister Marie of the Sacred Heart (June 12), and this may have been sent to La Musse.

3. On June 14, Sister Marie of the Sacred Heart wrote to Mme. La Néele: "Sister Thérèse of the Child Jesus is no longer doing badly, on the contrary" (see LT 191, note 8).

4. On June 29, Sister Marie of the Eucharist had sent her mother "a little hymn composed by Sister Thérèse of the Child Jesus": *To Throw*

Flowers! (P 30, June 28, 1896). The refrain sang of the offering of "first fruits" of sorrows and joys; this theme was already known by Léonie and Céline, who had heard it at Paray-le-Monial and wrote it down for themselves and for Thérèse, a sermon by P. Tissot: "You have a bouquet, but instead of carrying it to Him whom you love, you have it admired, inhaled by many persons, so it loses its scent, it gets overheated in your hands and withers . . . For the Beloved, there is no sharing, never any withered flowers; He must have the first fruits" (October 15, 1890). See CJ 25.7.8, where Thérèse refuses withered flowers for her Crucifix.

5. The marriage of Hélène Maudelonde at Lisieux, August 4, to M. Jules Houdayer, lawyer. The Guérins and Léonie returned to Lisieux on July 26.

6. Benedictine nun at Lisieux. The making of scapulars was among the works sold at the Carmel at this time.

LT 191   **From Thérèse to Léonie.**

July 12, 1896
→ LC 164

J.M.J.T.

Jesus †   July 12, 1896

Dear little Léonie,

I would have answered your *charming* letter last Sunday if it had been given to me. But we are five, and you know I am the littlest[1]. . .so I run the risk of not seeing the letters until after the others or else not at all. . .I saw your letter[2] only on Friday, and so, dear little sister, I am not late through my own fault. . .

If you only knew how happy I am to see you in these good dispositions. . .

I am not surprised that the thought of death is sweet to you since you no longer hold on to anything on earth. I assure you that God is much better than you believe. He is content with a glance, a sigh of love. . . As for me, I find perfection very easy to practice because I have understood it is a matter of *taking hold of Jesus by His*

Heart.[3] . . . Look at a little child who has just annoyed his mother by flying into a temper or by disobeying her. If he hides away in a corner in a sulky mood and if he cries in fear of being punished, his mamma will not pardon him, certainly, not his fault. But if he comes to her, holding out his little arms, smiling, and saying: "Kiss me, I will not do it again," will his mother be able not to press him to her heart tenderly and forget his childish mischief? . . . However, she knows her dear little one *will do it again* on the next occasion, but this does not matter; if he takes her again *by her heart*, he will not be punished.[4] . . .

At the time of the law of fear, before the coming of Our Lord, the Prophet Isaias already said, speaking in the name of the King of heaven: "Can a mother forget her child? . . . Well! even if a mother were to forget her child, I myself will never forget you."[5] What a delightful promise! Ah! we who are living in the law of love, how can we not profit by the loving advances our Spouse is making to us. . . how can we fear Him who allows Himself to be enchained by *a hair* fluttering on our neck[6]

Let us understand, then, how to hold Him prisoner, this God who becomes the beggar of our love. When telling us that it is a hair that can effect this prodigy, He is showing us that the *smallest actions* done out of love are the ones which charm His Heart

Ah! if we had to do great things, how much we would have to be pitied? . . . But how fortunate we are since Jesus allows Himself to be enchained by the *smallest things*. . .

It is not little sacrifices you lack, dear Léonie, is not your life made up of them? . . . I take delight at seeing you before such a treasure and especially when thinking you know how to profit from it, not only for yourself, but for souls. . . . It is so sweet *to help Jesus* by our light sacrifices, to help Him save souls that He bought at the price of His Blood and that are awaiting only our help in order not to fall into the abyss. . . .

It seems to me that if our *sacrifices* are the hairs which captivate Jesus, our *joys* are also; for this, it suffices not to center in on a selfish happiness but *to offer* our Spouse the *little joys* He is sowing on the path of life to charm our souls and *raise* them to Himself. . . .

I intended writing Aunt today, but I have no time; this will be on next Sunday.[7] I beg you to tell her how much I love her and dear

Uncle as well.

I am thinking very often of Jeanne and Francis.

You ask me for some news about my health. Well! dear little sister, I am not coughing anymore.[8] Are you satisfied?... This will not prevent God from taking me when He wills; since I am putting forth all my efforts to be a very little child, I have no preparations to make. Jesus Himself will have to pay the expenses of the journey and the cost of entering heaven....

Adieu, dear little sister, I love you I believe more and more....

Your little sister,
Thérèse of the Child Jesus
rel. carm. ind.

Sister Genevieve is very happy with your letter;[9] she will answer you the next time. All five of us kiss you....

* Autograph.
1. The youngest: "inferiority" which was not counterbalanced, within the family circle, by her seniority in profession with regard to Sister Geneviève (Céline) and Marie of the Eucharist (Marie Guérin), not even by her position as aide to the mistress of novices. See LT 173, note 6 and CJ 2.9.4, note 2.
2. This was July 10. On that day, Sister Geneviève received a letter from Léonie, written on July 9, who was insisting: "When you write me, my dear, give me precise news about little Thérèse; do not hide anything from me, I beg you; I want to know everything." This request could have brought about the search for the July 1 letter, which had remained in the hands of one or other of Thérèse's sisters or her cousin.
3. See LC 161, note 4.
4. A comparison used again and developed in LT 258; it is possible that Thérèse had borrowed it from *Avis spirituels pour la sanctification des âmes* (author unknown): "If we only knew how pleasing confidence is to God, we would practice it totally, we would act with Him as a thoughtless child does with its mother. I recommend this precious thoughtlessness of the child who loves his mother tenderly and expects everything from her. The mother prefers this thoughtless child who commits so many faults, and after each one returns to admit it and cry over it; she loves this child more than his brother who, less

culpable, retires into a corner and dares not appear when he had offended." (Chapter CCX, *Confidence in God's mercy must surpass fear of His justice*, pp. 355 ff., t. I, Ed. Jules Gervais, 15ᵉ ed., Paris, 1883.) See Ms. B, p. 198: "...instead of hiding in a corner and weeping over its misery."

5. Isaias 49:15.

6. See Canticle of Canticles 4:9; and LT 164, note 1.

7. See LT 192. The postscript of June 29, 1896, attributed to Thérèse in the first edition of the *Lettres* (CLXIX, p. 319) was written by Sister Marie of the Sacred Heart. See LC 170, note 6.

8. "Sister Thérèse of the Child Jesus is better, but she still looks unwell. She is no longer suffering in her chest, nor does she cough at all. There is a change for the better. Our Mother takes care of her so well that this is not surprising" (Marie of the Eucharist to Mme. Guérin, July 3, 1896; see DE, p. 807). On the development of Thérèse's illness, see Appendix. At this time, Sister Marie of the Sacred Heart was overfeeding her little sister according to her own tastes. See CJ 20.8.18. This overfeeding brought on attacks of indigestion.

9. Letter of July 9; see note 2.

LT 192   **From Thérèse to Mme. Guérin.**

July 16, 1896
→ LC lost

J.M.J.T.

Jesus †   July 16, 1896

Dear Aunt,

I would have liked to be the first to come to you, but there remains for me only the sweet and lovable duty of thanking you for the beautiful letter I received.

How kind you are, dear Aunt, to think of your little Thérèse. Ah! I assure you, you are not dealing with an ungrateful person.

I would like to tell you something new, but I rack my brains in vain, absolutely nothing comes except tenderness for my dear relatives...and this thing is far from being new since it is as *old as myself*....

Dear Aunt, you ask me to give you some news about my health just as I would to a Mamma; this is what I shall do, but if I tell you I am in excellent health, you will not believe me, so I shall allow the famous Doctor de Cornière to speak, to whom I had the *distinguished honor* of being presented yesterday in the speakroom.[1] This illustrious personage, after having *honored* me with a look, declared that I looked well![2] This *declaration* has not hindered me from thinking I will soon be allowed to go to heaven with the little angels,[3] not because of my health but because of another *declaration* made today in the Carmel's chapel by M. l'abbé Lechêne.... After having shown us the illustrious origins of our Holy Order, after having compared us to the Prophet Elias fighting against the priests of Baal,[4] he *declared*: "Times similar to those of Achab's persecution were about to begin again."[5] We seemed to be flying already to martyrdom....

What joy, dear little Aunt, if our whole family were to enter heaven on the same day. It seems to me that I see you smile...perhaps you think this honor is not reserved for us.... What is certain about this is that, all together or one after another, we shall one day leave the exile for the homeland and then we shall take delight in all the things for which heaven will be the *prize*[6] . . . for having *taken* some medicine on the days prescribed as well as for having been at Matins in spite of a sad face, or for having hunted for some rabbits[7] and gathered some oats. . . .

I see to my great sorrow that it is impossible for me to say anything which makes any common sense; it is certainly because I wanted to write many things to little Aunt, whom I love so much. . . .

Fortunately, Sister Marie of the Eucharist will make up for my poverty, she is my only consolation in my extreme indigence. . . . We are always together at our work,[8] and we understand each other very well. I assure you, neither of us encourages sadness; we have to be careful not to speak useless words, for after each *meaningful* sentence there always comes a little amusing refrain which we have to keep for the time of recreation.

Dear Aunt, I beg you to offer my love to all the dear inhabitants at La Musse, especially to Uncle, whom I ask to hug you tightly for me.

> Your little daughter who loves you,
> Thérèse of the Child Jesus
> rel. carm. ind.

* Autograph
1. Thérèse seems not to have been looked after up to this time except by Doctor la Néele. They "presented" her to the official doctor of the Community on the occasion of the latter's visit to a patient, no doubt Sister Marie-Antoinette, a young extern Sister, seriously stricken with tuberculosis (died on November 4, 1896).
2. A judgment confirmed by the contemporaneous photographs of Thérèse, VTL, no. 29 (see LC 165, note 5), and nos. 36, 37, 38. We notice, on the last one, a slight puffiness in her face.
3. See next to the last stanza of *To Throw Flowers!* This poem was sent to Mme. Guérin; see LC164, note 4.
4. See III Kings 18:20-40.
5. Since the election of Felix Faure to the presidency (January 17, 1895), who was supported by the conservatives and moderates, France was in its third administration. The first (under Ribot, January-October 1895) sought for a religious appeasement by substituting for the vex-

atious law called *d'accroissement* (December 28, 1880) the law called *d'abonnement* (April 16, 1895), which lowered the tax imposed on religious congregations to 30% of the value of their movable and immovable property. But the congregations carried on for the most part a passive fiscal resistance. The second administration (under Bourgeois, October 1895 - April 21, 1896) was noted for its anticlericalism: nine out of eleven of its members were freemasons. The third, in power in July 1896, was headed by Méline, a conciliator, vilified for this reason by all parties. Moreover, preparations for the fourteenth centenary of Clovis' baptism (December 25, 496) were the occasion of important religious demonstrations that aroused strong feelings on both sides.

6. A reference to the humorous hymn made up a few days earlier by Sister Marie of the Eucharist and the other novices during the washing (unpublished letters of the Guérin family, July 6-7, 12). There is a draught extant of it written by Thérèse, who may have shared in its composition. It outlines the day of a Carmelite nun in twenty-one couplets, according to the tune of *Le ciel en est le prix.*

7. This has a reference to Francis La Néele, an expert hunter. During his stay at La Musse, his sister-in-law, Marie of the Eucharist, had him supply game for the chaplain and the Carmelites dispensed from abstinence, Thérèse being one of them: "During the summer of this same year 1896, she was affected by a light dry and persistent cough. She was allowed meat for several weeks."

8. In the sacristy. Thérèse occupied her time in this task, painting, and as aide to Sister Marie of Saint Joseph in the linen room; see p. 845. Sister Marie of the Eucharist wrote in April: "I have changed assignments; I am now in the sacristy. This is a task I like very much.... I also do the choir, keeping it clean" (to Mme. Pottier, Céline Maudelonde, April 28, 1896).

LD   *From l'abbé Bellière to Mother Agnes of Jesus.*

July 21, 1896   The first letter from this seminarian since taking up military duty (November 12, 1895).

                                        Caen, Tuesday evening[1]

Reverend Mother Superior,[2]

It has been a very long time since I had the pleasure of chatting with you, but, if I am doing so today, it is for the purpose of begging once again.

I am a soldier, Mother, and this time has no value for the seminarian. I have had many a fall, many unheard of stupidities, in the midst of this world which has taken hold of me again. I just committed the most beautiful of all[3], but it is so powerful that it will be the last, for it is correcting me. I am plunged into a deplorable situation, and my dear sister, Thérèse of the Child Jesus, must tear me away from it, at all costs; she must do violence to heaven which will allow itself to be toutched by her prayers and her penance. Mother, she must or I am lost, and all the more since this will be for a greater good. Tell her she must. Pardon me for my insistence, and pray for me yourself, good Mother. Have your Community pray for me, my needs are great and *pressing*.

Pardon me, have pity on me, and help me, I beg you, in the name of the Virgin of Carmel and St. Joseph.

I dare to call myself, reverend Mother, your very obedient son.

You remember me who wrote you last November,[4] begging you to give me a sister among your religious. You were so kind. Be this more than then, if possible. If you only knew how I need divine help.

All yours, Mother, in Jesus Christ.

Maurice Bellière
Seminarian
Soldier, *5ᵉ de Ligne*
4ᵉ Compagnie
Caen

* Autograph.
1. Date written in by Thérèse on the autograph: "July 21, 1896" (date of writing). Letter kept among her personal papers.
2. L'abbé Bellière was unaware of the change in superiors.
3. "The most beautiful of stupidities" could have been his plan of renouncing his vocation to the priesthood to enter Military School; see LC 177, note 7.
4. October 15, 1895; see p. 918.

LC 165   *From P. Roulland to Thérèse.*

July 23, 1896   Letter dated in pencil by Thérèse. The envelope
is stamped: Meudon 10ᵉ 23 JUIL 96-Lisieux 3ᵉ
24 JUIL 96

Seminary of the
Foreign Missions   †
128, rue du Bac
     Paris

Sister,

By the graces God has given us, my family and myself, during
my stay in Normandy, you foresaw that the naturally painful separation could, nonetheless, be effected as well as possible. I was to leave
on Friday[1] at four in the afternoon. During the meal, we were all
happy until three o'clock, but afterward sadness began to settle in:
from time to time I had tears in my eyes. At four o'clock, I made
a sign to a friend: he went out to hitch up the horse, and ten minutes
later the wagon arrived in front of the room where we were gathered
together. All understood: my parcels were carried out, and I stood
up; in the kitchen, my father, my mother, two aunts, a cousin, and
a friend were on their knees. I gave all my blessing; I went out, closing the door behind me and was on my way. My mother came out;
a person who was in the wagon with me said: bid a last *adieu* to
your mother, and I did not do it. I wanted as much as possible not
to look back. St. Francis Xavier had left without bidding *adieu* to
his mother.

When passing through Lisieux, I saw the Carmel. I saw that house
which is so dear to me now. I blessed Sister Thérèse of the Child
Jesus and good Mother Marie de Gonzague.[2]

Arriving at Paris, I learned that my departure first set for August
26 would take place on July 29. I expect, then, soon the linens I used at my First Mass and which have been washed by you.[3] In all
simplicity, I tell you that at the moment I have everything I need;
later on when I shall need some linens, I will tell you with the same
simplicity. However, if you have a Life of St. Teresa, I would gladly accept it now to read during the trip. Am I not in some way a

child of Carmel, have I not for a sister in Jesus a daughter of St. Teresa?

I am leaving with the intention of not having more self-will in the hands of my bishop than a corpse would have; I leave happy because I know our apostolate, that is, yours and mine, will be blessed by God. On the mountain of Carmel, a soul will be praying for the success of the weapons of him who will be fighting in the field.[4] Each day, at the Holy Sacrifice, I will pronounce the name of Sister Thérèse of the Child Jesus. If as *you* hope you go to heaven before me, I will continue to pray for you. I will say: "I offer this Sacrifice for the repose of the soul of my sister in Jesus," begging the Blessed Virgin to do what she wills with the merits you will no longer need.

This is my address on the Missions:

P. Roulland, miss. ap., Su-Tchuen or.[5]

Foreign Missions, 128 rue du Bac

Paris

(a fifteen-cent stamp will suffice)

I beg Reverend Mother to accept my sentiments of deep respect and real gratitude.

And you, Sister, I shall never forget your last words: *A Dieu, mon frere.*[6]

In union of prayers and sacrifices for God and souls; *au revoir*, close to Jesus in the Eucharist, later on in heaven.[7]

A. Roulland

miss. ap.

Su-Tchuen or.

*   Autograph.
1.   Friday, July 17, since he wrote on the 16th to Mother Marie de Gonzague. See p. 1266.
2.   He wrote: "Mère Louis de Gonzague" (French title for St. Aloysius Gonzaga).
3.   The altar linens made by Thérèse; see LT 189.
4.   See LT 189 and the quotation from Exodus 17:11-13.
5.   "*Missionnaire apostolique au Su-Tchuen oriental.*" The missionary was aware of his assignment on the day of his ordination, June 28. He must have spoken to Thérèse about it on July 3 (see *below*, note

6), for she speaks of Su-Tchuen in her poem of July 16: *To Our Lady of Victories, Queen of Angels, Apostles, and Martyrs* (P 31, stanza 6). In the photograph called "Thérèse with the Scroll" (VTL, no. 29), the book resting on the branch of lilies is entitled: *The Mission of Su-Tchuen in the XVIIIth century-Life and Apostolate of Msqr. Pottier*, by . Guiot (Tequi, Paris, 1892). This detail and the comparison with other documents of the time would suggest that we place this photograph in July 1896 (and not on March 17, 1896, as VTL 2, p. 71 has it, based on inexact information from Sister Geneviève).

6. Words concluding the July 3rd visit: "That day I spoke with Sister Thérèse of the Child Jesus in the speakroom, before and after my Mass" (Père Roulland, PA, 55). On October 29, 1926, P. Roulland recalled a detail of this interview: "Before this Mass, the good Mother Prioress was kind enough to arrange an interview for me, in her presence, with 'my little sister'; and so that I might have the consolation of getting a glimpse of her, little as it was, otherwise than just behind the veiled grille of the speakroom, she was kind enough to tell me that Sister Thérèse, in her function as sacristan, would remain kneeling at the Communion grille as a sign that all had received. On her part, Thérèse added graciously: 'Our Mother will be the first to receive Communion.'"

7. Thérèse answered (see LC 166) no doubt on July 27 or 28, but her letter was not preserved. The following explanation was given: "When he was a missionary in China, a young native girl, gravely ill, was dying; the Reverend Father brought her one of his letters written by Sister Thérèse of the Child Jesus, and this young girl, having died, was buried with the precious letter." (Testimony of Mother Edbert-Marie of the Sisters of St. Thomas of Villeneuve, November 5, 1962.)

LC 166   *From P. Roulland to Thérèse.*

July 29, 1896
→ LT lost

†

My Sister in Jesus,[1]

I just received the Life of St. Teresa and the short note your Reverend Mother allowed you to write me.

I cannot give you any details. At Marseilles, I shall have more time. Today, Wednesday, at nine in the morning, I receive my faculties as Missionary; at eleven, I bid farewell to my confrères; at three, the farewell ceremony; at eight, departure from the seminary; at nine, departure from the station at Lyons; at Marseilles, this is my address until Sunday: *rue Nau 28*. I embark on Sunday[2] at four o'clock.

I never doubted, Sister, that your fervor was lasting; besides, I need your prayers today, tomorrow, and the rest of my life.

Today, Wednesday, at my last Mass in the Seminary, I said: "My God, set my Sister on fire with Your love,"[3] and I will continue this all my life.

I offered the Sacrifice in union with you.

A Dieu. In Apostolic union.[4]

I bless you.
A. Roulland
miss. ap.
Su-Tchuen or.

* Autograph.
1. This letter is on the second page of a double sheet; on the first, addressed to Mother Marie de Gonzague, Thérèse wrote in pencil: "July 29."
2. August 2; a day of "great sadness" for Thérèse. See Ms. C, p. 216.
3. According to Thérèse's own request in her first letter, LT 189. This prayer, taken seriously by them both, became a kind of password in their correspondence; see LC 171, 175; LT201, 221, note 12.
4. P. Roulland sent his photograph in exchange for that of Thérèse, sent in her own letter of July 27 (?); see LT 193, note 1.

LT 193   **From Thérèse to Pére Roulland.**

July 30, 1896   Letter addressed to Marseilles; see LC 167.
→ LC 166

J.M.J.T.

Carmel of Lisieux   July 30, 1896

Jesus †

Brother,

You allow me, do you not, to give you no longer any other name, since Jesus has seen fit to unite us by the bonds of the appostolate?

It is very sweet for me to think that from all eternity Our Lord has formed this union which must save souls for Him and that He created me to be your sister....

Yesterday, we received your letters; our good Mother brought *you* joyfully into the cloister. She is allowing me to keep my brother's photograph;[1] this is a *very special* privilege. A Carmelite does not even have the portraits of her closest relatives, but our Mother knows that your picture, far from reminding me of the world and earthly affections, will raise my soul to higher realms, and will make it forget itself for the glory of God and the salvation of souls. Thus, Brother, while I shall cross the ocean in your company, you will remain close to me, well hidden in our poor cell....

All that is around me reminds me of you. I have attached the map of Su-Tchuen[2] on the wall where I work,[3] and the picture you gave me[4] is resting always on my heart in the book of the Gospels which never leaves me. When I placed it there at random, here is the passage on which it fell: "He who has left all to follow me will receive a hundredfold in this world and eternal life in the world to come."[5] Mt 19:29 These words of Jesus are already realized in you, for you tell me: I leave happily."[6] I understand that this joy must be totally spiritual; it is impossible to leave one's father, mother, and country, without experiencing all the rendings of separation.... Oh, Brother! I am suffering with you, I am offering with you your great sacrifice, and I beg Jesus to pour out His abundant consolations on your dear relatives, while awaiting the heavenly union where we shall see them rejoicing in your glory which, drying their tears forever, will fill them with joy throughout a blessed eternity.

This evening, during my prayer, I meditated on some passages from Isaias which appeared to me so appropriate for you that I cannot refrain from copying them for you.

"Enlarge the place of your tent.... For you shall pass on to the right hand, and to the left, and your seed shall inherit the Gentiles, and shall inhabit the desolate cities.⁷.. Lift up your eyes and look around you; all those whom you see assembled are coming to you; your sons will come from afar and your daughters will come from all sides to find you. Then you will see this extraordinary multiplication; your astonished heart will be enlarged when the multitude of the shores of the sea and all that is great among the nations will have come to you."⁸

Is not this the hundredfold promised? And can you not cry out in your turn: "The spirit of the Lord is upon me, because the Lord has annointed me. He has sent me to preach his word, to heal those who are broken-hearted, to give freedom to those who are in chains and to console those who weep... I shall rejoice in the Lord, for he has clothed me with the garments of salvation and with the robe of justice he has covered me. For as the earth brings forth her bud, so shall the Lord God make justice to spring forth and praise before all the nations.⁹... My people will be a people of the just, they will be the shoots that I have planted.... I shall go into the most remote isles, to those who have never heard anyone speak of the Lord. I shall announce his glory to the nations, and I shall offer them as a gift to my God."¹⁰

If I wanted to copy out all the passages that touched me the most, I would have to have much time. I end, but beforehand I still have a request to make to you. When you will have a free moment, I would like you to write me the principal dates of your life. I would be able in this way to unite myself specially to you to thank God for the graces He has given you.

A Dieu, Brother...distance will never be able to separate our souls, death itself will make our union more intimate. If I go to heaven soon, I will ask Jesus' permission to go to visit you at Su-Tchuen, and we shall continue our apostolate together. In the meanwhile, I shall always be united to you by prayer, and I ask Our Lord never to allow me to rejoice when you are suffering. I would even wish that my brother always have consolation, and I trials; perhaps this is selfish?... But, no, since my only *weapon*[11] is love and suffering and since your sword is that of the word[12] and apostolic works.

Once again, *a Dieu*, Brother; please bless her whom Jesus has given you as a sister.

Thérèse of the Child Jesus
of the Holy Face
rel. carm. ind.[13]

*   Autograph.

1.   P. Roulland had written: "Since you permit a sister to cross the ocean with a brother, you will permit a brother to cross the grille of the cloister" (to Mother Marie de Gonzague, July 29, 1896; see VT, July 1963, p. 118). Thérèse kept this photograph on her desk, along with this note: "This photograph does not belong to me. Our Mother told me *to keep it for her* on our desk; she will take it when she needs it. Thérèse of the Child Jesus, rel. carm. ind." On the meaning of this notice, see LC 171, note 2. The photograph of the Carmelite, sent July 27, was 13 x 18 cms., a picture of "Thérèse with the rosary" (VTL, no. 37). On the back of the supporting cardboard, Thérèse had written the principal dates of her life.

2.   A geographical chart of this mission made by Père Launay in 1892.

3.   In which workroom? We must certainly exclude the paint workshop (see LT 192, note 8), open to the Sisters coming for art supplies. Did Thérèse place it in the sacristy where she was working alone? We do not know, but it is somewhat probable. There remains the linen room where she went as aide. It would not be unlikely that, when bringing her map of Su-Tchuen there (without revealing her spiritual association with P. Roulland), she may have tried to share her missionary zeal with Sister Marie of Saint-Joseph, her disciple; see LT 194, note 2. This is only a supposition.

4.   A picture-souvenir of his ordination, with this inscription on the back: "Here below, let us work together-In heaven, we shall share the reward."

5.   See Matthew 19:29.

6.   See LC 165. P. Roulland repeated this assurance to Mother Marie de Gonzague, August 1.

7.   See Isaias 54:2-3.

8. See Isaias 60:4-5.
9. See Isaias 61:1, 10, 11, 9. All these references appear on pp. 64-65 of Thérèse's scripture notebook. (See Mss. I, p. 37). The light variations and breaks are significative of the writer's care in adapting them to her correspondent.
10. See Isaias 66:19-20. This version differs notably from that of her scripture notebook mentioned above. "The most remote isles" appears again in Ms. B, p. 193.
11. Intentional underlining. See *Introduction*, p. 74. Probable reference to the poem *To Throw Flowers!* This was copied out by Thérèse at the end of Mother Geneviève's circular and sent to P. Roulland; see LC 167, note 3.
12. See Ephesians 6:17, quoted in the Carmelite Rule.
13. The fourth page of this letter is written by Mother Marie de Gonzague: "Dear child, man proposes and God disposes. I wanted to write you a long letter, and see how Jesus gives me a little suffering hindering me from writing. I am an old worn-out machine, my chest plays tricks on me from time to time, but I will offer up all to win souls our dear apostle will evangelize. You have a very fervent helper who will neglect nothing for the salvation of souls. The dear little thing is all for God!...

"We are following you, the ocean will not separate our souls.

"If you pass by Saïgon, do not forget the Carmel and tell the Reverend Mother Prioress and Sister Anne of the Sacred Heart that our hearts never leave them.

"*A Dieu en Dieu*. In heaven, we shall meet again, on the foreign soil, union of souls.

"Your old Mother, Sister Marie de Gonzague, r. c. ind.''

LC 167 *From P. Roulland to Thérèse.*

August 1, 1896   The date is on the first page, addressed to Mother
→ LT 193   Marie de Gonzague (see VT, July 1963, p. 119).

Sister,

I just read your letter; thank you. I would treat you as selfish if I did not know that a missionary's life, like that of a Carmelite, is necessarily accompanied by sufferings. But these crosses, if I remain faithful to the traditions of my forebears, I will carry with a smile.

There is one cross I beg God not to impose on me: that of being assigned to a mission seminary, that, especially, of returning as director at the Paris seminary, and nevertheless when my confessor left me at the station, he said: "*Au revoir, au revoir,* you hear what I am saying to you." On the other hand, he told me the Directors had very special reasons for sending me to Eastern Su-Tchuen. To this desire I add: "May the will [of God][1] be done.

During the crossing, I shall read the passage from Isaias, and God will give birth in my heart, I hope, to some of the sentiments which have set your own on fire.

I shall read, too, the note on the Mother Foundress of the Lisieux Carmel[2] and also the poem at the end.[3] I have already read and reread the last poem. I would like to be able to respond to it, but God wills me to be prosaic: I enjoy, however, the beauties of a poem coming from one's heart.

When I left Paris, I made my sacrifice in union with you, at Marseilles I shall do the same. My sorrows, my joys, these I will tell you, and we shall weep and rejoice together. I received your *Life of St. Teresa*; *we* shall read it during the crossing. You have recived, I hope, *The Soul of a Missionary*;[4] in it you will find the details of the departure ceremony. I recommend to your prayers a young girl from my region; she is not made for the world. Her great desire is to become an Augustinian. Let us force God to have her enter soon.

A Dieu, Sister; you are crossing the ocean and I am remaining at Carmel,[5] or rather we are crossing the ocean and we are remaining at Carmel.

A Dieu, Sister. United in the Sacrifice, we shall be united in heaven, and there I will present to you my good father and my generous mother.

I bless you.

> A. Roulland
> miss. ap.
> Su-Tchuen or.

This is my address: P. Roulland, miss. ap. au Su-Tchuen
Foreign Missions, 128 Paris
(postage: 15 cents)

*   Autograph.

1.   Words omitted.

2.   Mother Geneviève's circular or obituary account. At the beginning of this booklet, Thérèse wrote: "To Very Reverend Father Roulland, missionary apostolic to Eastern Su-Tchuen, and on the flyleaf: "The second edition of the circular letter addressed to all the monasteries of Carmel, 1891, on the occasion of the death of the Revered Mother Geneviève of St. Teresa, Foundress of the Lisieux Carmel." This new edition came out the preceding June 21.

3.   There were some blank pages at the end of the bound circular, and Thérèse wrote out eleven of her poems on them. This is the list she made up from memory eight months later: *The Answer of St. Agnes; Gloss on the Divine, of Our Father Saint John of the Cross; My Song for Today; To Live by Love; Remember!; Saint Cecilia; To the Sacred Heart; To the Holy Face; To Théophane Vénard; Prayer of Saint Joan of Arc in Prison; To Throw Flowers.* This list refers to Poems 22, 26, 5, 15, 21, 3, 20, 17, 44, to RP 3 (a fragment), and 30. Thérèse forgot to mention: *To Our Lady of Victories, Queen of Apostles and Martyrs,* the last poem read and reread by P. Roulland as he states in his letter. The erroneous mention of the poem: *To Théophane Vénard,* composed only on February 2, 1897, and enclosed in LT221 (March 19, 1897), would lead us to think she made up the list around Easter 1897, or even later. Six of these poems and part of *To Live by Love* were returned to the Lisieux Carmel.

4.   *L'Ame d'un Missionnaire, Vie du P. Nempon, Missionnaire apostolique du Tonkin occidental,* by G. Monteuuis (3rd ed., Victor Retaux et Fils, Paris, 1895). The copy has the inscription: "" *R. Ap. Reconnaissance. A. Roulland. e. de M. Miss. ap. Su-Tchuen or.*" See LT201.

5.   Reference to their exchange of photographs; see LT 193, note 1.

LC 168   *From Mme. La Néele to Thérèse.*

August 22 (?),   Date deduced from the content; see note 2.
1896

Dear little Thérèse,

How kind you are for having addressed such a charming poem
to me,[1] I do not know how to thank you for it. I cried when reading
it, but these were not tears of sorrow, there was something sweet
that made me shed them. So I eagerly come to express a big "thank-
you" for the pleasure you gave me. Alas! good Jesus is trying us
at this moment; our dear parents are laid up. There is a little improvement today, but I fear they will be sick a long time. We began
a novena to Our Lady of Lourdes the day before yesterday, and each
day I give them a little bit of Lourdes water. Since the novena began,
Papa has not had any sharp attacks. I am at Lisieux since Friday;[2]
I leave again Monday morning and will come back on Thursday.
You can see I am leading a nomadic life. Léonie is taking good care
of Papa and Mamma; she is really kind and devoted and renders
them great service. Thank little Marie of the Eucharist for the
beautiful letter she wrote me and for her good wishes; I wept again
when reading what she had written on the picture of her reception
of the Habit. Decidedly, it has been a day of tears. The holy and
famous Doctor[3] was delighted; he asks me to thank his dear little
sister Thérèse of the Child Jesus very much.

I shall, then, profit from the confidences Jesus has given to you,
and I shall abandon myself completely to His holy will. He knows
much better than I what is necessary for me, and if our prayers are
not answered, it is no doubt because the object of my desires would
be an obstacle to my salvation. I will tell you, dear little Thérèse,
that God has given me the grace of resignation; at the beginning of
my marriage, I was acting like the Israelites in the desert, I was complaining, I was rebelling, and this was not advancing me in the least,
on the contrary. Now I am resigning myself. I shall not tell you that
I do not feel a pang of sorrow when seeing a little child in its mother's
arms, but I am no longer tempted to complain, and I seem to hear
the Blessed Virgin say to me: "Go to Holy Communion, go to the
holy Table, and I shall give you my dear little Jesus, then you will

no longer be alone, you will be happier than the happiest of mothers." I notice, dear little Thérèse, my letter is very poorly written, I beg you to pardon me. Léonie is busy in her room, and I am being continually disturbed by my dear patients. Kiss little Marie of the Eucharist and the three other little sisters, and tell them Francis has just arrived, and he has found my dear parents better. Thank good Mother Marie de Gonzague for her affectionate wishes, and tell her I am praying for her cure.[4]

A Dieu, dear little Thérèse. I hug you tightly, begging you to pray for me, for our dear little Jesus can refuse you nothing.

Jeanne La Néele

*   Autograph.

1.   There were two poems: 1)one directed to Doctor and Mme. La Néele (P 33, August 21, 1896); 2)*Confidence of Jesus to Thérèse*, addressed to Mme. La Néele (P 34, same date). Thérèse is consoling her cousin for not having a child..

2.   Friday, the 21st. She left on Monday, the 24th. The letter was written on August 22 or 23.

3.   Title of the acrostic dedicated to Francis La Néele by Thérèse (P 35, August 21, 1896)

4.   See LT 193, note 13.

"Love...the key to my vocation" (Ms. B, p. 194)
(September - December 1896)
Age twenty-three

*With the "letter to Sister Marie of the Sacred Heart,"
or better still, the letters, the* Correspondence *reached a high
point in September 1896. Attached for the most part to the*
Story of a Soul *in 1898, and restored in 1956 in its authentic form under the title of* Manuscript B, *this inexhaustible
text has been considered, for some decades, as a jewel of
Christian literature. The reintegration of the first part (the
second, chronologically, as we shall show) into the corpus
of the* Letters *(LT 196) will help us better explain its origin.
Here, we shall shed some light on the biographical context.*

*First, we should recall some facts during the autumn of
1896. There are no incidents of any importance:*

*1) During the first days of September 1896, a priest from
Paris, Roger de Teil, informed the Community about "his
work, his desires"*[1] *for the Cause of the sixteen Carmelite
nuns of Compiègne, martyred in 1794. His zeal aroused the
enthusiasm of Thérèse.*

*2) September 7, in the evening, Thérèse entered on a
retreat of ten days: her last private retreat.*

*3) September 8, she commemorated in solitude the sixth
anniversary of her Profession which had made her "a
Carmelite, a Spouse, and a Mother" (Ms. B, p. 192) in the
order of grace. This feast was a free day in the Carmel.
Thérèse used part of her free time to explain in writing her
"little doctrine," as Sister Marie of the Sacred Heart had
asked her previously. These pages are especially a recalling
to mind of the graces received during the past five months,
culminating in the discovery of her personal vocation "in
the heart of the Church": "MY VOCATION IS LOVE!"
(Ms. B, p. 194.)*

4) *During the following days, there is an exchange of notes or letters with her older sister, Marie, and probably with Sister Marie of Saint-Joseph.*

5) *September 18, Thérèse returned to Community life. She even resumed (at this time or shortly afterward, see p. 1025) the regular observance from which she had been dispensed ever since spring because of her health. Furthermore, she practiced supererogatory mortifications. The incident of the iron cross could date from this time.*

6) *From October 8-15, the Community retreat. To the preacher, Père Godefroid Madelaine (who had already given a triduum, June 22-24), Thérèse confided her temptations against faith. On his advice, she carried the* Credo *permanently on her heart: she had chosen to write it out in her own blood.*

7) *October 31, the arrival of the first mail from China, from P. Roulland. "Our Mother's missionary" narrated, among other things, his visit to the Saïgon Carmel. He spoke on behalf of the Saïgon prioress, who was seeking personnel from France. Thérèse asked herself: Is there not here a providential sign for her? A novena for this intention soon brought her the answer (p. 1025).*

8) *November 4, the death of Sister Marie-Antoinette, extern Sister, taken at the age of thirty-five by tuberculosis.*

9) *On the family level, in preparation for the feast day of Mme. Guérin, anticipated on November 14, two group-photographs were taken: the five Martin-Guérin cousins in their work as sacristans (VTL, nos. 39 and 40).*

We do not know to what a degree or in what a perspective the Carmelites of Lisieux continued their interest in Diana Vaughan. September 29 was an important date in this affair. To say nothing of the birth of the Antichrist's great-

grandmother which was to have taken place on that same day at Jerusalem, according to the hair-raising "revelations" circulating, we must mention the antimasonic congress gathered at Trent. The most serious among the investigators finally opened their eyes: "a colossal hoax," stated the correspondent of the Kolnische Volkszeitung. And a few weeks later, Mother Agnes of Jesus was still asking: "Have you any recent documents concerning Diana Vaughan?" (To M. Guérin, December 6, 1896.) Was this the curiosity of the believer or the skeptic?

At least three of Thérèse's correspondents call for some remarks, for she was exercising a kind of spiritual maternity regarding each of them in varying degrees:

1) L'abbé Bellière, *age twenty-two. After the salutary experience of the barracks, he returned to the studious atmosphere of the seminary. Mother Marie de Gonzague judged that the hour had come to entrust him directly to Thérèse. The latter addressed her first lines to him on October 21, in a small, reserved handwriting. Up to his summer vocation of 1897, she wrote him bimonthly.*

2) Sister Marie of the Sacred Heart, *age thirty-six. After ten years or more of experience, she lost her illusions regarding P. Pichon's spiritual direction. Since 1894 she had come more and more under the influence of her goddaughter, Thérèse. Bothered by glaring faults, allergic to ascetical deeds of valor, she nonetheless coveted "the precious pearl," "the art of loving" (LC 169). Certain indications give us the impression that she has recently read the copybook of memories dedicated by Thérèse to Mother Agnes of Jesus at Marie's request (p. 886). In her turn, she wanted "to have something" from the retreatant (LC 169). Sufficiently great-souled to see that she has been given "lines that are not from earth but an echo from God's Heart" (LC 170)—would Thérèse have confided them to Mother Agnes?—Marie is also too great a soul to desire "what*

sparkles." She needs, with her sister's help, to overcome her prejudices and fears in order to come to "the blind hope" in the mercy of Jesus "who wills to give us heaven gratuitously" (LT 197).

3) Sister Marie of Saint-Joseph, *age thirty-eight. Having lost her mother when she was only nine, retaining in the cloister a nostalgia for her family, this religious was not without intelligence, good memory, a taste for music, tenderhearted. However, she was impulsive, at times uplifted or depressed, subject to violent fits of temper. The Sisters kept her at a distance. Thérèse was against this kind of ostracism that served only to shut this poorly loved soul within herself. With Mother Marie de Gonzague's approval, Thérèse took the initiative to break the vicious circle: she offered to help this difficult Sister in her work in the linen room. Sharing in her work, she also watched over her sleeping hours (LT 199). She channeled this Sister's belligerent nature into the spiritual combat (ibid., and LT 200). She snatched her away from her self-centered attitude by associating her in her own missionary zeal (LT 194, 195). Under a childish appearance, the notes that she wrote to Sister Marie of Saint-Joseph gave the same teaching embodied in the most sublime pages of* Manuscript B.

In her obsession to rejoin, beyond space and time, "those who are far away," Thérèse did not abandon "those who are near." She placed herself even closer to "Sick souls"; for them she wanted "to reserve her smiles, her love, her kind attention" (see DE, p. 393; Ms. C, p. 245).

Was Thérèse thinking of Sister Marie of Saint-Joseph when she was transcribing this verse from Isaias in the autumn of 1896: "If you pour out your soul to one who is hungry, and if you fill with consolation the soul who is afflicted, your light will rise up in the darkness, and your darkness will be like noon"?[2] She commented "enthusiastically" to Céline on this chapter (see CSG, pp. 93-96). In accord with her own experience at this time, this

*text took on a prophetic value in the autumn of 1896. Still
intermittent in September, her spiritual darkness went on
increasing.*[3] *Thérèse reached the threshold of her last winter,
her longest night. At the hour when "the bright flame of
faith" (Ms. C, p. 212) was eclipsed for her, another light
arose in her heart like a glimmer of the dawn, whose
brightness will not cease to increase in the following months:
"the flames of love" (Ms. C, p. 220).*

1. Sister Marie of the Angels, in a letter to the Carmel of Compiègne, September 7, 1896.
2. See Isaias 58:10. The only scripture text copied out by the hand
   of Thérèse in her little notebook, before the excerpts from
   Théophane Vénard's letters, copied out in November 1896. We
   shall notice that the great discoveries of Thérèse are supported
   by texts from Isaias:
   1) the Suffering Servant in 1890 (chapter 53); 2) her "little way"
   in 1894-1896 (chapter 66: "As a mother caresses her child");
   3) her universal mission in 1896 (chapter 66: "And even to the
   most remote isles"); 4) fraternal love in 1896-1897 (chapter 58).
3. See Ms. B, p. 198: "*At times*, it seems not to believe anything
   else exists except the clouds that envelope it" (emphasis is ours).

LT 194   **From Thérèse to Sister Marie of Saint-Joseph.**
                    (Fragment.)

September 8-17   The first of a series of eight notes which were
(?), 1896   not dated; approximate dating. See note 1.
→ LC lost

I am delighted with the little child,[1] and the *one* who carries her
in His arms is still more delighted than I.... Ah! how beautiful is
the little child's vocation! It is not *one mission* that she must
evangelize[2] but *all missions*.[3] How will she do this?... By *loving*,
by *sleeping*, by THROWING FLOWERS to Jesus when He is asleep.
Then Jesus will take these flowers, and, giving them an inestimable
value, He will throw them in His turn;[4] He will have them fly over
all shores and will save souls (with the flowers, with *the love of the
little child*, who will see nothing but will always smile even through

her tears!.... (A child, a missionary, and even a warrior,[5] what a marvel!)

* Autograph.

1. This was Sister Marie of Saint-Joseph. This exchange of notes would suggest that one of the Sisters was on retreat: either Thérèse (who made her retreat, September 7-18), and the numerous points of contact of this note with Manuscript B reveal a chronological proximity, even a simultaneity of redaction between these writings; or Sister Marie of Saint-Joseph was on retreat; she undoubtedly chose a period close to the anniversary of her Profession (October 15, 1882), before or after the Community retreat preached from October 8 to 15. The chronological imprecision, then, can hardly exceed one month.

2. A possible reference to Su-Tchuen, the mission of P. Roulland adopted by Mother Marie de Gonzague and, consequently, by the whole Community (LT 193, note 3); or to Saïgon: the eventuality of a departure for the Carmels of Saïgon or Hanoï was in the air of the Lisieux Carmel during this second half of 1896. There was a question of it for Mother Agnes on August 2 (see Ms. C, p. 216), then for Sister Geneviève (*ibid.*, and LT 207, note 6), and for Sister Marie of the Trinity (Ms. C, p. 217); finally, in November, for Thérèse herself (p. 1025). Such a departure was inconceivable for Sister Marie of Saint-Joseph because of her temperament.

3. See Ms. B, p. 192.

4. See Ms. B, pp. 195-196; and the poem *To Throw Flowers*! An admirer of Thérèse, Sister Marie of Saint-Joseph copied out these poems for herself and her family.

5. See Ms. B, p. 192; LT 198 develops the symbolism of the warrior; and LT 206.

LT 195 **From Thérèse to Sister Marie of Saint-Joseph.**
(Fragments.)

September 8-17 Approximate date; see LT 194, note 1.
(?), 1896
→ LC lost

J.M.J.T.

Little brother[1] thinks just like the little child....

The most *painful*, the most LOVING martyrdom is ours since Jesus alone sees it.

It will never be revealed to creatures on earth, but when the Lamb will open the *book of life*,[2] what a surprise for the heavenly court to hear proclaimed with the names of missionaries and martyrs those of poor little children who will have never performed dazzling actions....

I am continuing to take care of the very sick toques.[3]

* Autograph.
1. This was Thérèse.
2. See Apocalypse 20:12; quoted in Ms. B, p. 193.
3. These were the white linen wimples. Their repair was one of Thérèse's tasks in the linen room. This written information, relative to their work, confirms the fact that one of them was on retreat and not going to the linen room during this period.

LC 169   *From Sister Marie of the Sacred Heart to Thérèse.*

Jesus!   Sunday, September 13

Dear little Sister,

I am writing not because I have something to tell you but to get something from you, from you who are so close to God, from you who are His little privileged spouse to whom He confides His secrets.... The secrets of Jesus to Thérèse are sweet, and I would like to hear about them once again.[1] Write me a short note. This is perhaps your last retreat, for the *golden cluster*[2] of Jesus must make Him desirous of gathering it. Little Thérèse must be tempting, up above, Jesus and Mary, Papa and Mamma, and the four little angels, and all the saints of heaven, and all the angels whom she has taken as her relatives.[3] Ask Jesus to love me, too, as He does his little Thérèse. Ah! the little Thérèse, she has grown up, grown up, and still she is always the little one, she is always the Benjamin, she is always the darling whom Jesus (just as in the past her dear little father) holds by the hand. As for herself, she still goes on, as in days gone by, gazing on the stars of heaven and closing her eyes to all things here below.[4] But her heavenly Spouse does not mislead her anymore than did her father.... He does not lead her toward precipices, He does not let her fall. Far from it!... He rocks her gently on His Heart, He smiles at her abandonment, and He gathers for her thousands and thousands of treasures.... Is He not her entire fortune? So little Thérèse is disturbed about nothing but loving her Jesus. Ah! I ask her to pray very much for her little godmother who loves her so much so that she, too, closing her eyes on all things of the earth, may no longer dream of anything but of looking up above, of working for heaven, of exercising herself in the art of loving. That is the precious pearl[5] that little Thérèse possesses. Little godmother would really like to enjoy this treasure with her.

Marie of the Sacred Heart
r. c. ind.

Our mother permits you to answer me by return mail.[6] These two little roses represent goddaughter and godmother.[7]

---

*   Autograph.
1.   The word "again" would suggest some previous confidences. After the death of Sister Marie of the Sacred Heart (January 19, 1940), Mother Agnes of Jesus placed this letter (LC 169) in an envelope on which she wrote: "I believe that it is to this letter from Sister Marie of the Sacred Heart that our little Saint responded by means of the sublime pages that terminate the *Story of a Soul*. Many times, Sister Marie of the Sacred Heart had asked her *viva voce* to write 'her little doctrine' for her. Thérèse took advantage of her retreat by doing this." We do not exclude the possibility that this note was the result of l'abbe Combes' question in 1947: "As for chapter XI (see Ms. B, p. 190), what is puzzling is the date of *September 8*. Could we suppose that Sister Marie of the Sacred Heart had already asked the same thing *viva voce*, and that her letter only confirms her request?" (To Sister Marie-Henriette, July 21, 1947.) An examination of Mother Agnes' handwriting, subject to rather considerable variations, brings forth no decisive argument for dating the above-mentioned note. In every way, the supposition of André Combes was the only one consonant with the reality of the facts. However, it was not retained at the time, and one had recourse to that of an antidated composition of the second part of Manuscript B. P. François de Sainte-Marie still held to this second hypothesis, though in a qualified form, in the edition of

the *Manuscrits autobiographiques* (1956) in facsimile; see Mss. I, p.
46 and his note 3. Conrad de Meester agreed with l'abbé Combes'
intuition (without having any knowledge of his correspondence) by
the simple internal and external criticism of the facsimile; he explained
in a satisfactory manner the history of its redaction in his *Dynamique
de la confiance*, pp. 233-236. See LT 196, note 14.

2. On Thérèse's "Coat of Arms," two branches surrounding the Holy
   Face and the Child Jesus are an image of Thérèse, who had only one
   desire on earth: to offer herself as a little cluster of grapes to refresh
   the Child Jesus, amuse Him, allow herself to be pressed according
   to His whims, and to quench the ardent thirst He experienced during
   His Passion. See CH 25.7.12, note 1.

3. See Ms. B, p. 196. We note here that Sister Marie of the Sacred Heart
   does not have Ms. B. in her hands as yet. Thérèse, then, confided
   to her orally her approach to the "blessed inhabitants of heaven."

4. See Ms. A, p. 42.

5. See Matthew 13:46.

6. Thérèse followed instructions: the "evening" she speaks about (LT
   196) is Sunday night, September 13.

7. Sentence written in pencil.

LT 196	**From Thérèse to Sister Marie of the Sacred Heart.**
September 13 (?), 1896 → LC 169	This letter, dated "September 1896" by Sister Marie of the Sacred Heart, forms the first part of Manuscript B, p. 187.

J.M.J.T.

Oh, dear Sister! you ask me to give you a souvenir of my retreat,
a retreat that perhaps will be the last.... Since our Mother permits
it, it is a joy for me to come to speak with you, who are my Sister
twice over, with you who lent me your voice, promising in my name
that I wanted to serve Jesus alone when it was not possible for me
to speak.... Dear little Godmother, the child whom you offered to
the Lord is the one who speaks to you this evening,[1] she is the one
who loves you as a child can love its Mother.... In heaven only you
will know all the gratitude that overflows my heart.... Oh, dear
Sister, you would like to hear the secrets Jesus confides to your lit-

tle daughter; these secrets He confides to you, I know, for you are
the one who taught me to gather the divine teachings. However, I
am going to try to stammer some words, although I feel that it is
impossible for human words to repeat things that the human heart
can hardly sense.[2] . . .

Do not believe I am swimming in consolations; oh, no! my consolation is to have none on earth. Without showing Himself, without
making His voice heard, Jesus teaches me in secret.[3] It is not by
means of books, for I do not understand what I am reading, but
at times a word like this one that I drew out at the end of prayer
(after having remained in silence and aridity) comes to console me:
"Here is the Master I am giving you; he will teach you all you must
do. I want to have you read in the book of life wherein is contained
the science of Love."[4] The science of Love, oh! yes, this word re-
sounds sweetly in the ear of my soul. I desire only this science. Having given all my riches for it, I look upon this as having given nothing,
just as the spouse in the sacred canticles.[5] . . . I understand so well
that it is only love that can make us pleasing to God that this love
is the only good that I ambition. Jesus is pleased to show me the
only road which leads to this divine furnace, and this road is the
abandonment of the little child who sleeps without fear in his Father's
arms. . . . "Whoever is a *little one*, let him come to me"[6] said the
Holy Spirit through the mouth of Solomon, and this same Spirit of
Love has said again: "Mercy is granted to little ones."[7] In His name,
the Prophet Isaias reveals to us that on the last day: "The Lord will
lead his flock into pastures, he will gather together the *little lambs*
and will press them to his bosom,"[8] and as though all these promises were not enough, the same Prophet, whose inspired glance was
already plunged into the eternal depths, cried out in the Lord's name:
"As a mother caresses her child, so will I comfort you; I will carry
you on my bosom, and I shall rock you on my knees."[9]

Oh, dear Godmother, after language like this, there is nothing to
do but be silent and weep with gratitude and love. . . . Ah! if all weak
and imperfect souls felt what the littlest of all souls feels, the soul
of your little Thérèse, not one would despair of reaching the summit of the mountain of love, since Jesus does not ask for great actions but only abandonment and gratitude, since He has said in Psalm
XLIX: "I have no need of the he-goats from your flocks, for all

the beasts of the forest belong to me, and the thousands of animals that graze on the hills; I know all the birds of the mountains.... If I were hungry, I would not tell you, for the earth and all it contains are mine. Must I eat the flesh of bulls and drink the blood of goats?...

"*Offer to God sacrifices of praise and thanksgiving.*"[10] See, then, all that Jesus is asking from us. He has no need of our works but only of our *love*, for this same God, who declares He has no need to tell us if He is hungry, did not hesitate *to beg* for a little water from the Samaritan woman. He was thirsty.... But when He said: "Give me to drink,"[11] it was the *love* of His poor creatures that the Creator of the universe was asking for. He was thirsty for love.... Ah! I feel it more than ever, Jesus *is parched*; He meets with only the ungrateful and indifferent among His disciples of the world and among His *own disciples* He finds, alas! few hearts that give themselves to Him without any reservations, that understand all the tenderness of His infinite Love. Dear Sister, how blessed we are to understand the intimate secrets of our Spouse. Ah! if you were willing to write all that you know about them, we would have beautiful pages to read, but I know that you prefer to keep in the bottom of your heart "the secrets of the King." You say to me: "It is honorable to publish the works of the Most High."[12] I find you are right in keeping silence, and it is only in order to please you that I write these lines, for I feel my powerlessness in repeating in earthly words the secrets of heaven. And, then, after having written out pages and pages, I would find that I had still not begun.... There are so many different horizons, so many infinitely varied nuances, that the palette of the heavenly Painter alone will be able, after the night of this life, to furnish me with colors capable of painting the marvels that He reveals to the eyes of my soul.

Dear Sister, you have asked me to write you about my dream and "my little doctrine" as you call it.[13]... I have done this in the following pages,[14] but so poorly that it seems to me impossible for you to understand. Perhaps you are going to find my expressions exaggerated.... Ah! pardon me, this must be laid to my unpleasant style; I assure you that there is no exaggeration in my *little soul*, that all is calm and at rest there....

When writing, I am speaking to Jesus; it is easier for me to ex-

(margin notes: Ps 49: 9-14 ; Tobit 12:7)

press my thoughts...which, alas, does not prevent their being poorly expressed!

*   Autograph.

1.   Very probably Sunday evening, September 13; see LC 169, note 6.

2.   Probable reference to I Corinthians 2:9.

3.   See Ms. A, p. 179.

4.   *Petit Bréviaire du Sacré-Coeur de Jésus*, p. 58; one of the few books Thérèse kept with her always. See CJ 6.8.3, note 1.

5.   See Canticle of Canticles 8:7.

6.   See Proverbs 9:4. These words, read in a notebook of Céline's (Mss. I, p. 37) during the winter of 1894-1895, kept Thérèse's attention from then onward; see LT 173, note 6. She copied them out on a date that is still uncertain (1895-1897) on the back of a breviary picture; see its facsimile in CSG, p. 38.

7.   See Wisdom 6:7. This quotation appears in Céline's notebook, p. 43, although under this form: "Mercy is granted to little ones."

8.   See Iasias 40:11. Text quoted under a different form in Thérèse's notebook (p. 76), itself a copy from Céline's notebook (p. 78). Identical transcription to that of this letter (LT 196) appears on the back of "Souvenir of the short exile" of the four little brothers and sisters who died at an early age (see CSG, pp. 37-39). Through cross-checkings we can date this picture between August 1896 and March 1897. See LT 197, note 11. This quotation appears in part on the back of the picture mentioned in note 6.

9.   See Isaias 66:13, 12. Different translation in Thérèse's notebook (p. 74; similar to that of Céline's, p. 77). Identical formulation on the back of the picture of note 6.

10.   See Psalm 49:9-13.

11.   See John 4:7; see LT 141, note 15. Similar expression in the *Consecration to the Holy Face* composed by Thérèse for August 6, 1896, according to all probability.

12.   See Tobias 12:7.

13.   This double request had been made orally; see LC 169, note 1.

14.   These four words are written between the lines. The "following pages" means the four folios of Ms. B, properly so-called, written on September 8. The expressions used in this termination of the letter show quite obviously that the letter (LT 196 or "the first part" of Ms. B) was written *after* the "second part" of the manuscript.

LC 170   *From Sister Marie of the Sacred Heart to Thérèse.*

September   Date deduced from the content; see note 5. It was
17(?), 1896   written at three separate times.
→ LT 196
and Mrs. B,
second part

† Jesus

Dear little Sister, I have read your pages burning with love for
Jesus. Your little godmother is *very happy* to possess this treasure
and very grateful to her dear little girl who has revealed the secrets
of her soul in this way. Oh! what should I say about these lines marked with the seal of love?... Simply one word concerning myself.
Like the young man in the Gospel, a certain feeling of sadness came
over me[1] in view of your extraordinary desires for martyrdom.[2] That
is the proof of your love; yes, you possess love,[3] but I myself! no,
never will you make me believe that I can attain this desired goal,
for I dread all that you love.

This is a proof that I do not love Jesus as you do. Ah! you say
you are doing nothing, that you are a poor weak little bird,[4] but
your desires, how do you reckon them? God himself looks upon them
as works.

I cannot speak to you any longer; I began this note this morning,
and I have not had a minute to finish it. It is five o'clock.[5] I would
like to tell your little godmother, in writing, if she can love Jesus
as you do.[6] But only briefly, for what I have is sufficient for my
joy and my sorrow. For my joy, when I see to what a degree you
are loved and privileged; for my sorrow, when I have a foreboding
of the desire that Jesus has to pluck His little flower! Oh! I wanted
to cry when I read these lines that are not from earth but an echo
from the Heart of God.... Do you want me to tell you? Well, you
are possessed by God, but what is called...absolutely possessed, just
as the wicked are possessed by the devil.

I would like to be possessed, too, by good Jesus. However, I love
you so much that I rejoice when seeing you are more privileged than
I am.

A short note for little godmother.

* Autograph.
1. See Matthew 19:22.
2. See Ms. B, p. 193
3. See Ms. B, p. 197: "Is *pure love* really in my heart?"
4. *Ibid*., p. 198: "I consider myself as a weak little bird covered only with a light down."
5. The hour of evening prayer, which was followed immediately by collation (supper, during the fast at six o'clock). Sister Marie of the Sacred Heart hoped that Thérèse would find this note before her last hours of free time: the hour of recreation (6:45 to 7:40) from which she was dispensed because she was on retreat, and the evening silence (from 8:00 to 9:00). In this way, she would be able to answer "in writing," according to Sister Marie's request, before coming out of retreat on Friday morning, September 18. It is this acceleration of the last exchanges of notes which gives preference to the date of September 17 as opposed to "September 16, 1896" written by Mother Agnes on the autograph. On the envelope containing this letter, Mother Agnes wrote: "This is the letter of Sister Marie of the Sacred Heart, dated September 17, 1896. Sister Marie of the Sacred Heart did not date her letter to Thérèse, which must have been written on September 15 or 16, 1896."
6. From this word onward, there is a change in handwriting because of another interruption. The entire end of the note is in vertical handwriting used very rarely by Sister Marie of the Sacred Heart. It is the same movement, more hurried, as that of the postscript in the letter dated June 29, 1896, which was attributed to Thérèse; see LT 191, note 7.

LT 197   **From Thérèse to Sister Marie of the Sacred Heart.**

September 17,
1896
→ LC 170

J.M.J.T.

Jesus †   September 17, 1896

Dear Sister, I am not embarrassed in answering you.... How can you ask me if it is possible for you to love God as I love Him?...

If you had understood the story of my little bird, you would not
have asked me this question. My desires of martyrdom *are nothing*;
they are not what give me the unlimited confidence that I feel in
my heart. They are, to tell the truth, the spiritual riches that *render
one unjust*,[1] when one rests in them with complacence and when one
believes they are *something great*.[2]... These desires are a *consolation* that Jesus grants at times to weak souls like mine (and these
souls are numerous), but when He does not give this *consolation*,
it is a grace of *privilege*. Recall those words of Father:[3] "The martyrs suffered with joy, and the King of Martyrs suffered with
sadness." Yes, Jesus said: "Father, let this chalice pass away from
me."[4] Dear Sister, how can you say after this that my desires are
the sign of my love?... Ah! I really feel that it is not this at all that
pleases God in my little soul; what pleases Him is *that He sees me
loving my littleness* and my *poverty, the blind hope that I have in
His mercy*.... That is my only treasure, dear Godmother, why would
this treasure not be yours?...

Are you not ready to suffer all that God will desire? I really know
that you are ready; therefore, if you want to feel joy, to have an
attraction for suffering, it is your consolation that you are seeking,
since when we love a thing the pain disappears.[5] I assure you, if we
were to go to martyrdom together in the dispositions we are in now,
you would have great merit, and I would have none at all, unless
Jesus was pleased to change my dispositions.

Oh, dear Sister, I beg you, understand your little girl, understand
that to love Jesus, to be His *victim of love*,[6] the weaker one is,
without desires or virtues, the more suited one is for the workings
of this consuming and transforming Love.[7]... The *desire* alone to
be a victim suffices, but we must consent to remain always poor and
without strength, and this is the difficulty, for: "The truly poor in
spirit, where do we find him? You must look for him from afar,"
said the psalmist.[8]... He does not say that you must look for him
among great souls,[9] but "from afar," that is to say in *lowliness*, Mt. 5:3
in *nothingness*.... Ah! let us remain then *very far* from all that
sparkles,[10] let us love our littleness, let us love to feel nothing, then
we shall be poor in spirit, and Jesus will come to look for us, and
however far we may be, He will transform us in flames of love....

Oh! how I would like to be able to make you understand what I feel!.... It is confidence and nothing but confidence that must lead us to Love.... Does not fear lead to Justice (1)?... Since we see the *way*, let us run together. Yes, I feel it, Jesus wills to give us the same graces, He wills to give us His heaven *gratuitously*.[11]

Oh, dear little Sister, if you do not understand me, it is because you are too great a soul...or rather it is because I am explaining myself poorly, for I am sure that God would not give you the desire to be POSSESSED by *Him*, by His *Merciful Love* if He were not reserving this favor for you...or rather He has already given it to you, since you have given yourself to *Him*, since you *desire* to be consumed by *Him*, and since God never gives desires that He cannot realize.[12]...

Nine o'clock is ringing, and I am obliged to leave you.[13] Ah, how I would like to tell you things, but Jesus is going to make you feel all that I cannot write....

I love you with all the tenderness of my GRATEFUL *little childlike heart*.

> Thérèse of the Child Jesus
> rel. carm. ind.

(1) To *strict justice* such as it is portrayed for sinners, but no this *Justice* that Jesus will have toward those who love Him.[14]

* Autograph.
1. See Luke 16:11 and Ms. B, p. 195.
2. A possible reference to the *Imitation of Christ* II, 11:5: "Let him not think that of great weight which might be esteemed great." This letter recaptures in more than one point the spirit of this chapter of the Imitation, especially verses 4 and 5.
3. This was Père Pichon, S.J.; the quotation comes from his Conference of the 7th day, October 13, 1887, of his retreat preached at the Lisieux Carmel. Thérèse copied out this passage in 1889. See VT, April 1968, pp. 139-140.
4. See Matthew 26:39.
5. See Saint Augustine, *De bono viduitatis*, 21, 26.
6. Following the example of Thérèse and Céline, Sister Marie of the Sacred Heart was the third to make her offering to Merciful Love

during the summer of 1895; see p. 809. At first she was somewhat cautious, as she recalled later on, according to the testimony of her infirmarian: "Today, I was talking with Sister Marie of the Sacred Heart about the 'Act of Oblation'; she told me that when she was tedding the hay in the meadow that Saint Thérèse of the Child Jesus— standing next to her—had asked her if she wanted to offer herself as a victim to the Merciful Love of God and that she answered: 'Certainly not. I am not going to offer myself as a victim; God would take me at my word, and suffering frightens me too much. In the first place, this word victim displeases me very much.' Then little Thérèse answered that she understood me, but that to offer oneself as a victim to God's Love was not at all the same thing as offering oneself to His justice, that I would not suffer more, that it was in order to be able to love God better for those who do not want to love Him. She was so eloquent that I allowed her to win me over, and I am not sorry either!'" (Notebook of Sister Marie of the Incarnation, June 6, 1934, p. 137.)

7. This statement must be placed within the context of LT 196 and 197 and LC 169 and 170 and especially Ms. B; see, for example: "It is my weakness itself that gives me the audacity to offer myself" (Ms. B, p. 195). It is henceforth superfluous to point out that this statement is as far removed from any quietism as it is from pharisaical virtue (see *Collected Letters of Saint Thérèse of Lisieux*, p. 289, note 52). The assurance which appears in this entire letter reminds us of the Apostle's triumphant cry: "When I am weak, it is *then* that I am strong" (II Corinthians 12:10). We are at the very heart of the "little way."

8. In reality, the author of the *Imitation of Christ* (II, 11:14), quoting Proverbs 31:10.

9. Concerning the antithesis: "little souls-great souls," see LT 224 and 226. Must we point out that Thérèse admired greatness of soul in others? She acknowledged it in her father (Ms. A, p. 127), in her uncle (Auust 22, 1897, DE. p. 754), in Marie of the Sacred Heart, here and in an acrostic of 1894: "In everything, she is essentially very big and generous" (P 6), and in DE, p. 653: "You have a noble nature!"

10. See LT 243 which repeats, in an abridged form this same lesson on spiritual poverty for Céline.

11. A probable reference to Romans 3:24, a verse which Thérèse wrote at this same time, preceded by Romans 4:6, 4, on the back of a picture already mentioned: "Souvenir of the short exile" (see LT 196, note 8). This is the text: "Blessed are those whom God holds as just without works, for regarding those who do works the reward is not

looked upon as a grace but as something due. . . . It is, then, *gratuitously* that those who do no works are justified by grace in virtue of the redemption, whose author is Jesus Christ.''

12. Concerning desire as the sign of what is *realizable* and guarantee of being heard, see LD, October 21, 1887; *Act of Oblation to Love*; LT 201; Ms. C, p. 207 and 250; LT 253; CJ 13.7.15, 16.7.2, 18.7.1, etc. At the beginning of Thérèse's scripture notebook, Céline had copied this thought from Saint John of the Cross: "*The more God wills to give us, the more He increases our desires*. . . . God is so pleased with the hope of a soul that is unceasingly turned to Him, never lowering its eyes to another object, that one can say in truth of this soul: It obtains *as much as* it hopes for.''

13. The bell was ringing for Matins. On the reliquary in which this letter is enclosed, Mother Agnes of Jesus had engraved: ''This response that so perfectly reveals the foundation of her teaching was written in haste before MATINS on September 17, 1896, in the light of a little lamp.'' No doubt, such precise information was given in order to excuse the poor handwriting and the mistakes in spelling and punctuation.

14. A note added by Thérèse. In the text she had crossed out ''to Justice.'' This addition could have been made subsequent to the letter: its more careful penmanship contrasts with that of the lines: ''Nine o'clock is ringing'' down to the word ''heart,'' words almost unformed.

LC 171   *From P. Roulland to Thérèse.*
September 25-26   Approximate date; see note 1.
1896

R. Ap.

Procurature of   R. Roulland Miss. ap.
the Foreign Missions   oriental Su-Tchuen
Shanghai   Seminary of the Foreign
                    Missions
                Paris, 128 rue du Bac
                (Postage: 15 cents)

Sister,

At last I have walked on the soil of China, I reached my new country of adoption. Our good mother will give you some details of my voyage which, I may add, went very well:[1] today's ships are real palaces compared to the sailing-vessels that brought our Society's first missionaries to the Orient. We suffered mostly from the heat. I am now at the Procurature of the Society's headquarters, awaiting impatiently the happy moment when they will tell me to leave for Su-Tchuen: the Blue River current is too rapid at present and to sail upstream would be courting shipwreck. I shall not speak to you as yet about this very interesting province. However, I did see four Christians from my mission and was charmed by them. When they learned I was their priest, they genuflected before me one after the other, and I was somewhat embarrassed during this ceremony so novel to me. The Father Procurator, who was with me, told me afterward: "On your mission, Chinese society is much more refined than it is here, and your Christians will have a respect and attachment for you that is unknown here." We are at Shanghai, an important port about two hours from the ocean, situated on a large river that is bigger than the Seine and called the Wampoo. There are two separate sections in this city: the section inhabited by Europeans and the Chinese section. The greater number of Europeans is English, consequently, Protestant: so we see ministers out walking somewhat solemnly with their wives and children. These ministers, as well as those of the whole Celestial Empire, place many obstacles to the missionary's activity, thanks to their pecuniary resources. The Chinese can move about in the streets, making their living this way: the sidewalks are covered with them, and the middle of the streets is congested with rickshaws, little wagons carrying one person and drawn by Chinese yellow-tanned in complexion. Another means of locomotion is the sedan chair: a large wheel is in the center, and on the right and left a kind of chair for sitting. Other Chinese, with the aid of bamboo poles, carry enormous loads. They run for an hour, transporting a load for six or seven French sous. Still imbued with European ways, I was pitying their lot, but a priest quickly reprimanded me: "You must treat them haughtily and never smile at them, otherwise they will laugh at you and you will lose all authority." I made the resolution to cast no judgment on a people with customs so different from our own and to learn only the facts. And I did not have to go far to learn them. The Chinese section of the city is close to the Procurature; we went for a walk there. We passed through the gateway of the fortifications. The largest streets are hardly two meters in width: on the right and left are shops, always shops. I wondered where all these merchants found buyers, but I shall know this later on. In the shops I saw fabrics, pipes, objects of superstition, fish that had a very disagreeable odor, etc. The Chinese looked at us curiously as we passed by; in their eyes we are devils from the West. We entered a pagoda, a sort of temple where the devil is worshipped under every form. It was disturbing to see these Chinese prostrate before these hideous forms ranged around a large room with walls blackened by the smoke from candles. I had my parasol and would have gladly taken the pleasure of striking all these devils, but I would have paid dearly for this pleasure. At last, we reached the Catholic church; it was formerly a pagoda and today, in place of the old Buddha, a statue of the Immaculate Virgin, extends her arms to us. The priest in charge of the parish also administers a school. What must be very difficult is that in these cities with such narrow streets there is no air. Regarding this, the priest who was taking us around said, laughing, "It is a blessing there are not too many draughts, poisonous microbes cannot get around."

Let us leave the city and assist at Benediction in the countryside.

We approached a neighboring church, going along a highway, a small path one half meter in width, winding through fields sown with rice, cotton, and peas. Now we were able to breathe deeply. Chinese were working in the fields, for the weather was threatening and the rice and cotton were ready for harvesting. The greater number of these workers were Christians and had the priest's permission to work on Sunday. In the fields we saw tombs here and there. On the outskirts of the cities these tombs are close to each other. These are burial mounds ten times larger than the graves in France, or little houses one meter in height. Here, the coffin is simply placed on two trestles and covered with a roughly woven matting, or the coffin is simply placed on the ground. There is never any bad odor coming from the bodies because the boxes are very thick, well closed, and the bodies are covered in quicklime. We reached the priest's residence, a Jesuit from Caen, P. Pierre. He had a fever and begged us to give Benediction. We went to the church. The Christian women were there in large numbers on one side, the men not occupied in the fields were on the other side, and all were reciting the Rosary in the Chinese tongue in a chanting tone. After Benediction, they all recited an Act of Consecration to the Sacred Heart. We returned, somewhat tired but happy and loving China and the Chinese even more. Another interesting outing was the one to Zi-Ka-Wei, nine kilometers from Shanghai. It is this village, you recall, Sister,[2] which you pointed out to me when we were speaking about the Carmelite nuns at Shanghai.[3] It is a village, partly Catholic. The Jesuits have magnificent buildings there: a scholasticate, an orphanage for boys, one for girls; among the latter we saw poor little things, thin, fading away; soon they will go to heaven. The Carmel is very close to the orphanage, but I was so tired I did not go there. A Vicar Apostolic, Bishop Chouzy from Kouang-si, a prisoner of the Chinese, wrote recently to our Procurator: "We have been successful in our undertaking; this is thanks to the prayers of the Carmelites at Zi-Ka-Wei; thank them for us and tell them to pray still for our poor mission."

I can really see that the daughters of St. Teresa will share in heaven in the reward of the missionaries. Like the latter, they do not splash around in the pagan filth (an expression of a holy missionary), but by means of a life filled with sacrifices, spent among the most beautiful flowers of spirituality, they do violence to the Heart of our God by their holy prayers. Around October 15, feast of St. Teresa of Avila, I will put on Chinese clothes: my head will be shaved, with the exception of a circle on the top; to this hair will be attached a braid of false hair taken from I do not know where; I shall be given a long pipe, and I shall be Chinese. I shall leave for Su-Tchuen, confident in the future because it is God's, because in heaven a Mother will watch over me,[4] because in Carmel a Sister[5] will pray for me: we shall convert souls, we shall baptize little Chinese babies, and when you fly away to our common homeland, you will meet these little angels who will owe their eternal happiness to you. I shall reach my Bishop around December 25; I will write you around the end of January, and my letter will reach you at the end of March.[6]

You have sent me a box of large hosts;[7] the box is in my room, ready to embark once more. The hosts were used for celebrating Holy Mass on board, and we were all happy to use a host prepared by a Carmelite. During the crossing, I said Holy Mass several times, but I was so hot in those narrow cabins that my preparation and thanksgiving left so much to be desired that I had to renounce the joy of saying Mass. During this same crossing, I also read the obituary circular of the venerated Mother Geneviève; I read also some of the poems at the end of the booklet.[8] I beg you, Sister, place often at the feet of Jesus, in your brother's name, some of the sentiments that have set your soul on fire. On this condition, I will continue to say each morning: "My God, enkindle my Sister with Your love."[9] On December 25, you will send me your intentions, and I can guess what they are: You will thank the Lord for that day of graces among all days,[10] and probably for the day when God called you to Carmel. I am sending you the principal dates of my life.[11] I recommend to your prayers a young girl who wants to consecrate herself to Jesus and who is meeting with grave difficulties. My parents continue resigned, and my father's conversion is a serious conversion: *Deo gratias. A Dieu*, Sister, in apostolic union. I bless you.

A. Roulland, miss. ap.
Su-Tchuen

* Autograph.
1. P. Roulland dated his letter to Mother Marie de Gonzague September

24, 1896; see VT, July 1963, pp. 121-123. The letter addressed to Thérèse could not have been written except on the 25th or 26th; see LC 173, note 1. The envelope bears the stamp of Paris (30 OCT 96) and Lisieux (31 OCT 96). Thérèse answered on November 1 (LT 201). The sentence: "Our good Mother... went very well" is enclosed in parenthesis in pencil by Thérèse's hand, undoubtedly in order to be omitted when it was read in the Community; see *notes* 2 and 5.

2. The word "Sister" is crossed out in pencil and replaced by "Mother," by Thérèse's hand. P. Roulland was "Our Mother's missionary"; see LT 189, note 4, and, in a similar sense, LT 193, note 1.

3. In the speakroom, July 3; see LC 165, note 6.

4. The Blessed Virgin. P. Roulland loves to sign "child of Mary." He has his own mother, and we must wait until May 9, 1897 (LT 226) for Thérèse to invite him to consider himself the "son" of M. and Mme. Martin.

5. "Sister" is substituted by "Mother" by Thérèse's hand in pencil.

6. It arrived at Lisieux on March 19 (LC 173).

7. A box sent to Marseilles before the embarkment on August 2, 1896; regarding the "hosts from the Carmel," see CJ 1.5.2. The making of altar breads was one of the sources of income for the Lisieux Carmel.

8. Poems composed and copied out by Thérèse; see LC 167, note 3.

9. Concerning this prayer, see LC 166, note 3.

10. Among the "Days of Graces" in her life, singled out by Thérèse (see LT 193, note 1), appeared the "Day of graces among all days, December 25, 1886." See LT 201, in which Thérèse explains this grace of her "conversion."

11. According to Thérèse's request (LT 193). This is the list: " + R. Ap. Days of Graces granted by the Lord to His unworthy Missionary:
    Birth: October 13, 1870. Baptism: October 15, 1870. First Communion: July 3, 1881. Confirmation: June 8, 1883. Vocation saved by Our Lady of Perpetual Help: *September 8, 1890*. Entrance into the Major Seminary: October 1, 1890. Tonsure: June 29, 1892. Minor Orders: September 24, 1894. Subdiaconate: September 21, 1895. Diaconate: February 29, 1896. Priesthood and apostolic union: June 28, 1896. My father's conversion: July 9, 1896. Departure from France: August 2, 1896. First baptism of a pagan child: .... First conversion of a pagan adult: ...."

LD   *From l'abbé Bellière to Mother Marie*
          de Gonzague.

October 14, 1896   This mail contains a letter and a visiting card.
→ LD lost

Sommervieu, October 14, '96

Reverend Mother,

Dear Mother Agnes of Jesus, when giving over her charge to you, has also left you her heart, for I find her heart in yours. Thank you, good Mother, for the help you have given me in a moment of distress.[1] The storm has passed, calm has returned, and the poor soldier has become again the seminarian of former days.

Long live God! Mother, for the fight strengthens and sheds light. Today, I am happy with the joy of God. Thanks to you, thanks to my dear little Sister Thérèse of the Child Jesus. I do not know her, but I shall speak to her at the meeting up above where I shall come before her with the souls she will have helped me to save.

At this moment, the direct question of my vocation is being decided. Should I be a priest in the ordinary ministry or a missionary priest? My director has authorized me to have myself accepted by the Superior of the Foreign Missions among the number of aspirants. I trust, then, that the good Master will turn the scales on that side. When this good news has been definitely settled, I will let you know, Mother, as well as Sister Thérèse.

Let her pray for me and rejoice with me and save souls with me, a poor laborer.

And you, good Mother, if there remains a prayer for you to offer, please remember once again, to apply it to him, the poor soldier whom you have strengthened and the seminarian who wants God's glory by working for Him.

I remain, Reverend Mother, your very respectfully obedient and devoted son,

> M. Barthélemy-Bellière
> a. m.
> Student at the Major Seminary
> Sommervieu, Bayeux

> L'abbé M. Barthélemy-Bellière
> Sommervieu

Glory to St. Teresa

It will be a year ago tomorrow that the Lord united me by love to Sister Thérèse.[2] Tomorrow is her feast day as well as that of your holy Patroness, and unless there is a serious hindrance, I will offer my Holy Communion for her, you, and your Community; union of prayers.

---

* Autograph.
1. See LD, July 21, 1896. Not one response from Mother Marie de Gonzague or Mother Agnes to l'abbé Bellière was returned to the Carmel archives. The dossier was destroyed in part by l'abbé Adam (1878-1958), future vicar general of Bayeux, who had taken offense at the sentimental tone of this correspondence and made a virtue of its destruction. The letters from Thérèse had been turned over to the *Process of the Writings* by P. Aubrée, *missionnaire de La Délivrande*, sole legatee of P. Bellière.
2. See LD, October 23, 1895. Mother Marie de Gonzague had Thérèse answer the letter (LT 198).

LT 198   **From Thérèse to l'abbé Bellière.**

October 21, 1896   The first of the eleven letters from Thérèse to her
→LD, October 14   spiritual brother. She rewrote in May 1897, un-
1896   doubtedly from memory, the following sum-
                    mary: "October 25. Your letter of July had
                    caused me some sorrow. My joy is great when
                    receiving as a feast day bouquet the assurance

that God has answered me. "What does he know who has not been tempted?" "Blessed is the man who has suffered temptation." "I would give a thousand lives to save one soul," St. Teresa.

J.M.J.T.

Lisieux Carmel, October 21, '96

Jesus †

Monsieur l'abbé,.

Our Reverend Mother, being ill, has asked me to answer your letter. I am sorry you are deprived of the holy words this good Mother would have addressed to you, but I am happy to speak for her and to tell you her joy at learning the work Our Lord has just done in your soul. She will continue to pray that He will complete His divine work in you.

It is, I think, useless to tell you, Monsieur l'abbé, the great share I am taking in Our Mother's joy. Your letter of July disturbed me very much; attributing to my lack of fervor the combats you had to suffer, I did not cease imploring for you the maternal help of the sweet Queen of Apostles.[1] So my consolation was very great when I received as a feast day bouquet[2] the assurance that my poor prayers had been answered....

Now that the storm has passed, I thank God for having made you pass through it, for we read in our holy books these beautiful words: "Blessed is the man who has suffered temptation,"[3] and again: "What does he know who has not been tempted?"[4] In fact, when Jesus calls a soul to direct and to save multitudes of other souls, it is necessary that He have him experience the temptations and trials of life. Since He has granted you the grace to come out victorious from the fight, I trust, Monsieur l'Abbé, that our gentle Jesus will realize your great desires. I am asking Him that you may be not only a *good* missionary but a *saint* all on fire with the love of God and souls; I beg you to obtain also for me this love so that I may help you in your apostolic work. You know that a Carmelite who would not be an apostle would separate herself from the goal of her vocation[5] and would cease to be a daughter of the Seraphic Saint Teresa, who desired to give a thousand lives to save a single soul.[6]

I have no doubt, Monsieur l'Abbé, that you gladly join your prayers to mine so that Our Lord may cure Our venerated Mother.

In the Sacred Hearts of Jesus and Mary,[7] I shall always be happy to call myself,

> Your unworthy little sister,
> Thérèse of the Child Jesus
> of the Holy Face
> rel. carm. ind.

* Autograph.
1. Thérèse loves this title since her meeting with P. Roulland; see pp. 954, 975, note 3; 1014.
2. October 15, feast of St. Teresa of Avila.
3. See James 1:12.
4. See Sirach 34:10.
5. See St. Teresa of Avila, vol. II, *The Collected Works, Way of Perfection*, chapter 3.
6. *Ibid.* chapter 1. Thérèse copied this sentence: "I would give a thousand lives to save a single soul!" on the paper she holds in her hand for the photograph of July 1896 (VTL, no. 29; see LC 165, note 5). See also P 31, July 16, 1896, stanza 4. In the evening of October 15, at recreation, Thérèse drew out by lot this "Testament of Our Mother Saint Teresa: Her zeal for the glory of God and the salvation of souls." (Note copied by Thérèse, ACL.)
7. This formula repeats that of "the seal of union in apostolic love" sent the preceding year by l'abbé Bellière; see LD, October 23, 1895, note 3.

LT 199   **From Thérèse to Sister Marie of Saint-Joseph.**

October 20-30   Approximate date; see note 5.
(?), 1896

J.M.J.T.

Stay awake,[1] naughty little brother?[2]...*No, a thousand* times no!... I am not surprised at little brother's combats, but only that he loses his little bit of strength by surrendering his arms to the first corporal[3] who is in his way, and even that he pursues him on the stairs of the barracks to make him give up the very last piece of armor.

Why is it surprising then that a strong ray of sun (ordinarily borne with courage), falling on the little *disarmed* soldier, should burn him and give him a fever?...

For his punishment, his little brother condemns him to shut himself up in the prison of love and *to sleep* like a little saint; but first he must use his *musical* instrument of penance[4] *this evening*!...

If not, little brother will be sad.

(Above all, do not stay awake! Tomorrow, we shall pull our arms out of joint together![5]...)

---

*   Autograph.
1.   To work in the linen room; see note 5.
2.   Thérèse used the abbreviation "p.f." (*petit frère*) when referring to this Sister; she also uses this same abbreviation to refer to herself. See LT 195.
3.   The "corporal" has not been identified; we should take note that it is not a simple soldier.
4.   She means that the Sister should sing. Sister Marie of Saint-Joseph had a good singing voice; see LT 217, and page 1175.
5.   Undoubtedly to stretch the still damp linen: at this time, it was not ironed. This was hard work, especially after the two large washings of spring and autumn (Easter week and the week following October 15). Among other pieces, there were almost two hundred wimples (LT 195, note 3) to be placed in the pressing-machine. If it is true that Thérèse is referring to this operation, the note would be written in April or October of 1896. However, the spring of 1897 is to be eliminated: after April 18, 1897 (Easter date), Thérèse would no longer

have the strength for this work. Psychologically, the note seems to
have been written in October 1896.

LT 200/LC 171   From Thérèse to Sister Marie of Saint-Joseph.

End of October,   This note seems to follow LT 199.
1896 (?).

J.M.J.T.

All goes well. The little child is a brave one who deserves epaulettes of *gold*. But more than ever, he is not to *lower* himself to fight
with little stones;[1] this is unworthy of him. . . . His weapon must be
"Love."

The rest goes well, too, since the little child makes fun of *Messire
Satanas* and since he sleeps always on the Heart of the Great
General. . . . Close to this Heart, we learn courage, and especially
confidence. The hail of bullets, the noise of the cannon, what is all
that when we are carried by the General?. . .

*   CE
1.   A recall of the above incident "on the stairs of the barracks" (LT 199)?

LT 201   From Thérèse to P. Roulland.

November 1, 1896
→ LC 167 and 171

J.M.J.T.

Carmel of Lisieux   November 1, 1896

Jesus †

Brother,

Your interesting letter, which arrived under the patronage of All
Saints, gives me great joy. I thank you for treating me as a *real sister*.

With the grace of Jesus I hope to make myself worthy of this title so dear to me.

I thank you, too, for having sent us *The Soul of a Missionary*;[1] this book has interested me deeply. It allowed me to follow you during your distant journey. The *Life* of Père Nempon is perfectly titled, it really reveals the soul of a missionary, or rather the soul of all apostles truly worthy of this name.

You ask me (in the letter written at Marseilles)[2] to pray to Our Lord to remove from you the cross of being named director in a seminary or even that of coming back to France. I understand that this prospect is not pleasing to you; with my whole heart I am begging Jesus that He see fit to allow you to carry out the laborious apostolate such as your soul always dreamed about. However, I add with you: "May God's will be done." In it alone is rest to be found; outside this lovable *will* we would do *nothing* either for Jesus or for souls.

Mt. 6: 10

I cannot tell you, Brother, how happy I am to see you so totally abandoned into your superiors' hands. It seems to me it is a certain proof that one day my desires will be realized, that is, that you will be a great Saint.

Allow me to confide a secret to you that was just revealed to me by the sheet of paper on which are written the memorable dates of your life.

On September 8, 1890, your missionary vocation was saved by Mary, Queen of Apostles and Martyrs; on that same day, a little Carmelite became the spouse of the King of heaven. Bidding an everlasting *adieu* to the world, she had one goal, to save souls, especially the souls of apostles. From Jesus, her divine Spouse, she asked particularly for an apostolic soul; unable to be a priest, she wanted that in her place a priest may receive the graces of the Lord, that he have the same aspirations, the same desires as herself....

Brother, you know the unworthy Carmelite who offered this prayer. Do you not think, as I do, that our union confirmed on the day of your priestly ordination began on September 8?[3] ... I believed I would meet only in heaven the apostle, the brother whom I had asked from Jesus; but this Beloved Saviour, raising a little the mysterious veil that hides the secrets of eternity, has seen fit to give me in this exile the consolation of knowing the brother of my soul, of working with him for the salvation of poor infidels.

Oh! how great is my gratitude when I consider the kind attention of Jesus!... What is He reserving for us in heaven if here below His love dispenses surprises so delightful?

More than ever, I understand that the smallest events of our life are conducted by God; He is the One who makes us desire and who grants our desires.... When our good Mother suggested to me that I become your helper, I admit, Brother, that I hesitated.[4] Considering the virtues of the holy Carmelites around me, I thought that our Mother would have better served your spiritual interests by choosing for you a Sister other than myself; the thought alone that Jesus would have no regard for my imperfect works but for my good will made me accept the honor of sharing in your apostolic works. I did not know then that Our Lord Himself had chosen me, He who uses the weakest instruments to work marvels!... I did not know that for six years I had *a brother* who was preparing himself to become a missionary; now that this brother is really His apostle, Jesus reveals it to me in order no doubt to increase in my soul the desire of loving Him and making Him loved.

Do you know, Brother, that if the Lord *continues* to answer my prayer, you will obtain a favor which your humility prevents you from seeking? This incomparable favor, you guess it, is martyrdom....

Yes, I have the hope that after *long years* spent in apostolic works, after having given Jesus love for love, life for life, you will give Him, too, blood for blood....

When writing these lines, I am reminded that they will reach you in the month of January, the month during which we exchange happy wishes. I believe that those of your little sister will be the only ones of their kind.... To tell the truth, the world would treat as folly wishes like these; however, for us the world no longer lives, and "our conversation is already in heaven,'[5] our only desire is to resemble our adorable Master, whom the world did not wish to know because He emptied Himself, taking on the form and nature of a slave.[6] Oh, Brother! how blessed you are to follow so closely the example of Jesus.... When thinking you have dressed yourself in the clothes of the Chinese, I am naturally thinking of the Saviour clothing Himself in our poor humanity and becoming like one of us[7] in order to redeem our souls for eternity.

You will perhaps find me really childish, but it does not matter. I confess that I committed a sin of envy when reading that your hair was going to be cut and replaced by a Chinese braid. It is not the latter I desire but very simply a little tress of the hair now become useless. You will no doubt ask me, laughing, what I will do with it? Well, it is very simple, this hair will be a *relic* for me when you will be in heaven, the palm of martyrdom in your hand. You find, no doubt, that I am going about this far in advance, but I know it is the only means of reaching my goal, for your little sister (who is known only as such by Jesus)[8] will certainly be forgotten in the distribution of *your relics*. I am sure you are laughing at me, but this does not matter. If you consent *to pay* for the little amusement I am giving you with "the hair of a future Martyr," I shall be well recompensed.

On December 25 I will not fail to send my angel so that he may place my intentions near the host that will be consecrated by you. It is from the depths of my heart that I thank you for offering for Our Mother and me your Mass at dawn;[9] when you are at the altar, we shall be singing Matins for Christmas which precede the Midnight Mass.

Brother, you are not mistaken when saying that no doubt my intentions would be: "to thank Jesus for the day of graces among all days." It is not on this day that I received the grace of my religious vocation. Our Lord, willing for Himself alone my first glance, saw fit to ask my heart in the cradle, if I can so express myself.

The *night* of Christmas 1886 was, it is true, decisive for my vocation, but to name it more clearly I must call it: the night of my conversion.[10] On that blessed night, about which it is written that it sheds light even on the delights of God Himself,[11] Jesus, who saw fit to make Himself a child out of love for me, saw fit to have me come forth from the swaddling clothes and imperfections of childhood. He transformed me in such a way that I no longer recognized myself. Without this change I would have had to remain for years in the world. Saint Teresa, who said to her daughters: "I want you to be women in nothing, but that in everything you may equal strong men,"[12] would not have wanted to acknowledge me as her child if the Lord had not clothed me in His divine strength, if He had not

Himself armed me for war.

I promise you, Brother, to recommend to Jesus in a very special way the young girl about whom you speak to me and who is meeting with obstacles to her vocation. I sympathize sincerely with her suffering, knowing by experience how bitter it is to be unable to respond immediately to God's call. I hope she is not obliged like me to go even to Rome.... No doubt you do not know that your sister had the audacity to speak to the Pope?[13].... It is true, however, and if I had not had this audacity, perhaps I would be still in the world.

Jesus has said: "The kingdom of heaven suffers violence, and only the violent take it away."[14] It was the same for me concerning the kingdom of Carmel. Before becoming the prisoner of Jesus, I had to travel very far to take hold of the prison that I preferred to all the palaces of this earth. I had no desire to make a trip for my personal pleasure, and when my incomparable father offered to take me to Jerusalem if I wished to postpone my entrance for two or three months, I did not hesitate (in spite of the natural attraction which was drawing me to visit the places sanctified by the Saviour's life) to choose repose in the shadow of Him for whom I was longing.[15] I understood that really one day spent in the Lord's house was worth more than a thousand anywhere else.[16]

Perhaps, Brother, you want to know what obstacle I was encountering in the accomplishment of my vocation; this obstacle was none other than my youth. Our good Father Superior[17] formally refused to receive me before I was twenty-one, saying that a child of fifteen was not capable of knowing to what she was committing herself. His conduct was prudent, and I do not doubt that, in trying me, he accomplished the will of God, who willed to have me conquer the fortress of Carmel at the point of the sword; perhaps, too, Jesus permitted the demon to hinder a vocation which must not have been, I believe, to the liking of that villain *deprived of love* as our Holy Mother[18] called him; fortunately, all his tricks turned out to his shame, they served only to render a child's victory more striking. If I wanted to write you all the details of the combat I had to sustain, I would have to have much time, ink, and paper. Recounted by a clever pen, these details would have some interest for you, I believe, but my pen cannot give any charms to a long recital, so I ask your pardon for having already perhaps bored you.

You promise me, Brother, to continue each morning to say at the altar: "My God, enkindle my sister with Your love." I am deeply grateful to you for this, and I have no difficulty in assuring you that your conditions are and *always* will be accepted. All I ask Jesus for myself, I ask also for you; when I offer my weak love to the Beloved, I allow myself to offer yours at the same time. Like Joshua, you are fighting on the plain, and I am your little Moses,[19] and incessantly my heart if lifted to heaven to obtain the victory. Oh, Brother, how you would have to be pitied if Jesus Himself were not to hold up the arms of your Moses!... But with the help of the prayer you are making each day for me to the divine Prisoner of love, I hope you will never have *to be pitied* and that, after this life during which we shall have sown together in tears, we shall be joyful, carrying back our sheaves in our hands.[20]

I loved the little sermon very much that you addressed to our good Mother, exhorting her to remain on earth; it is not long, but as you say there is nothing to answer.[21] I see you will not have much trouble in convincing your listeners when you preach, and I hope an abundance of souls will be gathered and offered by you to the Lord. I notice I am at the end of my paper; this forces me to stop my scribbling. I want, however, to tell you that all your anniversaries will be faithfully celebrated by me. *July 3* will be particularly dear to me since on that day you *received Jesus* for the first time and on this same date I *received Jesus* from your hand and assisted at your first Mass in Carmel.

Bless your unworthy sister, Brother.

> Thérèse of the Child Jesus
> rel. carm. ind.

I recommend to your prayers a young seminarian who would like to be a *missionary*; his vocation has just been shaken by his year of military service.[22]

---

* Autograph.
1. The Life of P. Nempon; see LC 167, note 4. This missionary's heroism must have interested Thérèse; he died at age twenty-seven († December 13, 1889).
2. See LC 167.

Ex. 17 - 9 - 13

3. P. Roulland testified later: "I am pleased to admit that I am somewhat indebted to her for my missionary vocation" (PO, 1923). "On September 8, 1890, I was having some hesitancy concerning my vocation and entrance into the Major Seminary. While I was praying in the chapel of Our Lady of Ransom, I suddenly and definitively came to a decision. I learned later that on the same September 8, 1890, the day of the Servant of God's Profession, she had asked Our Lord to give her the soul of a priest, and she pointed out the link between these two events" (PA 2903).

4. Ms. C, p. 253.

5. See Philippians 3:20, quoted in the *Imitation of Christ* I, 8, *Reflections*; see LC 200. P. Roulland recalled these words in a letter to Mother Marie de Gonzague, October 13, 1897: "Sister Thérèse told me our conversation was in heaven. Today these words are completely realized. Sister is in heaven."

6. See Philippians 2:7.

7. *Ibid.*

8. See LC 171, note 2.

9. P. Roulland had written Mother Marie de Gonzague, September 24, 1896: "When you receive this letter, I shall be travelling on the Blue River; I shall reach my mission around Christmas. On that beautiful day I shall offer my second Mass, the Mass at Dawn, for your intentions and the intentions of my sister. . . . I shall say the Holy Mass between 6 and 7, that is, according to Lisieux time between eleven and midnight, the 24th." Sickness prevented the missionary from realizing his plan; see LC 173, note 5.

10. See the parallel account in Ms. A, p. 98.

11. See Psalm 138:10, quoted under this form by Sister Agnes of Jesus in her Christmas composition, 1889: "Behold that blessed night. . .about which it is said: 'It sheds light even on the delights of God!. . .'"

12. Saint Teresa of Avila, vol. II, *The Collected Works, Way of Perfection,* p. 70.

13. See LT 36 and Ms. A, p. 134.

14. See Matthew 11:12.

15. See Canticle of Canticles 2:3.

16. See Psalm 83:11.

17. Canon Delatroëtte († 1895); see vol. 1, pp. 287, 304-305.

18. According to our knowledge, this expression does not appear in the authentic writings of St. Teresa of Avila. We find it again in *The Triumph of Humility* (RP 7, June 21, 1896) written by Thérèse.

19. See Exodus 17:8-13.

20. See Psalm 125:5-6.
21. Here is the little sermon: "When I left France, Reverend Mother, you were sick; God, I hope, has answered my request and now you are well. It is good to go to heaven, but as late as possible. Holy Scripture tells us: '*Venit nox, quando nemo potest operari* (after death, we do not work anymore).' I foresee your answer. With Saint Paul you tell me: 'I want to die to be with Jesus. By the grace of God: His will and not ours.' To this you will find no answer." (Letter to Mother Marie de Gonzague, September 24, 1896).
22. We recognize here l'abbé Bellière.

LT 202   **From Thérèse to Mme. Guérin.**
November 16, 1896

J.M.J.T.

Jesus †   November 16, 1896

Dear Aunt,

It is very sad for your poor little daughter to be obliged to entrust
a cold pen with the care of expressing the sentiments of her heart....
Perhaps you will say with a smile: "But, little Thérèse, would you
express them more easily in words?" Dear Aunt, I have to admit
it, no, it is true, I do not find expressions that satisfy the aspirations
of my heart.

The poet who dared to say:
"What is well understood is clearly expressed,
And the words to express it come with ease,"[1]*

this poet did not feel what I feel in the depths of my soul!!!...

Fortunately, I have the deep Father Faber to console me. He
understood that words and sentences here below are incapable of
expressing feelings of the heart and that *full* hearts are the ones containing the most within themselves.[2]

Dear Aunt, I shall bore you with my quotations, and this even
more so because the letters of my four amiable sisters[3] are there to
give the lie to my words. Well! dear Aunt, be assured that in spite
of all their eloquence, they do not love you more than I who cannot
say this in choice words.... If you do not believe me now, one day,
when we are all reunited in the beautiful heaven, you will be forced
to admit that the *littlest* of your children was not little in her
tenderness and gratitude, that she was the *littlest* only in age and
wisdom.[4]

I beg you, dear Aunt, pray to God that I may grow in wisdom
just as the divine Child Jesus grew; I am not doing this, I assure
you. Ask your dear little Marie of the Eucharist, and she will tell
you that I am not lying; from day to day, I am becoming more wicked, and yet it will soon be *nine years* since I am in the Lord's house.

I should, then, be already advanced in the ways of perfection, but I am still at the bottom of the ladder. This does not discourage me, and I am as happy as the grasshopper; like it, I am always singing, hoping at the end of my life to share in the riches of my sisters who are much more generous than the ant. I hope, too, dear Aunt, to have a beautiful place at the heavenly banquet, and this is why: When the saints and the angels will learn I have the honor of being your little daughter, they will not want to make me sad by placing me far from you.... Thus I shall enjoy eternal goods because of your virtues. Ah! truly I was born under a blessed star, and my heart melts with gratitude to God, who has given me relatives such as are not to be found any longer on earth.

Since, dear Aunt, I am a *poor* grasshopper that has nothing but its songs (again, it can sing only in the bottom of its heart, not having a melodious voice),[5] I will sing my most beautiful tune on your feast day, and I will take care to have so touching a tone that all the saints, taking pity on my poverty, will give me treasures of graces that I shall be delighted to offer to you. Neither will I forget to fête dear Grandmamma with the riches of the saints; they will be so generous that my heart will have nothing more to desire, and, I assure you, this is not saying little, for my desires are very great.

I beg dear Uncle to kiss you very tenderly for me. If Francis, Jeanne, and Léonie will do this as well, I will sing a little tune to thank them (it goes without saying that dear Uncle will not be forgotten in my happy song).

Pardon me, dear Aunt, for saying so many things to you that have neither rhyme or reason, and believe I love you with all my heart.

Thérèse of the Child Jesus
rel. carm. ind.

* "*Ce qui l'on conçoit bien s'énonce clairement, Et les mots pour le dire arrivent aisément.*"

---

*   Autograph.
1.   Boileau, *Art poétique, chant* I, v. 153-154. According to the school notebook in which Thérèse transcribed the weekly program of her lessons and homework, the study of *Art poétique* held an important place in the teaching of Mme. Papinau, in 1886-1887.

2. We have not been able to find to this day the exact source of this quotation clearly indicated by the slanted handwriting from "The words and sentences." However, the sense of the *ineffable* and the *hidden* appears often in the work of Father Faber.

3. Her three sisters (whose letters were not preserved) and her cousin, who wrote of sending "two photographs representing your five little daughters in their work as bakers of altar breads and sacristans" (letter of Sister Marie of the Eucharist to Mme. Guérin, November 14, 1896). The photographs are in VTL I, nos. 39 and 40. The draft of the poem *Les Sacristines du Carmel* (P 36, November 1896) had two extra couplets addressed to Mme. Guérin.

4. A playful reference to Luke 2:40.

5. Must we conclude that Thérèse sang poorly? We cannot decide the question one way or the other. It is certain that not one of the Martin sisters was really gifted in music. Thérèse had a weak voice and often suffered from hoarseness since 1894 because of her illness. See Sister Marie of the Trinity's testimony (the incident took place on June 16, 1894, the day of her entrance): "When Sister Thérèse of the Child Jesus noticed I had a good voice for the choir, she expressed her satisfaction to me, saying: 'Now I am very much consoled at having a weak voice for the choir, and I thank Jesus for having given me a daughter who has a voice for both of us. . . . I offer Him your voice as if it were mine.' Then I told her I would always sing in her name as well as in my own, and I was touched when seeing the joy she felt" (note of Sister Marie of the Trinity to Mother Agnes of Jesus, June 16, 1942).

LC 172	*From l'abbé Bellière to Thérèse.*
November 28, 1896 → LT 198	First of eleven letters addressed directly to Thérèse by this seminarian.

Langrune - Saturday.

Good little Sister,

The Master is sending me a hard trial, just as He does to those whom He loves, and I am very weak. Undoubtedly, He will send me in a few days to the seminary of the African Missions.[1] My desire is at last going to be realized, but I have to struggle much, I have to break myself away from dear and great affections, from sweet and cherished habits of easy living, from a happy and blessed past that still attracts me strongly. I need strength, very dear Sister. Beg God that He give me, along with the full light, the virtue of the strong, beautiful abnegation and zeal for His glory, with humility which is the foundation of sanctity. The missionary must be a saint, and I am not one.

I left the Major Seminary. Perhaps I shall go back there for six more months; perhaps, too, I shall be leaving in a few days. I am awaiting a final decision.

Dear Sister, since you are my good angel, I entrust myself to your prayers again, always. The trial must be decisive, and I need all God's grace. As soon as the way is opened, I will let you know. At the moment, I am resting and waiting with my family at Langrune, Calvados.

Your last month's letter, Sister, encouraged me and did good. If your charity inspires you to write me again, this will be a great consolation for me and an added strength.

In the Heart of Jesus, let us remain united, very dear Sister, by charity, the apostolate, and suffering.

Your poor, very grateful and devoted brother,

Maurice Barthélemy-Bellière
Miss. Asp.

Pray for my poor mother also.[2]
Has your Mother Prioress been restored to good health?

* Autograph.
1. Seminary of Lyons. This plan did not go through.
2. His aunt and mother by adoption, Mme. Barthélemy.

"I have the hope that my exile will be short!" (see LT 220)
(December 1896 - April 1897)
Age twenty-three and twenty-four

"At the moment when my departure for Tonkin was being planned, around the month of November, you recall how we began a novena to Théophane Vénard in order to receive a sign of God's will? At this time, I returned to all the Community exercises, even to Matins. Well, precisely during the novena, I started coughing, and since then I have gone from bad to worse" (CJ 21-26.5.10).

From the vesicatory (a treatment Thérèse was receiving) to the next, the Correspondence *of the winter of 1896-1897 keeps us in touch with this gradual but irreversible decline of Thérèse.*

She went on fighting, however, even though from time to time she had to remain in her cell, with a footwarmer as her only source of heat (LT 208, note 1). This intermittent isolation explains in part the existence of fourteen notes, at times very brief, to her sisters (five to Mother Agnes, five to Sister Geneviève, three to Sister Marie of Saint-Joseph, one to Sister Marie of the Sacred Heart). Six other letters complete the collection: two "Christmas letters" to some novices, the other four to P. Roulland, l'abbé Bellière, and Brother Simeon at Rome.

Seven documents are dated by the writer. Four out of five times, Mother Agnes of Jesus gives the precise date of undated notes from her sister. Mother Agnes was to keep up this habit in the months following. This fact merits our notice, to the credit of the future witness of Last Conversations.

If there remains a margin of approximation for the date of the nine other notes, we can suggest at least very probable dates.

Biographical data are few for this period. Looked at superficially, some details seem to be even tainted with childishness. Thus at the approach of Christmas—ten years after the episode of the slippers at the fireplace in Les Buissonnets—Thérèse experienced the "childish desire" to leave a sad recreation and to go to the carriage gateway "to take in tree branches for the crib" (CJ 6.4.3). She gives up this pleasure in favor of Sister Marie of Saint-Joseph.

On February 2, 1897, in order to honor the martyrdom of Théopane Vénard (February 2, 1861), she wanted to offer God "a big suffering." While serving in the refectory, she broke a pane of glass. . .and cries over clumsiness (CSG, p. 158). But on that same day, in a canticle dedicated to her friend in heaven, she sang: "The entire universe in God's eyes is only a dot - My feeble love, my little sufferings— Blessed by Him, make Him loved afar!" (P 44, February 2, 1897.)

Afar in space and time: on February 8, in a piece composed for Sister Saint-Stanislaus, a jubilarian, she made her hero, Stanislaus Kostka, ask the great question that haunts her, the only question for her from now on: "I have a desire. . .a desire so great that I shall be unable to be happy in heaven if it is not realized. . . . Tell me whether the blessed can still work for the salvation of souls. . . . If I cannot work in paradise for the glory of Jesus, I prefer to remain in the exile and combat for Him!. . . " The affirmative answer of the Blessed Virgin Mary then gave rise to this entreaty: "I beg you, when I am close to you in the homeland, permit me to come back to earth" (RP 8, February 8, 1897). Saint Francis Xavier, then St. Joseph, are begged, in March, to sustain her request (see LT 221, note 11).

"To love Jesus and to make Him loved": such was her sole posthumous ambition (LT 218, 220, 221). This was a program that she attempted to realize hic et nunc *by pushing herself to the very end of her strength. On March 3, she*

undertook the Lenten fast with her Community.

March 25, for Sister Marie of the Eucharist's Profession (whose letters, in the past year, revealed the severe and beneficent influence of her young novice mistress), Thérèse composed the hymn Mes Armes (My Weapons), in which, without being actually named, appeared her two friends: Joan of Arc and Saint Cecilia. The poem ends: "Singing, I shall die on the field of battle—My weapons in my hands!" (P 46, March 25, 1897.)

There was no stoicism in this determination. On the contrary, a certain playfulness lights up the correspondence of her last winter. Thérèse could "laugh at everything" (LT 219). What was her secret? "What do death or life mean to me? Jesus, my joy is to love You...." (P 42, January 21, 1897.)

Read: Ms. C, p. 221.

LD	*From Sister Marie of the Eucharist to M. Guérin.*
December 4 (?), 1896	Uncertain date; see note 3.

J.M.J.T.

Jesus †

Dear little Father,

I am coming once again to make a little "knock, knock" on your bedroom door.[1] I am coming to recommend to you a poor beggar whom you have already laden with your kind deeds without her asking. This beggar is eating dishes from your table; the venerable matron, your wife, is trying hard to find delicate and appetizing dishes for this poor beggar.[2] The poor beggar had a vesicatory yesterday on her chest.[3] Because of the state of her illness, we were able to realize for ourselves the condition of her miserable hovel.[4] Picture to yourself a real hovel, the plaster walls scratched and black-

ened, a poor mean litter—this is the only name for it—made up of
a straw mattress softer than the best feather bed,* and covered with
her old clothes that served her as blankets. I will not enter into detail
about her garments, glad rags, bodices, etc.,[5] which lie on the floor
in a corner. The little doctor of the monastery who is speaking to
you at the moment[6] notices, when coming to see her patient, the
gratitude toward her generous benefactors, overflowing the poor beggar's heart. There is no mistake in applying here the words of a
modern poet: "And under the frightful rags imprisoning him there
beats a heart of gold." The poor beggar is not accustomed to good
things; so, yesterday, before a dish of veal in mushrooms, she left
aside the latter, not knowing too well what it was. . . . Our Mother,
coming in at that moment, told the patient that these little brown-
black berries were mushrooms. Our beggar, having lived in opulence
in her childhood, recalled that she used to love this kind of thing
very much. She was sorry for not having eaten them, but through
a feeling of innate pride, she did not want to admit that she had
not recognized this precious dish, and so she was profuse in interior
regrets and made up for it in the evening by swallowing them down
with avidity.[7]

You know, don't you, dear little Father, the poor beggar for whom
you have a special affection, so she is sending you her best kisses
and often thinks you are keeping her company in your own condition that saddens her and makes her offer up to heaven her most
fervent prayers.

You see, dear little Father, from my description, the riches of a
Carmelite's cell, but what compensates greatly for it is the affection
and devoted care given by her sisters, angels on earth.

I kiss and love you with my whole heart, along with my dear little
Mother.

Your little Marie of the Eucharist

---

* Autograph.
1. A preceding letter, very probable on December 1, 1896, from Marie
   to her father, began in this way: "Knock, knock! . . . Who goes there?"
   M. Guérin was sick during the first days of December.
2. We could easily find in the Martin-Guérin correspondence in the years

1893-1896 other examples of Mme. Guérin's care of the sick in the Carmel, especially for Mother Marie de Gonzague and her daughter Marie: gifts of bouillon, marmalade, and other prepared dishes. Up to this date, Thérèse had not benefited from this care.

3. There is no prescription regarding this in the Community copybook. We have reason to wonder whether there is question here of a vesicatory mentioned in these terms in the *Cahiers verts* at the date (uncertain) of May 21-26, 1897: "One day when she came to Mass and received Communion, although we had removed a vesicatory from her a short time before, I began to cry and was unable to attend the 'Little Hours.' I followed her into her cell and I shall always see her, seated on her little bench and her back supported by the poor board partition. She was exhausted and was looking at me in a sad and very sweet way! My tears redoubled, and guessing how much I was making her suffer, I asked her pardon on my knees. She answered simply: 'This is not too much to suffer for obtaining one Communion!...'" But to repeat the sentence is nothing, one would have to hear the tone of voice!" (DE, *Annexes*, p. 38.) A parallel version sets the incident in September 1896 (PA, 722, quoted in the *Annexes*, p. 433), but this date does not seem to be correct (see DE, p. 577). Thérèse could have undergone the vesicatory on December 3; see note 7.

4. Her cell; usually Carmelite nuns did not enter one another's cell. Thérèse used to receive the novices in a sort of antechamber to her cell.

5. She used the word *"requimpettes."* This word is not in the dictionaries of the Normandy patois; a possible deformation of the verb: *"se requinquer"*: to deck oneself out, to dress in one's Sunday best. The expression is employed here jokingly. The other word: *"petits corps"*: a kind of bodice of coarse linen making up part of the Carmelite's clothing.

6. Sister Marie of the Eucharist; see LT 136: "the little doctor from *rue de l'Oratoire*"; and DE, p. 756, L 58: "Very often a little doctor whom you know comes to give her advice" (Mother Agnes of Jesus to M. and Mme. Guérin, August 24, 1897).

7. From this passage it seems that Thérèse was sick enough "yesterday" from her vesicatory to take her meals in her cell. Usually, the Sisters, dispensed for reasons of health from the perpetual abstinence prescribed by the Carmelite Rule, abstained nonetheless on Friday and Saturday, according to the Church laws. They were permitted a more carefully prepared meal on Thursday (customs varied from one monastery to the other). Hence the *likelihood* of Thursday, December 3, for the veal in mushrooms.

*The straw in the mattress had lost all its strength.

LT 203 **From Thérèse to Mother Agnes of Jesus.**

December 4, 1896 Note dated by Mother Agnes. On the assump-
→ LC lost tion of work she was doing, we may suppose this
note followed the incident relating to the
vesicatory of December 3 (?); see *above* in note
3. Mother Agnes would have apologized to
Thérèse in writing; hence this answer.

J.M.J.T.

Little Mother is altogether too darling!...If she does *not know*
what *she is*, I myself know it well and I LOVE her!... Oh, yes! but
how pure my *affection* is!... It is that of a child who admires the
humility of its *Mother*. You do me more good than all the books
in the world!...[1]

* Autograph.
1. In a note on December 5 or 6, Sister Marie of the Eucharist wrote
   in the same way to Mother Agnes: "In your little hidden life now,
   how many lessons you give me, what candor, simplicity, above all
   love, you imprint in souls. Oh! one does not always need to use words
   to do good."

LD *From Mother Agnes of Jesus to M. and Mme.*
Guérin. (Extracts.)

December 6, 1896

J.M.J.T.

(December 6, 1896)

Jesus

Dear Relatives,
Our Mother is allowing me to write you without my showing her
the letter.... I am taking advantage of our Mother's permission by
confiding a little secret to you. Ever since the elections, with the

Superior's permission, I have been occupied in the direction of the little Sister in the white veil (Sister Marie-Madeleine).[1] It seemed to me for several really weighty reasons that she was in need of this. However, having become aware that she was not profiting enough from this for me to expose myself to such great perils, I recently gave it up. Sister Marie of the Eucharist, while washing dishes yesterday and the day before with this poor child, was speaking to her constantly about perfection, her own experience of infidelities that make the soul so downcast, her repugnance at going to confide in Sister Therese of the Child Jesus, her final victory, and her present happiness. The matter was settled. Sister Marie-Madeleine seemed to be won over, and, taking her angel-companion by the hand, she said with sincerity: "Well, no, I do not want to remain like this, sulking in my little corner. I will do as you do, and in spite of my invincible repugnance I will go to seek her whom our Mother has given us as mistress, so to speak. You will take me to her on Tuesday, the day of the Immaculate Conception." It was understood.

Here, then, were two happy children. Sister Marie of the Eucharist came to tell me all this, and I hid my feelings from her. I found she had worked a marvel, for I have not told you and I could not make you understand the degree to which Sister Marie-Madeleine is estranged from Sister Thérèse of the Child Jesus, feeling that she is read to the very depths of her soul, and, consequently, she is obliged to wage a real war against her nature. For a whole year, when I was Prioress, I had obligated her to go to Thérèse for a half-hour on Sunday, and I know what is involved.[2]

However, our little heroine had not taken the devil into consideration. Night brings on dark counsels, and the following morning, alas! The resolution of the poor tempted soul was *unshakeable*, she would not go seeking Sister Thérèse of the Child Jesus. "Not being obliged to this by authority," she said, "no, I will not go, do not talk to me about it anymore. When our Mother gives her to us openly as mistress, then I will go, but not before."

My preacher, then, was disconsolate, and I admit that I was too...during the silence before Matins, the tears came into my eyes when seeing and learning how difficult it is to do any good!

. . .

I hug you tightly.... I love you. Oh! I have no doubt these intimate details will interest you!...

See you soon!
Your poor child,
Sister Agnes of Jesus

* Autograph.
1. M. Guérin's "goddaughter" since her reception of the Habit; see LT 146, note 1.
2. See LC 157, note 8.

LT 204   From Thérèse to Mother Agnes of Jesus.

December 18, 1896
→ LC lost ?

December 18, '96

The Blessed Virgin is so content to have a little donkey and a little servant that she makes them run to the right and the left *for her pleasure*,[1] so it is not surprising that little Mother falls sometimes.[2]

Yes, but[3] when little Jesus will be big, when He will no longer need to learn "the little business of the shop,"[4] He will prepare a *little place*[5] for *little Mother* in His kingdom which is not of this world,[6] and then in His turn "He will come and go to serve her."[7] More than one little nose pulled by little Mother will have to stand up to look at her who had no other ambition but to be the donkey of little Jesus.

* ACL copy.
1. In these expressions borrowed by Mother Agnes from Sister Marie de Saint-Pierre of the Tours Carmel, Thérèse views the numberless interruptions which the task of econome imposed on her "little Mother" (since March 1896).
2. We have no knowledge of the circumstances of this impatience or blunder.
3. "Yes, but": an expression characteristic of Thérèse during her last months: see LT 219, 222, 229; CJ 18.4.3; 20.5.2, etc.
4. Recall of a *Noël d'Auvergne* that they used to love to sing at Les

Buissonnets; see LT 217.
5. See John 14:2.
6. See John 18: 36.
7. See Luke 12:37.

LT 205   **From Thérèse to Sister Marie of Saint-Joseph.**

December (?),   Uncertain date; see note 1.
1896
→ LC lost

How naughty to spend one's night in fretting, instead of falling asleep on the Heart of Jesus!...

If the night frightens the little child,[1] if she complains at *not seeing* Him who is carrying her, let her *close her eyes*, let her WILLINGLY make the sacrifice that is asked of her, and then let her await sleep...when she keeps herself peaceful in this way, the night which she is no longer looking at will be unable to frighten her, and soon calm, if not joy, will be reborn in her little heart....

Is it too much to ask the little child to close her eyes?...not to struggle against the chimeras of the night?...No, it is not too much, and the little child *will abandon* herself,[2] she will believe that Jesus is carrying her, she will consent not to see Him and to leave far behind the empty fear of being unfaithful (a fear not fitting for a little child).

An Ambassador

*   Autograph
1. We note some similarities of vocabulary between this note and LT 194 and 195. We are not excluding the possibility that it can be placed (LT 206 as well) during the retreat of September 1896 or during the retreat of Sister Marie of Saint-Joseph. But other indications (following note) give preference to December 1896. A careful examination of the autographs (in pencil) has not brought forward any decisive argument in favor of one or other assumption.
2. In December 1896, Thérèse composed for this Sister the poem *A l'Enfant-Jèsus* (P 38). We have found a copy of it made by Sister Marie of Saint-Joseph, entitled: *L'Abandon!* It is dated December 1896. The first stanza begins in this way: "Jesus, You know my name — And Your gentle glance calls me — It says to me: 'Simple abandonment

— I want to guide your boat!...' " The choice of the song that inspired it: "Where do you go when all is black!" is undoubtedly not meaningless. There could have been a chronological rapport between this note and the poem.

LT 206   **From Thérèse to Sister Marie of Saint-Joseph.**
December (?),   Uncertain date; see LT 205, note 1.
1896
→ LC lost

The little A.[1] has no desire to jump from the boat,[2] but he is here to show heaven to the little child. He wills that all the child's glances, all her attention be for Jesus. So he would be very happy to see the little child deprived of consolations too infantile and unworthy of a missionary and a warrior.[3]... I love my little child very much...and Jesus loves even more.

* CE
1. "Ambassador" as Thérèse signed herself in the preceding note. On August 4, 1929, returning six autograph notes to Mother Agnes of Jesus, Sister Marie of Saint-Joseph, exclaustrated since 1909, wrote: "As for the one which begins thus: 'The little Angel has no desire to jump from the boat....' I had lent it to a good, sick priest...who begged me to give it to him because he looked upon Thérèse as his Angel. He has died some time ago, and I will use all my efforts to return it to you." This autograph was not returned to the Carmel, but we may suppose that the copy of the Process (CE II, 172) was faithful. The reading "little Angel" would appear as a later idealization.
2. An obscure expression in the absence of the note from Sister Marie of Saint-Joseph. Is this "jumping" a veiled allusion to death which Thérèse 's illness allows one to fear? or at least her abandonment of her work in the linen room because of her health? Is the "boat" that of Sister Marie of Saint-Joseph as in the poem *A l'Enfant-Jésus* (see LT 205, note 2)? There is no answer to these questions.
3. See LT 194, note 5.

LT 207   **From Thérèse to Sister Geneviève.**
December (?),   Approximate date; see notes 4 and 6.
1896

J.M.J.T.

Poor thing, poor thing,[1] you must not have a heavy heart because
M. T.[2] has been caught in a trap![3]... When he will have wings,[4]
you will set up traps in vain, he will not fall into them, neither will
you, poor D.[5] He will stretch out his hand to you to attach two pretty
little white wings, and both of us will fly very high, very far; we shall
even go flapping our little silvery wings right to Saïgon.[6]... This
is the best we shall be able to do for Him since it is Jesus who wills
us to be two cherubs and not two foundresses. At the moment, this
is certain. If He changes His mind, we shall change ours also, that
is all![7]...

*   Autograph.
1. One of Sister Geneviève's nicknames taken from a romance that was
   sung at Les Buissonnets. We have not found the exact text. See LT
   228 and DE/G -8.2 and 4 (DE, pp. 602-603).
2. "*Monsieur Toto.*" Regarding "*Toto*" and "*Lili*" (Thérèse and
   Céline), see Lt 179, note 1.
3. "I had asked her some subtle questions regarding the Mission
   Carmels." (Note of Sister Geneviève in CMG IV, p. 380.)
4. After her death. This statement gives rise to a doubt on the date of
   this note, which could be given a few months later. Thérèse had no
   illusions concerning her state of health to Céline? In January 1897,
   it is true, the latter manifests "certain grave misgivings" regarding
   Thérèse; see LT 216, note 1.
5. "*Demoiselle Lili.*"
6. To the Saïgon Carmel which was looking for "foundresses" for that
   at Hanoï recently founded. On the back of the note Sister Geneviève
   wrote: "Regarding Hanoï, 1896."
7. The outcome of the November novena (p. 918) was regarded as a con-
   traindication to Thérèse's departure for the Far East. However, she
   did not abandon all hope; see LT 221, CJ 15.5.6, and Ms. C, p. 216.

LT 208   **From Thérèse to Sister Geneviève.**

Winter 1896-
1897

Approximate dating; see note 4. This note
presents again *"Monsieur Toto"* and
"Demoiselle Lili"; see LT 207.

J.M.J.T.

I beg you very humbly to spare poor *M.* his footwarmer
tomorrow[1]...but I beg you again *to see to it* that he *be awakened*
for the Hours.[2] He fears that his paper is useless,[3] since the awakener
is accustomed to seeing *demoiselle* coming to trounce *M.*, each morning, to gently bring him out from his dreams.[4]

Do not be upset, poor *demoiselle*, obliged to carry little jugs to
the *right* and to the *left*.[5] One day Jesus in His *turn*[6] "will go and
come to serve you"[7] and that day will come soon.

---

*   Autograph.
1.   A footwarmer heated with charcoal, the use of which Mother Marie
de Gonzague imposed on her during the winter of 1896-1897; Sister
Geneviève wrote: "She made use of it only out of obedience and great
necessity, this inexhorably causing her death, to my great displeasure,
when she judged it was not cold enough" (CSG, p. 64). As second
infirmarian Sister Geneviève was in a position to "spare" Thérèse
the use of it or not.
2.   Office of Little Hours (Prime, Tierce, Sext, None), recited at seven
in the morning during the winter.
3.   A Sister dispensed from the early morning rising attached a piece of
paper to the latch of her cell door. For the "second call" to rise,
around 6:40, a religious knocked at each of the doors having the paper.
4.   Sister Geneviève was giving Thérèse rubdowns with a haircloth: a painful treatment for a skin already made sensitive because of the
vesicatories. Thérèse admitted later: "Ah! to be 'trounced' as I was,
it is worse than anything else! (CJ 27.7.17). We still have to determine the time of these rubdowns. The *Cahiers verts* placed them "at
the end of Lent 1897" (see p. 1189, note 4), either at the end of March
or the beginning of April. But it is possible that there were several
series of rubdowns. We are poorly informed about the exact remedies
applied in 1896.
5.   See CSG, p. 103: "After a day of work, it seemed difficult for me
to go in the evening during the hour of rest or after Matins, bringing

relief to the tired Sisters. I was complaining about it, and she said: "Now it is you who are carrying little cups to the right and to the left, etc." In a letter to her father, dating from this same winter, Sister Marie of the Eucharist spoke of the overwork due "to the feast days and the sick."

6. The emphasis could have been a quick allusion to Arminjon; see LT 57, note 5.

7. See Luke 12:37 (already quoted in LT 204).

LT 209   From Thérèse to Sister Geneviève.
Winter 1896-1897 (?)

Do not forget to wake up M. T., tomorrow, poor D^elle L., humbled by everyone,[1] but LOVED by Jesus and M. T.

*   CMG.

1. "Thérèse was happy to see me fighting, step by step, with faults that kept me in a state of humiliation, for with my impetuous character I frequently had little outbursts with the Sisters, outbursts which bothered me very much because of my self-love. I found that my exterior conduct was misleading and that I was much better than I appeared, hence a certain frustration at not being judged according to my just deserts. To appear imperfect in the eyes of creatures seemed to me a mountain to be swallowed" (*Souvenirs autobiographiques*, 1909).

LT 210   From Thérèse to Sister Geneviève.
Winter 1896-1897 (?)

Will you look in tomorrow morning to see if M. T. has heard the clapper?[1] ...

*   Autograph.

1. A wooden instrument with a clapper that was used in the cloisters and corridors for the first rising at 5:45 during the winter.

LT 211
December 24,
1896

From Thérèse to Sister Geneviève.

The envelope has this address: "Message from the Blessed Virgin to my dear Child without a home in a foreign land."

Christmas 1896

Dear little Daughter,

If you only knew how much you delight my heart and that of my little Jesus, oh, how happy you would be!... But you do not know, you do not see, and your soul is in sadness. I would like to console you, and, if I do not do it, it is because I know the value of suffering and anguish of heart.[1] Oh, my dear child! if you only knew how my soul was plunged into bitterness when I saw my tender spouse St. Joseph coming back sadly to me without having found an inn.[2]

If you want to bear in peace the trial of not pleasing yourself,[3] you will give me a sweet home; true, you will suffer since you will be at the door of your house, but do not fear, the poorer you are the more Jesus will love you. He will go far, very far in search of you,[4] if at times you wander off a little. He prefers to see you hitting against the stones in the night than walking in broad daylight on a path bedecked with flowers that could retard your progress.[5] I love you, oh, my Céline, I love you more than you could understand....

I am delighted to see you desiring great things, and I am preparing still greater ones for you.... One day you will come with your *Thérèse into the beautiful heaven, you will take your place on the knees of my beloved Jesus,*† *and I will also take you in my arms and will shower you with caresses, for I am your Mother, your dear Mamma.*

Mary, Queen of little angels.[7]

---

* Autograph.
1. See her poem *Why I love you, oh, Mary!* (P 51, May 1897), stanza 16.
2. See Luke 2:7.

3. See LT 209, note 1.
4. See Imitation of Christ II, 11:4, quoted in LT 197.
5. See LT 149, note 4 and DE/G — 8.1.
6. The "knees of Jesus" or the "knees of God" (synonomous expressions): the place desired by *Toto* and *Lili* when in heaven, the place they chose because, being too poor, they had not been able to merit thrones" (DE/G — 8.2); see DE, p. 624.
7. See LT 192, note 3; and, in a very similar sense, the finale of this quatrain of Sister Marie of the Trinity, dedicated to Thérèse : "In the eternal Homeland — May the Face of Jesus — Transport us, oh, dear Sister — Among His 'Little Elect.' " (August 6, 1896.)

LT 212   **From Thérèse to Sister Marie of the Trinity.**

December 24,   Sister Marie of the Trinity explained the origin
1896   of this letter: "The Servant of God followed the
                      inclination of my soul in leading me to Jesus. She
                      told me she did not want to force others to follow
                      her way because God guides us in different ways
                      and each should walk according to the divine
                      will. At this time, being a little childish, I was
                      using a very strange method in the practice of
                      virtue: that of pleasing the Child Jesus by play-
                      ing all kinds of spiritual games with Him. This
                      method aided me in making serious progress, and
                      Thérèse encouraged me in using it by the follow-
                      ing letter that she placed in our cell on Christmas
                      Eve of 1896" (NPPA, *Red Notebook*, p. 53).

                                                    Christmas Eve 1896

Dear little Spouse,[1]

Oh! how pleased I am with you.... All year you have amused me very much by playing ninepins.[2] I was so pleased that the angelic court was surprised and charmed; more than one little cherub asked me why I had not made him a child...more than one asked me if the melody of his harp was not more pleasing to me than your joyful laugh when you knocked down a pin with the bowl of your love.

I answered my little cherubs that they were not to be sorry for not having been children since one day they would be able to play with you in the meadows of heaven; I told them, certainly, your smile was more sweet to me than their melodies because you could not play and smile except by *suffering*, by forgetting yourself.

Beloved little spouse, I have something to ask you, will you refuse me?... Oh, no! you love me too much for that. Well, I shall admit I would like to change the game; the ninepins amuse me, but I would now like to spin the top, and if you wish *you* will be my top. I am giving you one as a model. You see it is not beautiful, whoever does not know how to use it will kick it away with his foot. But a child will leap with joy when seeing it and will say: "Ah! how amusing, this can spin all day long without stopping."[3]

I, little Jesus, love you even though you are without any charms, and I am asking you always to spin in order to amuse me.... But strokes of the whip are necessary to make the top spin.... Well! let the Sisters render you this service and be thankful to them who will be the most assiduous in not letting you relent in your spinning. When I have been well entertained by you, I will take you up above and we shall play without any suffering....

Your little Brother Jesus.

* Autograph.
1. The Child Jesus is talking. The envelope has this address: "*Personal*. To my dear little Spouse, *Player at Ninepins* on Mount Carmel."
2. Sister Marie of the Trinity explained: "I pictured these ninepins in all sizes and colors in order to personify the souls I wanted to reach out to in my prayers" (CSHA, 1953, p. 237).
3. Thérèse is using here her novice's own words spoken a few days earlier: "In the month of December 1896, the novices received for the benefit of the missions different knicknacks for a Christmas tree. And there happened to be at the bottom of the surprise package an object that was very rare in Carmel: *a top*. My companions said: 'How ugly! What good is it?' I knew how to use it, and I picked up the top, saying: 'It is very enjoyable, this can spin all day long without stopping as long as you keep whipping it!' Then I began giving them a demonstration which surprised them. Sister Thérèse was watching me without saying anything" (CSHA, p. 237).

LT 213   **From Thérèse to l'abbé Bellière.**

December 26,   Summary of letter according to Thérèse's draft:
1896   "December 25. By way of exception our Mother
→ LC 172   allowed me to read your letter during Advent.
                         God does not ask sacrifices beyond our strength.
                         When He asks a sacrifice of all that is dear to
                         us, we can repeat with Him: 'My God, let this
                         chalice pass from me...nevertheless, may Your
                         will be done!' It is consoling to think that Jesus
                         trembled at the sight of the chalice He had
                         desired. It is suffering that saves souls. Our Lord
                         redeemed the world through suffering, by dying
                         on the Cross. At the foot of the Cross Jesus saw
                         His Mother. Picture of St. Francis of Assisi."

J.M.J.T.

December 26, 1896

Lisieux Carmel

Jesus †

Monsieur l'Abbé,

I would have liked to answer you sooner, but the rule of Carmel
does not allow the writing or receiving of letters during the time of
Advent. However, our revered Mother permitted me by way of exception to read your letter, understanding you needed to be particularly aided by prayer.

I assure you, *Monsieur l'Abbé,* I am doing all that is within my
power to obtain the graces necessary for you; these graces certainly
will be granted to you since Our Lord never asks sacrifices from us
above our strength. At times, it is true, this divine Saviour makes
us feel all the bitterness of the chalice that He is offering our soul.
When He asks the sacrifice of all that is dearest in this world, it is
impossible, without a very special grace, not to cry out like Him in
the garden of agony: "Father, let this chalice pass from

Mt 26:39

me...however, may your will be done and not mine."[1]

It is very consoling to think that Jesus, the Strong God,[2] knew our weaknesses, that He trembled at the sight of the bitter chalice, this chalice that He had in the past so ardently desired to drink.[3]...

Monsieur l'Abbé, your lot is really beautiful since Our Lord chose it for Himself and since He first wet His lips with the cup He is offering you.

A Saint has said: "The greatest honor God can give a soul is not to give it much but to ask much from it![4] Jesus is treating you then as a privileged one. He wills that you already begin your mission and that through suffering you may save souls. Is it not in suffering, in dying that He Himself redeemed the world?... I know you aspire to the joy of sacrificing your life for the divine Master, but martyrdom of the heart is not less fruitful than the pouring out of one's blood, and now this martyrdom is yours. I am right, then, in saying that your lot is beautiful, that it is worthy of an apostle of Christ.

Monsieur l'Abbé, you come seeking consolations from her whom Jesus has given you as a sister, and you have the right. Since Reverend Mother allows me to write you, I would like to respond to the sweet mission entrusted to me, but I feel the surest means of reaching my goal is to pray and to suffer....

Let us work together for the salvation of souls; we have only the one day of this life to save them and thus to give the Lord proofs of our love. The tomorrow of this day will be eternity, and then Jesus will restore to you a hundredfold the very sweet and very legitimate joys that you sacrificed for Him.[5] He knows the extent of your sacrifice, He knows the suffering of those dear to you increases your own, but He also suffered this martyrdom. To save our souls He left His Mother, He saw the Immaculate Virgin standing at the foot of the Cross,[6] her heart transpierced by a sword of sorrow.[7] So I hope our divine Saviour will console your good mother, and I am asking Him for this immediately. Ah! if the divine Master allowed those whom you are leaving for His love to glimpse the glory He is reserving for you, the multitude of souls who will make up your cortege in heaven, they would already be rewarded for the great sacrifice your separation will cause them.

Our Mother is still sick; however, she has been a little better for several days now. I trust the divine Child Jesus will restore to her the strength she will use for His glory. This reverend Mother is sending you the picture of St. Francis of Assisi that will teach you the means of finding joy in the midst of the trials and combats of life.[8]

I hope, *Monsieur l'abbé,* that you will continue to pray for me who am not an angel as you appear to believe, but a poor little Carmelite, who is very imperfect and who in spite of her poverty has, like you, the desire to work for the glory of God.

Let us remain close to the crib of Jesus through prayer and suffering.

Your unworthy little sister,
Thérèse of the Child Jesus of the Holy Face
rel. carm. ind.

* Autograph.
1. See Matthew 26:39.
2. See Isaias 9:5; this verse occurred frequently in the Christmas liturgy.
3. See Luke 22:15.
4. A sentence from P. Pichon? See LT 172, note 2.
5. See Matthew 19:29.
6. See John 19:25.
7. See Luke 2:35.
8. L'abbé Bellière answered Mother Marie de Gonzague: "Thank you for the kind words you directed to me yourself and through St. Francis. You have perfect joy, Mother, and your love shows it to me. May the Master see fit to give me a share in it." (Letter of January 18, 1897.)

LD   *From Sister Marie of the Eucharist to M. and Mme. Guérin.* (Extracts.)

December 31,   Date deduced from content; see note 1.
1896

I hope to be the first to wish you a good, happy, holy, and joyous year.[1] Adjectives could not express all I wish in the bottom of my heart....

It appears I have to leave space for your four little daughters to sign. You know their filial affection and their sincere wishes for you.

> Your very loving little daughter,
> Marie of the Eucharist

> Sister Agnes of Jesus, *goddaughter*[2]
> Sister Marie of the Sacred Heart
> Sister Thérèse of the Child Jesus
> Sister Geneviève of St. Teresa

...

Our Mother asks me to offer you with her religious sentiments her sincerest good wishes. All the Carmelites wish a good year to their Papa and Mamma, whom they hug very tightly.

*   Autograph.
1.   M. Guérin dated the letter in pencil: January 1, 1897; it was written, however, on December 31, 1896, because on that day Mme. Guérin thanked her daughter and announced her visit for the following day, January 1, at three o'clock.
2.   She was M. Guérin's goddaughter.

LT 214   **From Thérèse to Sister Geneviève.**
January 3,   Presumed date; see note 1.
1897 (?)
Happy Feast!!...

Monsieu Toto wishes a happy feast to *madmoisel* Lili.[1]

*   Autograph.
1. No date in CMG IV, p. 379, in which this note is written as the first
    among those "from 1894 to 1897—in Carmel." It is preceded by this
    explanation: "Note written in her left hand in a baby's spelling; it
    was offered to me by a baby, in bold relief chromolithograph, with
    a little flower."

    This chromolithograph, a calendar of 1896, is preserved in the
    Carmel archives. The December page has remained glued to it.

    On the envelope Sister Geneviève wrote: "A cutout
    chromolithograph, representing a little baby that Thérèse used to wish
    me a happy feast on August 6, in Carmel. There was attached to it
    a note written in her left hand to make the handwriting uncertain.
    It simulated also mistakes in spelling. It begins this way: 'Happy feast!
    Monsieur Toto souète, etc.'

    If we must rely on this very belated note, the "August 6" could
    be that of 1896 or 1897. We must exclude 1897, for at this time Thérèse,
    in the infirmary, was no longer able to write with ink, especially in
    her left hand. There remains "August 6, 1896"; however, the feast
    of St. Geneviève, January 3, appears the more likely date. It seems
    more normal that Thérèse would have used then an out-of-date calen-
    dar. Besides, the use of the nicknames *"Toto"* and *"Lili"* is more
    appropriate during the winter of 1896-1897.

LT 215   **From Thérèse to Sister Marie of the Sacred**
                        Heart.

Beginning of   Approximate date; see note 1.
1897 (?)

J.M.J.T.

Good Jesus loves you with all His Heart and I do also, dear Godmother!!!...

Thérèse of the Child Jesus[1]
rel carm.

*   Autograph.
1. The edition *Lettres*, 1948, presents this letter as being written "at the
    beginning of the year 1897." No fact of internal or external criticism

allows for more precision. It has on the back: "Sister Marie of the Sacred Heart," as though brought by a third party. Was Thérèse ill and kept in her cell? See a similar expression of her feelings in LT 222.

LT 216   **From Thérèse to Mother Agnes of Jesus.**
January 9, 1897

J.M.J.T.

January 9, 1897

Jesus †

Dear little Mother, if you only knew how much I was touched when seeing the degree to which you love me!... Oh! never would I be able to show you my gratitude here below.... I hope to go soon up above.[1] Since "if there is *a heaven, it is for me*,"[2] I shall be rich, I shall have all God's treasures, and He Himself will be *my good*, then I shall be able to return to you a hundredfold all I owe you. Oh, I am looking forward to it.... It troubles me so much to be always receiving without ever giving.

I would have liked not to have seen little Mother's tears flowing, but what I was happy *to see* was the good effect they produced, it was like magic. Ah, I am not vexed at anyone when my little Mother *is scowled at*,[3] for I see only too well that the Sisters are merely instruments placed *in the way* by Jesus Himself so that *little* Mother's way (in *little* Thérèse's eyes) resemble the one He has chosen for Himself when He was a traveller on the earth of exile.... Then His face was as though hidden, no one recognized Him, He was an object of contempt.. Little Mother is not an object of contempt, but very few recognize her because Jesus has hidden her face![5]...

Oh, Mother, how beautiful is your lot!... It is truly worthy of *you*, the privileged one of our family, of you who show us the way just as the little swallow that we see always at the head of his companions, tracing out, in the air, the way that must lead them to their new homeland.

Oh! understand the affection of YOUR little girl, who would like to tell you *so many, so many* things!

* Autograph.
1. The first explicit reference of her coming death in Thérèse's correspondence. We find, in the Community's copybook of prescriptions, two prescriptions of Dr. de Cornière, dated January 2, 1897. The second (no. 98665) is a camphor vesicatory of 12 cm., and it could have been for Thérèse. Sister Geneviève wrote Brother Simeon at Rome, January 10: "Sister Thérèse of the Child Jesus and I are trying to be saints, and we would really like to reach heaven soon. She is setting out for it, she is an angel. . . . Love consumes her life, and her delicate chest is giving us some serious worries."
2. A probable allusion to this verse of Soumet: "For whom would the heavens be if they were not for you?" taken from the tragedy *Jeanne d'Arc martyre*, third part of his *Jeanne d'Arc*, national trilogy dedicated to France (1846). Thérèse introduced this passage (which she erroneously attributes to d'Avrigny) into her play of 1895 *Jeanne d'Arc accomplissant as mission* (RP 3). The dubious variant at the beginning: "If there is a heaven" is the first reference, veiled to her trial of faith in her *Correspondance*.
3. We do not know the circumstances of this disagreement.
4. See Isaias 53:3.
5. "The Servant of God meant: since her little Mother was no longer prioress" (Note from CE II, p.59). There follows an illegible erasure of three or four words.

LT 217   **From Thérèse to Sister Marie of Saint-Joseph.**
January 1897 (?)   Approximate date; see note 2.

J.M.J.T.

Charming these little couplets.[1]. . . How naughty to go begging from others[2] when one has her purse all filled! But it is not naughty to sleep, to be good and happy, it is "the little trade of the shop"[3] and never must it be closed, even on Sundays and feast days. That is to say, the days that Jesus reserves to Himself for trying our souls.[4]. . . Sing your delightful refrains like a finch,[5] and I, like a poor little sparrow, sigh in my corner,[6] singing like the wandering Jew: "Death can do nothing for me, I can well see!"[7]

I do not hear any more talk about the famous tablecloth,[8] is there still any question of it?

* Autograph.
1. Couplets composed by Sister Marie of Saint-Joseph; they have not been preserved.
2. Thérèse herself, from whom Sister Marie of Saint-Joseph requested the composing of a poem in December 1896; see LT 205, note 2. There can be a question of another request. The very poor handwriting of this note would suggest its having been written during the first days of June. See LT 239, note 2.
3. See LT 204, note 4.
4. Same thought in CSG, p. 155.
5. Reference to Sister Marie of Saint-Joseph's good voice; see LT 199, note 4.
6. See Psalm 101:8.
7. The fifteenth of twenty-four stanzas of the *Complaint of the Wandering Jew*. These verses appear on a print dating from Thérèse's childhood at Les Buoissonnets. The Carmel Archives has quite a number of these prints; see CJ 31.7.1, note 1. On the *Wandering Jew*, see LT 239, note 2.
8. Repair work assigned to the Sisters in the linen room, Sister Marie of Saint-Joseph and Thérèse.

LC 173 *From P. Roulland to Thérèse.*
January 20, 1897

Kouy Fou R. + ap. January 20, 1897

Sister,

As you have done it, I shall write on all the lines[1] to save paper, and, with our kind Mother's permission I shall speak a few words with you about dear oriental Su-Tchuen. I reached the boundaries of this province, I recited the *Te Deum*, I offered God what I am and what I have. I thought of St. Teresa, who said: "To suffer or to die." Why did these words come to my mind? I soon had an explanation for it; I shall tell you my experience, and you will think the same way as I do. I finished my offering and was obliged to take to my bed; two days later we went down to Kouy Fou to a confrère's residence. My sickness increased; they called in a Chinese doctor, for the only European here is a priest. I was declared incapable of continuing my voyage; *adieu* then to my dear confrères, my companions. Ten days later, the fever broke out, a heavy fever, a kind of tribute I was paying to the climate. For ten days I was talking foolishly, but it seems all I said was only of a hilarious nature. The first doctor gave me up; a second, formerly persecuted for the faith, came and administered lots of quinine. The fever, easily fatal, became periodic, and an improvement began to set in. Today I am almost cured. That is the experience. I conclude: it is to the prayers of persons interested in me and especially to your own that I have not sung my *Nunc Dimittis* when entering my mission. And is it not evident that God willed to remind me that without the cross and suffering I shall do nothing for the glory of God and the salvation of souls? This is a missionary's opinion who has been in China for twenty-six years. He said: "Listen to this. The more tribulation you will have in the exercise of your ministry the better you will succeed." Thus, Sister, in our situation, we must not ask that I do not suffer, but that I know how to suffer. I shall find, moreover, many consolations both from God, who is helping us visibly, and from Christians, among whom are some excellent families. We have just learned of an incident which took place close to Kouy Fou. Fire broke out in a house close to that of a Christian converted in the past four months; fire brigades are still not organized in China. The fire was in control of the situation; most objects possible were snatched from the fire, and then its progress was watched. The flames pushed by the wind were falling on the Christian's house; he took some holy water and threw some on the conflagration. Instantly the flames veered in the opposite direction, and the house of the new convert was saved. Many, too, are deaths coming immediately after the reception of the sacraments.

In the solitude of your monastery, you have perhaps not heard anyone speak of the persecution that last year ravaged two-thirds of our province. Christians were pillaged and forced into exile; residences of missionaries, churches, mission buildings, all were pillaged and set on fire. One missionary in a college saw the pillagers come more than once close to the building and yet retire without having put their plans in execution. And here are the results of Satan's work: the three principal instigators of the troubles were recalled to Peking and fell into disgrace; the missions were completely indemnified; the mandarins and the people, seeing the missionaries so powerful at Peking, began to fear them: the former especially respect us and treat us as equals, and conversions are more numerous. Ah! if the French people could and would make that crowd of monsters who are working for its destruction go back into their hole; can it not do what a handful of apostles is doing?

At this moment, famine reigns here: the Chinese do not imitate the ant which, says the good La Fontaine, makes ample provision for a bad season, and they are caught when the harvest is bad. This year the rain did not cease falling for two months when the rice was in grain; the harvest rotted on the ground, and today there is nothing to eat. One-third of the population will die from hunger. A pagan family just killed two children because they had no rice to give them. This is why it is good to buy these poor little things. The girls are given away; the boys are sold at a cheap price. The priest of this residence just bought a child for fifteen fancs: his name is Paolo, he is four years old and has exceptional intelligence. He is often with the priest and speaks like an adult. He is even set up as my teacher; he comes to my side (he is here at this moment); he tells me a word and has me repeat it until I say it well. This child will receive a Christian education, and perhaps one day he will go to a seminary. His mother, without whose knowledge he was sold, must miss him, but he is very comfortable here. I was to baptize him, but my sickness prevented me from doing so. When shall I have my first baptism, my first conversion? Alas, I am only a little child: I do not know how to speak.[2] I shall spend a few months in a Christian family, learn the language, the customs, etc., and then the apostolate with a former confrère first. You want one of the little girls I shall baptize to be named Marie (Ma ly ia) Thérèse[3] (Te le sa). Choose between the two names, for the Chinese have only one. The name Louis is pronounced Louy-se. These signs[4] indicate the sound employed in conversation, and this is what I find the most difficult in the language.

I had told you that at Christmas I would celebrate a Mass for your intentions, and I was confined to bed.[5] I will carry out my promise as soon as I can. My first Mass I shall say for the Blessed Virgin's intentions; at the *memento* of the second, I will offer the divine Victim for my Carmelite sister according to the intentions she had formulated on Christmas eve. I will also make a *memento* for kind Mother, tell her this.

One privation of the missionary: he does not have Jesus in the Blessed Sacrament; subject to be called at each moment five or six leagues and more from his residence, he cannot leave Jesus without a guardian in a country like China. So in spirit I shall at times be in your chapel, and sometimes perhaps we shall meet together at the divine Master's feet, praying for our sanctification and that of souls.

I do not know when my letter will knock on Carmel's doors. Mail is not well established in China. The address is Chinese. If I can do so, I will send you my visiting card: Road where one meets mercy and teaching.⁶ Ask God that this may be so.

I have already distributed some of the chaplets you sent me: the color of the beads pleases the Christians who come asking for some. I will take care not to be prodigal, for China is far from France.

I come to an end. I was happy at my departure,⁷ happy at my arrival; the happiness of my confrères, their charity put me at ease. I feel I am at home as they say in the country of the apples.

A Dieu, Sister. I bless you with all my heart, you and good Mother. Your brother in Jesus,

Roulland
Miss. ap.
Su-Tchuen or.

Address: P. Roulland, *Miss. ap. au Su-Tchuen orient.*
Missions Etrangères, 128 rue du Bac Paris

(15 cent stamp)

*   Autograph.
1. Thérèse's letter of November 1, 1896 (LT 201) was especially cramped, but he must not have received that as yet; in his letter of January 19, to Mother Marie de Gonzague, he asked: "You have received my letter of September 26, I hope?" It is only on February 24, 1897 (LC 175) that he speaks explicitly of the "long letter" from Thérèse.
2. See LT 226, par. 2.

3. A desire expressed *viva voce* in the speakroom, July 3, 1896, or in a letter (lost) of July 27-28, 1896; see p. 975, notes 6 and 7.
4. Different diacritical signs follow, corresponding to the method used by P. Roulland to transcribe (indicating the sound which determines the meaning) the Chinese characters in Roman lettering. Since some of these signs have no equivalent in French printing, it is better to reproduce none of them in the names cited here.
5. See LT 201, note 9.
6. Thérèse had kept this card, black letters on a red background: a ceremonial card without which one could not be presented to a mandarin.
7. See LT 193, note 6.

LD   *From Brother Simeon to Sister Geneviève.*
                         (Extracts.)

January 25, 1897
→ LD

                                              Rome, January 25, 1897

Very dear Sisters[1] in Our Lord,

The Indulgence for your dear *Doyenne's* Golden Jubilee[2] is in my hands. I dared ask for and obtained the same blessing to be granted to the Very Reverend Mother Superior, her religious, and those assisting at the celebration. Sister Saint Stanislaus will be doubly happy! One is so blessed to please.

   . . .

I just read over again the splendid poem of your admirable sister.[3] It is a sublime song which could have been on the lips of the Great St. Teresa!! My confreres argue about this, but they are making copies of it. I shall send it to one of my nieces, Superior of *Bon Pasteur* at Lyons, who will enjoy it and benefit from it. I am convalescing from a serious illness lasting five months. In the month of June last, I had an attack of paralysis that impaired the entire left side of my person. This paralysis was creeping paralysis, and it brought me to the edge of the grave. I was given the last sacraments, there was no longer any hope. For the last two months

I am better, but only gradually, slowly. I am eighty-three, and one heals with difficulty at this age. I submit myself to God's holy will, to all He wills from His poor, very poor servant. Pray for me, dear Sisters, and have your companions pray for me. I can depend on it, can I not?

. . .

I thank you for the beautiful photograph you sent; its arrangement is very attractive and the personages could not have been better chosen![4] My compliments. I recognized you.[5]

. . .

Ask Madame, your very Reverend Superior, to accept my humble regards, as well as your good companions. Tell your holy Sister I am praying for her recovery. Pray for your very

> devoted servant,
> Brother Simeon

---

*   Autograph.

1.   Sisters Geneviève and Thérèse; in the letter Brother Simeon addresses only Sister Geneviève, for she only had written him on January 10; see note 2.

2.   Sister Saint-Stanislaus, aged seventy-three; she was celebrating fifty years of Profession, February 8, 1897. At the beginning of January, she had said: "What would please me very much would be for our little Sisters to write kind Brother Simeon to obtain the blessing of our beloved Holy Father." (Letter of Sister Geneviève to Brother Simeon, January 10, 1897.)

3.   The poem *Vivre d'Amour* (P 15, February 26, 1895), about which Sister Geneviève speaks in her letters of January 10 and 27.

4.   Sister Geneviève wrote on January 10: "With this letter I am sending you a photograph of a tableau made up in the Community. . . . Very dear Brother, our Mother is allowing me to tell you (in secret) that the religious who composed the tableau had me pose as St. Catherine and Sister Thérèse of the Child Jesus as Joan of Arc. . . . They say we are so lifelike that this photograph cannot go out of here. . . . Now you know your little friends. Oh! how we would love to know you too." (To Brother Simeon, January 10, 1897.) The photograph appears in VTL, no. 14. Touched up by Sister Geneviève, it was sent to some close friends outside the monastery, among whom it was passed off as a tableau. See LC 176, note 4 and CJ 10.8.4, note 1.

5. We should perhaps understand: "I identified you." On the assumption of a former meeting, see LC 134, note 2.

LT 218   **From Thérèse to Brother Simeon.**
January 27, 1897
→ LD January 25, 1897

J.M.J.T.

Carmel of Lisieux, January 27, '97

Jesus †

Monsieur le Directeur,

I am happy to join with my Sister Geneviève[1] in thanking you for the precious favor you obtained for our Carmel.

Not knowing how to express my gratitude, I want to show you how much I was touched by your kindness to us by means of my prayers at Our Lord's feet. . . .

A feeling of sadness is mingled with my joy when learning your health was impaired, so I am asking Jesus with my whole heart to prolong your life which is so precious for the Church the longest time possible. I know the divine Master must be eager to crown you in heaven, but I trust He will leave you still in this exile so that, working for His glory as you have done since your youth,[2] the immense weight of your merits may supply for other souls who will present themselves before God with empty hands.

I dare to hope, very dear Brother, I shall be of the number of these blessed souls who will share in your merits. I believe my course here below will not be long. . .when I shall appear before my Beloved Spouse, I shall have only my desires to offer Him, but if you have preceded me into the homeland, I trust you will come to meet me and offer for me the merits of your very fruitful works. . . . You see, your little Carmelites cannot write you without asking some favor and without making an appeal to your generosity!!!. . .

Monsieur le Directeur, you are so *powerful* for *us* on earth, you have already obtained our Holy Father Leo XIII's blessing for us

so many times that I cannot refrain from thinking that in heaven
God will give you a very great power over His Heart. I beg you not
to forget me in His presence if you have the joy of seeing Him before
I do.... The only thing I beg you to ask for my soul is the grace
of *loving* Jesus and of *making Him loved* as much as this is possible
for me.

If it be myself whom the Lord comes to look for first, I promise
to pray for your intentions and for all the persons who are dear to
you. However, I am not awaiting heaven for offering this prayer,
right now I am happy to be able to prove my deep gratitude in this
way.

In the Sacred Heart of Jesus, I shall always be happy to call myself,
Monsieur le Directeur,

> Your little grateful Carmelite,
> Sister Thérèse of the Child Jesus
> of the Holy Face
> rel. carm. ind.

* Autograph.
1. Sister Geneviève wrote on the same day as did also Mother Marie de
   Gonzague. Another letter from Sister Geneviève, February 11, gave
   a report on the Jubilee celebration for Sister Saint Stanislaus.
2. Brother Simeon entered religious life at age fifteen.

LC 174   *L'abbé Belli*ère to Thér*èse.*
January 31, 1897
                                    Sunday, January 31

†
R.A.[1]

Very dear Sister in Our Lord,

The kindness with which God treats me, and the kindness He has
given you work profoundly in my soul comforted by the attention
that your love inspires in you. I feel I am becoming better each time
a little of the piety lived at the Carmel reaches me, and I would like

to love Jesus as you love Him there. Sister, you had Him in your heart when you were composing this canticle of love that you saw fit to send me.[2] In it one breathes in a divine breath making one pure and strong. On the evening of the day when I had the joy of receiving the poem, it was the object of a long and sweet meditation in company with my director, who is so happy to know that my soul and work are entrusted to your solicitude. Since then it has served me in my acts of thanksgiving, the day before yesterday and today. I want to know the poem perfectly and use it as an ejaculatory prayer during the day and the night when I awaken. I have placed it in my New Testament, and since this holy book never leaves me, this canticle of love will always accompany me, even to the end of the world.

I would like to be able to sing like you, dear Sister, in order to tell Jesus the sentiments that your own inspire in me. But He, who is all good, sees fit to grant me only my rough and ready prose. His very tender Heart does not pay too much attention to form, and His grace descends continually.

Oh! yes, Sister: "Let us live by love." This is the means of finding happiness on earth. Without God, without His love, how cold it is around us. But when a holy fervor animates our hearts, what serenity and sweetness there is in life. It is in fact to repose on the stormy waves,[3] it is living the life of the Glorious King, the Delight of the Elect,[4] to begin on earth the happiness of heaven.

Calvary, then, becomes Tabor,[5] and there is no longer any sorrow, for, as the Saint says: when we love, there is no longer any sorrow, or if there is sorrow, it is a sorrow that we love.[6]

I beg the Sacred Heart to give us this love always greater, always stronger, and more generous, and that by means of it He may so draw us to Himself that we live definitively and indissolubly united to Him.

You know then, Sister, that I must postpone my departure until October;[7] yes, my superiors judged it was better to wait. This change of place might have divided this year which would have been disrupted at least with regard to my studies. My director here authorized me to leave, and those over there preferred that I wait. But, next year! will be the novitiate, proximate preparation, and afterward: *En avant*, God and Work.

When I baptize my first little black, I will ask your Reverend

Mother that you may be the godmother, for it will be yours, you will have drawn it more to God than I.

A Dieu, very dear Sister, pray always for my conversion, that the Master bring about some progress in me. I pray often and very fervently to Him for you.

Forever in His holy Heart, your poor brother,

M. Barthélemy-Bellière
a.m.

I recommend to your prayers especially the examinations that begin tomorrow, Monday, and end on the 14th.

* Autograph.

1. Abbreviation for *Regina Apostolorum* (Queen of Apostles).
2. The poem *Vivre d'Amour* (P 15). This poem had dispensed Thérèse from a new letter when she had written him the day after Christmas (LT 123). Since then l'abbé Bellière offered his wishes to the prioress on January 18; she answered him on January 27 or 28, sending him Thérèse's poem. By the same mail of January 31, he thanked Mother Marie de Gonzague: "Thank you especially for having sent me this song of divine love. You were right, Mother, it was to do me good, and it is often a sweet joy for me to read it over again. When adapting it to music, I seem to hear a tune from heaven" (letter of January 31, 1897).
3. The poem quoted, stanza 9.
4. *Ibid.*, stanza 3.
5. *Ibid.*, stanza 4.
6. Saint Augustine; see LT 197, note 5.
7. He had written to Mother Marie de Gonzague: "My superiors wanted me to postpone my departure for Africa until the month of October.

LT 219   **From Thérèse to Mother Agnes of Jesus.**

February 22,   Note dated by the recipient.
1897
→ LC lost

Thank you, little Mother! Your nose was broken,[1] *yes, but*!! it IS LONG!... There will always remain enough for you, whereas mine, if I were to break it, there would no longer remain any for me![2]... Ah! how blessed we are to be able to laugh at everything.... *Oh! yes!*...there is no *but* for that....

* Autograph.
1. A new disappointment, but we do not know the circumstances.
2. On Mother Agnes' long nose, see CJ 8.7.5, and on the "little nose" of Thérèse, see CJ 31.7.3.

LT 220   **From Thérèse to l'abbé Bellière.**

February 24,   Summary of this letter according to Thérèse's
1897   outline: "Feburary 25, Poems composed for the
→ LC 174   Carmelites. Recite every day this prayer: 'Mer-
                      ciful Father, in the name of our gentle Jesus, the
                      Blessed Virgin, and the saints, I beg you to enkin-
                      dle my sister with Your Spirit of Love and to
                      grant her the grace of making You loved very
                      much.' I am not worried about purgatory: 'What
                      does it matter to me to remain until the end of
                      the world in purgatory, if by my prayers I save
                      one single soul?)' (St. Teresa of Avila.)"

J.M.J.T.

(Carmel of Lisieux)

Wednesday evening, February 24, 1897

Jesus †

Monsieur l'Abbé,

Before entering into the silence of holy Lent,[1] I want to add a short note to our Reverend Mother's letter to thank you for the one you sent me last month.

If you experience any consolation when you think that in Carmel a Sister is praying incessantly for you, my gratitude is not less great than yours to Our Lord, who has given me a little brother whom He destines to become His priest and His apostle.... Truly, you will know only in heaven how dear you are to me; I feel our souls are made to understand one another. Your prose which you call "rough and ready" reveals to me that Jesus has placed in your heart aspirations that He gives only to souls called to the highest sanctity. Since He Himself has chosen me to be your sister, I trust He will not look upon my weakness or rather that He will use this weakness even to carry out His work, for the strong God[2] loves to show His power by making use of nothing.[3] United in Him, our souls will be able to save many others, for this gentle Jesus has said: "If two among you agree together on something which you ask from my Father, it will be granted them."[4] Ah! what we are asking Him is to work for His glory, to love Him and make Him loved.... How would our union and our prayer not be blessed?

Monsieur l'Abbé, since the canticle on love has pleased you, our good Mother told me to copy out several other poems for you,[5] but you will receive them only in a few weeks, for I have few free moments, even on Sunday because of my task as sacristan.[6] These poor poems will reveal to you not what I am but what I would like and should be.... When composing them, I have looked more at the substance than at the form, so the rules of versification are not always respected; my purpose was to translate my sentiments (or rather the sentiments of the Carmelite) in order to respond to my Sisters' desires. These verses are more suitable for a religious woman

[handwritten margin notes: Is. 9:5; 1 Cor. 1:27-29; Mt. 18:19]

than for a seminarian. I hope, however, they will please you. Is not your soul the fiancée of the Divine Lamb, and will it not soon become His spouse, on the blessed day of your ordination to the subdiaconate?

I thank you, *Monsieur l'Abbé,* for having chosen me as godmother of the first child you will have the joy of baptizing; it is, then, up to me to choose the names of my future godchild. I want to give it as protectors: the Blessed Virgin, St. Joseph, and St. Maurice, my dear little brother's patron. No doubt this child exists only in God's thought, but already I am praying for it and fulfilling in advance my duties as godmother. I am praying, too, for all the souls who will be entrusted to you, and above all I beg Jesus to embellish your soul with all virtues, and especially with His love. You tell me that very often you pray also for your sister; since you have this charity, I would be very happy if each day you would consent to offer this prayer for her which contains all her desires: "Merciful Father, in the name of our gentle Jesus, the Virgin Mary, and the Saints, I beg You to enkindle my sister with Your Spirit of Love and to grant her the favor of making You loved very much."[7] You have promised to pray for me *throughout your life*; no doubt your life will be longer than mine, and it is not permitted you to sing like me: "I have the hope my exile will be short!..."[8] but neither are you permitted to forget your promise. If the Lord takes me soon with Him, I ask you to continue each day the same prayer, for I shall desire in heaven the same thing as I do on earth: To love Jesus and to make him loved.

Monsieur l'abbé, you must think I am very strange; perhaps you are sorry to have a sister who seems to want to go and enjoy eternal repose and leave you working alone.... But rest assured, the only thing I desire is God's will, and I admit that if in heaven I were no longer able to work for His glory, I would prefer exile to the homeland.

I do not know the future; however, if Jesus realizes my presentiments, I promise to remain your little sister up above. Our union, far from being broken, will become more intimate. Then there will no longer be any cloister and grilles, and my soul will be able to fly with you into distant missions. Our roles will remain the same: yours, apostolic weapons, mine, prayer and love.

Monsieur l'Abbé, I notice I am losing count of time; it is late, in a few moments the divine Office will ring,[9] and nevertheless I still have a request to make. I would like you to write down for me the memorable dates of your life so that I may unite myself to you in a very special way to thank our gentle Savior for the graces He has granted you.

In the Sacred Heart of Jesus-Victim, who will soon be exposed for our adoration,[10] I am happy to call myself forever,

Your very little and unworthy sister,
Thérèse of the Child Jesus of the
Holy Face
rel carm. ind.

* Autograpph.

1. Lent was about to begin on Ash Wednesday, March 3.

2. See Isaias 9:5.

3. See I Corinthians 1:27-29.

4. See Matthew 18:19.

5. This is the list of the poems sent by Thérèse to l'abbé Bellière: *Les répons de St. Agnes, Jésus seul, Mon chant d'aujourd'hui, A Ste. Cécile, Vivre d'Amour, A Th. Vénard, Jésus mon Bien-Aimé, rappelle-toi, La volière de l'Enfant-Jésus, Au Sacré Coeur de Jésus, Jeter des fleurs, A mes petits frères du Ciel, Cant. pour la vénérable Jeanne d'Arc, Le triomphe de l'humilité, A mon Ange gardien, Me joie, Les sacristines du Carmel, Mes Armes, Qui a Jésus a tout.* According to the adopted numbering, it is question of the following poems: P 22, 32, 5, 15, 44, 21, 37, 20, 30, 45, 4; a fragment from RP 7; P 43, 42, 36, 46, and a fragment of P 16. The list conforms to the content and order of the poems returned to the Carmel of Lisieux (no doubt after the death of P. Bellière). See LC 177.

6. Sister Geneviève, stingy with her own free time, was struck by her sister's self-denial on these occasions: "I noticed when she was sacristan and her personal work was done, she purposely, on free days, walked near the sacristy so that one could ask her for some help. She made herself available to the one in charge of the linen room (Sister Marie of the Angels) so that the latter could ask for help, which never failed" (CSG, p. 105).

7. See the similar request made by Thérèse to P. Roulland, the preceding year: LC 166, note 3.

8. Poem *Vivre d'Amour*, stanza 9.
9. Matins was recited at nine in the evening; Thérèse was writing during the free hour of "silence."
10. February 28, March 1 and 2; Forty-Hours devotion.

LC 175   *From P. Roulland to Thérèse.*

February 24, 1897
→ LT 201

Kouy-Fou   R. + Ap.   February 24, 1897

Sister,

I am not writing you at length, for I am about to go up to Tchoug-Kin; I am not even answering your long letter which did me much good. I want only to send you some relics of a future martyr.[1] I left some with my parents on the day I left my family; I sent them some from Shanghai. Why should I not send some also to my sister? At the moment we are not in important danger of death, but from one day to the next we can receive thrusts from the knife. We would not be martyrs in the strict sense of the term;[2] however, by directing our intention, saying, for example: "My God, it is for Your love that we have come here, accept the sacrifice of our life and convert souls," would we not be martyrs enough to go to heaven?... And what, then, is the evil threatening us: this. The famine is at its height; fifteen leagues from here bandits burned a village; elsewhere, a young man, passing in front of a house, was seized, strangled, and cooked in a pot. This dish was offered to the person who recounted the matter to us and who saw the victim's two legs. Here there is a woman who was attacked in order to be robbed: each armed with a knife, two men ordered her to give up her clothes; the woman did so against her will, but she did not lose her presence of mind: at the right moment she seized the knives and stabbed the thieves. She came to tell the whole story to the mandarin, who gave her a reward. Here, bandits are hiding in the mountain and they slit the throats of the soldiers who are sent out to disperse them. A child came to deliver a letter: five leagues from here a large number of pagans and Christians are hiding in a cave of a mountain to escape the bandits chasing them; among these Christians are two religious who sent the child to ask the priest what they must do. It would be imprudent to leave these virgins with the very corrupt pagans, and they are called to Kouy-Fou. The cities I will come to while going up are in revolt. In a word, robberies, crimes, etc., are the order of the day, and the famine threatens more and more. If the first harvest (in two months) fails, what will happen? Now the dry weather has destroyed the buckwheat. To bring on the rain the mandarin has just published an edict: it is forbidden to eat meat. He believes he can make the gods propitious, in this way, as though these devils held the keys of the great celestial reservoir. A father was saying to me the day before yesterday: "It is possible I may die, it would be good for me to make my will." In a word, we are in God's hands. If the bandits kill me, and if I am not worthy to enter heaven immediately, you will draw me out of purgatory,[3] and I shall go to await you in paradise.

I have already done some ministry. A little girl of the Holy Childhood, one year old, just died; the priest in charge of Kouy-Fou sent me to bless the body. I left in a sedan chair. Arriving, I found the little girl lying on a bench; by her side, they were eating, smoking, warming themselves as though there was nothing; the children were playing as usual. The mistress of the house made me sit down, invited me to smoke, brought some tea, then some chinese dishes. I set to work close to the body. At this moment the coffin arrived: it was made up of some poor planks badly set together with some wooden pegs; this coffin cost two hundred sapekas (twenty *sous*). They placed the child in it; then I put on the surplice, the stole, and I took the Chinese hat and said the blessing. I admit I was happy to do it: I seemed to see the little soul come and smile at me and promise to pray for me and mine. (Naturally, when I speak of mine, I speak also of my Carmelite Sister.) You tell me, Sister, you offer Jesus my love with yours; well! at the Mass I offer your love with mine after Holy Communion. I am certain Jesus when seeing this offering will pardon me the little love I have for Him. At the *memento* for the dead I think of your dead relatives.

Some news we learned at this moment: the military mandarin from Kouy-Fou came to the city and punished on the spot the Chinese whom he found at fault. He fears: he has expedited his affairs in a more settled province. The Christian who gave this news to the priest who came up with me to visit a converted area added: "Father, do not leave; if any trouble comes up in your absence we would have no one to defend us." The priest assured him: "If there are troubles here, I will come back immediately." An old Christian and *holy* man has witnessed many crises: he saw a flood at his doors without any fear because he had had a Mass said and because he was sure of God's help. Today, he is in grave fear: what will become of us? More news: in another part of the country we learn there are disturbances.

What a gossip I am: I was to be short and see...I would have done better to tear up my sheet of paper. Above all say nothing outside; I want my family to know nothing of the dangers surrounding us. I will write you soon.[4] Offer my filial and affectionate respect to our good Mother; to you, Sister, this wish: that the very gentle Lord may enkindle your heart with His love.

A. Roulland
miss. ap.
Su-Tchuen oriental

*   Autograph.
1. A lock of his hair, according to Thérèse's request. The "relic" is preserved with the letter.
2. In this country, Europeans were victims of xenophobia or banditry rather than religious persecution. In her response on May 9 (LT 226), Thérèse agreed that "in the eyes of men this martyrdom does not bear this name."
3. See LT 226, Thérèse's strong reaction to this statement.
4. P. Roulland kept his word on April 29, 1897, (LC 178) even before he had received Thérèse's letter of March 19 (LT 221).

LC 176   *From Brother Salutaire to Thérèse.*
March 16, 1897

J.M.J.   Rome, March 16, '97

Dear Sister Thérèse of the *Child Jesus,*

I come to give you a surprise,[1] will you be pleased? I want you
to be pleased. Your goodness makes me hope so. Your holy fires
will enliven my coldness, and your ascents will aid my own feeble
flights.... You will not only be indulgent to my booklet: *Mes Dévotions,*[2] I am taking the liberty of offering to you, but it will be at
home near you in spite of its weak and discordant tones.... You
understand already that someone has sold you, and you can guess
who it is; but do not be displeased, for he has found a needy
buyer.... He has shared with me your rich literary compositions,[3]
and how I have enjoyed them. I am going to play the game with
you: who loses, wins.... yes, since I must admit the "how" of this
good undertaking, Brother Simeon showed me the delightful and
heavenly St. Catherine, with her beloved and lilied Jeanne d'Arc
carrying her white banner of victory.[4]... I could see with my eyes...
contemplate the resplendent and holy Virgin Mary of your dear and
youthful artist, Geneviève of St. Teresa; it is a striking tableau[5] il-
lustrated by angelic verses.[6] I am, then, among familiar faces, and
I can take liberties....

This long preamble may appear like a selfish approach, however,
let us get down to the matter at hand.

I intend publishing very soon a circular to favor the spread of my
book. Articles, letters, etc., are not lacking, but they are all fun-
damentally the same.... I intend sending you *one* of them that appeared in the *Gazetta del Clero* at Rome. It was written by a woman
from Lyons, very pious and very learned, whom I know only by
reputation...and this is how I know her: Our procurator, having
had some dealings with her regarding some books, had her accept
two copies of *Mes Dévotions,* for herself and her daughter, a Visitandine at Annecy. When answering, she thought it necessary to put
in a word for me: "Sister Eugénie and I want to thank with all our
heart your worthy Brother-Poet for his lovable book of religious

poems. At this moment I am reading it with great profit to my soul.''
I took advantage of this beautiful windfall (just as I am doing with
you), and I begged her to write a special article for me, suggesting
its form to her, since she had read my whole book with such great
interest. I am coming, then, to make the same request to you and
to engage you in writing out some lines so that you may contribute
to the good work, if you are willing. I am allowing myself, then,
to point out to you the character to be given your letter, for it should
be a letter in the form of an article that I need, should you see fit
to cooperate with my request. You are called by the beautiful name
of *Thérèse of the Child Jesus*. It is important that people perceive
this in your letter. . . . *Jesus of Thérèse* will be pleased with you. . . .
Jesus, that is your *theme*. . . . *Jesus*, how much this name appears
in the greatest part of my book. You will have noticed this easily.
Now you are doing the talking: "I have read with real interest the
delightful book *Mes Dévotions* with which you have recently enriched
the collection of pious manuals. . . . I must congratulate you on a
work so suitable for preserving the precious seeds that a Christian
education has sown in the impressionable heart of the child. It is
not possible to single out or to analyze in so many beautiful pages
the aspirations of love, the delightful tenderness of a soul for its
God.'' (Prelude for the subject.) "What a holy inspiration are your
pious affections on the Life of Jesus! To know Jesus, to love Him,
this is Religion. . . . This Life of Jesus! so compact, so well divided,
with its little stanzas that are so easy to learn and to retain, is not
all this simply an affectionate prayer in which the soul wills to remind the Divine Master of all He designed to do and suffer for it? . . .
Then the Mass, that act of love of a God for men, the Angel of the
Eucharist, the Union with Jesus, the Child loving Jesus, His Heart,
the Cross, victory of a God's love, Nazareth: these are the foun-
tains in which one may draw a thought, take out a stanze on the
love of Jesus for men. . . .[7]

You are not obliged to keep to my choice of sentences. . . . I am
only giving you some ideas in these sentences.

I am not, however, imposing myself on you. . . . I have perhaps
acted too quickly; you will please excuse me. You are so good, so
indulgent! I dared too much! I imposed too much on your kindness.

I beg you, dear Sister, not to make any references to the different passages in my letter, for I am writing this without the knowledge of Brother Simeon.... I wanted to give him a pleasant surprise. You can begin, then, the letter you will see fit to write me by these few words: "I just received an unexpected gift; instead of one thank-you, I believe I have to make two: one to the sender, the other to dear Brother Simeon, who is the first cause because of his intimate confidences to you. I am very happy since these confidences have procured for me the advantage of receiving a gift which is very pleasing to me." And if you judge it fitting, you begin immediately after the letter at the bottom of page three what I am suggesting to you, which you will send me as soon as possible. When sending your letter, you will thank me for the good and excellent news I gave you on Brother Simeon's health, etc.... I have entered into these details of arrangement to lighten the burden I am giving you and to lessen my mistakes.... If I am rushing you a little it is because I am in a hurry to print the circular in question.[8]... I am dealing with a generous heart, devoted to Jesus...a heart whose throbs charm her readers. My regards to your Geneviève, and my respects to your reverend Superior. Your fatiguing and grateful

	Brother Salutaire
Pardon me, please.	College Français St. Joseph

* Autograph.

1. This correspondent was unknown in the Carmel of Lisieux. A native of Herault, seventy-six years old, he was living at Rome since 1885, the year of the foundation of St. Joseph's College. He had enjoyed a brilliant career in teaching, giving among other courses some evening classes in French to the elite of Turin (1845-1853), which brought him into contact with Silvio Pellico. His biographical account describes him (in 1897) as a lovable and jovial old man: "Rarely a harsh or critical word, no sign of impatience, but a man with a happy propensity for the compliment, the expression of which was almost too familiar." (Biographical notice, p. 342.) This can be seen in his letter to Thérèse.

2. *Mes Dévotions ou l'Enfant aux autels de Jésus et de Marie:* a collection of poems composed by him and printed at Rome in 1896.

3. The poem *Vivre d'Amour* and several others composed by Thérèse, "if not the most beautiful, at least the most typical" (letter of Sister

Geneviève to Brother Simeon, February 11, 1897). Brother Simeon thanked her in these terms on March 5: "I thank you, dear Sister Geneviève, for the different poems you have sent me. Your good Sister is always drawing new treasures from her rich heart and her fecund intelligence!" Undoubtedly it is about this letter that Sister Geneviève was speaking in her *Conseils et Souvenirs*: It was read during recreation by Mother Marie de Gonzague in Thérèse's absence; the latter asked for it, then, out of renunciation, returned it to her sister without having read it (CSG, p. 139).

4. The banner does not appear on the photograph VTL, no. 14, even the retouched one. Sister Geneviève must then have sent the other pose of Joan of Arc with the banner (VTL, no. 11).

5. On February 11, 1897, Sister Geneviève spoke of this "reproduction of a painting in oil made by me; this work which is the dearest to me has been more the work of my heart than of my brush." Concerning this painting of the Virgin Mary, which was to hold an important place in Thérèse's piety when she was sick, see CJ 10.7.3, note 1.

6. The poem *La Rosée divine ou le lait virginal de Marie* (P 1, February 2, 1893), also sent to Brother Simeon.

7. In the lines preceding (Prelude for the subject), we read: "If this passage suits you, you could leave it as it is, but you have *carte blanche*: it is for this reason I stopped."

8. According to all probability Thérèse did not answer this letter. Besides it was during Lent. On April 25, thanking Brother Simeon for his letter of March 5, Sister Geneviève inserts this statement: "Thank you, very dear Brother Simeon for *all* you sent us, including *Mes Dévotions;* we cannot grow tired of reading and meditating on all that comes from Rome. Please accept...the most affectionate regards from your two little Carmelites."

LT 221   **From Thérèse to P. Roulland.**
March 19, 1897
→ LC 173

Jesus †   March 19, 1897

Brother,

Our good Mother just brought me your letters[1] in spite of Lent
(a time when we do not write in Carmel). She gladly allows me to
answer you today, for we fear our November letter went to pay a
visit in the depths of the Blue River. Your letters dated in September[2]
made a safe crossing and came to give joy to your Mother and little
sister on the day of the feast of All Saints, and that of January
reached us under the protection of Saint Joseph. Since you are
following my example and writing on all the lines, I do not want
to lose this good habit which, however, makes my ugly handwriting
even more difficult to decipher.... Ah! when shall we no longer have
any need of ink and paper to communicate our thoughts? You missed
up, Brother, on going to visit already that enchanted country where
one can make oneself understood without writing and even without
speaking. With all my heart I thank God for having left you on the
field of battle in order that you may win numerous victories for Him;
already your sufferings have saved many souls. Saint John of the
Cross has said: "The smallest movement of pure love is more useful
to the Church than all other works put together."[3] If it is so, how
profitable for the Church must be your pains and trials since it is
for the love of Jesus alone that you suffer them *with joy*. Truly,
Brother, I cannot pity you since in you are realized these words of
the *Imitation*: "When you find suffering sweet and when you love
it for the love of Jesus Christ, you will have found paradise on
earth."[4] This paradise is really that of the missionary and the
Carmelite; the joy that worldlings seek in the midst of pleasures is
only a fleeting shadow, but our joy sought and tested in works and
sufferings is a very sweet reality, a foretaste of the happiness of
heaven.

Your letter which was filled throughout with a holy joy really interested me. I followed your example, and I laughed heartily at the

expense of your cook, whom I can picture bashing in his cooking pot.[5] . . . Your visiting card also amused me. I do not know on which side to turn it, I am like a child who wants to read a book by turning it upside down.

But to return to your cook, would you believe that at times in Carmel we also have amusing incidents?

Carmel, like Su-Tchuen, is a country foreign to the world where one loses the world's most elementary usages. Here is a little example of this. A charitable person gave us a present recently of a *little lobster* tied up in a basket; no doubt it was a long time ago that this marvel was seen in the monastery. Our good Sister Cook remembered, however, that she had to place the little beast in water to cook it; she did this, sighing at being obliged to carry out such cruelty on an innocent creature. The innocent creature appeared to be asleep and allowed her to do what she wanted. But as soon as it felt the heat, its meekness turned into fury, and, knowing its innocence, it asked permission from no one to leap into the middle of the kitchen, for its kind executioner had not placed the cover on the pot. Immediately the poor Sister armed herself with tongs and ran after the lobster which was making desperate leaps. The fight continued for a long time. Finally for the sake of peace and quiet, the cook, still armed with the tongs, came in tears to find our Mother and tell her the lobster was possessed by the devil. Her face said much more than her words (poor little creature so gentle, so innocent just now, here you are possessed! Truly, we must not believe in the compliments of creatures.) Our Mother could not refrain from laughing when listening to the declarations of the severe judge demanding justice. She went immediately to the kitchen, took hold of the lobster, which, having made a vow of obedience to no one, put up some resistance; then, having placed it in its prison, she left, but only after having firmly closed the door, that is, the cover. In the evening at recreation, the whole Community laughed itself to tears over the little possessed lobster, and the next day each one was able to enjoy *a mouthful*. The person who wanted to regale us did not fail in his purpose, for the famous lobster, or rather its story, will serve us more than once as a feast, not in the refectory but in recreation. My little story may perhaps not seem amusing to you, but I can assure you that you would not have remained serious had you assisted at the performance.... However, Brother, if I am boring you, I beg you to pardon me. Now I am going to speak more seriously. Since your departure, I have read the *Life* of several missionaries (in my letter which you perhaps did not receive, I was thanking you for the *Life of P. Nempon*). I have read, among others, the *Life of Théophane Vénard*,[6] and it interested me and touched me more than I could express. Under its influence, I composed some couplets that are totally personal, however, I am sending them to you.[7] Our Mother told me she thought these verses would please my brother from Su-Tchuen. The couplet next to the last requires an explanation: I say that I would gladly leave for Tonkin if God were to call me there.[8] This will perhaps surprise you; is it not a dream that a Carmelite think of leaving for Tonkin? Well, no, it is not a dream, and I can assure you that if Jesus does not soon come looking for me for the Carmel of heaven, I shall one day leave for that of Hanoï, for now there is a Carmel in that city, the Saïgon Carmel recently founded it. You visited the latter, and you know that in Cochin-China an Order like ours cannot support itself without French subjects. But, alas, vocations are very rare and frequently superiors are unwilling to allow Sisters to leave whom they believe capable of rendering service to their own Community. Thus, in her youth, our good Mother was prevented by her superior's will from going to help the Saïgon Carmel. It is not up to me to complain about this. I thank God for having so well inspired His representative, but I recall that the desires of mothers are sometimes realized in the children,[9] and I would not be surprised to go to the infidel shore to pray and to suffer as our Mother would have liked to do.... I must admit that the news they send us from Tonkin is not reassuring, however: at the end of last year, some thieves entered the poor monastery. They came into the cell of the prioress, who was not awakened, but in the morning she did not find her crucifix next to her (at night a Carmelite's crucifix always rests near her head attached to the pillow); a little cupboard had been broken into and the little money making up the whole Community's treasure had disappeared. The Carmels of France, touched by the distress of the Hanoï Carmel, united together to give it the means of having a cloister wall built high enough to prevent thieves from entering the monastery.

Perhaps you want to know what our Mother thinks of my desire to go to Tonkin? She believes in my vocation (for really it has to be a special vocation, and every Carmelite does not feel called to go into exile), but she does not believe my vocation may ever be realized. For this it would be necessary that the sheath be as solid as the sword, and perhaps (our Mother believes) the sheath would be cast into the sea before reaching Tonkin. It is not really convenient to be composed of a body and a soul! This poor Brother Ass, as Saint Francis of Assisi called it, often embarrasses its noble Sister and prevents her from going where she would like..... However, I do not want to condemn him [the body] in spite of his faults; he is still good for something since he makes his companion win heaven and wins it for himself.

I am not at all worried about the future; I am sure God will do His will, it is the only grace I desire. One must not be more kingly than the king.... Jesus has no need of anyone to do His work, and if He were to accept me, this would be out of pure kindness; but to tell you the truth, Brother, I rather believe Jesus will treat me like a little lazy thing. I do not want this, for I would be happy to work and suffer a long time for Him. So I am asking Him to be content with me, that is, to pay no attention to my desires of loving Him in suffering or of going to enjoy Him in heaven. I hope, Brother, that if I were to leave this exile, you would not forget your promise of praying for me. You have always welcomed my requests with such great kindness that I am daring to make one more request from you. I do not want you to ask God to deliver me from the flames of purgatory; Saint Teresa said to her daughters when they wanted to pray for her: "What does it matter to me to remain until the end of the world in purgatory if through my prayers I save a single soul?"[10] These words find an echo in my heart. I would like to save souls and forget myself for them; I would like to save them even after my death.[11] So I would be happy if you were to say then, instead of the little prayer you are saying and which will be always realized: "My God, allow my sister to make you still loved."[12] If Jesus answers you, I shall be able to show you my gratitude.... You ask me, Brother, to choose between the two names Marie or Thérèse for one of the little girls whom you will baptize; since the Chinese do not want two protectors but only one, we must give them the more powerful one, so the Blessed Virgin wins. Later on, when you will baptize many children, you would please my sister (a Carmelite like me) by naming two little sisters Céline and Thérèse; these are the names we had in the world. Céline, almost four years older than I, has come to join me, after having closed the eyes of our good father; this dear Sister does not know about the intimate relationship I have with you. Since we speak often in recreation of our Mother's missionary[13] (the name you have in the Carmel of Lisieux), she was telling me recently of her desire that, by means of you, Céline and Thérèse might go to begin life again in China.

Pardon me, Brother, for my requests and my too lengthy chatter and please bless

> Your unworthy little Sister,
> Thérèse of the Child Jesus
> of the Holy Face

*   ACL copy.

1. Letters to Mother Marie de Gonzague, January 19 (see VT, July 1963, pp. 127-128) and to Thérèse.

2. See LC 171.

3. *Spiritual Canticle*, explanation of stanza 29, par. 2, *Collected Works*, p. 523. Thérèse wrote this thought on the first page of her *Consecration to the Holy Face* (August 6, 1896), and quotes it in her Ms. B, p. 197, and in LT 245.

4. See *Imitation of Christ* II, 12:11; see CJ 29.5.

5. This is the account of P. Roulland to Mother Marie de Gonzague: "We witnessed a sad accident which happened to the sailors' cook. Here it is: In the space reserved for them is their kitchen, a kind of hole deep enough to set the pot on the stove so that it is level with the floor. The pot was not covered, moving around was difficult, the cook came out of his cubicle and wanted to grab hold of a lever but missed and fell back sitting in the pot. The unfortunate man was quickly pulled up, but the results of the accident were there: the pot was caved in, the beans which were cooking were all over the kitchen, the water extinguished the fire. We saw only these damages, and we began to laugh heartily, but the cook showed us his burnt leg, and we began to sympathize with him; he was really upset, but I believe he was suffering more from losing face before the Europeans, who saw the accident, than from the wound. The next day he resumed his duties" (January 19, 1897).

6. *Vie et Correspondance de J. Théophane Vénard.* On November 21, Thérèse copied in her scripture notebook some extracts from the martyr's letters (four pages) and the hymn of l'abbé Chauvin in his honor (two pages). She borrowed from these sayings for her farewell to her own sisters (LT 245). This young saint was to be numbered among the great friends of Thérèse when she was sick and dying; see CJ 21-26.5.1, note 1.

7. Poem *A Théophane Vénard* (P 44); see LC 167, note 3.

8. See P 44, stanza 6: "I love, too, this infidel shore - which was the object of your ardent love - With joy I would fly to it - If God were to call me to it one day."*

9. See Ms. C, pp. 217-218, which took up and developed the same thoughts in the same words. See CJ 15.5.6.

10. *Way of Perfection, The Collected Works,* vol. II, chap. III, p. 50, par. 6.

11. On this same March 19, she had prayed to St. Joseph in view of this posthumous apostolate according to the testimony of Sister Marie of the Sacred Heart: "I recall also that on the feast of St. Joseph I was in his hermitage; Thérèse came there, and she was quite ill. I told her that she would have done much better to go directly to her cell than to take this roundabout way. She told me: 'I am coming to ask St. Joseph to obtain from God the grace for me to spend my heaven in doing good on earth.' I answered: 'You do not have to ask this from St. Joseph,' but she said: 'Oh! yes,' with a gesture which meant: I need him to support my request. She had also asked this from St. Francis Xavier in the *Novena of Grace*, March 4-12. (Notebook of Sister Marie of the Incarnation, p. 134; conversation written down, July 10, 1934.)

12. See testimony of P. Roulland: "Sister Thérèse had set her heart on spending her life and her heaven in making God loved. Here is a detail proving it: the purpose of our apostolic union was to save souls: union of prayers, sacrifices, works, for this purpose. We had agreed between us that each morning at the memento of the living I would say: 'Permit, my God, Sister Thérèse to make You loved by the souls who are dear to us.' Our union was not broken at her death. On her recommendation, I retained for the memento of the dead the sentence she dictated to me for the memento of the living. I add that I never failed to carry out this request." (Letter to Sister Geneviève, May 22, 1910.)

13. See LT 189, note 4.

Je l'aime aussi, cette plage infidèle
Qui fut l'objet de ton ardent amour
Avec bonheur je volerais vers elle
Si le Bon Dieu m'y appelait un jour

LT 222   **From Thérèse to Mother Agnes of Jesus.**
March 19, 1897   Dated by the recipient.
→LC lost?

J.M.J.T.

Thank you, little Mother. Oh! yes, Jesus loves you and I also!...
He gives you proof of this every day and I do not...yes, but when
I shall be up there, my little arm will be as though it were long and
little Mother will get news of it.[1]

*   Autograph.
1.   Concerning this hope, see LT 221, note 11.

LD   *From Sister Marie of the Eucharist to M. Guérin.*
(=LT 222 bis)   (Extracts.)
April 3, 1897   For the feast of St. Isidore, April 4. Letter
                        postdated by the writer; signed and annotated
                        by "the little Thérèse."

April 4, '97

J.M.J.T.

†Jesus

Dear little Father,

I must, dear little Father, allow your other daughters to wish you
a happy feast, and I would be swallowed up if I were not to leave
enough space.

Our Mother asks me to offer you her best feast day wishes, which accompany her little gift, your daughter's Candle.

> Signed: Sister Agnes of Jesus, who loves *her godfather* in a way impossible to love him more.
> Sister Marie of the Sacred Heart who cedes nothing to her in affection for her dear little Uncle. Sister Geneviève of St. Teresa, who has still more reasons than the others to love him.
>
> Thérèse of the Child Jesus, who is the littlest but who has not the least love!!!!!!!!!!!!!!!!!!!!!!!!!!!!!!!!!!!!!!!

All your twenty-five little Carmelites wish you a happy feast.
Sister Thérèse of the Child Jesus is not doing very well. The vesicatory took very well,[1] but now she has indigestion every day, her meals do not go down at all. M. de Cornière will come today.

This is not true;[2] I have a fever, every day at three o'clock sharp.

Little Thérèse

Our Father[3] wants Thérèse Pougheol[4] to enter on trial.

---

*   Autograph.
1.   The one mentioned in an undated letter from Marie to her mother: "Sister Thérèse of the Child Jesus had her large vesicatory 12 x 15; she is not doing too badly, and it took very well" (end of March - beginning of April 1897). To more information on April 3, M. Guérin answered on the same day: "May God preserve my little Thérèse for me, the precious pearl of my whole family. I am very sad to know she is ill." (See DE, p. 671.)
2.   This correction and all that follows is from Thérèse's hand.
3.   Canon Maupas, the superior.
4.   A friend of the Guérin-Martin families. She was a novitiate companion of Léonie at the Visitation at Caen in 1893 - 1894; she never entered the Carmel, but she returned to the Visitation again in 1901.

"I am not dying, I am entering into life" (LT 244)
(April - September 1897)
Age twenty-four

> Before the end of Lent, the fast of which Thérèse tried to observe since March 3, she "became gravely ill." She had been sick ever since 1894. However, the signs of her illness became evident to all eyes from now on: her face was flushed with fever, she had no appetite, she was so exhausted as to be hardly able to stand. There remained less than six months of life for her; these she spent more and more in her cell, then in the infirmary.

> Twenty years have gone by since April 4, 1877, when Thérèse had written her first letter, *seated on Pauline's knees and incapable "even of holding a pen" (see p. 110). The time was approaching when she will have to dictate her last message to her sister (see LC 196; NV 11.7.3), too weak even to hold a pencil. To her kind secretary, however, she did not have resources except in the last extremity. She wanted to die "her weapons in her hands" (DE, p. 639). Better than all other external testimony, the* Correspondence *of the last weeks manifests an indomitable courage stemming from her overflowing love for those whom she is getting ready to leave. Up to August 25, she found the strength to write forty-four "letters" to them. The last letters, it is true, are reduced to a few words written in pencil. We are reminded of Abbé Combes' statement: "What a striking symmetry between these little notes of the predestined child and the little notes at the end! From the first stammerings to the last, what an itinerary!" (See Introduction, p. 46.)*

> Because of the publication of the critical edition: Derniers Entretiens (Last Conversations), *it would be superfluous to present again the history of Thérèse's last illness.*[1] *A detailed diary (DE, pp. 148-186) has already compared the* Correspondence *(see the column: "What she writes") with her state of health, medical visits and remedies applied to her;*

with what she "thinks, says, does" (the principal source is the Yellow notebook*); with the different events in the family or the Community. A comparison of these writings and words is indispensable for this period. It is with this diary before our eyes that we should read the letters that follow.*

We shall take into account, too, some other writings of these same weeks:

1) *The epistolary dossier entitled "concerning her illness," made up of seventy-five letters or extracts, written between April 3 to September 30, 1897 (see* Last Conversations, *pp. 271-292). We are retaining here only the letters addressed to Thérèse (LC) and a few fragments (LD) which are necessary for recalling the context.*

2) *The writings of Thérèse: poems (at least five, including her Marian testament : Why I love You, oh, Mary) and particularly* Manuscript C, *many expressions of which are to be found in the correspondence.*[2]

Having set down these guidelines, we shall recall here, in broad outline, the stages of her last six months:

1) *April 4 - June 4: A period of transition in which Thérèse was gradually freed from her participation in the recitation of the Divine Office in the choir (CJ 18.5.4), from her work in the linen room (CJ 18.5.1), from Community recreations (DE, p. 416), her care of the novices (DE, p. 696). She made up for this separation from the novices by her little notes to them.*

From April 6, Mother Agnes began to write down some of her sister's words: these form the substance of the future Yellow Notebook. *Each worsening of Thérèse's illness upset Mother Agnes, and the former experienced the need of calming her by writing some lines. During the retreat from the Ascension to Pentecost (May 27 - June 6), both were en-*

gaged in one of the most revealing dialogues (six notes from Thérèse, and six from Mother Agnes).

Sister Marie of the Eucharist's reception of the Veil, June 2, was for Thérèse the last family celebration.

2) *June 6 - July 8: After a grave warning giving her the certitude of her approaching death, June 9, Thérèse experienced a remission. Although she still wrote some notes (LT 242 to 248), most of her time was taken up by the writing of* Manuscript C, *her last autobiographical copybook. Begun on June 3 by the orders of Mother Marie de Gonzague, written in part under the shade of the chestnut trees, this manuscript remained unfinished during the first days of July.*

3) *July 8 - August 25: When she began to spit up blood again, July 6, and was taken down to the infirmary, July 8, Thérèse seemed to be at death's door. An improvement in health put off this date. Appeals from outside brought new strength to her. These appeals were from the Sisters excluded from the infirmary, whom she had to console: Sister Marie of the Trinity, Sister Martha of Jesus, Sister Marie of Saint-Joseph; the seminarian Bellière, whom she had to help by means of an almost weekly letter during his vacation with his family before his departure for Africa; Léonie, the Guérins, P. Roulland, to whom she wanted to address a word of farewell. In all, she wrote eighteen messages (LT 249 to 266), which were so many victories of love over her physical exhaustion.*

4) *August 25 - September 30: Too weak to write[3] and soon even to speak, Thérèse enters into silence. She was still receiving letters (LC 196 to 202). The last three letters: from Africa, China, and Canada, arrived at Lisieux after her death: a sign of the millions of letters which would come to the Lisieux Carmel after the publication of the* Story of a Soul *(1898).*

1. A short resumé is to be found on p. 1187ff.
2. The convergence of themes is pointed out for the most part in the notes of *Derniers Entretiens*, pp. 409-589.
3. To be noted, however, is her last autograph on September 8, which will be published in *Prieres* (Prayers composed by Thérèse); see p. 57, note 1.

LT 223   **From Thérèse to Mother Agnes of Jesus.**

April 4-5, 1897

I fear I have grieved my little Mother.[1] I love her, nevertheless; oh, yes! but I cannot tell her all I am thinking. She has to guess.[2]

*   Autograph.
1. We do not know the reason for this.
2. Mother Agnes dated this note in pencil; the number 4 and 5 are superimposed on each other.

LC 177   *From l'abbé Bellière to Thérèse.*

April 17 or 18, 1897
→LT 220

Easter[1]

Alleluia!

My good and very dear little Sister,

Our Lord is allowing us to pitch our tent today on Thabor, which only yesterday was set up at the foot of the Cross on Calvary; yesterday, tears and mourning, today, joyful *Alleluias*. How can one better rejoice and sing than in a family? I come, then, to my sister and my Mother to thank Jesus for the joy He gives us after having accepted our penance during Lent, and I hasten to express immediately the pleasure you gave me by the poems you were so kind to copy out for me. They must have taken up much of the time of your recreations, and I am almost asking your pardon for being the cause of this work. However, I am not stressing this too much, for, really, they pleased me so much. You are not expecting me, dear Sister, to evaluate them properly; I do not dream of it either, estimating, with good reason, that I would fall short in any kind of accuracy. Realize simply that I was delighted and happy, and these are not banal compliments that I address to you but the expression of my feelings. You were composing for Carmelite nuns, but the angels must be singing with you, and men, unrefined as they are like myself, can find real charm in reading and singing this poetry from your heart. All the poems pleased me, especially perhaps: *My Song for Today, To Théophane Vénard* (with reason), *Remember, To my Guardian Angel*, etc. Pardon me, I notice I would be naming all of them. Yes, all were pleasing and precious to me; thank you simply but sincerely for your kindness. You know how to handle all nuances: gentleness with the Carmelite Sacristans, along with the male tones of the warrior in *My Weapons*. I love to see you speak of the lance, the helmet, the breastplate, the athlete, and I was smiling at the thought of seeing you armed in this way. However, Joan of Arc—whom you love, and whom I invoke, *each day*, under that title which I welcomed at the end of your poem: SAINT JOAN OF FRANCE—wore them, and so these arms you sing about are undoubtedly her most beautiful adornment. I am and will be, Sister, faithful to the little prayer that you point out to me; this is a solemn promise. I will offer it up always, even if. . .your exile may be short. I have understood you, Sister, I had underlined in your canticle of *Love* this verse: "I have the hope, my exile will be short,"[2] and this other verse: "*I feel it*, my exile *is about* to end."[3] I understand your desires, your impatience: you are ready, little Sister, to enter heaven, and your Spouse Jesus can at any moment extend His hand that will place you on the throne of glory; you are impatient like the Spouse of the Canticle. "Draw me,"[4] to Yourself, she says, coming to the feet of her Beloved, fainting away from the flame that is consuming her. When analyzing and meditating this Canticle of Canticles, I was applying it to the Carmelite and her Jesus, and it is undoubtedly for this reason that I wrote it up in this sense and that, here and there, some verses from *Vivre d'Amour* and other poems came to range themselves side by side with the Canticle. And you are right when you say that I am not permitted to sing like you! No, really,

I have first to make God forget by means of hard work and real penance my sinful past, and then to do something for God, to work in His vineyard.[5] Before being in a place of honor, Joan of Arc had to suffer, and more than anyone else I have to make reparation. And if I ever succeed in this, I shall then ask you: "Sister, beg God that *I may succumb to pain*; ask Him—and why not?—that I may die a *martyr!* This was my dream all my life; in the past, I wanted to die for France, today, I want to die for God. And you know: "If to die for one's Prince is an honorable fate," "When one dies for his God, what will death be?"[6]

I still have much to answer in your letter, and I am busy. I shall close. Pardon me, you ask for some dates, and I thank you for your kindness. I celebrate my birth and my baptism on June 10 (the date of the latter is June 25, but the religious person who took care of me at birth had to baptize me); my First Communion, June 7, my entrance into the Congregation of Saint Joseph, November 21, and into that of the Blessed Virgin and St. Louis de Gonzague, December 8, and at this same time, December 8, my reception of the cassock and my acceptance as a missionary aspirant; October 15, which saw your charity for me and the promise I made to remember you each day up to eternity in the memento of the Mass, along with other good works. Everything that has happened to me, good or bad, is found almost exclusively in June: it was in this month that I gave up military school, which I was preparing to enter,[7] in order to turn to Jesus, who was calling me to other conquests. And you, very dear Sister, celebrate memorable dates. Will you allow me to associate myself in them? Next January, I shall celebrate at least your twenty-fifth anniversary of birth, if I am not mistaken; and this will be in Africa, I hope.

I thank you, too, for your intentions as godmother, but will you also give some names in memory of yourself to a little Bedouin, if the first were to be a girl? I beg you to be so kind.

Since your exile still lasts, Sister, please continue for me the sweet consolation of your good and holy thoughts. You will never be able to measure the good they are doing me. The breeze coming from the Carmel to refresh my burning and tired head makes me better by giving me new fervor.

In the Heart of Jesus, the Mediator between our souls, I assure you once again, very dear and very good little Sister, of the prayers and respectful devotedness of your poor brother,

M. Barthélemy-Bellière

* Autograph.
1. According to the context, this letter seems to have been written on Holy Saturday, April 17.
2. *Vivre d'Amour*! stanza 9.
3. *Ibid.*, stanza 14.
4. See Canticle of Canticles 1:3 (and Ms. C, p. 254, commenting on this paragraph).
5. See Matthew 20:1.
6. Corneille, *Polyeucte*, Act IV, scene 3.
7. Should we see in this projected entrance into military school "the most beautiful foolishness," barely avoided, in June 1896? See LD, July 21, 1896.

LT 224   **From Thérèse to l'abbé Bellière.**

April 25, 1897   Summary according to Thérèse's outline: "The
→ LC 177   Life of Père de la Colombière and Blessed
                   Margaret Mary. I am a *little flower*, not a great
                   soul; however, the Almighty has done great
                   things for me. I asked for the favor of martyr-
                   dom. It is not he who wills, etc. He loves more
                   to whom much has been forgiven. Desire to
                   resemble Joan of Arc."

J.M.J.T.   April 25, 1897

Alleluia

Dear little Brother,

My pen or rather my heart refuses henceforth to call you "Monsieur l'Abbé," and our good Mother told me I could use when writing to you the name I always use when I speak of you to Jesus. It seems to me that the divine Saviour has seen fit to unite our souls in working for the salvation of sinners, just as He united, in the past, the souls of the Venerable Père de la Colombière and Blessed Margaret Mary. I was reading recently in the *Life* of this saint:[1] "One day, when I was approaching Our Lord to receive Him in Holy Communion, He showed His Sacred Heart as a burning furnace and two other hearts (her own and that of P. de la Colombière) that were about to be united and engulfed in It, saying: 'It is thus that My pure love unites three hearts forever.' He made me understand that this union was for His glory, and for this reason He willed us to be like brother and sister, equally endowed with spiritual goods. Then I pointed out to Our Lord my poverty and the inequality there was between a priest of such great virtue and a poor sinner like me, and He said: 'The infinite riches of My Heart will make up for everything and will equalize everything.' "

Perhaps, Brother, the comparison does not appear fair to you? It is true that you are not yet a Père de la Colombière, but I do not doubt that one day, you will be a real apostle of Christ like him. As for myself, the thought does not come into my mind to compare myself with Blessed Margaret Mary. I simply state that Jesus has chosen me to be the sister of one of His apostles, and the words that the "holy Lover of His Heart" addressed to Him out of *humility*, I repeat to Him *myself* in *all truth*; so I hope that His infinite riches will make up for all that I lack in accomplishing the work He entrusts to me.

I am really happy that God has used my poor verses to do you a little good; I would have been embarrassed in sending them to you if I had not remembered that a sister should have nothing to hide from her brother. It is truly with a fraternal heart that you welcomed and judged them.... You were undoubtedly surprised to find again *Vivre d'Amour*. My intention was not to send it to you twice; I had already begun to copy it when I remembered you had it already, and it was too late to stop.

Dear little Brother, I must admit that in your letter there is something that caused me some sorrow, and it is that you do not know me such as I am in reality. It is true that to find great souls one must come to Carmel; just as in virgin forests there grow flowers of a fragrance and brilliance unknown to the world, so Jesus in His mercy has willed that among these flowers there should grow littler

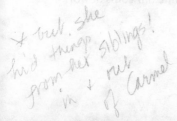

ones; never will I be able to thank Him enough, for it is thanks to this condescension that I, a poor flower without splendor, find myself in the same garden as the roses, my Sisters.[2] Oh, Brother! I beg you to believe me. God has not given you as a sister a *great* soul but a *very little* and a very imperfect one.

Do not think that it is humility that prevents me from acknowledging the gifts of God. I know He has done great things in me, and I sing of this each day with joy.[3] I remember that the one must love more who has been forgiven more,[4] so I take care to make my life an act of love, and I am no longer disturbed at being a *little* soul; on the contrary, I take delight in this. That is why I dare to hope "my exile will be short," but it is not because I am *prepared*. I feel that I shall never be prepared if the Lord does not see fit to transform me Himself. He can do so in one instant; after all the graces He has granted me, I still await this one from His infinite mercy.

You tell me, Brother, to beg for the favor of martyrdom for you; this favor I have often sought for myself, but I am not worthy of it, and truly we can say with St. Paul: "It is not the work of him who wills or who runs, but of God who shows mercy."[5] Since the Lord seems to will to grant me only the martyrdom of love, I hope He will permit me, *by means of you*, to gather the *other palm* we are striving after. I am pleased to see that God has given us the same attractions, the same desires. I made you smile, dear little Brother, when singing *My Weapons*. Well! I shall make you smile once more when I tell you that I dreamt in my childhood of fighting on the fields of battle.... When I was beginning to learn the history of France, the account of Joan of Arc's exploits delighted me; I felt in my heart the desire and the courage to imitate her. It seemed the Lord destined me, too, for great things.[6] I was not mistaken, but instead of voices from heaven inviting me to combat, I heard in the depths of my soul a gentler and stronger voice, that of the Spouse of Virgins, who was calling me to other exploits, to more glorious conquests, and into Carmel's solitude. I understood my mission was not to have a mortal king crowned but to make the King of heaven loved, to submit to Him the kingdom of hearts.

It is time to stop, and yet I must still thank you for the dates you sent me. I would really like you to add to them the years, for I do not know your age.[7] So that you may excuse my simplicity, I am sending you the memorable dates of my life,[8] and it is also with the intention that we be particularly united through prayer and gratitude on those blessed days.

If God gives me a little goddaughter, I shall be very happy to answer your request by giving it as protectors: the Blessed Virgin, Saint Joseph, and my Patroness.

Finally, dear little Brother, I come to an end, begging you to excuse my long scribbling and the rambling of my letter.

In the Sacred Heart of Jesus, I am for eternity,

> Your unworthy little sister,
> Thérèse of the Child Jesus
> of the Holy Face
> rel. carm. ind.

(It is understood that our relationship will remain secret, is it not? No one except your director must know the union that Jesus has formed between our souls.)

---

*   Autograph.

1. With hardly any changes, the quotation which follows conforms to the text written down by Thérèse on a sheet of paper. This copy is accompanied by the following references: "Extract from the Sacred Heart magazine. December 1896" and "Life of Blessed Margaret Mary by herself, p. 347. Life by her Contemporaries, p. 90." This latter reference corresponds to the publication: *Vie et Oeuvres de la Bienheureuse Marguerite-Marie Alacoque. Sa Vie inédite par les Contemporaines (Visitation de Paray-le-Monial, et Poussièlque,* Paris, 1867, 2 volumes). The *Messager du Sacré Coeur* of December 1896 carries an article on Margaret Mary and Claude de la Colombière, but it is under a form different from the text transcribed by Thérèse. Thus far we have not identified the "magazine" from which she took this quotation.

2. See Ms. A, pp. 14-15. We should note that Thérèse undoubtedly at this time was composing her poem *Une Rose effeuillée* (P 48, May 19, 1897) for Mother Marie-Henriette, Jubilarian of the Paris Carmel. Soon Thérèse will identify herself with this unpetaled rose.

3. See Luke 1:49, and Ms. C, p. 209.

4. See Luke 7:47.

5. See Romans 9:16, and Ms. A, p. 13.

6. See Ms. A, p. 72.
7. L'abbé Bellière inserted in his next letter (LC 186) the following list:
   Birth, baptism: June 10, 1874; my mother's death: June 17, 1874;
   my father's death: June 12, 1877; First Communion: June 7, 1885;
   Confirmation: June 9, 1885; Congregation St. Joseph: November 21,
   1889; Conversion: end of June 1892; Congregation Blessed Virgin:
   December 8, 1893; reception of cassock, missionary aspirant:
   December 8, 1894; fraternal apostolic union: October 15, 1895.
8. This list has not been found.

LC 178   *From P. Roulland to Thérèse.*
April 29, 1897

R. + Ap.

Ho-pao-tchang   April 29, 1897[1]

Sister,

Here I am, a little baby not knowing how to speak, learning the
language in a Christian family. My trip was blessed: only one accident that could have been tragic. One morning, I was in a sedan
chair, carried by three men. This chair was tied to two poles, and
the men were at the ends of the poles. I was seated then in my chair,
there were ricefields, to the left and right, filled with water and mud;
the path was seventy-five centimeters in width. . . . Suddenly, a cord
broke, and bearers, chair, and myself, were all thrown down. Had
I fallen to the right, I would have had a good bath; fortunately, I
fell to the left and came off with only a good fright. A little farther
on, we encountered, stretched out on the road, a corpse of a man
who had died from hunger. The Chinese love to think of death very
much, so they passed close to the corpse without being in the least
bit disturbed. Ho-pao-tchang has a Christian settlement of five hundred souls; the oratory is in open country, and all around are the
properties of the Christians, just like a real parish in France.

I was alone on Easter Sunday, the priest was spending the feast
day six leagues away. The Christians were good: they came in
numbers in the morning, bringing firecrackers (for here there is no

celebration without lots of noise). I promised them Benediction of the Blessed Sacrament. Immediately after my Mass, all the men and women fled away like thieves. I asked the reason for this: during Lent they had not eaten any meat, and they were hurrying up to enjoy some. Did they commit a sin of gluttony? Certainly not. After my dinner, they came back to greet me and to assist at Benediction; afterward, they came looking for me in my room. Before leaving they wanted to receive the priest's blessing. I went to the foot of the altar, and I made a large sign of the cross over the men, then over the women. What a beautiful day, Sister; even in the heart of China the missionary has great consolations.

Eight days later, I took, with P. Fleury, the road that brought me to the Louy home, a family from which I must learn the language. What beautiful things I could tell you about this family. I found there those beautiful traditions that, in the past, were flourishing[2] in our beautiful France. Yesterday evening, we counted twenty-two men and twenty women (the children are not included in this number) all living under the same roof. There is a head of the family whom all, brothers, children, and little children, obey as one. Each one has his work and there are never any arguments. Morning, noon, and night, prayers are said in common, and in the evening the rosary is recited. At a given signal, all run to sing the praises of God in their own language. Near this family is a pagan family that had an old woman who died on *Quasimodo* Sunday.* This old lady wanted to die as a Christian, but the family was opposed to the realization of her desire, and they were watching the Louy family when the letter came to see the patient. What did the latter do? They invited the pagan family to dinner, and when all of them arrived, one of the Louy family ran to the patient, taught her the principal truths of our holy religion, baptized her, and then returned at full speed. The pagans were aware of nothing. Before she died, the old lady told her family that she wanted to be buried like the Christians. They paid no attention to her last requests: gongs, flutes, firecrackers, all made an infernal noise all night long. These unfortunate people did not realize that their old mother was in heaven or on the way there.

In my family there are three virgins: two have the name of Thérèse. I said to them: "Now I am writing to my younger sister who has the same name as you." They said: "But Father told us he was alone." I got out of the difficulty by saying: "I cannot explain myself, I do not know your language."

You are praying for my intentions. Ever since I have been in the region of Ho-pao-tchung, I have offered your prayers to God to obtain the conversion of infidels in this country. Now, Sister, here is some good news which reached us: two hundred pagans at least have just acknowledged our God as their God, and they beg to be instructed in the truths of our holy religion. Who knows? These are perhaps my sister's prayers which have drawn down the grace of God on this region. I have begun my ministry by bringing God to the dying. I was happy to travel with Jesus in the midst of the pagans who did not suspect I had a treasure on my heart. How good is this Jesus to give Himself to all, even those deprived of their fortune. He remains in a house where I can hardly breathe. He gives Himself to sick people whom I must, out of prudence, touch only with precaution. What miseries in China! How great is God's mercy!

A Dieu, Sister; union of prayers, union of sacrifices, later union of glory in heaven.

A. Roulland edm
miss. ap.
Su-Tchuen or.

*What used to be the First Sunday after Easter, Low Sunday.

*   Autograph.
1.   This letter reached Lisieux on June 26 or 27. The envelope addressed to Thérèse had the stamp: Paris 26 June 97. When he wrote on April 29, P. Roulland had not yet received the letter from her of March 19 (LT 221).
2.   That is: *qui florissaient, étaient vivantes*. The verb *viger*, unknown in the Norman patois dictionaries, and traced to the Latin verb *vigere*, could have been a creation of the writer, whose years in the seminary were still quite recent.

LT 225   **From Thérèse to Sister Anne of the Sacred Heart.**

May 2, 1897   Professed in the Saïgon Carmel (1876), Sister
Anne had desired to come to the Lisieux Carmel
where she remained from 1883 to 1895.

J.M.J.T.

May 2, Feast of the Good Shepherd 1897

Jesus †

Very dear Sister,

You will undoubtedly be very much surprised to receive a letter
from me. So that you may pardon me for coming to disturb the
silence of your solitude, I shall tell you how it happens I have the
pleasure of writing you. The last time I went for spiritual direction
from our good Mother, we spoke about you and the dear Saïgon
Carmel. Our Mother told me she was allowing me to write you if
this pleased me. I accepted this suggestion with joy, and I am taking advantage of the free day[1] for the feast of the Good Shepherd
to come and speak for a few moments with you.

I hope, dear Sister, you have not forgotten me;[2] as for myself,
I think often of you. I recall with joy the years I spent in your company, and you know, for a Carmelite to think of a person whom
she loves is to pray for her. I ask God to bestow His graces upon
you and to increase each day His holy love in your heart. I do not
doubt, however, that you possess this love to an eminent degree.
The hot sun of Saïgon is nothing in comparison with the fire burning in your soul. Oh, Sister! I beg you, ask Jesus that I myself also
may love Him and that I may make Him loved. I would like to love
Him not with an ordinary love but like the Saints who did foolish
things for Him. Alas! how far I am from being like them! . . .

Ask Jesus, too, that I may always do His will; for this I am ready
to traverse the world[3] . . . I am ready also to die!

The silence[4] is about to end now; I must terminate my letter, and
I see I have told you nothing interesting. Fortunately, the letters from
our Mothers are here to give you all the news of our Carmel. Our

free day has been very short, but if it does not bore you, I shall come back to speak with you at greater length on another occasion.

Please, very dear Sister, offer my respectful and filial regards to your Reverend Mother.[5] She does not know me, but I often hear our good Mother speak of her. I love her, and I pray to Jesus to console her in her trials.

I leave you, dear Sister, remaining united with you in the Heart of Jesus; there I am happy to call myself forever,

> Your very little sister,
> Thérèse of the Child Jesus
> of the Holy Face
> rel. carm. ind.

---

*   Autograph.
1.   Day of extraordinary recreation during which the Sisters had permission to speak freely with each other.
2.   Sister Anne had retained few memories of Thérèse even though she had lived seven years with her in Lisieux. At the time of the canonization of Thérèse, when she was questioned about the Servant of God, she answered: "There is nothing to say about her; she was very good and very self-effacing, one would not notice her, never would I have suspected her sanctity." (In a letter from Saïgon Carmel to the Lisieux Carmel, December 21, 1947.)
3.   To go to Cochin-China. See CJ 21/26.5.2.
4.   Hour of optional siesta from noon to one o'clock in the summer, time of great silence in the monastery.
5.   Mother Marie of Jesus, who had succeeded Mother Philomena of the Immaculate Conception (d. 1895), foundress from the Carmel of Lisieux in 1861.

LT 226   From Thérèse to P. Roulland.
May 9, 1897
→ LC 175

J.M.J.T.

Carmel of Lisieux   May 9, 1897

Brother,

I received with joy, or rather emotion, the relics you were so kind to send me.[1] Your letter is almost a letter of *au revoir* for heaven. It seemed when I was reading it that I was listening to the account of your forerunners in the apostolate. On this earth, where all changes, one single thing remains, and this is the conduct of the King of heaven regarding His friends. Ever since He has lifted up the standard of the Cross, it is under its shadow that all must fight and carry off the victory. Théophane Vénard said: "The whole of a missionary's life is fruitful in the Cross";[2] and again: "To be truly happy we must suffer, and to live we must die."[3]

Brother, the beginnings of your apostolate are marked with the seal of the Cross; the Lord is treating you as a privileged one. It is more by persecution and suffering than by brilliant preaching that He wills to make His kingdom firm in souls. You say: "I am still a child who cannot speak." Père Mazel, who was ordained the same day as you, did not know how to speak either; however, he has already taken up the palm.[4] ... Oh! how the divine thoughts are above ours![5] ... When learning about the death of this young missionary whom I heard named for the first time, I felt drawn to invoke him; I seemed to see him in heaven in the glorious choir of Martyrs. I know that in the eyes of men his martyrdom does not bear this name, but in the eyes of God this sacrifice without any glory is not less fruitful than the sacrifices of the first Christians, who confessed their faith before tribunals. Persecution has changed in form, the apostles of Christ have not changed in sentiment, so the divine Master would not be able to change His rewards unless it were to increase them in proportion to the glory which was refused them here below.

I do not understand, Brother, how you seem to doubt your immediate entrance into heaven if the infidels were to take your life. I know one must be very pure to appear before the God of all Holiness, but I know, too, that the Lord is infinitely just; and it is this justice which frightens so many souls that is the object of my joy and confidence. To be just is not only to exercise severity in order to punish the guilty; it is also to recognize right intentions and to reward virtue. I expect as much from God's justice as from His mercy. It is because He is just that "He is compassionate ar   lled with gentleness, slow to punish, and abundant in mercy, f . He knows our frailty, He remembers we are only dust. As a father has tenderness for his children, so the Lord has compassion on us!!"[6] Oh, Brother, when hearing these beautiful and consoling words of the Prophet-King, how can we doubt that God will open the doors of His kingdom to His children who loved Him even to sacrificing all for Him, who have not only left their family and their country to make Him known and loved, but even desire to give their life for Him whom they love. . . . Jesus was very right in saying that there is no greater love than that![7] How would He allow Himself to be overcome in generosity? How would He purify in the flames of purgatory souls consumed in the fires of divine love? It is true that no human life is exempt from faults; only the Immaculate Virgin presents herself absolutely pure before the divine Majesty. Since she loves us and since she knows our weakness, what have we to fear? Here are a lot of sentences to express my thought, or rather not to succeed in expressing it, I wanted simply to say that it seems to me all missionaries are *martyrs* by desire and will and that, as a consequence, not one should have to go to purgatory. If there remains in their soul at the moment of appearing before God some trace of human weakness, the Blessed Virgin obtains for them the grace of making an act of perfect love, and then she gives them the palm and the crown that they so greatly merited.

This is, Brother, what I think of God's justice;[8] my way is all confidence and love. I do not understand souls who fear a Friend so tender. At times, when I am reading certain spiritual treatises in which perfection is shown through a thousand obstacles, surrounded by a crowd of illusions, my poor little mind quickly tires; I close the learned book that is breaking my head and drying up my heart,[9] and I take up Holy Scripture.[10] Then all seems luminous to me; a single word uncovers for my soul infinite horizons, perfection seems simple to me, I see it is sufficient to recognize one's nothingness and to abandon oneself as a child into God's arms. Leaving to great souls, to great minds the beautiful books I cannot understand, much less put into practice, I rejoice at being little since children alone and those who resemble them will be admitted to the heavenly banquet.[11] I am very happy there are many mansions in God's kingdom,[12] for if there were only the one whose description and road seems incomprehensible to me, I would not be able to enter there. I would like, however, not to be too far from *your mansion*; in consideration of your merits, I hope God will give me the favor of sharing in your glory, just as on earth the sister of a conqueror, were she deprived of the gifts of nature, shares in the honors bestowed on her brother in spite of her own poverty.

The first act of your ministry in China seemed delightful to me. The little soul whose mortal remains you blessed must have indeed smiled at you and promised you her protection as well as those who are dear to you. How I thank you for counting me among them! I am also deeply touched and grateful for your remembrance of my dear parents at Mass. I hope they are in possession of heaven to which all their actions and desires were directed; this does not prevent me from praying for them, for it seems to me these blessed souls receive a great glory from the prayers offered for them and which they can use for other suffering souls.

If, as I believe, my father and mother are in heaven, they must be looking at and blessing the brother whom Jesus has given me. They had so much wanted a missionary son!... I have been told that before my birth my parents were hoping their prayer was finally going to be realized.[13] Had they been able to pierce the veil of the future, they would have seen it was indeed through me their desire was fulfilled; since a missionary has become my brother, he is also their son, and in their prayers they cannot separate the brother from his unworthy sister.

You are praying, Brother, for my parents who are in heaven, and I often pray for yours who are still on earth. This is a very sweet obligation for me, and I promise you to be always faithful in carrying it out even if I leave this exile, and even more so perhaps since

I shall know better the graces necessary for them; and when their course here below is ended, I shall come to get them in your name and introduce them to heaven. How sweet will be the family life we shall enjoy throughout eternity! While awaiting this blessed eternity that will open up for us in a short time, since life is only a day, let us work together for the salvation of souls. I can do very little, or rather absolutely nothing, if I am alone; what consoles me is to think that at your side I can be useful for something. In fact, zero by itself has no value, but when placed next to a unit it becomes powerful, provided, however, that it be placed on the *right side*, after and not before!....[14] That is where Jesus has placed me, and I hope to remain there always, following you from a distance by prayer and sacrifice.

If I were to listen to my heart, I would not end my letter today, but the end of silence is about to ring.[15] I must bring my letter to our good Mother, who is waiting for it. I beg you, then, Brother, to send your blessing to the *little zero* God has placed near you.

Sister Thérèse of the Child Jesus
of the Holy Face
rel. carm. ind.

* CE
1. A lock of P. Roulland's hair.
2. A sentence copied out by Thérèse in pencil on the back of the sheet of paper mentioned in LT 224, note 1.
3. *Pour être heureux il faut souffrir - Et pour vivre il nous faut mourir*: verses extracted from the *Chant d'un missionnaire arrivant au Tong-King*, composed by Théophane Vénard in July 1854; *op. cit.*, p. 208.
4. They had just learned on May 1 at the Lisieux Carmel of the murder of this missionary, twenty-six years old (see CJ 1.5.2). P. Mazel had been killed by looters on April 1 because he was a European. Following the text already quoted down in pencil the victim's *curriculum vitae*. She concluded with the prayer: "Blessed Martyr, pray for me!" (See DE, p. 417.)
5. See Isaias 55:9.
6. See Psalm 102:8, 14, and 13; see Ms. A, p. 15 and 165.
7. See John 15:13.
8. If we must give credence to *Novissima Verba*, pp. 80-81, Thérèse on

July 16 referred Mother Agnes to this letter in which she felt she had explained herself on the subject of God's justice. The authenticity of this *saying* appears difficult to uphold psychologically. Mother Agnes would be assuming that in May 1897 Mother Marie de Gonzague (the only one aware of this correspondence with P. Roulland) had written out a copy of Thérèse's letter, or that in July Thérèse is thinking of the future communication of her letters to Mother Agnes by her correspondents. Two assumptions equally improbable. It is more likely that the *saying* in question (NV, July 16, no. 3) is a later interpolation of Mother Agnes. See DE, p. 578.

9.   See VT. July 1964, p. 107, quoting a text from Father Faber to which Thérèse seems to be referring: *All for Jesus or The Easy Ways of Divine Love*, ch. 6, par. 4.

10. The Gospel especially; see CJ 15.5.3.

11. See Matthew 19:14.   M K . 10:14

12. See John 14:2.

13. On January 3, 1873, Mme. Martin wrote Mme. Guérin: "I was expecting a boy! I was thinking this for the last two months because I felt her to be stronger than my other children" (CF, p. 141, January 3, 1873).

14. In *L'arithmétique de Mademoiselle Lili* (see LT 179, note 1), "Lili taught Toto that zero is nothing all alone, but when placed at the right hand of other numbers it gives them a value ten times greater" (*Numérotation - La récolte de noyer par Mlle. Lili*). Recalling this passage of Thérèse's letter, P. Roulland later summed up the Saint's posthumous activity in these words: "She multiplies the missionary's work by ten" (to Canon O. Germain, October 29, 1924).

15. See LT 225, note 4.

LT 227   **From Thérèse to Sister Geneviève.**

May 13, 1897   (Fragment ?)

Jesus is pleased with little Céline to whom He gave Himself for the first time thirteen years ago.[1] He is more proud of what He is doing in her soul, of her littleness and her poverty, than He is proud of having created millions of suns and the expanse of the heavens!...

*   Autograph.

1.   It was really seventeen years ago, May 13, 1880; see Ms. A, p. 57. Thérèse is confusing it with her own First Communion (1884). Sister

Geneviève corrected the autograph by writing over it the number "17." She dated this note also: May 13, 1897.

LT 228	**From Thérèse to Sister Geneviève.**
April-May 1897	Approximate date; see note 3. "I was giving her massages according to the doctor's orders, and this was a martyrdom for her; she told this to Mother Agnes later on, but she was asking for them from me. No doubt, on this occasion, I was willing to postpone the massage until the next day" (Sister Geneviève's note, CMG IV, p. 381).

I fear Mother[1] will not be pleased, she values the massages very much, *especially on my back*. If M. Clodion[2] comes on Sunday[3] to shake his long hair over my back, he will wonder why we have not done what he had said.... Perhaps it would be better to wait until Monday; however, *Pauvre, Pauvre*,[4] do as you like; all will be ready tomorrow. Above all, do not speak to this *Pauvre Monsieur*, do what seems good to you[5] and remember we must be *rich, very rich, both of us!*...[6]

* CMG.

1. "Our Mother," Mother Marie de Gonzague.
2. "*Clodion le chevelu*," nickname for Doctor de Cornière: "He used to wear his hair long...*à la Jeanne d'Arc, en artiste*" (note of Sister Geneviève, CMG IV, p. 381). See DE, p. 708.
3. Too slight a clue to serve as a basis for the definite dating of the letter. Vouched for are the doctor's visits on January 2 (Saturday); April 3 (Saturday, see p. 1076); April 25 (Sunday, see DE, pp. 671-672); May 23 (Sunday, copybook of prescriptions). The note seems to have been written in the spring, but its dating remains uncertain. See LT 208, note 4.
4. See LT 207, note 1.
5. "*Monsieur Toto* (Thérèse) was receiving massages in the morning before the Little Hours, therefore, during the great silence which lasted until the end of Prime, according to the Rule of Carmel.
6. "A reference to a spirited witticism she had written down" (note of Sister Geneviève, CMG IV, p. 382). The story in question can be read in CSG, p. 175.

LT 229   **From Thérèse to Mother Agnes of Jesus.**
May 23, 1897

J.M.J.T.

I really fear I have grieved my little Mother.[1] . . . Ah! I who would
have liked to be her little joy, I feel, on the contrary, I am her little
sorrow.

Yes, but! when I shall be far away from this sad earth where
flowers fade, where birds fly away, I shall be very close to my dear
Mother, to the angel whom Jesus sent before me to prepare the way[2]
the way leading to heaven, the elevator[3] lifting me without fatigue
to the infinite regions of love. . . . Yes, I shall be very close to her
and this without leaving the homeland, for I will not be the one *to
come down*, but my little Mother will be the one *to come up* where
I shall be. . . . Oh! if I could, like her, express what I am thinking,
if I only knew how to tell her how much my heart overflows with
gratitude and love for her, I believe I would already be her little joy
even before being far away from this sad earth.

Dear little Mother, the good you have done to my soul, you have
done to Jesus, for He said: "What you have done to the *least* of
my brethren, you have done to me. . . ."[4] And I am the one who
is the *least*! . . .

Ex. 23:20 (margin annotation)

* Autograph.
1. We do not know the reason for this; perhaps it was the state of
   Thérèse's health. See DE, medical diary, p. 150.
2. See Exodus 23:20. A text taken from the liturgical Office of the Holy
   Angels, October 2, the date of Pauline's entrance into Carmel (1882).
   It appears, too, on the front of little Madeleine Aubrée's death-picture;
   she died at the age of two (September 26, 1891). This picture is mentioned in *Derniers Entretiens* (CJ 20.6 and DE, p. 441). The picture
   represents an angel going up to heaven, a child in his arms. There
   is a kind of paraphrase of this in the poem *A ma Mère Chérie, le Bel
   Ange de mon enfance*, dedicated by Thérèse to Mother Agnes of Jesus
   (P 19, September 7, 1895).
3. The first appearance of this word under Thérèse's pen, soon to be
   repeated in Ms. C, p. 207 (written between June 4 and 9) and in LT
   258. Concerning this symbol and the question of who used it first,

Mother Agnes or Thérèse, see A. Combes, *Le Problème de l'Histoire
d'une Ame*, pp. 103-109; François de Sainte-Marie, Mss. II, p. 67;
Conrad de Meester, *Dynamique de la Confiance*, pp. 65-67. The
critical edition of *Derniers Entretiens* (DE, pp. 572-574) poses the question of the existence of the "note" mentioned in CJ 21/26.5.11 (DE,
p. 388). Deeper research, required for this *Correspondence*, has
strengthened the data in favor of a negative conclusion.

4. See Matthew 25:40.

LC 179   *From Mother Agnes of Jesus to Thérèse.*

May 23, 1897   Date deduced from the content.
→ LT 229

At the very moment when I was taking up my pen[1] to breathe out
a sigh, I received your little note, oh, my dear Angel! It made the
little vessel overflow, yes, but it also made a change in me, for the
little vessel, filled with very bitter water, was able instantly to flow
over only with a very sweet and pleasant liquid. And I was just saying to myself: I would really like my little angel to tell me, before
she leaves, what she will do for me up above. I must have this among
my little consolations,[2] and there was your little note telling me this
very thing. Well, die now. I know that up above you will be occupied
with your little Mother. Die quickly so that my heart may no longer
have any attachment here below, so that all I love may be up above.
Here I am beginning to shed big tears while writing this, and I can
no longer see. . . . I do not know what is the matter with me today.
NEVER had I been so sure of your approaching end. Poor little
Angel, or rather blessed little Angel, if you only knew what awaits
you! Oh! how well you will be received! What a celebration for the
whole assembly of the Saints. How tenderly the Immaculate Virgin
will press you to her heart. You will be like a little child whom each
passes on to the other to rock and caress, and the little Innocents[3]
will come with pride to take you by your little hand, and they will
show you how to use your wings, they will teach you their games.

Oh! ask them to make, too, a little place for me in their ranks.

*   Autograph.

1. The adjective "little" comes up fourteen times in this note. It is not

less frequent in the ones that follow. This fact merits our attention insofar as it has influence on the vocabulary of *Derniers Entretiens (Last Conversations)*. The word "little" appears 347 times in the "Yellow Notebook." Mother Agnes could have introduced it in her transcriptions of Thérèse's words far beyond the actual use the latter made of it. In every way, Thérèse adapted herself to the language of her "little Mother."

2. The intimate memories that will give her consolation after the death of Thérèse, and especially the notes she is beginning to take down in the last two weeks; see DE, p. 116.

3. See DE, pp. 424-425, 21/26.5.9, note 1. It is possible that Mother Agnes has in mind the four little Martin children who had already died in childhood.

LT 230

May 28, 1897

From Thérèse to Mother Agnes of Jesus.

Note dated by Mother Agnes of Jesus, who explained the circumstances in this way: "One day (she was already sick but not confined to bed), a Sister came to ask her immediate help in a work of painting. I was present and objected in vain that Thérèse was feverish and extremely tired. The Sister was insisting. Then some agitation appeared on the face of Sister Thérèse of the Child Jesus, and in the evening she wrote me these lines" (NPPA, Humble sentiments about herself, p. 5)

J.M.J.T.

Dear little Mother, your little girl has again shed sweet tears just now,[1] tears of repentance but more so of gratitude and love.... Ah! this evening I showed my *virtue*, my TREASURES of *patience*!... And I who preach so well to others!!!!!!!!!!!!!!! I am happy you saw my imperfection. Ah, the good it does me for having been bad!... You did not scold your little girl, nevertheless, she deserved it; but your little girl is accustomed to this, your gentleness speaks more to her than severe words; you are the image of God's *mercy* for her. Yes, but...Sister St. John the Baptist,[2] on the contrary is *usually* the image of God's *severity*. Well, I just met her, and instead of passing coldly by my side, she embraced me, saying: (absolutely as though I had been the best girl in the world) "Poor little Sister, I felt sorry for you, I do not want to tire you out, I was wrong, etc., etc...." I, who felt contrition in my heart, was astonished at her not reproaching me in any way. I know that basically she must find me imperfect; it is because she believes I am going to die that she has spoken this way to me, but it does not matter. I heard only gentle and tender words coming from her mouth, and I found her very good and myself very bad.... When reentering our cell, I was wondering what Jesus was thinking of me, and immediately I recalled these words He addressed one day to the adulterous woman: "Has no one condemned you?"[3] And I, tears in my eyes, answered Him: "No one, Lord.... Neither my little Mother, image of Your tenderness, nor Sister St. John the Baptist, image of your justice, and I really feel I can go in peace, for You will not condemn me either!...."

John 8.10

Little Mother, why, then, is God Jesus so *gentle* towards me? Why does He never scold me?... Ah! truly, it is enough to make me die of gratitude and love!...

I am happier for having been imperfect than if, sustained by grace, I had been a model of meekness.... This does me much good to see Jesus is always so gentle, so tender to me!... Ah! from this moment, I know it: yes, all my hopes will be realized...yes, the Lord will do for us marvels that will infinitely surpass our *immense desires*![4]

Little Mother, Jesus does well to hide Himself, to talk to me only from time to time, and "through the lattices" (Canticle of Canticles),[5] for I feel I would be unable to bear any more, my heart would break, being powerless to contain so much joy.... Ah! you, the sweet Echo of my soul,[6] you will understand that this evening the vessel of divine Mercy overflowed for me!... You will understand that you have been and always will be the Angel charged with leading me[7] and announcing to me the mercies of the Lord!...

> Your *very little* girl,
> Thérèse of the Child Jesus
> of the Holy Face
> rel. carm. ind.

a "lace" allusion

*   Autograph.
1. The illness accentuated Thérèse's emotivity during her last months; see DE, p. 452.
2. There is no necrological circular on this Sister, and we know little about her. Fifty years old in 1897, she impressed others by her noble bearing. In charge of the linen room before Sister Marie of Saint-Joseph, she watched the comings and goings of the novices coming to see Thérèse, whose cell was only a few yards away from the linen room. "Our heart used to beat fast as we passed by the linen room," wrote Sister Geneviève (1948). At times, approaching very stealthily, she would without warning open the door of Thérèse's antechamber, pretending urgent business. "The novices, witnesses to these matters, were indigant, but they were edified at the same time by the conduct and counsels of their prudent mistress, who remained calm" (Mother Agnes of Jesus, NPPA, Prudence). These facts should be placed between the autumn of 1894 and March 1896, the date on which Sister Marie of Saint-Joseph was placed in charge of the linen room.
3. See John 8:10.
4. The handwriting of "immense" reveals a certain emphasis; a possible allusion to the correction from "infinite desires" to "immense desires" in her formula of the *Act of Offering to Love*, upon the request of P. Lemonnier in 1895; see p. 905. According to the testimony of Mother Agnes of Jesus, this change was difficult for Thérèse (PO, 1524).
5. See Canticle of Canticles 2:9.
6. Title given formerly to Céline; see LT 89 and 94.
7. See LT 229, note 2.

LC 180   *From Mother Agnes of Jesus to Thérèse.*

May 30, 1897   This note crossed that of Thérèse, LT 231. That evening, Thérèse revealed to her sister her spitting up of blood in April 1896.

My poor dear little Angel, I have certainly caused you some grief; nevertheless, I assure you that I find it a grace from God to me to know what has happened to you, for I would have learned these details after your death, and I believe I would never have been consoled. I have a character so strangely formed; it would have always seemed to me that because of my struggles you had hidden yourself from me,[1] and so I would have always believed that our intimacy, so sweet, so ENTIRE, in my eyes during your life was not to the degree I had supposed it to be. What do you expect? I am not mistress of my sad feelings,[2] this is the weakness of my little character. Oh! how I thank God for this evening's recreation.[3] Yes, I see that He loves me and pities my poor little heart. I want to bear any type of struggle during your life, but afterward every memory must be sweet to me and I must have no longer anything *to learn*. That nothing was said to me at the time I do not find wrong, but have pity on my maternal weakness and beg that on another occasion I may be made aware of everything. Oh, little Angel, you have a strange little Mother. During Compline there was in my heart a kind of real abyss of bitterness, a very special kind, a kind I had never experienced before. Oh! how I pity God when souls have no confidence in Him. This is the greatest outrage one can commit against His paternal tenderness. As for you, dear Angel, your motive was one of TOTAL TENDERNESS. Oh! I have no doubt of it, and I terminate this note, repeating again to Jesus: "Oh! thank You! You had pity on my weakness. No, I would not have been able to bear this after the death of my little Angel, I would have died of sorrow...."

Above all, do not be worried,[4] for I have understood everything.

* Autograph.
1. This is exactly what happened. Sister Marie of the Trinity testified that on April 3, 1896: "Thérèse made her promise to keep secret this sad news (which she called joyful!) so as not to worry Mother Agnes of Jesus" (NPPA, *Carnet Rouge*, p. 64). In CJ 12.8.4, the conflicts between Thérèse, already sick (in 1896?) and desirous of observing the Rule to the end, and her sisters "begging her to take care of herself" are apparent. Thérèse herself will admit that she "has hidden a little corner of the envelope" (LT 231). After the words: "hidden from me," the autograph has: "and you would no longer have done me," crossed out by Mother Agnes.
2. The handwriting in this note shows the weight of the shock she suffered that night; it was an hour of truth. See DE, pp. 34-38.
3. There were no Community recreations between Ascension (May 27) and Pentecost Sunday (June 6). Mother Agnes spent the time of this evening recreation, between the evening meal and Compline (at twenty

minutes to seven) with Thérèse. The preceding day, Thérèse had undergone the treatment of *"pointes de feu"* (CJ 29.5).

4. Because of the fear of a possible displeasure on the part of Mother Marie de Gonzague when she learned the secret had been divulged by Thérèse. This last sentence gives rise to a doubt as to whether the prioress' "permission" had been given, which was mentioned in CJ 30.5.1. See Thérèse's answer in LT 232.

LT 231	**From Thérèse to Mother Agnes of Jesus.**
May 30, 1897	This note crossed the preceding note from Mother Agnes (LC 180).

J.M.J.T.

May 30, '97

Do not be grieved, dear little Mother, because *your* little girl *has seemed* to hide something from you. I say *seemed*, for you know very well, if she has hidden a little corner of the *envelope*,[1] she has never hidden from you a single line of the *letter*, and who then knows better than you this little letter that you love so much? To others I can show the envelope on all sides since they can see only this, but to you!!!... Oh! little Mother, you known now that it was on Good Friday[2] that Jesus began to tear a little the envelope of *your* little letter. Are you not happy because He is getting ready to read this letter that you have been writing for the last twenty-four years?! Ah, if you only knew how well it will be able to tell Him of your love throughout all Eternity.[3]

* Autograph.

1. The *Copy of the Writings* has two notes: one in the margin, written by Sister Marie of the Sacred Heart: "She had hidden from Mother Agnes of Jesus, who was no longer the prioress, the spitting up of blood she had experienced"; the other written by Sister Madeleine of Jesus: "She was making reference to the physical sufferings she had not confided to her; by *envelope* she meant her *body* and by *letter*, her *soul*" (CE II, p. 61). On the symbolism of the envelope and letter, current in the literature of the time, see LT 232, LC 182; CJ

30.5.2.
2. April 3, 1896.
3. Mother Agnes copied out this note with some light changes in her *Yellow Notebook*, CJ 30.5.1.

LC 181   *From Mother Agnes of Jesus to Thérèse.*

May 30, 1897
→ LT 231

I fear once again, little Angel, I have grieved you by my harsh note; yours, oh, yours is so gentle. Ask Jesus to make me like you.

Soon you will be flying away far from this earth, and my heart deep down is thrilled with a supernatural joy; while my eyes are shedding tears, I feel myself totally transported interiorly with an inexpressible sentiment of happiness. Oh, white dove, it is time that the Master of the dovecote set you in your place! It is time that the little angels be no longer deprived of your company; it is time that God may receive new glory through your entrance into the heavenly homeland. After this, I want to suffer on earth as long as God wills it, I really want to sigh in my turn like a sad little turtledove exiled in the valleys here below. I want tears for myself. Yes, I am VERY HAPPY. Finally my little Angel is about to return to her country; she is going to prepare a place for her little Mother, she will make her holy, she will teach her from on high how to master her very sad feelings, she will give her all kinds of things, having herself forever such a great abundance of them!

Oh, Jesus, I love You! I, too, will go to see You. In the meanwhile, I am sending You ALL THAT I LOVE.

* Autograph.

LT 232   **From Thérèse to Mother Agnes of Jesus.**

May 30, 1897   This note, too, crossed that of Mother Agnes
→ LC 180   (LC 181).

(second note)

J.M.J.T.

I placed my first note in the hands of Sister Geneviève[1] just as she was giving me yours. I regret[2] now having posted my missive, but I shall pay double postage to tell you that I really understand your sorrow. I wanted, more than you perhaps, to hide nothing from you, but it seemed to me that I had to wait. If I did any wrong, pardon me, and believe that *never* did I fail in my confidence in you!... Ah! I love you too much for that!... I am very happy that you have understood. I do not recall having hidden anything else of the *envelope* from my little Mother, and I beg her, after my death, not to believe what anyone will say to her. Oh! little Mother, *the letter is yours.* I beg you, continue writing it until the day when Jesus will tear up completely the little envelope that has caused you so much grief ever since it was made!...

---

*   Autograph.
1.   Sister Geneviève, as infirmarian, transmitted these written messages.
2.   "*Je regrette*": an attempt at a phonetic transcription of "*jai raigrette.*" See also LT 242. Mother Agnes also used this expression. Thus she annotated in pencil a draft of a poem Thérèse had submitted to her: "It seems to me I now prefer '*les bienheureux*'; I regret (*jai raigrette*) having crossed it out" (May 1897, poem *Pourquoi je t'aime, ô Marie!* For the next to the last stanza Thérèse offered a choice between: "*tous les élus du Ciel*" and "*les bienheureux du Ciel.*" It is probable that the two sisters were mimicking the intonation of l'abbé Baillon, the Community's extraordinary confessor at this time. He had a way of asking his penitents: "Raigrettez-vous?"

LC 182   *From Mother Agnes of Jesus to Thérèse.*

May 31, 1897   Date deduced from the content; see note 1.

This evening, I said my entire little chaplet on my knees before the Blessed Virgin's May altar;[1] it seems to me, at the end of it, she had a very special smile. Oh, my little Angel, I feel that if you pray for me, I shall really begin a new life; I feel I have received a very great grace. I do not even want to be sad if our Mother refuses you;[2] the Blessed Virgin has made me understand that all the most beautiful Lives of the Saints are not of more value than is an act of obedience and renunciation. Even if our Mother, after your death, were to tear up your little life,[3] it seems to me, if I am as I am this evening, that I shall feel nothing but a more powerful attraction for heaven. I shall fly higher, that is all: Above the clouds, The sky is always blue. We touch the shores, On which God reigns!....[4]*

Do not feel sorry for me any longer,[5] our union has never been more intimate; oh, I feel it. This evening, near the Blessed Virgin there was a very bright candle that had overflowed and the wax formed, on the side, *the veritable mold of a very little lamb pleading.* I thought that the light was you and the little lamb was myself, who, leaning on your brightness and turning toward Mary, would be pitied by her. I do not know what I am saying to you, dear Angel. My heart and my soul, my entire little person is a world this evening. I hope you understand me and that, after your departure from the valley of tears, you will come often to embellish this little world, and walk in it with the little angels, and *with a luminous breath* make it *a little sun*[6]

Enfant, quand vous serez au-dessus des nuages
Vous jouant avec paix dans les prairies des Cieux
Quand du livre de vie vous tournerez les pages
     Sur moi toujours baissez les yeux.

Voyez donc si mon nom dans ce livre de grâce
Au vôtre lumineux ne s'est pas enlace

Au-dessus des nuages, Le Ciel est toujours bleu.
On touche rivages Où règne le bon Dieu!

> *Et si dans l'avenir je devrai prendre place*
>   *Petit Ange à votre côté.*

> *Le bon Jésus parfois dans sa tendresse immense*
> *De nos petits péchés se plait à ne rien voir*
> *N'est-ce pas douce enfant c'est bien cela qu'il pense*
>   *En Lui quand on met son espoir!...* *

I composed, dear little Angel, these little verses to give solace to my heart. Oh! how I love you! This is not what I would have liked to say to you. Now you will know only in heaven what your soul places poetically in my own. Oh! what joy to be your little sister, your little Mother, and to feel I am *loved* by you. I thank you for all the thoughtfulness you have for me. I have, however, been very unfaithful in my little religious life, but I am going to begin my conversion to be like you; when God sees this, He will forgive my little sins, I hope.

Oh! take me away with you from this earth.... My soul escapes from its frail envelope when thinking that white and gilded wings are growing on you; they are already prepared, all that is needed is a light breeze from on high to set them in motion.

> *Child, when you are above the clouds,
>   Playing peacefully in the meadows of heaven,
>   When you turn the pages of the book of life,
>   Lower your eyes always on me.

> See, then, if my name in this book of grace
> Is not interwoven with your own luminous one,
> And if in the future I shall have to take my place,
>   Little Angel, at your side.

> Good Jesus at times in His immense tenderness
> Is pleased to see nothing of our little sins.
> Is this not really, sweet Child, what He thinks
>   When we place our hope in Him!...

* Autograph.
1. This detail suggests our adopting the date of May 31, Thérèse's preceding letter being written on May 30.
2. The implication here is the permission of continuing her autobiography. At this stage, Mother Agnes seems to envisage the request as being made by Thérèse herself to the prioress.
3. The first copybook dedicated to Mother Agnes (MS. A), the existence of which Mother Marie de Gonzague was still unaware at this date.
4. The poem *L'Abandon est le fruit delicieux de l'Amour*, stanza 17, composed at the request of Sister Thérèse of Saint Augustine. The copy made by Thérèse was dated May 31.
5. Regarding the incident of the preceding day.
6. See Victor Hugo, *Louis XVII*, stanza 10: *Prends les ailes d'azur des cherubins vermeils - Tu viendras avec nous bercer l'enfant qui pleure - Ou dans leur brûlante demeure - D'un souffle lumineux rajeunir les soleils.* (Take the azure wings of the bright red Cherubim - You will come with us to rock the child who weeps - Or, in their burning abode, - With a luminous breath to rejuvenate the suns.) See *Last Conversations*, p. 217. This poem is at the beginning of a copybook of choice pieces copied out by Pauline at the Visitation boarding school at Le Mans, 1875 - 1876. There is a doubt concerning the page which follows, distinct from the preceding page. The paper and handwriting belong more to the appearance of the LC 183 note. The content harmonizes more with that of this day (LC 182). Without settling the question, Thérèse's response seems to go in this direction.

LT 233   **From Thérèse to Mother Agnes of Jesus.**

June 1, 1897   Date written in by Mother Agnes.
→ LC 182

J.M.J.T.

It is far too touching, far too melodious!... I prefer to be silent to attempting in vain to sing what is taking place in my little soul!... Thank you, little Mother!...

* Autograph.

LT 234

June 2, 1897

From Thérèse to Sister Marie of the Eucharist.

A year later, Sister Marie of the Eucharist wrote her parents: "I am sending you, with this letter, the note that Sister Thérèse of the Child Jesus wrote me last year on the day of my reception of the Veil.... It is a relic for me; I found this note at our place before the Mass for the reception of the Veil" (Letter to M. and Mme. Guérin, June 2, 1898).

J.M.J.T.

June 2, 1897

To my dear little Sister, a souvenir of the beautiful day on which the Bridegroom of her soul deigns to place His seal on the head[1] He is preparing to crown one day before all the Elect....

Formerly, the entire heaven joined together on June 2 to contemplate this mystery of love: Jesus, the gentle Jesus of the Eucharist giving Himself for the first time to Marie.[2] This beautiful heaven made up of the Angels and the Saints is here again today; it is here contemplating with delight: Marie giving herself to Jesus before the world astonished at a sacrifice it cannot understand. Ah! if it were to understand the *look* that Jesus cast upon Marie on the day of His first visit, it would also understand the *mysterious seal* she wishes to receive today from Him who has wounded her with love.... It is no longer the graceful veil with the long snowy fold that must envelop Marie of the Eucharist; it is a somber veil that reminds the Spouse of Jesus that she is exiled, that her Bridegroom is no longer a Bridegroom who must lead her into festivities but to Mount Calvary. Henceforth, Marie must look no longer at *anything* here below, at *anything* except the *Merciful God*, the *Jesus* of the EUCHARIST!...

Little Sister Thérèse
of the Child Jesus
of the Holy Face
rel. carm. ind.

*   Autograph.

1.   A reference to one of the Responses for the ceremony: *Posuit signum in faciem meam* (He has placed His seal on my face), taken from the Divine Office for the feast of St. Agnes.

2.   Marie Guérin made her First Communion on June 2, 1881.

LT 235   **From Thérèse to Marie of the Eucharist.**

June 2, 1897   A picture added to the preceding note. Mother
                       Agnes explained later on: "Sister Thérèse of the
                       Child Jesus had this picture in her breviary and
                       found it pretty, but during her last illness when
                       looking at the Child Jesus whom she had found
                       so beautiful, she no longer saw it in the same
                       light and began to cry, thinking everything was
                       unattractive on this earth, that only in heaven
                       she would see Jesus in His real beauty. She gave
                       this picture to Sister Marie of the Eucharist,
                       without telling her about her feelings." (Note at-
                       tached to the picture.)

Souvenir of the beautiful day of my dear little Sister's reception of the Veil. June 2, 1897

May Thérèse's little Jesus always caress Marie of the Eucharist.

*   Autograph.

LT 236   **From Thérèse to Sister Marie of the Trinity.**

June 2, 1897   Date indicated on the copy of the Process.

God *wills* that you bear your trial alone.[1] He is proving this in many ways.... But, my dear little doll,[2] I am suffering with you!!!... And I love you very much....

Do not be grieved. I will go looking for you tomorrow for a few minutes, and the day after the washing, I will go with you to the breads.[3]

*   Autograph.
1. Sister Marie of the Trinity has left no clarification concerning this remark.
2. Thérèse used the abbreviation "p." (poupée). See LT 249, CJ 22.9.4, and DE, p. 564. The nickname of "doll" was no doubt linked with a recent recreation in the novitiate. At the end of May, Sister Marie of the Eucharist wrote her mother: "That she was not to forget the large doll about which she had spoken to her. That the doll and the lace were to be wrapped with "Personal" marked on it" (to M. Guérin, May 1897.)
3. In the room where they baked the altar breads.

LC 183   *From Mother Agnes of Jesus to Thérèse.*

June 2 (?), 1897   Date deduced from Thérèse's response; see LT 237.

J.M.J.T.

Oh, my little Angel! I no longer have any words with which to express my tenderness for you. Do not scold me; see how the apostles were sad when good Jesus was telling them that He was going to leave them soon.[1] ... *Yes, but*! ... They will return *filled with joy*[2] when the blow has passed ... thus will it happen for little Mother.

Is it worth while my asking our Mother for the continuation of the little Life?[3] I fear that if she agrees, this will tire you out, even that it may be impossible for you to do it. Your condition is worsening so much! Then I would have perhaps committed a blunder. You will tell me about this tomorrow. You know that our Mother cried very much after the visit.[4] ... As for me, she immediately cast me aside. However, provided you occupy yourself with me in heaven! ... When I think you are about to die. Ah! I would have been really happy to have something from you this year. I mean the continuation of your little life. I no longer know what position to take: I would like to let you leave and, at the same time, keep you here. I still did not know how much I loved you! Sister Marie of the Eucharist really tired me out just now with her chatter[5] over her scruples, I almost had a lump in my throat from it. ... I can imagine what you suffered from her.[6] ... But all that is over! And what

a beautiful crown has been made for you. But, no, since you do not
want a crown;[7] then what glory you have given to God. I wonder
what will take place in heaven at your arrival? It already seems to
me that Papa, in his sweet and melodious voice,[8] is singing to you
from on high: "Come to us, young daughter. There is a sparkling
pearl missing in my crown."[9] As for Mamma, the elect and the angels
rise and proclaim her blessed,[10] and regarding our little ones, their
companions, the Holy Innocents, cover them with kisses, strew
flowers under their feet, and do not know what to do to congratulate
them. You be the judge of whether they are strutting around![11] Ah!
certainly there is a big to-do!

Arise, dear dove, the winter is past for you,[12] the fountain of your
tears is dried up, come and taste the delights of the eternal fountain
of love.

Above all, do not answer me, this would break my heart.

---

* Autograph.
1. See John 16:6.
2. See Luke 24:52. These lines were written during the octave of the
   Ascension; Mother Agnes' correspondence contains frequent
   references to the Liturgy.
3. "*la petite vie*": the autobiography of Thérèse. See CJ 11.6.2.
4. Undoubtedly the visit with the Guérin family on the occasion of Sister
   Marie of the Eucharist's reception of the Veil, that same morning.
5. Mother Agnes used the word "*diries*," a word proper to Normandy,
   meaning: chatterings, boring verbiage, words without end (Moisy dictionary, p. 209).
6. See Sister Marie of the Eucharist's own testimony, reporting Thérèse's
   words: "Ah! how many times she spoke these words to me: "I beg
   you, be busied a little less with yourself, occupy yourself with loving
   God, and forget about yourself. All your scruples, these are just a
   lot of self-seeking. Your griefs, your sorrows, all that is centered on
   yourself, it is like spinning around on the same pivot. Ah! I beg you,
   forget yourself, think of saving souls.' She used to be repeating this
   every time I was with her for direction" (notes used by Mother Agnes
   of Jesus in her own testimony, p. 2).
7. See LT 143, note 6.
8. See LC 60, note 1 and LD, around July 20, 1893.
9. A. van Hasselt, *Le Chant des Anges*. M. Martin copied out this poem
   and "used to repeat it with an inexpressible tone of voice" (G/NPHF,

p. 463). On September 14, 1894, the day of Céline's entrance into Carmel, Thérèse had placed on her sister's bed their father's autograph copy of it.

10. See Proverbs 31:28.
11. Figure of speech: *faire jabot* or *se rengorger* means: to strut about, put on airs, blow oneself up, etc. An expression familiar to the Martin family. See CJ 27.5.6.
12. See Canticle of Canticles 2:10-12.

LT 237   **From Thérèse to Mother Agnes of Jesus.**

June 2, 1897   Date inserted by Mother Agnes.
→ LC 183

No, the little dove does not want to leave its little Mother, it wants to fly and take rest in the delightful little world of her heart. Tomorrow, I will say thank-you to my little Mother. I say nothing this evening in order not *to break her heart* and because it is too late. Baby[1] is going to sleep.

* Autograph.
1. The expression "baby" will appear in LT 254, 255, 257. It is of frequent occurrence in *Last Conversations* (see DE, pl 871). On the real significance of this nickname, see the important note in DE, pp. 442-444.

LT 238   **From Thérèse to Léonie.**

June 3, 1897   An inscription on the back of a picture for
                         Léonie's thirty-fourth birthday. At this time,
                         Léonie tells us: "I was thinking rather of orien-
                         tating myself to the secular life" (Sister François-
                         Thérèse, PA, Bayeux, p. 611).

Dear little Sister, how sweet it is for me to think that one day we
shall follow together the Lamb throughout the whole of eternity![1] . . .

> Souvenir of June 3, 1987
> Sister Thérèse of the Child Jesus
> of the Holy Face
> rel. carm. ind.

* Autograph.
1. See Apocalypse 14:4.

LC 184   *From Mother Agnes of Jesus to Thérèse.*

June 3 (?), 1897   Uncertain date; see note 1.

I cannot tell you all that is happening in my soul regarding
yourself, it is ineffable.

In spite of your vagabond walks will I be able to talk to you for
a little one quarter of an hour?[1]

* Autograph.
1. The writer added later: "it was written by Sister Agnes of Jesus";
   and in the margin: "note given to Thérèse" and "evening 2."
   However, these two last words do not resemble the usual dating of
   Mother Agnes. They seem rather to be the continuation of a first
   marginal line, illegible, over which is written "note given," etc.

LT 239   **From Thérèse to Mother Agnes of Jesus.**
June 3 (?), 1897   Response written on back of preceding note.

I must walk right up to my last moment[1] —This is what will end
my torment—Like the poor wandering Jew.[2]

* Autograph.
1. The first edition of the *Lettres*, pp. 395-396, placed this note in May,
   the time when Thérèse, upon the advice of the infirmarian, was taking "each day a little walk of a quarter of an hour in the garden"
   (DE, p. 649). June 3 seems to be the closing date for this exhausting
   exercise. Thérèse is "very sick" on June 5 (DE, p. 677). On June 7,
   she has recourse to a wheelchair (*ibid.*). We offer this date, however,
   because of the style of LC 184, which is quite similar to the series
   of notes during these dates.
2. The note in French: "*Il faut que je marche jusqu'à mon dernier instant - Comme le pauvre Juif errant.*" See LT 217, note 7. However,
   the Complaint runs: "*Jésus, la bonté même - Me dit en soupirant -
   Tu marchera toi-même - Pendant plus de mille ans - Le dernier juge-
   ment - Finira ton tourment.*" ("Jesus, goodness itself - Told me with
   a sigh - You yourself will walk - More than a thousand years - The
   last judgment - Will end your torment." (Twenty-second stanza of
   the "*Complaint.*")

LT 240   **From Thérèse to Sister Marie of the Trinity.**
June 3 (?), 1897   Probable date; see note 1.

J.M.J.T.

Dear little flower of Jesus, I understood everything very well; know
that it is not necessary that you speak to me at length about it. The
little eye that is in your calyx indicates to me what I must think of
the whole little flower.[1] . . . I am very happy, very much consoled,
but you must no longer *desire to eat earth*; the forget-me-not must
half-open or rather lift its corolla so that the *Bread of Angels* may
come like a divine Dew to strengthen it and to give it all that it is
lacking.[2]

Good night, poor little flower, believe that I love you more than you can imagine!...

   *   Autograph.
   1.   This note develops the symbolism of the forget-me-not, dear to Sister
      Marie of the Trinity (see LT 187). We understand here that the novice's
      look alone informs Thérèse of her dispositions. This sentence sug-
      gests a meeting: a short one in which Marie of the Trinity could not
      "speak at length": perhaps the "few moments" promised in the
      preceding note (LT 236)? Sister Marie of the Trinity dated the
      autograph in pencil "June '97." The *Process of the Writings* placed
      it between the note of June 2, (LT 236) and that of June 6 (LT 242).
   2.   Sister Marie of the Trinity wanted to deprive herself of Holy Com-
      munion to punish herself for a failing.

LT 241   **From Thérèse to Sister Martha of Jesus.**
June 1897 (?)   Uncertain date; see note 4.
→ LC lost

J.M.J.T.

Dear little Sister, yes, I understood all.... I am begging Jesus to
make the sun of His grace shine in your soul. Ah! do not fear to
tell Him you *love Him, even without feeling it*. This is the way *to
force* Jesus to help you, to carry you like a little child too feeble
to walk.

It is a great trial to look on the *black* side, but this does not depend on you completely. Do what you *can*; detach your heart from
the *worries* of this earth, and above all from creatures, and then be
sure Jesus will do the *rest*. He will be unable to allow you to fall
into the dreaded *mire*.... Be consoled, dear little Sister, in heaven
you will no longer *take a dark view of everything* but *a very bright
view*.... Yes, everything will be decked out in the divine *brightness*
of our Spouse, the Lily of the valleys.[1] *Together* we shall follow Him
everywhere He goes.[2]... Ah! let us profit from the *short moment*
of life...*together* let us please JEsus, let us save souls for Him by
our sacrifices.... Above all, let us be *little*, so little that everybody
may *trample* us underfoot,[3] without our even having the appearance
of feeling it and suffering from it....

See you soon, dear little Sister; I take delight in seeing you.[4] . . .

* Autograph.
1. See Canticle of Canticles 2:1.
2. See Apocalypse 14:4.
3. See Imitation of Christ III, 13:3; and the *Prayer to obtain Humility* composed for Sister Martha during the following weeks in view of her birthday (LT 256).
4. The 1948 edition of *Lettres* places this note "perhaps in 1894" (pp. 287-288), "during a private retreat" of Sister Martha. She presents it as having been written "during a retreat" in PO 2072, without specifying the year; in PA, 1285, she says simply: "one day." Her chronology is generally fluid. In her outline (NPPA), she joins together these statements: "I am not surprised at the defects of the little child. But how bad it is to spend one's time in fretting over things instead of sleeping on the Heart of Jesus." We recognize here some elements from the notes LT 199 and 205, written by Thérèse to Sister Marie of Saint-Joseph. The disappearance of the autograph removes all possibility of dating it by the handwriting. The choice made here rests on some probabilities: 1) the prophylactic measures adopted in 1897 because of Thérèse's illness affected especially Sister Martha and Sister Marie of the Trinity (see DE, p. 580), who felt they were deserted by Thérèse; 2) the advice given here by Thérèse is that of an accomplished spiritual guide. In 1894, Thérèse's role consisted rather in attracting Sister Martha to certain "practices," which she tabulated on paper. See p. 864. However, the date proposed is not definitive; the question remains open.

LC 185   *From Mother Agnes of Jesus to Thérèse.*

June 4 (?),   (Fragments)
1897   Date deduced from the contents; see note 1 and 2.

J.M.J.T.

My dear little Angel, I feel very sorry for having made you undertake you know what,[1] however, if you only knew how much this pleases me! . . . You know that the saints in heaven can still receive glory until the end of the world and that they favor those who honor them.... Well, I shall be your little herald, I shall proclaim your feats of arms. I shall take care to make God loved and served by means of all the lights which He has given you and which will never be extinguished. Then you will favor me with you caresses, will you not, little Angel? You will come to spread around me the little gilded dust from your golden wings; I shall have to feel your presence everywhere.

This morning we sang your poem *Holy Innocents*.[2] Sister Thérèse of St. Augustine left, weeping when we sang the couplet: "Like them, I also want to kiss Your sweet Face, oh, my Jesus." I blushed with pride rather than with sorrow. To tell the truth, I love you so much that I can cry only with one eye. To know that my little Angel is soon going to leave this sad prison in order to enter into infinite glory, what joy for a Mother's heart. Look, I really believe that later on I shall be the one who consoles the girls. They will come, each in turn, to express their sympathy for you and have me listen to their varied lamentations which will really touch them.[3]... After all, I can see that they love you very much; yes, but not as much as I do, for if they were to see what is taking place in my heart, they would be amazed, so strong and limitless like the ocean is the ebb and flow of tenderness that I feel in my heart for my dear Angel.

There is still one thing I wanted to tell you. You well know, my little girl, that it is not usual for my character to have accepted the trial of these recent days so well; this morning, I was astonished at this, and God said to me: "But your little girl has prayed for you, that is the secret of your strength." I come, then, to thank you and to press you to my little heart. If you are already so powerful on earth, what shall I see, what shall I feel when you will be up above?... Mother Subprioress[4] says that you will not go to purgatory for one second; alas, who can doubt this?... However, my little Angel, count on many little gifts from me.[5] Immediately after your death, I shall have you go to purgatory to console the little souls who are there with my little prayers. So you will ask the Blessed Virgin to descend that you may descend there with her, carrying my little glasses of refreshment; I shall have more than one kind of these refreshments to offer you, you will see; it will be my turn to give you little joys.

* Autograph + photocopy.
1. The continuation of Thérèse's autobiography. Mother Agnes obtained Mother Marie de Gonzague's consent for this on June 2 or 3. Her statement would suggest that Thérèse had already begun this work.
2. The poem *A mes Petits Frères du Ciel*, composed by Thérèse. The poem was probably sung when the Community was doing the laundry; the "washing" about which Thérèse spoke in LT 237 and for which the date of June 5, Saturday, the Eve of Pentecost, must be excluded. Mother Agnes was recalling the eleventh stanza, last verse.
3. Sentence inserted by Sister Geneviève (from: "They will come") to replace a passage which she suppressed.
4. "Mother Subprioress," who was Sister Marie of the Angels.
5. Prayers and sacrifices, as Thérèse was to ask from them later on; see DE, pp. 582-583.

LT 242 **From Thérèse to Sister Marie of the Trinity.**

June 6, 1897 Note written on Pentecost Sunday.
→ LC lost

J.M.J.T.

Jesus † June 6, 1897

Dear little Sister, your nice little letter delights my soul. I really see I am not mistaken in thinking God is calling you to be a great saint while you remain *little* and become more so each day.[1] I understand very well your sorrow at not being able to speak to me, but be assured I am suffering also at my helplessness, and never have I felt so keenly that you hold an *immense place* in my *heart*!...

One thing that pleases me is to learn that sadness is not making you melancholic. I was unable to refrain from laughing when reading the end of your letter. Ah! this is how you make fun of me? And who, then, has spoken to you about *my writings*?[2] To which folios are you making reference? I see clearly that you are trying to draw me out. Well, one day you will know it, if not on earth, then in heaven; but certainly it will hardly disturb you, we shall have other things to think about then....

You want to know if I am joyful at going to paradise? I would

be very much so *if* I were going there, but. . . I do not count on the
illness, it is too slow a leader. I *count only on love*. Ask Good Jesus
that all the prayers being offered for me[3] may serve to increase the
Fire which must consume me. . . .

I believe you will not be able to read this;[4] *I am sorry,*[5] but I had
only a few minutes.

* Autograph.
1. Compare with Ms. C, p. 207, written on that same date.
2. Her autobiographical copybook, Ms. C.
3. In particular, the novena to *Notre Dame des Victoires*, which the Community was making for Thérèse, June 5-13; see LT 244, note 2.
4. However, the note in ink was very legible.
5. "je regrette": see LT 232, note 2.

LT 243   **From Thérèse to Sister Geneviève.**

June 7, 1897   That day, Pentecost Monday, Sister Geneviève
→ LC lost?   photographed her sister (VTL, nos. 41, 42, and
                   43). In spite of her exhaustion, Thérèse had to
                   pose for a long time to satisfy Céline's demands.
                   According to an oral tradition, Céline was im-
                   patient. The present note seems to answer the
                   apologies expressed by the novice, *viva voce* or
                   by writing.

J.M.J.T.

June 7, 1897

Beloved little Sister, let us never speak what appears great in the
eyes of creatures. Solomon, the wisest king who ever was on earth,
having considered the different works that occupy men under the
sun, painting, sculpture, all the arts, understood that *all* these *things*
were *subject to envy*; he cried out that they were only vanity and
affliction of spirit![1]. . .

The only thing that is not *envied* is the last place; there is, then,
only this *last place* which is not vanity and affliction of spirit. . . .

However, "the way of man is not within his power,"[2] and we surprise ourselves at times by desiring what sparkles.[3] So let us line up humbly among the imperfect, let us esteem ourselves as *little souls* whom God must sustain at each moment. When He sees we are very much convinced of our nothingness, He extends His hand to us. If we still wish to attempt doing something *great* even under the pretext of zeal, Good Jesus leaves us all alone. "But when I said: 'My foot has stumbled,' your mercy, Lord, strengthened me!... Ps. XCIII."[4] YEs, it suffices to humble oneself, to bear with one's imperfections. That is real sanctity![5] Let us take each other by the hand, dear little sister, and let us run to the last place...no one will come to dispute with us over it....

* Autograph.
1. See Qoheleth 1:14, Vulgate.
2. See Jeremias 10:23.
3. See LT 197, paragraph 4.
4. See Psalm 93:18.
5. See Ms. C, p. 207, written during these same days: "I must bear with myself, such as I am with all my imperfections." Sister Marie of the Trinity comments in these words on this sentence of LT 243: "What canonized Saint has ever spoken in this way: 'We ourselves,' she said to me, 'we are not saints who cry over our sins; we take delight in them because they serve to glorify the mercy of God'" (note of Sister Marie of the Trinity to Mother Agnes, March 8, 1925).

LC 186　　　　*From l'abbé Bellière to Thérèse.*
June 7, 1897
→ LT 224

†　　　　　　　　　　　　　　　　　　　June 7, 1897
R. Ap.

To Sister Thérèse of the Child Jesus
　　　　　　　　Peace!

Good and very dear Sister,

I have never sung with greater enthusiasm than yesterday the first stanza of your Canticle of Love.[1] On no other day, I believe, was it more appropriate, because it formed the substance of the day since it found its place in the Gospel.[2] But for me there was an added grace: Yesterday, at the very hour when the Holy Spirit descended upon the Apostles with His Light and His Strength, I received His orders from my director's mouth. In other words, I received an almost definitive decision on my vocation, and I listened to these words: "You have a genuine vocation in which I firmly believe and in which God is manifesting His providence in a singular manner. With a thousand chances of perdition, He is giving you ten thousand chances of salvation. Furthermore, He wills that you be a missionary; the career is open; go." And I shall leave, dear little Sister; I shall spend this vacation with my family and, on October 1, I shall arrive at Algiers to make my novitiate at the *Maison-Carrée* with the White Fathers. The only obstacle I foresee would come from the Bishop; I need his authorization, and sometimes he makes objections, and this even more so because, this year, a number of requests were addressed to him from different Congregations. I had the joy of contributing to the choice of the White Fathers' African Missions on the part of one of my confrères, whom I am taking there.

Regarding the decision given to me, I am at peace and happy, for my director assured me that even if I had not manifested my desire for the missions to him, he would have sent me there. And so if later on it were to happen that I experienced some failures and discouragement, which is almost inevitable at the beginning, I would be joyful like St. Paul in the midst of his tribulations,[3] for I would be conscious of doing God's will, and I would also have you near me, Sister, by means of your fraternal charity which will not be the least support for my poor soul. You promised me this even after the exile: you will be there, and I have no fear.

Let us adore God, Sister, and you thank Him with me. Less than anyone else, and I beg you to believe this, I deserved this honor which I consider only in trembling, and I am somewhat frightened by this love of God. However, I want confidence to prevail and I want to give myself without any reservations. Moreover, this is what is being asked from me. Father told me: "You must give yourself to God totally, who is asking all from you; you cannot be in His service by halves, you will be a good priest or nothing.'' This is my own sentiment, and I want to give without counting, being very sure ''That when one loves, one does not count,''[4] so that when I set foot on African soil, I may continue: ''I have given all...lightly I run. I have nothing any longer but my only riches, To live by Love!''*

> *   *''Que lorsqu'on aime on ne calcule pas*
>   *J'ai tout donné...légèrement je cours*
>   *Je n'ai plus rien que me seule richesse*
>   Vivre d'Amour!''*

This will be an additional rapprochement with my little Sister. You were saying to me recently: ''I feel our souls were made to understand one another,'' and it seems so to me too; since I am a little bit superstitutious regarding Providence, I cannot refrain from setting up these points of similarity (but also how many dissimilarities!). Permit me to present some to you in all simplicity: the same desires: souls, the apostolate...you are before all else an apostle, it seems to me; the need of dedication to a sacred cause. You love the cause of God and the Church, but also that of France, the Pope, true? And if you had been given the chance of carrying the sword for one or the other, you would have done it. I admit that I myself had thought first of terrestrial arms; this was only conquered (after a struggle with blessings and graces) by Christ to whom I capitulated, while retaining in my heart an ardent love for these objects. And, understand, if a war were to come, if the Pope were to call his valiant ones, it seems to me I would be among the first. One of my joys over there will be also to work for France, insofar as this will be within my power and my duty.

     When very young, dear little Sister, you were severed from maternal caresses. Look, I did not know my mother; furthermore, she died on account of me. Up to the age of ten or eleven, I was unaware of this misfortune, receiving from an aunt the devotedness and endearments which I believed were maternal because they were so gentle and beneficent. So I was calling ''mother'' this sister of my mother, and my heart will suffer just as much as it would have suffered if I had left my mother for the distant apostolate. I recommend her to you, good little Sister; each day I think of your father and mother who are also dead. My father is dead too. My whole family is now entirely spiritual, but, I believe, I am not less attached to it.

I would not be surprised if we had the same devotions. The Sacred Heart converted me after how much folly and cowardliness; the beautiful years, those which Jesus loves more, I wasted, sacrificing to the world and its follies the "talents" God was lending me. But the Blessed Virgin, *Notre Dame de la Délivrande*, whom you undoubtedly know,[5] was also a great help to me. St. Joseph received me into his guard of honor, and I ask much from the kindness of Saints Paul, Augustine, Maurice, Louis de Gonzague, Francis Xavier, and Saints Joan of Arc, Cecilia, Agnes. You have sung about all of them. Geneviève was a brave one, and she comes between your birth and your baptism (January 3). Teresa, especially since I know that she is the holy patroness of my dear little Sister; Mary Magdalene, the sinner who was so much loved by Jesus. There are also the dear apostles or martyrs, such as, P. Perboyre, Vénard, de Bretenières, Chapdelaine, etc. Certainly you know all these inhabitants of heaven.[6]

And now, dear Sister in God, I thank you for sending me your holy dates, and I am happy this letter will reach you on the anniversary of a memorable one.[7] Pardon me for having saddened you in my last letter; excuse me, I am so rude, so abrupt. At least, do not condemn my good will, my heart. Thank you, too, for the names of the future goddaughter; they are ones I would have chosen myself. I accept with the same simplicity the comparison of P. de la Colomcière and of Blessed Margaret Mary with some reservations, for I would like to interchange the roles, if I did not fear grieving you. It is sweet and divine this outpouring of the Heart of Jesus and His loved ones.

How I must bore you, distract you, my brave and dear little Sister, with all this verbiage, in which it seems to me I am talking about myself outrageously; pardon me. Truly, I assure you, I am a miserable person, and you have to be around for God to love me. I count on His rewarding you, and I will ask this from Him with fervor.

Very dear and good Sister, I am forever your grateful but un-worthy brother,

M. Barthélemy-Bellière

Have no fear, Sister, I am too jealous of the grace God is giving me and the benefit of your letters to allow an outsider to enter into our secret.

*   Autograph.
1.   The poem *Vivre d'Amour*! (P. 15.)
2.   The Liturgy for Pentecost Sunday was using at this time John's Gospel 14:23-30; Thérèse had quoted John 14:23 in the first stanza of her poem *Vivre d'Amour*!
3.   See II Corinthians 7:4.
4.   *Vivre d'Amour*! Stanza 5; the verses that follow are from this stanza.
5.   A Chapel in Normandy, between Caen and the coast. Regarding a pilgrimage of Thérèse to *Notre-Dame de la Délivrande*, Sister Geneviève has left two contradictory statements:

> 1) In 1943, she wrote: "In July 1887, our good father took us, Léonie, Thérèse, and myself, to the exhibition at Le Havre. We went there by way of Honfleur, stopping first at *Notre-Dame de Grâce*. It seems to me it was not the first time we went to Honfleur to pray to the Madonna. He brought us also to *Notre-Dame de la Délivrande*, about this same time." (G/NPHF, p. 555. We should note here: the trip to Le Havre took place in *June* 1887.)

> 2) In 1958, after having recalled her own pilgrimages with Léonie and the Guérin family, Sister Geneviève wrote: "I cannot believe that Thérèse ever went without me, without all of us to *Notre-Dame de la Délivrande*, nor can I state that Papa ever set foot there. Yes, this is what I can unfourtunately state, he never set foot there" (to P. Piat, February 21, 1958). In this letter, the witness, eighty-nine years old, manifests so many lapses of memory that we cannot rely on these memories. After careful examination, the question remains open regarding Thérèse's hav-ing visited this chapel.

6.   In the autumn of 1896, Thérèse read the *Life* of several missionaries, besides those of P. Nempon and Théophane Vénard, but we do not

know which ones. Let us point out the existence in the Carmelite monastery of Lisieux an old biography of Blessed Perboyre (1802-1840; beatified in 1889, hence the second title of Sister Martha of Jesus: *Martha of Jesus and of Blessed Perboyre*), and a biography of P. Chapdelaine.

7. He is referring to June 9, the second anniversary of her *Act of Oblation to Merciful Love*. This is a date which Thérèse had not given to P. Roulland, the preceding year; see the facsimile in *Fêtes et saisons*, June 1972, p. 35.

LT 244	**From Thérèse to l'abbé Bellière.**
June 9, 1897	This note was never sent because of an improve-
→ LC 186	ment in Thérèse's condition; see diary, DE, p. 154.

J.M.J.T.

June 9, 1897

Dear little Brother, I received your letter this morning, and I am profiting from a moment when the infirmarian is absent to write you a last note of *adieu*. When you receive it, I shall have left the exile.[1] . . . Your little sister will be united forever to her Jesus; then she will be able to obtain graces for you and to fly with you into distant missions.

Oh, dear little Brother, how happy I am to die! . . . Yes, I am happy not because I shall be delivered from sufferings here below (suffering, on the contrary, is the only thing that seems desirable to me in this valley of tears), but because I really feel that such is God's will.

Our good Mother would like to keep me on earth; at this moment they are making a novena of Masses for me to Our Lady of Victories.[2] She has already cured me in my childhood, but I believe the miracle she will work will be none other than that of consoling the Mother who loves me so tenderly.

Dear little Brother, at the moment of appearing before God, I understand more than ever that there is only one thing necessary, that is, to work *solely* for *Him* and to do nothing for self or for creatures.

Jesus wills to possess your heart completely, He wills you to be a great saint. For this you will have to suffer very much, but then what joy will inundate your soul when you will reach the blessed moment of your entrance into Eternal Life!... Brother, I shall go soon to offer your love to all your friends in heaven, begging them to protect you. Dear little Brother, I would like to tell you many things that I understand now that I am at the door of eternity; but I am not dying, I am entering into Life, and all that I cannot say to you here below, I will make you understand from the heights of heaven....

A Dieu, little Brother, pray for your little sister who says to you: *A bientôt, au revoir au Ciel!*...

> Thérèse of the Child Jesus
> of the Holy Face
> rel. carm. ind.

* Autograph.
1. On June 9, Thérèse was assured that her death was very close; see CJ 15.6.1 and 27.7.18.
2. *Notre-Dame des Victoires* at Paris, dear to the Martin and Guérin families. See Ms. C, p. 215 and DE, p. 675. The Novena of Masses was offered by l'abbé Elie Pottier (1856-1940), pastor of *Notre-Dame des Victoires* from 1888 to 1898.
3. May 13, 1883; see LC 26 and Ms. A, p. 65.

LT 245

From Thérèse to Mother Agnes of Jesus, Sister Marie of the Sacred Heart, and Sister Geneviève.

June (?), 1897   Approximate date; see note 5.

Recto
at top   Do not weep over me, for I am in heaven with the Lamb and the consecrated Virgins![1]...

below   I see what I believed
                  I possess what I hoped for
                  I am united to Him whom I loved
                  with all my power of loving.[2]

on each side   The smallest movement of pure Love is more useful to the Church than all other works put together![3] It is, then, of the greatest importance that the soul exercise herself much in Love in order that, consuming herself rapidly, she hardly stops here below and arrives promptly in seeing her God Face to Face.[4]

(St. John of the Cross.)

Verso

I find nothing on earth that makes me happy; my heart is too big, nothing that is called happiness in this world can satisfy it. My mind takes flight to Eternity, time is about to end![5]... My heart is peaceful like a tranquil lake or a serene sky;[6] I do not long for the life of this world, my heart is thirsting for the waters of eternal life![7]... In a little while my soul will leave the earth, will end its exile, will terminate its combat.... I am ascending to heaven...I am touching the homeland, I am carrying off the victory!... I am about to enter into the abode of the elect, to see beauties that the eye of man has never seen, to listen to harmonies the ear has never heard, to enjoy delights the heart has never tasted.[8]... Here I am, brought to that hour which each of us has so much desired![9]... It is very true that the Lord chooses the little ones to confound the great ones of this world.... I do not depend on my own strength but on the strength of Him, who on the Cross has overcome the powers of hell.[10] I am a springtime flower that the Master of the garden is plucking for His pleasure.... We are all flowers planted on this earth that God gathers in His own time, a little earlier, a little later.... I, a little short-lived creature, am going there the first![11] One day we shall find one another again in Paradise, and we shall enjoy true happiness![12]...

Thérèse of the Child Jesus borrowing the thoughts of the angelic Martyr, Théophane Vénard.

*   Autograph (picture)
1.   Adaptation of the third lesson of Matins for the second feast of St. Agnes (January 28).

2. Antiphon for the *Benedictus* of the same Divine Office.

3. Saint John of the Cross; see LT 221, note 3.

4. The *Living Flame of Love*, stanza 1, explanation of the sixth verse; see *Collected Works*, p. 594, par. 34. This sentence concludes the third passage marked with a cross by Thérèse in the copy that she later kept at her bedside during her illness. See DE, pp. 492-495.

5. *Théophane Vénard*, letter of January 3, 1861, to Msgr. Theurel. As Thérèse mentions in her signature, the *verso* of this picture is made up of passages borrowed from the letters written by the martyr during his imprisonment, between his arrest (November 30, 1860) and his decapitation (February 2, 1861). All these extracts, and others not used here, had been copied out by her on November 21, 1896, in a notebook (see p. 1074). When calligraphing them for her sisters, she introduced some slight variants appropriate to her own situation. The carefulness of her handwriting makes its expert evaluation difficult. Its firmness would suggest, however, an anterior date: April - May? It is by association with the scene of her *adieux* (June 9 - 13? See DE, p. 432), that this inscription is mentioned at the same epoch. The picture could have been given earlier or later to its recipients.

6. *Ibid.*, December 28, 1860, letter to Msgr. Theurel.

7. *Ibid.*, January 2, 1861, letter to his family.

8. *Ibid.*, January 20, 1861, letter to his sister; see I Corinthians 2:9.

9. *Ibid.*, January 3, 1861, letter to Msgr. Theurel.

10. *Ibid.*, December 3, 1860, letter to his family.

11. *Ibid.*, January 20, 1861, letter to his father.

12. *Ibid.*, January 2, 1861, letter to his family.

LD　　　　　　*From Mother Agnes of Jesus to Sister Marie of the Sacred Heart.* (Fragment.)

June (?), 1897　　　Approximate date; see note 1.

. . .

I, too, am very sad at heart. But what do you expect? It is God who is afflicting us, God who loves us and *who loves her* much more than we love her. Ah! how sad this earth is!

This dear little one did everything to please us this evening;[1] we must be careful not to show her any sadness to grieve her little heart.

* Autograph.
1. The paper, handwriting, and ink present many similarities to those of the letter of Mother Agnes to her uncle and aunt Guérin, June 7; see DE, p. 676. We do not know to what incident the note is making reference; *perhaps* to the reunion of Thérèse's three sisters for her "adieux"? See CJ 4.6.1 and DE, p. 431.

LC 187   *From Sister Geneviève to Thérèse.*

June-July (?),   Approximate date; see note 2.
1897

Here, my dear, is what I drew from the Gospel[1] after asking the Blessed Virgin to console me.[2]

"It will be for you (Thérèse) a cause of joy and happiness, and *at his birth* many will rejoice.... For he will be great before the Lord, and he will convert *a great number of the children* of Israel to the Lord their God, in order to unite the hearts of fathers to those of their sons, to lead back the unbelieving to the wisdom of the just so as to prepare for the Lord a perfect people.[3]..."

Oh, Thérèse, my own Thérèse!...

* Autograph.
1. Opening the gospels at random.
2. "Sister Thérèse of the Child Jesus was very sick when I wrote her this note" (note of Sister Geneviève). We may suppose the worsening of her condition of June or that of July 6-7.
3. See Luke 1:14, 16, 17.

LT 246   **From Thérèse to Sister Marie of the Trinity.**
June 13, 1897

May the divine little Jesus find in your soul an abode all perfumed with the roses of Love, may He find there the burning lamp of fraternal charity,[1] which will warm His little cold members and which will delight His little Heart by making Him forget the ingratitude of souls who do not love Him enough.

Sister Thérèse of the Child Jesus
of the Holy Face
r.c.i.
(June 13, 1897)[2]

* CE.
1. See Ms. C, p. 219, on fraternal love, written around June 12 - 15. "It seems to me that the lamp represents charity which must enlighten, rejoice, etc."
2. Trinity Sunday, feast of Sister Marie of the Trinity. According to NPPA (Red Notebook, p. 42), this text was written on the reverse side of a Christmas holy picture, now lost.

LT 247   **From Thérèse to l'abbé Bellière.**
June 21, 1897
→ LC 186

J.M.J.T.

Carmel of Lisieux   June 21, 1897

Jesus †

Dear little Brother,

I thank Our Lord with you for the great grace He has seen fit to grant you on the day of Pentecost; it is also on this beautiful feast (ten years ago) that I obtained not from my director but from my father the permission to become an apostle in Carmel.[1] This is still one more rapprochement between our souls.

Oh, dear Brother, I beg you, never believe "you bore or distract me" when speaking much about yourself. Would it be possible that a sister not take interest *in all* that has to do with her brother? As for what distracts me, you have nothing to fear; on the contrary, your letters unite me more to God by making me contemplate closely the marvels of His mercy and His love.

Sometimes Jesus is pleased "to reveal his secrets to the littlest one,"[2] and the proof is that after reading your first letter of October 15, '95, I thought the same thing as your director: You cannot be a saint by halves, you will have to be one totally or not at all. I felt that you had to have a courageous soul, and it was for this that I was happy to become your sister....

Do not think you frighten me by speaking "about your beautiful, wasted years." I myself thank Jesus, who has looked at you with a *look of love* as, in the past, He looked at the young man in the Gospel.[3] More blessed than he, you have answered faithfully the Master's call, you have left all to follow Him, and this at the *most beautiful age* of your life, at eighteen. Ah! Brother, like me you can sing the mercies of the Lord,[4] they sparkle in you in all their splendor.... You love St. Augustine, Saint Magdalene, these souls to whom "many sins were forgiven because they loved much."[5] I love them too, I love their repentance, and especially...their loving audacity![6] When I see Magdalene walking up before the many guests, washing with her tears the feet of her adored Master, whom she is touching for the first time, I feel that *her heart* has understood the abysses of love and mercy *of the Heart of Jesus*, and, sinner though she is, this Heart of love was not only disposed to pardon her but to lavish on her the blessings of His divine intimacy, to lift her to the highest summits of contemplation.

Ah! dear little Brother, ever since I have been given the grace to understand also the love of the Heart of Jesus, I admit that it has expelled all fear from my heart. The remembrance of my faults humbles me, draws me never to depend on my strength which is only weakness, but this remembrance speaks to me of mercy and love even more.

When we cast our faults with entire filial confidence into the

Mk 10:21

Ps 88:2

LW

1 Jn 4:18

also 1 John
× see Moltmann – Justification
is more then Reconciliation

lo

devouring fire of love, how would these not be consumed beyond return?[7]

Jn 14.2

I know there are some saints who spent their life in the practice of astonishing mortifications to expiate their sins, but what of it: "There are many mansions in the house of my heavenly Father,"[8] Jesus has said, and it is because of this that I follow the way He is tracing out for me. I try to be no longer occupied with myself in anything, and I abandon myself to what Jesus sees fit to do in my soul, for I have not chosen an austere life to expiate my faults but those of others.

I just read over my note, and I wonder if you are going to understand me, for I have explained myself very poorly. Do not think that I condemn the repentance you have for your faults and your desire to expiate them. Oh, no! I am far from doing so, but, you know, we are now *two*, the work will be done more quickly (and I with *my way* will do more than you), so I hope that one day Jesus will make you walk by the same way as myself.

Here she does not say "little" way just "WAY"

Pardon me, dear little Brother, I do not know what is the matter with me today, for I am not saying what I would like to say. I have no more space for answering your letter; I shall do it another time. Thank you for your dates, I have already celebrated your twenty-third birthday.[9] I am praying for your dear parents whom God has taken out of this world, and I am not forgetting the mother whom you love.[10]

> Your unworthy little Sister,
> Thérèse of the Child Jesus
> of the Holy Face
> rel. carm. ind.

* Autograph.
1. May 29, 1887; see Ms. A, p. 107.
2. See Matthew 11:25.
3. See Mark 10:21.
4. See Psalm 88:2, basic theme of Ms. A, taken up again at the beginning of Ms. C, in the course of its redaction.
5. See Luke 7:47.
6. See Ms. C, pp. 258-259; the same reference for the two last paragraphs of this letter.

7. See CJ 11.7.6. See P. Tissot: "Were you to have committed the greatest possible offences, as soon as you enter the Wound of the divine side, hardly have you touched this sacred Door when love, like a devouring fire, comes forth, hastens, and in its ardor consumes even the smallest infidelities!... It is an abyss that the greatest iniquities cannot fill up: cast your sins into this abyss of love and soon they will be pulverized and nothing of them will remain!" (*Meditation* of October 15, 1890, transcribed into the scripture notebook of Thérèse; see LC 164, note 4.)

8. See John 14:2.

9. June 10.

10. His aunt, Mme. Barthélemy.

LT 248   **From Thérèse to Léonie.**

End of June (?),   Conjectured date; see note 1.
1897

J.M.J.T.

Dear little Léonie,

I am *very much touched* by your eagerness to please me. I thank you with all my heart, and I am delighted with the little blanket you made for me.[1] It is exactly what I wanted....

I will offer up my Communion for you tomorrow....

I *love you* and I kiss you.

Your little Sister,
Thérèse of the Child Jesus
rel. carm. ind.

*   Autograph.

1.   "A little blanket for the infirmary," suggests the first edition of the *Lettres*, p. 437. However, this note must have been written before Thérèse's coming down to the infirmary (July 8) and even before Léonie's departure for La Musse with the Guérin family (July 2). It was during the first days of July that Thérèse stopped writing in ink. This note, written in pencil, has a steady handwriting, clearly anterior to that of letters 253 (July 13, 1897) and 255 (July 16). Its borderline

date seems to be July 1. We could also accept a date several weeks before July 1.

LT 249	**From Thérèse to Sister Marie of the Trinity.** (Fragments.)
Mid-July (?), 1897	Approximate date; see note 3. "One day, when I was no longer able to stand the sorrow and struggle of being kept at a distance from her like a stranger, I went to the infirmary and gave vent to my complaints before one of her sisters: 'Your sisters and your cousin,' I told her, 'cannot love you more than I do, and they have the consolation of coming to see you whenever they want. I find this is not just.' My bitter complaint grieved the Servant of God, and she sent me away, reproaching me severely for my lack of virtue. In the evening, she had this note sent to me" (NPPA, Red Notebook, p. 100).

J.M.J.T.

Dear little Sister,

I do not want you to be sad. You know what perfection I dream about for your soul.

. . .

I have pity on your weakness. . . with you, it is a matter of having to speak *immediately* what you are thinking

. . .

infirmary should have made you understand that it would be more difficult to obtain permission to come after Matins[1] . . .

. . .

Now it is not

. . .

understood your struggle and would have consoled you gently, if you had not said it aloud, but that you

. . .

Adieu, dear little doll;[2] I will have to bring you to heaven very quickly! I want to have it totally[3]

* Autograph in ten fragments. This note and all the following ones are written in pencil.

1. At this hour, Mother Agnes (who favored Sister Marie of the Trinity) was relieved of her duties regarding Thérèse by Sister Geneviève, who slept in the cell contiguous to the infirmary; see DE, p. 46. It is undoubtedly Sister Geneviève against whom the "complaints" mentioned in the *Red Notebook* were directed.

2. Thérèse used the letter "p," an abbreviation for *"poupée"*; see LT 236, note 2.

3. This note in pencil, very much mutilated, deleted in part, comes from the same type of note paper as in LT 252 and the same loose sheets of the original notes collected by Mother Agnes at her sister's bedside, July 11-12; see DE, pp. 61-62. It had to be written at a date very close to this. The Red Notebook, pp. 100-101, gives this version: "Dear little Sister, I do not want you to be sad. You know what perfection I am dreaming about for your soul, and that is why I spoke to you severely.... I would have understood your struggle and have consoled you gently if you had not spoken of it aloud and had kept it in your heart as long as God permitted it. I have only to remind you that our affection must be hidden...." The Process reproduced an abridged transcription of it (PA, 2461). The first edition of the *Lettres* presents an amalgamation of the fragments of the autograph and the *Red Notebook*.

LT 250   **From Thérèse to Sister Marie of Saint Joseph.**
July (?), 1897   Approximate date; see note 1.

J.M.J.T.

I hope Sister Geneviève has consoled you;[1] it is the thought that you are no longer grieved which makes mine disappear!... Ah! how *happy* we shall be in heaven; then we shall share in the divine perfections,[2] and we shall be able to give to all without being obliged to deprive our dearest friends!... God has done well not to give us this power on earth; perhaps we would have wished not to leave it, and then it does so much good to recognize that He alone is perfect,

He alone must be enough for us when it pleases Him to take away the branch supporting the little bird! The bird has wings, it is made for flying![3]

* Autograph.
1. No doubt for not having access to the infirmary, over which Sister Geneviève was guardian? The handwriting of this note is very bad.
2. We may have noticed the repetition of the verb "to share" since the autumn of 1896: LT 202, 226 (twice), and 263 (twice).
3. The "branch" is evidently Thérèse, the "bird" is Sister Marie of Saint-Joseph. The latter suffered from the need of having to be satisfied with a few silent visits to the infirmary. See DE, pp. 558-559.

LT 251   **From Thérèse to Sister Marie of Jesus.**

June-July (?),   Approximate date; see note 2.
1897
→ LC lost

J.M.J.T.

The little spouse of Jesus must not be sad, for Jesus would be sad too. She must always sing in her heart the canticle of love, she must forget her *little* sorrows to give solace to the *great* sorrows of her Spouse.

Dear little Sister, do not be *a sad little girl* when seeing you are not understood, that you are judged badly, that you are forgotten, but lay a trap for everybody by taking care to do like others, or rather by doing for yourself what others are doing for you, that is, *forget all* that is not Jesus, *forget* YOURSELF for His love!... Dear little Sister, do not say that this is difficult; if I speak in this way, it is your fault, for you told me that you loved Jesus *very much*, and nothing seems impossible to the soul that loves.[1]...

Be assured that your note *pleased* me very much![2]...

* Autograph.
1. See *Imitation of Christ* III, 5:4.
2. We meet this expression in CJ 15.6.2 and 8.7.6. Certain characteristics of the handwriting of this note in pencil show a strength that we do

not find any longer in her writings from July 13 onward. There would be nothing against our situating the note some weeks earlier.

LT 252   **From Thérèse to Mother Agnes of Jesus.**

July 13, 1897   Date written in by Mother Agnes.

I love you very much, little Mamma, you will see this very soon!...
Oh yes!...

*   Autograph.

LT 253   **From Thérèse to l'abbé Bellière.**

July 13, 1897   This note takes up again several thoughts of the
                       June 9 farewell note (LT 244) which had never
                       been sent.

J.M.J.T.

July 13, 1897

Jesus!

Dear little Brother,

Perhaps when you read this note, I shall no longer be on earth but in the bosom of eternal delights! I do not know the future; however, I can tell you with certainty that the Bridegroom is at the door, and a miracle would be needed to keep me in the exile, and I do not think Jesus will perform this useless miracle.

Oh, dear little Brother, how happy I am to die! Yes, I am happy, not at being delivered from sufferings here below (suffering united to love is, on the contrary, the only thing that appears to me desirable in this valley of tears). I am happy to die because I feel that such is God's will, and that much more than here below I shall be useful to souls who are dear to me, to your own in particular. You were asking in your last letter to our Mother that I write you often during your vacation.[1] If the Lord wills to prolong my pilgrimage for several weeks more and if our good Mother allows it, I shall be able to scribble some notes to you like this one; but it is more probable that I shall do more than write my dear little Brother, more even than speak to him in the fatiguing language of this earth I shall be *very close* to him, I shall see all that is necessary for him, and I shall leave no rest to God if He does not give me all I shall want!... When my dear little Brother leaves for Africa, I shall follow him no longer by thought, by prayer; my soul will be always with him, and his faith will be able to discover the presence of a little sister whom Jesus gave him, not to be his support for barely two years but *right up to the last day of his life.*

All these promises, Brother, may perhaps appear to you a little bit chimerical; however, you must begin to realize that God has always treated me like a spoiled child. It is true that His Cross has followed me from the cradle, but this Cross Jesus has made me love with a passion. He has always made me desire what He wanted to give me.[2] Will He begin, then, in heaven to carry out my desires no longer? Truly, I cannot believe it, and I say: "Soon, little Brother, I shall be near you."

Ah, I beg you, pray very much for me, prayers are so necessary for me at this moment; but *above all* pray for *our Mother*. She would have liked to hold me back here below for still a long time, and to obtain it this venerable Mother has had a novena of Masses offered to *Notre-Dame des Victoires*, who had already cured me in my childhood; but I, feeling that the miracle would not take place, asked and obtained from the Blessed Virgin that she console my Mother's heart a little, or rather that she make her consent to Jesus' taking me away to heaven.

A Dieu, little Brother, *à bientôt au revoir* in this beautiful heaven.[3]

> Thérèse of the Child Jesus
> of the Holy Face
> rel. carm.

*   Autograph.
1.   "If you only knew the good the letters of your dear daughter do me; they make me good, strong, more pious, more humble, more detach-

ed. Allow me to beg that they be more numerous during my vacation. I am going to have much to struggle against in myself first, and
against sweet affections that I shall have to break with difficulty''
(letter of l'abbé Bellière to Mother Marie de Gonzague, June 7, 1897).
Since this letter, l'abbé Bellière had again written to the prioress on
June 20, her feast day, Saint Louis de Gonzague.

2. Identical sentence on this day in CJ 13.7.15.

3. This letter must have been held back for a few days for l'abbé Bellière
received it only on Saturday, July 17, accompanied by a letter from
Mother Marie de Gonzague; see LC 189.

LT 254   **From Thérèse to P. Roulland.**

July 14, 1897   The last letter to the missionary.
→ LC 178

J.M.J.T.

Carmel of Lisieux   July 14, 1897

Jesus †

Brother,

    You tell me in your last letter (which pleased me very much): "I
am a *baby* who is learning to talk." Well, I, for the last five or six
weeks, am a baby too, for I am living only on *milk*;[1] but soon I shall
sit down at the heavenly banquet,[2] I shall quench my thirst at the
waters of eternal life![3] When you receive this letter, no doubt I shall
have left this earth.[4] The Lord in His infinite mercy will have opened
His kingdom to me, and I shall be able to draw from His treasures
in order to grant them liberally to the souls who are dear to me.
Believe, Brother, that your little sister will hold to her promises, and,
her soul, freed from the weight of the mortal envelope, will joyfully
fly toward the distant regions that you are evangelizing. Ah! Brother,
I feel it, I shall be more useful to you in heaven than on earth, and
it is with joy that I come to announce to you my coming entrance
into that blessed city, sure that you will share my joy and will thank
the Lord for giving me the means of helping you more effectively

Erickson's STAGE 9

in your apostolic works.[5]

I really count on not remaining inactive in heaven. My desire is to work still for the Church and for souls. I am asking God for this and I am certain He will answer me. Are not the angels continually occupied with us without their ever ceasing to see the divine Face and to lose themselves in the Ocean of Love without shores?[6] Why would Jesus not allow me to imitate them?

Brother, you see that if I am leaving the field of battle already, it is not with the selfish desire of taking my rest. The thought of eternal beatitude hardly thrills my heart. For a long time, suffering has become my heaven here below, and I really have trouble in conceiving how I shall be able to acclimatize myself in a country where joy reigns without any admixture of sadness. Jesus will have to transform my soul and give it the capacity to rejoice, otherwise I shall not be able to put up with eternal delights.

What attracts me to the homeland of heaven is the Lord's call, the hope of loving Him finally as I have so much desired to love Him, and the thought that I shall be able to make Him loved by a multitude of souls who will bless Him eternally.

Brother, you will not have time to send me your messages for heaven, but I am guessing at them, and then you will only have to tell me them in a whisper, and I shall hear you, and I shall carry your messages faithfully to the Lord, to our Immaculate Mother, to the Angels, and to the Saints whom you love. I will ask the palm of martyrdom for you, and I shall be near you, holding your hand so that you may gather up this glorious palm without effort, and then with joy we shall fly together into the heavenly homeland, surrounded by all the souls who will be your conquest!

Au revoir, Brother; pray very much for your sister, pray for *our Mother*, whose sensitive and maternal heart has much difficulty in consenting to my departure. I count on you to console her.

I am your little sister for eternity,
Thérèse of the Child Jesus and
of the Holy Face
rel. carm. ind.

*   CE.

1. Thérèse was on a milk-diet ever since the week of Pentecost; see
    medical diary, DE, p. 154.

2. See Luke 13:29.

3. See LT 245, note 7.

4. This is what made P. Roulland write, October 13, when he received
    this letter: "I was expecting news at any moment; it is here. My sister
    has already left earth a long time" (to Mother Marie de Gonzague,
    October 13, 1897).

5. With regard to this paragraph and the three following, see DE, pp.
    256-270, the words of July 12-18; also DE/Meu, p. 777; letter 35,
    DE, p. 721; etc.

6. See Arminjon, *op. cit.*, p. 302, himself quoting P. Blot, *In heaven
    we shall know one another*. See CJ 17.7.

LC 188   *From l'abbé Bellière to Thérèse.*

July 15, 1897
→ LT 247

Langrune, July 15

†

To Sister Thérèse

My very good and very dear Sister,

It is almost a month since I received your dear letter.[1] If I had
not been very much taken up since I have been on vacation, I would
have come already looking for some kind words from you, warming and comforting words. You know the milieu of vacations is made
more for chilling and shaking a poorly strengthened soul than for
effecting the good which is so much desired and so necessary, particularly on the eve of an immense grace.[2] That is to say, dear Sister,
more than ever the outpouring of your religious soul into my soul
exiled on vacation is becoming more needful for me. Come, then,
very quickly to speak some good things to me. Do you realize you
are opening up new horizons for me? In your last letter especially,

I find some insights on the mercy of Jesus, on the familiarity He encourages, on the simplicity of the soul's relations with this great God which had little touched me until the present because undoubtedly it had not been presented to me with this simplicity and unction your heart pours forth. And I have thought just like you, but I reach only imperfectly this delightful simplicity which I find astonishing because I am a sad, proud person and because I depend still too much on created things.

No, dear little Sister, you did not explain yourself poorly. You are right. I understood your theories well, and, as you say it so well and so kindly, since we are two at work, I am relying fully on Our Lord and on you. This is the surest way. I consider, as coming from Jesus Himself all that you say to me. I have full confidence in you and am guiding myself according to your way which I would like to make my own.

Tomorrow, Sister, I shall be closely united with you and your Community,[3] especially in the Holy Communion that I shall receive with this intention. One of my friends, a newly ordained priest,[4] my companion for several years, will sing your Solemn Mass. He will be very blessed. And I asked our good Mother for permission to come there in a few years on the eve of my leaving for Central Africa in order to consecrate on the altar of the Carmel the Body of Our Lord, which I would then place with joy on your tongue. At that time, in fact, I shall return to France to spend a few days.

Today, I asked our Mother for a favor, and I hope that you will agree with it, for I have done it myself reciprocally;[5] as always I am appealing to your heart. Allow me to recommend to your heart some temporal favors my mother is praying for.

Dear, very dear little Sister, I leave you in the Heart of Jesus where I find you very often and where I am making a *rendezvous* with you forever.

Forever, I am your attached and grateful brother,

Maurice Barthélemy-Bellière
a.m.

A letter soon, right? I beg you.

*   Autograph.
1. L'abbé Bellière had not yet received the letter of July 13; see LT 253, note 3.
2. Entrance into the novitiate of the White Fathers in October.
3. For the feast of Our Lady of Mount Carmel, July 16.
4. L'abbé Troude, nephew of Sister Marie-Philomène; see CJ 15.7.3 and DE, p. 867.
5. Mother Marie de Gonzague asked him for his photograph; he promised to send her one; see DE, p. 705. In exchange he asked for her own and that of Thérèse. He wrote the prioress in the same letter: "You want to recognize me at the great rendezvous, but. . . I shall have to go in search of you and I will have to recognize you too at that time. If then, good and very dear Mother, you can send me your picture and that of Sister, you will make my mission easier at that hour while affording me a real joy right now" (to Mother Marie de Gonzague, July 15, 1897). The prioress refused to send her photograph but sent him one of Thérèse; see LT 258.

LT 255   **From Thérèse to M. and Mme. Guérin.**
July 16, 1897

J.M.J.T.

Jesus   July 16, 1897

Dear Uncle and dear Aunt,

I am very happy to prove to you that your little Thérèse has not yet left the exile, for I know this will please you. However, it seems to me, dear Relatives, your joy will be greater still when, instead of reading a few lines written with a trembling hand, you will feel my soul near your own. Ah! I am certain God will allow me to pour out His favors lavishly upon you, my little sister Jeanne, and her dear Francis. I shall choose for them the most beautiful cherub of heaven, and I shall beg good Jesus to give him to Jeanne so that he may become "a great pontiff and a great saint."[1] If I am not answered, it will really have to be because my dear little sister no longer has the desire to be a mother here below, but she will be able to rejoice at the thought that in heaven: "The Lord will give her the joy of seeing herself the *mother of many children*,"[2] as the Holy Spirit promised when singing by the mouth of the Prophet-King the words I have just written. These children would be the souls that her well-accepted sacrifice would bring to birth in the life of grace.[3] But I really hope to obtain *my cherub*, that is to say a little soul who is *her replica*,[4] for, alas! not one cherub would be willing to be exiled even to receive the gentle caresses of a mother!...

I notice in my letter that never shall I have the space to say all I would like. I would like, dear Relatives, to speak to you in detail of my Holy Communion this morning which you made so touching or rather so triumphant by your bundles of flowers.[5] I am allowing dear little Marie of the Eucharist to tell you all the details, and I want only to tell you that she sang, before Communion, a little couplet that I had composed for this morning.[6] When Jesus was in my heart, she sang this couplet from *Vivre d'Amour*: "To die by love is a very sweet martyrdom."[7] I cannot express to you how high and beautiful her voice was; she had promised me not to cry in order to please me, and my hopes were surpassed. Good Jesus must have *heard* and understood perfectly what I expect from Him, and it was exactly what I wanted!

My sisters, I know, have spoken to you about my cheerfulness.[8] It is true that I am like a finch except when I have a fever; fortunately, it usually comes to visit me only at night during the hour when finches sleep, their heads hidden beneath their wings. I would not be so cheerful as I am if God were not showing me that the only joy on earth is to accomplish His will. One day, I believe I am at the door of heaven because of the puzzled look of M. de C.,[9] and the next day he goes off very happy, saying: "Here you are on the road to recovery." What I think (the little *milk baby*)[10] is that I shall not be cured, but that I could *drag on* for a long time still. *A Dieu*, dear Relatives, I shall speak to you only in heaven about my affection, as long as I *shall drag on* my pencil will not be able to express it.

Your little daughter,
Thérèse of the Child Jesus
r.c.i.

* Autograph.
1. See LT 152, note 3.
2. See Psalm 112:9.
3. See confidences of Mme. La Néele to Sister Marie of the Eucharist shortly after she had read *Story of a Soul*: "I am telling no one what Thérèse has said to me when reading her *Life*. I have said it only to my dear husband from whom I keep nothing hidden. I am telling you, my dear, but do not speak of it, for I think the best things lose their fruit when not remaining preciously closed within oneself. I have seen the truth of this saying of our little saint: 'I shall spend my heaven in doing good. . . .' The favors she is granting me are much more precious than if she were to send me the little fair-haired child she promised. She consoles me spiritually, she suggests that I offer up my little sufferings for a priest, and what good this thought has done me! I shall not be able to be the mother of a priest (what I was dreaming about all my life), but I shall be able to bring forth spiritually a servant of God by uniting my sorrows to the merits of Jesus Christ. I shall have no joys from this, I shall have only sufferings, but what does it matter, Jesus will be content. Pray for me, my dear, for this spiritual joy will not last forever" (fragment of an undated letter; end of 1898?).
4. The same promise to Dr. La Néele on the occasion of his visit to her, August 17; see DE, p. 757.
5. See DE, p. 702. She received Communion from l'abbé Troude; see LC 188, note 4.
6. "You who know my extreme littleness" (P 53); concerning this composition, see DE, p. 469.
7. P 15, stanza 14.
8. See Sister Marie of the Eucharist's letter to her father, July 12; DE, p. 695.
9. Doctor de Cornière.
10. See LT 254, note 1.

LT 256   **From Thérèse to Sister Martha of Jesus.**

July 16 (?),
1897

J.M.J.T.

Dear little Sister, I remember just now that I did not celebrate your birthday.[1] Ah, believe me, it is an oversight that *is breaking my heart*, I was getting such a great joy over it. I wanted to offer you the prayer on humility;[2] I am not entirely finished copying it, but soon you will have it. Your little twin,[3] who would be unable to sleep if she were not to send you this note.

> Thérèse of the Child Jesus
> rel. carm. ind.

*   Autograph.
1.   Sister Martha of Jesus was thirty-two years old on July 16, 1897.
2.   See LT 141, note 3.
3.   Thérèse and Martha were *quasi*-twins in Profession by two weeks: September 8 and 23, 1890.

LT 257   **From Thérèse to Léonie.**

July 17, 1897   The last letter to her sister.
→ LC lost?

J.M.J.T.

Jesus †   July 17, 1897

Dear Léonie,

I am very happy to be able to speak with you again. A few days ago I was thinking I no longer had this consolation on earth, but God seemed willing to prolong my exile a little. I am not disturbed by it, for I would not want to enter heaven one minute earlier by my own will. The only happiness on earth is to apply oneself in always finding delightful the lot Jesus is giving us. Your lot is so beautiful, dear little sister; if you want to be a saint, this will be easy for you since at the bottom of your heart the world is nothing to you. You can, then, like us, occupy yourself with "the one thing necessary,"* that is to say: while you give yourself up devotedly to exterior works, your purpose is *simple*: to please Jesus, to unite yourself more intimately to Him.

Lk. 10.41

You want me to pray in heaven to the Sacred Heart for you.[2] Be sure that I shall not forget to deliver your messages to Him and to ask all that will be necessary for you to become a *great saint*.

A Dieu, dear sister; I would like the thought of my entrance into heaven to fill you with gladness since I shall be able to love you even more.

Your little sister Thérèse
of the Child Jesus

I shall write you at greater length another time; I cannot do so now, for baby has to go to sleep.[3]

* Autograph.
1. See Luke 10:41.
2. Léonie was at La Musse with her uncle and aunt since July 2; her request, then, was made either in a letter to Thérèse (lost) or in a letter to Sister Marie of the Eucharist, expressed by Mme. Guérin, July 11 (DE, p. 693).
3. These six last words were erased on the autograph, according to the advice of Sister Marie of the Sacred Heart to her sister, Easter 1910. Léonie had not received this letter when she wrote to Sister Geneviève, July 18; see DE, p. 712. When no longer able to write, Thérèse entrusted her sisters with messages for Léonie. We know the tenor of the last message through the testimony of the recipient: "You know that a few days before her holy death Thérèse had written to me by means of our dear Sister Marie of the Sacred Heart that if I wanted 'to live by love and humility, she would come to get me'. . .and I am begging her to help me and not to forget her promise" (Sister Françoise-Thérèse Martin to Sister Geneviève, August 6, 1910).

LC 189   *From l'abbé Bellière to Thérèse.*

July 17, 1897   Date deduced from the content; see note 1.
→ LT 253

☩

Oh! my poor little Sister, what a blow to my poor heart.[1] It was so little prepared, do not ask it this joy you feel at the approach of bliss. It remains attached to its heavy chain, it is tied more tightly to its cross. You are about to leave, dear little Sister, and my heart remains alone once again, no mother, no family. It was concentrating on its Sister's love, making a sweet habit of her holy intimacy. It was happy (oh! how happy) to feel near it this friendly hand that was consoling, strengthening, or uplifting it. My heart was advancing with a smile on the way of the cross because it no longer felt alone, it was happy and waiting with impatience to cast itself into the desert because it had confidence in being sustained. It was about to break with its one earthly affection, depending on her—whom Jesus had lent it as an angel on earth—to compensate for this. And now Jesus withdraws this good at the moment when it appears the most desirable. Oh! how difficult it is, how painful for a soul poorly strengthened in God! However, *fiat! fiat!* since you will be happy, little Sister, forever. Yes, it is right. . . I am a selfish person. Leave little Sister, do not make Jesus wait any longer, He is impatient to gather you up. Let me battle on, carry the cross, fall beneath it, and die from the pain. You will be here just the same; you promised it and I am counting on it. This is my last hope for now and the future. You will be with me, near me. Your soul will lead mine, will speak to it, will console it, unless Jesus, irritated by my complaints, does not will it. But you, little Sister, His spoiled child, now become His spouse, queen with Him, you will win my case and draw me to Him, on the last day; you know by which way, the most speedy, martyrdom, if He wills it. I am thanking the Master just the same. He is teaching me, by means of a new lesson, to detach myself from everything that is passing and to look only at Him.

Leave, then, dear little Sister of God, my own little Sister too. Tell Jesus I would like to love Him very much with my entire being. Teach me to do this as you do. Tell Mary I love her with my whole soul, and my saints, whom you know, tell them of my love, and you who are going to become my Saint of predilection, you my own Sister, bless me, save me. Leave me, too, I beg you, something belonging to you, your crucifix, if you will.[2]

A Dieu, dear Sister, *a Dieu*, and I will see you soon. As long as the exile may be, it will be short compared with eternity.

Au revoir! au Ciel!

Your brother forever,

                              Maurice Barthélemy-Bellière
                              A Dieu!

*   Autograph.

1.   In the same mail, dated simply "Saturday," l'abbé Bellière wrote to Mother Marie de Gonzague: "I just received your sad letter, and my own sorrow must be equal to yours. Look, I am crying like one who is struck by a great calamity" (July 17, 1897; see DE, p. 709).

2.   A similar request was made to Mother Marie de Gonzague in the same mail. (The "page added," quoted in DE, p. 705, would really seem to make up part of letter 26, July 17, rather than letter 23, July 15.) The seminarian's request was answered, see LT 263.

LT 258   **From Thérèse to l'abbé Bellière.**

July 18, 1897
→ 188 & 189

                              J.M.J.T.

Jesus †   July 18, 1897

My poor and *dear* little Brother,

Your sorrow *touches me deeply*, but see how good Jesus is. He is allowing me to be able to write you again in order to try to console you, and no doubt this will not be the last time. The gentle Saviour is hearing your complaints and your prayers, and this is why He leaves me still on earth. Do not believe I am disturbed by this; oh! no, dear little Brother, on the contrary, for I see in this conduct of Jesus how much He loves you!....

I undoubtedly explained myself poorly in my last note, since you tell me, very dear little Brother, "not to ask from you this *joy* I feel at the approach of *bliss*." Ah, if for a few moments you could read into my soul, how surprised you would be![1] The thought of heavenly bliss not only causes me not a single bit of joy, but I even ask myself at times how it will be possible to be happy without any suffering. Jesus no doubt will change my nature, otherwise I would miss suffering and the valley of tears. Never have I asked God to die young, this would have appeared to me as cowardliness; but He, from my childhood, saw fit to give me the intimate conviction that my course here below would be short. It is, then, the thought alone of accomplishing the Lord's will that makes up all my joy.

Oh, little Brother, how I would like to be able to pour into your heart the balm of consolation! I can only borrow the words of Jesus at the Last Supper. He cannot take offense at this since I am His little spouse and, consequently, His goods are mine.[2] I say to you, then, as He said to His intimate friends: "I am going to my Father but because I have spoken to you these things, sorrow has filled your heart. But I speak the truth to you: it is expedient for you that I depart. And you, therefore, have sorrow now; but I will see you again, and your heart will rejoice, and your joy no one will take from you.'[3]

Yes, I am certain of it, after my entrance into life, *my dear* little *Brother's* sadness will be changed into a *peaceful joy* that no creature will be able to take from him. I feel it, we must go to heaven by the same way, that of suffering united to love. When I shall be in port, I shall teach you, dear little Brother of my soul, how you must sail the stormy sea of the world with the abandonment and the love of a child who knows his Father loves him and would be unable to leave him in the hour of danger. Ah! how I would like to make you understand the tenderness of the Heart of Jesus, what He expects from you. In your letter of the 14th,[4] you made my heart thrill sweetly; I understood more than ever the degree to which your soul is sister to my own, since it is called to raise itself to God by the ELEVATOR of love and not to climb the rough *stairway* of fear....

I am not surprised in any way that the practice of familiarity with Jesus seems to you a little difficult to realize; we cannot reach it in

not "little" way

one day, but I am sure that I shall help you much more to walk by this delightful way when I shall have been delivered from my mortal envelope, and soon, like St. Augustine, you will say: "Love is the weight that draws me."[5]

I would like to try to make you understand by means of a very simple[6] comparison how much Jesus loves even imperfect souls who confide in Him:

I picture a father who has two children, mischievous and disobedient, and when he comes to punish them, he sees one of them who trembles and gets away from him in terror, having, however, in the bottom of his heart the feeling that he deserves to be punished; and his brother, on the contrary, throws himself into his father's arms, saying that he is sorry for having caused him any trouble, that he loves him, and to prove it he will be good from now on, and if this child asks his father *to punish* him with a *kiss*, I do not believe that the heart of the happy father could resist the filial confidence of his child, whose sincerity and love he knows. He realizes, however, that more than once his son will fall into the same faults, but he is prepared to pardon him always, if his son always takes him by his heart.[7] ... I say nothing to you about the first child, dear little Brother, you must know whether his father can love him as much and treat him with the same indulgence as the other....

[W]

But why speak to you of the life of confidence and love? I explain myself so poorly that I must wait for heaven in order to converse with you about this happy life. What I wanted to do today was to console you. Ah! how happy I would be if you were to welcome my death as Mother Agnes of Jesus welcomes it. Undoubtedly, you do not know that she is my sister twice over and that she has served me as mother in my childhood. Our *good* Mother feared very much that her sensitive nature and her very great affection for me would make my departure very bitter for her; the contrary has happened. She speaks of my death as of a celebration, and this is a great consolation for me. I beg you, dear little Brother, try like her to convince yourself that instead of losing me you *will find* me, and that I will no longer leave you. Ask the same favor for the Mother whom you love and whom I love still more than you love her, since she is my visible Jesus. I would give you with joy what you are asking if I had not made the vow of poverty, but because of it I cannot even dispose of a picture. Our Mother alone can satisfy you, and I know she will grant your desires. Precisely in view of my approaching death, a Sister took my photograph for our Mother's feast day. The novices cried out when seeing me that I had taken on my grand look;[8] it seems that usually I am smiling more, but believe, little Brother, that if my photograph is not smiling at you, my *soul* will not cease *to smile at you* when it is near you. *A Dieu, dear and much loved Brother*; believe that I shall be for all eternity your *true little* sister Thérèse of the Child Jesus. r.c.i.

* Autograph.
1. The "trial of faith" which Thérèse was suffering from for the last fifteen months had not relented: "It is upon heaven that everything hinges" (CJ 3.7.3).
2. See Ms. C, p. 255.
3. See John 16:5-7, 22. On the place of the Gospel according to Saint John during the last weeks of Thérèse, see DE, p. 697, note 67.
4. July 15, LC 188, par. 1.
5. Saint Augustine, *Confessions* 13:9.
6. See LT 191.
7. See LC 161, note 4.
8. She refers here to the third pose—nine seconds—of June 7, 1897, VTL, no. 43. Thérèse held herself stiffly in order to control her exhaustion.

LC 190   *From Mme. Guérin to Thérèse.*

July 20 (?),   Date deduced from the content; see note 3.
1897
→ LT 255

My beloved little Thérèse,

We are still fragrant from the perfume of your nice letter. God's dear little finch! do you know the angels can envy your happiness! They enjoy the vision of God and praise Him, but you, poor little exile, you are suffering for Him, and your complaints are expressed in a song of love and joy! Do you know, my darling, that you are drawing tears from our eyes when we see you so joyful in the midst of suffering! God wills to embellish your crown still more. He looks at you with the same love with which He looked at His Son when He was on earth. He gave Him the Cross to carry, and good Jesus was crucified. Is He not more than ever at this moment the model of His dear little Spouse? You long so much to be with God, dear little Thérèse, and this desire is augmenting your martyrdom, but with your divine Bridegroom you repeat each day: "Father, may your will be done, not mine."[1] And the heavenly Father leaves you still in our midst because He knows you do some good and are still useful here below. And all your dear ones rejoice in this delay that God is granting them. We feel more than ever how much a Carmelite's life is a life of penance which is shared with her family. It would be so sweet to be able to lavish our cares on you, to relieve your sufferings, to visit you often. This is a hard privation for your dear little Léonie. But God provides all things, is this not so? He consoles those who cannot give you any care, and He has placed such a kind Mother near you! We shall not be able to express our gratitude to her; we pray God to take care of her and give her in joy and graces all she is doing for you. If she will permit it, you will kiss her for me today, little Thérèse. You say very nice things for our Jeanne. How much I thank you for thinking of her in this way; you are her true little sister. I recommend to your prayers the pilgrimage of our three dear children.[2] It really touched me to see that my little Marie had sung at the moment when good Jesus came to visit you. Poor darling, she must have had to receive a great grace for her voice not to betray the emotion of her heart. I fear I am tiring you, dear little *milk baby*, for I know your strength is not great; pardon me if I overtired you, and as the finch puts its head under its wing, give yourself up, dear little one, to a gentle sleep under the wing of your good angel.

I kiss you with all my heart, beloved little Thérèse. Your Uncle wanted to write you, but he is sick this morning.[3] This illness will not have any aftereffects, and I think he will be able to write tomorrow.[4] Jeanne also will write you. In the meanwhile, both kiss you with all their heart. Francis wants to be remembered to you.

Your devoted Aunt,
Céline Guérin

* Autograph.
1. See Luke 22:42.
2. Pilgrimage of Dr. La Néele, his wife, Jeanne, and Léonie to Lourdes, August 19-25.
3. Morning of the 19th or more likely the 20th. Mme. Guérin did not have Thérèse's letter (LT 255) on July 18, at five o'clock when she wrote to Sister Geneviève (DE, p. 711).
4. M. Guérin was unable to write until July 24-25 (LC 192).

LC 191   *From l'abbé Bellière to Thérèse.*
July 21, 1897
→ LT 258

                                        Langrune, July 21, 1897

               †
R. Ap.

To Sister Thérèse

Good and very dear little Sister,

I won...oh! how easy it was...I have your photograph, and henceforth you live in my mind, after having up to the present lived only in my heart. I am expressing myself poorly. Try to understand, however, that your letters, your thoughts, take on a body, a form; they are no longer strictly abstract, they are *you* now. I had really tried to build up your features in my imagination, and I must tell you I was not too far from the reality, at least regarding the general outline, so that when seeing you for the first time, I recognized you. In spite of the fact that you had "taken on your grand look" as you express it, dear Sister, I found you...as I, moreover, very well knew you...very good, very loving, and, yes, smiling despite what you say. Thank you for your condescension in having given me this joy of possessing you almost really near me, always with me. What will it be, then, when your soul will animate these features, smile at my soul, and be fully alive...this will be paradise...and shall I find any longer a reason for being unhappy? What possible suffering is there when a corner of heaven illumines a whole life! But, do you know, I fear that Jesus will tell you all the sorrows I have caused Him, all my misery, and that your tenderness will grow cold. If you only knew how miserable I am! If this has to be, at His first words close His lips, and come, for without you I cannot stand up. But what do I read at the bottom of your portrait: "The Lord *has commanded* his angel to watch over you and to keep you in *all* your ways."[1] Long live God! I breathe, you will stay with me, you are compelled, it is God's command. You will then embark with me for Africa, first in the novitiate. You know what one does there, you will be my pilot, "beloved pilot...I have your motto written on my sail: *Vivre d'Amour*."[2] And in three years, we shall leave for the desert, we shall be missionaries, there you will find yourself in your element. Suffering will not be absent, but I shall be your representative then, since you will no longer suffer. And you do not know if you will be able to dwell in heaven, my brave little Sister, because one no longer suffers there? Use me as a compensation. If I become worthy of it, obtain suffering for me...in love...so that I may be separated from you the least possible in heaven...on the last day.

I thank Jesus, who wills to keep you still among us. Yes, how truly He loves us! I prayed insistently to Him, I called out, I cried out.... He allowed Himself to be conquered by our sorrow and our tears... I was resigned, however. At the first instant, there was the impetuosity of sorrow coming forth very strongly, and then calm was restored. I finally thought like you...yes, it is expedient that you go...and besides you will be closer to me. But look: your presence...your activity at least...will not be more felt than now, and I, little accustomed to things supernatural, I am unable to form any concept that you will really be more present to my activity. It is no use for me to complain any longer...I am ready for your departure...perhaps it is because it seems less imminent, since you are still alive.

You are happy, dear Sister, to see me enter into Love by means of confidence. I believe, with you, that this is the only way that can lead me to the Port. In my relationship with men, I have done nothing through fear. I have never been able to submit to violence, the punishments of my professors left me cold, while reproaches given with affection and gentleness drew tears from me, brought out apologies and promises that I usually kept. It is almost the same with God. If I was shown an angered God, His hand always armed to strike, I became discouraged, I did nothing. But if I see Jesus waiting patiently my return to Him, granting me a new grace after I have asked pardon for a new sin, I am conquered, and I climb again into the saddle. Now, what holds me back at times is not Jesus but myself. I am ashamed of myself, and, instead of throwing myself into the arms of this Friend, I hardly dare drag myself to His feet. Often a first inspiration draws me into His arms, but I stop suddenly at the sight of my wretchedness, and I do not dare. Am I wrong? Tell me, little Sister. I believe the divine Heart is much more saddened by the thousand little acts of cowardice, indelicacies, that His friends commit than by the grave sins that stem from our nature. You understand me, and you will make me generous, irreproachable to Jesus. Would that I had to as high a degree, at least, for Jesus, the "point of honor" that I have *vis-à-vis* men!

You speak to me, dear Sister, about Mother Agnes of Jesus, your own blood sister. I remember her often, along with you, in my prayers, for I am not forgetting what I owe her...thank her cordially in my name. I prayed with all the more love when *I knew* the bond that united you to her. Listen to my confession: It is by means of you and your family that I have known there was a Carmel in Lisieux. Some of my confrères from Lisieux were talking one day among themselves about a Martin family that had given three daughters to the Carmel and about some distant relatives. One of the daughters had entered there at age fifteen, another after having taken care of her holy father in an admirable way right up to the end. I was present...and later on when I thought of asking for a Sister in Carmel, searching around where I might write, I recalled there was a Carmel at Lisieux...and behold the coincidence. Your sister received me and it is you...about whom I had only heard others speak...who was given to me. When I received your "dates," I was struck by their proximity, and I drew some conclusions. Was I mistaken? Are you not the one who in the world was named *Mademoiselle* Geneviève Martin? I beg your pardon for my indiscretion, but you have taught me to keep nothing hidden. So there it is. Once again, pardon me.

Soon, dear little Sister, some news from you; if you could only see how happy I am to get any news from you; however, I would no longer be happy, if I were to know that this had caused you fatigue.[3] Listen only to your affection.

Forever, with all my heart, I am, dear and very dear little Sister, your very fortunate brother,

Maurice Barthélemy-Bellière

*   Autograph.
1. See Psalm 90:11. It is not likely that Thérèse, very weak, had written this quotation at the bottom of her photograph.
2. P 15, stanza 8.
3. In fact, this correspondence required no little courage on Thérèse's part, her weakness was always increasing. See the "medical diary," DE, pp. 164-166.

LT 259   **From Thérèse to Sister Geneviève.**
July 22, 1897

J.M.J.T.

July 22, 1897 - Feast of
St. Magdalene

Jesus †

"Let the just man break me out of compassion for sinners, let the oil with which one perfumes his head not weaken mine."[1]

———————————

I cannot be broken, tried, except by the just, since all my Sisters are pleasing to God. It is less bitter to be broken by a sinner than by a just man; but out of compassion for sinners in order to obtain their conversion, I ask You, oh, my God! that I be broken for them by the just souls who surround me.[2] I ask You, too, that the *oil* of praise so sweet to nature may not weaken my head, that is, my mind, by making me believe I possess virtues that I have hardly practiced several times. Oh, Jesus, Your name is like *oil* poured out;[3] it is in this divine perfume that I want to bathe myself entirely, far from the eyes of creatures....

    *   Autograph.
1. See Psalm 140:5.
2. We do not know anything about the incident to which Thérèse is making reference in these hidden words.
3. See Canticle of Canticles 1:3.

LT 260	**From Thérèse to M. and Mme. Guérin.**
July 24-25 (?), 1897	Date deduced from the content. This note must have crossed that of M. Guérin (LC 192).
→ LC 190	

J.M.J.T.

Little Thérèse thanks her dear Aunt very much for the nice letter she sent her; she thanks also her dear Uncle for the desire that he had to write her, and her little sister Léonie, who delights her because of her abandonment and her *real* affection.[1]

Little Thérèse is sending some gifts to all her own. (Alas! these are some flowers[2] as ephemeral as she is....)

(*Very serious explanations* for the distribution of the flowers.)

There is *a Pansy* for Uncle, *a Pansy* for Aunt (not counting all those blooming for them in the garden of my heart).

The two rosebuds are for Jeanne and Francis, the one that is alone is for Léonie....

With these flowers little Thérèse would like to send all the Fruits of the Holy Spirit[3] to her dear relatives, particularly that of *Joy*!

    *   CMG.
1. See the letter of Léonie to Sister Geneviève, July 18 (DE, p. 712).
2. It is not unlikely that these flowers were entrusted to the sacristan, August Acard, who, on July 25, accompanied the chaplain, l'abbé Youf, to the chateau of La Musse for a few days of rest; see DE, p. 727. We have a note from M. Guérin, relative to this note: "A little note sent to La Musse with some flowers. The marks of two pins

are on it. Isidore Guerin." Thérèse's note has disappeared. According to CMG III, p. 265, it was written in pencil.

3. It was because of this comment that this note was placed "a few days after Pentecost," in the first edition (LT 1948, p. 407, note 2). But Thérèse's symbolism, as we have already remarked, stems generally from something concrete. There is a reference several times to fruit in *Last Conversations*, pp. 108-109.

LC 192   *From M. Guérin to Thérèse.*
July 24-25, 1897
→ LT 255

La Musse, July 24 & 25, '97

My dear little Angel,

I would have liked to answer earlier the admirable letter you sent us a few days ago, but I was unable to do so because of the state of my health. For several days now, I have been suffering from an attack of the gout that, even this morning, has redoubled in intensity; but this afternoon, feeling much better, I am taking advantage of it by paying a little visit to your bed of pain. Your letter was the cause of an inexpressible surprise and joy; it moistened my eyes with tears. What was the nature of these tears? I cannot analyze it. A crowd of different sentiments brought them about. The pride of having such an adopted daughter, admiration for so great a courage and so great a love of God, and I cannot hide it, my darling, sadness against which human nature is defenseless when faced with a separation that appears eternal to it. Faith and reason protest, and we give in to their arguments, but they cannot stop the painful groanings of the body when seeing itself deprived of one of its most precious members. You were your good mother's little pearl; you were your aged father's little queen; and you are the most beautiful little flower of the lily-wreath crowning, scenting, and giving me a forestate of the perfections of heaven. Whatever may be the sorrow haunting and restraining me at certain moments, it has never come to my mind to dispute over you with the love of your Bridegroom, who is calling you. Would one seek to hold back in the mire, into which is sinking and hardly living, a dear one who extends her arms to the Saviour after whom she has sighed for a long time? This would be a poorly understood affection, a selfishness. Each time one of my five little Carmelite daughters crossed the threshold of the cloister, I experienced an inner rending similar in every way to what one feels at the loss of a beloved person. The wound was gradually healed, and when it is opened again at the final separation, it will be less painful. And, then, when one is growing old, the feelings are purified, one experiences better one's nothingness, sees better the purpose and brevity of life and the measureless happiness of eternity, understands better that real family joys and love for one's own will receive their complete development and indestructibility only when they are intermingled with the divine love that will consume them in the same ardor. This is what we think, we who have faith. But the world longs for the mud in which it moves about, having no idea whatever of the splendor and beauty of the heavens. When I think of you, a flower so pure and so chaste, I begin to despise humanity. The distant sound of these maledictions has never struck your ears; you do not even suspect the frightful and hideous depth of the wounds gnawing away at humanity, and, when you do see them from the height of heaven, with what deep pity you will be moved at the sight of your own dear ones who are still living in the midst of this stench. Yes, you will pray for us, for me above all, the least good, the most soiled because he has already lived much, seen, and brushed against all the infamies of a corrupt world, and because he is of a more passionate nature, and he will owe his salvation only to the holy souls who have always helped him with their prayers.

They say that the swan, always mute and silent during its life, gives forth a sublime song when it sees death approaching. Your letter, my darling, is no doubt the last song you have dedicated to us.[1] We shall preserve it as a precious deposit. The pious thoughts it inspires in us will perhaps teach us to feel a little bit the flame of divine love which is consuming you and to which you desire to be united more intimately. Dear little white bird, who has seen the burning bush ever since its tender childhood, who has been fascinated by its brilliance, and who has drawn near in such a way that it will soon be intermingled with It! *A Dieu*, my beloved child, precious pearl, whom your good mother entrusted to me;[2] the remembrance of your virtues and your innocence will never leave me, and I hope that your prayers will make me worthy of being reunited with all my own in the eternal abode. The one who has perhaps the right to call himself your second father and who kisses you from the very bottom of his heart,

Isidore Guérin

* Autograph.
1. The note LT 260 had not yet reached La Musse.
2. His sister, Mme. Martin (née Zélie Guérin).

LT 261   **From Thérèse l'abbé Bellière.**

July 26, 1897
→ LC 191

J.M.J.T.

Jesus †   July 26, 1897

Dear little Brother,

How much your letter pleased me! If Jesus has listened to your prayers and prolonged my exile because of them, He has also in His Love answered mine, since you are resigned to losing "my presence, my perceptible activity," as you express it. Ah! Brother, allow me to say it: God is reserving for your soul very sweet surprises; you have written, it is "little accustomed to supernatural things," and I, who am not your little sister for nothing, I promise to have you taste after my departure for eternal life the happiness one can find in feeling a friendly soul next to oneself. It will not be this correspondence, more or less distant, always very incomplete, which you seem to long for, but it will be a fraternal conversation that will charm the angels, a conversation that creatures will be unable to reproach since it will be hidden from them. Ah! how good it will seem to me to be freed from these mortal remains that would oblige me, if, *to suppose the impossible*, I were to be with several persons

in my dear little Brother's presence, to look upon him as a stranger,
one without any meaning for me!... I beg you, Brother, do not imitate the Hebrews who missed "the onions of Egypt";[1] I have for
some time served you only too much these vegetables that make one
shed tears when coming close to them with the eyes when they are
still uncooked.

Now I dream of sharing with you "the *hidden* manna"
(Apocalypse)[2] that the Almighty has promised to give "to the victor." It is precisely because it is *hidden* that this heavenly *manna*
attracts you less than "the onion of Egypt"; but I am sure, as soon
as I shall be permitted to offer you an entirely spiritual nourishment,
you will not miss the one I would have been giving you if I had remained on earth for a long time. Ah! your soul is too great to be
attached to any consolations here below. You must live in heaven
by anticipation, for it is said: "Where your treasure is, there is your
heart also."[3] Is not *Jesus* your *only Treasure*? Since He is in heaven,
it is there your heart must dwell, and I tell you very simply, dear
little Brother, it seems to me it will be easier for you to live with
Jesus when I shall be near him forever.

You must know me only imperfectly to fear that a detailed account of your faults may diminish the tenderness I have for your
soul! Oh, Brother, believe it, I shall have no need "to place my hand
on the lips of Jesus." He has forgotten your infidelities now for a
long time; only your desires for perfection are present to give joy
to His Heart. I beg you, do not *drag* yourself any longer to *His feet*;
follow that "first impulse that draws you into His arms." That is
where your place is, and I have learned, more so than in your other
letters, that you are *forbidden* to go to heaven by any other way
except that of your poor little sister.

I am in total agreement with your opinion: "The divine Heart is
more saddened by the thousand little indelicacies of His friends than
by even the grave sins that persons of the world commit"; but, dear
little Brother, it seems to me that it is *only* when His own, unaware
of their continual indelicacies, make a habit of them and do not ask
His pardon, that Jesus can say these touching words which are placed
for us in His mouth by the Church during Holy Week: "These
wounds you see in my hands are the ones I received in the house
of those who *loved me*!"[4] Regarding those who *love* Him and who

come after each indelicacy to ask His pardon by throwing themselves into His arms, Jesus is thrilled with joy. He says to His angels what the father of the prodigal son said to his servants: "Clothe him in his best robe, and place a ring on his finger, and let us rejoice."[5] Ah! how little known are the *goodness*, the *merciful love* of Jesus, Brother!.... It is true, to enjoy these treasures one must humble oneself, recognize one's nothingness, and that is what many souls do not want to do; but, little Brother, this is not the way you act, so the way of simple and loving confidence is really made for you.

I would like you to be *simple* with God, but also...with me. You are surprised at my sentence? It is because, dear little Brother, you ask my *pardon* "for your *indiscretion*," which consists in desiring to know if in the world *your sister* was named Geneviève; I find the request very natural, and to prove it to you, I am going to give you some details on my family, for you have not been very well informed.

God gave me a father and a mother more worthy of heaven than of earth; they asked the Lord to give them many children and to take them for Himself. This desire was answered: four little angels flew away to heaven, and five children left in the arena took Jesus for Bridegroom. It was with a heroic courage that my father, like a new Abraham, climbed *three times* the mountain of Carmel to immolate to God what was most dear to him.[6] First, there were his two eldest; then the third of his daughters,[7] on the advice of her director and conducted by our incomparable father, made an attempt in the convent of the Visitation. (God was content with her acceptance, *later* she returned to the world where she lives as though in the cloister). There remained to the Elect of God only two children, one eighteen years old, the other fourteen. The latter, "the little Thérèse," *asked permission to fly to Carmel, which she obtained from her good father, who pushed his condescension even to taking her first to Bayeux, then to Rome, in order to remove the obstacles which were holding back the immolation of her whom he called his queen. When he had brought her to port, he said to the only child* who remained with him:[8] "If you want to follow the example of your sisters, I consent to it, do not worry about me." The angel who was to support the old age of such a saint answered that, *after his departure for heaven*, she would also fly to the cloister, which filled with joy him who lived only for God.[9] But such a beautiful life was to be crowned by a trial worthy of it. A short time after my departure, the father whom we cherished with such good reason was seized with an attack of paralysis in his limbs, which was repeated several times,[10] but it could not remain there, the trial would have been too sweet, for the heroic Patriarch had offered himself as a victim to God;[11] so the paralysis, changing its course, settled in the venerable head of the victim whom the Lord had accepted.... I lack the space to give you some touching details. I want only to tell you that we had to drink the chalice to its very dregs and to separate ourselves for three years from our venerated father, entrusting him to religious but strange hands. He accepted this trial, the entire humiliation of which he understood, and he pushed heroism even to not willing that we ask for his cure.[12]

A Dieu, dear little Brother; I hope to write you again if the trembling of my hand does not increase, for I was obliged to write my letter on several occasions. Your little Sister, not *"Geneviève"* but *"Thérèse"* of the Child Jesus of the Holy Face.

   * Autograph.
  1. See Numbers 11:5.
  2. See Apocalypse 2:17.
  3. See Matthew 6:21.
  4. See Zacharias 13:6.
  5. See Luke 15:22.
  6. See Genesis 22:2.
  7. Léonie.
  8. Céline.
  9. This incident took place on June 15, 1888; see LT 53, note 3.
 10. It was really on May 1, 1887, that M. Martin had his first attack of paralysis; see LD, May 3-4, 1887.
 11. See Story of a Soul, p. 154, note 182, the circumstances of this offering, according to the interpolated text by Mother Agnes in the first edition, HA 1898.
 12. "I told him," wrote Sister Geneviève (Céline), during this visit on March 15, 1889, "that we were making a novena to St. Joseph for his cure and that he might return to Lisieux: 'No, you must not ask for this, but only God's will' " (CMG IV, p. 196).

LD   *From P. Pichon to Sister Marie of the Sacred*
                Heart, Mother Agnes of Jesus, and Sister
                Geneviève.

July 26, 1897   "After he received a letter saying she was very
                 sick, he believed it was ended" (note of Sister
                 Marie of the Sacred Heart on the autograph).

                                                    † Montreal
                                                July 26, St. Anne

My dear Children, always mine forever, is it true that Jesus has
taken our Thérèse from us? Is it true the beloved angel has taken
her flight to the homeland? My eyes and my heart search for her
up above, this dear daughter of my soul, and I do not know whether
to smile or to weep. But, no, over such deaths we do not weep. Jesus,
gathering up a flower from our garden, has a right to our Thanks,
to our Alleluias!

Be that as it may! The blow is felt and it has carried even to
America. If you only knew how much is my own, your sorrow, your
sacrifice, and the feeling of emptiness in your heart.

God alone! God alone! How good Jesus is to attach us more and
more to heaven, to all that does not perish! In God, the union of
our souls is sheltered from the blows of death. This union will be
perfected on the tomb of our Thérèse. Our souls united to this angel
who has flown up above will be more and more fixed on heaven
and absorbed in God. In God we possess always those whom we
lose. In God death is a birth, and passing away is a gain.

Tell me that on the threshold of eternity the dear child still thought
of her exiled father,[1] his distant apotolate. Tell me that in the cortege of Jesus she will not forget me and will patronize my little
ministry.

I have already offered and will offer every day my chalice and
my host. If she needs ransom, let us hasten to help her. One must
be so pure to appear before God.

My very dear Children, do you feel what sacrifices my poor eyes[2]
impose on me? They are dimming little by little and they can say
like St. Paul: "Quotidie morior! I die daily!"[3]

Your letters are good for me, better than ever if that is possible.

Thank my beloved Mother Marie de Gonzague[4] for her few lines, alas! too short. Thanks to my very faithful children, Sister Marie of the Sacred Heart and Sister Geneviève. I read with so much joy each of their pages. I read even all that the blessed Lamb[5] does not write me. . . . And each of you I bless tenderly in the Sacred Hearts.

Almire Pichon

The letter from the lion[6] reached me only during these last days. And nevertheless it had the date of May 8: I believed I should read July 8.[7] My retreats follow one another; this is the 488th. Pray, pray with all your heart for two sacerdotal retreats which I shall open at Quebec, August 10 and 24. Pray.

I await details on the last days of the dear little lamb.[8]

The dear anniversary of the 29th[9] will unite us in the same spirit, and the Patriarch will smile on us from heaven.

* Autograph.
1. We know Thérèse wrote a last time to P. Pichon around this time; however, not before July 12-14, since letters took an average of ten days to reach Canada, and P. Pichon had received nothing from her by July 26. Could her letter to him have arrived around August 5-8? Was it at this time that Thérèse was bidding him her farewell? In a long letter "she was telling him all that God had done for her, all she thought of His Love and Mercy. She submitted also to the Reverend Father her hopes and very specially her desire to do good on earth. She was using Psalm XXII, making her comments on it" (note in the first edition of *Lettres*, pp. 433-434). "Sister Marie of the Sacred Heart, who placed this letter with the other mail for Canada, wanted to read it and found it so beautiful that she wanted to copy it out. This copy was never made, and, Thérèse having been informed about the matter, had a feeling of regret because of her little sisters, and said: "Ah!. . . it was my whole soul. . ." (note of Sister Geneviève, 1947-1948). Was P. Pichon conscious of the value of this spiritual testament? We are surprised that he makes no comment on it in his letter on October 4 to Thérèse, whom he believed was still alive. Perhaps this letter had gone astray, as happened to the letter of Sister Marie of the Sacred Heart, October 1897; see LC 202.
2. See LD, January 1, 1896.
3. See I Corinthians 15:31.

4. Mother Marie de Gonzague, who was perhaps a co-recipient of this letter.
5. Mother Agnes of Jesus, who wrote P. Pichon only occasionally.
6. Sister Marie of the Sacred Heart; see LT 75, note 1.
7. This was in fact the correct date. July 7 and 8, Thérèse was thought to be dying. The family and friends had been alerted; see DE, pp. 678-679,
8. See LC 202, note 5.
9. Death of M. Martin.

LD   *From l'abbé Bellière to Mother Marie de Gon-*
              zague and Thérèse.

July 29, 1897
→ LT 261

                                             Thursday evening

Dear Mother and beloved Sister,

I am lending you this ugly fellow for a few days;[1] since my little sister would be pleased to see her brother, I am sending her a facsimile—on loan—this mannequin is not something to be kept. On Sunday, I will try to pose in order to please you, and I will send you my photograph as an ecclesiastic.[2] I shall then beg you to return the soldier, this being the only one which remains at home—besides, my mother is holding on to it. I am sending it, then, to please my dear sister before her departure for heaven.

Thank you for the joy brought by today's letters; soon there will be letters from the son and brother, and as always in the Hearts of Jesus and Mary.

                         M. Barthélemy-Bellière
                         a.m.

Today, I also received authorization from the bishop to leave and the order to leave for the novitiate, September 29 (embarking from Marseilles). This will be a new pact, on this feast of St. Michael, a pact against Satan with his ancient enemy, *"Quis ut Deus!"*[3]

* Autograph.
1. His photograph in military garb. See Thérèse's reflection on July 30: "When looking at the pictures of P. Bellière and P. Roulland, she said: 'I am prettier than they are!' " (CJ 30.7.4). See LT 263.
2. This was sent on August 17; see LC 194. Neither of these photographs has been preserved in the Carmel archives.
3. "Who is like God?" See Apocalypse 12:7.

LT 262   **From Thérèse to Sister Geneviève.**

August 3, 1897

Oh, my God, how gentle You are to the little victim of Your Merciful Love! Even now when You join exterior suffering to the trials of my soul,[1] I cannot say: "The agonies of death have surrounded me,"[2] but I cry out in my gratitude: "I have descended into the valley of the shadow of death, nevertheless, I fear no evil because You are with me, Lord!"[3]

To my beloved little Sister Geneviève of St. Teresa, August 3, 1897. Psalm XXII, 4.

* Autograph.
1. See CJ 3.8.8: "Since July 28, there were great sufferings."
2. See Psalm 17:5.
3. See Psalm 22:4. Perhaps it was during these same days that Thérèse commented on this Psalm 22 for P. Pichon; see LD, July 26, 1897, note 1.

LC 193   *From l'abbé Bellière to Thérèse.*
August 5, 1897
→ LT 261

Thursday evening

†
R. Ap.

My very dear and very good Sister,

Taken up with a thousand occupations, I would despair of finding a moment to talk with you if I were not to steal a few moments this evening. If I was lamenting my helplessness each day, my thoughts were often centered on you and my heart found yours in that of our mutual Friend, good Jesus, who wills to preserve you for us, knowing how we shall miss you and how effective even your earthly influence is. However, dear little Sister, truthfully, I am prepared for everything the Master wills from me, and all the more so because I *fully* believe in your word and in your plans for the other life. In spite of what you say about them, dear little one, "the raw onions" were a delicious dish of which I never grew tired.

No doubt Jesus is the Treasure, but I found Him in you, and He was becoming more approachable, and it is still by means of you that He will come to me, true? This is to tell you that from heaven as from here, I expect ALL from you, and my confidence will be powerful enough to await in case of need a direct and manifest activity from this friendly soul whom Jesus made the sister of my soul, in a very close union.

My dear and very dear little Sister, I am acquainted enough with you to realize that my misery would never bring an end to your tenderness here below, but in heaven sharing in the Divinity, you will acquire its prerogatives of justice, sanctity...and every stain will have to become an object of horror to you. That is why I was afraid, but since I hope you will remain the spoiled Child, you will do for me what you wanted to do on earth, and I believe and hope and expect from you this *loving confidence* that I still lack and ardently desire, deeming that with it one is fully happy here below and does not find the exile too long.

How kind you are, little Sister, in this simplicity and this openness which charm me while embarrassing me! I am so little accustomed to finding this among men that I am astounded at times but intensely delighted. The details that you ingenuously give me touched me sweetly...especially, oh, yes, especially, the one revealing an additional kindness on the part of my dear sister: the death-souvenir and picture of her venerable father, *on the very anniversary day* of his death. Thank you from my heart, and also thank you for the details concerning yourself. How well your dear father had named you: his "Queen." Oh! yes, and you have remained Queen throughout: both on the eve of receiving the last crowning and the final anointing...Queen forever. How good God was to your family, but how admirable it is also!

Blessed are those who hear the voice of God, blessed those who obey Him so perfectly...beloved of God through suffering and glory in heaven!

So you have always been Thérèse, little Thérèse and not Geneviève. You were perhaps predestined by means of this name: long live Saint Teresa, then, in my dear little Sister Thérèse. Will you tell me also how you became my sister...by choice or by lot?

In spite of all the joy, all the happiness, your letters give me, I do not want the writing of them to cause you any discomfort; dear little Sister, spare yourself, I beg you.

You will see a new name in my signature; since Monday I am a religious of Saint Francis in the Third Order, and my second Patron, that of Africa, that of the tertiaries, has become mine more particularly.

Accept, then, dear little sister of my soul, your brother's expression of respectful love,

Louis de France

* Autograph.

LT 263   **From Thérèse to l'abbé Bellière.**
August 10, 1897   The last letter to her spiritual brother, to whom
→ LC 193   she will later send only a holy picture; see LT
                       266.

J.M.J.T.

Carmel of Lisieux   August 10, 1897

Jesus †

Dear little Brother,

I am now all ready to leave; I received my passport for heaven, and my dear father is the one who obtained this grace for me. On the 29th he gave me the assurance that I was soon to join him; the next day, the doctor, surprised at the progress the sickness had made in two days, told our good Mother that it was time to grant my desires by having me receive Extreme Unction. I had this happiness, then, on the 30th, and also that of seeing Jesus-Victim leave the tabernacle for me, whom I received as *Viaticum* for my *long* voyage!... This Bread of Heaven fortified me; see, my pilgrimage seems to be unable to end. Far from complaining about it, I rejoice that God permits me to suffer still for His love; ah! how sweet it is to abandon oneself into His arms without fear or desire.

I admit to you, little Brother, that we do not understand heaven in the same way. It seems to you that sharing in the justice, in the holiness of God, I would be unable as on earth to excuse your faults. Are you forgetting, then, that I shall be sharing also in the *infinite mercy* of the Lord? I believe the Blessed have great compassion on our miseries, they remember, being weak and mortal like us, they committed the same faults, sustained the same combats,[1] and their fraternal tenderness becomes greater than it was when they were on earth, and for this reason, they never cease protecting us and praying for us.

Now, dear little Brother, I must speak to you about the *inheritance* you will receive after my death. Here is the share our Mother will give you: i) the relic I received on the day of my reception of the

Habit, and it has never left me since then; ii) a little Crucifix which is incomparably more dear to me than the large one, for the one I have now is no longer the first one I had been given. In Carmel, we exchange objects of piety at times; this is a good way to prevent us from becoming attached to them. I return to the little Crucifix. It is not beautiful; the face of Christ has almost disappeared. You will not be surprised at this when you realize that since the age of thirteen this souvenir from one of my sisters[2] has followed me everywhere. It was especially during my trip to Italy that this Crucifix became precious to me; I touched it to all the famous relics I had the happiness to venerate, and to tell you the number would be impossible for me. Furthermore, it was blessed by the Holy Father. Ever since my illness, I hold our dear little Crucifix almost always in my hands; when looking at it, I think with joy that, after having received my kisses, it will go to claim those of my little Brother. Here, then, is what your *inheritance* consists of, and in addition our Mother will give you the *last* picture that I have painted.[3] I am going to end, dear little Brother, where I should have begun, by thanking you for the *great pleasure* you gave me in sending your photograph.

A Dieu, dear little Brother; may He give us the grace to love Him and save souls for Him. This is the wish that your unworthy little Sister Thérèse of the Child Jesus of the Holy Face has.

r.c.i.

(It is by choice that I became your sister.)

I congratulate you on your new dignity. On the 25th when I am celebrating my father's feast day, I will have the joy of celebrating that of my brother *Louis de France*.[4]

---

* Autograph.

1. Thoughts similar to those of Arminjon, *op. cit.*, pp. 310-311; see also CSG, p. 31.
2. Léonie; see also LD, September 5, 1890, note 2.
3. See LT 266.
4. See LC 193, last paragraph before the end.

LT 264   **From Thérèse to Sister Marie of the Trinity.**

August 12, 1897   Lines in pencil on the back of a picture of the
                   Holy Family

To my dear little Sister - Souvenir
of her twenty-third birthday -
August 12, 1897.

May your life be all of humility and
love in order that you may come to
where I am going: into the arms of
Jesus!...

Your little sister, Thérèse of the
Child Jesus of the Holy Face.

*   Autograph.

LC 194   *From l'abbé Bellière to Thérèse.*

August 17, 1897
→ LT 263

                                                    Tuesday evening

†
R. Ap.

Very dear little Sister,

The moment has come, then, you are about to leave for heaven,
you are going to see God and the Blessed Virgin. How blessed you
are. Beloved Sister, go, satisfy yourself in Love. Heaven, already
so dear to your soul, already the life of your soul, will be the complement, the perfection of earth. Jesus will at last be yours, all yours,
and soon there will be an exchange of sweet and ardent affection
which will last as long as eternity. Love henceforth without any
obstacle, in its plenitude, seeing it, hearing it, breathing it in, feel-

ing it on all sides invading and powerful, shared with those who are awaiting you, and with them also mutual.

Already they are initiating you to the happiness of up above, since your beloved father has not been able to control his impatience, since his is warning you of the Bridegroom's approach.

You are expected, then, and the angels are preparing your place. What can the poor creature do from now on? Can he dream of holding you back and saddening your friends in heaven? They are holding out their hands to you. Go ahead, leave, fall asleep in their arms, in the arms of Jesus, who seems to be only waiting for your consent to draw you to Himself. But when a dear friend goes to another very dear friend, it is customary, is it not, to entrust the first with messages for the second. Tell Jesus, then, dear little Sister, that He animate my good mother with His grace. Having a presentiment of what must happen, she has begun to tell me that she would not give me her consent; undoubtedly, I shall not retreat, but your loving heart feels how painful it is to crush a soul so dear. Jesus can arrange all that; plead my cause, dear little Sister. I also recommend myself very specially *to the* BLESSED VIRGIN, to the saints whom you know, to Cardinal Lavigerie, to the saints whose relics I shall have the happiness of venerating after you. Oh! good little Sister, how I recognized the sharing of your heart in this "inheritance" that I shall welcome from you; how choice these dear objects are; how grateful I am for the affection that inspired this choice. Thank you, oh! thank you from the bottom of my heart for that dear Crucifix (oh! how much it will be for me after having meant so much to you). Right up to my death it will be my best friend, yes, dear for so many reasons; how good you are for having thought of leaving it to me, along with this relic, too, the companion of your entire religious life—from heaven you will see what my veneration for it will be—and even that picture, the *last* impression left by you of your piety, all these will make up my dearest treasure. Simply but with my whole heart, thank you, dear little Sister.

Tomorrow, or rather Thursday, I shall leave for Lourdes with my mother. Be assured I shall pray for you with a special fervor. I hope to be a stretcher-bearer. Join me on my pilgrimage; I shall be ceaselessly united with you at the feet of the very gentle Mother of Mercy.

Right up to the last day, if you CAN DO it, will you, dear little Sister, give me some thoughts from yourself? This also will be my inheritance; but, please, do not tire yourself. I would like upon my return, the 25th, to know you are still with us.

However, Jesus is calling you; go to God. Your little brother is perhaps sending you his last *adieu and au revoir* in heaven, for always and forever he remains,

Brother Louis

*   Autograph.

LC 195   *From M Guérin to Thérèse.*

August 18, 1897   M. Guérin was taking the cure at Vichy from August 8 to 30; his wife was with him until the 25th.

Vichy, August 18, '97

Dear little Angel,

I want to speak with you today. Whatever may be the great pleasure I would have had in answering the little Benjamin's[1] affectionate letter, I thought it was to you that I should write, for you are abandoned on your bed of pain and your image haunts me at each moment of the day. In the midst of the turmoil in which we live, my mind withdraws apart and lifts itself to more serene regions where one can judge pettiness and grandeur more sanely. Here is what I have seen in one of these real and experienced visions.

Before and around me, I see a great crowd of every age and nationality, walking feverishly in all directions and passing each other in rich carriages. There are splendid avenues, banks of rare flowers, and shaded groves, succeeding one another to infinity, and then come stores with articles of dress, jewelry, and art, attracting and arousing the covetousness of the passers-by. When I arrived here, I thought I was going to meet a crowd of the crippled, the gout, and the doddering, and yet I find that everybody is healthy in appearance, and

I am meeting people who eat and drink well. When looking further, I recognize some sick people, but their number is surpassed by that of walkers and runners out for pleasure. From morning till night, everybody wears his richest and most attractive apparel, and I see nothing but plumes and flowers waving in the wind. Beautiful women out for walks solicit the gaze of spectators gathered on each side of the avenue, their eyes sparkling with unsatisfied pleasure; they enter the Casino, only to come out soon, and then run to concerts that succeed one another on all sides, and then on to the distractions of Eden, of the theatre, and the dance. A burning fever consumes these beautiful plants. A few years more, and these bodies, so well cared for, so much adorned, leaving a perfumed trail behind them, will be wrinkled and emaciated, and worms, perhaps, will crawl on their velvety cheeks. From the midst of this crowd, drunk with pleasure, there is not a single cry, not a single aspiration coming from their heart to the God, who had made the creature so beautiful, who has endowed him with the genius to bring forth marvels of art and civilization. If the creature breathes out some aspirations, these are rare, and God alone knows; but I seem to see the diaphanous robes of the guardian angels flying far away, and Satan, baton in hand, beating time for the infernal dances.

But over there, I behold a modest building surmounted by the Cross,[2] and approaching closer, I see neither gilding nor sculpture, and I hear neither songs of joy or the sound of violins, but I am aware of a kind of gentle whispering, and I smell a fragrance of incense. Its inhabitants are not dressed in striking and soft robes, silver and crystal do not sparkle on their table, and soft beds are absent; they are dressed in coarse woolens and hair shirts, they nourish themselves on unrefined foods, and they sleep on beds hard as planks. Their youth, their fortune, allowed them to shine in the world and to enjoy the pleasures of life, but they preferred mortification and suffering. Like others, they are thirsty for pleasure. They love, but with a chaste and pure love a perfect and divine Being, who gives them His graces and enkindles in them a love that others cannot even suspect.... And further over, on a bed of pain lies a pure young girl already consumed by the fires of this divine love to which she longs to be united totally and forever. She does not desire death, but she loves it as a liberator. She asks for suffering in order to be more conformed to her Master, and she offers up everything: her prayers, mortifications, sufferings, not in expiation for sins she committed but for those of this crowd that is running, while dancing to the strains of infernal violins, to cast itself blithely into hell. . . .

And above this feverish crowd, I saw the brown robes of my little Carmel, floating in space and being carried away by angels, and I heard the very gentle voices of my five little daughters who were crying out to heaven: "Grace, Lord! Mercy and pardon!" My eyes were moist, as they still are, when I was writing this vision of the day before yesterday, and from the bottom of my heart, I, too, cried out: "Thank You, one thousand times thank You, Lord, for having given me such angels here below; thank You, Lord, for having made me experience, in preference to so many others, the beauties of Your love and the holiness of Your law.

This, my darling, is what I have seen, really seen, and it was your candid face that was shining the most in this cortege of Virgins, interceding and making reparation.[3]

As you are well aware, your aunt and I are not burnt by the thirst for pleasure, like the world around us. We can isolate ourselves and live a life almost as serene as that at Lisieux. We go out very little, at the hours for drinking the waters, morning and evening, at the hours for the baths, and when we come out from the church, our very close neighbor, we go in the evening to the park in order to listen to one or two pieces of music, and then we return home to retire between nine and nine-thirty. Time seems somewhat long for us, far from our dear Lisieux, and we count the days separating us from it. I am still only on the ninth day of the cure, and twenty-one are necessary! What good will I get from it? I feel the waters are working, for the gout has given up in despair successively in all parts of my body. If God does not cure me, so much the worse! If He does cure me, so much the better! Whatever happens, I shall lovingly kiss His hand. Though I do not have a great love for life, I have not reached my little Thérèse's perfection, who would be happy at the coming of the *Thief*.[4] I do not see my usefulness here below too well, but I believe the "Thief" will come by night to steal my fruits only when they are ripe and when my lamp, flickering at the least breeze, is well lighted.[5]

Between now and then, I thank Him and glorify Him for the glory with which He has made my house renowned, for the unknown ways in which He has been pleased to guide my steps during so many years, for the traps He has removed from my path, and for the very magnificent gifts He has bestowed on me in my beloved ones. It will be twenty-seven years ago on Sunday since He has entrusted me with the most precious pearl in my jewelry box.[6] It was necessary to fashion and polish her from her birth, and, if I have contributed little to this, her very gentle and good mother has cut off the rough edges, and you, my dear, have contributed by giving her all her splendor.[7]

Thank you, my very dear child, I kiss you; how I love you from the very depths of my soul and bless you. Share this with my Benjamin and your sisters.

Your uncle,
Isidore Guérin
Affectionate regards to
good Mother Prioress

*   Autograph.
1.   Sister Marie of the Eucharist, who wrote him on the 17th (DE, pp. 745-747).
2.   The Carmel of Lisieux.
3.   The reading of the word "*intercessrices*" is uncertain.
4.   The Lord, a reference to Matthew 24:43-44. Thérèse speaks frequently of the "Thief" in *Last Conversations*; see DE, p. 438.
5.   See Luke 12:35.
6.   His own daughter, Sister Marie of the Eucharist; see LT 265.
7.   Through her role as mistress of novices.

LT 265   **From Thérèse to Sister Marie of the Eucharist.**

August 22, 1897   On the same day, Sister Marie wrote her mother: "This morning for my birthday Thérèse gave me a picture which she wanted to sign. She had great difficulty in doing so, and she thought she was unable to finish it" (DE, p. 753, letter 57).

To my dear little Sister Marie of the Eucharist - souvenir of her twenty-seventh birthday - Thérèse of the Child Jesus

* Autograph.

LT 266   **From Thérèse to l'abbé Bellière.**

August 25, 1897   Inscription on the back of a picture, the *last* one that Thérèse painted; see LT 263.

Last souvenir of a soul, sister of your own soul.[1]

Thérèse of the Child Jesus

* Autograph.
1. An expression which seems to recall LC 193, par. 2. The date "August 25, 1897," on this picture, could have been written by another hand, but it is difficult to know: Thérèse's handwriting was very much changed.

LC 196   *From l'abbé Bellière to Thérèse.*

August 28, 1897
→ LT 266 and
LT lost?

August 28, 1897

†
R. Ap.

Dear little Sister of Jesus,

You must have realized that today I was especially united to you and in whom we encountered one another: your saintly mother[1] looked upon you with more complacence than usual, seeing that you will be soon reunited with her and her bliss. . .timidly, I presented myself to her, asking for a blessing and praying to her for you. Undoubtedly, dear little Sister, you heard her voice, closer and more urgent, calling you, laying claim to you, and you answered: "Soon."

The moment is approaching, dear Sister of my soul; you are about to leave for your real home. At Lourdes, I did not ask for your cure...I prayed to the gentle Queen of Virgin and Martyrs to aid you in your final preparations and to open heaven to you. I do not know how to pray, so I asked to be a stretcher-bearer for the poor sick people, and I was doing this for your sake. Often when carrying them to the Grotto, to the baths, my thoughts went to you and ascended to Mary, saying: "Mother, this is for Sister Thérèse." And if a little suffering came to me, it was for you. On Sunday, especially, I offered even the sufferings of the sick for you, and when the Blessed Sacrament passed close by me, blessing this crowd of unfortunate people gathered round It, I prayed fervently for you. That is what my prayer was. And when I saw these sick people, whom a few hours before I had carried in my arms, almost without any life, shocking at times in their illness, when I saw them made well, cured,[2] and now forming the escort of honor for Jesus, I was thinking of you, suffering on your poor bed, and I asked from your Bridegroom for a consolation, a last preparation, an additional act of tenderness for you. My prayer, then, was especially a prayer of action. But affective prayer, which God also loves, *which I do not know*, you will teach me, little Sister, when you will be near me. I really knew that you had not yet left this earth, for I had not felt this in my heart. *Thanks*, little Sister, for your feast day souvenir and for the thought dictated from your heart. My thanks to Mother Agnes, who wrote it.[3] Thank you for the few lines written out, the last ones, dear and precious, with the holy prayer that you loved so much;[4] thank your for this recent act of tenderness.

Beloved little Sister, the language of earth is tiring you...your unworthy and poor brother is capable only of distracting you from Jesus...he says to you once more: *A Dieu*, see you again, union of apostolate and love for Jesus forever.

You see that I am resigned, and at times I long for that more intimate union that Jesus is preparing for us.

In His loving Heart forever, your brother,

Louis

I would like to bring you some souvenir from Lourdes...your

poverty holds me back. . .I have nothing. . .except my prayer which is worthless, without generosity and without merit.

   *   Autograph.
   1.   Mme. Martin, who died twenty years before (August 28, 1877).
   2.   Doctor La Néele, who was on this pilgrimage, wrote that there were forty thousand pilgrims, and about fifty cures, "which, in the memory of man, had never been seen at Lourdes" (letter to M. Guérin, August 26, 1897).
   3.   This message dictated by Thérèse to Mother Agnes has not been found; see p. 903, note 1.
   4.   We have no information on "these lines"; do they have something to do with LT 266 or a last note? Neither has the prayer been identified.

LC 197   *From Mme. La Néele to Thérèse.*

September 5,   Date deduced from the content; see note 2.
1897

Dear little Thérèse,

I am writing you only a few lines, fearing to fatigue you. I am sending you, with this little basket of flowers, all my affection; you know, dear little Sister, that you have a large place in my heart, so I am often, very often, in spirit near you. When I realize you are suffering, it breaks my heart, so I am asking the Holy Spirit to enlighten your two doctors[1] that they may comfort you. I shall not tell you, dear little Angel, the joy I had at seeing my husband enter the Carmel to examine you.[2] This is a treat from Providence; good Mother Prioress sent Francis your photograph[3] to thank him, she said. However, I believe the roles have changed, and it is we who thank, from the bottom of our heart, this good Mother, who is so considerate and kind. I was very much moved when receiving your portrait, dear little Sister, and I had such a lump in my throat from my tears that I could not speak.

A Dieu, my darling, I embrace you tightly, very tightly, and may the Blessed Virgin keep you under her protection.

> Your little sister who loves you,
> Jeanne

My affectionate regards to Reverend Mother, and, once more, my gratitude.

Francis will arrive at Lisieux at five this evening.

Mamma will send you some good chicken in white sauce tomorrow before ten.[4]

---

*   Autograph.

1. Doctor de Cornière, the Community's doctor, and Doctor La Néele, who was called in occasionally to replace him.
2. He entered the cloister to examine his cousin on August 17, 30, and 31; he entered again that same evening; see CJ 5.9.4.
3. The photograph of August 30, taken in the outside cloister (VTL, no. 45).
4. After the serious intestinal attack, August 22-28 (see medical diary, DE, pp. 172-175), Thérèse began to eat a little, the first days of September. The Guérin family tried to satisfy the patient's desires, for example, the one for a chocolate eclaire; see DE, p. 766.

LC 198   *From Léonie to Thérèse.*

Beginning of   Approximate date; see note 2.
September (?),
1897

Thérèse of the Child Jesus -
from her little Léonie, who loves her so much.

I came back from the fish-market; perhaps these little mussels will give an appetite[1] to my very dear little patient.[2]

*   Autograph.
1.   "*appetisser*": "*mettre en appétit*," a verb used in Normandy (Moisy, p. 30).
2.   This note—the wrapping paper containing the mussels—dates either from the first days in September (see *above*, note 4) or from the first days of June, before Thérèse was placed on the milk-diet; see LT 254, note 1.

LC 199   *From Mme. La Néele to Thérèse.*

September 15-16, 1897   The envelope of this letter has the stamps of Caen and Lisieux, both of September 16. The letter could have been written the day before.

Dear little Thérèse,

I do not know what to send you in order to please you; when I go out, I look in the store windows with great attention, always in search of an object which may please you. Yesterday, I saw this picture at Dudouit's,[1] and I thought of sending it to you to show I am thinking of you all the time. Each day, I pay you a little visit, I take your photograph,[2] and I remain a while looking at you and thinking of you. It is a meditation, then I send you a long kiss, very tender and affectionate. Francis told me that you would send us a little angel when you were up above;[3] I am sure that our little Marie-Thérèse-Françoise will resemble you. I depend on it, for good Jesus can refuse you nothing. I beg you, do not forget to send me this little angel.

I shall not tire you out any longer, dear little Sister; if you could read into my heart, you would be surprised to see there all the affection I have for you. May the Blessed Virgin keep you, my darling, and may she protect you. With a sad and heavy heart I am sending you a kiss; how fortunate your sisters are to be taking care of you, and to be near you!

Francis joins me in kissing you and sending his regards to Reverend Mother Prioress.

                    Your little sister who loves you,
                        J. La Néele

* Autograph.
1. A religious bookstore at Caen. The picture in question could have been a subject in lace, with many violets, entitled: "*La grâce du pauvre malade*" (see DE, p. 770, note 30).
2. See LC 197, note 3.
3. See LT 255, notes 3 and 4.

LD

September 30, 1897

From Mother Agnes of Jesus to M. and Mme. Guérin and Léonie.

A note sent to the recipients in the chapel of the Carmel where they were praying during Thérèse's agony in the evening.

J.M.J.T.

Beloved Relatives and
Dear Léonie,

Our Angel is in heaven. She gave up her last sigh at seven, while pressing her Crucifix to her heart, saying: "Oh! I love You!" She had just raised her eyes to heaven, what was she seeing!!!

Your little daughter
who loves you more than ever
Sister Agnes of Jesus
r.c.i.

* Autograph.

LC 200   *From P. Roulland to Thérèse.*

September 13,   The missionary had not yet received the letter of
1897   July 14 (LT 254), and this letter reached Lisieux
                   after Thérèse's death.

Yum tchang   R. + Ap.   September 13, 1897[1]

Sister Thérèse of the Child Jesus

Sister,

I am six leagues from the place where I am learning the language:
I have just finished quite a work, a difficult work because it is the
first time I am doing it. Our parishes are larger than those of France;
they are made up of stations more or less distant from each other.
The Christians of these stations cannot come to see the priest: so
the priest goes to see them. Twice each year he makes his visit, and
at this moment I am helping a missionary to pay his visits. I have
been here for more than two weeks and the work is completed; I
leave tomorrow morning for Ho-Pao-Tchang. This is how the days
are spent: morning, meditation during which the Christians recite
morning prayers in the chapel; Mass at which all assist; thanksgiving frequently interrupted by the arrival of Christians who come to
greet the priest and with whom he must talk. Breakfast followed by
the recitation of the Breviary; afterward, I hear about fifteen confessions. At eleven, I am free, and then I take my pipe (do not be
scandalized), I take my pipe and go to dinner; after the meal, I take
my recreation by walking back and forth in the yard; exercises of
piety (shortened: ask God to pardon me); recitation of the Breviary,
the rosary. Then when the sun has set, I call the young people and
the children, and we all go off happily on a walk in the district. I
am the doctor and have a lot of practice: the pagans do not dare
to come, so they ask me for remedies through the intermediary of
the Christians; after supper, I go in search of a group of Christians,
and then I become a pupil, and they teach me sentences, correcting
me when I make mistakes, becoming furious when I begin speaking
Latin with the theologian who is with me because they do not understand anything. You can see, Sister, the missionary is happy in China.

During these two weeks, I preached four times: Opening of the retreat, the necessity of saving one's soul, nativity of the Blessed Virgin, the Holy Name of Mary. These were not too unsuccessful, and I hope to make myself understood later.

This is the first time, then, that I am in contact with souls. Well! Sister, I can tell you that there are some beautiful souls among the Chinese Christians; no doubt, we must not demand the perfection which we encounter among the daughters of St. Teresa, but let us not forget that God is merciful, He does not demand from the Chinese what He expects from the Carmelites. One young girl of twenty came with her mother to see me. "Father," she said, "I do not know your teaching; my father is a bad Christian; I do not dare to pray at home; my father wants me to marry a pagan, so I have run away with my mother, and here I am, I will do what the priest will tell me. I shall marry, if he wishes, but with a Christian." The priest will give her some money; the young girl will remain here, work, learn our teachings, and next year she will be wedded and will become with God's grace a mother. I have blessed two marriages: a young man of fifteen married a girl a little over twelve years of age. I would like to talk to you about this ceremony, but I do not dare; perhaps I did this in my last letter, so I beg your pardon. During this visit, there were a good number of conversions; the Christians were delighted. The first visit was good, filled with consolations, *Deo gratias*. It was the grace of God that did everything, but the prayers rising to heaven from the Carmel of Lisieux, and especially your own, have made God not take into account the unworthiness of His servant. A thank-you to your good Mother, to all your Sisters, and to you, Sister; you are working for God, and God will reward you.

These Christians whom I am visiting are not mine. The bishop has not assigned me this region; I am lazy; I shall be called back in October to his Excellency.

My health is very good; the work of adaptation to the climate is still not completed; let us hope that God will not leave you to carry crosses alone; what would be left to me when God will call me to Himself? Do not forget that you are my younger sister; I must die before you.

Offer my deep respects and gratitude to your Mother Superior, whom I allow myself to call my mother.

To you, Sister, I shall say thank-you in heaven where we shall one day be reunited, I hope.

If good Mother allows you, write me: your letters do me some good;[2] our conversation is in heaven.[3] Do you understand?

When I shall get my assignment, I shall write you. *Au revoir* in the Hearts of Jesus and Mary.[4]

A. Roulland edm
miss. ap.
Su-Tchuen or.

*   Autograph.

1. The envelope bears the stamp of Paris, November 9, 1897. Mother Marie de Gonzague answered him on November 11, telling him of the death of Thérèse.

2. The same statement regarding this correspondence in a letter to Mother Marie de Gonzague, October 13, when he received LT 254; see CG I, p. 73, note 62.

3. See Philippians 3:20; see LT 201, note 5.

4. To this letter was added a list (not found) of Chinese Christians admitted into the Confraternity of Our Lady of Mount Carmel, according to the letter of October 13, 1897, to Mother Marie de Gonzague.

LC 201   *From P. Bellière to Thérèse.*

October 2, 1897

Saturday[1]

†

R. Ap.

Dear and very dear little Sister,

Be happy; the soul whom you love so much and for whom you have offered so many prayers and good actions has finally realized— or at least almost entirely—its dearest desires. Your brother, little Sister, is a day-old missionary. To whom does he owe this, tell me? First, to Jesus, who has chosen him, but after Him, to my good little Sister of the Lisieux Carmel, Sister Thérèse of the Child Jesus. You have won entirely, for you have done everything. Through my own way of acting, I seemed to be disturbing what you have done, but your Jesus is so good. He loves you so much that He could refuse nothing to your suffering which was asking mercy for me. Thank you, from the bottom of my heart, good little Sister; I owe you this immense honor of being to day the missionary of Jesus. And see how good He is. He has willed that you be present at this triumph of grace since He has preserved you until now.[2] You will leave soon, little Sister, you will come soon to your brother who awaits you here. Jesus is waiting for you and so am I. Come quickly. If you only knew how beautiful Africa is; how much the poor Arabs are to be consoled. If you only knew above all (oh! how selfish I am) how your brother needs to know that you are near him. He does not know how it is he is in so holy a house! Who brought him there? How was he snatched away from so many tight and charming bonds? He understands nothing and would never have thought of finding such joy; he wonders even if he is dreaming at times.

You have prayed much, much for my poor Mother, did you not? She was admirable. Ask your reverend Mother, her letter will complete this one.[3] Oh! that hour of departure, that last blessing, in the midst of the sobs of my friends who were present, of my Mother strong up to the end, sending me to God, I shall never forget it. If you only knew these tricks of the devil, these temptations, these thousand means he was using against my resolution! Once again he has lost; long live God! Now I am at work, I must go ahead, and I am happy already. It is difficult at the beginning, but so much the better; when it is very difficult, I think that it is more so for you. Thus, we sleep on a simple straw mattress; in May, we shall be sleeping on a plank. This brings me closer to you, and I am happy, very happy.

When you leave for heaven, tell me. I am waiting for you with impatience; henceforth, what remains for me except the immediate activity of your dear soul near, very near to mine, for I am always in need of some support. When you get to know me at that moment, you will see how miserable I am. After your departure, there will be your inheritance[4] which will be one of my dearest treasures. Your last picture is here,[5] your photograph is here,[6] surrounded by some others, the number of which is very much restricted, my Mother and some friends and also your good father in a somewhat beautiful frame, and that is all, my books, my Crucifix, while I am waiting for yours. Here I have no relics, except a piece of linen from Blessed Margaret Mary. I am also awaiting yours. You see, it is a matter of your inheritance: is this bad? Is this cupidity? It is yourself, especially, whom I await. What is the condition of your health? Will you be coming soon?

Today I am sending my guardian angel to yours, and I made the same prayer to him as you were singing recently,[7] asking him to tell you that I am entering my retreat tomorrow and coming out of it on the 10th, with the reception of the Habit (a white robe, with a rosary around the neck—this is the Arabic dress: a woolen garment, a cloak, and a hat, the rosary added, black and white). If you are still on earth, I shall have the joy of throwing you some flowers on October 15; if not, receive these flowers right now of my respectful and fraternal affection in my real gratitude forever.

F. Louis[8]

Pardon me, if in any way I have caused you an inconvenience; I do not wish to do so.

* Autograph.
1. October 2. The envelope has the stamp of *Maison Carrée* (Alger) 4 OCT 97 and that of Lisieux, 8 OCT 97.
2. Upon receipt of this letter, Mother Agnes answered without delay, giving an account of the death of her sister on September 30 "at 7:30, Thursday evening." The news reached P. Bellière on October 13 (data deduced from his answer on October 14, 1897, to Mother Marie de Gonzague).
3. The letter to Mother Marie de Gonzague was written "Friday evening," October 1. Already on September 28, l'abbé Bellière had mailed "*en gare de la Roche*" (stamped PTT) a card worded: "Good Mother and dear little Sister: It is done, I have left; it was frightful and I was broken-hearted. But God is good, and He gave us His abundant grace.

   "Pray much for my poor mother; she offered her sacrifice with an admirable faith in spite of her immense sorrow.

   "She said she could refuse nothing to God. *A Dieu*, then, I leave tonight for Marseilles and tomorrow for Algiers.

"It is done; long live God! Forever in the Heart of Jesus, I am your loving, affectionate, and devoted son and brother. F. Louis, a.m. And my Sister Thérèse? Oh! what a saint!"

The letter bears the stamp of Lisieux "3ᵉ 29 SEPT 97." We do not know if Mother Marie de Gonzague shared it with Thérèse, who "in the morning, appeared to be in her agony" (CJ 29.9.1).

4. See LT 263.
5. See LT 266.
6. See LT 258.
7. Probable reference to the poem *A mon Ange Gardien* (P 43, st. 3); see LT 220, note 5.
8. On this Christian name, see LC 193.

LC 202   *From P. Pichon to Thérèse.*
October 4, 1897

†

Quebec
October 4, '97[1]

My beloved Child in Our Lord,

I am not the least assiduous *of yours* at your bedside, and you are so present to me at the Holy Altar. Today, in spite of my 2,300 retreatants (young and old women, Children of Mary), you will be the privileged one of my pen,[2] just as you are of the Cross, and not one of my daughters of Lisieux will be jealous of this.

On the day when you leave for heaven (for I suspect you are very strong in wanting to leave us), hold out your hands to Canada to receive all my messages. Then from up above, let your prayer shine even to the country of the Hurons and the Iroquois. In the meanwhile, I depend on all your sufferings. I need so many helpers in order to save souls. I would like it to be legion. Oh! How beautiful is the harvest on this side of the ocean.

See: I suffer the weakness of asking Our Lord that you may suffer less, and yet I want you to be so privileged by His love. Set this in order! It is a contradiction.

I place in your hands all my blessings. Keep the greater part and distribute the rest among my dear daughters, beginning with my dear Mother Saint Aloysius de Gonzague.[3]

Almire Pichon

Thank you, thank you, to my eldest[4] for her dear letters.[5]

*   Autograph.
1.   The day of Thérèse's burial; P. Pichon was unaware of her death. The envelope has the seals of Quebec, October 4, and Lisieux, October 14.
2.   In view of the feast of Saint Teresa, October 15.
3.   "Mother Saint-Louis de Gonzague," that is, Mother Marie de Gonzague.
4.   Sister Marie of the Sacred Heart.
5.   No mention of the last letter of Thérèse, July-August 1897; see LD, July 26, 1897, note 1. Sister Marie of the Sacred Heart, in answer to this letter, informed him of Thérèse's death. This letter was lost since P. Pichon wrote on January 26, 1898: "Your letter announcing the departure for heaven of our Thérèse...what has become of it? Would it not have had the same lot as those whose postage was insufficient? They are discarded at Paris or Ottawa. And you have dared to suspect me of indifference, to accuse me of forgetfulness. Oh, my dear child, you will know in heaven if I forget or if I am insensible." (Letter to Sister Marie of the Sacred Heart. The Brook.)

COMPLEMENTARY
DOCUMENTS

EXTRACTS FROM LETTERS ABOUT THÉRÈSE

The two volumes of General Correspondence *give an appreciable number of "lettres diverses" (LD). For a clarification of what these letters are, the reader is referred to* General Correspondence, *volume I, pp. 96-99. The present section of LD gathers together all the known extracts speaking about Thérèse from her birth to her death. To avoid any arbitrariness of choice among these letters, we have retained fragments which are insignificant in appearance as the reader will soon observe.*

However, very significant passages will be found in the first forty or more pages of this section of LETTERS ABOUT THERESE. Needless to say, a mother's words and letters about her own child are always informative. In these forty pages, we read about the birth and early years of the future Saint Thérèse of the Child Jesus. Mme. Martin had only four and a half years to live after the birth of this last child (she died of cancer of the breast, August 28, 1877), but during those years she corresponded frequently with Mme. Guérin, her sister-in-law, at Lisieux, and her daughter Pauline, in boarding school at Le Mans. Her first letters express a joy at the birth of little Thérèse, but soon this joy is turned into anguish over the possibility of an early death for her child. And Thérèse would have died were it not for the constant attention of her mother. As the child improved in health and grew strong, Mme. Martin writes with pride about her character development: the good and the bad. She describes her lovable nature, her humor, her fits of anger, and her invincible stubbornness. Above all, she stresses the child's intelligence, precocity, something she has not seen in all her other children. Because of her own simple method of religious education, Thérèse manifested a love

*for God, an interest in heaven, an insistence in saying her prayers,
and a desire to practice virtue which she hardly understood. These
letters, then, help us to understand better this future saint whom
so many have come to love and venerate.*

*Pauline was the recipient of many of these letters because she was
deprived of Thérèse's presence, being away at boarding school. We
can see Thérèse's own attachment to her sister Pauline, and the latter's interest and love for Thérèse, which were never to diminish up
to the end of Thérèse's life, September 30, 1897.*

1872

July 21

From Mme. Martin to M. and Mme. Guérin: "I must share with
you an event which will probably take place at the end of this year,
but it hardly interests anyone but myself at this moment. However,
I would be delighted if I knew I could rear this little being who is
about to come to live in our home; the latter will not leave it as long
as it and I have any life.

I am better than the last time; I have a good appetite and never
have any fever. I trust this child will come forth well; misfortune
is not always at the same door; however, may God's will be done!"
(*Correspondance familiale*, p. 135.)

September 29

From Mme. Martin to Mme. Guérin: I beg my brother not to forget
the two kilograms of good candy that I need for the baptism of "little
Thérèse." I am already thinking of the year's end regarding the child
who will come as my New-Year's gift. How will I rear it? I have
nightmares about this every night. However, I must hope that I shall
come out better than I believe and shall not have the grief of losing
it. (CF, pp. 138-139.)

December 15

From Mme. Martin to Mme. Guérin: Now I am expecting my little
angel any day, and I am very much embarrassed because as yet I

have not found a wet-nurse. I have seen several, but they were only imperfectly suitable, and my husband has never been able to decide on taking one. This is not because of the cost, it is because we fear bringing into our house an unsuitable person as all wet-nurses to-day are in general.

As for taking a second maid who would give me trouble and would not take care of the child the way I would like, I prefer to be at peace. If God were to give me the favor of nursing it, it would be a pleasure to take care of it. I am madly in love with children; I was born to have them, but it will soon be time for this to end. I shall be forty-one years old on the 23rd of this month; this is an age when one is a grandmother!

I shall probably not write you before the birth of the baby; I trust this will be around Christmas, and I really count on being the one to announce it to you. (CF, pp. 139-140.)

1873

January 3
From Mme. Martin to Mme. Guérin: My little daughter was born yesterday, Thursday, at 11:30 at night. She is very strong and very well; they tell me she weighs eight pounds. Let us put it at six, that is already not bad. She seems to be very pretty.

I am very happy. However, at first I was surprised, for I was expecting to have a boy! I imagined this for two months because I felt the child to be much stronger than my other children.

I suffered hardly for half an hour; what I suffered beforehand is not to be counted. She will be baptized tomorrow, Saturday. We shall be missing all of you to make the celebration complete. Marie will be the godmother, and a little boy close to her age, godfather. (CF, p. 141.)

January 16
From Mme. Martin to Mme. Guérin: I am fully recovered now, the little one is doing well also; she promises to be very strong. However, I do not dare count on this, I always fear enteritis.

I had begun to nurse her, and, fearing this was not sufficient, I wanted to make use of the feeding-bottle. Everything went well until Sunday, but the famous feeding-bottle spoiled it all; it was impossible to have her take the breast again. I used every means: I let her fast and she cried pitifully. I had to give in.

She drinks perfectly. I am giving her toast with water, with half milk; this is her entire nourishment, and I have decided to give her no other for the next three or four months. When I try to make her eat, I shall ask you to tell me what food you gave your little daughters at the beginning.

The little one is not at all difficult during the day, but often she makes us pay dearly at night for her good day. Last night, I held her in my arms until eleven-thirty, and I could do so no longer because of fatigue; afterwards, she did nothing but sleep, fortunately.

This child, like my last one, is named Thérèse; *everyone tells me she is beautiful, she is already smiling. I noticed this on Tuesday for the first time. I imagined I was mistaken, but yesterday doubt was no longer possible; she looked at me attentively, then she gave me a delightful smile.*

When I was carrying her, I noticed something which never happened with my other children: when I sang, she sang with me. . . . I am confiding this to you, no one would be able to believe it. (CF, pp. 142-143.)

January 17
From Mme. Martin to M. Guérin: I am extremely worried with regard to my little Thérèse. I fear she has intestinal trouble; I notice the same alarming symptoms as my other children had who died. Will I have to lose this one?

Tell me how I should feed her, whether breaded water with half milk is suitable? All she is doing is sleeping this morning for three hours and a half. I make her drink while sleeping, so she has taken almost nothing.

I do not know if it is weakness that causes this sleep, and I am very worried. As for myself, I hardly sleep more than two hours, for I am almost constantly with my little one, who, for some time, is very much agitated for part of the nights.

If you could write and encourage me by your advice, this would really please me, for I need this very much. (CF, pp. 143-144.)

March 1

From Mme. Martin to M. Guérin: Since you left Alençon, my little Thérèse was perfectly well. She was visibly getting stronger, and I was proud of her. But today things have really changed; she was very sick, and I have no hope whatsoever of saving her. However, she is sleeping well; last night I took her in my arms only once; she drank and fell asleep afterwards until ten o'clock this morning. But at present, here she is still awake ten o'clock this night.

The doctor left a minute ago; I do not have great confidence in his remedies, and I don't know why.

I must now tell you a story; it dates from the first sickness of the little one. On the night you arrived, I had just mailed a letter to Sister [Sister Marie-Dosithée, Mme. Martin's sister] at Le Mans, in which I was saying that my little Thérèse was dying, that she had only a few days to live.

Sister gets busy praying to Saint Francis de Sales with extraordinary fervor, and she makes a promise: if the child is cured, I will call her by her second name, Françoise. The promise is made, and she goes in search of Marie and Pauline, who are very sad, and she tells them: "Do not cry anymore, your little sister will not die." And she told them what she had done. The Superior added: "You must write your sister immediately, so that she can begin calling her Françoise."

When I received the famous letter, I was really upset. Sister told me that she had made this promise, really thinking I would agree with it, that she had told Saint Francis that if I were not to consent to calling the child by his name, he was free to take her, and, in this case, she added, I had nothing to do but make a coffin.

This struck me deeply, in spite of myself, and yet I have not decided to give my little daughter any other name but that of Thérèse. I have written, then, to Le Mans that Saint Francis had not cured her, for she was already much better before my letter arrived. And this is true, for if you recall on Sunday morning the child was, so to speak, recovered and did nothing but sleep the whole day; however, Saint Francis had not been prayed to as yet.

However, what do you say to all this? Was I culpable? Would I have had to call her Françoise? I myself had not been the inspirer of this promise, and, besides, what does it matter to Saint Francis de Sales whether she is called by one name or another? My refusal could not be a reason for him to have her die!

If I had not had the misfortune of giving her, among her names, the name of Françoise, Sister would not have had this idea. Already, before the child was born, she had written me, believing it would be a boy, that I should not give him the name of Joseph but François, as though she suspected the good Saint Joseph of having taken away my children!

I answered that whether he died or did not die, he would be named Joseph.

However, I am confiding to you that there has remained with me a vague worry concerning "this coffin which must be made it I were unwilling to consent to Sister's promise." I beg you, write me by return of mail, for if you delay my little Thérèse will probably be dead. I prefer to call her Françoise or any other name and not to make a coffin; it makes me shiver even to think of it!

You will write me a long letter and you will tell me how I must name her so that she does not die. Were anyone to see this letter, he would believe I have lost my head! I would like Sister to have no inkling of what I am writing you, for I do not want to cause her any grief; she is so good and she loves us so much! But this time, she astounds me.

Frequently I think of mothers who have the joy of nursing their children, and I must see mine all dying one after the other! (CF, pp. 143-145.)

March 9
From Mme. Martin to Mme. Guérin: I am taking advantage of a moment of quietness to answer your last letter. I am busy and so unhappy for the past two weeks that I have no rest day or night: my little daughter is sick, she has enteritis, and I fear losing her.

However, she is always happy; as soon as she has a short moment of respite, she laughs heartily. In spite of this her face has changed, I find her very pale since last Thursday, and yet she has not grown thin.

I would have much to tell you if I had a little more time, but I am alone looking after the little one, who is actually sleeping, so I am hurrying as much as possible.... Pray to God that He may keep my little Thérèse for me; I still have a little hope, for she is not so sick as not to be cured. Tell Jeanne and Marie to pray for their little cousin; God listens to the prayers of children. (CF, pp. 146-148.)

March 16 (?)
*From Mme. Martin to Mme. Gu*érin: Since I wrote you, I have had many sorrows; my little daughter was getting worse and worse. Last Monday, I sent for another doctor, M. Belloc. He came around five o'clock in the evening. After he examined the child, he asked me what I was giving her. I told him what I had done; he thought it was good but not sufficient for giving her nourishment in the state to which she had been reduced.

He believes that one can feed a child without milk for two or three days but not more. Then he told me: "This child needs breast feeding immediately, this is the only thing that can save her."

I did not know how to do it, for I could not think of feeding her myself, and I had no wet-nurse in mind. I explained my difficulty to him, and he gave me a prescription: I must give her one spoonful of rice water and one of limewater in two spoonfuls of milk, twice a day.

When I saw this prescription, I said to myself: "My little daughter is lost, she will not last on two-thirds of milk in her state." Mme. Leriche came in to see her tonight; she was very much disturbed by her condition and she went to bed without any supper and did nothing but cry. She was looking at her own child and she said: "If he were in this condition, I would die!"

Well, this evening I was seeking a way of finding a wet-nurse at all costs when I remembered a woman whom I knew very well and who was suitable in every way. But her own child was exactly one year older than mine, and I judged her milk was too old.

It was eleven o'clock and I left to see the doctor. I spoke to him about the wet-nurse of one year, and he thought it over for a while. He said: "You must take her immediately, it is the only recourse you have now for saving your child, and if it does not save her, you will have nothing with which to reproach yourself."

Had it not been so late, I would have left immediately to see the wet-nurse. The night seemed long for me. Thérèse wanted nothing to drink, and all the gravest signs that preceded the death of my other little angels were evident, and I was very sad, convinced that the poor darling was unable to receive help from me in her weakened condition.

I left, then, early in the morning to see the wet-nurse who lives in Semallé, close to two leagues from Alençon. My husband was away, and I did not want to talk of my undertaking to anyone else. On the road I met two men who filled me with a certain fright, but I said to myself: "Even if they were to kill me, it would mean nothing to me." Death was in my soul.

Finally, I arrived at the wet-nurse's home, and I asked her if she were willing to come with me to live at our house right away. She told me she could not leave her children and her home, that she would stay with us one week and would then bring the little one with her. I consented, knowing that the child would do very well at her home.

We left after half an hour and we reached my home at ten-thirty. The maid said: "I was unable to make her drink, she does not want to take anything." The wet-nurse looked at the child, shaking her head, and she seemed to be saying: "I have made a useless trip!"

I went quickly up to my room, and knelt at the feet of Saint Joseph, asking him for the favor of curing the little one, while resigning myself to God's will if He wanted to take the child. I do not cry often, but my tears flowed when I was saying this prayer.

I did not know if I should go down, but I decided to do so. And what did I see? The child was sucking wholeheartedly, and did not give up until one o'clock in the afternoon. Then she threw up a few mouthfuls and fell back on the wet-nurse as though she were dead.

We were five around her, all were struck. There was a worker who was weeping, and I felt my blood turn to ice. The little one was apparently not breathing; we bent over her in vain trying to find some signs of life and we saw none. However, she was so calm, so peaceful, that I thanked God for having had her die so easily.

Finally, after fifteen minutes passed by, my little Thérèse opened her eyes and began to smile. From that moment on she was totally cured; her healthy appearance returned and her gaiety as well. Since then all goes better.

But my dear little one has left; it is very sad to have taken care of a child for two months and then be obliged to entrust it to strange hands. What consoles me is to realize that God wills it this way since I did all I could to rear it myself. I have nothing with which to reproach myself in this matter.

I would have preferred to keep the wet-nurse at my home, and so would my husband. He did not want others, but he really accepted this one, whom he knew as an excellent woman.

I hope with all my heart that you will never have children in this condition; one does not know what to do and fears not giving them what is suitable. It is a continual agony. One has to experience it in order to know what this torture is. I do not know if purgatory is worse than this; we suffer there, it is true, at least we know what to do. Here, then, is a difficult trial come to an end. (CF, pp. 148-151.)

March 30

From Mme. Martin to Mme. Guérin: You have already begun to notice, dear sister, that life is not a bed of roses; God wills this to detach us from earth and draw our thoughts to heaven.

Yesterday, I was filled with these sentiments when going, accompanied by the doctor, to see my little Thérèse, who is still very sick. I noticed a beautiful chateau and some magnificent properties, and I said to myself: "All this is nothing; we shall not be happy until all of us, we ourselves and our children are reunited up above." I then made the offering of my child to God.

Ever since Thérèse was with the wet-nurse, she was always doing well, she had even grown very much; however, since Friday, her intestinal trouble, which was only dormant, has gone to her chest and throat. When the doctor saw her, the child had a high fever; however, he told me he did not think she was in danger.

Today, she is doing better, but I have grave fears; I believe we shall be unable to take care of her. My first little boy was like this; he was coming along well, but he had a persistent enteritis that he was unable to shake off.

Well, I have done all in my power to save Thérèse's life; now if God wills to dispose matters otherwise, I shall take care to bear up with the trial as patiently as possible. I really need to raise up my courage; I have already suffered very much in my life, and I would really like, my dear friends, you to be happier than I am. (CF, p.

152.)

April 11 (?)

From Mme. Martin to Pauline: I know it amuses you very much to make a pattern for the *point d'Alençon*.

If it does not please you, you will not do it. If you prefer to knit, ask your aunt to have some nice blue and white wool bought for you, and you will make some stockings for Thérèse. And if you are not interested in this either, buy some tapestry wool and make a nice little covering for a stool or whatever you want, or else two paintings for my bureau, I need some.... Marie is better, soon she will be cured, and when you come we shall all go to see your little sister when Marie is able to go in the wagon.

If you were to come now, you would have to return without seeing Marie or little Thérèse and almost even your mamma. We would always have to talk in a whisper. I had to send Céline to Mlle. Philomène for the whole day because she makes too much noise. So you would be unhappy. (CF, 157.)

April 20

From Mme. Martin to Mme. Guérin: The wet-nurse brought our little Thérèse today, and she is very well and strong. (CF, p. 160.)

May 14

From Mme. Martin to Pauline: I just brought Marie up to her room; I help her walk by holding her under her arms as they do for your little Thérèse. However, I hope she will walk soon without any support. (CF, p. 168.)

May 22

From Mme. Martin to Pauline: We shall go a week from Monday by wagon to see Thérèse; she is very strong at present. I saw her on Thursday last; her wet-nurse brought her, but she did not want to stay with us and let out piercing cries when she no longer saw her wet-nurse. So Louise was obliged to carry her to the market where "little Rose" was selling her butter. There was no other way to control her.

As soon as she saw her wet-nurse, she looked at her, laughing, then did not breathe a word; she remained like that at the sale of the butter with all the good women right up to noon! As for myself, I cannot carry her for a long time without getting tired, for she weighs fourteen pounds. She will be very nice and even very pretty later on. (CF, p. 170.)

May 22
From Marie to Pauline: I am awaiting your vacation with great impatience; I take so much delight in seeing you again, if you only knew! We shall enjoy ourselves a lot; we shall go in the wagon to the home of Thérèse's wet-nurse and gather daisies and cornflowers. How amusing this will be, true, little Pauline?

May 29
From Mme. Martin to Mme. Guérin: I imagine you are in good health and your dear little ones as well? Here, all are well; little Thérèse is growing splendidly, she weighs almost fifteen pounds. The wet-nurse has begun to make her eat during this past week. I am well satisfied with this woman, you hardly meet another like her for taking care of children. (CF, p. 171.)

July 1
From Mme. Martin to Pauline: The wet-nurse brought little Thérèse on Thursday. She did nothing but laugh, and little Céline was the one who pleased her. She screamed with laughter with her. I would say that she wants to play already, stiff as a little post and I believe she will be walking soon. She will have a nice disposition; she appears intelligent and has the good face of the predestined.

At present, she is eating well; I assure you she finds my porridge good! I made a lot so that Céline may have some too, but Thérèse did not think she had enough, the only thing left was what stuck to the pot.

We have decided that we shall go to see her only next month when you are here. We do not want to have this joy without Pauline.... I would not be able to stay away so long without kissing my baby, but the wet-nurse will bring her on Thursday. (CF, pp. 172-173.)

July 20
From Mme. Martin to Mme. Guérin: As for Thérèse she is a big baby; she is tanned by the sun. The wet-nurse brings her on a wheelbarrow into the fields, on top loads of grass. She hardly ever cries; "little Rose" says one cannot see a more darling child. (CF, p. 176.)

October 27
From Mme. Martin to M. and Mme. Guérin: Thérèse is always well, she is very strong and big. She holds herself up straight against the chairs; I think she will walk in her first year. (CF, p. 180.)

November 1
From Mme. Martin to Marie and Pauline: I have not seen little Thérèse since the day we went together to Semallé. I really miss her; I shall have to decide to go there, but this is very hard for me because it is so far! Fortunately, she does not have a long time to stay there. (CF, p. 182.)

November 29
From Mme. Martin to M. Guérin: Thérèse is always growing marvelously; I shall take her from the wet-nurse on March 11. I had promised her for one year, and I must keep my promise. Without having made it, I would take her back two months earlier. (CF, p. 185.)

November 30
From Mme. Martin to Marie and Pauline: I saw Thérèse on Thursday in spite of the bad weather, and she was better than the last time. However, Louise was not pleased, for the little one did not want to look at her or go with her; I was very much annoyed. Working women were coming to me each moment, and I was giving her to one and then another. She really wanted to see them, even more willingly than to see me, and she kissed them several times. Country women dressed like the wet-nurse, this is the world she needs!

Mme. T. arrived when a working woman was holding her. When I saw her, I said: "Let us see if the baby is going to want to go to you." She, all surprised, answered: "Why not? Let's try..." She held out her arms to the little one, but the latter hid herself, giving out cries as if she had burnt her. She did not want Mme. T. to look at her. We laughed a lot about this; she is afraid of people dressed *à la mode*!

I trust she will walk by herself five or six weeks from now. We have only to place her standing near a chair and she supports herself well there and never falls. She takes her little precautions for this. . . . Little Thérèse will not return before New Year's, but on that date they will bring her to me because of you. (CF, pp. 187-188.)

December 13
From Mme. Martin to M. and Mme. Guérin: Céline would like a little carriage for her doll. . . . As for Thérèse, she is with the wet-nurse; let us wait until next year. . . . I shall tell you, too, that my little Thérèse is walking almost alone; she has only two teeth. She is very gay and very darling. (CF, pp. 189-190.)

1874

January 11
From Mme. Martin to M. and Mme. Guérin: Little Thérèse is walking alone since Thursday; she is sweet and darling like a little angel. She has a charming disposition, I see this already. She has such a sweet smile. I am longing to have her at home. (CF, p. 192.)

February-March
From Léonie to her mother: Are little Céline and Thérèse well? I am awaiting the Easter vacation with great impatience.

March 23 (?)
From Mme. Martin to Marie and Pauline: I saw the wet-nurse's husband today; he told me that Thérèse should come on Thursday. Now I would like to have her immediately. I already have a sky-blue outfit in mind for her, with little blue shoes, a blue cincture, and a pretty white bonnet. She will be charming. I take delight in advance in dressing this doll, but I would not be so happy if I needed thirteen meters of material as I do for Marie!

I shall write you again on Sunday to give you some news about Thérèse. (CF, pp. 192-193.)

March 29

From Mme. Martin to M. Guérin: Little Thérèse arrives definitely on Thursday; she is a charming child; she is very sweet and very advanced for her age. (CF, p. 194.)

June 1

From Mme. Martin to M. Guérin: Céline and Thérèse give much promise; there is only one thing which disturbs me regarding Céline, and this is that she is frightfully thin; she is growing very quickly. I always have the fear she will turn out like my Hélène.

As for my Thérèse, it is not the same thing; I never had a child so strong, except the first one. She appears to be very intelligent. I am very happy to have her; I believe she will be the last. She will be beautiful, and she is already graceful. I admire her little mouth which the wet-nurse told me is *"grand comme un z'yeu!"* (CF, p. 196.)

June 24

From Mme. Martin to Mme. Guérin: Thérèse is almost beginning to talk. She is becoming more and more darling, but she is not just a little burden, I assure you, for she is continually at my feet, and it is difficult for me to work. So to make up for the time lost, I continue my lace-work up until ten o'clock at night, and I rise at five o'clock. I still have to get up once or twice during the night for the little one. However, the more trouble I have the better I am! (CF, pp. 197-198.)

June 25

From Mme. Martin to Marie and Pauline: Your father just put up a swing, and Céline is filled with joy; but you should see the little one using the swing, it makes you laugh. She conducts herself like a big girl, and there is no danger she will let go the cord; then when it does not go fast enough, she cries. We tie her in front with another rope, and in spite of this I am uneasy when I see her perched on the swing.

A funny incident happened to me recently regarding the little one. I have the habit of going to Mass at five-thirty; at the beginning, I did not dare to leave her, but seeing that she never woke, I ended up by deciding to leave her. I put her in my bed, and I brought the cradle so close that it was impossible for her to fall out.

One day, I forgot to put the cradle in place. I came and the little one was no longer in my bed; at the same moment, I heard a cry, and I looked, and I saw her seated on a chair that was opposite the head of my bed. Her little head was lying on the crossbar, and there she was sleeping an uncomfortable sleep, for she was cramped.

I was unable to understand how she fell seated on this chair, since she was in bed. I thanked God that nothing had harmed her. It was really providential; she should have rolled out on the floor. Her good angel watched over her, and the souls in purgatory to whom I pray each day for the little one protected her. This is how I explain it. . . explain it the way you want! . . . The little baby has just passed her little hand over my face and kissed me. The dear little thing does not want to leave me, she is continually with me; she loves going into the garden very much, but if I am not there, she does not want to remain and cries until someone brings her back to me. . . . I am very happy that she has so much affection for me, but sometimes it is troublesome! (CF, pp. 200-201.)

July 24

From Mme. Martin to Mme. Guérin: Soon the joy of seeing us; I hope the political situation will not prevent us, this year nor next year. Never have I been so calm in this respect, I no longer busy myself with external events, only with my little Thérèse! (CF, p. 203.)

August 9

From Mme. Martin to M. and Mme. Guérin: Little Thérèse was very sick this week. It is true that it was only her teeth, but what a state she was in! Her mouth was pitiful to see and her tongue was swollen and covered with pustules so that she was unable to take anything. I saw the doctor, who advised me to force her to drink some milk. It is impossible to tell you the difficulties I had. Night and day, I had to be near her; she was suffering terribly, and this lasted one week. She is much better, and she is beginning to eat a little porridge; however, she is still very weak and does nothing but sleep. It is very fortunate that this did not happen during your stay here; we would have had a sad joy!

During the Easter vacation, Marie said to me: "You think, Mamma, that I shall have no more little sisters? This makes me sad; I am so happy when I have little children."

But this time, she has enough! These poor little ones spent a very trying week; they did not have a moment of rest. So Marie is very much afraid of having more little sisters, and she tells me she will never marry because it is a source of too many troubles! (CF, p. 204.)

October 12

From Sister Marie-Dosithée to M. and Mme. Guérin: To tell you the truth I do not know how she [Mme. Martin] can put up with a kind of life like hers; to take care of Louise she has taken some Sisters to watch over her, but in addition to her work all day long she must go to bed at eleven, often get up midnight, at two o'clock to prepare something for the patient to eat, and besides this she gets up for her little daughter; tell me, whether she is not killing herself!

November 8

From Mme. Martin to Mme. Guérin: You ask me, dear sister, what I want for my children's New Year's gifts.... For Thérèse I want a Noah's Ark; this will amuse her better than anything else, and will render me a great service. She does not go to bed before eight in the evening, and I do no know what to occupy her with in the evening, and she prevents me from working. However, she is very reasonable, and she does not have to have much for passing the time.... I beg you, think only of the two little ones; regarding them, this gives me great pleasure, for children of that age are so happy on that day. (CF, p. 209-210.)

December 24

From Mme. Martin to Mme. Guérin: You do not mean it! sending gifts for my five children, all expensive things; and not content with that, you send me some too. This is not reasonable.

Well, now that I have scolded you, I must decide to thank you. I begin by saying you are too kind to us, that I am, in spite of my annoyance, very thankful and I love you very much.

You have always made Thérèse and Céline very happy. When their father unpacked the toys, I would have loved you to see Thérèse! We had told her: "There are toys inside that your aunt from Lisieux is sending." She was clapping her hands! I was leaning on the case to help my husband open it, and she made little anxious cries, telling me: "Mamma, you are going to break my beautiful toys!" She pulled me by my dress to make me stop. But when she saw the pretty little house, she remained dumb with pleasure. (CF, p. 211.)

December 25-28
From Sister Dosithée to M. and Mme. Guérin: Marie and Pauline are going to vacation. They are very happy to see their parents again, and their little sisters; they will find Thérèse grown up, this will please them.

1875

January 17
From Mme. Martin to Marie and Pauline: I would have liked to amuse you with some reflections on Thérèse, but this will be for another time. She talks incessantly of Marie and Pauline, who are at Le Mans. (CF, p. 220.)

March 14
From Mme. Martin to Mme. Guérin: Little Thérèse is always well, she has a prosperous look about her; she is very intelligent and carries on amusing conversations with us. She already knows how to pray to God. Every Sunday she goes to Vespers and if, unfortunately, we were to omit taking her, she would cry without finding any consolation.

A few weeks ago we had taken her out for a walk on a Sunday afternoon. She had not been to *"la Mette"* as she calls it. When we returned, she began crying loudly, saying that she wanted to go to Mass; she opened the door and took flight in the direction of the church, in the rain which was coming down in torrents. We ran after her to take her back home and her sobs lasted a good hour.

She said out loud to me in church: "I was at Mass here! I really prayed to God." When her father returns in the evening, and she does not see him saying his prayers, she asks: "Why, Papa, are you not saying your prayers? Have you been to church with the ladies?" Ever since the beginning of Lent, I go to Mass at six o'clock, and I often leave her when she is awake. When I am leaving, she tells me: "Mamma, I will be very good." Actually, she does not budge and she falls asleep. (CF, pp. 228-229.)

April 4
From Sister Dosithée to Mme. Guérin: I had a beautiful little visit which I was not expecting on Easter Monday: Zélie brought me her little Thérèse, she thought it would please me to see her. She is a very darling little girl, exceptionally obedient, she did everything we told her without having to beg her, and she was so quiet that we could have had her remain all day long seated without budging; I was very happy to see her.

April 29
From Mme. Martin to M. and Mme. Guérin: I was forgetting to give you some news about my sister whom I have just seen. She is well at the moment. I brought her little Thérèse, who was very happy to get on the train. When we arrived at Le Mans, she was tired, she cried, but she remained in the visiting room all the time, good like a big girl. However, I do not know what was the matter with her; when we entered, she was heavy-hearted, and her tears came without any noise, she was choking. I do not know if it was the grilles that frightened her. Afterwards, all went well. She was answering all the questions as if she had passed an examination.

The Superior came to see her and gave her some gifts. I said: "Ask the good Mother to bless you." But she did not grasp it and answered: "Mother, will you come to our house?" This made everybody laugh.

I am alone with her at the moment; the maid and the other children have accompanied Léonie to Catechism. I gave her my box of *sous* so that she let me work, for she cried a lot when seeing her sisters leave. She spread out all the money on my bureau, but, hearing her father, she said: "Mamma, Papa is coming, gather the *sous* up quickly!'' (CF, pp. 230-231.)

May 19
From Mme. Martin to Mme. Guérin: My little Thérèse is sick, she has a stubborn cough with a fever. It does not strike me as a simple cold, I fear she has measles. Decidedly, there is something brewing to make the day of Léonie's First Communion a day of mourning. (CF, p. 232.)

July 4
From Mme. Martin to Mme. Guérin: As for Thérèse, when she is five or six, we shall no longer be able to leave her, she will have to accompany us, for I do not believe she will be like Léonie, willing to give up her place, either for gold or silver...

   She has a cold at present and this happens often with her. (CF, p. 234.)

July 11
From Mme. Martin to Mme. Guérin: I shall take care to go to your home around August 14, eve of the Assumption; this is the earliest I could leave.... I hear nothing any longer spoken of except Lisieux from morning to night; even baby meddles into it and also wants to go there to see the godmother of Céline and little Jeanne. Léonie said to her: "I will bring you all the cakes they give me, little darling, I will not eat one of them." Dear little Léonie really has a kind heart, and she loves her little sisters in a special way. (CF, pp. 235-236.)

August 22
From Mme. Martin to Mme. Guérin: You will tell Jeanne that her little fishing boat pleased her little cousin Thérèse very much; she has placed it in the big room and often during the day she goes to admire it, saying that it is her little cousin who sent it to her, and, in return, when the latter comes, she will give her a large piece of chocolate. (CF, p. 238.)

August 31
From Mme. Martin to Mme. Guérin: Yesterday, my husband ran

to the station to see my brother on the train; I would have liked to go there too....

I was very sorry that the little girls did not go with him to greet their uncle. It was their fault. I had repeated in vain: "Get dressed early." But they knew better, so they were not ready in time. They wanted to dress when it was time to leave for the station. Louis chatted with my brother for nearly ten minutes. I so deplored this disappointment that I was really saddened by it and so was Marie. However, I hope to make up for it on Friday, at five-thirty, upon the return of my brother. We shall all be at the station: father, mother, and the five daughters. (CF, pp. 239-240.)

October 10

From Mme. Martin to Pauline: Thérèse is sick for the last two days; she has a fever and a tired stomach. I hope it is nothing. She asks always where Pauline is and says: "I would like her to come home, in our house." Then there are "whys" which never come to an end. (CF, p. 248.)

October 14

From Mme. Martin to Pauline: Thérèse is still sick, poor thing! She has a fever and I was really disturbed this morning, but I am less so now, for I noticed that she had a large tooth ready to break through. She has a very swollen gum, and it is quite sure that this causes her temperature. (CF, p. 250.)

October 17

From Pauline to her parents: It appears Thérèse is sick, this troubles me, I am always afraid of seeing her die; the sadness I would get from this cannot be described, for I love my little baby so much.... I kiss you with all my heart and my little sisters as well.

October 24

From Mme. Martin to Pauline: It is night. Céline and Thérèse spent the evening with me. Céline, who has no pleasure except to cut up everything that comes into her hands, has taken two bulletins of Saint Joseph and cut them into pieces.... Little Thérèse is cured; this illness did her nothing but good. Now she is eating better than she usually does. (CF, p. 251.)

October 24
From Marie Martin to Marie-Louise Morel: The hour is coming when I must busy myself with Céline, for I have been put in charge of teaching her...only for a short time. She is still too young and delicate to go to the boarding school, and I assure you that I am very happy and proud because of my assignment. She already knows how to read and write passably. Now she is learning a little catechism and bible history; it amuses me very much to teach her, and it is a real pastime for me when she is not naughty. But, too often, Thérèse comes to disturb our *serious studies* with her presence. Without making any noise, she enters my room to obtain the pleasure of upsetting my inkwell and pens, get hold of books that fall under her hands, then runs off like a little thief. When she returns, it is to tease her sister by repeating in a little mocking voice some words that poor Céline is learning with so much trouble. However, our baby is a pretty rascal; this funny little child Thérèse is attractive, impish, and darling, all in one. (Typed copy, 1966; Visitation of Le Mans.)

October 31
From Mme. Martin to Mme. Guérin: As for my little Thérèse, without being very strong, she has a good temperament, eats perfectly, nothing makes her ill. Last night, however, Marie made her sick for me. She was making her eat while telling her a story that interested her. Seeing that the story would never end and the little one eating all the time, I told Marie: "Do not give her anymore, I beg you."

But it was too late and around midnight the poor little thing was sick. I held her in my arms for an hour and I caught a cold. This is a good lesson for Marie! (CF, p. 253.)

November 7
From Mme. Martin to Pauline: Little Thérèse is very attractive; she is wearing for the first time today a pretty blue hat.

Two days ago, Marie put her to bed without having made her say her prayers, and she had placed her in the large bed. When I went up to my bedroom, I put her to bed in her own without warming it up, I did not have a burner. Sound asleep as she was, and although well wrapped up in her nightgown, she became aware of this, and she began to cry out persistently for a warm bed. I heard this music all the time I was saying my prayers. Tired of it, I scolded her and she kept quiet.

When I went to bed, she told me she had not said her prayers. I answered: "Sleep, you will say them tomorrow." Yes, but she did not give up her ideas. To end it, her father made her say them. But he did not know how to say all she was accustomed to reciting, and, then, he had "to ask the grace of. . ." He did not understand what she meant by this. Finally, he said something quite close to it in order to satisfy her, and she fell asleep until the next morning. (CF, pp. 256-257.)

November 21

From Mme. Martin to Pauline: The little one is at my side; the others just left for Vespers. She asks me why I am always writing? whether we are going to leave soon for church? On Sunday, I had taken her to solemn Vespers, but it is much too long for so young a child, so I shall bring her only to Benediction.

She begs me to tell Pauline to return home, that it is long enough since she has been at Le Mans, and this is very annoying. And here she is asking me why I did not take her to Lisieux!. . .

I interrupted my letter uselessly in order to prepare Thérèse, who wanted to go out. When we had both got dressed up, the rain was falling so heavily that I was obliged to undress the little one. This made up three quarters of an hour of interruption; now Marie has returned from Vespers and is entertaining baby, and they are getting along well together. . . . I hear Thérèse calling me: "Mamma!" She does not go upstairs alone without calling at each step: "Mamma! Mamma!" So many steps, so many "Mamma's!" And if, unfortunately, I forget to answer a single time: "Yes, my little girl!" she remains there without going forward or backward. (CF, pp. 259-260.)

December 5

From Mme. Martin to Pauline: The baby is a matchless rascal; she comes to caress me, wishing me dead: "Oh! how I wish you were dead, dear little Mother!" We scold her, and she says: "It is so that you may go to heaven, since you say we must die to go there.'' She wishes also death of her father when she is in her transports of love.... Céline is playing blocks with the little one, and from time to time they argue. Céline gives in, in order to have a pearl in her crown. I am obliged to correct the dear baby who gets into frightful tempers; when things do not go according to her way, she rolls on the floor like one in despair, believing that all is lost. There are moments when it is too much for her, and she chokes up. She is a very excitable child, however, she is very darling and very intelligent, she remembers everything. (CF, pp. 263-264.)

December 27
From Marie Martin to Marie-Louise Morel: There are also some happy children at home on Christmas day! Thérèse and Céline received many gifts from the Child Jesus, who never fails to pay His visit each Christmas night and to bring good children dolls and candy! All these beautiful things were not lacking for our two little girls, and it would be difficult to tell you about their joy and enthusiasm. On Christmas morning, still very sleepy, they came down in their nightgowns, concerned about nothing but running like two little fools through the house, looking for their slippers. They finally end up by finding them placed in front of the fireplace. There were at least half a dozen of slippers, boots, galoshes, all this was filled with bags of candy, little sugar sabots, little Jesus-cakes! But what appeared the most comical was to see a beautiful doll coming out of one of the shoes and waiting patiently the arrival of the mammas. This is what gave the greatest pleasure to Thérèse and when she noticed the famous doll, she threw everything aside to fly to it. Unfortunately, her transports of joy do not last long, and now that she knows *her charming daughter* she is beginning to neglect it. Today, annoyed to see it does not walk fast enough, she broke the end of its two feet, an arm is already dislocated, and soon, I think, it will be ended with this poor doll. But I am wrong, when it is really dead, she will have a burial, and truly the burial of a doll is very amusing. Thérèse has experienced this more than once. (Typed copy, 1966; *Visitation of Le Mans*.)

December 28
From Mme. Martin to Mme. Guérin: Little Thérèse is already beginning to read. She absolutely wants Marie to give her classes like Céline, and since Monday she knows almost all her letters. I believe she will learn easily. She speaks often of her uncle and aunt of Lisieux. (CF, p. 266.)

December 28
From Marie to Mme. Guérin: I believe Thérèse wants to become learned, for during the last three days she pursues me incessantly so that I teach her to read. The day before yesterday, I took an alphabet and I amused myself by showing her the letters, while believing this was useless. But what was my surprise when, the next day, I saw her come with her book, reading to me, without making a single mistake, all the letters I pointed out to her at random. This little one really has an incredible facility; I believe that in six months she will be able to read with ease, for she has an extremely precocious intelligence. (CF, p. 266, note 1.)

1876

January 7
From M. Guérin to Mme. Martin: Kiss the other little darlings, Céline and Thérèse, for us.

January 9
From Mme. Martin to Mme. Guérin: I am sure you are not pleased with me, for I was too long a time in thanking you for the beautiful New Year's gifts that you sent and that were received with such cries of joy that I had to hold my head in both hands and suffered right up until the evening.... Céline was leaping with joy before her beautiful case which was so complete. And Thérèse! You should have seen her!... Her fortune is made! She wants nothing more in this world; she is amusing herself constantly with her pretty carriage... We were delighted by Jeanne's little letter.... Kiss her for me and tell her that aunt and her little cousins think often of her, even little Thérèse, who wants absolutely to name her doll Jeanne Guérin. (CF,

pp. 267-268.)

January 16
From Mme. Martin to Pauline: Thérèse is asking if you are coming back soon? She is always darling and an imp! (CF, p. 270.)

January 30

From Mme. Martin to Pauline: We went to Pay a visit to Mme. Z. and Marie accompanied me as well as the two little ones; we stayed there close to an hour.

This woman has a little daughter seven months older than Thérèse; she is a real little demon!.... I brought the children to Vespers at the hospice, and from there we went to the Square where booths have been set up for the Candlemas fair.... Marie was looking at little girls as old as Céline and Thérèse, envying their dresses and asking me to dress them like that. It is a case of saying one is never satisfied! They are dressed, both of them, as you were never dressed, but this is still not enough because she sees something better! However, I have no desire to climb higher, this is a real slavery, we become really slaves to fashion! (CF, pp. 271-272.)

February 6
From Sister Marie-Dosithée to Marie: You would like your little sister to be as well dressed up as many other children whom you see; you do not know, then, that everybody is demented and each one wants to climb and appear always more than he is.... I congratulate you on your success in the education of your little sisters; you set about it the right way, so you succeed; God will bless your efforts, and these children will be your consolation.... Give me all the smallest details about yourself and your sisters, everything is interesting when we love.

February 27
From Mme. Martin to Pauline: Only myself and Thérèse will go to the comedy!... This evening, there is a great reunion of the Catholic Club. (CF, p. 276.)

March 5

From Mme. Martin to Mme. Guérin: As for Thérèse, she has begged Marie to give her lessons, and on two or three occasions she has made such progress that she should soon be able to read, if she were to give her a lesson every day. (CF, p. 279.)

March 12

From Mme. Martin to Pauline: "A gardener is coming to us, tomorrow; the children are delighted, for this good man pleases them very much. Marie has taken a fancy to him. He tells strange stories about his good wife who, after her death, came to frighten him, "to upset" him, as he says, and who asked him to close the door. When little Thérèse sees him, she repeats the good man's words in her own way: *"Tu m'nabre, ma bonne femme, tu m'nabre."* We are obliged to make her keep quiet!...

Céline is well enough now; little Thérèse is very well. She is always very sweet, and she was telling me this morning that she wanted to go to heaven and that, for this, she was going to be nice like a little angel. (CF, pp. 281-282.)

March 26

From Mme. Martin to Pauline: Half way to the chateau [the mayor's residence], I saw some urchins who had taken bunches of jonquils from it; my intention was to buy some from them for the little girls. At the same moment I was thinking this, I saw one of them who was scattering two large bouquets on the road. Céline gathered them up; she was very happy and so was Thérèse.... Thérèse is a little rascal, who is the joy of the whole family, she is extremely intelligent.

Last night she woke us up, calling her father and telling him she was "hit." Her father answered: "Go to sleep, Thérèse," and she kept repeating: "Papa, I am hit." Finally, he got up to see what this hitting was. Actually, her little head was touching the wood of the bed, and each time she moved, she was giving herself a bang; tonight, I arranged her little bed in such a way that she no longer hit herself!

She is incessantly asking if tomorrow is Easter, in order to see "little Pauline"; the day before yesterday, she began calling to me in the garden, telling me with all her heart that it was too long, that she wanted it to be right now. (CF, p. 284.)

April 23
From Sister Dosithée to Marie: Thérèse could be learning how to read, it would not be too early.

May 7
From Mme. Martin to Mme. Guérin: Céline is working always with Marie; Thérèse is learning with great facility; she is very intelligent. How happy I am to have her! I believe I love her more than all the others; no doubt it is because she is the youngest. (CF, p. 287.)

May 14
From Mme. Martin to Pauline: As for the little ferret, I do not know too well how she will turn out; she is so little, so thoughtless, she has an intelligence superior to Céline's, but she is less gentle and has in her an almost invincible stubbornness; when she says "no," nothing can make her give in. I could put her all day in the cellar and she would sleep there rather than say "yes."

However, she has a heart of gold, she is very affectionate and very honest; it is funny to see her running after me to make her confession. "Mamma, I pushed Céline once, I struck her once, but I will not do it anymore." (It is like this for everything she does.) Thursday evening, we were out walking near the station, she wanted absolutely to go into the waiting room to go and get Pauline; she was running ahead with a joy that was pleasing to see, but when she saw that we had to return without getting on the train to go and get Pauline, she cried all they way home.

Here she is at this moment very much taken up with cutting papers, this is her greatest pastime. She has made her choice among all the papers that fell from my bureau, for I had sorted out some letters. Fortunately, she has the good habit of coming to show them to me before touching them in order to be sure she can cut them up. She is well settled now in her little chair and is cutting, singing with all her heart.

It has been a long time since I was interrupted with this letter. Since then I have been to High Mass; afterwards, we took a long walk in the fields.... When returning, we met a poor old man who had a good appearance. I sent Thérèse to give him a little alms: he was very much touched and thanked us so much that I saw he was very unfortunate.... Another thing: Poor Thérèse is in great grief. She broke a little vase, as big as your thumb, which I gave her this morning. As usual, when an accident happens to her, she came very quickly to show it to me; I appeared somewhat displeased, and her little heart was sad.... A moment afterwards, she ran to find me, saying: "Do not be sad, little Mother, when I earn some money, I assure you that I will buy you another one." As you can see, I am not close to holding her to it! (CF, pp. 289-291.)

May 21
From Mme. Martin to Pauline: I am very tired this evening, we left at half past twelve to go to the cemetery; it was oppressively warm. Little Thérèse could no longer walk and I was obliged to carry her when returning. I put her to bed and she had a nice snooze for two hours, Céline as well. During this time I was at Vespers while your father watched over them.... Tomorrow afternoon, the children will go out again for a walk with their father, but I will not go with them, for I have an order of lace to make up for Tuesday and I have no time to lose.... I received, Friday, a box of candy from Lisieux, coming from the baptism of little Hélène Maudelonde. Thérèse was happy; you should have seen her jumping and clapping her hands. Yesterday evening, we were speaking about a rich proprietor, and Louise who always envies the rich, was saying: "If only I had that!" But the little one very quickly declared that she much preferred the box of candy to all that. How blessed one is at this age! It is a pity to leave it!

Marie loves her little sister very much, she finds her very darling; she could be hard to please, for the poor little thing greatly fears causing her any trouble. Yesterday I wanted to give her a rose, knowing this makes her happy, but she began begging me not to cut it, Marie had forbidden it, she was red with emotion; in spite of this I gave her two, and she did not dare appear in the house. I told her in vain that the roses were mine; she said: "No, they are Marie's." She is a child who becomes easily overexcited. As soon as she had done some wrong, everybody must know it. Yesterday, without willing to do so, she knocked off a little corner of wallpaper, and she was in a state to be pitied, and her father must be told very quickly. He came home four hours later, we were no longer thinking of it, but she went quickly to Marie to say: "Tell Papa quickly that I tore the paper." She is there like a criminal awaiting condemnation, but she has in her little mind that we will pardon her more easily if she accuses herself. (CF, pp. 293-294.)

June 4
From Mme. Martin to Mme. Guérin: I am very late in answering your nice letter and in thanking you for the box of candy which you sent me and which made up Thérèse's complete happiness! (CF, p. 295.)

June 11 (?)
From Mme. Martin to Pauline: Did your sister tell you that last week there was a mad dog which did much harm in the city?... Your father and your two little sisters just missed being bitten; they passed very closely to the dog. They left for a walk, and the dog was following them. (CF, p. 298.)

July 16
From Mme. Martin to Pauline: Yesterday, I sent you the photographs of Céline and Thérèse; I knew you wanted them very much, and so I really wanted to advance the moment so that you might see them before your vacation.... I am sorry I entrusted the two photos to M. Vital, I fear he will make you wait for them. Céline is not good, one eye is half-closed; she had to be taken three times. Thérèse also, who did not succeed any better for all that. The poor little thing was afraid of the photographer. She who is always smiling was pouting as when her tears are on the verge of falling; we had to reassure her.

The little one asks every day if Pauline will be returning soon. (CF, pp. 302-303.)

October 22
From Mme. Martin to Pauline: As for Thérèse, she is always the same little rascal; she speaks often about Pauline and says she is annoyed at not seeing her return from Le Mans. This evening, she

thought we were going to wait for you at the station because your father was going out to bring Marie to Mlle Pauline's; Thérèse struggled "to go also to get Pauline."

I had several little things to tell you about her that would have amused you very much, but I don't recall them just now. Yes, here is one: Yesterday morning, Céline was bothering her father to take her with Thérèse to the Pavilion as he had done the evening before. He said to her: "Are you jesting? Do you think I will take you there every day?" Thérèse was in a corner, playing with a wand and totally absorbed by her toy. All of a sudden, with an air of indifference, she said to her sister: "We must not get sassy so that Papa bring us every day." (CF, pp. 311-312.)

October 29

From Mme. Martin to Pauline: Little Thérèse asked me the other day if she would go to heaven? I told her "yes" if she were very good; She answered: "Yes, but if I were not good, I would go to hell...but I know what I would do. I would fly to you who would be in heaven. What would God do to take me? You would hold me tightly in your arms." I saw in her eyes that she positively believed that God could do nothing to her if she were in the arms of her mother. (CF, p. 314.)

October 31

From Pauline to her mother: I beg you to kiss for me Papa, Marie, my little sisters and our dear Louise [the maid].

November 5-6

From Pauline to her mother: I beg you to kiss for me Papa, my little sisters, and Louise.

November 8

From Mme. Martin to Pauline: Even Thérèse wants at times to join in performing the practices [little acts of virtue counted on beads]. She is a charming child, sharp as a needle, very vivacious, but she has a sensitive heart. Céline and she love one another very much; the two are sufficient for entertaining each other; every day, as soon as they have eaten, Céline goes to get her little rooster, and she catches

Thérèse's hen with one swoop. I cannot succeed in doing this, but she is so quick that at the first bound she has it. Then both of them come with their animals to sit at the fireplace, amusing themselves in this way for a very long time. The other day, Céline slept with me, Thérèse slept upstairs in Céline's bed, and she had begged Louise to take her downstairs to dress her. Louise went up to get her and found the bed empty. Thérèse had heard Céline and had gone down with her. Louise said: "You don't want to come down to dress?" "Oh, no! poor Louise, we are like the two little hens, we cannot be separated." And saying this, they hugged each other, and both clung together.

Then in the evening, Louise, Céline, and Léonie left for the Catholic Club, leaving poor Thérèse, who understood she was too little to go there. She said: "If you only wanted me to sleep in Céline's bed!" But, no, we did not want that...she said nothing and remained alone with her little lamp; in a quarter of an hour she was sleeping a deep slumber. (CF, pp. 317-318.)

November 12

From Mme. Martin to Mme. Guérin: I am worried about my little Thérèse; she has difficulty in breathing for several months and this is not natural. As soon as she walks quickly, I hear a strange whistling in her chest. I consulted a doctor, he told me to give her an emetic; I did it and she is even worse. I think a vesicatory would do her some good, but it is frightening to think of it.

My God, if I were to lose this child, how sad I would be! And my husband adores her!... It is incredible all the sacrifices he makes for her day and night. I shall see the doctor again, but Louise does not want him to give her a vesicatory; however, it seems to me that this is the best, for she is very sick at this moment. (CF, p. 323.)

November 19

From Mme. Martin to Pauline: Céline said to me this morning, seeing that I was giving much to Thérèse: "Tell me, Mamma, if you love me the most." I told her that I loved both of them very much, and to please her I told her I loved her a little more. This did not satisfy her entirely, and she answered: "Love me like you love Pauline; you know that you love her more than a little more than

Marie.'' I said: "Naughty thing, don't go and tell this to Marie!'' Oh! no, there is no danger. (CMG I, p. 104.)

She begged me to hug you very tightly, and Thérèse, who heard her, said: "I, too, and tell her I love her with all my heart.'' So I have carried out my messages.

Tomorrow morning, your father will go to Héloup to buy some apples; he is going to make cider again this year, it is a savings by half. The children are delighted, even Marie: for they will see again the good man who amuses them so much, with this good wife who comes back at night to tell him to close his door! (CF, pp. 324-325.)

December 3

From Pauline to her mother: I hope that Céline's little indisposition did not have any bad effects, she is so often sick...what a difference in temperament with our big Thérèse...I think often of these dear babies, they are my delight during vacation...Last Wednesday...we worked for the poor...Sister Marie Aloysia gave me a big dress to work on...so my little shirts are not finished, I will try, however, to bring Thérèse's shirt.

December 3

From Mme. Martin to Pauline: Two weeks ago, Thérèse, who found Céline happy at being ill, and desired so much to be in her place, was seized like her with a very strong fever, with all the symptoms of measles; thanks be to God, at the end of four days, she was cured.

At this time, all children are sick and many are dying. Little Moisy was taken like your sisters; on Sunday, she was better since she wanted them to take her down to the table and, on Tuesday morning, she was dead; she was Thérèse's age.

We asked Thérèse when she was sick: "Are you content now to be sick like Céline?'' But, no, her envy was passed! She answered, crying: "I wanted to be sick as big as the head of a pin but not like that.''

I had several of her funny sayings to tell you in order to amuse you, but I no longer remember them. I must write them down instantly. Another time, I will do it to fill my four pages. (CF, pp. 326-327.)

December 7
From Mme. Martin to Mme. Guérin: You speak to me already about New-Year's gifts!... For Thérèse, it will be whatever you wish; as for toys, she has carriages and dolls.... I hear Thérèse who is crying very loudly saying: "How unhappy I am!" And it is because Céline told her: "her dolls are badly reared and that she lets them carry out their whims!" (CF, pp. 329-330.)

December 17
From Pauline to her mother: It seems that Marie is rejoicing very much at seeing me on the first of the year and that Thérèse is making her little preparations, and I also am delighted to see once more these dear little sisters!... I ask you to kiss for me Papa, my little sisters and Louise.

December 17
From Mme. Martin to Mme. Guérin: I am, however, far from disillusioning myself, and I hardly sleep at night when I think of the future.... Now Marie is grown up, she has a very, very serious character, and has none of the illusions of youth. I am sure that when I am no longer here, she will make a good housekeeper and will do everything possible to rear her little sisters well and give them good example.

Pauline is also charming, but Marie has more experience: she has besides much influence over her little sisters. Céline shows the best dispositions, she will be a very pious child. It is rare to show at her age such inclinations to piety. Thérèse is a real little angel. As for Léonie, God alone can change her, and I am convinced that He will do it. (CF, pp. 332-334.)

1877

January 8
From Mme. Martin to Mme. Guérin: My little Thérèse is sick, and I am worried about it. She has frequent colds giving her breathing problems. This lasts usually two days. I must consult the doctor, but he will tell me to give her vesicatories and this frightens me. This

evening, I found her almost cured when I returned from Le Mans. (CF, p. 344.)

January 11
From Mme. Martin to Pauline: I want to relieve you of all worry about your little sister whom you left as sick. When I arrived on Monday evening, she came to meet us with the maid but not as far as the station; she ate with us and was very happy; the sickness had disappeared. I cannot account for these indispositions which take hold of her so often and which never last longer than one or two days. Immediately afterwards they no longer appear. (CF, p. 345.)

January 21
From Pauline to her mother: You will all go out walking today, for it is magnificent weather. I am sure Thérèse and Céline will be very happy and more cheerful than usual.... I ask you to kiss for me and give my affectionate regards to my dear little Father, Marie, Thérèse, Céline, Léonie, Grandma, and Louise.

January 21
From Mme. Martin to Pauline: We assisted at Vespers at the Hospice, and we all went for a walk in the country; the weather is so good this afternoon, and it was such a long time since we had gone out! So this did us a lot of good. (CF, pp. 351-352.)

January 28
From Pauline to her mother: I am sorry I can't write her [Marie]; however, this does not prevent me from always thinking of her very much and loving her with all my heart, and Léonie also, the babies, and my dear little Louise.

January 28
From Sister Marie-Dosithée to M. and Mme. Guérin: I thank the dear little nieces [Guérins] for their kind prayers, and I beg our Lord to bless them just as I begged Him to bless their cousins [Martins].

February 4
From Pauline to her mother: And are Thérèse and Céline always

the two family bouquets?... I love them always more and more.

February 6
From Mme. Martin to Mme. Guérin: I took the children on Sunday [to the Palace of Justice Square] to please them, and I recognized all that was at the fair at Lisieux, even the wooden horses.... All are well here. (CF, p. 357.)

February 13
From Mme. Martin to Pauline: Little Thérèse, whom we took [to the sermon] was really bored. She said: "It was more beautiful than usual, but it bores me just the same." We had had a superb sermon, and it is too bad that she understands nothing; it was Greek to the poor baby. She was heaving sighs! The child is too little for such long ceremonies, but it is annoying to stay at home because of her on a day like this. Well, she was able to recoup with the torchlight tattoo!

It is nine o'clock. The little ones have gone to bed. This is good for me, for they were making a lot of noise.... I don't know anything amusing about Thérèse, except this little detail which comes to mind:

One morning, I wanted to kiss her before going downstairs; she seemed to be in a deep sleep, and I did not dare awaken her when Marie said to me: "Mamma, she is pretending to sleep, I am sure." Then I bent over her forehead to kiss her, but she hid immediately under her blanket, saying with the air of a spoiled child: "I don't want anyone to see me." I was less than pleased and I made her feel it.

Two minutes later, I heard her crying and soon to my great surprise I saw her at my side. She had left her little bed all by herself, had come down the stairs barefooted, hampered by her nightgown which was longer than herself. Her little face was bathed in tears: "Mamma," she said, throwing herself at my knees, "Mamma, I was naughty, pardon me!" Pardon was quickly granted. I took my cherub in my arms, pressing her to my heart and covering her with kisses.

When she saw she was so well received, she said: "Mamma, if you swaddled me up as when I was little! I will eat my chocolate here at the table." I went to the trouble of going for her blanket, and I wrapped her up as when she was little. I appeared to be playing at dolls. (CF, pp. 358-360.)

February 20
From Mme. Martin to Mme. Guérin: I see you enjoyed yourselves very much on Mardi-gras, especially Jeanne and Marie. I would have loved to see them in their costumes as little peasants; the children here have spoken so much about it! (CF, p. 361.)

February 24: Death of Sister Marie-Dosithée Guérin.

March 1-3
From Pauline to her mother: I beg you, dear little Mother, to kiss Papa, my dear little sisters, and Louise, very tenderly for me.

March 4
From Mme. Martin to Pauline: This evening, Léonie came to ask me to show her aunt's souvenirs; at the same time, Céline and Thérèse looked at them and kissed them.

If only I could tell you something interesting; undoubtedly, it is about your little sister that I should speak to you?

She is always very darling and is as intelligent as is possible. She is interested in knowing what day it is; so, in the morning, hardly has she opened her eyes when she asks what day it is. This morning, again, she said to me: "Today is Sunday, tomorrow is Monday, then Tuesday." And so forth, she knows all the days and no longer makes mistakes.

But the strangest thing is her chaplet of "practices" which never leaves her for one minute; she records even a little too much. The other day, thinking in her little head that Céline deserved a reproach, she said: "I said a naughty thing to Céline, I must mark a 'practice.' " But she saw immediately that she was mistaken; I told her that on the contrary she had to push a bead back. She replied: "Oh! well, I can't find my chaplet."

The other day she was at the grocer's with Céline and Louise; she was talking about her practices and was arguing strongly with Céline. The woman said to Louise: "What does she mean? When she is playing in the garden we hear her talking about these practices. Mme. Gaucerin puts her head out the window in order to understand what this debate means over practices.''

The poor little one makes up all our happiness; she will be good. We already see the seed, and she speaks only about God. She would never fail to say her prayers. I would like you to see her reciting little fables, never have I seen anything so pleasing. She finds by herself the expression she must give and the tone, but it is especially when she recites: ''Little child with blond hair, where do you believe God is?'' When she comes to the words: ''He is up in the blue heaven,'' she raises her eyes above with an angelic expression, so beautiful that we never tire of having her say it. There is something so heavenly in her eyes that we are enraptured by it!...

Céline and Thérèse are inseparable; you could not find two children who loved each other better. When Marie comes to get Céline for her class, poor Thérèse is all in tears. Alas, what is to become of her, her little friend is leaving!... Marie takes pity on her, bringing her along also, and the poor little one sits on a chair for two or three hours. We give her beads to thread or a piece of cloth to sew. She doesn't dare to budge and often heaves big sighs. When her needle becomes unthreaded, she tries to rethread it, and it is curious to see her, unable to succeed and not daring to disturb Marie; soon we see two large tears flowing down her cheeks.... Marie consoles her quickly, rethreads the needle, and the dear little angel smiles through her tears. (CF, pp. 367-369.)

March 22
From Mme. Martin to Pauline: I have confidence in God, and I am asking Him now for the favor of allowing me to live.... The two little ones do not worry me, both are so good, they are choice characters; certainly they will be good. Marie and you will be able to rear them perfectly. Céline never commits the slightest voluntary fault. The little one will be good too, she would not lie for all the gold in the world, she has a mind such as I have never seen in any of you. (CF, pp. 377-378.)

April 29
From Mme. Martin to Pauline: At this moment I don't have any

idea of what I am doing: Grandmother is talking to me while I am writing, the maid just came in with the little ones, and they are making lots of noise.... Good! here I am again pestered by the little ones; this time I am leaving my letter aside, for I have a headache. My God! how unfortunate I am that it is raining, otherwise all would be sent off on a walk! (CF, pp. 384-385.)

April 30
From Pauline to her mother: I beg you, dear little Mother, kiss Papa, Marie, and all the little ones.

May 10
From Mme. Martin to Pauline: Our two darlings, Céline and Thérèse, are angels of benediction, little angelic characters. Thérèse makes up the joy, the happiness of Marie and her glory, it is incredible how proud she is of her. It is true she has answers that are very rare for her age; she gives advice to Céline who is twice her age. Céline was saying the other day: "How is it that God can be in a host so small?" The little one said: "This is not surprising since God is all-powerful!" "What does all-powerful mean?" "It means to do whatever He wills!" (CF, pp. 392-393.)

May 30
From Pauline to her mother: I beg you, dear little Mother, to kiss Papa, my little sisters, and Louise for me.

June 11
From Mme. Martin to Mme. Guérin: Even if Louis were to come [to Lourdes], I assure you the two younger ones could very well remain with the maid; she loves them very much, of this I am sure. (CF, p. 405.)

June 17
From Mme. Martin to her husband: We leave tomorrow morning [from Angers to Lourdes] at half past seven. I close, for night is coming on. Kiss the two little girls for me. (CF, p. 408.)

June 25

From Mme. Martin to Pauline: We arrived at Alençon only at half past six; the train was close to a half hour late. Your father was waiting for us for an hour, with the two little ones, and he was happy to see us again. (CF, p. 416.)

July 8

From Mme. Martin to Mme. Guérin: The maid must definitely leave soon; I still have no one in mind. Oh! if God were to do me the favor of curing me, I would no longer want any servants. Marie is good regarding the management of the house, taking care of the bedrooms, attending to her little sisters. Pauline and Léonie would also help and we would be happy as I have never been before.... The little ones know that the two older ones must leave [for Lisieux]; but if one of the three were to come, it would be tears and lamentations which would force me to take all five!

The littlest one would be the most eager. She will remember all her life how we left her at Alençon two years ago, and when she speaks of it, her tears flow immediately. My Thérèse is a charming little creature, and I assure you she will turn out well. (CF, pp. 421-422.)

August 9

From Marie to Mme. Guérin: Mamma weeps at times and looks at all of us, one after the other, then she says: "Ah! my poor children, I shall be unable to go out for a walk with you, I who wanted to make you so happy!... Little daughters, if I could go with you, admit it, how happy we would be!" Our poor little mother forgets about herself in such a way that she is happy when seeing us leave. To please her, Papa arranges boat trips for my sisters. But what joy is there in going out when we know our mother is so sick?... I have given you news about everybody, dear Aunt, except my two little girls, Céline and Thérèse. However, I want to speak about them, I have so many interesting things to tell you. I must speak about the beautiful distribution of prizes that took place the day after your departure, at the "Holy Mary Visitation at Alençon" (this is what our boarding school is called!)

I assure you it was very beautiful. I had decorated my bedroom with wreaths of periwinkle intermingled with bouquets of roses. At intervals, wreaths of flowers were hanging. A carpet covered the floor and two armchairs awaited the Presidents of the *August Ceremony*, M. and Mme. Martin.

Yes, Aunt, Mamma wanted to assist at the prizes also. Our two little ones were dressed in white, and you should have seen with what triumphant faces they came in to receive their prizes and crowns. Papa and Mamma distributed the rewards, and I called out the names of my pupils.

At times I wanted to laugh at my beautiful "Distribution," and I remained as serious as I possibly could, especially when giving the speech which Pauline and I had composed the evening before.

You can see, dear Aunt, this little celebration made us forget for a moment our bitter preoccupations. Poor children, they are now filled with joy, vacation has begun. However, a very sad vacation, alas! because of our dear Mamma, who is so sick. (CMG IV, pp. 399-401. This "distribution of prizes" took place on July 31 or August 1.)

August 28: Death of Mme. Martin.

September 10
From Pauline to Mme. Guérin: It is a consolation for us to think that in a few months we shall be with you. I was touched by the sacrifices Papa has made to carry out this plan.... Our black dresses are made; Thérèse will have a crepe veil, the dressmaker thinks she is big enough to wear one. Yesterday, we went to pray at Mamma's tomb. I could not describe the pangs that came over me in the presence of this beloved tomb. (G Copy.)

September 16
From Pauline to Jeanne and Marie Guérin: I am delighted to go to Lisieux to see you for a very long time. Céline and Thérèse especially do not know how to express their joy.

November 25
From M. Martin to his daughters: You, Marie, continue to devote yourself more and more to your sisters, take care that when seeing

you, they may have before their eyes a good model to imitate.... A Dieu, my dear children, I press you all to my heart; how I love you. (PST, p. 112.)

November 29
From M. Martin to his daughters: I have hastened to return to you... A big kiss to all five of you. (PST, p. 112.)

November 26-30 (?)
From Pauline to M. Martin: Thérèse has a bad cold, and Uncle has given her a bottle of syrup to take; she is coughing a lot, but this does not stop her from laughing and amusing herself. Yesterday, she recited her little fables in a charming way; we were at dinner at Aunt's and she knew how to behave.

Today, she slept the whole day. If she is not cured tomorrow this will not be our fault; we have lavished on her syrups and marshmallow paste which does some good, I think, for our little Thérèse's trouble. (CMG III, p. 55.)

Winter 1877-1878
From Pauline to M. Martin: Your baby is always good, she cannot have changed much since your recent departure. She is always our Benjamin, our dear child, just as she is for you. (CMG III, p. 55.)

1878

June 18
From Pauline to M. and Mme. Guérin: We thank you for all the trouble you are going to in taking care of our little sisters.... Very tender kisses for our dear little cousins and our little sisters, right? We are thinking of them.

June 22
From Marie to Mme. Guérin: To think that you have Thérèse with you for a week and to leave her with you for such a long time, is this not too much an abuse of your kindness?... As for our five little sisters and cousins, we kiss them all tenderly and we take delight

in seeing them again.

1879

Summer 1878 or 1879 (?)
From Marie Guérin to Jeanne: Céline and Thérèse came to have breakfast with us. We were made up: Thérèse was a flower merchant, Céline was a lady, and I was a nurse. We played *guinemache*. I pasted little men on paper; I pasted all of them. (No date. "Guinemache": misspelling for "guigne-muche," a game of hide-and-seek, in Norman patois.)

June (?)
From Pauline to Mme. Guérin: How are you, my good relatives and all the little girls? Is Thérèse very good, poor little thing? I love her so much that her blond hair is always present in my memory; I am deprived at not being able to place some big kisses on her little pink cheeks.... A thousand caresses for the little ones, the best of them for our dear big Léonie. Papa sends regards to you and to his little daughters. (No date.)

June (?)
From Pauline to Mme. Guérin: Is Thérèse always darling? Let her take advantage of her last days of vacation. She must resume catechism and bible history on Monday, reading, writing, etc., etc. Poor little thing, how unhappy she is with her naughty sister Pauline! (Two days after preceding letter.)

1882

May 19
From P. Pichon to Marie: Thank you for the care you took in making me acquainted with your family on earth and that in heaven. It is somewhat my family too.

June 3
From P. Pichon to Marie: Your little photos really moved and delighted me.... I don't have the time to tell you how precious the dear photographs are to me.

September 1
From P. Pichon to Marie: Share with your sisters and especially your beloved Agnes of Jesus my best blessings.

Towards Christmas
From Sister Agnes of Jesus to Céline: Virtue is not so difficult. Give in to your little sister, be very gentle with her companions...after all, is this difficult to do? (No date.)

December 31 (?)
From Sister Agnes of Jesus to M. Martin: A thousand kisses and good wishes to all.... I have no time to write each one in particular. I love them all as *incomparable* sisters.

1883

March 13
From Mother Geneviève of Saint Teresa to M. Martin: Henceforth, Monsieur, and more than ever, your interesting family and that of M. Guérin will be united to the family of Carmel. My best to your dear daughters.

June 12
From P. Pichon to Marie: I bless with you and like you our dear little Thérèse.

During the summer
From M. Martin to his friend M. Nogrix: I tell you that Thérèse, my little Queen, that is what I call her, for she is a fine slip of a girl, I assure you, is totally cured; the numerous prayers took heaven by storm and God, so kind, willed to capitulate. Recently, I spoke to you of my five daughters. (PST, p. 113. After May 13, 1883.)

August 24-25
From Sister Agnes of Jesus to Céline: Always be very gentle, very good with Thérèse, with Léonie, not to mention Marie, who must be treated as a little Mother. (No date.)

August 31 (?)
From Sister Agnes of Jesus to M. Martin: A week ago, your four treasures gave you their love and offered you the richness of their good wishes.... Today, it is my turn. (No date.)

September 11-16
From P. Pichon to Marie: Don't keep for yourself all my blessings. I want some left for Thérèse, Léonie, and Céline.

October (?)
From Sister Agnes of Jesus to Céline: I saw Thérèse today, and I await Thursday with impatience to see you in your turn.... Be Thérèse's guardian angel, you are big enough to take on this sweet task. (No date.)

1884

May 6
From P. Pichon to Marie: Thursday you will be happy twice over: for your Pauline and your little Thérèse, and I at least three times over, for my three children.... Share my blessings with your two dear sisters.

May 7
From Sister Agnes of Jesus to M. Martin: Your angel Theresite must not come alone to throw herself at your feet to beg pardon and blessing on the eve of the greatest day.... Tomorrow! Ah! I admit that in pronouncing this word *tomorrow*, I have trouble holding back my tears. I am picturing the celebration on earth...my beloved Father leading by the hand his two little daughters to the altar.

June 15
From P. Pichon to Marie: My paternal congratulations to your dear Thérèse. (Day after Thérèse's Confirmation.)

June 23-29 (?)
From Sister Agnes of Jesus to Mme. Guérin: All sorts of caresses to the dear little boarders.

August 24
From Mother Geneviève to M. Martin: Tomorrow [the Carmel] will beg the God of all goodness...to preserve you, Monsieur, for many long years to the affection of your beloved daughters.

November (?)
From P. Pichon to Marie: I bless all your sisters, above all dear Thérèse who thinks of down there. (Montreal.)

December (?)
From P. Pichon to Marie: If you fall again into anger, you will have to double your repentance. To allow your thunder to burst over Thérèse, no, I do not want it! I forbid it.

December 31
From Sister Agnes of Jesus to M. Martin: All my heart and my first kisses of the year to my little Léonie and to the Benjamins.

1885

February
From P. Pichon to Marie: I bless dear Pauline, Léonie, Céline, and Thérèse, and I bless you in them.

July 28 (?)
From Sister Agnes to Marie: Oh! what mysteries remain at this moment under my pen! I could say, like Thérèse: "I understand and I would like to express everything, but it passes like a flash of lightning."

August 22
From M. Martin to Marie: I am sending you a dozen gold shells; you will give two to Céline and two to my little Queen; kiss them firmly on their two cheeks. (PST, pp. 115-116. From Paris.)

August 24
From P. Pichon to Marie: Tell your Thérèse that all the children of the whole universe do not rival her in the affection your father has for her.... I bless one hundred times your sisters, Pauline, Léonie, Céline, and Thérèse.

August 27
From M. Martin to Marie: Tell my little Pauline that I often think of her. Carry out the same message to Léonie, Céline, and Thérèse.... I assure you that I would like to have all five of you; without you, the greatest part of my happiness is missing.... Your father...who kisses you many times, as also the other four from the same nest. (PST, p. 117. From Munich.)

August 30
From M. Martin to Marie: All the charming letters that reached me at Vienna pleased my very much. You will thank for me Léonie, Céline, Thérèse, and my "real Pearl" in Carmel for their feast day wishes.

It seemed I saw all of you around me in the belvédère, and my little Queen, in her attractive and sweet voice, lisping her little congratulations to me. This so moved me that I wanted to be at Lisieux for good and to kiss you because I love you.... Finally, Marie, my big one, my first, continue to lead your little battalion as well as you can.... The one who loves all of you and carries you in his heart. (PST, pp. 118-119. From Vienna.)

September 3
From Marie to M. Martin: What will I say more, dear little Father? We are all well. Thérèse took a walk in the garden yesterday with Tom [her dog] for more than half an hour because he had not gone out in the morning. She seemed happy to see herself followed so faithfully by her "hairy beast." (CMG III, p. 102.)

September 7
From M. Martin to Marie: Kiss my little Pearl for me, as well as Léonie, Céline, my brave one, and the Queen of my heart. (PST, p. 120. On the Black Sea.)

September 11
From M. Martin to Marie: Tell Céline, the brave one, my Queen of France and Navarre, to let me know also what would please them.... I kiss you, dear Marie, Pauline, Léonie, Céline, and Thérèse. (PST, p. 112. From Constantinople.)

September 16
From M. Martin to Marie: Hug tightly for me Léonie, Céline, my Queen, and my beautiful little Pearl. Alas! it is impossible through her grilles. (PST, p. 124. From Constantinople.)

September 25
From M. Martin to Marie: Come, my dear daughters, always be my joy and consolation on earth and continue to serve the Lord well.... Adieu, then, dear children.... (PST, pp. 125-126. From Naples.)

September 25-30
From Marie to Céline: I made you some cuttings, and tomorrow will be Thérèse's turn. I have much work. I love you and I will not tease you anymore but a little bit just the same. Look at my rambling; it is because I don't know too well what I am writing. Thérèse could be jealous. I must say a word to her. (No date.)

September 27
From M. Martin to Marie: Tell Céline and my little Queen that I think a lot about them and that, if you are pleased, I shall reward them.... I kiss also Léonie, Céline, and my little Queen.... I leave you all in God's grace and pray each day for you at St. Peter's. (PST, pp. 126-127. From Rome.)

October 5
From Mother Geneviève of St. Teresa to Marie: My sincere regards to Mlles. Léonie and Céline, a nice kiss for my dear little daughter

Theresita.... I offer Mlles. Léonie and Céline two little [illegible words] very devout and to my little Theresita the garden with the gardener.

October 6
From M. Martin to Marie: I kiss all five of you with all my heart. (PST, p. 128. From Milan.)

December 31
From Sister Agnes of Jesus to M. Martin: What mercy on His part for having drawn me to Himself when so young and *the first*! I say the first, for I love to think that His divine glance will draw still several other doves from your nest. (No date.)

December 31 (?)
From Sister Agnes of Jesus to Marie: May this year be for you the *great Year*!... I ask *Marie* to hug tightly for me my beloved little Léonie, my dear little Céline, and my Theresita. (No date.)

1886

June (?)
From Sister Agnes of Jesus to Céline: To the Benjamin the most tender kiss.... Beloved Mother [Mother Marie de Gonzague] of the whole family at Les Buissonnets sends her heart with mine. (No date.)

June (?)
From Sister Agnes to Marie: Kiss the Benjamin of my heart for her Mother and for me. (No date.)

August 15
From Sister Agnes of Jesus to Céline: Adieu, see you soon, do not tell Thérèse that I have written to you. (No date.)

August 24
From Sister Agnes of Jesus to M. Martin: Dear little Father, do you know you can be proud? Not for me or anyone in particular, but

because of God's choice and His marked predilection for us five.

December 30
From Sister Marie of the Sacred Heart (Marie) to M. Martin: Yes, beloved Father, we will glorify you as you like to be glorified, by becoming saints.... Remain, however, a long time still with your children whose whole joy you make up.

1887

January 16
From Sister Marie of the Sacred Heart to her cousin Sophie Bohard: The little sisters have grown up. Céline will be eighteen years old in the month of April, and Thérèse is in her fifteenth year! She is very well now; for a year she no longer is attending the Abbey; she is taking special lessons. (Copy from the Angers Carmel.)

A little before March 19
From Sister Marie of the Sacred Heart to Céline: I kiss my three darlings. Let them rejoice when thinking that Jesus is waiting for them also!... At the cloister door, approach very close so that our Mother may see you. You will have to remove your cloaks beforehand. (Marie was about to come out of the cloister for the ceremony of the reception of the Habit, March 19.)

April 27
From Sister Agnes of Jesus to Céline: To the *little Benjamin*, very close to the Carmel, a little kiss which says all!

June 16
From Sister Agnes of Jesus to Sister Marie of the Sacred Heart: Little dove, ask our Mother permission to show the little ones the cherry and the note. (No date; see LD, p. 229.)

June 28
From Sister Marie of the Sacred Heart to Marie Guérin: I have had no mishaps since my last letter, but Céline has a very sad one to tell

you: the death of her little bluebird which died last night. Papa told us this morning that the remaining one appears very joyful at being rid of his wife, he is making never-ending chirps. But I believe the poor little husband was crying; birds are not like people, they cannot show their sorrow in another way. Thérèse almost said a funeral prayer for the defunct. It seems she encouraged Céline to resignation; finally, to soften bitter regrets they have decided to have it stuffed. (No date; "Tuesday." According to this letter, we must rectify note 3 of General Correspondence I, p. 277. The trip to Le Havre took place in June not July.)

July-December
From Sister Marie of the Sacred Heart to M. Martin: How return to you all that you do for us? By becoming saints.... Oh! this is what we all aspire to, your daughters in the cloister and the two who remain in the world.

August 21
From Jeanne Guérin to Céline: Adieu, dear little Céline; I kiss you with all my heart and beg you to give Thérèse a good kiss for me. *P.S. from Mme. Guérin to Céline:* I send my regards to my dear little nieces, and I ask you to remember me to their good father.

August 23
From Sister Marie of the Sacred Heart to M. Martin: May God keep you for long years for your children who love you so much, for you are their ray of sunshine in this life.... Your Diamond joins the two last jewels in kissing you with all her heart.

August 24
From Sister Agnes of Jesus to M. Martin: I wish for nothing for you on earth except to see all five of us in the Lord's house! In this I believe I am pleasing you because you desire nothing more. (No date.)

November 9
From Sister Agnes of Jesus to M. Martin: Céline wrote us from Paris about all the kindness, the touching attention that you have for your

two Benjamins.... I rejoice to learn that all three of you are today in the little House of the Blessed Virgin.

November 20

From Jeanne Guérin to Céline: If we are feeling the cold, our heart is not feeling it; neither the fogs nor the snow prevent us from seeing in the midst of a great city two dear little cousins, whom a great distance separates from us, but who will return soon. My thoughts go often to you.... Adieu, dear little Céline. I kiss you with all my heart and my Theresita as well.

November-December

From P. Pichon to Sister Marie of the Sacred Heart: My beloved visit to Les Buissonnets...your very excellent father, your Céline, your Thérèse, what things to tell you! (Fragment without any date.)

December 31

From Sister Agnes of Jesus to M. Martin: Our Mother sends you this little picture for your New-Year's gift. It is the Child Jesus, the one who is taking all your children from you! I ask Him to wish you a good Year for me.

1888

January 22

From P. Pichon to Sister Marie of the Sacred Heart: May the Lion (Marie) rival in roaring the Lamb (Pauline) and the little lamb (Thérèse).

March (?)

From Sister Agnes of Jesus to Sister Marie of the Sacred Heart: As for the cell, I have no sorrow whatsoever, on the contrary. What bothered me at first was to see you change your nice little cell for my ugly one.... But I experience a certain interior pleasure in changing, especially at the moment of Thérèse's entrance; in the eyes of the Community this will do very well. (No date. In preparation for Thérèse's entrance, they were freeing a cell in the "Mother Prioress corridor," which obliged Sister Agnes to go into the "St. Elias corridor," in another wing of the monastery.)

April 9: Entrance of Thérèse to Carmel.

April 9
From Sister Marie of the Sacred Heart to M. Martin: What Céline tells us is worthy of you! Ah! what a father we have!... How Jesus will have to return to you a hundredfold for the lily hardly in bloom, the lily filled with freshness and purity that you are offering Him today. (No date.)

April 10
From M. Martin to the Nogrix family: Thérèse, my little Queen, entered Carmel yesterday! God alone could demand such a sacrifice, but He is helping me so powerfully that, in the midst of tears, my heart superabounds with joy. (PST, p. 128.)

April 27
From Sister Marie of the Sacred Heart to Céline: Thank our father for what he brought this afternoon, and tell him his queen and his diamond and his real pearl love him with all their hearts and even more. (No date.)

After June 15
From M. Martin to his three Carmelite daughters: I insist on telling you, my dear children, that I am urged to thank and to have you thank God, for I feel that our family, though very lowly, has the honor of being numbered among our Creator's privileged ones. (PST, p. 129; after Céline informed him of her vocation.)

Around June 20 (?)
From Sister Agnes of Jesus to M. Martin: The hearts of your three little daughters are so filled with affection and tenderness for you that it is impossible to express it. Yesterday, I saw something sad in your features and some tears in your eyes. Do not weep, dear Father, or better still shed tears of joy, for it is not to a mortal spouse that you have sacrificed us, but to a God "who does not die!" Never

have our three hearts belonged more to you!

July 1
From Sister Agnes of Jesus to M. Martin: I am not going to forget *your big fish....* With regard to yourself, everything has been begun. It is up to us now to continue. Besides, this is our vocation, the special vocation of Carmelites.... The Diamond and the Queen send their kisses. ("The Fish": M. de Lesseps in whose salvation M. Martin had been interested.)

July 23
From Sister Marie of the Sacred Hearts to M. Martin: Thérèse of the Child Jesus is sending a note to Céline, and on this same occasion your diamond comes to say a little *bonjour*. (No date.)

July 27
From Céline to Pauline Romet: Marie, Pauline, and Thérèse are well, they are always happy and content; together we talk over the good old times.

August 23
From Sister Marie of the Sacred Heart to M. Martin: We warm ourselves at this divine hearth (the Heart of Jesus), and the coldness of life soon disappears: the springtime of heaven begins. Yes, in Carmel, it is thus the diamond, the real pearl, and the Queen are living, filled with the Lord's gifts and the favors, too, of their dear father.... Are you happy, dear little Father, with the beautiful medalion of hair that our Mother sent you?... With your white beard, we shall place the blond hair of your queen, and thus your youth and your old-age will be united to the beginning and the end of this chain of love which is called your children. (Medalion of hair: hair of Marie, worked according to the custom of the time and arranged with M. Martin's beard when he was still young.)

October 7
From Céline to Mother Marie de Gonzague: This evening, Léonie and I were in the sacristy to enlist for some work, when the Pastor of St. Pierre's said to us: "Your sisters are very happy." "Oh! yes,

M. le Curé." "And you are also, for you have an incomparable
Father, isn't he good?" (No date.)

October 14
From P. Pichon to Sister Marie of the Sacred Heart: Let St. Teresa
answer me tomorrow, and you will all be well provided for. For my
four children, my Mass and all my little spiritual treasures.

November 1
From Sister Marie of the Sacred Heart to M. Martin: It is not a long
time since you left and already the time to see you again weighs on
me. They love you so, your jewels, diamond, real pearl and Queen.

November 25
From Sister Marie of the Sacred Heart to M. Martin: The last time
we saw you, I recall that you said to us: "Children, fear nothing
concerning me, for I am God's friend...." Yes, little Father, this
is very true! You are God's friend.... He has proven this by choosing us as His spouses, in having us enter this blessed Carmel where
all our days pass by in peace and joy...

November 29
From Sister Agnes of Jesus to Pauline Romet: Sister Thérèse of the
Child Jesus hugs you *very, very tightly* also.

December 30
From Sister Agnes of Jesus to Pauline Romet: I repeat to you all
my good wishes, the Benjamin joins me in offering hers, which are
the same. All three of us kiss you as a dear Aunt.

December 31
From Sister Marie of the Sacred Heart to M. Martin: Your diamond
even here below would like to crown you! And the crown, after all,
is it not begun? Are there not three flowers already in the hand of
the divine Worker? In Carmel, are not we three working on your
crown?

1889

March 11
From P. Pichon to Sister Marie of the Sacred Heart: Later I will write to Léonie and to the dear little lamb.

End of March (?)
From Sister Agnes of Jesus to Céline: You do not tell us the impression produced by our letters. I am very much disturbed. Alas! how this poor little Father understands all.... Aunt came this afternoon, my letter was almost finished. Papa did not want to read our letters! (No date.)

April 2 (?)
From Sister Agnes of Jesus to Céline: We expect you on Thursday. How both of you must be suffering. And Papa!... It is heart-rending!... The little angel is waiting till Thursday to tell you her thoughts.... She is suffering much! But she is generous. We do not dare write to Papa. (No date.)

April 5 (?)
From Sister Marie of the Sacred Heart to Céline: Come tomorrow; you will spend Sunday with them [the Guérins].... This will be the last time you will see us in the speakroom; we are going to build (the Turn quarters.) (No date.)

April 29
From Céline to Jeanne Guérin: I would like Marie to make some chocolate rice for the feast of the Good Shepherd; we must give our poor Carmelites all the sweets possible.

May (?)
From Sister Marie of the Sacred Heart to Marcelline Husé: Little Sister Thérèse of the Child Jesus would be happy to have some flowers, some peonies if they are in bloom, and some hawthorn. (No date.)

1890

January 7
From Céline to Vital Romet: The Carmelites and ourselves think often of her [Pauline Romet, deceased], each day she is the subject of our prayers, for we love to recommend her to God and to recommend ourselves to her so that she may protect us.... The Carmelites and Léonie join me in offering you their regards and prayers.

February 16-19
From Sister Agnes of Jesus to Céline: Yesterday, we were speaking of Joan of Arc during recreation, of the joy of her old father, who followed her, they say, to the anointing of Charles VII. Sister Marie of the Sacred Heart thought immediately of Papa, whose glory has passed away! But Thérèse of the Child Jesus, with a heavenly look which you know in her, replied: "Yes, but the humiliation will pass away, too, and one day he will follow us, or rather we will follow him into heaven; *then one of his white hairs will illuminate us...*" (No date.)

End of March (?)
From Sister Agnes of Jesus to Céline: Sister Thérèse of the Child Jesus is better. (No date; no information concerning the illness.)

May 1
From Sister Agnes to Céline: I shall think so much about you during these days of solitude! Sister Thérèse of the Child Jesus told me of your joy over the painting and the book; do not fear that I think you are ungrateful, you did well to ask her, and, besides, I would not have been able to go to the speakroom, being very busy with my paintings for Caen.

July 22
From Sister Marie of the Sacred Heart to Jeanne Guérin: I have no time to write anyone but you, but would you tell Marie and Céline that Thérèse of the Child Jesus would be delighted to have some aspen, and, if you find some, two bouquets of peonies like they used to have at Mlle. Léonie's [Helloy, seamstress]. If there are still some

cornflowers, this will please her too, as well as some slips of fuchsia, one slip of each kind. (Tuesday, July 24; inexact date: in 1890, Tuesday fell on July 22.)

August 20-25 (?)
From Sister Marie of the Sacred Heart to Céline: I am returning the empty quinquina bottles; you would be very kind in giving us two more. These will be the last we are asking for; they are for the little lamb and little Thérèse.

1891

January 19 (?)
From Sister Agnes of Jesus to Céline: Yesterday evening, we offered our little paintings to Our Mother, who was very happy. Sister Thérèse of the Child Jesus did all of them, I inscribed them only. Our dear Mother is happy to give you this little pleasure of sending them yourself to Father. (No date.)

January 21
From Sister Agnes of Jesus to Mme. La Néele: Your three little sisters think of you *very, very often.*

April 15
From Céline to Mme. La Néele: Yesterday, I was at the Carmel, and my visit was spent only in talking about you, and I talked at length! If you only knew how happy they were, I could not satisfy them.... I spoke much about Francis also; I cannot tire of speaking of him. I told everything, even the electric batteries.... I have supplied myself with books on physics and chemistry.... My battery is a great distraction for me, it appears to me even in my dreams!

End of July-beginning of August
Sister Agnes of Jesus to Céline: All three of us hug you very tightly.

December 6
From Mme. Guérin to Mme. La Néele: [Mother Geneviève] loved

us very much when she was on earth, and now I trust she will look upon us still with kindness, being part of her family since she was the mother of three *of our children*.

1892

February 10
From Sister Marie of the Sacred Heart to Céline: In the speakroom, I envied the lot of Sister Thérèse of the Child Jesus, not because poor little Marie annoys me; oh, no, but she is so young! She has not suffered, and you have suffered and trial matures souls. (Dated by Céline: in the speakroom that same day, Thérèse was talking with Céline and Sister Marie of the Sacred Heart, with Marie Guérin.)

March
From Sister Agnes of Jesus to Céline: Thérèse of the Child Jesus *remained* before your masterpiece as though she had a vision of heaven. (No date; painting of the Assumption made by Céline for the Hôtel-Dieu of Bayeux.)

Beginning of May
From Sister Agnes of Jesus to Céline: Papa is about to return!... Tell us the day and the hour.... Thank Uncle and Aunt in my name and in that of Thérèse of the Child Jesus; I fear Sister Marie of the Sacred Heart is not mentioning our gratitude to both of them. (No date.)

May 8
From Mme. Guérin to Mme. La Néele: We will pray for you, and I will write to the Carmelites when I know you have left [for Auray].

May 10
From Mme. Guérin to Mme. La Néele: We often speak of you.... The Carmelites are making a novena for you; you are not forgotten, I assure you, my little Jeanne.

July (?)
From Sister Marie of the Sacred Heart to M. Martin: How God must love you, you who gave your children to Him with such generosity.

July (?)
From Sister Agnes of Jesus to Céline: Your photos, especially the little one, are *masterpieces.* How noble Papa looks, especially in the little one. Sister Marie of the Sacred Heart and Thérèse of the Child Jesus cannot look at him enough.

July 27
From Marie Guérin to Léonie: Kiss the Carmelites for me when you see them.

August 2
From P. Pichon to Sister Marie of the Sacred Heart: I bless you, dear child, and with you your saintly Mother [Marie de Gonzague], the Lamb, the little Lamb, from my very paternal heart. (From St-Joseph-de-Lévie.)

August 14
From Sister Agnes of Jesus to Céline: Hug little Marie *very, very tightly* for her little Carmelite SISTERS, and an especially big one from her dear Mother.... All four of us kiss our little Céline, Mother first and very tenderly.

August 18
From Mme. Guérin to Léonie: If you see the Carmelites, tell them Jeanne would have liked to write them, but she was still too weak.

1893

March 5 (?)
From Mother Agnes of Jesus to Céline: Dear little Céline, your poem is delightful! I am sending you that of the angel.... (No date; the angel is Thérèse, her poem: "The Divine Dew.")

June 20 (?)

From Mother Agnes of Jesus to Céline: What a delightful painting, it is a masterpiece. I had the painting placed by the cloister door by Auguste in order to get it after Matins. When Mother Marie de Gonzague entered her cell, I went to get it, and a half hour later I had the angel Thérèse of the Child Jesus awakened, who jumped with delight from her bed. She came very quickly and found it very *heavenly*. (No date. Painting of the Nativity given, it seems, for the feast day of Mother Marie de Gonzague, June 21.)

July 25

From Sister Marie of the Sacred Heart to Céline: To answer your nice letter, I will write only a note, for I hardly have any time, and I know that Thérèse of the Child Jesus is sending you a beautiful letter.

July 25

From Mother Agnes of Jesus to Céline: Our little postulant (Sister Marie-Madeleine) was received by the Community. We must now set the day for the ceremony. Tell me simply if it would not be better to insist that Aunt be godmother. I am afraid to give you any trouble, little Céline, but I cannot refrain from thinking this would be better, especially having Uncle as godfather. . . . Sister Thérèse of the Child Jesus says it would be ridiculous to do otherwise, and I see that Mother Marie de Gonzague thinks so too.

August 31

From Sister Marie of the Sacred Heart to Céline: I did not know that Thérèse was writing you, otherwise I would have been happy to send you a note. Impossible at present, they are waiting for the letter.

1894

LD   *From Mother Agnes of Jesus to Sister Marie-*
             Aloysia Vallée.

January 29-30   This letter was found in the archives of the
1894   Visitation at Le Mans when this present work
                 was already composed. We are giving it here in
                 the Appendix. It should be read between LT 156
                 and LT 157.

J.M.J.T.   Lisieux Carmel
                                            January 29, 1894
                                            Feast of St. Francis
                                            de Sales

Beloved Sister,

I wish a happy feast and a good year to all my beloved at the Visitation.... It is about time, for within a few days there would no longer be any time. Pardon me, I beg you, I have a thousand excuses.... Ah! it is always as usual, my heart flies to you very, very often! How useless it is to take up the pen! It can say nothing at all. I assure you that I don't take to letters, and I write as few of them as possible....

Dear Sister, dear Mistress, *beloved Mother,*[1] how are you? Give me some news about yourself, I hunger and thirst for it. Are you always praying for your poor child?... In one month it will be a year that she has cared for the Carmel's sheep and lambs![2]... What a story! What a fantasy! What a whim on the part of Jesus! It is really strange!... Let us thank Him, I am remaining very little, a lamb, and I do not know or wish to take on any other appearance. So true is this that our Father Superior[3] never begins the letters he writes to me otherwise than by these words: "Reverend Mother, dear daughter in our Lord Jesus Christ, and always, in spite of your dignity, *simple little lamb*." Dear Sister, did you think of this little lamb who loves you, on the 21st?... Ah! what a feast day in Carmel![4] It was made up of all colors; I no longer knew where I was, or rather I felt so happy, yes, really happy when seeing the spirit of faith, the union of hearts that reigned in Carmel! I don't believe I was proud; in the morning, I made my little plans with Jesus, and, according to what we agreed upon, never could they say too much to me or do too much for me. You understand, don't you?... It would take too long to describe the days of the 20th and 21st. I say only that Sister Thérèse of the Child Jesus decided to play the role of Joan of Arc listening to her voices.[5]... It was DELIGHTFUL! Sister Marie of the Sacred Heart played the role of St. Catherine, and she was ravishingly beautiful and spoke *heavenly* things, as well as her companion St. Margaret and the great Archangel Michael.

January 30.... Alas, the angel, Joseph de Sales,[6] tells me that you are sick, beloved little *Mother*. This saddens me and sets aside all my thoughts of continuing my discourse of yesterday. I must have a letter as soon as you are well. Our Lord will not be displeased with my *asking for* this consolation in spite of Lent.[7]

Regarding consolation, I hope to give you a very little one by sending you a painting of your beloved Jesus. If it still takes twenty-eight days, this will help you in practising patience while waiting for it.[8]

This humble sketch[9] was painted by Thérèse of the Child Jesus and given to me *for you* on the 21st by this dear little Angel. I assure you, she was very secretive about it, for I suspected nothing.... But, alas! when taking up the brush, she believed she was doing something marvelous, wanting to copy the Divine Child, whom she saw in her heart, so easy to render, she thought, *for she saw* Him so *clearly*! The brush misguided her! And the result cost her much in tears; this was not what she wanted to give her dear Aunt Maria-Aloysia.... Really, this painting is a real daubing, but when we think it was made according to an inspiration,[10] we are more indulgent, especially towards a child who has never learned sketching or painting. Well, I am sending it to you, in spite of the contrary opinion of Mother Marie de Gonzague, who does not like it.... She has painted such pretty things in flowers and landscapes, and the little Jesus could have been so attractive according to a model! But such as He is, it is always *a little Jesus*, and you will give Him a nice welcome, I am sure. May the Divine Child see fit to smile on your sufferings and lighten them for you, if this does not trouble the dream of His Heart for you....

Adieu, very dear Sister and Mother. I love you more and more in Jesus! Pray for me. Sister Marie of the Sacred Heart is not forgetting you.

Your child,
Sister Agnes of Jesus
r.c.ind.

I am sending you *the explanation of the painting*[11] that Sister Thérèse of the Child Jesus gave me. The most beautiful part remained within her heart and mind.... (Do not believe what she is saying about her *poor* little Mother.)

My good Father is doing well. Céline takes care of him with a devotedness and tenderness very easy to understand, for he is an incomparable Father and a real saint!

Mother Marie de Gonzague sends her regards to my dear Mothers of the Visitation.

* Autograph.
1. See LT 160, note 6, at the end.
2. This sentence would suggest that Mother Agnes had not written to Sister Maria-Aloysia since her election as prioress on February 20, 1893. But the archives of the Visitation of Le Mans preserve an envelope of Mother Agnes to this religious, carrying the stamps of LISIEUX 9 MAI 93, LE MANS 10 MAI 93. The letter has not been found.
3. Canon Delatroëtte.
4. January 21, feast of Saint Agnes.
5. See p. 726.
6. A religious of the Le Mans Visitation; see LT 160, note 8.
7. Lent was to begin February 7, Ash Wednesday. Usually, religious did not write during this period without necessity.
8. Behind this vocabulary, understood by the two interested parties, Mother Agnes of Jesus was making a reference to the absence of spiritual consolation on the tangible level.
9. The painting as commented on in LT 156.
10. Thérèse, however, had been helped by a painting; see LT 156, note 1.
11. The letter of LT 156.

April 4
From Sister Marie of the Sacred Heart to Céline: I would like you to ask the Superior of the Visitation for some of Léonie's hair if they must cut it.... Sister Thérèse of the Child Jesus will tell you what she wants to do with it. (Wednesday.)

June 28
From Marie Guérin to Mme. La Néele: At Carmel, they are waiting for Francis to come on Sunday to speak with Thérèse, who has a persistent sore throat, husky voice, and is suffering in her *chest*. They would have liked Francis to examine her, but this is a very delicate matter because of Dr. de Cornière.

October 11
From Marie Guérin to Céline (Marie of the Holy Face): Poor little Father is so positively sick from it that for two days he has passed into a state of continual emotion. Pray for him and for me, who will represent as well as I can the virgins of the family. It is a sweet consolation for me to represent my big sisters of the Carmel, and I will put forth my efforts to represent them as worthily as possible. (October 9-11: the transfer of the remains of the Martin-Guérin families from Alençon to Lisieux.)

October 20
From Mme. Guérin to Céline (Marie of the Holy Face): We kiss you with all our heart, darling, with real feast-day kisses. Kiss your sisters for us. It is permitted on this feast day.

October 31
From Mme. La Néele to Céline (Marie of the Holy Face): This morning, during my meditation, I seemed to hear Our Lord say to me: "And you, you do not want to do as she (Céline), you do not want to love suffering? You see your four little sisters of Carmel, they love sorrow, they seek the cross, and they embrace it with delight. You do not want to be a saint?".... I hug you a thousand times very tightly, your sisters too. Francis asks me to give all his fraternal regards to his four little sisters.

1895

January 30
From Sister Thérèse-Dosithée (Léonie) to Sister Geneviève (Céline):
No, it is not in my power to describe all I have in my innermost heart
for my four treasures in Carmel and for you in particular.

February 4
From Mme. La Néele to Sister Geneviève: Until tomorrow, my dear,
I kiss you a thousand times as I love you, and your sisters as well.
(No date; eve of Céline's reception of the Habit.)

February
From Mme. La Néele to Sister Geneviève: Your reception of the
Habit has left us an ineffaceable memory.... I embrace you very
tightly as I love you, as well as my three other little sisters.

February
From Mme. Guérin to Sister Geneviève: Give some good big kisses
to your sisters for me. I imagine this is allowed still these days which
are so close to the big celebration. (No date.)

March 3
From Marie Guérin to Mme. La Néele: For having had patience and
resignation for several years, we shall have a little Credidi, who will
be a saint. Did not Thérèse ask this on the day of her reception of
the Habit (read: taking of the Veil)? The saints always make us wait
and want something for a very long time. (*Credidi:* nickname for
Jeanne, and, by extension, for the baby she always wanted.)

May 17
From Marie Guérin to Sister Geneviève: Kiss my three big sisters
for me.

June 12
From Mme. La Néele to Sister Geneviève: I then had the thought
of making a novena to Our Lady of Lourdes, and at the same time
offer each day a prayer to my holy Uncle [M. Martin]. Certainly,

he is in heaven, certainly, he will hear our prayers and especially those of his four Carmelites?.... Thanks in advance, little Céline, pray very hard, I beg you, you and your sisters.

July 10

From Mme. Guérin to Sister Marie of the Sacred Heart: If you and your sisters still have a short quarter of an hour before my return, think of me and use it for me. Thank little Thérèse for having interceded in my favor. Adieu, good Marie, I kiss you with all my heart; kiss your sisters for me.

July 18

From M. Guérin to Mother Agnes of Jesus: I am awaiting the return of Léonie. We must be resigned and esteem ourselves as very blessed that out of five, God has chosen four, of whom the fifth, less well gifted, will nevertheless be one of the elect in heaven.... I embrace you tightly, beloved little Pauline, as well as all my little birds in Carmel.

August 5

From Marie Guérin to Sister Geneviève: Tell Pauline I hug her very tightly, very tightly.... Kiss Marie and Thérèse also. (No date.)

August 18

From Mme. Guérin to Sister Marie of the Eucharist (Marie Guérin): Give my affectionate regards to Mother Marie de Gonzague, assure her of my love, as well as your dear cousins, among whom I beg you to share my best kisses, my *most affectionate* kisses.

August 19

From Sister Marie of the Eucharist to Mme. La Néele: Our Mother wishes you a happy feast; Mother Marie de Gonzague sends you, too, her best wishes, my sisters do so too. (No date.)

August 20

From Mme. Guérin to Sister Marie of the Eucharist: I know that good Mother Marie de Gonzague and your dear cousins will give you on this day [August 22: Marie was twenty-five] a good kiss for your papa and mamma, your sister and even your brother-in-law.... My kisses and best regards to the dear cousins.

August
From Mme. Guérin to Sister Marie of the Eucharist: Kiss good little Mother Prioress [Mother Agnes] for me; I cannot express to her how much I love her, as well as all of you, my darlings. Share my kisses if you can, do not forget your angel [Thérèse].

September 15
From Sister Marie of the Eucharist to Mme. Pottier [Céline Maudelonde]: Mother Marie de Gonzague and your cousins send their regards to their little Céline.

December 15
From M. Guérin to Sister Marie of the Eucharist: All the dwellers on rue Banaston kiss you a thousand times, my other children in Carmel as well.

December 18
From Mme. Guérin to Sister Marie of the Eucharist: Tell Pauline she did me much good yesterday in the speakroom.... Kiss your cousins. (No date.)

December 28
From Sister Marie of the Eucharist to M. and Mme. Guérin: On this great feast in Carmel, the little novices are mistresses today; they do anything they want.... The office is run by all the little novices. Sister Geneviève and Sister Marie-Agnes have the black veil. Sister Thérèse of the Child Jesus has the white veil, and is versicler with me.... Christmas is celebrated in Carmel as I never saw it celebrated before.... The Community is no longer recognizable, it is a free day and all are joyful.

1896

February 15
From Mme. Guérin to Sister Geneviève: Speak above all to God about our treasures who are our dear children, all of you whom your good Mother [Mme. Martin] entrusted to me. May she obtain the favor for me to be always for her Léonie, insofar as I am able, a guide and a support.

February 16
From Sister Marie of the Eucharist to Mme. Pottier: I wish you in advance a happy birthday. All your little cousins of Carmel send you good kisses.

February 20
From Brother Simeon to Sister Geneviève: Please remember me to your dear Sister Thérèse of the Child Jesus, thank her for the good prayers she is saying for me. I trust you are joining her in her intentions for me to obtain for me the carrying out of God's will in everything and for a holy death.

March 16
From Mme. Guérin to Sister Marie of the Eucharist: My affectionate regards to Mother Marie de Gonzague and my good kisses to your dear cousins.

June
From Sister Marie of the Sacred Heart to Sister Geneviève: Here is all that I possess, try to make me something wonderful.... Your poor mamma who has a great need of the strokes of the brush of her two babies in order to sparkle a little bit. (N.B. Marie was asking her sister to decorate a picture for her for the feast of Mother Marie de Gonzague, June 21, 1896: Thérèse and Céline together were her "Babies.")

June 17
From Sister Marie of the Eucharist to Mme. Guérin: It will be [Saturday] at three o'clock that we shall celebrate. Afterwards, we shall

act out a little comic piece, and the next day another more serious one. I am playing two contrasting characters: St. Michael and an Asmodée. Diana Vaughan is the one who gave us the idea of composing this play.

June 19
From M. Guérin to Sister Marie of the Eucharist: It is not only you that I have in mind in these considerations, but also my four other little daughters for whom I have an affection almost equal, because they were entrusted to me by their good mother, because I have acquired certain rights over them throught a little sharing in their vocation, in their education, and through the care we took of them.... Adieu, my dear Benoni, your mamma and I hug you as we love you, my four little daughters as well, and this is not saying a little.

June 21
From Sister Marie of the Sacred Heart to M. and Mme. Guérin: We have been overwhelmed by you who are unique in the world in love for your children!... They are paying you, too, in similar coin, for their hearts overflow with tenderness for you, especially the one who writes you these lines.... Yesterday and today, two little plays by the novices. Yesterday, the Benjamin [Marie Guérin] dressed up as a gardener with blouse and wig enacted the part of the innocent one to perfection. Today, transformed into St. Michael, she combatted Satan and his devils.... It was a current event. Asmodée was there, speaking about Diana Vaughan, etc., etc.; it was composed by Sister Thérèse of the Child Jesus.... These are the amusements of the Carmelites.

June 22
From Sister Marie of the Sacred Heart to M. and Mme. Guérin: Since you want us to taste the products from La Musse: your dear little daughter and all those who have the humiliation of eating meat will eat some wild rabbits. Thus you see that Francis is going to have some work. (N.B. Thérèse was then on a meat diet.)

June 28
From Mother Agnes of Jesus to M. Guérin: Have you seen, dear

Uncle, the blank pages at the end of the circular [of Mother Geneviève]?... I count on you to fill them in with the *delightful* poems composed by Sister Thérèse of the Child Jesus.

July 3
From Sister Marie of the Eucharist to Mme. Guérin: Tomorrow, we celebrate in Carmel the feast of St. Isidore, April 4. We are going to have a formal Office for him. This week, Sister Thérèse of the Child Jesus officiates; Mother Agnes of Jesus and Sister Geneviève are versiclers; Sister Marie of the Sacred Heart is reader of the Martyrology; and Sister Marie of the Eucharist recites an antiphon and a Nocturn lesson at Matins. The whole family will do something, then, for the feast of St. Isidore, we shall celebrate this great saint in a special way.... Sister Thérèse of the Child Jesus has no more Kola-wine; this has done her much good, and if she could have some more, our Mother would be pleased, but I don't know if you will be able to get some. She is better, but she still does not look good. She no longer suffers in her chest, nor does she cough at all. There is a real improvement. This is not surprising because our Mother takes such good care of her.

July 6-7
From Sister Marie of the Eucharist to Mme. Guérin: At the moment, we are doing the haying. So we are turning the hay over and over again. Our meadow is not as big as that at La Musse as you can well imagine. (See photo VTL, no. 35.)

July 12
From Sister Marie of the Eucharist to Mme. Guérin: We [the novitiate] have composed in honor of my girl [an expected postulant who did not enter] a kind of little poem to give her some courage and ourselves as well, for it is washday, and some little compositions help us much in our work. Our poetry is very comical.

July 16
From P. Roulland to Mother Marie de Gonzague: I shall be passing through Lisieux around eleven tonight, today Friday; I will send you a blessing, to you and to my sister in Jesus. If I were to see her,

I would scold her, for I see that in spite of my protestations she has taken sorrows for herself and leaves me consolations.... What I am happy to inform Sister Thérèse of the Child Jesus is that we have begun our apostolate. The soul the most dear to me in the world, the soul of my father, is reconciled to his God.... From Paris, I will give you more details which will certainly interest Sister Thérèse.

August 15
From Sister Marie of the Eucharist to Mme. Guérin: I would never have believed I would be Fêted in Carmel. Sister Thérèse of the Child Jesus made me a painting with some verses corresponding to my innermost feelings ["Jesus alone"]. I am sending it to you because I know this will please you.... You could copy it out if you want. When there is an opportunity, I will ask you to return it to me.... I am sending you, too, the poem "To Live by Love" done by Sister Thérèse of the Child Jesus. A year ago when I entered our cell, I found it on my bed, surrounded by flowers.

September 24
From P. Roulland to Mother Marie de Gonzague: My last letter dated from Marseille was short: It was...a last blessing given to my Mother and my dear Sister.

October 6 (?)
From Sister Marie of the Eucharist to Mme. Pottier: All your cousins kiss you. Pray for us, we are entering on retreat on Thursday until the feast of St. Teresa.

October (?)
From P. Pichon to Sister Marie of the Sacred Heart: To your Reverend Mother always well-beloved, to the Lamb, to the Benjamin [Thérèse], to the pupil of the Holy Face, and to you, my old one, my soul and my heart remain tenderly devoted and paternally attached in the Most Sacred Heart of Jesus.

November 24-25
From Sister Marie of the Eucharist to M. and Mme. Guérin: Our Mother sends you her respectful regards. All the little daughters of

Carmel eat with kisses their uncle, their aunt, their cousin, cousins and sisters.

December 1
From Sister Marie of the Eucharist to M. Guérin: If I had had the space, I would have told you the story of a thief in Carmel. Yesterday evening, in the sacristy, Sister Thérèse of the Child Jesus heard movement in the room next to the one where she was. She came looking for us; five or six went armed; you will laugh at our arms of defense: a broom, some forks, heavy sticks. Not seeing them return, Sister Marie of the Sacred Heart left with me with tongs and shovels. There was one who had taken a fistful of ashes to throw on the head of the thief. All these arms were useless; we looked everywhere, and no thief.... As this was during recreation, the incident was not without some excitement.

December 28
From Mme. Guérin to Sister Marie of the Eucharist: Kiss your cousins and tell them of my regrets at not seeing them before next year.

December 31
From Mme. Guérin to Sister Marie of the Eucharist: We do not see signs of affection, my darling, nor those of your cousins, you have made a generous sacrifice of them to Jesus, but it is said that Jesus never allows Himself to be outdone in generosity. So He wills that these signs be given to us with affection by the dear children whom He has left in the world, Jeanne, Léonie, and Francis. All three have redoubled in affection for us, and it is to you, dear little one, and to your four little sisters that we owe this.... Your nice letters are always for us our greatest joys; and it is always when turning to your dear Carmel that we have our fervent thanksgiving ascend to God.... We are thinking of going to see you tomorrow around three.... Kiss your cousins, thank them for us for their good wishes and offer them ours which are *very sincere* and *affectionate*. Tell them that I take delight in seeing all of you.

1897

Beginning of January
*From Sister Marie of the Eucharist to Mme. Pottier (C*éline
Maudelonde): All your little cousins send you their kisses and most
affectionate wishes.

January 10
From Sister Geneviève to Brother Simeon: If it were not for the joy
this new occasion gives me for expressing how much your two little
Carmelites think of you, I would be ashamed to write you in order
to claim the same and great favor.... Sister Thérèse of the Child
Jesus and I are very proud to know you. But be careful, very dear
Brother, I fear that your ambassadresses are writing you again to
beg the same privilege.... There is still something which would please
us, the two little Romans. We brought back from Rome a great devotion to the gentle virgin St. Cecilia, and we remember a painting
placed, I believe, near the room of the baths where she suffered
martyrdom. This painting represents an Angel crowning Cecilia and
Valerian with lilies and roses. It struck us very deeply, and it would
be a sweet consolation for us to have a photograph of this painting;
it exists, for we remember having seen it. Since then we have tried
to get it; we have even written to the religious of the Convent, guar-
dians of the tomb, but they did not answer. Then we thought that
it would be only through a friend that this consolation could be given
to us.... I am sending in this letter a set of verses composed by her
[Thérèse]; this is only one flower detached from the beautiful bouquet that she is leaving to her religious family.

January 18
From l'abbé Bellière to Mother Marie de Gonzague: I come to thank
you for the sympathy you have for my poor soul, and for having
taken to heart, you too, Mother, with my good and dear sister
Thérèse of the Child Jesus, the cause of my vocation and my salvation.... It is at the Crib, at Calvary, and at the Tabernacle...that
you will find me, good Mother, asking God that He restore your
health completely, and praying to Him fervently for you, my Sister,
and your Community.... I beg you here, Reverend Mother, to ac-

cept the expression of my respectful and filial gratitude which you will see fit to share with Sister Thérèse, I beg you.

January 19
From P. Roulland to Mother Marie de Gonzague: On November 12 I entered the waters of the Blue River, remarkable for its dirty water.... Finally, we reached the limits of oriental Su-tchuen; if you permit it, good Mother, I shall speak to Sister Thérèse about our beautiful Mission. (LC 173, January 20, followed.)

January 23
From Mother Agnes of Jesus to Mme. La Néele: All your little sisters send you good kisses, especially Sister Marie of the Eucharist.

January 27
From Sister Geneviève to Brother Simeon: Oh! why have you done *so much* for your two little Carmelites?... You have been sick, and this places a shadow over this picture.... Your little daughters are not allowing you yet to sing your *Nunc Dimittis!*... When you see God...you will tell Him in a whisper: "that Thérèse and Céline would like to be with Him."

January 27
From Mother Marie de Gonzague to Brother Simeon: You will permit old Mother to join her two childlike angels in expressing her respectful and warm gratitude.

January 31
From l'abbé Bellière to Mother Marie de Gonzague: It was not enough to give me as helper - and what a helper! - one of your saints. You yourself see fit to join in these works which the all-good Jesus inspires and encourages. May you be blessed, Mother, for what you are doing.... The help you are giving me with my dear Sister gives me confidence.... Yes, when in the midst of the battle on the plain I shall feel exhausted, I shall return to the Mountain and the sight of a Mother and a Sister who are praying for me will restore my courage.... Allow me to thank my Sister also.

February 11

From Sister Geneviève to Brother Simeon: In the evening [February 8], the novices enacted a little play composed by Sister Thérèse of the Child Jesus; it was the entrance of St. Stanislaus into the Company of Jesus.... One of our novices had the good thought of offering to our amiable Jubilarian [Sister St. Stanislaus] a photograph of the Virgin Mary and a poem on the same subject. This photograph is the reproduction of a painting in oil done by me; this work which is the dearest to me was more that of my heart than of my brush. The poem is the first Sister Thérèse of the Child Jesus composed [The Divine Dew]; both of us were inspired together.... This picture is the reproduction of the work of your two children.... In the package you will find the copy of some poems of Sister Thérèse of the Child Jesus. I have indicated the tunes, and they are better when sung. I think that I have collected, if not the most beautiful, at least the most typical. The king will always remain: To Live by Love. She composes them at the request of the Sisters, according to their devotion. She composes plays, and all have a special seal.

February 20 (?)

From Mme. Guérin to Sister Marie of the Eucharist: Kiss your dear cousins.

March 5

From Brother Simeon to Sister Geneviève: Please thank her [Sister Saint Stanislaus] for the sacrifice she made in my favor by giving up the beautiful picture painted by you and for the magnificent poem of the worthy Sister Thérèse of the Child Jesus. I will preserve this souvenir which will remind me of the dear Jubilarian and her beloved Sisters Geneviève of St. Teresa and the inspired Thérèse of the Child Jesus. (See LC 176.)

End of March - beginning of April

From Sister Marie of the Eucharist to Mme. Guérin: I am sending you the few words that our Mother addressed to me on the day of my Profession; then, in the evening, we have the custom of always singing to the newly Professed, and to fete me they sang "My Weapons" composed by Sister Thérèse of the Child Jesus; then,

Mother Subprioress added for our Mother and for me some quatrains that I am sending you also. I beg you to return as soon as possible "My Weapons." I will copy them out if you wish; I have sent you the original to please you, but several Sisters asked me for it in order to copy it out, that is why I beg you to return it soon. Be very careful of it, please, as I value it like my two eyes.

April 1

From l'abbé Bellière to Mother Marie de Gonzague and Thérèse: L'-Abbé M. Barthélemy-Bellière received the precious and lovable souvenir. Deeply touched by the kindness of which he is the object, he awaits the Alleluia to tell his good and dear Mother and Sister of his gratitude, which is equalled only by that of his respectful attachment and total devotedness. (N.B. He is speaking here on his reception of the circular for Mother Geneviève of St. Teresa and the poems of Thérèse. He will write at Easter time.)

April 18

From l'abbé Bellière to Mother Marie de Gonzague: [In October 1895] I presented myself as a beggar to Mother Agnes, who received my request with kindness and gave me as Sister her whom you call our angel—and truly she has been this for me - and I feel that I owe much to her care. You, dear and good Mother, ratified what had been done.

April 25

From Sister Geneviève to Brother Simeon: When she [Thérèse] will be with Jesus, she will call me. . . . Please accept. . . the most affectionate regards from your two little Carmelites.

April 28

From Sister Marie of the Eucharist to Mme. La Néele: I leave you, sending you my biggest kiss as well as that of all your little sisters.

May 20

From Brother Simeon to Sister Geneviève: Do not be surprised at my long delay in answering your good letter of April 25. I was away from Rome. I was very sorry about the sad news you gave me concerning your excellent Sister. I really prayed for her. I love to trust that she is doing better and that her health will give you no more worries. I am saying some prayers that things may be such. . . . Give my regards to your holy Sister and your holy companions, recommending me to their prayers.

June 7
From l'abbé Bellière to Mother Marie de Gonzague: My Director, who calls me "big child," continues to direct me even in Africa; Mother, see fit to continue yours, and the customary help of my dear Sister Thérèse.

June 20
From l'abbé Bellière to Mother Marie de Gonzague: Today is a celebration in the Carmel of Lisieux, celebration for Mother, celebration for her children. . . . If I unite myself with all my heart to your whole family, I am united especially to my good and dear Sister, who, I know, is delighted and happy to honor her venerated Mother.

July 12
From Brother Simeon to Sister Geneviève: The sad news your letter brings me on the sad condition of your admirable sister is sorrowful and consoling. To die from love of Jesus, who died out of love for us, what is more sublime, more heroic, more worthy of envy!! I am praying and having others pray, however, that God preseve her and cure her for your consolation and the glory of your Lisieux Carmel.

The Holy Father is not receiving at the moment; we are having suffocating heat and can hardly breathe. I asked for the Apostolic Blessing and the Indulgence *in articulo mortis* for your holy Sister. The Holy Father granted all. It was through the intervention of the Prelate, his secretary, that the favor arrived just now.

July 21
From l'abbé Bellière to Mother Marie de Gonzague: Thank you, thank you, thank you, you first who have given me this new mark of kindness and very much real happiness by means of this photograph [of Thérèse], which is one of my most precious jewels. However, I have a sort of reticence in my gratitude, I am missing

the photograph of my dear Mother. Thanks to my Good Angel [Thérèse], who was so pleased to give it to me with you. Thanks to the religious who had the good inspiration and the honor of taking this beautiful portrait, and the one who inspired and wrote the words below, if this were not my Sister herself.

August 5

From l'abbé Bellière to Mother Marie de Gonzague: Keep Sister Thérèse for us for a long time.

August 15

From Sister Marie of the Eucharist to M. and Mme. Guérin: I send you all my love and my biggest kisses. All the little girls of the Carmel do the same, especially the little patient.

August 17

From l'abbé Bellière to Mother Marie de Gonzague: The sacrifice of the dear victim is then close to completion. What sorrow for a human creature whose angel guardian this dear soul was, and nevertheless what a consolation to know such a friend in heaven.

In two days, I am going to Lourdes. I don't know what I must ask from the Queen of Miracles - the cure of this dear saint or her prompt union with Jesus. . . . Do you know, Mother, that my good confrère, l'Abbé Troude, was blest, I envied him in a singular way. . . . I trust that his joy of July 16 will one day be granted to me. Alas! the dear Sister whom Jesus had given to me will no longer be there. Mother! oh, you will be there still and in spite of the absent one I shall still be blest.

August 28

From l'abbé Bellière to Mother Marie de Gonzague: Thank you, Mother, for these good wishes and the occasion chosen to offer them to me [feast of St. Louis], for these of my dear Saint, of which you were the inspirer in expressing them. She would have loved to send me some kind words germinated in her holy soul, and I would have been happy to receive them. Her Jesus did not will it. Long live Jesus just the same! and His will be done! Has He consoled your heart, dear Mother, are you resigned to the thought of the separation? As for myself, it seems to me that I am resigned. At Lourdes, I did not ask for her cure. Was that wrong? I prayed for the intentions of the Saint and of Our Lord, and for yours too, Mother. May the good Lady of Lourdes see fit to put the last touch to the masterpiece you are preparing for Jesus; this is what I asked her above all and that she bless Mother and her children by uniting them in her Heart.

September 19

From l'abbé Bellière to Mother Marie de Gonzague: In the midst of all the sorrow surrounding me, I no longer know where to rest my head or my heart except in your own and that of my dear Thérèse and within you family. My mother is in despair; she no longer wants to give me her consent and she spends her days and nights in crying. . . . I am so overwhelmed that I cannot write personally to my good little Sister. Speak to her, Mother, of my union with her which is more and more close and intimate. This suffering brings me somewhat closer to her (however, from quite a distance), and I am happy about this. St. Maurice will be our means of union, and I associate myself wholeheartedly to the devotion of my Sister during this month. May the brave warrior, through the intervention of this other little warrior of Carmel, give me her strength, her victory, and her love for God. I thank Divine Providence that has sent my holy Patron to my little Thérèse, and I pray to him for her. What will happen to her, the dear Saint? Often, very often, I picture her there almost lifeless and always brave. What a crown for this angel who has nothing human about her! . . . I am yours forever in the Heart of Our Lady of Sorrows, dear and good Mother and Sister.

PRINTED DOCUMENTS

This section presents the texts of two poems and a prayer mentioned in the *General Correspondence* which greatly influenced the thought and conduct at certain moments of Thérèse's life.

1. THE LITTLE FLOWER OF THE DIVINE PRISONER

The text of a poem printed on a picture given to Thérèse by Céline on the occasion of the former's reception of her First Communion. Thérèse writes about the influence this poem had on her (see *Story of a Soul*, pp. 71 and 76).

> Between two cold bars, there grew a humble plant
> That charmed away the cares of a poor prisoner.
> It was the sole happiness of his suffering soul,
> The only pastime of his dismal abode!
> Under the dark walls of his somber retreat,
> His hand had planted it...his tears had watered it!
> And as reward for his cares, he saw the poor little thing
> Give him, in return, its scents and its flowers.
>
> Ah! my Sovereign Master, within your Tabernacle,
> For eighteen hundred years, Prisoner because of love,
> In spite of our coldness, by a constant miracle,
> In our midst You have set up Your abode.
> And there, more forsaken, more solitary still
> Than the poor captive whose abandonment I pity,
> Your tenderness implores for Your perverse children,
> Those hearts whose gift these ingrates refuse You.

Alas! since they forever are bent on fleeing from You,
Since they leave You alone, O God of my heart!
Lower, out of pity, Your eyes on my lowliness,
I shall be, my Jesus, Your little flower.
Listen to the incessant prayer of my soul;
You inspire it, Lord, so answer it.
Ah! tell me, a lowly flower, how to please You,
How my soul, in Your hands, will forget itself forever.

The answer of Jesus

Well! It is in FAITH...in a NAKED FAITH
That My hand would plant this little flower,
That, living for ME ALONE...unknown by men,
Would have no other Sun but a ray from My Heart.

For this tender flower I would have as Root
That trust in Me which never grows weak;
Infinite hope in My divine Bounty,
That surrender of the child who knows I love it.

As Stem, it must have, without desire and without fear,
A tranquil, a joyful, a prompt acquiescence
To the lightest call of My Holy Will,
With no hesitation...with no reasoning.

It would delight Me, if, taking as its foliage
Contempt for esteem and human observation,
It could veil from the eyes that behold it
The gifts it has received from My divine hands.

As Flower for it I would want a constant joy
That neither dreams nor sorrows could trouble,
That even as prey to suffering and to bitterness
It would still know how to rejoice in My joy.

Finally, its Fruit would be that virtue so pure

That sees nothing but GOD ALONE. . .here below as in heaven
That no longer has regard for any creature,
That seeks only in ME the goal of its longings.

Thus, realizing the expectation of My designs,
It will have merited that sweetest of favors:
And on My Sacred Heart, grafting My humble plant,
In uniting it to MYSELF, I shall make up its happiness.

2. THE TOY OF JESUS

A simple leaflet without references to publisher or author. The
latter was Père Jean Léonard, Abbot of Frontfroide (1815-1985),
founder of the Cistercian Congregation of Sénanque. The Carmel
archives have several copies of this leaflet.

Thérèse became acquainted with it by means of Sister Agnes of
Jesus, at the end of October or beginning of November 1887. The
theme of the "little ball" or "little toy" owes its origin to this poem.
It was used frequently by Thérèse in her writings; see LT 34, note 2.

You are suffering, Jesus, my little brother,
And to dry Your tears, You have no toy.
I come to offer myself to You; You will want, I hope,
To play with this poor object.

In your hands, I would like to possess the suppleness
Of a ball pliant to the whim of Your desire.
Throw me, break me, I want to be insensible
To everything except Your good pleasure.

The harder You will throw me against the ground,
The higher, my gentle Jesus, I shall bounce to You;
I do not fear Your strikes, O my Friend, my Brother,
Amuse Yourself always with me.

You will that at times it be the creature
Who casts me off with contempt, disdain.

Then, very promptly, I roll without complaint,
Jesus, towards Your gentle hand.

When lifting me up with Your amiable smile,
You say: "I am content!" I bounce with delight,
Suffering becomes a game when Your adorable Heart
Can rejoice in my suffering.

Oh! throw! throw again! My proud nature
Has need of buffets to lift itself to You;
My soul, in Your hands, rebounds more joyfully
When You come to humble me.

If You will, throw me to reach souls,
In order that in touching them, I draw them to You.
I shall whisper to them that their hearts seek You,
To You the honor, nothing for me.

Formerly, from the heavens You hastened towards suffering,
It was the supreme desire of Your Heart.
I want to resemble You, O my childhood Friend,
For Your love, to suffer too!

3. A PRAYER OF GENERAL DE SONIS

A simple leaflet preserved by Thérèse in her *Christian Manual*.
We see in the fourth paragraph, the symbol of the "grain of sand,"
frequently used in the *General Correspondence* of 1888-1890. See
LT 45, note 4.

My God,
Here I am before You, poor, little, destitute of everything.
I am nothing. I have nothing. I can do nothing.
I am here at Your feet plunged into my nothingness.
I would like to have something to offer You, but I am only
misery.
You, You are my All. You are my riches.

My God, I thank You for having willed that I be nothing in Your presence. I love my humiliation, my nothingness. I thank You for having withdrawn from me certain satisfactions of self-love, certain spiritual consolations. I thank You for disappointments, worries, humiliations. I know that I needed them, and that these goods could have held me back from You.

I love to be broken, consumed, destroyed by You.

Reduce me to nothing more and more.

May I be in the building, not like the stone worked and polished by the laborer's hand, *but like the grain of obscure sand hidden by the dust of the road.*

MY GOD, I thank You for having allowed me to glimpse the sweetness of Your consolations. I thank You for having deprived me of them. All that You do is just and good. I bless You in my poverty. I regret nothing, except for not having loved You enough. I desire nothing except that Your will may be done.

You are my Master, I am Your possession. Turn me and turn me over again. Destroy me and work me. I want to be reduced to nothing for love of You.

O Jesus! How gentle is Your hand even at the height of the trial! May I be crucified but crucified by You! Amen.

BIOGRAPHICAL GUIDE FOR PROPER NAMES

ACARD, AUGUSTE-FERDINAND (1864-1931)

Gardener, workman, and sacristan at the Carmel of Lisieux from 1889 to 1912. See *Last Conversations*, p. 186.

AGNES OF JESUS, MOTHER (1861-1951)

Marie Pauline Martin, sister and "little Mother" to Thérèse; born at Alençon, second child of the Martin family; made her studies at the Visitation convent at Le Mans from 1868 to 1877; upon her mother's death, she undertook the care and education of Thérèse, who was four and a half; she entered Carmel of Lisieux on October 2, 1882, received the Habit on April 6, 1883, and made Profession on May 8, 1884, the same day that Thérèse received her first Commuinion.

She was elected Prioress on February 20, 1893; was reelected on April 19, 1902, and, with the exception of eighteen months, from May, 1908 to November, 1909, she was to remain in this office until her death in 1951.

AIMÉE OF JESUS, SISTER (1851-1930)

A Carmelite nun of Lisieux. She entered Carmel on October 13, 1871, received the Habit on March 19, 1872, and was professed on May 8, 1873. She was physically strong and very gentle, and upon the request of Sister Thérèse, she held the latter in her arms when she could barely be touched. Sister Aimée was the only one not present at Sister Thérèse's death on September 30, 1897, because she did not hear the infirmary bell summoning the members of the community. She testified at the Process.

ANNE OF JESUS, VENERABLE (1545-1621)

A spanish Carmelite nun, née Ana de Lobera. She was companion to St. Teresa of Avila in the early days of the Carmelite Reform, and was to become one of the foundresses of Carmel in France in 1604. Sister Thérèse had a dream in which she saw and spoke with Venerable Anne of Jesus. Cf. *Story of a Soul*, p. 191.

BELLIÈRE, MAURICE, REVEREND (1874-1907)

Spiritual brother to Sister Thérèse. He was born at Caen; began his studies for the priesthood in October, 1894. The following year, October 15, 1895, he wrote the Carmel of Lisieux asking that one of the nuns pray for his vocation. Mother Agnes, Prioress, assigned her sister Thérèse as his spiritual sister. He left for Algiers to enter the novitiate of the White Fathers. He was ordained on June 29, 1901, and assigned to the mission at Nyassa. He returned to France in January, 1906, because of poor health and died at Caen the following year.

CLODION LE CHEVELU

A nickname given to Dr. de Cornière by Thérèse because of the way he wore his hair; historically, Clodion was the chief of a Franklin tribe (d. 447).

DE CORNIÈRE, ALEXANDRE-DAMASE (1841-1922)

This was the doctor who took care of Thérèse. He was born at Bonnebosq (Calvados); made his medical studies at Caen and Paris, and began to practice medicine at Lisieux in 1869. He was doctor at the Carmel for a period of almost thirty years, 1886-1920. He took care of Thérèse during her last illness, with the exception of the month of August when he was away on vacation. (She was then attended to by Dr. La Néele, a relative of Thérèse through marriage). Dr. de Cornière was the father of seven children; was a fervent Christian and took care of many poor people free of charge. He died at Lisieux.

DE CORNIÈRE, JOSEPH, REVEREND (1874-1939)

The oldest son of Dr. de Cornière, born at Lisieux. He made an attempt to become a Redemptorist in Holland (1892) and in South

America (1893). He was invited by the Guérin family to La Musse for the summer vacations of 1893 and 1894. He was ordained a priest for the Bayeux diocese where he worked until his death.

DENIS DE MAROY, JOSEPH, REVEREND (1871–1962)

Born at Paris, ordained at Bayeux on September 18, 1897, he said his first Mass at the Carmel of Liseiux the following day, September 19.

Cf. *Last Conversations*, p. 192.

DUCELLIER, ALCIDE, REVEREND (1849–1916)

Born at Chicheboville (Calvados), ordained priest in 1874, he worked as one of the assistants at St. Peter's in Lisieux from 1877 to 1884. He heard Thérèse's first confession around 1880 and remained her confessor until her entrance at the Benedictine Abbey for her studies in October, 1881. He preached the sermon for Pauline's reception of the Habit; also preached for Céline's reception of the Habit and the Veil. Spiritual director to Mother Agnes of Jesus. Testified at the Process.

FAUCON, PIERRE, REVEREND (1842–1918)

Born at Ondefontaine (Calvados), he was ordained a priest on June 29, 1868. Father Faucon was extraordinary confessor at the Carmel from 1886–1891; he heard Thérèse's last confession on September 29, 1897. He testified at the Process.

FOURNET, ELISA-ERNESTINE (1816–1901)

Born at Liseiux, daughter of Pierre-Antoine Petit and Marie-Roslaie Monsaint, she married Pierre-Celestin Fournet on November 11, 1839 and had four children, one of whom, Céline, was the future Mme. Guérin, aunt to Thérèse. On May 12, 1866, the Fournets sold their pharmacy to M. Isidore Guérin. Céline Martin and her sister Thérèse gave the name of "grandmamma" to Mme. Fournet.

GENEVIÈVE OF ST. TERESA, SISTER (1869–1959)

Sister to Thérèse and one of her novices.

Céline, born at Alençon, the seventh child of the nine of the Martin family, she made her first Communion on May 13, 1880 at the

Benedictine Abbey where she made her studies from 1877–1885. She stayed with her father, Louis Martin, during his long illness at Caen, Lisieux, La Musse (1889–1894). She entered Carmel on September 14, 1894, taking the name of Sister Marie of the Holy Face; she received the Habit on February 5, 1895, her name being changed to Sister Geneviève of St. Teresa in memory of the foundress; she was professed on February 24, 1896, and received the Veil on March 17, 1896. Céline made her novitiate under Thérèse's guidance. She was assigned as infirmarian-aide and later on became infirmarian to her sister during the last months of her life. In 1916, she took the name of Sister Geneviève of the Holy Face. Sister Geneviève played an important role in the spread of St. Thérèse's message, both through her writing and her portraits of St. Thérèse. She was the one who took the many photos of Thérèse that we still have today. She testified at the Process.

GENEVIÈVE OF ST. TERESA, MOTHER (1805–1891)

Claire Bertrand, born at Poitiers, entered the Carmel of that city on March 26, 1830. She became Mistress of novices in 1837, and was sent as foundress to Lisieux on March 16, 1838. She was elected Prioress for five terms. Dr. de Cornière attended to her during her last illness and admired her for her courage. Thérèse witnessed her death in the infirmary (cf. *Story of a Soul*, p. 169), in the very same bed she was to occupy later on in her last illness in 1897.

GUÉRIN, CÉLINE (1847–1900)

Aunt of Thérèse.

Born at Lisieux to Pierre-Celestin Fournet and Elisa-Ernestine Petit. She married Isidore Guérin on September 11, 1866, and had three children, two girls, Jeanne and Marie, and a boy who was stillborn; upon the death of Mme. Martin, sister to Isidore Guérin, the Martin family moved to Lisieux from Alençon, and Mme. Guérin played a mother's role to her five nieces: Pauline, Marie, Léonie, Céline, and Thérèse. These visited the Guérin home each week with their father, Louis Martin. At the time of her illness, Thérèse was supplied by Mme. Guérin with choice dishes to tempt her to eat more. She died in Lisieux.

GUÉRIN, ISIDORE (1841–1909)
Uncle of Thérèse.
Born at Saint-Denis-sur-Sarthon (Orne) to Isidore Guérin and Louise-Jeanne Mace, who had three children, one of whom, Zélie, was to become the mother of St. Thérèse. Isidore made his studies as a pharmacist in Paris (1862) and received his license to practice in 1866. He set up his business at Lisieux, place St. Pierre, buying the Fournet pharmacy, whose daughter, Céline, he married on September 11, 1866.

He was named deputy guardian of his nieces on September 16, 1877, upon the death of their mother, and he estabished them in Les Buissonnets at Lisieux. Isidore inherited the chateau at La Musse in August of 1888 and sold his pharmacy to Victor Lahaye (see Lahaye below). He took on the role of father to his nieces when their own father, Louis Martin, had a paralytic stroke, taking him into his own home in order to tend to his needs in his old age. A militant Christian, he established the work of the nocturnal adoration in Lisieux in June, 1895. He was to play an important role in the publication of *Histoire d'une Âme* in 1898. His old age was saddened by the death of his wife, February 13, 1900, and his younger daughter, Marie, in 1905. She had entered the Carmel of Lisieux and was one of Thérèse's novices, taking the name of Sister Marie of the Eucharist.

HERMANCE OF THE HEART OF JESUS, MOTHER (1833–1898)
Madeleine Pichery, born at Honfleur; she entered the Lisieux Carmel on May 14, 1858, received the Habit on November 24, 1858, and was professed on December 2, 1859. In 1866, she became foundress of the Carmel at Coutances, returning to the Lisieux Carmel in 1882 because of sickness. She was quite a trial to the infirmarians because of her difficult character. Sister Thérèse predicted her death.

HUGONIN, FLAVIEN-ABEL-ANTOINE, BISHOP (1823–1898)
Bishop at Bayeux and Lisieux during the lifetime of Thérèse.
Born at Thodure (Isère), he was made bishop of Bayeux on July 13, 1866. He was the one who confirmed Thérèse, June 6, 1884, and was later to receive M. Martin and his daughter, Thérèse, October 31, 1887, when she was seeking permission to enter Carmel at the

age of fifteen. Two years later, he gave her the Habit, January 10, 1889; he presided at Céline's taking of the Veil and Marie Guérin's reception of the Habit on March 17, 1896. He was later on to grant the imprimatur for the publishing of *Histoire d'une Âme (Story of a Soul)*, March 7, 1898.

LA NÉELE, FRANCISQUE-LUCIEN-SULPICE, DOCTOR (1858–1916)

Doctor of Thérèse during the absence of Dr. de Cornière, and her cousin through his marriage to Jeanne Guérin.

Born at Paris, he made his studies with the Jesuits; pharmacist and medical doctor. Married Jeanne Guérin on October 1, 1890. Sold his pharmacy, November 26, 1891, and opened a doctor's office at Caen, 24 rue de l'Oratoire. He was called in to take care of Thérèse during her own doctor's absence, and he visited her three times during the months of August and September of 1897.

LA NÈELE, JEANNE-MARIE-ELISA (1868–1938)

First cousin to Thérèse.

Daughter of Isidore and Céline Guérin, born at Lisieux. Married Dr. Francis La Néele on October 1, 1890. Thérèse helped her in accepting the sacrifice of not having children of her own. She testified at the Process. After her husband's death, she adopted one of her grand-nieces. She died at Nogent-le-Rotrou.

MARIE DE GONZAGUE, MOTHER (1834–1904)

Prioress of the Carmel of Lisieux.

Marie-Adèle-Rosalie Davy de Virville, born at Caen. She entered the Carmel on November 29, 1860, received the Habit, May 30, 1861, and made Profession on June 27, 1862.

Elected Subprioress in 1866 and 1869, she then served six terms as Prioress, leaving upon the community the mark of her strong personality. She was elected again after Mother Agnes of Jesus had served out her first term from 1893–96, and she was in office until April 19, 1902. Mother Marie de Gonzague died of cancer on December 17, 1904, with sentiments of great devotion to Thérèse.

MARIE OF JESUS, SISTER (1862–1938)

Eugénie-Henriette-Amélie Courceau was born in Rouen. She entered the Carmel of Lisieux on April 26, 1883, received the Habit on October 15, 1883, and was professed on December 5, 1884. She tried the patience of Thérèse during the hours of prayer through a strange habit she had of clicking her teeth together (cf. *Story of a Soul*, p. 249). In 1897, she occasionally helped the infirmarians, and thus she witnessed some of the sessions of painful cauterization which Thérèse was subjected to.

MARIE OF THE TRINITY AND THE HOLY FACE (1874–1944)

A novice of Thérèse.

Marie-Louise-Joséphine Castel, born at Saint-Pierre-sur-Dives (Calvados), the thirteenth in a family of nineteen children. She entered the Carmel of Paris, l'avenue de Messine, April 30, 1891; she received the Habit on March 12, 1892, however, poor health forced her to leave on July 8, 1893. The Carmel of Lisieux received her as a postulant on June 16, 1894. Thérèse did all in her power to help her realize her vocation. Her Profession took place on April 30, 1896. As infirmarian-aide, Sister Marie of the Trinity was aware of Thérèse's hemoptysis in April, 1896, but she did not take care of Thérèse in 1897 in the infirmary because of her youth and the fear she would contract the disease. She wrote down her memories of the novice mistress; her testimony at the Process was important.

MARIE OF THE EUCHARIST, SISTER (1870–1905)

First cousin of Thérèse and one of her novices.

Marie Guérin, born at Lisieux, was the second daughter of Isidore and Céline Guérin. She made her studies at the Benedictine abbey of Lisieux with Thérèse. She entered Carmel on August 15, 1895, received the Habit on March 17, 1896, and was professed on March 25, 1897. Thérèse helped her novice overcome her scruples. Marie's correspondence with her family remains a precious source of information on the last months of Thérèse, giving minute details of the progress of her illness. She died of tuberculosis at the age of thirty-five in spite of the cares of her brother-in-law, Dr. La Néele, and the use of new treatments introduced at this time.

MARIE OF THE INCARNATION, LAY SISTER (1828–1911)

Born Zephirine Lecouturier at Firfol, near Lisieux. She entered Carmel on August 10, 1852, received the Habit August 3, 1853, and was professed November 14, 1854. This Sister was the one mentioned by Thérèse (cf. *Story of a Soul*, p. 227) who stopped to chatter with her about all sorts of things: hay, ducks, hens, in order to distract her when she was sick in June, 1897.

MARIE OF ST. JOSEPH, SISTER (1858–1936)

Born Marie-Josephine-Lucie Campain at Valognes (Manche). She entered the Carmel on April 28, 1881, received the Habit on October 15, 1881, and was professed on October 15, 1882. She had a very difficult temperament and was a trial to the community. In 1896, Thérèse volunteered her services to help this Sister in the linen room where no other Sister was able to remain. Marie of St. Joseph left the Carmel in June 1909.

MARIE OF THE ANGELS AND THE SACRED HEART, SISTER (1845–1924)

Mistress of Novices at the time of Thérèse's entrance.

Born Jeanne de Chaumontel at Montpinçon (Calvados), she entered Carmel on October 29, 1866, received the Habit on March 19, 1867, and was professed on March 25, 1868. Marie of the Angels was Subprioress from 1883 to 1886, and was placed in charge of the novices from October, 1886, to February, 1893. From 1893 to 1899 she was again Subprioress; besides, she took charge of the novitiate after the death of Thérèse and remained in this charge until 1909. She testified at the Process.

MARIE OF THE SACRED HEART, SISTER (1860–1940)

Sister and godmother of Thérèse.

Louise-Joséphine-Marie, born at Alençon, was the oldest of the Martin children. She acted as godmother to Thérèse on January 4, 1873. Father Pichon, S.J., aided her in finding her vocation. She entered the Carmel of Lisieux on October 15, 1886, received the Habit on March 19, 1887, and was professed on May 22, 1888. For a short time she was a novice with Thérèse, who had entered on April 9, 1888. She was the one who had suggested that Thérèse write her "childhood memories" and requested that Thérèse write her retreat inspirations out for her. Thus we owe to her Mss. A and B of the *Story of a Soul.*

She suffered for many years and right up to her death from rheumatism in the joints.

MARIE-ELIZABETH OF ST. TERESA, SISTER (1860–1935)

Marie-Antoinette-Eugénie Hamard, born at Couterne (Orne), entered the Carmel of Lisieux on July 7, 1890, but not as one of the cloistered nuns; she was an extern. She made her profession on October 15, 1891. Sister Marie-Elizabeth knew Thérèse through the latter's duties at the turn and in the sacristy; on several occasions, she entered the infirmary to take care of Thérèse while the nuns were attending Sunday Mass. She represented the community at the burial of Thérèse, who was buried in the city cemetery, October 4, 1897. Sister testified at the Process.

MARIE-MADELEINE OF THE BLESSED SACRAMENT, LAY SISTER (1869–1916)

One of Thérèse's novices.

Born Méline-Marie-Françoise Le Bon at Plouguenast (Côtes-du-Nord), she entered Carmel on July 22, 1892, received the Habit on September 7, 1893, and was professed in November, 1894. On this occasion, Thérèse wrote her poem entitled: "*Histoire d'une bergère devenue Reine.*" ("Story of a shepherdess become Queen.") She testified at the Process.

MARIE-PHILOMÈNE OF JESUS, SISTER (1839–1924)

Noémie-Colombe-Alexandrine Jacquemin, born at Langrune (Calvados), entered Carmel on October 13, 1876, but she had to leave it in order to take care of her dying mother; she entered again on November 7, 1884, and made her Profession at forty-six, March 25, 1886.

MARTHA OF JESUS, LAY SISTER (1865–1916)

Novice of Thérèse.

Désirée-Florence-Martha Cauvin, born at Giverville (Eure), entered Carmel on December 23, 1887, received the Habit on May 2, 1889, and was professed on September 23, 1890. She wanted to remain in the novitiate with Thérèse. The latter aided her in freeing herself from the too strong influence of Mother Marie de Gonzague (cf. *Story of a Soul*, p. 236). She testified at the Process.

MARTIN, MARIE-LÈONIE, SISTER OF THÉRÈSE (1863–1941)

The third of the Martin children, born at Alençon, of a delicate and difficult temperament, she was the cause of much anxiety to her mother. She made several attempts at the religious life: the Poor Clares at Alençon (October, 1886), the Visitation at Caen (from July, 1887 to January 6, 1888). At the age of thirty, she was postulant once more in this order (June 24, 1893), but had to leave in 1895. She lived then with her Uncle Guérin. After the death of Thérèse, she entered definitively the Visitation at Caen (January 28, 1899) and took the name of Sister Françoise-Thérèse. She carried on a great correspondence with her sisters at Lisieux Carmel until her death. She testified at the Process.

MAUPAS, ALEXANDRE-CHARLES, REVEREND (1850–1920)

Ecclesiastical Superior of the Lisieux Carmel.

Born at Mesnil-Auxouf (Calvados). Attended the seminaries of Vire, Sommervieu, and Bayeux. Ordained priest on June 29, 1874; eventually became assistant at St. Jacques' parish at Lisieux in 1895, where he succeeded his cousin, Reverend Delatroëtte. He replaced the latter also as Superior of the Carmel. He administered the last sacraments to Thérèse on September 30, 1897. He testified at the Process.

MAZEL, FREDERIC, REVEREND (1871–1897)

A missionary and fellow student of Father Foulland. He was assassinated in China on April 1, 1897.

PICHON, ALMIRE, REVEREND (1843–1919)

Born at Carrouges (Orne), he entered the novitiate of the Company of Jesus on October 30, 1863, was ordained priest on September 8, 1873. In 1882, he became spiritual director of Marie Martin. In August, 1883, he met Thérèse. Father Pichon preached a retreat at the Carmel of Lisieux in October, 1887, and again in May, 1888,

Thérèse being a postulant. He reassured her after she had made a general confession (cf. *Story of a Soul*, p. 149). He was sent to Canada as a missionary (1884–1886; 1888–1907) and Thérèse corresponded with him. He did not keep any of her letters. Father Pichon testified at the Process.

POTTIER, CÉLINE (1873–1949)

A childhood friend of Thérèse.

Marie-Céline-Ernestine Maudelonde, daughter of Marie-Rosalie Fournet (sister of Mme. Guérin) and Césard-Alexandre Maudelonde, was exactly the same age as Thérèse; they played together as children (cf. *Story of a Soul*, p. 54). She married Gaston Pottier on June 19, 1894, and had two children.

PROU, ALEXIS, REVEREND (1844–1914)

Born at St. Pazanne (Loire Atlantique), he entered the Franciscans when already a subdeacon (September 4, 1869) and was ordained priest on June 29, 1871. Guardian or Superior of the Franciscan house of St. Nazaire, he preached a retreat at the Carmel of Lisieux (October 8–15, 1891), which was the occasion of important graces for Thérèse (cf. *Story of a soul*, p. 173).

ROULLAND, ADOLPHE, REVEREND (1870–1934)

Spiritual brother to Thérèse.

Born at Cahognolles (Calvados), he entered the Foreign Missions seminary at Paris. On May 30, 1896, he asked Mother Marie de Gonzague that one of her religious be associated with him in his missionary apostolate. Thérèse was assigned to this by the Prioress. He was ordained a priest (June 28, 1896), and he said his first Mass and met Thérèse at the Carmel on July 3, 1896. He sailed for China on August 2, 1896. Father Roulland carried on an important correspondence with his spiritual sister. He was recalled to France in 1909, and he testified at the Process.

ST. JOHN OF THE CROSS, SISTER (1851–1906)

Alice-Emilie Bourgeret, born at Torigny-sur-Vire (Manche), entered the Carmel on April 21, 1876, received the Habit on December 8, 1876, and was professed on January 17, 1878. She used to visit Thérèse in the infirmary, and her visits were not too consoling to Thérèse because she seemed somewhat unsympathetic towards the patient. Cf. *Last Conversations*, p. 167.

SAINT-RAPHAEL OF THE HEART OF MARY, SISTER (1840–1918)

Born Laure-Stéphanie Gayat at Le Havre, she entered Carmel on February 24, 1868, received the Habit on June 26 of the same year. She made her Profession on July 6, 1869. Thérèse was her helper at the turn and had to practice much patience with her because of her difficult character.

SAINT-STANISLAUS OF THE SACRED HEARTS, SISTER (1824–1914)

Thérèse's infirmarian; oldest member of the community.

Marie-Rosalie Guéret, born at Lisieux, was one of the first Carmelites of the foundation (founded in 1838); she entered on April 6, 1845, received the Habit on January 15, 1846, and was professed on February 8, 1847. She carried out many functions during her long life, being sacristan, infirmarian, etc. Thérèse was her helper in the sacristy. Sister St. Stanislaus was her infirmarian during the beginning stages of her illness.

ST. VINCENT DE PAUL, LAY SISTER (1841–1905)

Born Zoé-Adèle Alaterre at Cherbourg, she entered the Carmel on February 2, 1864, received the Habit on December 8, 1864, and was professed on December 14, 1865. She made Thérèse suffer much as a novice by reproaching her for her slowness in carrying out her duties. After the death of the Saint, she was the first to benefit from one of her miracles: she was cured of cerebral anemia after kissing the feet of the dead Thérèse.

THÉRÈSE OF ST. AUGUSTINE, SISTER (1856–1929)

Julia-Marie-Elise Leroyer, born at Cressonnière (Calvados) entered the Carmel on May 1, 1875, received the Habit on October 15 of the same year, and was professed on May 1, 1877. Thérèse experienced a natural antipathy for the good religious (cf. *Story of a Soul*, p. 222), but her exterior charity persuaded Sister Thérèse of St.

Augustine of just the opposite. After the death of St. Thérèse, this Sister wrote her memories of a holy friendship which brought out some of her last conversations with Thérèse. She testified at the Process.

TROUDE, PAUL-FRANÇOIS, REVEREND (1873–1900)

Born at Langrune (Calvados), fellow student of Reverend Bellière (first spiritual brother of St. Thérèse), he was ordained a priest on June 29, 1897. He was a nephew to Sister Marie-Philomène, and he celebrated Mass on the feast of Our Lady of Mount Carmel, July 16, 1897, in the chapel of the Lisieux Carmel. A contemporary of St. Thérèse, he died only a few years after her.

VÉNARD, THÉOPHANE, MARTYR (1829–1861)

Born at St. Loup-sur-Thouet (Deux-Sèvres), he was a young priest from the Foreign Missions at Paris, who was beheaded in Hanoi. He was beatified by Pius X on May 2, 1909. Thérèse had read his biography and letters. She composed a poem in his honor on February 2, 1897, and she kept his portrait before her eyes during her illness, having it pinned to the curtains of her bed. Very frequently in her last conversations she made direct references to him.

YOUF, LOUIS-AUGUSTE, REVEREND (1842–1897)

Chaplain of the Lisieux Carmel.

Born at Caen, he attended the seminaries of Villiers, Bayeux, and was ordained a priest in 1869. He became assistant of St. Jacques' parish in Lisieux· and chaplain of the Carmel from July, 1873 till his death, a week after that of Thérèse, October 7, 1897. He was Thérèse's ordinary confessor all through her religious life.

CHRONOLOGY

This chronology gathers together biographical data concerning Thérèse, scattered throughout the two volumes of *General Correspondence*. It draws attention to some of her writings: letters, poems, prayers, etc.

ALENÇON

(1873–1877)

1873

January 2: 11:30 p.m., birth of Marie-Françoise-Thérèse Martin, at 36, rue Saint-Blaise (today, no. 42).

January 4: baptism in the church of Notre-Dame; godmother: her eldest sister, Marie (13 years old).

January 14: first smile at her mother (p. 1200).

January 17: first symptoms of enteritis (ibid)

March 1: Thérèse is "very sick" (p. 1201).

March 11: at the last moment, she is saved by the wet nurse, Rosalie Taillé (p. 1204).

March 15 or 16: taken to the home of "little Rose" Taillé at Semallé (p. 1204).

April 20: "in good health and very strong" (p. 1206).

July 20: "big baby...browned by the sun" (p. 1208).

October 27: "very strong and big" (1208).

1874

January 8: "walks alone...sweet and darling" (1209).

April 2: definitive return to Alençon; "very much advanced for her age" (ibid)

June 24: "begins to say almost anything" (1210).

1875

March 29: trip by train to Le Mans with her mother (p. 1214).

May 19: "persistent cough" (ibid)

October 24: "little humorous child...attractive, mischievous, and darling" (p. 1217).

November 5: does not want to sleep until she says her prayers (p. 1218).

November 21: "So many steps, so many 'Mamma!'" (ibid).

December 5: "gets into frightful states of fury...very nervous" (p. 1219).

December 28: "knows almost all the letters of the alphabet" (1220.) "At the age of two," thinks: "I will be a religious."

1876

May 14: "has an almost invincible stubbornness...very honest" (p. 1223).

Around July 16: first photo (p. 1225).

November 8: "wants at times to join in the practices (of virtue)" (p. 1226).

Mid-November: "all the symptoms of the measles" (p. 1228).

December 24: Mme. Martin consults Dr. Notta about a tumor on the breast; "it is too late" for an operation (CF, p. 336).

During 1876: "At the age of three, I began refusing nothing that God was asking from me" (DE, p. 717).

1877

February 24: death of Sister Marie-Dosithée Guérin, Visitandine at Le Mans, sister of Mme. Martin.

March 4: Thérèse "wants to know what day it is" (p. 1232).

April 3: "I shall be a religious in a cloister" (p. 108).

April 4: first letter of Thérèse (p. 110).

April 9: family outing at Semallé (p. 111).

May: "makes her prayer leaping with joy...roguish and not silly" (p. 113).

June 18–23: pilgrimage of Mme. Martin, Marie, Pauline, and Léonie to Lourdes (p. 117).

August 1 (?): "distribution of prizes" for Céline and Thérèse (p. 1236).

August 28: death of Mme. Martin at 12:30 a.m.

August 29: burial; Thérèse chooses Pauline (sixteen years old) as her second mother (p. 117).

September 9: M. Guérin finds at Lisieux a house for the Martin family: "les Buiussonnets" (p. 118).

CHRONOLOGY

LISIEUX

Les Buissonnets (1877–1888)

November 15: arrival of Thérèse and her sisters at Lisieux, conducted by Uncle Guérin.

November 16: settling in at Les Buissonnets (p. 129).

1878

April: for the first time, she understands a sermon (on the Passion).

June 17–July 2: trip of M. Martin, Marie, and Pauline to Paris (p. 131). Thérèse is placed in the charge of her aunt Guérin.

August 8: sees the ocean for the first time at Trouville (p. 134).

1879

During the year: first visit to the chapel of Carmel (Ms. A, p. 36).

Summer (or 1880): prophetic vision of her father's illness (p. 126).

End of the year (or beginning of 1880): first confession (ibid).

1880

Beginning of the year: writes without help (p. 136).

May 13: First Communion of Céline (p. 126).

August 9: reads "La Soeur de Gribouille" (p. 137).

December 1: first letter (preserved) written alone (p. 140).

1881

July 10: M. Martin gives a Magpie to Thérèse (p. 144).

October 3: entrance at the Benedictine Abbey at Lisieux as day-boarder (p. 146).

1882

January 12: enrollment in the Work of the Holy Childhood (DE, p. 483).

February 16: Pauline receives her vocation to Carmel (p. 148).

April 17: Marie takes P. Pichon as her spiritual director.

May 31: Thérèse is received as "Child of the Holy Angels" (p. 224).

Summer: learns by surprise of Pauline's coming departure; feels she is called to Carmel (p. 148).

October 2: entrance of Pauline to Carmel (Sister Agnes of Jesus). New school year of Thérèse with the Benedictines. Céline receives lessons in drawing. Thérèse "burns with envy" to imitate her but keeps silent (p. 210).

October 15: celebrations for the third centenary of St. Teresa of Avila's death.

December: headaches, insomnia, "pimples and plasters" (p. 154).

1883

January 31: Mother Geneviève of Saint Teresa is elected prioress of the Carmel (p. 160).

March 25 (Easter): during a stay at Paris of M. Martin, Marie, and Léonie, beginning of Thérèse's nervous illness at the Guérin home; trembling, hallucinations (p. 161).

April 6: Pauline's reception of the Habit (Sister Agnes); a little better, Thérèse kisses her sister in the speakroom (p. 164).

April 7: relapse at Les Buissonnets (p. 161).

April 8: death of grandmother Martin at Valframbert, Orne (p. 167).

May 13 (Pentecost): sudden cure by "the ravishing smile of the Blessed Virgin" (p. 163).

May: visit with Sister Agnes and the other Carmelites; beginning of her scruples regarding the illness (lasting till May 1888) and of the smile of the Virgin (till November 1887) (pp. 174, 175).

Second half of August: vacation at Alençon, in the chateaux and the surroundings, with her father and sisters (p. 174).

August 22: first meeting with P. Pichon at Alençon.

October 1: reentrance at the Abbey, second class.

1884

January: entrance of Henri Chéron as assistant to M. Guérin in his pharmacy (ChrIG, p. 33).

February–May: with Sister Agnes' aid, fervent preparation for her First Communion (pp. 181 ff.).

April 2: received as Communicant in the Catechism examination (p. 196).

May 4: Thérèse enters the Abbey as boarder for four days.

May 5–8: preparatory retreat, instructions by l'abbé Domin (p. 198).

May 8: First Communion of Thérèse at the Abbey: Profession of Sister Agnes at the Carmel. Interior peace for one year (p. 203).

May 22 (Ascension): receives Communion for second time (ibid).

June 14: Confirmation by Bishop Hugonin, bishop of Bayeux, at the Abbey (ibid).

June 21 (?): Sister Agnes' poem in set rhymes on the cat Mira.

June 26: arrival at Les Buissonnets of Tom, Thérèse's spaniel (p. 238).

July–August: Whooping cough.

July 16: taking of the black Veil by Mother Agnes of Jesus.

Beginning of August: vacation at Saint-Ouen-le-Pin at the Guérins (p. 204).

August 8: Thérèse sketches the farm of Saint-Ouen (p. 207).

September 25: enrollment in the Holy Rosary Confraternity (DE, p. 483).

October 4: Marie goes to Le Havre with her father to meet P. Pichon leaving for Canada.

October 6 (?): Thérèse goes to the Abbey for the school year (p. 204).

December 14: nominated counsellor of the Association of the Holy Angels at the Abbey (p. 224).

1885

April 26: enrolled in the Confraternity of the Holy Face at Tours (DE, p. 483).

April 29 (?)–June 5: stay of the Guérins at Deauville, maison Colombe (p. 225 and ChrIG, p. 34).

May 3–10: Thérèse on vacation at Deauville; sketches the "*Chalet des Roses*"; headaches; "the donkey and the little dog" (pp. 213, 222).

May 17–21: retreat in preparation for Solemn Communion; instructions by l'abbé Domin. Beginning of her scruples, lasting till autumn 1886 (p. 226).

May 21: Solemn Communion.

July: Thérèse has her linnet (p. 239).

End of July: "really happy" on vacation at Saint-Ouen-le-Pin (p. 228).

August 4: Céline completes her schooling at the Abbey.

August 22: departure of M. Martin for Constantinople, trip lasting seven weeks (pp. 229, 1242–43).

September 3–30 (?): vacation of the Guérins at the *Villa Rose*, at Trouville (p. 234).

September 20–30 (?): vacation of Céline and Thérèse at Trouville (ibid and p. 226).

Beginning of October: Thérèse begins classes alone at the Abbey (p. 226).

October 10–17 (?): return of M. Martin to Lisieux (p. 237).

October 15: enrollment of Thérèse in the Apostolate of Prayer (DE, p. 483).

1886

February 2: Reception as aspirant into the Children of Mary (p. 239).

February 3: Mother Marie de Gonzague elected prioress of the Carmel; Sister Marie of the Angels, subprioress and mistress of novices.

February–March: headaches, M. Martin removes Thérèse definitively from the Abbey; special lessons with Mme. Papinau (p. 226); Thérèse arranges a study for herself in the attic (p. 239).

June 15–July 31: vacation of the Guérins at Trouville, chalet des Lilas (p. 240).

June 30 (?): arrival of Thérèse at Trouville; nostalgia at the end of three days (p. 242).

August: Thérèse learns of Marie's coming departure for the Carmel (pp. 227, 246).

September 21: resumption of lessons with Mme. Papineau.

September 29: trip of M. Martin and Marie to Calais, Douvres, Paris, to meet P. Pichon returning from Canada (p. 248).

October 3 (?): return of the above to Les Buissonnets.

October 5 (?): trip of M. Martin and his daughters to Alençon for a few days (p. 227).

October 7: Léonie enters without any warning the Poor Clares at Alençon (ibid).

October 15: entrance of Marie (Sister Marie of the Sacred Heart) to the Carmel of Lisieux (pp. 227, 249).

End of October (?): Thérèse freed from her scruples (p. 227).

December 1: return of Léonie to the family (p. 251).

December 25: after the midnight Mass, grace of "conversion" at Les Buissonnets; beginning of the "giant's race" (p. 259).

1887

For Céline and Thérèse, life at Les Buissonnets, this year, is "the ideal of happiness" (p. 263).

January–May: Céline gives drawing lessons to Thérèse (p. 261).

March 19: reception of the Habit of Sister Marie of the Sacred Heart; sermon by P. Pichon (pp. 262, 1245 and 318).

Night of March 19 to 20: Pranzini murders two women and a young girl at Paris.

Around this time: Thérèse returns two afternoons a week to the Abbey in order to become a child of Mary (p. 270).

April 12: sketches the church of Ouilly-le-Vicomte, near Lisieux (p. 261).

May 1: M. Martin has his first paralytic stroke, partial paralysis of one side (p. 267).

May: reading of the Arminjon Conferences (p. 262).

May 29 (Pentecost): Thérèse receives permission from her father to enter Carmel at age fifteen (p. 262).

May 31: reception as child of Mary at the Abbey (p. 270).

June 16: outing at Touques, sketch of Thérèse gathering flowers (p. 270).

June: pilgrimage to Honfleur; trip to the exposition of Le Havre; Thérèse buys two bluebirds for Céline (pp. 1246 and 277).

June 21: Sister Agnes of Jesus leaves the novitiate quarters.

June 20–July 31: stay of the Guérins at Trouville, *Chalet des Lilas* (p. 271 and ChrIG, p. 35).

June 20–26: vacation of Thérèse with the Guérins at Trouville.

Spring–Summer: spiritual talks with Céline in the belvédère of Les Buissonnets (Arminjon's Conferences).

July: awakening to an apostolic dimension when she sees an image of the Crucified (pp. 262, 277).

July 13: Pranzini is condemned to death. Thérèse prays and makes sacrifices for his conversion (p. 262).

July 16: Léonie enters the Visitation at Caen.

September 1: Thérèse read in *La Croix* the account of Pranzini's execution (August 31) and his conversion.

October 6–15: retreat preached at Carmel by P. Pichon (p. 290).

October 8: Thérèse asks permission from her uncle Guérin to enter Carmel at Christmas; he wants to delay her entrance (p. 286).

October 12: Céline takes P. Pichon as her spiritual director (p. 291).

October 18-21: three days of "a very painful martyrdom" for Thérèse regarding her vocation (p. 294).

October 22: under the influence of Sister Agnes of Jesus, M. Guérin consents to Thérèse's entrance to Carmel (p. 297).

October 24 (?): useless approach to M. Delatroëtte, superior of the Carmel, who was opposed to her entrance because of her age (p. 300).

October 31: visit of Thérèse and her father to Bishop Hugonin at Bayeux; answer is delayed (p. 287).

November 4-6: departure for Rome with her father and Céline; stay at Paris; special grace of peace at Notre-Dame-des-Victoires regarding the authenticity of Mary's appearance to her (pp. 303-309).

November 7-13: Switzerland, Milan, Venice, Bologna, Loreto (pp. 312 ff.).

November 13-24: stay at Rome with excursion to Naples, Pompeii (pp. 330 ff.).

November 20: audience with Leo XIII; Thérèse presents her petition to the Pope (pp. 350 ff.).

November 24-December 2: return trip: Assisi, Florence, Pisa, Genoa, Nice, Marseilles, Lyons, Paris (pp. 365 ff.).

December 2: arrival at Lisieux (p. 379).

December 16: letters to Bishop Hugonin and M. Révérony, to ask entrance at Christmas (pp. 380-382).

December 28: answer of Bishop Hugonin to Mother Marie de Gonzague: she may receive Thérèse (p. 389).

1888

January 1: answer is transmitted to Thérèse, but the Carmel postpones her entrance for three months (p. 389).

January 6: Léonie leaves the Visitation at Caen (p. 395).

February 15 (Ash Wednesday): M. Martin gives Thérèse a baby lamb which dies on that same day (pp. 395-96).

March: "one of the most beautiful months of my life" (p. 390).

Beginning of April: photo of "Thérèse with her hair coiled up" to make her look older.

April 9: entrance of Thérèse to the Carmel (p. 413). That same day, Céline receives offer of marriage (p. 435).

AT THE CARMEL

April: assigned to work in the linen room, sweeping a corridor. Postulancy: "more thorns than roses" (p. 418).

May 22: Profession of Sister Marie of the Sacred Heart (Marie); Thérèse crowns her with roses (p. 419).

May 23: Marie takes the Veil; sermon by P. Pichon (ibid); celebration of the fiftieth anniversary of founding of the Lisieux Carmel.

May 24-28: sermons of P. Pichon, two instructions each day.

May 28: Thérèse makes general confession to P. Pichon (p. 419); she takes him for her spiritual director (p. 436).

June 15: Céline tells her father about her vocation to Carmel (p. 435).

June 21: prioress' feast day; Thérèse plays the role of St. Agnes (ibid).

June 23-27: flight of M. Martin to Le Havre (pp. 418, 473).

June 26: outbreak of fire in the house next to Les Buissonnets (p. 438).

Beginning of July: stay of M. Martin, Céline, and Léonie at Auteuil (p. 445).

August 6: trip of the three of them to Alençon (pp. 452-53).

August 12: relapse of M. Martin at Les Buissonnets (p. 394).

August 22: death of M. David, cousin of Mme. Guérin; important inheritance for the Guérins (pp. 453, 455, 122).

October 8-15 (?): preached retreat; P. Blino? (p. 462-63).

End of October: Thérèse is approved for reception of the Habit by the conventual Chapter (p. 469).

October 31-November 2: Céline and M. Martin go to Le Havre to bid farewell to P. Pichon leaving for Canada (p. 473). At Honfleur serious relapse of M. Martin. Return by way of Paris (p. 490).

November: because of M. Martin's condition, they postpone Thérèse's reception of the Habit (p. 476).

December 8: sale of the Guérin pharmacy to M. Lahaye (ChrIG, p. 37).

December (?): M. Martin gives 10,000 Francs for the new altar of Saint-Pierre's Cathedral.

1889

January 5-10: retreat for reception of the Habit (p. 497-98).

January 10: reception of the Habit. Snow. Last celebration of M. Martin (ibid).

January: new task for Thérèse: refectory, sweeping (p. 526). Two photos of Thérèse as a novice (p. 531).

Around January 22: M. Martin's condition becomes disquieting (p. 530); "drags out for some ten days," then he is confined to bed (p. 533).

February 12: "Our great riches": M. Martin is hospitalized at Bon Sauveur at Caen; he will remain there three years (pp. 527, 534).

February 13: Reelection of Mother Marie de Gonzague as prioress for three years (p. 525).

February 19: Léonie and Céline stay at a boarding house in Caen to be near their father (p. 534).

April 4: letter to Céline: "To suffer in peace" (p. 553).

April 20: The Guérins buy a house (p. 566) at Lisieux.

May 2: Sister Martha of Jesus receives the Habit (p. 525).

May: renovation in the Turn quarters (p. 532); the speakroom is used as a confessional; Céline and Léonie will be one year without *seeing* their Carmelite sisters (p. 649).

May 5: centenary of the convocation of the Etats Generaux (1789); big celebration at Lisieux (p. 561).

May 14: return of Léonie and Céline to Les Buissonnets (ibid).

May 23–31: they accompany the Guérins to the Exposition at Paris (p. 565).

May 30: letter of Thérèse to Marie Guérin on frequent Communion (p. 567).

June 7: the Guérins move to Les Buissonnets for a few weeks (p. 564).

June 18: "interdiction" of M. Martin; the tribunal of Lisieux appoints an administrator over his possessions; one of the saddest trials for Thérèse (CMG IV, p. 200).

July 6-20: stay of the Guérins with Léonie and Céline at the chateau de La Musse (pp. 572, 578).

July: Thérèse receives a Marian grace in the hermitage of Saint Mary Magdalene; week of "quietude" (p. 571).

July 12: Marcelline Husé, servant of the Guérins, enters the Benedictines at Bayeux (p. 706).

July 20: on their return from La Musse, Céline and Léonie go to live with the Guérins, rue Paul Banaston (p. 578).

August 27: death of the Carmel's sacristen (p. 582); Thérèse is assigned for a few weeks to sweep the outside chapel (p. 571).

October: no preached retreat because of the renovations (p. 563).

Around October 21: some furniture from Les Buissonnets is given to the Carmel; Tom comes into the cloister yard and recognizes Thérèse (pp. 564-65). This was her spaniel.

December 25: Cancelling of the lease for Les Buissonnets (p. 593). In the Carmel, Thérèse plays the role of the Blessed Virgin in "The First Dream of the Child Jesus" (p. 594).

December 31: M. Martin's clock is set up in the Carmelite choir (p. 599).

1890

During the year: Thérèse reads the Works of Saint John of the Cross and discovers the texts of Isaias concerning the Suffering Servant.

January: Profession postponed; Thérèse reads the "Foundations of the Spiritual Life" (p. 593).

April 4 (Good Friday): Mother Geneviève, foundress of the Carmel, receives Extreme Unction (p. 637).

May 6–17 or 18: pilgrimage of the Guérins with Léonie and Céline to Tours and Lourdes (p. 615).

May (?): interview of Thérèse with P. Blino (p. 623).

June 8: engagement of Jeanne Guérin to Dr. La Néele (p. 627).

July: the new quarters of the Turn are completed; the speakrooms are used as before; arrival of two Turn Sisters (Sister Marie-Elizabeth and Sister Marie Antoinette). The novitiate is arranged on the first floor.

July 10–31: stay of the Guérins at La Musse, with Léonie and Céline (pp. 627, 642).

July 18: letter to Céline: "the hidden beauties of Jesus" (p. 630).

Beginning of August: Thérèse is admitted for Profession by the conventual Chapter (p. 647).

August 28–September 8: retreat for Profession made in aridity (p. 643).

September 2: goes into the chapel for the canonical examination: "I came to save souls and especially to pray for priests"; arrival of a blessing from Leo XIII for Thérèse and her father (pp. 643, 660).

September 5: Céline has the crown and the crucifix of Thérèse blessed by M. Martin at Bon Sauveur, Caen (pp. 668–69).

September 7: during a vigil of prayer, Thérèse doubts her vocation (Ms. A, p. 166).

September 8: her Profession. Thérèse asks for herself "love without limits," "martyrdom of body and heart"; for Léonie, her vocation; for her father, a cure, but under conditions (pp. 643 ff.).

September 23: Profession of Sister Martha of Jesus (p. 682). Great disappointment of Thérèse regarding her father (p. 683).

September 24: reception of the black Veil, in M. Martin's absence; tears (p. 685). Marie Guérin is assured of her Carmelite vocation (p. 702).

October 1: marriage of Jeanne Guérin and Francis La Néele (p. 679).

October: preached retreat by Godefroid Madelaine, Premonstratentian (p. 711).

October 8–16 (?): pilgrimage of Léonie and Céline to Paray-le-Monial (pp. 708, 711).

December: Sister Marie of the Sacred Heart gives Céline the notes of P. Pichon's retreat (1887–1888) to copy out.

1891

Towards February 10: appointed as aid to the Sacristan (p. 703).

January: severely cold weather (p. 742).

April–July: prayer for Hyacinthe Loyson, ex-Carmelite.

June 29–August 13: stay of the Guérins, with Léonie and Céline, at La Musse (p. 728).

July 5: Sister Marie of the Sacred Heart leaves novitiate quarters (p. 727); Thérèse has no one but Sister Martha as companion (p. 703).

July (?): episode of "the keys for the Communion grille"? (p. 729).

July 22: Diamond Jubilee of Mother Geneviève (p. 731); Céline painted a picture of the Agony of Christ for her infirmary.

September 11: Silver Jubilee of M. and Mme. Guérin (p. 735); Thérèse is on retreat.

October 7–15: retreat preached by P. Alexis Prou, Franciscan. A great grace for Thérèse (p. 737).

October 10: death of l'abbé Révérony, vicar general of Bayeux.

November 3: "Two question to be resolved," editorial of M. Guérin in *Le Normand*, against H. Chéron (p. 811).

November 23–25: celebrations for the third centenary of Saint John of Cross' death, sermons by P. Déodat, Franciscan; entrance of Bishop Hugonin into the cloister, "thousand caresses" given to Thérèse (pp. 737, 763).

November 26: Francis La Néele sells his pharmacy at Caen, keeping only the medical office (p. 740).

December 5: death of Mother Geneviève, foundress (p. 737).

December 23: Mother Geneviève is interred in the Sanctuary of the Chapel.

December 28: beginning of the influenza epidemic; Thérèse takes care of the sacristy; can receive Communion daily (pp. 737, 747).

1892

January 2: Thérèse is nineteen years old; death of Sister Saint Joseph (Ms. A, p. 171).

January 4: death of Sister Fébronie, subprioress (ibid).

January 7: death of Sister Madeleine of the Blessed Sacrament (ibid).

Beginning of the year: l'abbé Baillon is appointed extraordinary confessor (p. 768).

February: the elections (1889–1892) are postponed (p. 737); Mother Marie de Gonzague remains as prioress.

April 20: marriage of Henri Maudelonde; a dance missed for Céline (pp. 733, 747).

April 26: the double daisy; letter to Céline (p. 747).

May 10: return of M. Martin to his family at Lisieux (p. 738).

May 12: last visit of M. Martin in speakroom of the Carmel (ibid).

July: Céline goes to live in house on rue Labbey, with her father, Léonie, and two servants (p. 751).

July 23: entrance of Sister Marie-Madeleine of the Blessed Sacrament (p. 703).

July 23–August 23: stay of the Guérins at La Musse (ChrIG, p. 40).

August 3: P. Pichon secretly urges Céline to take part in a religious foundation in Canada (Mss. II, p. 57).

August 11–23: vacation of Céline at La Musse (p. 752).

August 15: letter to Céline about "the apostolate of prayer" (pp. 752–53).

October: private retreat of Thérèse (p. 763).

November: preached retreat by P. Déodat, Franciscan (ibid).

Around December 8: enlightens Sister Martha (pp. 757–58).

At end of this year, it was "above all the Gospel" which nourished her prayer (p. 738).

1893

February 2: first poem by Thérèse: "The Divine Dew" (pp. 758, 785–86).

February 20: election of Mother Agnes of Jesus as prioress; mistress of novices: Mother Marie de Gonzague; Thérèse is associated with her in the formation of her companions (pp. 778 ff.). She leaves the sacristy and is assigned in the work of painting small objects, etc.

April 25: letter to Céline: "the drop of dew" (p. 783).

April–May: "portrait" of Thérèse and of the whole Community by Sister Marie of the Angels.

June: Thérèse paints a fresco in the Oratory (p. 777); assistant to the bursar (p. 823).

June 24: Léonie enters again the Visitation at Caen (p. 815).

June 27–August 18: stay of the Guérins at La Musse, with Céline, M. Martin, and Tom, the spaniel (pp. 791, 818).

July 16 (?): prayer: "Glances of love towards Jesus"; Thérèse and Sister Martha count their "practices," acts of virtue (p. 805).

September 7: reception of the Habit by Sister Marie Madeleine; M. Guérin is "godfather" (p. 812). For a year, Mother Agnes "obliges" this novice to consult with Thérèse (p. 823).

September 15: Céline takes lessons in painting with Krug (p. 825).

September: Thérèse was supposed to leave the novitiate quarters; she asks to remain there (p. 819). Tasks: painting, second portress (?).

October 7–15: retreat preached by P. Lemonnier (p. 832).

December: reading in the refectory of the Life of Saint Jeanne de Chantal (p. 835). Thérèse joins with Sister Martha in carrying out the "practices," counting acts of virtue (p. 805).

1894

January 2: Thérèse is twenty-one years old; begins to fast (p. 820).

January: adopts definitively vertical handwriting (p. 838); in view of the feast of St. Agnes (January 21), she paints: "The Dream of the Child Jesus" (pp. 839–40) and composes her first play: "The Mission of Joan of Arc" (RP 1). During the whole month, "practices" with Sister Martha (p. 805).

January 27: Leo XIII declares Joan of Arc Venerable.

February 20: Mother Marie de Gonzague is sixty years old, second poem of Thérèse for the occasion.

February–March: "practices" with Sister Martha during Lent (p. 805).

Spring: Thérèse begins suffering in the throat.

April 6: reception of the Habit by Léonie (Sister Thérèse-Dosithée) at Caen (p. 854).

April–May: composition of four poems (P 3 to P 6), including "My Song for Today" (p. 874).

May 8: big celebrations in Lisieux in honor of Venerable Joan of Arc; the Guérins and Martins decorate their houses with flags (ACL).

May 27: M. Martin has a paralytic attack, and he receives Extreme Unction (pp. 857–58).

June 5: he has a serious heart attack (857).

June 16: entrance of Sister Marie of the Trinity (p. 856), who is entrusted to Thérèse.

June 20: P. Pichon explains to Céline his plans for "Bethanie" (p. 869). He had in mind a religious group of women, and Céline would be the foundress.

July 1: they consulted Dr. La Néele regarding Thérèse: huskiness in throat, pains in chest (p. 870).

July 4: departure of the Guérins for La Musse, with M. Martin and Céline (p. 860).

July 7: letter on the Trinity to Céline (ibid).

July 17: centenary of the martyrdom of the Carmelites of Compiègne (p. 873).

July 29: death of M. Martin at La Musse (p. 874).

August 2: his burial at Lisieux (p. 877).

August 7 or 8: Céline asks the Superior for permission to enter Carmel (ibid).

August 20: P. Pichon gives up his plans and "gives Céline to Carmel" (p. 879).

August: Thérèse changes her cell (room).

September 14: entrance of Céline to Carmel (Sister Marie of the Holy Face), entrusted to Thérèse.

October 7–15 (?): retreat preached by P. Lemonnier (p. 904).

October 11: transfer from Alençon to Lisieux of the remains of Mme. Martin and her four children, her father, and her mother-in-law (p. 1260).

October 20: worrisome hoarseness of Thérèse (p. 892); advice of Dr. La Néele.

November 20: Profession of Sister Marie-Madeleine (p. 895); on this occasion (?), photo "of the Lourdes grotto" (VTL, no. 9).

In the autumn: Thérèse examines the notebooks of Céline; finds there decisive scripture texts for her "little way" (p. 897).

December: composition (for Christmas) of the play: "The Angels at the Crib of Jesus" (pp. 606, 905).

December 18: reception of the Habit by Sister Marie of the Trinity.

End of December: Mother Agnes orders Thérèse to write her childhood memories (p. 886).

December–January: composition (for January 21, 1895) of "Joan of Arc accomplishing her mission" (p. 886).

1895

Year of the writing of her first copybook (Manuscript A) of the *Story of a Soul* (p. 774).

January 17: election of Felix Faure as President of the French Republic (p. 970).

January 21: Thérèse plays the role of Joan of Arc (RP 3); she just misses being burned alive (PA 1003). Shortly afterwards: five photos (VTL, nos. 11 to 15).

End of January: Céline was given the name of Sister Geneviève of St. Teresa (p. 898).

February 5: reception of the Habit by Sister Geneviève (id.). Thérèse had furnished the outline of the sermon (DCL).

February 25: last personal letter from P. Pichon to Thérèse (p. 900).

February 26 (Mardi gras): spontaneous composition of the poem "To Live by Love" (P 15).

April: "I shall die soon" (p. 897).

April 25–28: ten photos of the Community (p. 903).

June 9 (Trinity Sunday): during the Mass she receives the inspiration to offer herself to Merciful Love (p. 887).

June 11: makes this offering to Love, with Sister Geneviève.

June 13: "conversion" of Diana Vaughan (p. 948).

June 14 (?): when beginning the Way of the Cross, Thérèse experienced a "wound of love" (p. 906).

June 27–August 6: stay of the Guérins at La Musse (p. 907).

June–July: suggests the offering to Merciful love to Sister Marie of the Sacred Heart (p. 999).

July 20: Léonie leaves the Visitation (p. 885).

July 29: Sister Anne of the Sacred Heart returns to the Saïgon Carmel (p. 942).

August 15: entrance of Marie Guérin (Sister Marie of the Eucharist) to the Carmel (p. 943).

October 7–15 (?): retreat preached by P. Lemonnier; he examines the text of the Act of Oblation to Merciful Love (p. 905).

October 8: death of M. Delatroëtte, superior.

October 17: Mother Agnes entrusts a spiritual brother, l'abbé Bellière, to Thérèse; a seminarian, future missionary (p. 918).

October 21: for the feast of Céline, poem "Jesus, my Beloved, Remember!" (P 21).

November 10: death of Sister Saint-Pierre (p. 942).

November 30: proposes to Sister Marie of the Trinity the Act of Oblation to Love (p. 905).

December 25: "The Little Divine Beggar of Christmas" (p. 922).

1896

January (?): paints her coat of arms; composes "The Flight into Egypt" (RP 6) for the 21st and "The Answer of Saint Agnes" (P 22).

January: M. Maupas made the new superior of the Carmel (p. 962).

January 20: Thérèse gives Mother Agnes of Jesus her copybook of childhood memories (Manuscript A).

February 23: long letter to Céline: "All is ours" (pp. 924 ff.).

February 24: Profession of Sister Geneviève (ibid).

March 14: hospitalization of Sister Marguerite-Marie at Bon Sauveur at Caen (p. 942).

March 21: difficult election of Mother Marie de Gonzague as prioress (ibid). Thérèse is confirmed in her role as auxiliary mistress of the novitiate; other tasks: sacristy, painting, linen room (p. 943).

April 2–3: first spittings up of blood (p. 947).

April 5 (Easter): shortly afterwards, entrance into "the thickest darkness," trial of faith which will last till her death (ibid).

April 30: Profession of Sister Marie of the Trinity (ibid).

May 7: reception of the Veil by Sister Marie of the Trinity (ibid).

May 10: dream of Venerable Anne of Jesus (p. 948).

May 30: Mother Marie de Gonzague entrusts a second spiritual brother to Thérèse, P. Roulland, M.E.P. (p. 948).

June 10–July 26: stay of the Guérins, with Léonie, at La Musse (p. 964).

June 21: feast day of Mother Marie de Gonzague well solemnized (pp. 958; 1265 ff.). Thérèse composed "The Triumph of Humility" (RP 7) according to the *Memoirs* of Diana Vaughan (p. 948).

June 22–24: triduum preached by P. Godefroid Madelaine (p. 986).

June 28: poem "To Throw Flowers!" (p. 989); ordination of P. Roulland (p. 957).

June 29: "Legend of a very little Lamb," to Mother Marie de Gonzague (p. 958).

July 3: first Mass of P. Roulland at the Carmel; talk with Thérèse in the speakroom (p. 975).

Shortly afterwards, several pictures of Thérèse alone (p. 970) or of the Community, including that of the haying (p. 1266).

July 12: "does not cough any longer" after several weeks of a strengthening diet (pp. 967 ff.); letter to Léonie "take Jesus by His Heart" (p. 966).

July 15: presented to Dr. de Corniére in the speakroom (p. 970).

July 16: poem "To Our Lady of Victories" (p. 975).

August 2: departure of P. Roulland for China; there is question of the departure of Mother Agnes for Saïgon (pp. 990, 977).

August 6: "Consecration to the Holy Face" (p. 996).

August 15: poem "Jesus alone" (p. 1267).

July–August: martyrdom of desires, reading of Isaias, St. Paul; request for "twofold love"; talk with Sister Marie of the Sacred Heart on this subject (pp. 949, 985).

September 7–18: personal retreat (pp. 985 ff.).

September 8: writing of Manuscript B, second part, to Jesus (p. 985).

September 13–16: letter to Sister Marie of the Sacred Heart (LTG 196 = Ms. B, first part) to dedicate this text to her (pp. 991–996).

September 17: letter to Sister Marie of the Sacred Heart (LT 197), confirmation and complement of Ms. B (p. 998).

October 8–15: retreat preached by P. Godefroid Madelaine; after speaking with him (or in June?), Thérèse writes the Credo with her blood (p. 986).

October 21: first letter to l'abbé Bellière (p. 1009).

November 4: death of Sister Marie-Antoinette, turn sister (p. 986).

November: reading of the Life of Théophane Vénard (p. 1074); novena to this martyr for Thérèse's cure and her departure for Indochina (p. 1025); but a definite relapse (ibid).

December 3 (?): vesicatory (p. 1029).

December 20–25: Christmas tree (p. 1026).

December 24: letters to Sister Geneviève and to Sister Marie of the Trinity (the nine-pins and the top).

December 25: fourteenth centenary of the baptism of Clovis (p. 971).

1897

"This year, the discovery of fraternal charity" (p. 988).

January 21: poem "My Joy!" (p. 1027).

February 2: poem "To Théophane Vénard" (p. 1026), composed spontaneously.

February 8: play "Saint Stanislaus Kostka" (RP 8) for the jubilee of Sister Saint Stanislaus (p. 1026).

March 3: beginning of Lent; she tries to fast.

March 4–12: personal novena to Saint Francis Xavier to obtain favor of "spending her heaven in doing good on earth" (p. 1074).

March 19: same request to St. Joseph (ibid).

March 25: Profession of Sister Marie of the Eucharist; poem "My weapons" (pp. 1027, 1271).

Beginning of April (end of Lent): falls gravely ill (p. 1077).

April 6: beginning of "Last Conversations" (ibid).

April 19: Leo Taxil reveals his impostures, in particular regarding Diana Vaughan (DE, p. 187).

May: she is freed from all duties and Office in the Choir (ibid); "walks for a missionary" (p. 1116); poem "Why I Love you, O Mary!" (p. 1078).

May 19: poem "An Unpetalled Rose" (p. 1086).

May 23: "elevator" (p. 1098).

May 27–June 6: retreat from Ascension to Pentecost; exchange of notes with Mother Agnes (pp. 1078–79).

May 31: poem "Abandonment is the delightful fruit of Love" (p. 1109).

June 2: reception of the Veil by Sister Marie of the Eucharist (p. 1111).

June 3: at the request of Mother Agnes, Mother Marie de Gonzague orders Thérèse to continue her autobiography: writing of Ms. C (p. 1079).

June 7: long pose for three photos (p. 1121).

June 9: "the night of nothingness" (Ms. C, 211); "I am entering into life" (p. 1128).

July 2–August 6: stay of the Guérins and Léonie at La Musse (p. 1135).

July 6–August 5: some twenty blood-spittings.

July 8: brought to the infirmary (p. 1079).

Beginning of July: leaves Manuscript C unfinished (ibid).

July 14: last letter to P. Roulland (p. 1141).

July 16: "Prayer to obtain humility" (p. 1148).

July 17: last letter to Léonie (ibid). "I feel my mission is about to begin" (DE, p. 269).

July 24–25: last note to the Guérins (p. 1160).

July 30: Extreme Unction.

Beginning of August (?): last letter to P. Pichon (p. 1168).

August 8–30: stay of M. and Mme. Guérin at Vichy (p. 1177).

August 10: last letter to l'abbé Bellière (p. 1173).

August 15–27: great sufferings, temptation to suicide.

August 19: last Communion, offered for H. Loyson (DE, p. 173).

August 30: last photo of Thérèse alive (pp. 1183–84).

September 8: last autograph lines to Blessed Virgin.

September 30: around 7:30, death of Thérèse (p. 1186) after an agony of two hours.

October 4: burial in the Lisieux cemetery.

TABLE OF REFERENCES

to the Bible, the Imitation of Christ
Saint Terèsa of Avila, and St. John of the Cross

I. TABLE OF REFERENCES TO THE BIBLE

This table contains all the references made by Thérèse in her letters (LT), excluding those that appear in the letters of her correspondents (LC and LD). Therefore, the abbreviation LT will not be repeated before the number of her letter, in the right column in bold print.

Implicit quotations or references to biblical data are preceded by an asterisk *. For example, in LT 148, Thérèse makes reference to the ark and the dove in * Genesis 8:8–9, without quoting the bible text.

GENESIS		NUMBERS	
* 3:18	127	* 11:5	63
* 8:8–9	148	N 11:5	261
* 15:1	145	JUDGES	
15:1	182	* 16:17	50
15:1	183	I KINGS	
* 22:2 p.1165 Compared Louis to 261		* 8:27	169
* 22:12 Abraham	167	* 18:20–40	192
EXODUS		TOBIAS	
* 17:8–13	107	12:7 Jn 55	196
17:8–13✓	135✓	N 13:13 –	172
17:8–13✓	201✓	JOB	
* 23:20	229	* 42:10–12	146

PSALMS

17:5	262
* 18:6	141
* 22:2	142
22:4	262
* 41:2	142
49:9–13 ᴊᴍ SS	196
* 75:10	145
N 79:2	169
* 83:6	190
83:11	201
* 88:2	247
89:4	71
89:4	71
89:4	87
* 90:12	161
93:18	243
* 101:8	217
102:8, 14, 13	226
N 112:9	255
* 117:23	91
* 125:5–6	201
125:6	185
* 125:6	168
126:1	147
* 127:6	152
136:1	157
136:1–2	85
* 136:1–4	149
N 136:4, 2	165
* 138:10	201
* 138:12	144
140:5	259

PROVERBS

SS 9:4	196
* 31:10	197

QOHELETH (ECCLESIASTES)

* 1:2	58
* 1:14	243

CANTICLE OF CANTICLES

1:3	259
1:3–4	137
1:7	142
1:13	108
1:13	144
1:13	165
* 1:13	185
* 1:14	110
2:1	141
2:1	183
* 2:1	241
N 2:3	201
* 2:7	182
* 2:9	157
2:9	230
2:11, 10	158
* 2:16	122
* 3:2	145
* 4:6	120
4:6	130
4:6	141
4:6	142
* 4:6	156
4:9	164
* 4:9	191
* 5:1	142
N 5:2	108
5:2 See 211	158
* 5:2	160
N 5:10	108
5:10 See 1.3	137
N 5:11	108

✓ 6:10–11	165	60:22	64
7:1	149	61:1, 10, 11, 9	193
7:1	165	63:1–5a	108
* 7:1	182	63:3	108
7:1	183	63:3, 5	165
8:1 *see 2, 11*	158	63:5	108
8:7 *SS.*	(196)	66:13–12 SS	196
		66:19–20	193

WISDOM

		JEREMIAH	
* 3:6	165	* 2:13	169
4:1	130	✓ 10:23	243
4:1	149	**MICAH**	
6:7 SS	196	* 6:3	190
11:22	161	**ZECHARIAH**	

SIRACH (ECCLESIASTICUS)

34:10	198	* 9:17	156

ISAIAH

		* 9:17	183
* 9:5	213	* 13:6	190
9:5	220	13:6	261
40:11 *S.S.*	(196)	**MALACHI**	
49:15	191	* 3:20	141
53:1–5	108	**MATTHEW**	
53:3	108	5:8	105
53:3	116	5:11	107
* 53:3	117	5:12	107
53:3	137	5:48	107
53:3	140	6:9	101
53:3	145	6:9	127
* 53:3	156	6:9	127
* 53:3	183	6:21	127
53:3	216	6:21	134
53:4	108	6:21	261
54:2–3	193	* 6:30	141
* 55:8	87	8:20	137
55:8	107	* 8:20	144
55:8	142	* 8:24	144
* 55:9	226	8:24	165
60:4–5	193	8:26	144
		* 8:26	167
		* 8:26	171

9:37–38	(135)
10:34	57
11:12	201
* 11:25	127
11:25	190
11:25	247
12:50	130
12:50	142
12:50	172
* 13:44	145
18:12	142
18:19	220
* 19:14	226
* 19:29	72
19:29	180
19:29	193
* 19:29	213
* 20:22	100
* 20:23	167
25:34–36	145
25:40	229
26:39　SS	197
26:39	213
* 26:63	145
26:64	117
26:64	161
* 27:46	178

MARK

4:38	144
* 10:21	247
* 14:3–6	169
* 14:36	178

LUKE

* 1:49	224
* 2:7	211
2:14	149
* 2:35	213
* 2:40	202

5:5	161
7:47	130
7:47	224
* 7:47	247
10:41	257
* 10:41–42	141
* 11:5–8	99
* 12:37	204
* 12:37	208
* 12:48	83
* 13:29	254
15:22	261
15:31	142
* 16:11	197
* 19:4	137
19:5 Mt. 8:20	137
19:48	145
21:29 ff	143
* 22:15	213
22:28–29	165
22:29	165
22:30	117
* 23:11	169
* 24:26	186

JOHN

* 1:1	165
* 1:38 Mt 8:20	137
* 2:7–9	166
* 4:6	144
4:7	141
4:7　SS	196
* 4:10	141
4:35	135
7:37	142
8:10	230
* 9:4 (at Ps. 89.4 71)	
* 11:16	98
* 12:1–8	169

Table of References

* 14:2 *see Mt 6.21*	127
* 14:2	204
* 14:2	226
14:2	247
* 14:3	173
14:6	165
14:23 *See Mt. 12:50*	142
14:23	165
* 15:13	226
16:5-7, 22	258
17:17	165
17:21	165
18:36 *18.16 Typo*	117
* 18:36	204
18:38	165
* 19:25	213
* 20:17	165
21:5	161
21:15	152

ACTS OF THE APOSTLES

20:35 *see Is 55.8*	142
20:35	169

ROMANS

* 3:24	197
8:26	165
9:16	224

I CORINTHIANS

1:27-29 *See Is. 9.5*	220
2:9	68
* 2:9	94
* 2:9	124
* 2:9	173
2:9	182
* 2:9	196
7:31	85
7:31	120
7:31	130
7:31	137
* 13:12	57

II CORINTHIANS

* 4:17	173
* 6:2	129
* 8:9	109
* 12:15	109

GALATIANS

2:20	184

EPHESIANS

* 6:17	193

PHILIPPIANS

2:7	201
2:7	201
3:20	201

COLOSSIANS

* 3:4	141

JAMES

1:12	105
1:12 *sirach 34,10*	198

I JOHN

* 3:2	141

APOCALYPSE

* 2:17	183
* 2:17	261
7:13-15	108
* 14:3-4	186
* 14:4	238
* 14:4	241
* 20:12	182
* 20:12	195
21:4	68
21:4	83
21:4	117
* 21:4	190

2. QUOTATIONS FROM THE IMITATION OF CHRIST IN THE LETTERS OF THÉRÈSE

*	I, 1: refl.	71		12:11	221
	1:3	58	III,	5:4	65
	2:3	95	*	5:4	251
	2:3	145	*	13:3	241
	2:3	176	* III,	34:1	135
*	8: refl.	201		47: refl.	173
*	11:4	57	*	47: refl.	87
*	11:4	65	*	49	145
*	17: refl.	107	*	49:2	81
*	II, 8:1	135	III,	49: 7	145
	11:4	145		49:7	176
*	11:4	197		51:2	165
*	11:4	211	*	58:9	64
*	11:5	197			

3. QUOTATIONS FROM ST. TERESA OF AVILA

Life
ch. XXX   143

Way of Perfection
ch. I   198
ch. III   198
ch. III   221
ch. VIII   201
ch. XXXIV   178
ch. XLII   49
ch. XLII   56

Interior Castle
*   VII, IV   65
*   Exclamations
   n° 13   82

Poetry
   Bookmark   27
*   Bookmark   81

Correspondence
   Letter,
   September 1578   150

4. QUOTATIONS FROM ST. JOHN OF THE CROSS

Ascent of
Mount Carmel
  str. VIII — 108
Dark Night
  Book I, ch. 4 — 188
Spiritual Canticle
* str. I — 145
* str. III — 149
  str. IX and XI — 85
* str. XI — 109
  str. XIV — 135
  str. XXI — 188
  str. XV — 137
* str. XXVIII — 157
  str. XXIX — 221

  str. XXIX — 245
* str. XXXI — 141
* str. XXXI — 164
Living Flame
  str. I, v. 6 — 245
Poems
  Glosa — 142
Maxims
  Prayer of the
  enamored soul — 137
  Prayer of the
* enamored soul — 182
  n° 80 — 188
Sayings of St.
John of the Cross — 81
— 188

SELECTED INDEX OF THÉRÈSE'S LETTERS
Significant Nouns

Abandon (ed) Vol. I 289, 332, 353, 557, Vol. II 861, 863, 1014, 1033, 1134, 1173

Abandonment Vol. II 796, 828, 850, 903, 994, 1152, 1160, reservations 995

ABBEY AT LISIEUX Vol. I 663

Abode Vol. II 762, 795, 811, 816, 863, 1132, tent 863

ABRAHAM Vol. II 871, 908

Absolution Vol. I 658

Abyss Vol. II 925, 966

ACHAB Vol. II 969

Actions Vol. II 855, 882, 966, 991, 994

Adoration Vol. II 728, 1061

Adornment Vol. II 861, 925, 929

Advice Vol. I 457

Affection Vol. I 282, 333, 468, 477, 481, 482, 483, 493, 576, Vol. II 707, 715, 740, 743, 760, 763, 811, 816, 830, 836, 846, 866, 871, 878, 896, 899, 907, 908, 921, 977, 1030, 1046, 1146, 1153, 1160 Hug Vol. I 459, 460, Vol. II 712 Kiss (es) Vol. I 110, 112, 119, 133, 140, 143, 152, 191, 223, 234, 236, 237, 239, 242, 244, 249, 276, 282, 299, 308, 333, 366, 396, 421, 429, 433, 435, 452, 457, 459, 460, 461, 491, 510, 545, 547, 556, 590, 600, 631, Vol. II 744, 760, 796, 839, 843, 916, 921, 1135, 1153, 1174, Mary's 925

Affliction Vol. II 1121

AFRICA Vol. II 1140

AGNES OF JESUS Vol. I and Vol. II see **MARTIN, PAULINE**

AGNES, SAINT Vol. I 335, 435, 440, 512, Vol. II 927

Agony (ies) Vol. I 442, 450, 541, Vol. II 862, 908, 934

Air (empoisoned) Vol. II 883

ALENÇON Vol. I 275, 461

All Vol. I 449, 450, 467, 504, 514, 530, 542, 546, 552, 553, Vol. II 707, 741, 871, 894, 930

ALL Vol. I 602, 641

ALL SAINTS Vol. II 1013, 1069

Alone Vol. I 133, 289, 366, 449, 457, 684, Vol. II 803, 862, 902, 1122

Altar Vol. I 482, Child Jesus altar 589

Angel (s) Vol. I 233, 427, 454, 455, 510, 672, 684, *see also* **MARTIN, MARIE** Vol. II 713, 725, 732, 781, 785, 816, 828, 833, 838, 839, 849, 850, 851, 894,

896, 908, 916, 925, 926, 927, 928, 929, 961, 969, 1016, 1022, 1043, 1110, 1142, 1163, 1165, *See also* **MARTIN, CÉLINE**

Archangel Vol. I 233

Anguish Vol. I 449, 577, Vol. II 1038

ANNE, SAINT Vol. II 759, 830

Anxiety (ies) Vol. I 568, 577, Vol. II 908

Apostolate Vol. II 753, 956, 977, 978, 1014, 1092

Apostolic Vol. II bonds 956, 977; soul 1014; work (s) 1010, 1015; union 957

Apostle (s) Vol. I 578, Vol. II 781, 804, 851, 882, 927, 956, 1011, 1014, 1015, 1042, 1059, 1084, 1092, 1133

Arid (ities) Vol. I 577, 654, Vol. II 801, 861, 994

Ark Vol. II 816, 835, 843

Arrows (fiery) Vol. II 927

Artists Vol. I country of 342, models 662, *see also* **THÉRÈSE** Vol. II 926, models of flowers 916, painting 1121, Thérèse's 848

ASCENSION Vol. I Feast 567, Thursday 423

ASH WEDNESDAY Vol. I 395

Aspirations Vol. II 765, 1014

ASSISI Vol. I 366

ASTRAKHAN FUR Vol. I 480

Atom Vol. I 500, 504, 505, 580

Attentiveness Vol. II 801

Attention Vol. II 739, 1034

Attraction (s) Vol. I 587, Vol. II 882, 999, 1017, 1085

Audience Vol. I *see* **POPE**

AUGUSTINE, SAINT Vol. I 406, Vol. II 1133, 1153

AUNT Vol. I and Vol. II *see* **GUÉRIN, CÉLINE,** Vol. II *see* **THÉRÈSE**

Axe Vol. I 450, 467

BABYLON Vol. I 546, 553, Vol. II 899

Ball Vol. I *see* **THÉRÈSE**

Banquet Vol. I 445, 451, Vol. II 795, 1022, 1094, 1141

Baptism (second) Vol. I *see* **Profession;**

Vol. II 929

Bath Vol. I *see* **LOURDES**

BAYEUX Vol. II 1165

Beauty (ies) Vol. I 390, 500, 504, nature's 618, *see also* **JESUS** and **MARTIN, CÉLINE**

Bees Vol. II 741

Beggar Vol. 596, Vol. II 808

Bell Vol. I *see* **THÉRÈSE**-promptness

Belles-de-nuit Vol. I *see* **JESUS**

BELLIÈRE, L'ABBÉ Vol. II 1018, 1041, 1042, 1043, 1059, 1060, 1061, 1083, brother 1059, 1084, 1085, 1086, 1127, 1128, 1133, 1134, 1139, 1151, 1152, 1153, 1154, 1163, 1164, 1165, 1166, 1173, 1174, dignity 1174, Louis de France 1174, presence 1164

Beloved Vol. I 390, *see also* **JESUS** and **MARTIN, LOUIS**

Belvedere Vol. I 468

BENOIT, MONSIEUR Vol. I 431

BETHANY Vol. II 894

BETHLEHEM Vol. II 804

Birds Vol. I 238, dove 191, 232, finches 276, nightingale 233, robin 232, swallow 232, waterfowl 434, *see also* **GUÉRIN, MARIE** and **MARTIN, PAULINE,** Vol. II 715, 760, 999, 1098, 1138, dove (s) 813, 816, 827, 843, 1114, finch 1047, 1146, magpie 916, sparrow 1047, swallow 1046, swan 928

Birthday Vol. I 395, 556, 560, 610, Vol. II 724, 765, 1134, 1148, 1175, 1181

Bishops Vol. II 882

Bitterness Vol. I 449, 530, 577, Vol. II 961, 1038, 1041

Black side Vol. II 1117

Blanket Vol. II 1135

Bless (ing) (s) Vol. I 298, 299, 389, 405, 494, nuptial *see* **Profession invitation,** Vol. II 707, 712, 957, 1054, 1095, 1133

Blessed Vol. II 926, 1173

Blood Vol. I 440, 547, 630, *see also* **JESUS,** Vol. II 713, 741, 936, 1015, *see also* **JESUS**

Blue Beard Vol. II 765

Boat Vol. I 398, 400, Vol. II 803, 804, 1034

Body Vol. II 1072, brother ass 1072, envelope 1104, 1106

BONZAGUE, SISTER LOUISE DE Vol. I 110

Book (s) Vol. II 926, 991, 994, 1010, 1014, 1030, 1070, 1093, 1094

Boys Vol. II 873

Branch Vol. I *see* **Lillies**; Vol. II 1138, of eglantine 916

Bread (s) Vol. II altar 1111, of angels 1116, of heaven 1173

Bride (of Jesus) Vol. I *see* **THÉRÈSE**, Vol. II *see* **MARTIN, CÉLINE**

Brother (s) Vol. II 729, 928, 1015, *see also* **BELLIÈRE, ROULAND** and **SIMEON**

Burden (some) Vol. I 449, 546, 612

CAEN Vol. I 536, Vol. II 728, 759, 762, 810, 881, 883

CALAIS Vol. I 248

Call Vol. II 861, 896, 1017, 1142

Calm Vol. II 870, 872, 889, 907, 908, 995, 1033

CALVARY Vol. I 529

CANA Vol. II 866

CANADA Vol. I 468, 619

Candle (s) Vol. I 424, pink 671

Canticle (s) Vol. I 553, Vol. II 863, 873, 927, 951, 994, 1059, 1138

Care (s) Vol. II 709, 811, 830, 834, 843, 882, 889, 902, 927, 960, 1020, Mary's motherly 925

Caress (es) Vol. I 600, Vol. II 743, 833, 1038, 1146

CARMEL Vol. I 249, 273, 276, 289, 298, 332, 342, 353, 365, 366, 387, 388, 392, 396, 399, 400, 405, 423, 429, 449, 451, 452, 453, 456, 476, 481, 482, 483, 491, 493, 563, 620, 658, 661, 680, Vol. II 724, 740, 743, 781, 846, 847, 866, 881, 882, 915, 969, 1018, 1054, 1059, 1068, 1070, 1071, 1073, 1084, 1085, 1090,

1133, 1174

Entrance Vol. II 1017

Feast of Our Lady of Mount Carmel Vol. I 244

Kingdom of Carmel Vol. II 1017

Mountain of Carmel Vol. II 934, 1165

Nest of Carmel Vol. I 479

Order of Carmel Vol. II 927, 969

Rule of Carmel Vol. II 753, 831, 1041

CARMELITE (S) Vol. I 423, 493, Vol. II 739, 753, 759, 817, 834, 835, 909, 915, 916, 933, 956, 977, 1010, 1014, 1043, 1054, 1059, 1069, 1071, 1072, 1073, 1090

Carp Vol. I 451, *see also* **Fish**

Carriage (s) Vol. I 239, 366

Cart Vol. I *see* **Colloquialisms**

Castles Vol. I *see* **Colloquialisms**

Cat (laugh) Vol. II 909

CECILIA, SAINT Vol. 434, 440, 442, 553, Vol. II 827, 828, 850, 927

Celebration (s) Vol. I clothing 510, profession 683, 684, Vol. II 853, 925, 926, 927, 928, 929, 930, 1153

Cell Vol. II 926, 977, 1071, 1101

Cellar Vol. I 652, of the Child Jesus 433

Centimes Vol. I 461

Ceremony Vol. I 615, Vol. II 843

Certitude (inner) Vol. II 871

Chalice (s) Vol. I 400, 541, 553, 600, 622, Vol. II 826, 837, 838, 1042, 1166

Champagne Vol. I 509

CHANTAL, SAINT Vol. II 835

Chapel Vol. I 482

Chaplet Vol. I 191, Vol. II 805

Chapter room Vol. I 671, Vol. II 928, deliberation 959

Chariots of Aminadab Vol. II 861

Charm (s) Vol. I divine 631, hidden 667

Charm (s) Vol. II 765, 1017, 1040

Cheerful (ness) Vol. I 276, 423, Vol. II 759

CHERUBIM Vol. I 542, Vol. II 882, Four Dead **MARTIN** children 936

CHERUBS Vol. II 1035, 1039, 1040,

1145, 1146, Four dead **MARTIN**
children 927, 928, 930

Child Vol. I 289, 298, 353, 382, 482, 483,
491, 529, Vol. II 743, 761, 764, 795,
803, 804, 838, 839, 849, 863, 878, 907,
966, 990, 993, 994, 1030, 1033, 1034,
1038, 1039, 1040, 1060, 1070, 1092,
1094, 1117, 1152, 1153, 1165

...**Jesus** Vol. I 388, 390, 433, 680, Vol.
II 1016

Childhood Vol. I 661, 679, Vol. II 715,
732, 743, 760, 765, 846, 850, 851, 865,
1016, 1085, 1127, 1140, 1152, 1153

Children Vol. I 392, 493, 504, Vol. II 713,
741, 833, 850, 884, 894, 903, 908, 910,
916, 926, 927, 928, 929, 930, 991, 1021,
1040, 1071, 1073, 1093, 1094, 1146,
1153, 1165

CHILDREN OF MARY Vol. I 239, 273,
275, 482, consecration 482

Chimeras Vol. II 1033

CHINA Vol. II 1073, 1094, distant
regions 1141

CHINESE Vol. II 1015, 1072, braid 1016

Chocolate Vol. II 759

Choir (of martyrs) Vol. II 1092

CHOIR Vol. II 926

CHRIST Vol. I and Vol. II *see* **JESUS**

Christians Vol. II 871, 883

CHRISTMAS Vol. I 298, 380, 381, 382,
387, 388, Vol. II 1016

CHRISTOPHER, SAINT Vol. II 804

Church (es) Vol. I 317, 366, Vol. II 707,
728, 828, 830, 1054, 1069, 1142, 1164,
fold 728

Cincture Vol. I pink 143, Scotch 434

City Vol. I 468

Clapper Vol. II 1037

Clay Vol. II 871

CLOISTER (meaning enclosure) Vol. II
926, 977, 1060, 1165, wall 1071

Clothes Vol. II 1015, 1016

Clouds Vol. I 577, Vol. II 739, 784, 811,
958, 959

Coats-of-Arms Vol. II 926

COCHIN, CHINA Vol. II 1071

Cold (ness) Vol. 480, 577, 631, 652

Colloquialisms Vol. I Cart 281, 421,
Castles 396, Cost 622
Heaven 236, Hole 152, Pegs 152, Pro-
verb 236, Vol. II Stones 1038

Color (s) Vol. II 741, 814, 995

COLOMBIÈRE, VEN. PÈRE DE LA
Vol. II 1084

Combat (images) Vol. II 1017, Armor
1012, Barracks 1012, Battle 1069, 1142,
Conqueror 1094, Corporal 1012, Helmet 933, sheath 1072, war 1017, warrior (s) 928, 990, 1034, weapon (s) 979,
1013, 1060, 1085, *see also* **Sword**

Combats (noun) Vol. II 1010, 1012, 1043,
1073

Commandment Vol. I 622

Common sense Vol. II 970

COMMUNION Vol. I 396, 576, Vol. II
921, 1135
HOLY Vol. I 478, 567, 568, 569, 576,
Vol. II 811, 833, 917, 1084, 1146
First Vol. I 152, 191, 204, 223, 423,
435, 482, 555, Vol. II 865, 900
Second Vol. I 224

Community Vol. I 496, 544, Vol. II 707,
847, 915, 916, 1070, 1071

Companion (s) Vol. I 483, Sr. Martha
520, 682, Thérèse faithful 449, Vol. II
805, 1046, 1072, Léonie 909

Compassion Vol. II 872, 1159, 1173

Complacence Vol. II 999

Concert (s) Vol. II 863, 921, 926

Confession Vol. I 152

Confessors Vol. II 927

Confidante Vol. I 289, *see also* **MAR-
TIN, PAULINE**

Confidence Vol. I 353, 365, 387, 388, 442,
in God 332, lack of 568, Vol. II 729,
1000, 1013, 1093, 1165, filial 1133,
1153

Consolation (s) Vol. I 234, 453, 454, 455,
457, 479, 504, 511, 545, 576, 615, 616,
617, 618, 652, 655, 667, 684, Vol. II

741, 763, 781, 794, 795, 796, 809, 835, 836, 843, 846, 866, 908, 929, 970, 977, 979, 994, 999, 1010, 1014, 1034, 1042, 1059, 1148, 1152, 1153, 1164

Consolers Vol. II 862

Contemplation Vol. II 1133

Contempt Vol. I 612, Vol. II 936, 1046

Conversation (s) Vol. I 494, 500, 611, Vol. II 908, 929, 1015, 1163

Conversion Vol. II 1016, 1159

Conviction Vol. II interior 916, intimate 1152

CORNIÈRE, DR., alias CLODION, MONSIEUR Vol. II 969, 1097, 1146, 1173

Cortege Vol. II 925, 926, 1042, royal 927

Cost Vol. I *see* **Colloquialisms**

Country Vol. I 133, 651, 654, girl *see* **GUÉRIN, MARIE**; Vol. II 959, 977, 1069, 1070, 1093, 1142

Couplet (s) Vol. II 1074, **THÉRÈSE'S** 1146

Courage Vol. I 289, 290, 353, 467, 501, 537, 546, 557, 580, 662, Vol. II 871, 896, 908, 1012, 1013, 1085, heroic 1165

Court Vol. I 641, heavenly 679, 680, Vol. II heavenly 725, 732, 926, 991, 1039

Cousin Vol. I 112, 119, 223, 239, 242, 308, 458, 480, 491, Vol. II 739, 740, 829, 846, 847, 866

COUTANCES Vol. II 728

Cowardliness Vol. II 1152

Cradle Vol. I *see* **JESUS**; Vol. II 1016, 1140 *see also* **JESUS**

Cream Vol. II 759

Creation Vol. I 552

Creator Vol. I 679

Creature (s) Vol. I 499, 501, 504, 553, 576, 577, 580, 588, 612, 615, 618, Vol. II 713, 748, 753, 762, 784, 785, 796, 813, 814, 826, 841, 862, 902, 961, 991, 995, 1070, 1117, 1127, 1152, 1163, eyes of 928, 933, 1121, 1160

Crime (s) Vol. II 762, 882, criminals 729

CROSS (BYZANTINE) Vol. I 421

Cross (es) Vol. I 454, 478, 529, 537, 557, 596, 630, Feast finding of 616, Vol. II 707, 761, 816, 838, 871, 872, 935, 960, 1014, 1042, 1092, ST. TERESA'S 909

Crown (s) Vol. I 399, 400, 454, 491, 496, 510, 577, 661, 667, of thorns 684, Vol. II 763, 794, 801, 816, 829, 838, 894, 910, 926, 934, 1093

Crucible Vol. I 563, Vol. II 728, 861, 878

Crucifix Vol. II 1071, **THÉRÈSE's first 1174**

Cry Vol. I 578

CUISINE d'ITALIE Vol. I 451, du MONDE 451

Cup Vol. II 872, 1042

Cure Vol. II 810, 1166

Curls Vol. I *see* **Lamb**

Darkness Vol. I 504, 511, 618, 658, Vol. II 752, 801, 804, 808, 861

Daughter Vol. I 191, 236, 298, 317, 382, 396, 405, 427, 452, 455, 456, 459, 462, 477, 478, 491, 495, 496, 502, 504, 505, 544, 596, 597, 615, 652, 654, 655, 661, 671, 674, 680, of Teresa 591, Vol. II 816, 921, 1011, 1072, 1165, of Teresa 1016

DAVID, MONSIEUR Vol. I 453, 455

DAVID (PSALMIST) Vol. I 553, Vol. II 1093, 1146

Dawn Vol. II 795, 804

Day (s) Vol. I 232, 233, 398, 406, 421, 449, 456, 461, 468, 479, 482, 483, 493, 494, 496, 500, 511, 514, 530, 537, 542, 546, 552, 553, 555, 556, 558, 561, 580, 600, 601, 620, 622, 631, 674, 675, 680, Vol. II 865, 882, 915, 1016, 1036, 1038, 1040, 1042, 1060, 1069, 1075, 1085, 1090, 1091, 1110, 1111, 1115, 1120, daylight 1038, of eternity 933, wedding CÉLINE 925

Death Vol. I 400, 576, of M. David 455, 456, of lamb 396, of silkworms 274, 275, Vol. II 709, 809, 882, 978, 1047, 1072, 1092, 1106, 1153, 1154, evening of life 741, 749, Papa's 884, Thérèse's

1173, voyage 1173

Debt (of gratitude) Vol. I 589, Vol. II 715, 739, of gratitude 956

Deeds (heroic) Vol. II 908

DELATROËTTE CANON Vol. I 392, Vol. II 902, 1017

Delight (s) Vol. I 546, 618, 630, Vol. II 808, 816, 827, 841, 863, 894, 903, 915, 936, 966, 969, 1016, 1085, 1110, 1118, 1139, 1142

Deliverance Vol. II 925

Demon Vol. II 810, 1017

Departure Vol. II 896, 1071, 1142, 1153, 1163, 1165, entrance into Carmel 1166

Depth (s) Vol. I 455, 501, Vol. II 994, 1021

Desert Vol. I 663, Vol. II 795, 841, 861

Desire (s) Vol. I 387, 388, 423, 468, 480, 481, 500, 541, 568, 580, 622, 651, Vol. II 722, 728, 741, 765, 784, 816, 830, 836, 865, 884, 902, 903, 956, 957, 999, 1000, 1010, 1014, 1015, 1017, 1022, 1034, 1043, 1054, 1059, 1060, 1071, 1072, 1073, 1085, 1093, 1094, 1101, 1116, 1140, 1142, 1145, 1154, 1160, 1164, 1165, 1173

Destiny Vol. I 266, 450

Detachment Vol. I 400, 577

Devil Vol. I 567, 568, 569, Vol. II 1070, MESSIRE SATANAS 1013

Dew Vol. II 795, 796, 800, 801, 843, 927, 1116

DIAMOND Vol. I *see* **MARTIN, MARIE**

Diamond (s) Vol. I 467, 563, 683, Vol. II 725, 785, 926, 927

Director (s) spiritual Vol. II 796, 1132, 1165, direction 1090

Discernment Vol. II 960

Disciple (s) Vol. II 753, 862, 882, 995

Discourses Vol. II 813

Disposition (s) Vol. I 425, 454, 455, Vol. II 965, 999

Distractions Vol. I 387, 388

Doctor Vol. II 1173

Doctors (of the Church) Vol. II 926, 927

Doctrine Vol. II 995

Doll Vol. I *see* **GUÉRIN, MARIE**; Vol. II *see* **GUÉRIN, MARIE** and **MARIE of the TRINITY**

DOMIN, M. L'ABBÉ Vol. I 663

DOMITIA, SAINT Vol. I 143

Donkey Vol. I 143, Vol. II *see* **MARTIN, PAULINE**

Door Vol. II of eternity 1128, of heaven 1146

Doubt (s) Vol. I 575, Vol. II 722, 759, 831

Dove Vol. I and Vol. II *see* **Birds**

DOVER Vol. I 248

Dowry Vol. I 679

Dream (s) Vol. I 233, 440, 537, 552, 568, 622, 630, Vol. II 732, 760, 838, 839, 841, 848, 957, 995, 1071

Dress Vol. II 902, 903

Dwelling Vol. II 896

Eagle Vol. I *see* **MARTIN, MARIE**

Ear Vol. I *see* **JESUS**

Earth Vol. I 234, 239, 289, 396, 399, 400, 429, 445, 452, 457, 479, 491, 500, 501, 510, 530, 542, 546, 557, 561, 564, 576, 577, 580, 616, 618, 621, 622, 641, 662, 679, *see also* **MARTIN, MARIE** Vol. II 712, 713, 724, 728, 739, 761, 781, 784, 785, 809, 816, 826, 828, 831, 833, 839, 850, 851, 853, 863, 866, 882, 894, 896, 908, 910, 921, 925, 926, 928, 933, 935, 936, 959, 960, 961, 965, 991, 1017, 1018, 1022, 1046, 1054, 1060, 1069, 1092, 1094, 1098, 1116, 1117, 1120, 1121, 1127, 1137, 1139, 1140, 1141, 1146, 1148, 1151, 1164, 1165, 1173

Earthenware Plates Vol. II 909

EASTER Vol. I 556, Monday 401, Vol. II 899

Ecstasy (ies) Vol. I 620, 675, divine 455, Vol. II 809

Education Vol. II 872

Egoist Vol. I 467

EGYPT Vol. I 461

ELECT Vol. I 462, 479, Vol. II 933,

1110, 1165

Elevator Vol. II 1098, 1152

ELIAS Vol. II 926, 969

Emotion Vol. II 743, 908, 909, 1092, feeling (s) 760, 853, 865, 884, 921, 930, 1021, 1153, pity 1136, sulking mood 966

Enclosure Vol. II *see* **CLOISTER**

Energy Vol. II 909

ENGADDI Vol. I 652

Entrance Vol. I *see* **CARMEL**; Vol. II 1128, 1141, 1149, 1152, *see also* **CARMEL**

Envy Vol. II 1015, 1021

Espousals Vol. I 435, 500, Vol. II 843

Eternal Vol. I 233, 396

Eternity Vol. I 399, 440, 542, 546, 553, 558, 577, 587, 588, 601, 602, 611, 661, Vol. II 707, 714, 724, 742, 781, 785, 786, 828, 839, 899, 925, 934, 951, 960, 961, 962, 977, 978, 1014, 1015, 1042, 1086, 1095, 1104, 1115, 1128, 1154

EUCHARIST Vol. I 555, Vol. II 839, HOST 956, 1016, wheat of the Elect 933

Evil Vol. I 567, 621

Exaggeration Vol. II 995

Excuse (s) Vol. I 152, Vol. II 829

Exile Vol. I 445, 454, 455, 546, 577, 578, 613, 616, 641, 661, 663, 675, 684, Vol. II 724, 728, 763, 784, 785, 816, 826, 835, 841, 843, 853, 871, 925, 935, 961, 970, 1014, 1054, 1060, 1072, 1085, 1094, 1127, 1139, 1145, 1148, 1163

Experience Vol. II 764, 936, 1017

EXTREME UNCTION Vol. II Thérèse's 1173

Eye(s) Vol. I 427, 455, 457, 462, 496, 500, 557, 577, 580, 675, *see also* **JESUS** and **THÉRÈSE**; Vol. II 713, 728, 741, 748, 753, 759, 760, 765, 781, 784, 803, 808, 826, 853, 855, 896, 995, 1033, 1116, of creatures 1121, 1160, of God 846, 849, 1092, of men 1092, *see also* **THÉRÈSE**

FABER, FATHER Vol. II 1021

Face (s) Vol. I 276, 667, *see also* **HOLY FACE** and **JESUS**; Vol. II 709, 762, 781, 809, 814, 828, 838, 839, 843, 848, 862, 933, 970, divine 1142

Faith Vol. II 722, 865, 908, 1092, 1140

Faithful Vol. I 332, 393, 547, Vol. II 871

Falsehood Vol. II 960

Family Vol. I 611, 616, 658, colony 642, Vol. II 759, 795, 811, 830, 831, 835, 894, 896, 928, 929, 969, 1046, 1093, 1165, Carmelite 933

Father Vol. II 977, 1153, 1165

FATHER Vol. I and Vol. II *see* **MARTIN, LOUIS** and **GOD**

FATHER SUPERIOR Vol. II *see* **DELATROËTTE, CANON**

Fault (s) Vol. I 152, 493, 662, Vol. II 785, 795, 965, 966, 1072, 1092, 1133, 1138, 1153, 1164, 1173

Favor (s) Vol. I 459, 480, 510, 542, 555, Vol. II 764, 811, 830, 882, 1000, 1015, 1054, 1060, 1095, 1145, 1153, of martyrdom 1085

Fear (s) Vol. I 236, 458, 568, 569, 575, Vol. II 936, 966, 994, 1000, 1033, 1133, 1152, 1173

FEAST (day) Vol. I 143, 229, 230, 232, 299, 467, 478, 590, 591, 596, 597, Our Lady of Mount Carmel 244, St. ELIZABETH of HUNGARY 332, 333, Vol. II 712, 713, 714, 715, 727, 731, 739, 740, 741, 743, 744, 753, 759, 760, 762, 811, 826, 831, 832, 839, 848, 894, 921, 934, 1044, 1070, 1132, (day) 888, 895, 916, 951, 956, 1010, 1022, 1047, 1154, 1174, of All Saints 1069, of Good Shepherd 1090, of St. Luke 917, Precious Blood 727

Feeling (s) Vol. II *see* **Emotion**

FÉLICITÉ (servant) Vol. I 249

Fervor Vol. I 641, Vol. II 888, 902, 1010

Fiancé (e) Vol. I 556, 667, Jesus 467, 496, 504, 511, 514, 519, 530, 641, 642, 651, 652, 654, Vol. II 816, 843, 925, 926, 929, 1060, Céline's 928

Field (s) Vol. I 542, Vol. II 753, 784, 796, 801, of battle 827, 863, 1069, 1085, 1142, of scripture 861

Fight Vol. II 853, 1010

Fire (s) Vol. I 233, of Hell 399, 401, Jesus on 553, of love 557, Vol. II 801, 908, 933, 956, 1010, 1090, 1093, 1121, 1134

Fireworks Vol. I 510

Fish (es) Vol. I 281, 425, 544, 556, April 266, Vol. II 851, 881, 916, delicacies 882, lobster 1070

Flame (s) Vol. I 529, Vol. II 999, of Purgatory 1072, 1093

Flock Vol. II 958, 959, 960, 961

Flower (s) Vol. I 152, 191, 238, 496, 541, 560, 591, Vol. II 708, 712, 713, 714, 725, 741, 742, 748, 781, 784, 796, 801, 827, 838, 839, 894, 902, 916, 952, 989, 1038, 1084, 1098, 1146, 1160, language of 713, 741, 748, models of 916

　Bouquet Vol. I 560, 561, 589, 622, Vol. II 753, 781, 927

　Bud Vol. I 622, Vol. II 748

　Calyx Vol. I 449, Vol. II 713, 714, 784, 801

　Corolla Vol. II 741, 749, 784, 1116

　Daisy Vol. II 725, 748, 749

　Forget-me-not (s) Vol. II 952, 1116

　Heather Vol. II 753

　Lily (ies) Vol. I 449, 495, 496, 542, 611, 616, 618, immortelle *see* **MARTIN, CÉLINE**, *see also* **JESUS**; Vol. II 725, 894, 926, 927, bouquet 930, 1010, *see also* **MARTIN, CÉLINE** and **THÉRÈSE**

　Pansy Vol. II 1160

　Petals Vol. I 611, 613, 618, Vol. II 926

　Rose (es) Vol. I 143, 190, 281, 282, Vol. II 714, 725, 784, 894, 926, 1085, 1132, rosebuds 1160

　Stamen Vol. I 449

　Verbena Vol. I 459

　Violet Vol. I 427

　　see also Vol. I **JESUS** and **THÉRÈSE**, *see also* Vol. II

MARIE OF THE TRINITY and **THÉRÈSE**

Flowerpot (s) Vol. I 587

Folly (ies) Vol. II 882, 1015

Food Vol. II 882, 933, hunger 916

Fool (s) Vol. II 882

Foot (feet) Vol. I 429, 480, 481, *see also* **JESUS**; Vol. II 761, 765, 804, 816, 850, 1040, 1122, of the Cross 1042, *see also* **JESUS**

Forehead Vol. I 234, Vol. II 732

Forgetfulness Vol. I 630, Vol. II 844

Foundress (es) Vol. II 1035

FOURNET, MADAME Vol. I 454, 596, Vol. II 833, 834, 895, 921, 1022

FRANCE Vol. I 289, 308, 431, 461, 462, 510, Vol. II 728, 729, 957, 1014, 1085

FRANCIS DE SALES, SAINT Vol. I 557

FRANCIS LA NÉELE Vol. II *see* **LA NÉELE, FRANCIS**

FRANCIS XAVIER, SAINT Vol. I 398

Francs Vol. I 619

Freedom Vol. II 959

Friend (s) Vol. I 238, 239, 478, 630, meaning Jesus 449, 499, 642, Vol. II 708, 784, 808, 826, 827, 836, 837, 841, 847, 882, 1092, 1093, 1128, 1137, 1152, 1164

Fruit (s) Vol. I 557, Vol. II 828

Fun Vol. I 140, 244, 431

Furnace Vol. II 994, 1084

Future Vol. II 743, 843, 866, 871, 1060, 1072, 1094, 1139

GALILEE Vol. II 804

Gall Vol. I 400

Game (s) Vol. II 872, 1040

Garden Vol. I 232, 557, Vol. II 708, 784, 795, 838, 1085, Gethsemane 862, of agony 908, 1041, of my heart 1160

Gem (s) Vol. I 457

General Vol. I *see* **MARTIN, CÉLINE**

Generosity Vol. II 908, 929, 1054

GENEVIÈVE, MOTHER Vol. II 731, 749, 781, 927, 935

GENEVIÈVE OF THE HOLY FACE,

Sister Vol. I and Vol. II *see* **MARTIN, CÉLINE**

GENEVIÉVE, SAINT Vol. II 927

GENOA Vol. I 431

GERMAIN, BISHOP Vol. I 353

Gift (s) Vol. I 390, 395, 457, 460, 461, 496, 589, 602, 654, 667, of the HOLY SPIRIT 429, present 421, Vol. II 731, 743, 747, 760, 809, 814, 848, 863, 882, 894, 916, 933, 936, 1160, of God 1085, of Nature 1094, *see also* **present**

GILBERT, TH. Vol. I 459

Gingerbread Vol. I 496

Girl Vol. I *see* **THÉRÈSE**, Vol. II 861, 1017, 1046, 1072, 1101, 1138, *see also* **THÉRÈSE**

Glance Vol. I and Vol. II *see* **Look**

Glory (ies) Vol. I 454, 530, 537, 552, 591, 612, 630, 661, 675, Vol. II 742, 810, 816, 828, 833, 839, 863, 896, 910, 927, 928, 929, 934, 951, 959, 977, 978, 1042, 1043, 1054, 1059, 1060, 1084, 1092, 1094

Goal Vol. I 561, 651, Vol. II 729, 816, 865, 872, 1011, 1014, 1016, 1042, purpose 865

GOD Vol. I 230, 233, 248, 273, 276, 289, 298, 317, 332, 335, 353, 354, 365, 380, 382, 387, 388, 393, 398, 399, 423, 435, 445, 450, 452, 454, 455, 457, 458, 462, 467, 476, 479, 482, 491, 510, 530, 544, 547, 564, 575, 576, 577, 587, 596, 600, 618, 621, 630, 640, 674, 679, Father 602, 622, Will of 332, 353, 365, 381, 382, 400, 468, 684, Vol. II 707, 712, 714, 722, 725, 729, 739, 743, 763, 764, 765, 781, 801, 811, 813, 830, 831, 833, 835, 843, 846, 851, 853, 861, 862, 863, 865, 866, 870, 871, 878, 882, 884, 888, 889, 902, 903, 908, 909, 915, 916, 929, 956, 965, 966, 967, 994, 999, 1000, 1010, 1014, 1015, 1022, 1042, 1054, 1055, 1059, 1069, 1071, 1072, 1084, 1085, 1086, 1090, 1092, 1093, 1094, 1095, 1101, 1110, 1111, 1120, 1122, 1127, 1134, 1137, 1140, 1142, 1145, 1146, 1148, 1159, 1163, 1165, 1166, 1170, 1173, Almighty 1164, Commands 959, Creator 753, 995, Divine musician 863, FATHER 894, 896, 1041, 1060, 1152, Fidelity 794, Generosity 843, Holiness 1173, Heart 714, Will of 709, 794, 1139, 1146, 1152, Perfect 1137, Vision of 896

See also Vol. I and Vol. II **HOLY SPIRIT** and **JESUS**

GODCHILD Vol. II 1060

GODMOTHER Vol. I 334, 395, 396, 400, Vol. II 1045, 1060

Gold Vol. II 861, 878, epaulettes 1013

Gondola Vol. I 318

GONZAGUE, MOTHER MARIE DE Vol. I 152, 191, 290, 308, 354, 396, 401, 450, 510, 511, 575, 591, 619, 658, 662, 663, Vol. II 811, 814, 834, 847, 861, 866, 871, 873, 878, 917, 956, 958, 959, 960, 977, 993, 1010, 1011, 1015, 1018, 1038, 1041, 1042, 1043, 1059, 1069, 1070, 1071, 1072, 1083, 1090, 1091, 1095, 1097, 1098, 1139, 1140, 1142, 1153, 1154, 1173, 1174, shepherdess 959, 960

GOOD FRIDAY Vol. II 1104

Good (s) Vol. II 872, 1022, 1030, 1137, 1152, spiritual 1084

GOSPEL Vol. I 450, Vol. II 732, 753, 800, 804, 808, 862, 894, 977

Grace (s) Vol. I 399, 401, 423, 449, 454, 467, 482, 491, 496, 510, 514, 521, 530, 547, 557, 568, 580, 588, 589, 596, 617, 618, 621, 640, 641, 662, as call to Carmel 298, 299, 308, 380, 382, 392, Vol. II 707, 709, 712, 729, 731, 732, 781, 805, 813, 830, 835, 851, 853, 865, 866, 894, 896, 902, 926, 933, 936, 999, 1000, 1010, 1014, 1016, 1022, 1041, 1055, 1061, 1072, 1085, 1090, 1093, 1095, 1101, 1117, 1127, 1132, 1133, 1146, 1173, 1174

Grades Vol. I *see* **School**

Grain of sand Vol. I *see* **THÉRÈSE**, Vol. II 851

GRANDMAMMA Vol. II *see* **FOURNET, MADAME**

Grapes Vol. I 589

Gratitude Vol. I 493, 495, 544, 545, Vol. II 712, 763, 765, 810, 829, 834, 839, 849, 917, 961, 993, 994, 1015, 1021, 1022, 1046, 1054, 1055, 1059, 1072, 1086, 1098, 1100, 1101, 1170

Grille Vol. I 459, Vol. II 846, 849, 916, 1060

GUÉRIN FAMILY

GUÉRIN, CÉLINE (AUNT) Vol. I 133, 140, 223, 238, 239, 242, 244, 249, 275, 276, 281, 282, 308, 317, 332, 333, 342, 365, 366, 429, 453, 454, 455, 459, 477, 478, 480, 490, 491, 496, 544, 545, 576, 589, 596, 597, 600, 602, Feast 342, 365, Vol. II 712, 715, 731, 743, 744, 759, 763, 764, 765, 810, 811, 832, 833, 834, 837, 848, 849, 863, 873, 878, 894, 895, 907, 908, 909, 910, 915, 921, 966, 969, 970, 1021, 1022, 1160

GUÉRIN, ISIDORE (UNCLE) Vol. I 239, 249, 281, 288, 289, 298, 308, 318, 333, 388, 401, 406, 429, 453, 454, 480, 491, 496, 544, 545, 556, 576, 589, 597, 600, 602, 616, 684, Vol. II 712, 739, 764, 765, 813, 833, 834, 837, 863, 894, 907, 908, 915, 916, 921, 967, 970, 1022, 1160

GUÉRIN, JEANNE (COUSIN), (DAREL) Vol. I 223, 242, 244, 249, 273, 274, 275, 276, 281, 282, 308, 318, 333, 342, 343, 429, 459, 480, 545, 576, 589, 602, 616, 619, Vol. II (MADAME LA NÉELE) 712, 739, 753, 759, 810, 811, 829, 830, 833, 881, 910, 915, 916, 917, 967, 1022, 1145, 1160, Fifine 915

GUÉRIN, MARIE-DOSITHÉE SISTER, Vol. II 816, 853

GUÉRIN, MARIE (SR. MARIE OF THE EUCHARIST) (COUSIN) (LOUPLOUP) Earlier Name SR. MARIE OF THE BLESSED SACRAMENT Vol. I 116, 119, 133, 205, 223, 241, 242, 244, 249, 273, 275, 281, 282, 317, 333, 334, 342, 365, 429, 458, 480, 555, 567, 568, 569, 575, 576, 589, 600, 602, 618, 622, 631, 641, 642, bird 281, country girl 641, doll 480, 481, imp 429, 459, louploup 481, mistress of the house 545, Vol. II 712, 759, 821, 861, 863, 873, 907, 909, 915, 916, 970, 1021, 1110, 1111, 1146, 1181, angel 909, 915, angelic 908, Benjamin 921, control 909, doll 1111, gaiety 909, 915, imp 917, melancholy 759, postulant 915, rascal 915, treasure 909, valiant woman 909, voice 915, 1146

Guide (divine) Vol. I 493, 651

Gypsy Vol. I *see* **MARTIN, MARIE**

Habit (reception of) Vol. I 461, 483, 491, 495, 496, 512, 519, 671, Vol. II 902, 1174, Léonie's Visitandine 835, 843, 844

Hair Vol. I 429, 496, Vol. II 743, 855, 966, 1016, 1097

Halo Vol. I 421

Hand (s) Vol. I 112, 232, 233, 244, 299, 399, 400, 442, 454, 456, 457, 499, 500, 537, 553, 577, 596, 600, 619, 651, 667, 683, 684, His gentle little 440, 442, 456, Vol. II 728, 810, 826, 837, 838, 841, 878, 908, 928, 1014, 1015, 1018, 1054, 1122, divine 816, 909, of angels 927, God's 1122, *see also* **JESUS; MARTIN, CÉLINE** and **THÉRÈSE**

Hanoi Vol. II 1071

Happiness Vol. I 308, 332, 493, 504, 577, Vol. II 809, 843, 844, 855, 862, 916, 956, 962, 966, 1069, 1148, 1163, 1173, 1174

Harp Vol. II 899, 1039

Head Vol. I *see* **THÉRÈSE**, Vol. II 1110,

see also **JESUS** and **THÉRÈSE**

Headache Vol. I *see* **THÉRÈSE**

Health Vol. I 223, *see also* **Illness**; Vol. II 759, 871, 899, 967, 969, 1054

Heart Vol. I 233, 421, 423, 442, 445, 457, 479, 496, 504, 530, 537, 541, 547, 553, 555, 557, 569, 575, 576, 577, 580, 596, 602, 630, 631, divine 600, good 684, pure of 618, quiet of 641, strength of 588, Vol. II 708, 709, 712, 713, 715, 725, 728, 732, 743, 744, 749, 760, 762, 763, 764, 765, 781, 782, 784, 794, 795, 796, 804, 810, 813, 814, 815, 816, 827, 828, 830, 832, 833, 836, 837, 839, 841, 846, 847, 848, 850, 851, 855, 861, 862, 865, 882, 894, 896, 935, 936, 956, 958, 959, 960, 961, 966, 995, 1033, 1035, 1038, 1042, 1084, 1085, 1114, 1117, 1128, 1133, 1138, 1140, 1149, 1152, 1153, 1164, *see also* **JESUS' Heart**

THÉRÈSE's Heart Vol. I 239, 317, 332, 333, 335, 342, 353, 380, 381, 387, 393, 406, 429, 435, 440, 452, 454, 455, 456, 461, 467, 477, 481, 482, 483, 491, 495, 500, 502, 505, 514, 529, 545, 546, 556, 561, 563, 567, 587, 590, 591, 597, 611, 612, 613, 629, 642, 652, 661, Vol. II 723, 853, 854, 866, 878, 884, 902, 908, 915, 916, 917, 921, 929, 951, 961, 977, 993, 999, 1000, 1014, 1016, 1018, 1021, 1022, 1038, 1054, 1069, 1073, 1083, 1084, 1085, 1093, 1095, 1098, 1101, 1120, 1133, 1135, 1142, 1146, 1148, 1152, 1160

All my heart—meaning Thérèse's Vol. I 112, 116, 119, 133, 143, 147, 190, 191, 205, 232, 237, 242, 275, 276, 281, 282, 290, 308, 460, 496, 510

Into my heart—meaning Thérèse's Vol. I 152, 191, 289, 298, Vol. I and Vol. II

Heaven Vol. I 191, 233, 421, 442, 454, 459, 462, 468, 479, 491, 493, 494, 510, 514, 546, 547, 553, 561, 563, 564, 580, 601, 602, 620, 621, 654, 661, 662, 672, beatitude 630, fatherland 675, home 468, Jesus king of 452, language of 684, *see also* **colloquialisms**, Vol. II 729, 732, 739, 743, 753, 781, 784, 785, 794, 811, 814, 816, 826, 828, 830, 831, 835, 839, 849, 850, 851, 853, 854, 882, 884, 896, 910, 925, 926, 929, 933, 951, 952, 956, 960, 961, 967, 969, 970, 978, 993, 995, 1000, 1014, 1015, 1016, 1018, 1021, 1034, 1038, 1040, 1042, 1046, 1054, 1055, 1059, 1060, 1069, 1071, 1072, 1085, 1092, 1093, 1094, 1095, 1096, 1098, 1110, 1117, 1120, 1128, 1137, 1140, 1141, 1142, 1145, 1146, 1148, 1149, 1152, 1153, 1164, 1165, 1173, beatitude 1142, blessed city 1141, bliss 1152, *see* **homeland** Vol. I and Vol. II

HEBREWS Vol. II 1164

Hell Vol. I 399, 401

Hermit Vol. I **THÉRÈSE** 590, 651, *see also* **MARTIN, MARIE,** Vol. II 927

HEROD Vol. II 882

Heroism Vol. I 577, Vol. II 1166

Hidden Vol. II 862, 933, 977

History (French) Vol. I 238, Vol. II 1085

Hole Vol. I *see* **Colloquialisms**

Holidays Vol. I 143, 244

HOLY FATHER Vol. I 332, *see also* **POPE**; Vol. II 1174 *see also* **POPE**

HOLY SPIRIT Vol. I 429, 680, Vol. II 994, 1146, 1160

HOLY WEEK Vol. II 1164

Home Vol. I 237, 244, 684, Vol. II 804, 808, 816, 841, 894, 896, 916, 1038

Homeland Vol. I 530, meaning heaven 445, Vol. II meaning heaven 724, 784, 796, 816, 827, 828, 833, 839, 849, 853, 861, 865, 896, 933, 970, 1046, 1054, 1060, 1098, 1142

Honor (s) Vol. II 816, 894, 933, 969, 1015, 1021, 1042, 1094

Hope (s) Vol. I 233, 454, 580, Vol. II 713, 743, 829, 848, 999, 1015, 1054, 1060, 1101, 1142, 1146

Horizons Vol. I 529, infinite 455, 457, 546, Vol. II 724, 754, 995, 1094

HOST Vol. II *see* **EUCHARIST**

Hotel Vol. I 427

HOULGATE Vol. I 143

House Vol. I 140, 239, 401, of love 642, Vol. II 761, 813, 841, 882, 899, 961, 1017, 1021, 1038

Hug Vol. I and Vol. II *see* **Affection**

HUGONIN, MONSEIGNEUR Vol. 1 380, 381, 387, 388, 405, 406

Human Vol. II 871

Humanity Vol. II 1015

Humble Vol. II 855

Humiliation (s) Vol. I *see* **Profession Invitation**, Vol. II 816, 909, 1166

Humility Vol. I 575, 580, 662, Vol. II 761, 836, 839, 851, 1015, 1030, 1084, 1085, 1148, 1175

Hundredfold Vol. II 712, 916, 978, 1042, 1046

Husband Vol. II 865, 866

HUSE, MARCELLINE Vol. I 318, 481, Vol. II now Sister Marie Joseph of the Cross

Idler (s) Vol. II 882

Illness Vol. I Léonie's 616, Papa's 482, 542, Vol. II as leader 1121, torment 1116, *see also* **THÉRÈSE**

Illusion Vol. I 557, Vol. II 760, 1093

Image (s) Vol. II 741, 761, 838, 861, 925, 1100, 1101

IMITATION OF CHRIST Vol. II 1069

Immolation Vol. II 1165

Imp Vol. I *see* **GUÉRIN, MARIE**

Imperfect Vol. II 1122, *see also* **THÉRÈSE**

Imperfection Vol. II 1016, 1122, *see also* **THÉRÈSE**

Impulse Vol. II 1164

Indelicacy (ies) Vol. II 1164, 1165

Infidels Vol. II 1015

Infidelities Vol. II 855, 1164

Infirmarian Vol. II 883, 1127

Infirmary Vol. II 1136

Infinity Vol. I 546, Vol. II 725, 801

Infirmaties Vol. I 641

Influenza Vol. I 600

Ingratitude Vol. I 630, Vol. II 708, 1132

Inheritance Vol. II 1173, 1174

Ink Vol. II 796

Inn Vol. I (bad) 427, Vol. II 1038

Innocence Vol. II 927, 929, 936

Instrument (s) Vol. II 960, 1015, musical 782, 1012, God using 814, 827

Insult Vol. I 612

Intention (s) Vol. II 707, 1055, 1084, 1086, 1093

Interior Vol. II 762

Intimacy Vol. II 1133

Intimates Vol. II 882

Intrepide No. 2 Vol. I *see* **MARTIN, CÉLINE**

Invitation Vol. I *see* **Profession Invitation**

Iron Vol. II 871

ISAIAS (PROPHET) Vol. I 630, 631, Vol. II 966, 978, 994

ISRAELITES Vol. I 461

ITALY Vol. I 318, 342, 365, 457, Vol. II 1174

Itinerary Vol. I 618, 651

Jealous Vol. I 529, Vol. II 827, 855

JEANNE GUÉRIN *see* **GUÉRIN, JEANNE**

Jerusalem Vol. II 871, 1017

JESUS Vol. I 289, 298, 380, 381, 398, 399, 435, 440, 442, 449, 450, 452, 456, 457, 467, 468, 478, 482, 483, 493, 494, 496, 499, 500, 501, 504, 505, 510, 511, 512, 514, 519, 520, 529, 530, 537, 541, 542, 544, 545, 546, 547, 552, 553, 555, 556, 557, 558, 563, 564, 567, 568, 569, 575, 576, 577, 579, 580, 587, 589, 611, 612, 615, 616, 620, 622, 630, 631, 662, 675, 682, 683, 684, 685, Vol. II 707, 709, 712, 713, 714, 725, 728, 729, 733, 740, 743, 748, 749, 752, 753, 761, 762,

764, 781, 784, 786, 794, 795, 800, 801, 803, 804, 808, 809, 813, 814, 816, 826, 827, 828, 831, 832, 833, 836, 838, 839, 841, 843, 846, 848, 849, 851, 852, 854, 855, 862, 865, 871, 872, 878, 882, 884, 888, 894, 897, 899, 902, 916, 917, 926, 928, 930, 932, 936, 956, 965, 991, 993, 994, 995, 1015, 1032, 1033, 1034, 1035, 1036, 1037, 1038, 1040, 1042, 1043, 1045, 1046, 1047, 1054, 1055, 1059, 1060, 1069, 1071, 1072, 1073, 1083, 1084, 1090, 1091, 1092, 1093, 1094, 1095, 1096, 1098, 1101, 1104, 1106, 1110, 1111, 1116, 1117, 1121, 1122, 1127, 1128, 1132, 1133, 1134, 1138, 1145, 1146, 1149, 1151, 1152, 1153, 1160, 1163, 1165

Absence Vol. II 933

Arms Vol. II 801, 989, 1164, 1165, 1175

ALL Vol. I 641

Beloved Vol. I 553, 591, 602, 655, 667, unique 641, Vol. II 752, 761, 762, 784, 795, 804, 808, 826, 827, 838, 863, 882, 951, 1018

Blood Vol. I clothing stained in 630, face of 580, name of 537, 553, 591, 611, Vol. II 753, 838, 966

Bridegroom Vol. I 461, Vol. II 925, 926, 927, 933, 1110, 1139, 1165

Child Vol. I 388, 390, 433, 680, Altar of 589, Cellar of 433, Vol. II divine 903, 1021, 1043

Cradle Vol. I 390, 602, Vol. II 828, 835, crib 838, 839, 1043

Descriptions of Vol. I gentle violence 387, Lily of our souls 618, Lily without name 611, need for love 622, on fire 553, quench thirst 587, 591, 630, thirsty 622, touch of love 684, weeps 567, 568, Vol. II asleep 862, 989, beggar of love 894, 966, brightness 1117, divine quest 764, flower of the fields 933, foolish 882, heavenly painter 995, knight of suf-

fering 933, lamb 713, 926, 933, 991, lily of the valleys 933, 1117, prisoner 966, prisoner of love 957, reality 951, spiritual director 796, strong God 1042, treasure 1164, wedding 925

Divine guide Vol. I 651, divine spouse 661

Ear (s) of Vol. I 611

Eyes of Vol. I 553, 652, 667, belles-de-nuit 613, Vol. II 739

Face Vol. I 553, 618, 630, 652, 675, 680, 685, Vol. II 933, 1046, 1174
Vol. I adorable 580, beloved's 667, blood-stained 580, hidden 671, image of the holy 611, luminous 580, of the most beautiful and whitest of lilies 618, picture of 591, unknown and beloved 685, Vol. II adorable 781, divine 1142, sorrow 961, 1138

Fiancé Vol. I 467, 496, 504, 511, 514, 519, 530, 578, 591, 641, 642, 651, 652, 654

Foot (Feet) of Vol. I 299, 483, 557, Vol. II 961, 1054

Friend Vol. I 449, 499, 568, 642

Hand (s) of Vol. II 796, 961, 936, 1035

Head Vol. II 762, 764, 804, 882

Heart Vol. I 458, 478, 501, 503, 568, Vol. II 709, 844, 863, 897, 930, 933, 934, 951, 961, 966, 1011, 1013, 1033, 1045, 1055, 1061, 1084, 1086, 1091, 1132, 1133, 1149, 1152, 1164

King Vol. I 452, 457, 460, 493, 611, 641, Vol. II 715, 732, 762, 925

Kingdom Vol. II 800

Kiss Vol. II 952

Knees Vol. II 959, 1038

Lips Vol. I 591, Vol. II 1042, 1164

Little Vol. I 152, 190, 191, 299, 335, 382, 387

Look Vol. I 588, 613, glance 530, 620, veiled 684, Vol. II 902

Lord Vol. I 455, 557, Vol. II 866, 884,

908, 909, 936, 960, 966, 977, 979, 993, 1010, 1014, 1015, 1016, 1017, 1021, 1041, 1042, 1054, 1055, 1059, 1060, 1084, 1085, 1092, 1093, 1101, 1123, 1140, 1141, 1142

Majesty (gentle) Vol. II 959

Master Vol. I 435, 567, Vol. II 865, 929, 994, 1015, 1042, 1054, 1092, Master's call 1133

Mouth Vol. II 862, 1164

Savior Vol. II 908, 1014, 1015, 1017, 1041, 1042, 1061, 1083, 1151

Spouse Vol. I 529, 546, 652, 675, 684, divine 661, of blood 658, of tears 684, of virgins 661, Vol. II 709, 715, 722, 724, 728, 732, 739, 748, 794, 828, 832, 841, 861, 951, 956, 966, 1014, 1054, 1085, 1110, 1117, of blood 862

Statue of little Vol. I 671

Tears of Vol. I 580, 591, 630, 631, 667, Vol. II 732, 741, 935

Titles Vol. I Flower of flowers 613, King of heaven 452, King of Kings and Lord of Lords 679, Man and son of Mary 680, Passion 679, Second Person of the Adorable Trinity 680, Son of Man 680, Word of God 680, Vol. II Great general 1013, King of glory 882, King of heaven 956, 966, 1014, 1085, 1092, King of kings 863, King of martyrs 999, Love 1133, 1165, 1175, of the Eucharist 1110, Shepherd 959, 961, Sun of justice 785, Word of God 862

Victim Vol. II 951, 1061, 1173

Viaticum Vol. II 1173

Voice Vol. II 804, 994

JEW Vol. II 1047, 1116

Jewels Vol. I 456, 683

JOAN OF ARC Vol. II 927, 1085, warrior's costume 927

JOB Vol. II 811

JOHN OF THE CROSS, SAINT Vol. I 632, Vol. II 752, 761, 927, 953, 1069

JOHN THE BAPTIST, SISTER SAINT Vol. II 1100, 1101, severity 1101

JOSEPH, SAINT Vol. II 709, 930, 1038, 1060, 1069, 1086, spouse 1038

JOSEPH DE SALES, SISTER (Visitandine) Vol. II 849

JOSHUA Vol. II 1018

JOURNEY Vol. II 803, 967, 1014

Joy (s) Vol. I 190, 229, 234, 238, 239, 241, 276, 299, 308, 318, 333, 343, 365, 399, 400, 427, 449, 454, 461, 478, 493, 495, 496, 501, 504, 511, 537, 542, 546, 553, 555, 558, 561, 563, 564, 577, 587, 596, 616, 620, 621, 629, 651, 662, 671, 684, of color 671, Vol. II 743, 744, 794, 795, 809, 811, 816, 827, 831, 832, 835, 841, 843, 844, 846, 848, 853, 862, 865, 866, 882, 888, 896, 899, 908, 915, 925, 927, 928, 929, 956, 957, 958, 960, 966, 969, 977, 978, 993, 999, 1010, 1013, 1033, 1040, 1043, 1054, 1055, 1060, 1069, 1085, 1090, 1092, 1093, 1098, 1101, 1128, 1141, 1142, 1145, 1146, 1148, 1152, 1153, 1160, 1164, 1165, 1174, of angels and saints 961, of Jesus 930, joyful 1120

Justice Vol. II 1000, 1093, 1101, 1173, God's 707, 1093

Kind (ness) Vol. I 241, 382, 387, 396, 405, 433, 482, 495, 509, 510, 544, 600, Vol. II 715, 829, 871, 961, 1054, 1072

King (s) Vol. I 493, *see also* **JESUS** and **MARTIN, LOUIS** Vol. II 927, 1072, 1085, 1093, 1121 *see also* **JESUS** and **MARTIN, LOUIS**

Kingdom (s) Vol. I 479, 493, 679, head of the 462, Vol. II 862, 925, 934, 1032, 1085, 1092, 1093, 1094, 1141, of Carmel 1017

Kiss (es) Vol. I and Vol. II *see* **affection**

Knowledge Vol. I 575, Vol. II 759, 803, 915

Lace Vol. I 461, Vol. II 902

Lady Vol. I 274, 281, 679, 680

Lamb Vol. I 395, 396, *see also* **MARTIN, PAULINE** and **THÉRÈSE** Vol. II 958, 959, 961, 962, *see also* **JESUS**

Lamp Vol. I 429, 459, 480, Vol. II 1132

LA MUSSE Vol. II 881, 907, 970, Chateau 810

Land Vol. II 803, foreign 724, 827, 929, native 709, 732

LA NÉELE, FRANCIS Vol. II 739, 759, 810, 830, 881, 910, 915, 917, 967, 1022, 1145, 1160

Language Vol. I 318, 620, 684, Vol. II 760, 795, 853, 865, 908, 994, expressions 1021, of this earth 1140

LA PRIEURE, MADAME Vol. I 483

LAST SUPPER Vol. II 1152

Laugh Vol. II 1039, (ing) 1070, 1120

LAZARAS Vol. II 882

LECHÊNE, M. L'ABBÉ Vol. II 969

LEFRANÇOISE, MOTHER MARIE DE SALES Vol. II 854, 884, 889, 897, 899, 903

LE MANS Vol. II 849, 902

LENT Vol. I 395, Vol. II 846, 899, 1058, 1069

LEO XIII Vol. I and Vol. II *see* **POPE**

LE ROY, MOTHER JEANNE-FRAN-ÇOISE Vol. II 854, 884, 889, 897, 899, 903

LES BUISSONNETS Vol. I 275, 276, 555, 564

Life Vol. I 233, 281, 399, 400, 401, 423, 427, 452, 454, 455, 457, 467, 482, 491, 494, 537, 546, 553, 564, 568, 569, 577, 587, 588, 591, 602, 621, 631, 658, 662, eternal 479, of Carmel 392, 590, Vol. II 709, 713, 724, 739, 741, 743, 784, 785, 795, 804, 813, 826, 827, 835, 839, 841, 847, 862, 865, 866, 881, 882, 884, 896, 926, 933, 934, 951, 959, 960, 978, 995, 1014, 1015, 1017, 1018, 1022, 1042, 1043, 1054, 1060, 1061, 1071, 1073, 1084, 1085, 1086, 1092, 1093, 1095, 1117, 1133, 1140, 1152, 1153, 1165, 1175, arena 1165, brevity 896,

eternal 927, 1128, 1141, 1163, lives 883, 1011, religious 816, 831, 915

Light Vol. I 442, 459, 491, 504, 511, 577, 580, 588, 613, 618, 652, 658, Vol. II 732, 753, 801, 813, 831, 861, 903, 1016

Lily (ies) Vol. I *see* **Flowers**, immortelle *see* **MARTIN, CÉLINE**, *see also* **JESUS**; Vol. II *see* **Flowers**, *see also* **MARTIN, CÉLINE** and **THÉRÈSE**

Linen (s) Vol. I 396, 662, Vol. II 917, 956

Lion Vol. I *see* **MARTIN, MARIE**

Lips Vol. I 553; Vol. I and Vol. II *see also* **JESUS**-lips

LISIEUX Vol. I 119, 229, 241, 298, 317, 365, Vol. II 871, 883, 915, 1073

Little one (littlest one) Vol. II 897, 961, 965, 966, 1021

Littleness Vol. II 999, 1096, 1117, 1120

Look (s) (Glance) Vol. I 588, 600, *see also* **JESUS**; Vol. II 724, 749, 785, 801, 804, 835, 846, 909, 965, 969, 994, 1016, 1034, 1154, *see also* **JESUS, MARTIN, CÉLINE** and **THÉRÈSE**

LORD Vol. I and Vol. II *see* **JESUS**

LORETTO Vol. I 335

LOUIS, SAINT Vol. I 431

LOURDES Vol. I 616, 618, 620, Vol. II 866

Love (noun) Vol. I 433, 440, 482, 504, 529, 530, 537, 542, 546, 557, 558, 568, 575, 576, 577, 588, 602, 611, 616, 618, 622, 630, 631, 641, 642, 651, 654, 658, 661, 662, 667, 682, 683, 684, sickness of 641, Vol. II 723, 725, 753, 782, 785, 795, 796, 801, 804, 808, 810, 813, 816, 826, 830, 838, 839, 852, 853, 855, 866, 882, 889, 896, 908, 909, 917, 929, 933, 934, 936, 953, 956, 961, 966, 970, 979, 989, 994, 995, 999, 1010, 1012, 1013, 1015, 1016, 1018, 1039, 1042, 1059, 1060, 1069, 1084, 1085, 1090, 1093, 1098, 1100, 1101, 1104, 1110, 1121, 1128, 1132, 1133, 1134, 1139, 1146, 1152, 1153, 1175, acts of 806, 813, 829, sighs of 965

LOYONS, HYACINTHE PÈRE Vol. II
  728
LUKE, SAINT Vol. II 917
LYONS Vol. I 461
Lyre (of my heart) Vol. I 611, Vol. II 782,
  796, 813, 828, 851
MADELEINE, MARIE, SISTER Vol. II
  894
MAGDALENE, MARY SAINT Vol. II
  732, 882, 883, 1133
MAGDELAINE, LOUISE Vol. I 110
Magnet Vol. I 365
Majesty Vol. I *see* **MARTIN, LOUIS**;
  Vol. II *see* **JESUS**
Mamma Vol. I and Vol. II *see* **MARTIN**
  PAULINE
Man (men) Vol. I 462, 479, 530, just man
  455, *see also* **Profession Invitation**,
  Vol. II 1121, 1122, 1159
Mantle Vol. I 618
MARCELLINE Vol. I 481
MARGARET MARY, SAINT Vol. I
  299, Vol. II 729, 816, 888, 1084, 1085,
  lover of His heart 1084
MARIA (servant) Vol. I 318
MARIE ALOYSIA, SISTER (Sister
  Marie Aolysia) Vol. I 110, Vol. II 848
MARIE DE GONZAGUE, MOTHER
  Vol. I and Vol. II *see* **GONZAGUE**
MARIE OF JESUS, SISTER Vol. II
  spouse 1138
MARIE OF ST. JOSEPH, SISTER Vol.
  II 989, 990, 1012, 1013
MARIE OF THE TRINITY, SISTER
  (Marie Castel) Vol. II 872, 952, 953,
  1137, 1175, flower 1116, rabbit 872
Marks Vol. I *see* **School**
Marriage Vol. II 865, 932
MARSEILLES Vol. II 1014
MARTHA, SAINT Vol. II 784, 882, 883
MARTHA OF JESUS, SISTER Vol. I
  519, 520, 682
MARTIN FAMILY
  MARTIN, CÉLINE (SISTER
    GENEVIÈVE OF THE HOLY
FACE) Vol. I 112, 147, 168, 191,
  204, 205, 242, 248, 266, 274, 275,
  276, 299, 307, 308, 317, 318, 334,
  342, 393, 396, 401, 423, 450, 459,
  467, 529, 542, 551, 552, 555, 557,
  575, 577, 578, 587, 588, 590, 591,
  601, 602, 610, 611, 615, 616, 617,
  618, 619, 621, 629, 662, 667, 683,
  684, 685, beauty 683, diamond 683,
  general 530, lily immortelle 449,
  530, 537, 541, 561, intrepide No. 2
  476, jewel 683, Vol. II 708, 709, 713,
  722, 723, 724, 728, 729, 731, 740,
  741, 747, 748, 749, 752, 753, 760,
  761, 762, 783, 785, 786, 794, 795,
  800, 801, 803, 804, 808, 809, 813,
  814, 826, 827, 828, 841, 846, 847,
  850, 851, 852, 853, 854, 861, 862,
  863, 870, 884, 1038, 1054, 1073,
  1137, 1170, angel 794, beloved 933,
  936, beloved daughter 927, beauty
  929, bride 926, 927, candor 878,
  child 878, 935, demoiselle 914,
  demoiselli Lilli 1035, 1036, 1037,
  docility 878, exiled princess 933,
  fiancée, spouse 925, 926, 927, 928,
  929, 930, lily 713, 725, 732, 784,
  796, look 878, lyre 827, madmoisel
  Lili 1044, Mary's daughter 925,
  Moses 753, nature 871, of the Holy
  Face 826, Papa's 882, Papa's brave
  one 929, plant 741, shepherdess 933,
  Sr. Geneviève 899, 835, 967, Sr.
  Geneviève's hand 1106
MARTIN CHILDREN (4 dead) Vol.
  II 927, 928, 930, 936, 969
MARTIN, HÉLÈNE Vol. II 928
MARTIN, JOSEPH (two) Vol. II 928
MARTIN, LÉONIE (LOLO) Vol. I
  191, 249, 267, 276, 299, 308, 396,
  423, 462, 542, 547, 602, 616, god-
  mother 618, princess 462, little
  Visitandine 631, Vol. II 709, 733,
  815, 816, 817, 831, 832, 835, 836,
  843, 844, 853, 854, 855, 861, 884,

888, 889, 896, 897, 899, 902, 908, 909, 951, 965, 966, 967, 1022, 1149, 1160, 1174, acceptance 1165, poor spouse 889, voice 816

MARTIN, LOUIS (PAPA, FATHER) Vol. I 133, 140, 229, 230, 232, 233, 234, 236, 237, 244, 248, 249, 275, 276, 298, 318, 335, 354, 380, 382, 387, 388, 395, 396, 406, 421, 425, 431, 433, 434, 451, 452, 457, 461, 476, 479, 482, 493, 510, 537, 555, 563, 564, 600, 616, 621, 622, 630, 658, 667, 671, 684, beloved 232, 482, illness 482, 542, King, 421, 424, 431, 434, 435, 452, 461, 476, 479, 494, 509, 510, Jesus' postman 424, 433, majesty 462, Vol. II 707, 724, 732, 743, 762, 763, 816, 843, 850, 863, 882, 884, 896, 928, 929, 930, 1017, 1073, 1094, 1165, 1166, 1173, Feast day 1174, illness 837, my King 796, new Abraham 1165, old man 927, 928, paralysis 1166, Patriach 929, 1166, saint 1165, victim 1166

MARTIN, MARIE (SISTER MARIE OF THE SACRED HEART) Vol. I 112, 133, 140, 143, 152, 190, 204, 224, 242, 244, 249, 273, 307, 335, 354, 395, 396, 451, 478, 578, 671, 674, angel 429, 661, diamond 421, 425, 430, 433, 434, 451, 456, 461, godmother 248, 289, 308, 654, gypsy 421, hermit, 427, Lion 501, 514, 563, 564, Vol. II 709, 727, 733, 739, 811, 815, 817, 830, 866, 873, 878, 883, 928, 993, 999, 1000, godmother 993, 994, 999

MARTIN, PAULINE (SISTER AGNES OF JESUS) Vol. I 110, 116, 133, 140, 143, 152, 190, 191, 238, 242, 248, 273, 288, 289, 307, 332, 334, 335, 353, 354, 392, 396, 398, 399, 400, 401, 406, 451, 480, 542, 619, 658, 667, confidante 308, lamb 440, 441, 442, 445, 500, 511,

512, 579, 612, 613, 620, 662, light lark 612, little belloni 580, luminous light 613, mademoiselle 542, mama 504, 620, 651, pearl 421, 425, 433, 434, 452, 456, 457, 461, Veronica 580, Vol. II 781, 782, 1153, donkey 1032, gentleness 1100, Mamma 1139, Mother 861, 866, 902, 915, 917, 928, 1030, 1046, 1058, 1080, 1090, 1100, 1104, 1106, 1109, 1114, nature 1153, provisor 759, tears of 1046, vessel of divine mercy 1101

MARTIN, THÉRÈSE Vol. I and Vol. II *see* **THÉRÈSE**

MARTIN, ZÉLIE Vol. I madame 680, mother 495, 496, Vol. II beautiful lady 927, 928, mamma 930, mother 724, 853, 884, 927, 1094, 1165, Patriach's happy spouse 781, 929

Martyrdom Vol. I 530, 537, 552, 577, Vol. II 725, 741, 801, 871, 872, 927, 928, 969, 991, 999, 1015, 1016, 1042, 1085, 1092, 1142, 1146

Martyrs Vol. I (of love) 588, Vol. II 828, 927, 1092, 1093

Marvels Vol. I 308, Vol. II 725, 760, 839, 990, 1015

MARY (BLESSED VIRGIN) Vol. I 248, 450, 482, 483, 568, 602, 617, 618, 662, 684, month 567, mother 482, 569, statue 619, Queen 679, 680, Vol. II 709, 732, 761, 804, 817, 835, 851, 865, 871, 925, 926, 928, 929, 930, 932, 936, 1011, 1032, 1060, 1072, 1086, 1093, 1140, Immaculate Mother 1142, Immaculate Virgin 1042, 1093, Liberatrix 925, lily 709, Mama 929, mantle 729, Mother 932, Our Lady of Mt. Carmel 866, Queen 925, 926, of apostles 1010, of apostles and martyrs 1014

Mass (es) Vol. II 956, 1016, 1018, 1094, 1127, 1140, nuptial 929

Massages Vol. II 1097

Material Vol. I 434

MATINS *see* Vol. I and Vol. II *see* **OF-**

FICE (DIVINE)
MAUDELONDE GIRLS (MARGUER-
ITE, CÉLINE, HÉLÈNE) Vol. I 239,
244, 459, Vol. II 722, 847, friend 865
MAUDELONDE, HENRY Vol. II 732
MAUDELONDE, MADAME Vol. I
244, Vol. II 722, 847
MAURICE, SAINT Vol. II 1060
MAZEL, PÈRE Vol. II 1092
Meadow (s) Vol. II 747, 748, 784, 958,
959, 960, 1040, heavenly 961
Meditations Vol. I 555
Meekness Vol. II 1101
Melody Vol. I (Cecilia's) 440, Vol. II 782,
794, 808, 827, 828, 933, 1039, 1040,
melodious 1109
Melon Vol. I 509
Memory (ies) Vol. I 431, 557, 561, 596,
600, 602, 611, 674, Vol. II 715, 743,
759, 765
Merits Vol. I 510, Vol. II 729, 794, 801,
929, 936, 956, 999, 1054, 1094,
medicine 970, oats 970
Mercy (ies) Vol. II 808, 813, 908, 999,
1084, 1085, 1093, 1101, 1122, 1133,
1141, 1173
Message (s) Vol. I 242, 249, 424, 454, 462,
547, Vol. II 827, 909, 1142, 1149
Messenger Vol. I 454
Midnight Vol. I 602
Milk Vol. II 936, 1141
Mind Vol. I 428, 480, 630, Vol. II 760,
763, 902, 1035, 1084, 1093, 1094
Ministry Vol. II 1094
Miracle Vol. II 851, 1127, 1139, 1140
MIRLITIR Vol. II 765
Miser Vol. I 601
Misery (ies) Vol. I 575, 619, Vol. II 1173
Misfortune Vol. I 425, 537, 542
Mission Vol. I 461, 588, 641, Vol. II 707,
712, 744, 748, 753, 759, 784, 785, 794,
810, 847, 850, 989, 1042, 1060, 1085,
1127
Missionary (ies) Vol. II 956, 990, 1010,
1014, 1015, 1018, 1034, 1069, 1071,

1073, 1092, 1093, 1094
Mistakes Vol. I 537, 575, *see also*
THÉRÈSE
Mistress Vol. I 545, *see also* **MOTHER
ST. PLACIDE**
Mistress of Novices Vol. II hunters 872
Model (s) Vol. II 827, 1040, 1101, In-
nocents 927
Monastery Vol. II 1070, 1071
Money Vol. II 916
MONSIEUR L'ABBÉ Vol. II *see* **BELL-
IÈRE, L'ABBÉ**
MONSIEUR LE DIRECTEUR Vol. II
see **SIMEON, BROTHER** and
THÉRÈSE
Monster Vol. I 451
Mortal (s) Vol. II 882, 1173, mortal re-
mains (THÉRÈSE) 1163
Mortifications Vol. II 1134
Moss Vol. I 459
MOTHER Vol. I *see* **GONZAGUE,
MARY, MARTIN, ZÉLIE,
MOTHER ST. PLACIDE;** Vol. II
743, 763, 764, 894, 966, 977, 993, 1145,
1146, Mamma 969, masterpiece 764,
ABBÉ BELLIÈRE'S AUNT 1134, *see
also* **GONZAGUE, MARY, MAR-
TIN, PAULINE, MARTIN, ZÉLIE**
and **THÉRÈSE**
MOTHER ST. PLACIDE Vol. I 482, 483
MOUNT CALVARY Vol. II 1110
Mountain (s) Vol. I 317, 332, 618, 651,
652, of Carmel 680, of love 658, Vol.
II 753, of Carmel 934, 957, 1165, of
love 994
Muddle Vol. I 273, *see also* **THÉRÈSE**
Music Vol. I 342, 440, 442, 661, Vol. II
827, 896
Myrrh Vol. II 795, 804, 936
Mysterious Vol. I 663, 684
Mystery Vol. I 547, 557, 577, 600, 642,
658, Vol. II 713, 722, 741, 753, 761,
781, 804, 809, 839, 855, 862, 929, 961,
1110
Name Vol. I 461, 546, 611, 641, Vol. II

765, 781, 782, 848, 854, 882, 894, 927, 956, 977, 991, 993, 1014, 1060, 1073, 1083, 1092, 1095

Nature Vol. I 317, 553, 557, 618, Vol. II 748, 813, 1094, 1152, 1159, *see also* **MARTIN, CÉLINE** and **MARTIN, PAULINE**

Naughty Vol. I 276, 281, 429

NAVARRE *see* **QUEEN OF FRANCE AND NAVARRE**

NEMPON, PÈRE Vol. II 1014, 1071

Nephew (s) Vol. I 459, Vol. II 830

Nest Vol. I 232, 479, 563, Vol. II 760, 761

Nets Vol. I 576, Vol. II 805, 851

NEW YEAR Vol. I 390, 490, 491, 493, 494, 600, 601, 602, Vol. II 765, 836, 896

Niece Vol. I 453, 454, 459, Vol. II *see* **THÉRÈSE**

Night Vol. I 273, 318, 427, 429, 491, 561, 580, 588, 600, 630, 654, Vol. II 741, 784, 804, 813, 838, 839, 841, 851, 995, 1016, 1033, 1038, 1071, 1146

Ninepins Vol. II 1039, 1040

Nobility Vol. I 680

Nook Vol. I 642

Nothing Vol. I 289, 396, 398, 400, 427, 457, 478, 491, 499, 501, 504, 510, 512, 542, 547, 552, 557, 612, 622, 641, 652, 658, 671, Vol. II 709, 713, 722, 724, 741, 752, 753, 762, 796, 801, 803, 809, 814, 841, 843, 848, 851, 871, 872, 909, 989, 994, 999, 1014, 1022, 1059, 1095, 1127, 1163

Nothingness Vol. I 641, Vol. II 999, 1094, 1122, 1165, lowliness 999

NOTRE-DAME-DES-VICTOIRES Vol. I 308, 568, Vol. II 1127, 1140

Nourishment Vol. II 933, 1164

NOVEMBER 19th Vol. II 715, 743

Novena Vol. II 1127, 1140

Novitiate Vol. I 537, Vol. II 727, 902, 915, novice (s) 1154

Nuptials Vol. I 675, Vol. II 827, Mass 929

Obedience Vol. I 619, Vol. II 956

Obstacle (s) Vol. I 289, Vol. II 849, 878, 1017, 1093, 1165

Ocean (s) Vol. I 423, 546, 629, Vol. II 724, 796, 803, 957, 977, of love 1142

OFFICE (DIVINE) Vol. I 490, Vol. II 930, 1061, Hours 1036, Matins 837, 970, 1016, 1136

Oil Vol. II 1159, 1160

Ointment (s) Vol. II 882, 883

Onions Vol. I 461, Vol. II of Egypt 1164

Ordination Vol. II 1014, 1060

Orphan (s) Vol. I 602, 684

ORPHELINE DE LA BÉRÉSINA Vol. I 461, 476, 493

Pain (s) Vol. I 388, 449, 453, 454, 478, 511, 545, 557, 577, Vol. II 999, 1069

Painful Vol. I 449, 453

Painting Vol. II 1121 *see also* **THÉRÈSE** artist

Palace (s) Vol. I 457, Vol. II 841, 1017

PALL Vol. II 956, 957

PALLU, MARGUERITE (OF BELLAY) Vol. I 143

PALLU, MARIE-THÉRÈSE (OF BELLAY) Vol. I 143

Palm (s) Vol. I 440, 442, 530, 577, Vol. II 927, 934, 1016, 1085, 1092, 1093, 1142

PAPA Vol. I and Vol. II *see* **MARTIN, LOUIS**

PAPINOT (PAPINAU) MME. Vol. I 241, 244, 659

Paradise Vol. I 455, Vol. II 863, 1069, 1120

Pardon Vol. II 729, 849, 1133, 1134

Parents Vol. I 493, Vol. II 916, 1134, Thérèse's 816, 1094

PARIS Vol. I 308

Park Vol. I 459, *see also* **Play**

PASCHAL TIME Vol. II 846

Passage Vol. I (subterrainian) 652, 658, 667, Vol. II 800

Passion Vol. I 577, Vol. II 1140, of Jesus 851

Passport Vol. II for heaven 1173

Paternal Vol. I *see* **GUÉRIN, ISIDORE**
Path (s) Vol. I 613, 651, 675, Vol. II 808, 839, 846, 961, 966, 1038
Patron (ess) Vol. II 927, 1060, 1086, patronage 1013
PAUL, SAINT Vol. I 479, 641
Peace Vol. I 504, 510, 511, 553, 561, 568, 575, 641, 658, 685, Vol. II 826, 846, 861, 866, 896, 903, 916, 961, 1038, 1070, 1101, serenity 872
Peach Vol. II 813, 814
Pearl (s) Vol. I 133, *see also* **MARTIN, PAULINE**; Vol. II 725, 732, 784
Pegs Vol. I *see* **Colloquialisms**
PELLETIER, M. L' ABBÉ Vol. I 652
Pen Vol. I 110, 273, 282, 289, 454, 556, 576, 684, Vol. II 712, 832, 1017, 1021
Penance Vol. II 956, 1012
PENTECOST Vol. I 429, 621, Vol. II 1132
Perfect Vol. I 406, Vol. II *see* **GOD**
Perfection (s) Vol. I 641, Vol. II 795, 907, 909, 965, 1022, 1093, 1094, 1136, 1137, 1164
Perfume (s) Vol. I 541, of roses 191, of love 611, Vol. II 781, 782, 839, 883, 1160
Permission Vol. II 1136, 1165
Persecution Vol. II 1092
PETER, SAINT Vol. II 851, 925
PHILOMENA, MOTHER (Prioress of Saigon Carmel) Vol. II 847
Photograph Vol. II 872, 915, 977, 1174, of THÉRÈSE 1154
PICHON, PÈRE ALMIRE Vol. I 248, 297, 468, 684, Vol. II 878, 999, docile instrument of Jesus 878
Picture (s) Vol. I 140, 190, 392, 406, 457, 478, 512, of the Holy Face 591; Vol. II 852, 951, 1043, 1154, Roulland's 977
PIERRE Vol. I 459
PIGEON LADIES Vol. I 274
PILATE Vol. II 862
Pilgrimmage Vol. II (life on earth) 1140, 1173

Pilgrims Vol. I 353
Pinpricks Vol. I 442, 499, 530, 552
Place Vol. II 724, 813, 1121, last 1122
Plans Vol. I 424
Play Vol. I 110, 239, 281, outings 281, park 281, rings 244, Vol. II playing 827, 828
Pleasure (s) Vol. I 230, 239, 244, 281, 282, 343, 365, 395, 425, 451, 457, 458, 482, 496, 514, Vol. II 744, 827, 828, 902, 915, 956, 1069, 1090, 1174, Mary's 1032, Thérèse's 1016
Poem (s) Vol. II 850, 1059
Poet (BOILEAU) Vol. II 1021
Pontiff (s) Vol. II 926, 928, 1145
POPE LEO XIII Vol. I 332, 335, 342, 353, 365, audience 366, kissing his foot 353, Vol. II 707, 1017, 1054
Port Vol. I 398, 400, 577, Vol. II 803, 804, 888, meaning Carmel 1165, meaning heaven 1152
Portrait (s) Vol. I 396, Vol. II 977
POTTIER, MONSIEUR Vol. II 866
POTTS DISEASE Vol. I 428
Poverty Vol. I 641, 642, Vol. II 814, 970, 999, 1022, 1043, 1084, 1094, 1096, vow of 1153, poor 903, 999
Power Vol. I 190, 600, 616, 674, Vol. II 959, 1041, 1055, 1059, 1122, 1128, 1137, God's 814, Jesus 826, Thérèse's 762
Powerful Vol. II 1054, 1095
Powerless (ness) Vol. I 457, 641, Vol. II 995, 1101
Practice (s) Vol. I 190, 191, Vol. II 727, 1152
Prayer (s) Vol. I 190, 191, 237, 393, 457, 476, 483, 596, 642, Vol. II 728, 731, 753, 763, 764, 800, 810, 817, 829, 830, 832, 833, 836, 847, 888, 899, 908, 925, 961, 979, 994, 1011, 1014, 1018, 1041, 1043, 1055, 1059, 1060, 1086, 1094, 1095, 1121, 1140, 1148, 1151, Thérèse's 801, 866, 978, 1010, 1015, 1054, 1072
Preaching Vol. II 1092

Predestination Vol. II 866

Present (s) Vol. I *see* **gift**; Vol. II 930, 935, 1070

Presentiment Vol. II 713, 839

Priest Vol. I 578, 588, 602, 631, Vol. II 708, 753, 882, 883, 1014, 1059, 1084, of Baal 969

PRIMOIS, MESDEMOISELLES Vol. I 555

Princess Vol. I 679, 680

Prison, Prisoner (s) Vol. I 546, 620, Vol. II 966, 1017, 1070

Privilege (d) Vol. I 541, 621, Vol. II 732, 785, 794, 881, 977, 999

Procession Vol. I (Corpus Christi) 242, Vol. II 927, 929

Profession Vol. I 652, 662, 663, Marie of the Sacred Heart's 401, 427, 429; Vol. II Léonie's 902 *see also* **THÉRÈSE**

Profession invitation Vol. I humiliation 680, man 680, nuptial blessing 680

Profundity Vol. I 641

Promise (s) Vol. I 387, Vol. II 907, 916, 966, 994, 1060, 1072, 1140, 1141

Proof Vol. I 684

Proof (s) Vol. II 707, 837, 862, 896, 902, 1014

Proverb Vol. I *see* **Colloquialisms**

Provisions Vol. I 461

PSALMS Vol. I 491, 553

Pure (purity) Vol. I 496, 618, Vol. II 732, 851, 871, 1093

PURGATORY Vol. I 500, Vol. II 925, 1072, 1092, 1093

QUEEN Vol. I and Vol. II *see* **THÉRÈSE**

QUEEN OF FRANCE AND NAVARRE Vol. I *see* **THÉRÈSE**

Quiet Vol. I (of heart) 641, Vol. II 1070

Rain Vol. I 652, Vol. II 713, 784

RAPHAEL, SAINT Vol. I 237

Rapture Vol. I 455

Rascal Vol. I 110, 429, 510, Vol. II *see* **GUÉRIN, MARIE**

Ray (s) Vol. I 233, 343, 613, Vol. II 713, 741, 784, 785, 838, 848

Reality Vol. I 455, 536, 552, 587, 671, Vol. II 1069, 1084

Reception Vol. I into Children of Mary 482, 483, 491, 495, 496, 512, 519, 671, Vol. II 902, 1173, Marie of the Eucharist, of veil 1111

Recovery Vol. II 899, 1146

Recreation Vol. II 915, 970, 1070, 1073

Reed Vol. I 427

Refectory Vol. I 496, Vol. II 835, 926, 1070

Refuge Vol. I 630

Relative (s) Vol. I 455, 544, 555, 589, 600, Vol. II 765, 836, 894, 908, 969, 977, 978, 1022, 1145, 1160

Relic (s) Vol. I LES BUISSONNETS 564, ST. AGNES 335, Vol. II 749, 1016, 1092, 1173, 1174

Religion Vol. II 855, 865

Religious Vol. II 888, 915

Remedy (ies) Vol. II 915, 917

Reparation Vol. I 631

Resignation Vol. I 468, Vol. II 707, 908

Resolutions Vol. I 563

Rest Vol. I 400, 561, 615, Vol. II 896, 995, 1014, 1140, 1142

Resurrection Vol. II 899

Retreat Vol. I 152, 223, 289, 427, 429, 462, 499, 501, 510, 511, 619, 658, PENTECOST 621, Vol. II 831, 861, Thérèse's 761, 993

RÉVÉRONY, MONSEIGNEUR Vol. I 353, 366, 380, 382, 388, 393, 652

Reward (s) Vol. I 600, 621, Vol. II 794, 809, 828, 836, 896, 909, 929, 933, 1092

Ribbons (white) Vol. I 435

Rich (es) Vol. I 461, 467, 529, 544, 557, 561, 641, Vol. II 993, 994, 999, 1022, 1084

Ring Vol. I 133, 435, *see also* **Play**

Risk Vol. II 908, 965

River (s) Vol. I 546, 553, 618, Vol. II 784, 841, 899, Blue 1069

Road Vol. I 236, 440, 529, 641, 658, 661, Vol. II 808, 826, 827, 865, 878, 899,

961, 1094, 1146, weariness of 896
Robe (white) Vol. I 662
Rocks Vol. I 398
ROME Vol. I 342, 365, 381, 382, 387, 388, 399, 401, 457, 460, 461, 493, 667, Vol. II 707, 709, 724, 830, 1017, 1165
ROMET, PAULINE Vol. I 140
ROULLAND, PÈRE ADOLPHE Vol. II 956, 957, 977, 1014, 1015, 1016, 1017, 1018, 1141, brother 1069, 1071, 1072, 1073, 1092, 1093, 1094, 1095, son 1094
Route Vol. I 651, 652
Rule Vol. II 1059, Carmelite 753, 831, 1041
SACRÉ COEUR DE MONTMARTRE Vol. I 308
Sacrifice (s) Vol. I 289, 427, 456, 588, 591, 620, monotony 620, Vol. II 805, 816, 837, 855, 870, 888, 907, 915, 916, 926, 966, 977, 1033, 1041, 1042, 1092, 1110, 1117, 1146
Sacristan Vol. II 1059
Sad (ness) Vol. I 274, 289, 423, 448, 467, 468, 511, 551, 552, 557, 602, Vol. II 841, 861, 902, 970, 999, 1038, 1054, 1120, 1136, 1138, 1142, 1152
SAIGON Vol. II 847, 1035, 1090, CARMEL 1071, 1090
Saint (s) Vol. I 237, 248, 406, 421, 433, 450, 454, 456, 493, 510, 520, 537, 542, 557, 684, Vol. II 731, 785, 813, 830, 833, 908, 909, 925, 926, 928, 929, 961, 1010, 1012, 1014, 1022, 1042, 1084, 1090, 1110, 1120, 1128, 1133, 1134, 1142, 1145, 1149
Salvation Vol. I 547, 588, Vol. II 728, 753, 933, 956, 977, 1014, 1042, 1084, 1095
SAMSON Vol. I 429
Sanctity Vol. I 542, 557, 558, 622, Vol. II 935, 1059, 1122, sanctification 960
Sanctuary Vol. I 567, Vol. II (of the heart) 826, 839
SATAN Vol. II *see* **DEVIL**
Sauce Vol. I 451

Sayings Vol. II 881, 882, ships 872
Scandal Vol. I 289
Scapular Vol. II 866
School Vol. I 140
Science (of rejoicing) Vol. I 641
Scribbling Vol. I 289, 561, 569, 580, Vol. II 1018, 1086
Scripture (s) Vol. II 861, 1094
Scruples (martyrdom of) Vol. I 568
Sea Vol. II 803, 804, 872, 1072, 1152
Seal Vol. II 732, 843, 926, 934, 1110
SEBASTIAN, SAINT Vol. II 928
Secret (s) Vol. II 722, 724, 841, 848, 960, 993, 994, 995, 1014
Seed (s) Vol. II 878, 936
Self-love Vol. I 529, Vol. II self-seeking 902
Seminarian (s) Vol. II 1018, 1060, Seminary 1014
Sentiment (s) Vol. II 763, 851, 921, 1021, 1059
Separation Vol. I 239, 467, Vol. II 760, 871, 907, 977, 1042
Sermon Vol. I 244, 274, 288, Vol. II 1018
Servant (s) Vol. II 761, 811, 1032
Service Vol. II 813, 1040, 1071
SÉVIGNÉ, MADAME DE Vol. I 458
Sewing Machine Vol. I 423, Vol. II *see* sewing work under **THÉRÈSE**
Shadow (s) Vol. I 494, 504, 551, 552, 558, 618, 685, Vol. II 732, 782, 785, 796, 839, 851, 1017, 1069, 1092
Sheaves Vol. II 878, 936, 1018
Sheep Vol. II 728, 795, 958, 960, 961, sheepfolds 960
Shepherdess Vol. II 958, 961, 962, *see also* **GONZAGUE** and **MARTIN, CÉLINE**
Shore (s) Vol. I 233, 398, 400, 546, heavenly 455, Vol. II 803, 896, 899, 989, 1071, 1142
Shovel Vol. I 431
SHRINE Vol. I *see* **TOURS**
Sick Vol. I *see* **Headache**, Vol. II Thérèse 871

Silence Vol. I 499, 510, 620, Vol. II 708, 752, 764, 808, 851, 853, 961, 994, 995, 1059, 1090, 1095

Silkworm Vol. I 274

SIMEON Vol. I 662

SIMEON, BROTHER Vol. II brother 1054, Monsieur le Directeur 1054

Simplicity Vol. II 784, 785, 1085

Sin (s) Vol. I 567, 568, Vol. II 813, 1016, 1134, 1164

Sinner (s) Vol. I 440, 500, Vol. II 762, 795, 804, 882, 1000, 1084, 1159

SION Vol. I 553

Smile (s) Vol. I 234, 631, 667, 684, Vol. II 732, 741, 801, 915, 1021, 1040

Smoke Vol. I 529, 587

Snow Vol. I 396, Vol. II 959

Soldier (s) Vol. I 530, 591, Vol. II 1012

Solitude Vol. I 455, 612, Vol. II 709, 724, 752, 846, 1085, 1090

SOLOMON Vol. II 994, 1121

Son Vol. II 1094, 1153

Song (s) Vol. I 654, Vol. II 765, 782, 827, 1022

Sorrow (s) Vol. I 239, 276, 427, 450, 453, 454, 456, 467, 478, 500, 537, 541, 545, 546, 555, 567, 578, 590, 591, 630, 663, 682, 684, Vol. II 763, 764, 804, 826, 837, 908, 960, 1106, 1120, 1151, *see also* **JESUS** and **THÉRÈSE**

Soul (s) Vol. I 233, 392, 399, 400, 435, 440, 448, 449, 450, 454, 455, 468, 496, 499, 500, 501, 503, 504, 511, 530, 537, 542, 547, 552, 557, 567, 569, 575, 576, 577, 578, 580, 587, 588, 591, 602, 615, 618, 620, 621, 622, 629, 630, 631, 641, 642, 651, 652, 654, 658, 663, 667, 671, 682, 683, 685, Vol. II 708, 713, 722, 724, 728, 731, 732, 733, 753, 760, 761, 762, 763, 764, 765, 781, 784, 795, 796, 800, 801, 803, 804, 805, 808, 810, 814, 826, 827, 828, 843, 846, 847, 848, 850, 855, 861, 862, 865, 871, 872, 873, 894, 896, 909, 916, 925, 927, 933, 936, 957, 960, 961, 966, 977, 989, 999, 1000,

1010, 1011, 1014, 1016, 1018, 1041, 1042, 1047, 1054, 1055, 1059, 1060, 1069, 1110, 1117, 1120, 1122, 1128, 1132, 1133, 1134, 1136, 1139, 1141, 1142, 1146, 1153, 1159, 1163, 1164, 1165, 1174, 1181, guest of our soul 863

Souvenir Vol. I 204, 205, 224, 249, 392, 491, 519, 674, 682, Vol. II 727, 848, 936, 953, 993, 1110, 1111, 1174, 1175, 1181

Sparrow *see* **Birds**

Speakroom Vol. I 459, Vol. II 843, 969

Spirit Vol. I 365, 458, 482, Vol. II 959, 960, 1060, 1121, meaning Louis Martin 882

Splendor Vol. I 455, 661, Vol. II 861, 929, 933

Spouse (s) Vol. I 553, 630, 652, 672, 674, 684, *see also* **JESUS** Vol. II 707, 804, 808, 813, 816, 826, 827, 828, 831, 833, 838, 839, 841, 843, 855, 861, 862, 866, 894, 899, 903, 925, 928, 929, 930, 994, 1014, 1040, 1060, 1110 *see also* **JESUS, ST. JOSEPH, SR. MARIE OF JESUS** and **THÉRÈSE**

Spring Vol. I 445, 501, Vol. II 724, 760, 843, 882

Stain Vol. I 662

Star (s) Vol. II 785, 933, 1022

Statue (s) Vol. I 248, of CHILD JESUS 589, 671, OUR LADY OF LOURDES 619

Stockings Vol. I 133

Storm (s) Vol. I 442, Vol. II 826, 851, 872, 881, 888, 1010

Story Vol. II 850, 916, 999, 1070

Stranger Vol. I 457, 500, Vol. II 1164

Strength Vol. I 435, 450, 467, 501, 504, 511, 529, 600, Vol. II 801, 830, 831, 855, 908, 999, 1012, 1016, 1041, 1043, 1133

Submission Vol. I 388

Suffering (s) Vol. I 273, 399, 400, 423, 467, 478, 499, 501, 504, 530, 537, 541, 542, 547, 552, 553, 557, 558, 563, 564,

662, 680, Vol. II 709, 728, 739, 741, 804, 827, 871, 872, 873, 896, 929, 935, 936, 951, 961, 962, 979, 999, 1017, 1038, 1040, 1042, 1043, 1069, 1072, 1092, 1127, 1139, 1142, 1152, 1170

Summit (s) Vol. I 651, 652, 658, Vol. II 909, 994, 1133

Sun Vol. I 281, 427, 429, 455, 546, 557, 652, Vol. II 713, 741, 784, 785, 795, 827, 1012, 1090, 1096, 1117, 1121, sunlight 927

SUNDAY Vol. I 318, Vol. II 1047, 1059, 1097

Support (s) Vol. II 908, 929, 961, 1140

Surprise (s) Vol. I 365, 510, Vol. II 991, 1015, 1163

SU-TCHUEN Vol. II 977, 978, 1070, 1071, map 977

Swallow Vol. II *see* **Birds**

Swan Vol. II *see* **Birds**

Sweetness Vol. I 449, 499, 504, 577, 684, Vol. II 795

SWISS MOUNTAINS Vol. I 317

Sword Vol. I 552, 558, Vol. II 933, 979, 1017, 1042, 1072

Tabernacle Vol. I 567, 568, 630, 642, Vol. II 764, 784, 816, 833, 925, 1173

Tablecloth (s) Vol. I 423, Vol. II 1048

TABOR Vol. II 795

Talent (s) Vol. II 785, 902, 915

Teachers Vol. I 482, 483

Teaching (s) Vol. I 613, Vol. II 994

Tears Vol. I 450, 467, 479, 500, 542, 611, 658, 675, 683, 684, 685, dress from 667, *see also* **JESUS**, Vol. II 724, 731, 828, 848, 871, 878, 908, 935, 936, 958, 959, 961, 962, 978, 989, 1018, 1100, 1127, 1133, 1139, 1152, 1164 *see also* **JESUS, MARTIN, PAULINE** and **THÉRÈSE**

Temper Vol. II 966

Temptation (s) Vol. I 567, 618, Vol. II 861, 889, 902, 1010

Temptests Vol. I 442

Tenderness Vol. I 590, 596, 602, Vol. II 715, 740, 743, 760, 764, 830, 837, 841, 862, 908, 915, 958, 969, 1000, 1101, 1152, 1164, 1173, *see also* **JESUS** and **THÉRÈSE**

TERESA OF AVILA, SAINT Vol. I 289, 589, 591, 621, Vol. II 801, 830, 831, 837, 849, 853, 888, 909, 927, 933, 956, 1011, 1016, 1017, 1072, cross 909, daughter 1016, intercession 830, life 830

Thanksgiving Vol. I 621

THÉRÈSE

Self-Descriptions Vol. I Ball 335, 353, 499, 500, 504, 514, Bridge of Jesus 671, Cat 308, Grain of sand 406, 427, 440, 441, 537, 547, 551, 552, 580, 612, 613, 663, Little 318, 423, 429, 568, 575, 600, 641, Little daughter 597, 615, 652, 654, 655, 661, 671, 674, Little fiancée 651, 667, Little flower 233, 661, Little girl 110, 191, 224, 233, 399, Little hermit 590, 651, Little lamb 563, 579, 620, Little niece 454, Little novice 575, muddle-headed 450, nightingale 233, poor 342, poor atom 580, poor little thing 612, Princess 679, prisoner in Carmel 620, Queen 232, 421, 424, 425, 430, 431, 434, 452, 456, 457, 460, 461, 462, 476, 477, 479, 493, 494, 510, Queen of France and Navarre 431, 452, 457, 461, 462, robin 232, Saint 493, 510, 520, second lamb 298, servant 387, swallow 232, the last, 616, the littlest 616, Thérèsita 335, 406, timid dawn 233, thread on foot 612, Toy 335, 353, 499, 511, 512, 514, unworthy little sister 576, your Benjamin 600, your sister 615, Vol. II Ant 1022, Aunt 830, Baby 1114, 1149, milk baby 1146, Benjamin 715, 765, 833, 916, child 967, 993, 998, 1017, 1140, daughter 715, 743, 744, 763, 764, 810, 811, 994, 1022,

dog 872, Grasshopper 1022, Jesus'
plaything 903, least 1098, little A
1034, little brother 1000, 1012, Little Carmelite 1014, Little daughter
994, 1021, Little lamb 961, Little
thief 928, Little victim of your merciful love 1170, Magpie 916, Monsieur le Directeur 1055, niece 765,
pauvre monsieur 914, 1097, Queen
796, 882, 1165, Roulland's helper
1015, Roulland's little Moses 1018,
Roulland's little sister 1016,
Roulland's sister 1018, Senior of the
novitiate 915, spouse 903, toy 903,
victim 1170, zero 1095
Other references Vol. I artist 140, 248,
274, 459, answering back 152, bell
(promptness) 427, 456, eye (s) 274,
442, 611, fatigue 308, forehead 234,
head 435, 442, headache 223, heart
see Heart, hunchbacked 244, idle
fancies 236, intelligence 140,
laughter 110, 275, 429, lessons 241,
loulou 429, mistakes 140, 354, swing
244, Vol. II aspirations 1021, artist
848, 1121 (sculpture), audacity 1017,
back 1097, birth 1094, cheerfulness
1146, confidence 883, 888, 999,
1106, efforts 902, 967, eyes 1046,
1101, fever 1146, flower 1085, girl
765, 1100, 1104, gravity 915, grief
848, hand 1145, 1164, 1166, 1174,
hand (trembling) 1166, handwriting
759, 810, 832, 837, 841 (codfiches),
1018, 1069, 1086, head 1093, 1159,
heart *see* Heart, helplessness 1120,
illness 1116, 1121, 1174, imperfect
1101, imperfection 1100, indigence
970, life 1022, 1085, 1086, look 853,
mind 1159, mistake 813, not die
young 1152, presence 1140, 1163,
profession 707, 903, retreat 761,
993, revenge 816, sewing work 956,
991 (toque), sick 871, sorrow 970,
1084, 1098, 1138, soul 902, 903, 908,
921, 930, 956, 994, 1038, 1094,
1098, 1140, 1145, 1152, 1154, 1181,
spiritual direction 903, 908, taste
916, tears 762, 1100, 1101, unfaithful 1033, verse 1071, 1084, Viaticum
1173, view 1117, voice 921, 960,
1022, way 1134, 1164, wedding 902,
will 933, youth 1017

**THÉRÈSE of ST. AUGUSTINE,
SISTER** Vol. I 191

Thirst Vol. I 445, 501, mysterious 591,
see also **JESUS**

Thorns Vol. I 553, 576, 611, 618, 684,
Vol. II 724, 936

Thought (s) Vol. I 289, 318, 342, 459,
468, 479, 542, 552, 621, Vol. II 728,
783, 785, 829, 888, 896, 902, 929, 951,
953, 958, 960, 965, 996, 1015, 1069,
1084, 1092, 1093, 1137, 1140, 1142,
1146, 1149, 1152, of God 1060, of
Thérèse 908

Thread on your foot Vol. I 612

Throne Vol. I 233, 479, 661, 675, Vol. II
724, 882, 928, 934

TIFFENNE, MADAME Vol. I 555

Time Vol. I 152, 236, 238, 242, 273, 289,
298, 308, 353, 365, 395, 429, 456, 459,
460, 461, 467, 468, 482, 483, 490, 493,
502, 552, 563, 568, 569, 578, 580, 591,
596, 600, 601, 602, 618, 630, 662,
mirage 630, Vol. II 763, 765, 800, 816,
836, 871, 882, 899, 902, 910, 916, 921,
927, 961, 969, 1017, 1054, 1061, 1069,
1117, 1134, 1140, 1142, 1146, 1151,
1164, 1166, 1173, moment 1116, 1117,
1122, 1127, 1128

TISSERANT WATER Vol. II 883

Title (s) Vol. I 457, 461, 476, 493, 537,
552, 679, Vol. II 872, 933, 1014

TOBIAS Vol. I 237

TOM (THÉRÈSE'S DOG) Vol. I 237

Tomb Vol. I 232, 421, 455

Tongue Vol. I 428, Vol. II 850

TONKIN Vol. II 1071, 1072

TOTO, MONSIEUR (M.T.) Vol. II

1035, 1036, 1037, 1044

TOURS Vol. I 616

Traveler (s) Vol. II 872, 908, 1046

Travels Vol. I 230

Treasure (s) Vol. I 450, 457, 467, 500, 558, 587, Vol. II 715, 724, 741, 764, 781, 808, 837, 839, 851, 861, 966, 999, 1022, 1046, 1071, 1100, 1141, 1165

Treat (s) Vol. I 494, 496, 589, Vol. II 715, 760, 829

Tree (s) Vol. I 450, 459, 467, Vol. II 761, 831

Trial (s) Vol. I 276, 289, 353, 380, 382, 387, 388, 398, 400, 478, 537, 545, 555, 576, 600, 684, Vol. II 739, 762, 795, 808, 816, 837, 861, 862, 866, 870, 871, 872, 878, 888, 889, 902, 908, 909, 959, 960, 961, 979, 1010, 1043, 1069, 1091, 1111, 1117, 1166, 1170

Tribulation (s) Vol. II 871, 896

Tricks Vol. I 110, Vol. II 1017

TRINITY Vol. I 680, Vol. II 862, 882, 925, 929, 933

Trip Vol. I 229, 237, 239, 244, 342, 431, 469, 617, 618, 651, 654, Vol. II 709, 849, 1017, 1174

Trouble (s) Vol. I 239, 398, 399, 400, 459, 503, 512, 555, Vol. II 959

TROUVILLE Vol. I 273, 276

Truth Vol. I 452, Vol. II 862, 903, 908, 960, 961, 999, 1015, 1072, 1084

Turmoil Vol. I 450, Vol. II 861

Turn Vol. I 461

UNCLE Vol. I and Vol. II *see* **GUÉRIN, ISIDORE**

Uncreated Vol. I 671

Underground Vol. I 652

Union Vol. I 468, 675, Vol. II 740, 760, 830, 831, 835, 865, 929, 933, 952, 977, 978, 1014, 1059, 1060, 1084

Unity Vol. I 468, Vol. II 740, 760

Universe Vol. I 467, 542, Vol. II 753

Unknown Vol. I 620, 621, 680, 685

Unworthiness Vol. I 482, Vol. II 707

Valley (s) Vol. I 427, 454, 491, 675, Vol.

II 795, 811, 861, 958, 1127, 1139, 1152

Value Vol. II 760, 855, 989, 1038, 1095

Vanity (ies) Vol. I 452, Vol. II 1121

VATICAN Vol. I 457

Veil Vol. I 429, 613, 659, Vol. II 781, 851, 1014, 1094, 1110, reception of 1111

VÉNARD, THÉOPHANE Vol. II 1071, 1092, 1129

VENICE Vol. I 317, 318

VESPERS Vol. I *see* **OFFICE** (DIVINE)

Viaticum Vol. II Thérèse's 1173

Vibration (s) Vol. I 641, Vol. II 863

Victim Vol. II 999 *see also* **MARTIN, LOUIS** and **THÉRÈSE**

Victory (ies) Vol. I 569, Vol. II 933, 1017, 1018, 1069, 1092, victorious 1010

VINCENT DE PAUL, SISTER ST. Vol. I 503

Virgin (s) Vol. II 709, 713, 729, 732, 748, 781, 828, 838, 851, 927, 933, 951, 1085

Virtue (s) Vol. I 467, 482, 600, 622, 641, 675, Vol. II 796, 801, 836, 839, 894, 903, 909, 915, 999, 1015, 1021, 1060, 1084, 1093, 1100, 1159

VIRVILLE, MONSIEUR DE Vol. I 396

Visit (s) 238, 276, 459, 556, 616, 684, Vol. II 722, 1069, 1110

VISITANDINE Vol. I 299, Vol. II 902

VISITATION Vol. I 276, Vol. II 816, 835, 849

Vocation Vol. I 289, 380, 382, 387, 482, answer 380, 381, Vol. II 753, 831, 878, 881, 882, 902, 989, 1016, 1017, 1018, 1071, 1072

Voice (s) Vol. I 661, Vol. II 927, 933, 956, 993, 1085, *see also* **GUÉRIN, MARIE; JESUS; MARTIN, LÉONIE** and **THÉRÈSE**

Void Vol. I 576, Vol. II 712, 884

Vows Vol. I 667, Vol. II 902, 1153, indissoluable bonds 928

Wagon Vol. I 396

Washing Vol. I 451, Vol. II 917

Walk Vol. I 459

Water (s) Vol. I 442, 622, Vol. II 796,

861, 866, 882, 995, 1141

Wave (s) Vol. I 442, Vol. II 803, 862, 888

Way (s) Vol. II 761, 827, 862, 899, 1000, 1022, 1046, 1055, 1093, 1098, 1117, 1152, 1153, 1165, Thérèse's 1134, 1164

Weak (ness) Vol. I 442, 514, 557, 613, 641, Vol. II 851, 1042, 1059, 1093, 1133, 1136, 1173, frailty 1093

Weather Vol. I 429

Wedding Vol. I 510, 537, 667, 672, 679, 680, 683, Vol. II 866, 926, 927, 928, *see also* JESUS and THÉRÈSE

Wicked Vol. II 894

Will Vol. I 500, 537, God's 298, 468, 577, 684, His 658, 662, Vol. II 871, 1015, 1042, 1071, 1093, God's 794, 839, 846, 894, 903, 908, 1014, 1017, 1060, 1127, His 1072, 1090, Jesus 871

Wind Vol. I 442, 529, 652, Vol. II 732, 803, 804, 889

Window (s) Vol. I 233, 468, 557, Vol. II 841

Wine Vol. I 433, 630, 652, 658, Vol. II 838, 862, 866, 933, wine press 862

Wing (s) Vol. I 232, 233, 511, 512, Vol. II 851, 936, 1035, 1138, 1146

Winter Vol. I 480, Vol. II 843

Wise (wisdom) Vol. II 961, 1021

Wish (es) Vol. I 477, 494, Vol. II 724, 765, 829, 830, 832, 835, 836, 926, 1015

Woman (men) Vol. I 459, Vol. II 909, 927, 995, 1016, 1059, 1101

Word (s) Vol. I 307, 342, 442, 491, 553, 579, 580, 591, 641, 662, 685, WORD OF GOD 680, Vol. II 714, 753, 765, 781, 785, 795, 801, 808, 828, 837, 862, 872, 979, 1069, 1070, 1084, 1093, 1094, 1100, 1101

Work (s) Vol. I 449, 511, 561, 569, Vol. II 714, 739, 762, 785, 848, 896, 909, 970, 979, 995, 1010, 1015, 1054, 1059, 1069, 1072, 1084, 1095, 1121, 1127, 1134, 1142, 1149, God's 814

World (s) Vol. I 276, 289, 390, 459, 530, 546, 557, 587, 591, 674, 679, 685, Vol.

II 724, 732, 761, 801, 816, 843, 846, 861, 865, 866, 872, 881, 882, 883, 894, 960, 977, 995, 1014, 1015, 1016, 1017, 1030, 1032, 1041, 1042, 1070, 1072, 1084, 1090, 1110, 1114, 1149, 1152, 1164, 1165, monopolizer 882

Wound (s) Vol. I 546, 683, *see also* JESUS, Vol. II 936, 961

Writing (s) Vol. I 600, Vol. II 1120

YOUF, MONSIEUR Vol. I 658

Youth Vol. II 760, 1054, 1071, Thérèse 1017

ZACHAEUS Vol. II 761

Zeal Vol. II 1122

General: Thérèse's writings were all done when she was the age of young mothers

NOT his death but her father's departure "Our Fr who art in Heaven" p. 724

Points for Last Chapter

The Institute of Carmelite Studies promotes research and publication in the field of Carmelite spirituality. Its members are Discalced Carmelites, part of a Roman Catholic community—friars, nuns and laity—who are heirs to the teaching and way of life of Teresa of Jesus and John of the Cross, men and women dedicated to contemplation and to ministry in the Church and the world. Information concerning their way of life is available through local diocesan Vocation Offices, or from the Vocation Director's Office, 1525 Carmel Road, Hubertus, WI 53033.

1. Child-Care: Thérèse wanted to spend her heaven doing good on earth. All "good on earth" depends on the weakest link in the succession of generations: children.